EDWARDIAN ARCHITECTURE

Robert Angell: premises in Old Compton Street, W1.
Coloured glazed brick and faience.

EDWARDIAN ARCHITECTURE

A Biographical Dictionary

A.STUART GRAY

Photographs by Jean Nicholas Breach. Drawings by Charlotte Halliday.
Foreword by Nicholas Taylor.

Wordsworth Editions

First published 1985 by Gerald Duckworth & Co. Ltd,
The Old Piano Factory, 43 Gloucester Crescent, London NW1.

This edition published 1988 by Wordsworth Editions Ltd,
8b East Street, Ware, Hertfordshire, under licence
from the proprietor.

ISBN 1-85326-908-5

Printed and bound in Portugal by Printer Portuguesa Industria Gráfica.

CONTENTS

ACKNOWLEDGMENTS

I wish especially to thank Tony and Leslie Birks-Hay for their enthusiasm, patience and skill in putting this book together; Jean and Nicholas Breach for taking and producing over 400 photographs involving thousands of miles of travel; Charlotte Halliday for her drawings; Nicholas Taylor for his kind foreword and exhaustive examination of the text; Andrew Saint, Susan Beattie and John Brandon-Jones for reading the text and making valuable suggestions; Marjorie Morrison, Margaret Richardson and Anne Riches for their help; Rosalind Macdonald for preparing the first draft from my manuscript and Evelyn Lacey for the final draft; Letitia Blake for collating the index.

My special thanks are also due to Mary Adshead (Mrs Stephen Bone), Ian Allan, John Archer, Chris Arnold, David Attewill, Arthur Bailey, Hugh Bankart, Bateman and Bateman, P. A. Bezodis, Bomer and Ransom, Charles Bradford, John Brookholding-Jones, John Michael Bunney, Doreen Cadwallader, Alban Caröe, A. B. Chatwin, the Chief Architect of the Metropolitan Police, David Clarke, Joanna and Robert Coates, Hazel Cook, Eric de Maré, Arthur Cooksey, Elizabeth Cooper, Mrs Cruse, Sir Anthony Denny, Bt, E. T. Downing and H. F. Morley, Dame Bridget D'Oyly Carte, Paul Dalou Drury, William Eden, A. R. Fox, Andor Gomme, Brigid Grafton-Greene, Harold Greenwood, William Guttridge and Charles Tarling, Mark Harris, E. Vincent Harris, Lord Horder, Allan James, Edward Jamilly, Norman Jewson, Henry Kay, W. H. Kininmouth, George Knight, Lanchester and Lodge, Christine Loeb, R. N. Mackellar and Partners, J. D. McArthur, Prof. E. W. N. Mallows, Hugh Martin-Kaye, Mervyn Miller, Alexander Moira, H. V. Molesworth-Roberts, E. Morphew, John Moss-Eccardt, George Mould, Aubrey Orchard-Lisle, Dawn Orr, Ethel Parker, Dick Peddie and McKay, Michael Penty, Richard Mountford-Piggott, Godfrey Raphael, E. N. Roberts, Henry Rushton, Godfrey Samuel, Richard Scott, Colin Sorensen, Gavin Stamp, David Stokes, Rodney Tatchell, Ruth Treadgold, Elvira Wade, Adrian Waterlow, A. B. Waters, Lesslie Watson and especially to Norman Watkins. I am also grateful to the Newspaper Collection of the British Library, the British Architectural Library and Drawings Collection, the GLC Archives and Photo Library, and the Westminster City Library.

For their kind permission in allowing photographs to be taken, I would like to thank the Master and Fellows of Balliol College, Oxford, the Master and Fellows of Emmanuel College, Cambridge, the Master and Fellows of Gonville and Caius College, Cambridge, the Principal and Fellows of Lady Margaret Hall, Oxford, the Master and Fellows of Trinity Hall, Cambridge; the municipal authorities and staff of Belfast City Hall and Cardiff City Hall, the municipal authorities, Northallerton, the staff of Bristol Central Library, Glasgow College of Art, and St Deiniol's Library, Harwarden; the management and staff of the Piccadilly Hotel, Harrods, Waring and Gillow, and Selfridges; the Headmaster of Christ's Hospital, Horsham, the Headmaster of Downside, the Headmaster of Gresham School, Holt, the Headmaster of Mill Hill School, and the Master of Wellington College; the owners of the following houses: Happisburgh Manor; Marshcourt, Stockbridge; Woodside, Graffham, Petworth; Hill House, Helensburgh; Greywalls, Gullane; The Close, Brompton, Northallerton; The Orchard, Chorleywood; Pasture House, North Luffenham; Brantridge Forest, Balcombe; The Clock House, Cowfold; Great Maytham, Rolvenden; The Inn, Roseneath; Conkwell Grange, Bradford-on-Avon; Heathcote, Ilkeley; Oakdene, Rotherfield; The Cearne, Limpsfield; 37 Hartopp Road, Four Oaks, Sutton Coldfield; Lea and Stoneywell Cottages, Charnwood Forest; the clergy and staff of the following cathedrals and churches: Liverpool Anglican Cathedral; St Sophia, Lower Kingswood; St Martin, Blackheath, Wonersh; St Mary Star of the Sea, Hastings; Brockhampton Church; St Mary the Virgin, Great Warley; St Barnabas, Shackleswell Road, Hackney; St Andrew, Roker Park, Sunderland; St Cyprian, Clarence Gate; Kempley Church, near Ross; St Peter, Falcon Avenue, Edinburgh; Kirkby in Ashfield Church; and the Mother Superior and nuns, All Saints, London Colney; and finally, the staff at Greenwich Power Station, the staff of Midhurst Sanatorium, and the owners of The Cloisters, Letchworth.

The recent reorganisation of local government in the UK has led to changes in the extent and names of some counties. These have not been incorporated in this book, which generally uses the old county names in use in the Edwardian era.

The marginal numbers refer to pages on which illustrations are to be found.

FOREWORD
by Nicholas Taylor

'Yes, I want the world,' said the prematurely dying Baroque architect Edwin Rickards to his novelist friend Arnold Bennett in 1919 (page 311 of this book). The wistfulness of the once ebullient architect's deathbed yearning (the same sadness as in Elgar's Cello Concerto of the same year) arose from an acute sense of loss: he and his friends had indeed had the whole world at their feet before the cataclysm of 1914 had swept their young clients away, and before that ominous modern phenomenon, the inflation of building costs (two-and-a-half times between 1914 and 1920), had killed off the exuberance of Edwardian architecture for good. In spite of all the inner economic decay which hindsight now reveals to us — the progressive decline of agriculture since the 1870s, the techno-logical competitiveness of the French and the Germans, the growing maritime strength of the Germans and the Americans, the failure to translate native inventiveness into the production skills of the 'managerial revolution' — in spite of all this, and in spite of the increasing social unrest of trade unionism and feminism, Edwardian England generally reeked of popular confidence in the permanent prosperity of everlasting empire.

To immerse oneself in this architectural encyclo-pedia is to immerse oneself in a forgotten psychology of magniloquent optimism: vast flights of steps, statues of local heroes, portentous classical inscriptions, astonishing sculptural groups of 'Strength, Prudence, Abundance and Prosperity' (on the United Kingdom Provident Institution), 'Science inspiring the Allied Trades' (on the Royal Automobile Club), 'The Fatherless Widow, The Winged Messenger of Peace, The Horrors of War, The Dignity of War, Truth, Justice and Fame' (on the new War Office) or 'Britannia seated between the Higher Mathematics and the Lower Mathe-matics, supported by Mercury and Truth, with the Owl of Wisdom in one corner' (an unusual late entry of 1925 on the National Provincial Bank in the City of London). In the wake of 'victory' the British Empire in the twenties actually covered a wider spread of the earth's surface and population than ever before, but by now it was a burden of statesmanship — the prewar spirit of greed and thrill had quietened down. To us in the 1980s the Edwardian era seems now as psychologically remote as the Neolithic must have been to the Tudor, so great have the changes been, not just materially and socially but in popular outlook. Monumental buildings are left to us stranded out of context. It needs therefore something of the

sheer prodigality of this biographical dictionary by Stuart Gray to provide a living bridge to the Edwardians for those of us who can otherwise reach them only through their own books, magazines, obituaries, drawings, directories, documents. I say 'living bridge' advisedly because Stuart, being the age he is, has the personal contact with the period that those of us born since 1939 cannot possibly have: look up Watkins, William Henry on page 372 ('Watkins of Bristol') and there in the modest last sentence as the filling in the sandwich of Watkins Gray International is Stuart himself.

'Have you met Mr Gray yet?' Margaret Richardson asked me at the RIBA Drawings Collection some time in the 1970s, knowing instinctively that Stuart and I were birds of the same (encyclopedic) feather. Margaret explained that he was a brand-new architectural historian of astonishing enthusiasm, a recently retired architect who had decided to research exhaustively the period of his Edwardian childhood: the heyday of those monumental father-figures — Sir Edwin Lutyens, Sir Reginald Blomfield, Sir Herbert Baker, Sir Edwin Cooper — who had toured the drawing boards of the Royal Academy Schools when he sat there as a student in the nineteen-twenties. As soon as I got to know Stuart Gray, particularly in the context of his beloved Hampstead Garden Suburb, I grew to realise, behind the mild and modest and slightly abstracted owlishness, his irrepressible youthful-ness and perceptiveness and sense of curiosity (and dry sense of fun). Readers of this book, wherever they dip, will enjoy Stuart's almost uncontrollably lateral mind as he forages crab-wise across the complicated network of interlocking partnerships and pupillages, competition entries and clients, innovations and bankruptcies.

On the analogy of Tillyard's book *The Elizabethan World Picture*, what Stuart Gray builds up here is an elaborate social-and-architectural mosaic of the Edward-ian world picture. In his introductory sections he is particularly strong on department stores and luxury hotels and Lyons' corner houses, not to forget mansion flats and underground stations. There is an appropriate (if awful) pun in Sellar and Yeatman's *1066 and All That* when Gray's Elegy in a Country Churchyard is misprinted as Gray's Energy — and Gray's energy is what this book is. The gift of having been so close to it all, unlike younger historians, means that he can unerringly relate architects and buildings to clients and their requirements. Architectural historians who have a narrow training in art history tend not to be very good as historians (Mark Girouard is a notable exception). The Edwardian period demands breadth of historical perception just because, beneath all those rhetorical sculptures and murals, it was a decade of rapid technical change, Reyner Banham's 'first machine age'. Electricity, telephones, typewriters, motor cars, refrigeration plant, reinforced concrete, synthetic materials, air conditioning — time and again on these pages the most professional architectural historian will be rocked back on his heels as something familiar and taken-for-granted in daily life erupts from the page as a fresh revelation in an architectural context. Who, for example, designed the Centre Court at Wimbledon? Did you know that it is a pioneering example of exposed board-marked concrete? Did you know (and this is where Gray scores an ace) that the man who designed it spent his spare time making innumerable imaginary reconstructions of Solomon's Temple at Jerusalem, which is why he was so good at making accurate models for the All-England committee which showed the exact ratio of sunshine and shadow on the court at different times of the year? Mind you, you may not even have known that the architect concerned, C. Stanley Peach, was the great electricity generating station specialist — every time I go to Lord's I bitterly lament the disappearance of the great tapering Baroque chimney which he and the young Sir Charles Reilly designed at Lodge Road.

Take another subject: did you know who the prime mover was behind the compulsory installation of safety curtains in British theatres (heaven knows, we look at the things often enough)? Page 315 of this book introduced me to the unique contribution of the architect Edwin Otto Sachs, and to the Russian artillery colonel who invented uralite (the main asbestos component in the curtains). Take another familiar feature of the London scene, the splendid Ben-Hur-like Peace quadriga unveiled in 1912 on top of Decimus Burton's Wellington Arch at Hyde Park Corner. Did you know that it was sculpted by a man, sixty-seven when it was finally completed, who spent his first twenty-four years of working life as an Army veterinary surgeon in India, Abyssinia, Egypt and the Cape? (And his name, in case you forget, was Captain Adrian Jones.)

On the more strictly architectural aspects of architectural history, Stuart Gray is equally good as a detective. At last the full story of the genesis of Selfridge's store seems to be definitive (page 70): the sketch by Daniel H. Burnham of Chicago, the façade detail by the obscure American globetrotter Francis F. Swales, the working out of it all by our own Frank Atkinson (who then died), the continuation of Atkinson's work by Sir John Burnet, Tait and Lorne, and then the totally unexpected involvement of Burnham's successors Graham, Anderson, Probst and White, the architects of the Wrigley Building and the Merchandise Mart in Chicago (for whom Stuart Gray himself worked). Likewise the Savoy Hotel story is sorted out: sandwiched between the famous names of A. H. Mackmurdo and T. E. Collcutt is

the man who actually did the bulk of the work, Collin Beatson Young (and who was he?). And I certainly never knew that the characteristic red-tiled and green-tiled aesthetic of the London underground stations was the work of Leslie William Green, who wore himself out at the age of thirty-three. Nor did I remember that the finance for them came first from Whitaker Wright, who committed suicide in the Old Bailey, and then from the American Charles Tyson Yerkes (pronounced Yerkeys) who two years later likewise died bankrupt — the chaotic substructure of ebullient Edwardian risk-taking.

But it would be a mistake to see this book as merely an assemblage of fascinating detail. Throughout the mammoth task of proof-reading the twenty introductory sections and then the 348 biographical entries from Edwin Austin Abbey to William Young, I was greatly moved by the stead-fast balance of Stuart Gray's judgement and the authority of his interpretations. Just as the special quality of Pevsner's Buildings of England series comes out ultimately in the set-pieces of analysis such as Durham Cathedral or Wells Cathedral, so the real test of Stuart Gray is in entries such as 'Belcher, John RA', 'Joass, John James', 'Shaw, Richard Norman RA' and 'Stokes, Leonard Aloysius Scott'. As an architect of great experience, he contributes a special undertaking of the actual technique of placing design on paper and the peculiar effects demanded from particular materials. The Joass entry is a striking example, as these extracts show: 'At Mappin & Webb's and at the St James's Street building, the Greek Mount Pentelikos marble, which has the warm whiteness of English alabaster, afforded an opportunity for the precision Joass liked; it provided him with a chance to express lightness in contrast to the heaviness of Waring & Gillow's next door in Oxford Street, and the solidity of the neighbouring Ritz Hotel in Piccadilly. But in the absence of a new idiom in which to formulate the clothing of a steel frame in a logical way, Joass expressed himself here in enigma and paradox ... The coupled columns, taken from Michelangelo's library staircase walls where they *appear* to be doing no work, here appear to be doing *too much*. Above, the bay windows seem to usurp the function of the piers which are already weakened by niches, in their turn forsaken by Bertram Mackennal's *putti*. These, as *The Builder* pointed out at the time, 'appear to have climbed out of their niches to seek shelter under the cornice ... The building exhibits in full measure the tensions it is now fashionable to detect in works of art, sustained even in the chimney stacks which could pass as the work of half a century later ... The square blocks and petrified swags with "necropolitan" connotations — easy to dash off on the drawing board with the T-square and set-square which replaced the compasses and French curves of the previous quarter-century — produced results [in imitators] which at times verged on the ridiculous ...' I wish I could have written that, with its subtle mixture of aesthetic evaluation ('enigma and paradox'), understanding of materials (the precision of Mount Pentelikos marble) and techniques of draughtsmanship (T-square and set-square as against 'compasses and French curves'), leavened with a long-lost Edwardian student joke ('necropolitan').

This book is at its best in the streets of London. It is biased in favour of London as against the provinces, in favour of public buildings as against country houses, in favour of classicism as against Arts and Crafts. (I hasten to add that there is nonetheless in its pages a host of provincial architects, country houses and Voysey-Gimson guildsmen.) But such bias is in my view wholly understandable and indeed desirable. The much less careful bias of the Modern Movement in favour of 'pioneers' has led to excellent early twentieth century classical architecture being ignored (some of it extremely original) — the whole complex of palaces at the Cardiff Civic Centre, for example, or Rickards's Deptford Town Hall. Furthermore, in the heyday of Edwardianism, London *was* the hub of the Empire — perhaps its central pivot being Sir Aston Webb's *rond-point* in front of Buckingham Palace, where Sir Thomas Brock's memorial to Queen Victoria, superbly grand in its outline, however banal its detail might be, still serves as a focal point for popular pageantry and assembly. However absurd the rhetoric of such a memorial — seated statues of Motherhood, Truth and Justice, pedimental groups of Science and Art and Naval and Military Power, water basins flanking figures of Industry, Agriculture, War and Peace, each accompanied by a lion — and however disgusting at a time of widespread poverty and degradation the use of 2,300 tons of best Carrara marble for such a thing might be, the fact is that the Edwardian architects and sculptors knew without inhibition how to set the scene for joyful popular behaviour.

We have only to look at the joylessness of our recent public buildings on the South Bank to see how the spark has gone, however earnest and socially proper our intentions. It is in the celebration of joy that the Edwardians still have much to teach us.

W. E. Riley: this London Fire Brigade Station at Euston, NW1, demonstrates powerfully the influence of the Arts and Crafts movement, and particularly of W. R. Lethaby, on the architects of the young London County Council. This photograph was taken before the effect was shattered by the painting of gutters, heads and down pipes *white*.

INTRODUCTION

In the century of tremendous endeavour which followed the introduction of steam power much of the landscape of Britain had been radically altered and the pattern of many people's lives had been drastically changed. From the vantage point of 1901, what had been achieved and what remained to be done?

While inland navigation canals had been completed before the advent of the railways, all the great railway undertakings begun in the reign of Queen Victoria had reached completion by 1897, the year of her Diamond Jubilee. The Severn Tunnel, over 4¼ miles long, shortening the link between the South Wales coalfields and Bristol, Southampton and London was completed in 1886. That most magnificent engineering feat, the Forth Bridge, with its 50,000 tons of Bessemer steel, had forged a railway link with eastern Scotland in 1890, and the opening of the Ship Canal in 1894 had made Manchester a seaport. The Great Central, the last mainline railway to establish a terminus in London, opened Marylebone Station in 1899.

In Glasgow, Manchester, Liverpool, Leeds and Birmingham civic pride had found expression in proud city halls affording some relief from, and indeed some atonement for, the grim scenery of docks, warehouses, mills and workers' houses which had been imposed upon those towns and seaports. By the turn of the century every town had been provided with a main water supply and a public supply of coal gas. After the great reforms of Chadwick they had their own sewerage installations. While these did credit to the engineers who devised them, subsequent accretions and abandoned apparatus had rendered them unsightly.

In London, the rebuilding of the Palace of Westminster had provided a new home for the two Houses of Parliament; the Foreign Office and India Office had risen in Whitehall; the hall of the Great Exhibition of the Industry of all Nations of 1851, built in Hyde Park, now stood on Sydenham Hill; and the Royal Courts of Justice had moved from Westminster to a new palace in the Strand in 1881. Together with the Albert Hall and the museums and colleges on the site of the exhibitions of 1862, 1883 and 1886 at South Kensington, these were further evidence of the vigour of a generation which gloried in ambitious enterprises on a grand scale.

New seaside resorts with their mammoth hotels had developed out of fishermen's hamlets, and large drapery establishments and department stores on the French and American pattern had arrived.

Beginning as a string of converted houses, these awaited a grand rebuilding.

Under the influence of Edward, Prince of Wales, the fashion for country house entertaining had received a new impetus. To the already large number of country seats had been added buildings which rivalled in elaboration the great mansions of the past, and established families continued to maintain, while new families sought to acquire, the status of landed gentry.

A great number of new churches had been built for the several denominations. After Catholic emancipation in Britain and the suppression of religious houses in France numerous seminaries were established in Britain, while the restoration of ancient cathedrals, abbeys and parish churches was carried out with often ruthless vigour.

Since Robert Owen's New Lanark of 1813, Colonel Ackroyd's Ackroyden of 1846, and Titus Salt's Saltair, near Leeds, of 1850, new communities had been founded at William Lever's Port Sunlight in Cheshire in 1888 and at George Cadbury's Bournville, near Birmingham, in 1895, and were now to appear at Joseph Rowntree's New Earswick, near York, in 1902, at Letchworth Garden City in 1903, founded on the principles expounded by Ebenezer Howard, and at Dame Henrietta Barnett's Hampstead Garden Suburb founded in 1907.

275
11
359
24
25
26
27

Meanwhile, hospitals, Poor Law institutions and

These cottages in Holly Grove, Bournville, Birmingham, exhibit picturesque elements deriving from Shaw and Nesfield.

prisons attempted to cater for the casualties among a population which had experienced upheaval and growth to an alarming degree. But the little which had been done to improve the housing, health and education of the people had been achieved principally by private charity and by the churches. While Lord Shaftesbury's Acts leading to the Housing of the Working Classes Acts of 1885 and 1890 marked a beginning in the task of remedying appalling deficiencies and abuses, much was still required of public authorities as yet ill-constituted for the task until the Local Government Act of 1888 provided for the formation of local authorities.

Following the Forster Education Act of 1870 a substantial amount had been achieved before the end of the century to provide schools. Town halls and county courts, municipal baths and fire stations were next on the list, together with sanatoria, convalescent homes and more hospitals. The Public Libraries Acts of 1892 and 1893 enabled local authorities to administer the public libraries which benefactors like Andrew Carnegie and Passmore Edwards were willing to donate.

The advent of electricity heralded an era of further change. Generating stations had to be built to provide the new source of artificial light, and power for the new electric tramcars and lifts. The London underground railways, which used steam traction when they were first built in 1864, could now use the electric power which also made possible deep tube railways requiring a chain of surface buildings. Similarly, a network of exchange buildings was called for by the public telephone service, introduced in 1879 and at first installed by private companies until (with the exception of the service at Kingston-upon-Hull) it was eventually acquired by the Post Office in 1911.

The face of domestic architecture in London was also changing. As leases on the old ducal estates were renewed, the more favoured areas of London emerged in a new dress, reflecting a variety of revived styles. Sir George Gilbert Scott's advice to diversify the vista of long, straight streets was being followed, and cheerful gabled houses with ingenious plans and terracotta or carved brick fronts replaced the plain stock brick of Harley Street, Sloane Street and Mayfair. As hydraulic, and later, electric passenger lifts, became available, blocks of many-storeyed mansion flats made their appearance. These needed fewer servants to carry the coals and hot water and dispose of the slops and ashes than the tall mansions bordering Hyde Park and flanking Cromwell Road which had grown up in the middle years of the nineteenth century — and which Guy Dawber was to call 'the dreary South Kensington order'. The rebuilt houses and new flats were just right for the Japanese prints and blue china introduced by Whistler and Godwin and the artists of the Aesthetic Movement, for the Morris screens, bead curtains, bullrushes and peacock feathers purveyed by Mortimer Menpes, and for beaten copper fittings by W. A. S. Benson and the silk fans painted by Charles Conder.

Above: the former Magistrates' Court, Tooley Street, London SE1. *Above right:* Branch Library, Lillie Road, Fulham, London SW6 (demolished). *Below right:* Public Baths, Fulham, by Dighton Pearson. These illustrate the diversity of treatment of public buildings at the turn of the century, as recommended by Sir George Gilbert Scott forty years earlier.

A new generation of architects in search of a new architecture in tune with the age carried the social idealism of Morris and the Arts and Crafts Movement into the last decades of the nineteenth century. Their work expressed the Arts and Crafts ideals of simplicity, honest construction and traditional styles used in an original way, bringing a new brilliance to British domestic architecture which earned recognition at home and abroad. But they were seldom successful in the application of these ideas to large-scale buildings.

In garden-making there appeared that art which concealed art, blending the house with the formal garden and the formal garden with the wild garden, encouraged by two great gardeners — William Robinson and Gertrude Jekyll.

In these spheres, at the dawn of the new century, engineers, architects, painters, sculptors, craftsmen and gardeners continued to make their contribution.

At the beginning of the age of iron, the steam hammer and the foundry, there had been hopes that new materials would produce a new architecture, and a prominent role was at first given to exposed iron beams and supports. Although at this stage these structural members were given forms associated with stone and wood, a few thought the time to be near when buildings of pre-fabricated units — of which the Crystal Palace of 1851 was the supreme example — would come into general use. But two factors were to hinder the realisation of this ideal and to separate further the functions of the engineer and the architect. First, the need to protect the iron structural members against fire, and second, the invention of Bessemer steel in 1856 and its formation into rolled sections for girders and columns. Consequently, the iron parts of a building no longer had to be hammered or cast into special shapes for special purposes. But if exposed, the new rolled steel sections — bolted or riveted together with gusset plates — did not go well with brick and stone, and reinforced concrete was still in its infancy. Hopes that a new architecture would soon emerge from the use of these new materials were disappointed. Failing the appearance of a new idiom, how were architects to design?

The 'Battle of the Styles' had ended in a truce. Lord Palmerston had had his way and Sir George Gilbert Scott and Matthew Digby Wyatt were obliged to design the new building for the Foreign and India Offices in an Italian High Renaissance style. Henceforth it was to be Classic for secular, Gothic for ecclesiastical buildings, with a choice of either for colleges. G. E. Street's Royal Courts of Justice built in the 1870s was to be the last great secular building in the mediaeval style.

The next generation had introduced a compromise and students had extended their studies from Gothic to Renaissance, from the cathedrals of France to the merchants' houses of Holland, the cloth halls of Belgium, the *Rathaüser* of Germany

13

Regency House, Warwick Street, W1. Mannerist devices
hinting at the steel-framed structure. Architects: Metcalf
and Greig.

and the *châteaux* of the Loire. The smaller scale
and details of these buildings was to prove more
appropriate to the terracotta now being skilfully
made in England than Alfred Waterhouse's imitation of mediaeval masonry on the Natural History
Museum (1873–81) — the first large-scale use of
terracotta.

Following the architectural histories of James
Ferguson (1808–86), Professor Banister Fletcher's
*History of Architecture on the Comparative
Method* first appeared in 1896, emphasising the
influence of climate, geology, and geography in
the shaping of regional architecture, while Thomas
Harris and William Lethaby urged the development of a style appropriate to new purposes and
new materials.

For the majority, however, the answer continued
to be one of eclecticism, of adapting instead of
adopting, as Sir George Gilbert Scott had
advocated when he wrote in 1858:

> The peculiar characteristic of the present day,
> as compared to former periods, is this: that
> we are acquainted with the history of art.
>   In all periods of genuine art no one thought
> much of the past — each devoted his energies
> wholly to the present. These energies were
> consequently CONCENTRATED and none of
> their thoughts dissipated or diverted from the
> one object before them; and mainly to this
> we owe the perfection which each phase of
> art in its turn attained.
>   The first natural effect of working with
> this vivid PANORAMA of the past placed
> constantly in our view is to induce a capri-
> cious eclecticism — building now in this
> style, now in that — content to pluck the
> flowers of history without cultivating any
> of our own.
>   In a great deal which is just now said
> about eclecticism, there is much confusion
> through the word being used in two differ-
> ent senses. In the sense of expressing the
> liberty of the same architect choosing for
> each building just what style he may fancy
> — now one, and now another — it is mani-
> festly vicious. In the sense, however, of
> borrowing from all we know of art,
> elements wherewith to enrich, amplify
> and render more perfect that style which
> we have laid down as our nucleus,
> eclecticism is a principle of the highest
> value ...

Many adopted that particular form of eclecticism
mistakenly called 'Queen Anne', but closer to
Dutch Baroque, introduced with characteristic
originality by Richard Norman Shaw, whose
imitators were thus eclectics at second hand.

The eclectics were having most of the fun. Their
style, dubbed Free-Classic, was accepted for both
public and private buildings. The chief exponent
was John Belcher, aided by his lieutenants, first

Arthur Beresford Pite and then J. J. Joass. The building most representative of this rich eclectic style was that 'jewel of London City buildings', the Hall of the Incorporated Institute of Chartered Accountants (1889) in Moorgate Place. The placing of the sculpture and the blocked or rusticated columns and architraves here were to become part of the stock-in-trade of the period, heralding the grand manner of Edwardian neo-Baroque.

The first of the mammoth prestige office buildings, Belcher's Electra House (1902, now the City of London College), in Moorgate, has that ebullience verging on vulgarity that was to characterise the age. Here it found expression in the cupolas springing or sprouting from the top hamper of the building — although these were by no means exclusive to Belcher. The competition designs for Berlin Cathedral had shown a dozen variations on this theme. In Britain such turrets, deriving from the western towers of St Paul's Cathedral or the twin cupolas of Greenwich Hospital, had already appeared on William Young's Glasgow Municipal Chambers (1883—9) and they are to be found on his New (now Old) War Office in Whitehall (1900). The most vulgar and indeed senseless example is on the Queen Victoria Memorial in Calcutta (1905—20) by Sir William Emerson, where there are nine; the largest in the British Isles is on the Belfast City Hall (1898—1906) by Sir Brumwell Thomas, the most astonishing on the Lady Ashton Memorial (1906) in Lancaster by Belcher and Joass. The Mersey Docks and Harbour Board buildings by Briggs, Wolstenhome and Thornely on the Liverpool waterfront sport five. Lanchester,

15

Belcher and Joass: the Royal Society of Medicine, Henrietta Street, W1. One of those buildings at the end of the decade showing at once Beaux-Arts and Mannerist tendencies.

Briggs, Wolstenholme and Thornely: the offices of the Mersey Docks and Harbour Board, Pier Head, Liverpool. A quincuncial arrangement of domes.

W. Aubrey Thomas: The Royal Liver Building, Pier Head, Liverpool. An early example by L. G. Mouchel of reinforced concrete construction on the Hennebique principle.

W. Aubrey Thomas: Tower Buildings, Pier Head, Liverpool. Reinforced concrete logically expressed and logically encased in glazed tile.

Stewart and Rickards's winning design for the Wesleyan Central Convocation Hall, Westminster, was intended to have them, and Heathcote Statham, that enthusiastic editor of *The Builder*, suggested them for the National Gallery (RA, 1894) and published drawings of such towers as they had appeared on St Peter's in Rome before they were swept away in 1696 (*Bldr* 9.10.09). Countless banks and insurance companies adopted variations of the Greenwich cupolas as a symbol of their financial integrity.

The Edwardian neo-Baroque style was capable of considerable flexibility, as is demonstrated by the London West End buildings of those Masters of the Narrow Frontage, Treadwell and Martin, who composed many variations on the theme of ground-floor shop and upper-storey flats, terminating in a gable. In their buildings fifteenth-century Gothic, Art Nouveau and Free-Classic sometimes met *on the same façade* and the carving was unmistakably of the period, while those Masters of the Diversified Frontage, Read and Macdonald — pupils of Sir Ernest George — made inimitable London scenery with Stewart's Tea Rooms (1904) at the corner of Old Bond Street and Piccadilly.

Perkins and Pick: the National Westminster (formerly Parr's) Bank, St Martins, Leicester. Banker's Baroque. ▷

171 Strand, WC2. Another steep gable proclaiming the presence of a fine baroque façade on its flank.

◁ Karslake and Mortimer: 54 Pall Mall, SW1. A shy little façade packed with interest, bravely maintaining its place in the street.

△ Seventeenth-century houses in Green Street, Bath. The taller gabled house gives the clue to the narrow frontages of the Edwardian decade.

That most Edwardian of architects, W. D. Caröe, succeeded in achieving both dignity in his church buildings and joviality in his secular work, while the imagination of Leonard Stokes, a pupil of Street and Bodley, took a different path. His 'balanced line', his modernisms and his evolutionary ideas carried him beyond the class of the Free-Classicists, even including that Master of the Public Library, Henry T. Hare, who established his own version of the style in the many public libraries he won in competition. Norman Shaw, who over a long career had shown his genius for employing a variety of styles with equal originality, emerged from retirement to pull out all the stops on the grand fantasia of the Piccadilly Hotel, the first new building of the Regent Street Quadrant.

A great number of architectural competitions held between 1901 and 1910 contributed to the many buildings carried out in Edwardian neo-Baroque since such a system of selection encouraged competitors to observe the taste of the assessors. But competitions were not alone in fostering a style. The training of the architect until the First World War was usually by the system of pupillage supported by attendance at the schools of art and culminating in his joining an architect's office as an assistant. If in London, he attended the Royal Academy Schools, then large enough to have a lower, middle and upper school where Academicians and Associates were 'visitors' while a permanent Master presided as mentor — from 1870 Richard Phené Spiers, succeeded in 1906 by Charles de Gruchy. Prizes and (after 1881) travelling studentships were awarded for designs in accordance with one or other of the prevalent styles and at the same time students were required to study and measure assiduously the architecture of previous centuries at home and abroad, as the Architectural Association Sketch Books testify. The intending architect was considered fortunate if he was articled to an architect who was a member of the Royal Academy.

In addition to the Royal Academy Schools, London had the schools of the Architectural Association and University College, Gower Street, the drawing school and workshops of King's College, Strand, and the South Kensington Schools. In other cities, however, the art schools and technical schools provided only limited instruction in architecture until the foundation of a school of architecture in Liverpool in 1904.

Much of the inspiration, and indeed many of the architects — J. J. Burnet, William Young, James Miller, and J. J. Joass among them — were to come from Glasgow or by way of Glasgow, which had its masterpiece of the narrow frontage in 'The Hatrack', an 1899 building by James Salmon junior at 142 Vincent Street, while the monumental frontage of McGeogh's (1905) by Burnet was prominent in West Campbell Street until it was demolished in 1971. Collaboration between the architect and designer Charles Rennie Mackintosh and the School's English Principal, Francis Newbery, produced the new Glasgow School of Art (1897–1907), revealing to the full the genius of Mackintosh.

C. F. A. Voysey, Edgar Wood, Baillie Scott and C. R. Mackintosh were fortunate to find patrons thankful to be freed from the complicated, over-furnished houses of Victorian times and willing to build in the new simplified manner. The work of these architects showed plain wall surfaces, openings uncluttered by mouldings, and easily cleaned

C. R. Mackintosh: Glasgow School of Art, the Library.

19
250
251
252
253

internal finishes in houses of long, low proportions enhanced by simple furniture, tiles and stencilled patterns. Their pioneer work was illustrated abroad in *Deutsche Kunst und Dekoration* and *Innen-Dekoration* and was the subject of a careful and penetrating study by Hermann Muthesius.

The ranks of the innovators also included A. H. Mackmurdo, Charles Harrison Townsend, George Walton, Barry Parker, C. R. Ashbee and Charles Holden. It was Mackmurdo who first introduced the sinuous line and 'swirl and blob' which became the characteristic of Art Nouveau, and Townsend produced an original style which had affinities with the work of the American architect H. H. Richardson. But perhaps the most lasting example of progressive ideas in architecture, owing much to Philip Webb and Lethaby, was the work of the architects of the new London County Council which succeeded the Metropolitan Board of Works in 1889 and went on to become the most advanced housing authority in Britain.

Adherents to the historical styles had chosen to return to the style evolved by Wren after his stay in Paris in 1665. The chief exponents of this new 'Wrenaissance' style were Sir Mervyn Macartney, who collaborated with John Belcher on *Later Renaissance Architecture in England* and visited every surviving example of the style; Horace Field who produced a study of his own with Michael Bunney; and Sir Reginald Blomfield, also a redoutable historian who first extended the term Renaissance to include seventeenth and eighteenth-century developments of Renaissance art.

Meanwhile the reputation of the Ecole des Beaux-Arts and the *ateliers* run by practising architects attracted those who could afford to go to Paris. Their lure was first felt not in Britain but in the USA, where Paris came to be preferred to Rome as a centre for the study of the arts. The first architectural pilgrim from America was Richard Morris Hunt, who joined the *atelier* of Hector-Martin Lefuel and assisted on the drawings for the Pavillon de la Bibliothèque at the Louvre. The stream of American students who followed included Charles Follen McKim who helped to extend the new Franco-American Classic style when he supported the classicist Daniel Burnham, architect of the Chicago World's Fair, against the Chicago School of Louis Sullivan.

One of the chief exponents of the neo-neo-Classical movement in Paris was Jean-Louis Pascal, among whose pupils were Henri-Paul Nénot (1853–1934), architect of the much admired New Sorbonne, and J. J. Burnet of Glasgow. The new classic style entered Britain by several routes — through the work of Burnet in Glasgow which culminated in London in the Edward VII Galleries of the British Museum; through that of Frank T. Verity, also Paris-trained, who adapted for London the style of the *appartements* of the Champs Elysées; and — also direct from Paris to London at the command of the hôtelier César Ritz — through Charles

Dunbar Smith and Cecil Brewer: The National Museum of Wales, Cardiff. A more sedate style now follows the Baroque effulgence of the City Hall.

Mewès ('Le Patron') and his alumnus Arthur J.
Davis, who imparted to the Ritz Hotel, the Royal
57 Automobile Club and the *Morning Post* building
the style of Ange-Jacques Gabriel and François
Joseph Bélanger.

Another port of entry for the new classicism, this
time via the USA, was Liverpool — then the terminal of the transatlantic liners. Here, encouraged by
Professor C. H. Reilly, it appeared later in the
Cunard Building, Pier Head (1914), by Willink and
Dod with A. J. Davis as consultant. In Cardiff it
was already to be seen at the University Registry
by H. W. Wills who had worked in McKim's office
in New York; at Glamorgan County Hall (1909)
20 by E. Vincent Harris; and finally at the National
Museum of Wales by Smith and Brewer (1910),
all more severe than the ebullient baroque of the
21 Cardiff City Hall and Law Courts of 1899—1902
by Lanchester, Stewart and Rickards. Furthermore, the illustration of the historical styles by
Country Life under Edward Hudson and *The
Architectural Review* under Mervyn Macartney,
and the example of Edwin Lutyens, delayed the
advent of a new architecture for a generation and
influenced even the progressive London County
Council.

In the early years of the twentieth century the
Arts and Crafts Movement was suspected of
tendencies towards Art Nouveau and architects
retreated to the security of the historical styles and
designed houses and flats in which the decorations
and furnishings could be comfortably entrusted
to Maple, to Waring & Gillow or to White Allom.

While it had not directly given rise to a new architecture, the Arts and Crafts Movement had led to
a rational approach to 'the Arts connected with
Building' — the title of a series of lectures delivered
at Carpenters Hall, London, by Robert Schultz
Weir, E. Guy Dawber, F. W. Troup, C. F. A.
Voysey, M. H. Baillie Scott and others (published
by Batsford, 1909). Under Lethaby's guidance,
furniture making, carving, lettering and silversmith-
ing, weaving, printing and bookbinding were taught
by the best exponents of their crafts at the Central
School of Arts and Crafts (now the Central School
of Art and Design), a seminary of the Movement.

In their endeavours to produce a new architecture,
some brother-upholders of the Art Workers' Guild
had turned for inspiration to places free of the
sophistication of Roman building. J. F. Bentley
for his great Westminster Cathedral turned to
Byzantine Ravenna and St Mark's, Venice; Schultz
Weir and Troup to the remains of Byzantium.
Beresford Pite revived the neo-Greek and Mannerist styles while Ernest Gimson and Ernest and
Sidney Barnsley retreated to the architecturally
unexplored Cotswolds where C. R. Ashbee and
his followers were also occupied in the revival
of craftsmanship in emulation of William Morris.

Lanchester, Stewart and Rickards: Rickards's superb
Royal Arms, and supporters, carved by Henry Poole
on the Cardiff Law Courts. The quality of the column
detail proclaims the good architect.

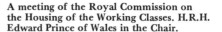
A meeting of the Royal Commission on the Housing of the Working Classes. H.R.H. Edward Prince of Wales in the Chair.

Housing the people in London

The growth and movement of population in the nineteenth century had created two kinds of slum. On the one hand there were the tall, outworn, one-family terrace houses let out into rooms and the purpose-built tenements of the Glasgow Gorbals district; on the other, the massed cottages of the London rookeries and the back-to-back houses of the mill towns.

The extensive London slums, with their appalling squalor and their comparative proximity to Parliament, were the first object of attack. Powers for their removal and rebuilding began with the Common Lodging House Act of 1851. Other Acts followed extending these powers, but none were 22 really adequate until the Royal Commission of 1884 resulted in the 1885 Act granting powers to demolish whole areas.

The new London County Council set about the renewal of the most shocking of all rookeries, 'The 22 Nichol', the Boundary Street area of Shoreditch which Arthur Morrison describes in *The Child of the Jago*. Here 5,179 persons lived on fourteen acres and the annual death rate was 40 per 1,000 when the average for London in 1890 was 18.4 per 1,000.

The area was reconstructed as Arnold Circus, named after a London County Councillor. The first scheme had been for straight parallel streets but a radial plan was finally executed. The new buildings, in a style deriving from Germany, were an improvement on the early Peabody and other Trust buildings. Their cheerful brickwork and painted 'sash' windows restored the domestic character of the area and the great lofts under steeply pitched tiled roofs, reminiscent of those which had been required by law in mediaeval Germany for the storage of the harvest against war and siege, were here used for drying clothes.

The new LCC buildings were the work of a group

of gifted young architects at County Hall under Thomas Blashill, who retired in 1899 to be succeeded by W. E. Riley. They took their inspiration from Philip Webb and W. R. Lethaby, and in the years preceding the First World War produced some of the most advanced housing, fire stations and other public buildings in the country.

23 Arnold Circus, completed in 1900, was followed by Churchway, St Pancras; Garden Row and Roby 312 Street, Clerkenwell; Webber Row, Southwark; 313 Union Buildings, Holborn; Dacre Buildings, London Fields and Bruce Buildings, Caledonian 23 Road, N7, and, best known of all, the Millbank Estate in Pimlico. Three prisons were to have been demolished to provide sites for the LCC new housing, but in the end only half of one prison site

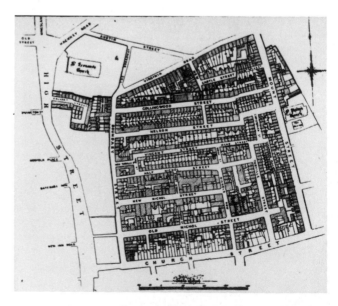
The infamous 'Nichol', the Boundary Street area of Shoreditch, E2, before re-modelling.

(Millbank Prison) was made available, the other half being reserved for the new Army Medical College, by Woodd and Ainslie. The Millbank Estate was completed by 1903. Stirling Buildings and Siddons Buildings were completed in Tavistock Street, WC2, the same year.

Bruce House in Drury Lane, named after the chairman of the Housing Committee, was opened in 1906. The Council's best example of a Lodging House, this was built on the site of the slums around Clare Market, cleared during the construction of Kingsway and Aldwych. How advanced all these designs were over others can be judged from Murphy Buildings, Borough Road, by Joseph, Son and Smithem, built at the same time.

In contrast to the five- and six-storey blocks, the Council developed, at White Hart Lane, Tottenham, and Totterdown Fields, Tooting, estates of two-storeyed cottages of the type then being built at Letchworth Garden City and Hampstead Garden Suburb.

The final instrument to enable councils to purchase property for housing was the Housing, Town Planning etc. Act passed in 1909. The spirit of social idealism in forming the Bill that gave rise to it was

Arnold Circus, Shoreditch, E1, the first London County Council re-housing of the slums.

△ The Millbank Estate, SW1. London County Council housing on the site of Millbank Penitentiary. The steep roofs, originating in Germany for the storage of food, are here introduced for the drying of laundry.

expressed by the Rt Hon John Burns, MP, when he said:

> The object of the Bill is to provide a domestic condition for the people in which their physical health, their morals, their character, and their whole social condition can be improved by what we hope to secure in this Bill. The Bill aims in broad outline at, and hopes to secure, the home healthy, the house beautiful, the city dignified and the suburb salubrious. It seeks and hopes to secure more houses, better houses, prettier streets, so that the character of a great people in towns and cities and in villages can be still further improved and strengthened by the conditions under which they live. It hopes to get rid of the regulation roads that are so regular ... to diminish what have been called 'bye-law' streets with little law and much monotony ...

312

Letchworth: the first garden city

The foundation of Letchworth is closely linked with the life and ideas of Sir Ebenezer Howard. Born in 1850, the son of a baker in the City of London, Ebenezer Howard started his career as a copy clerk in a stockbroker's office at the age of fifteen. He used to practise his shorthand by taking down the sermons of Dr Parker, a noted preacher of the day, at the Poultry Congregational Chapel.

Howard worked in City offices at a time when the smoke-laden air was a cause of concern and those who could escape did so, at least temporarily. In 1871 Howard went to Iowa and then to Nebraska where he started farming. Preferring city life, he soon gave up farming to join a shorthand-writing office in Chicago, finding time to invent a shorthand typewriter. When he returned to London in 1876 Howard joined a firm of official parliamentary reporters.

It was during this period that Howard began to develop an interest in the question of public ownership of land and the building of ideal communities. From his reading of Tom Paine's *Age of Reason* he moved on to the ideas expounded by George

Bellamy in *Looking Backward* and by Henry George in a talk he gave in London on land reform. He had also met Thomas Davidson, the Scottish-born American who attempted to form a co-operative settlement near London. By 1898 Howard's own ideas had taken shape and he brought out his *To-morrow, a Peaceful Path to Real Reform* (published by Swann, Sonnenschein), followed by a revised version the same year, *Garden Cities of To-morrow*.

The Times viewed Howard's ideas with some favour, observing that 'the only difficulty is to create such a city, but that is a small matter to Utopians'. The *Fabian News* (December 1898), however, commented: 'We have got to make the best of our existing cities, and proposals for building new ones are about as useful as would be arrangements for protection against visits from Mr Wells's Martians'. This and other remarks showed that the Fabians had mistaken Howard's by now well-known diagram for a working plan.

In 1899 the Garden City Association was formed to promote Howard's ideas, a site was selected at Letchworth, in Hertfordshire, between Hitchin and Baldock, and the First Garden City Limited was formed in 1903, just five years after the appearance of Howard's book. The first directors included the Quaker cocoa refiners, Joseph Rowntree of York and Edward Cadbury of Bournville, W. H. Lever (later Lord Leverhulme), founder of the model village of Port Sunlight near his soap and vegetable oils factory in Cheshire, and T. H. W. Idris, the mineral water manufacturer. Thomas Adams from Midlothian was appointed secretary and manager.

The principles on which Letchworth is based are well known. In simple terms the aim was to establish a community with the right proportion of agricultural land, factory and residential areas, public and educational buildings and parks, all held in trust for the lessees who would share in the appreciation of land values. Howard was fortunate in finding the right architects to put his ideas into practice. Richard Barry Parker and his brother-in-law and partner Raymond Unwin had already begun to build a model village for Joseph Rowntree at New Earswick, near the family's chocolate factory at York. Plans for Letchworth were also invited from Halsey Ricardo and W. R. Lethaby, and from Geoffry Lucas and Sydney Cranfield, but the Parker and Unwin plan was preferred and was carried out almost as originally planned.

The first and principal problem was to attract manufacturers to the factory sites and householders to the houses. To this end Thomas Adams and St Loe Strachey, editor of the *Spectator* and owner of the *Country Gentleman* and *Land and Water*,

359

The White Cottage, Croft Lane, Letchworth Garden City, Hertfordshire.

Nos. 3 to 19, Meadow Way Green, Letchworth Garden City, Hertfordshire.

24
25
organised a Cheap Cottages Exhibition in 1905; 120 cottages were built, the Great Northern Railway rushed up a temporary station and excursion tickets were issued. The impression that Letchworth was for rural cottages only was dispelled by an Urban Cottages Exhibition held in 1907.

Examples from both exhibitions prove an interesting record of experimental materials and methods of the period and of the work of architects who later made their reputations.

The factory sites were slow in being taken up and W. H. Gaunt, who had been concerned with the development of Trafford Park Industrial Estate, Manchester, was appointed manager of this department. Although a genial man, Gaunt did not conceal his dislike of the prettiness of roofs covered in hand-made tiles and his own preference for Welsh slates. Discouraged by Gaunt's attitude, Thomas Adams left to found what was to become the world-renowned firm of town planners, Adams, Thompson and Fry.

After Unwin left in 1907 to plan the Hampstead Garden Suburb, Barry Parker remained at 296 Norton Way South to plan the residential areas of Letchworth, assisted by Cecil Hignett, Robert Bennett and Wilson Bidwell, R. B. Hall, C. H. James, Felix Lander, John Tickle and Samuel Pointon Taylor (later Chief Architect to HM Office of Works).

Part of Barry Parker's office, later his home, is now a public museum of architectural work and town planning — one of the very few architects' homes to become a museum of the architect's work.

The Hampstead Garden Suburb

Although carefully planned residential estates built on the periphery of cities and towns were by no means new, the Hampstead Garden Suburb was unique in setting out to provide for people with a wide range of occupations and incomes.

26
27

The idea originated with Henrietta Octavia Barnett (*née* Rowland; 1851–1936), the daughter of an importer of East Indian produce whose name is remembered because of his Rowland's Macassar Oil. A disciple of the reformer Octavia Hill, Henrietta Rowland married the Rev. Samuel Barnett, vicar of St Jude's, Whitechapel, who founded Toynbee Hall, the first University Slum Settlement, and the East London Art Gallery, Whitechapel, E10.

The Barnetts spent their weekends at Heath End House, Hampstead Heath, which they re-named St Jude's Cottage. From their windows they could see stretching away to the north and west the still untouched fields of Middlesex, many of which provided fodder for London's large population of horses.

As honorary secretary to the Hampstead Heath Extension Council Mrs Barnett was instrumental

in the acquisition of 80 acres of the Wylde's Estate as an extension to the Heath. She was well aware of the threat to the Heath from the advance of London housing, but the first news of a still worse encroachment is said to have reached her in the unlikely circumstances of a sea trip to Russia. An American fellow-passenger (very probably Charles Tyson Yerkes) told her that the Charing Cross to Hampstead Tube Railway was to be extended to Golders Green, with an intermediate station near the Bull and Bush public house in the heart of Hampstead Heath.

Mrs Barnett set about writing 12,000 letters to influential people and organisations calling attention to the disastrous consequences if the Heath extension with its trees, hedgerows and streams were to be hopelessly defaced because of what she dramatically called 'the landlord's greed and the people's helplessness'. At the same time she outlined her alternative proposals. The outcome of her persistence was the foundation of the Hampstead Garden Suburb Trust and the purchase of 243 acres from Eton College in 1907. Mrs Barnett had consulted Raymond Unwin, whose books and pamphlets she had read, and Unwin moved from

Sir Edwin L. Lutyens, RA: Central Square, Hampstead Garden Suburb, NW11, showing the Free Church, the Manse, the Institute and the houses of North Square.

Letchworth to Wylde's Farm, North End, Hampstead, where he set up house and office and planned the new Garden Suburb, incorporating Mrs Barnett's carefully worked out ideas.

26
27
282

These included the provision of groups of cottages, a village green, a clubhouse on the green, an institute, two churches, one Anglican, the other non-denominational, and tea-houses, shops, homes for the elderly, playgrounds, allotment gardens and sites for schools. There were also to be larger houses, some of manor-house dimensions, since it was Mrs Barnett's intention that the various social classes should benefit from proximity, as in the traditional English village with its squire, parson, doctor, lawyer, banker, brewer, miller and tenants. But public houses were to be excluded — no doubt Mrs Barnett's experience of the squalor and misery associated with drink in her husband's parish work in Whitechapel had a part in this decision.

Unwin's first plan followed the idea of the naturally grown village and this was retained for the

Sir Edwin L. Lutyens, RA: houses in North Square, Hampstead Garden Suburb, NW11. It was intended that this arrangement with the stone arch should occupy each of the four corners of the Square.

northern end of the site. At an early stage, however, Edwin Lutyens, already known for his country houses, was appointed consultant and asked to plan the central area with its institute and churches. Here Lutyens changed Unwin's informal plan to a formal one. While Parker and Unwin's cottages were based on the Hertfordshire and Essex cottage of the sixteenth century, its thatched roof replaced by tiles and its iron casements replaced by wood, Lutyens, with hipped roofs, red and silver-grey bricks and white windows and cornices, recalled the doctors' and bankers' houses of the reign of William and Mary and Queen Anne. His clever arrangement of such houses in North Square and on the slope of Erskine Hill, combined with his Institute and two churches, amazed his contemporaries.

26
242
243

Unwin and his team at Wylde's Farm were in their own way no less skilful. Unwin had played an important part in the preparation of a special Act of Parliament passed in 1906 which offered an escape from the rigorous bye-laws instituted, with good reason, in the nineteenth century to establish standards of sanitation and safety. This enabled him to vary the building line and plan economical closes and culs-de-sac. He also obtained consent for the abolition of the ugly party-wall which featured as a fire precaution above the roofs of terrace houses of the period. Taking full advantage of the new Act, Unwin achieved variety by setting some houses on the frontage line and others far behind it, and by placing houses so that they enjoyed views at the back as well as at the front. At the same time Unwin exercised control both over his team of assistants and over the independent architects working with him, so that in just seven years – the seven good years of the Hampstead Garden Suburb – the whole estate had become a single work of art.

Among those working in Unwin's office was the talented young Charles Paget Wade, who illustrated much of the work, and A. J. Penty who had recently left his father's practice in York. Working independently but in close association with Unwin were Michael Bunney and C. C. Makins, C. M. Crickmer, Geoffry Lucas, W. H. Ward, Herbert A. Welch, and G. L. Sutcliffe, also from his father's office in Yorkshire, who was architect to the Co-Partnership Tenants, one of the development companies. Lessees of single plots or builders building to sell were offered a list of recommended architects.

27
283

128
157
381
342

Facing the Heath Extension is a feature unique in any modern suburb — the Great Wall with its gazebos, fitted with sliding 'Yorkshire' windows looking out over the Heath where ancient hedgerows still divide fields now used for family recreation and club games. Unique too are the arcaded terraces of shops and flats on the Finchley Road at Temple Fortune, NW11, known as Temple Fortune House and Arcade House, and reminiscent of the architecture of German towns. These are almost certainly by Penty. Before the mean neo-

27

283

Barry Parker and Sir Raymond Unwin with A. J. Penty and Charles Wade: the Great Wall, Hampstead Garden Suburb, NW11.

Georgian building was inserted at this point white gates indicated this important entrance to the Suburb.

27 The northern part of the estate where the cottages lie was sadly deprived of its focal point, the Clubhouse in Willifield Green, when it was destroyed by an air-borne mine in 1940. This was a splendid design by Charles Wade who also did the surrounding cottages (those facing the Clubhouse site have been imperfectly restored). 'The Orchard' is also rebuilt in a different form.

The planning and planting of the first 243 acres have never been equalled on a suburban estate. As the American town planner Lewis Mumford remarked during his 1961 visit, very little of the lesson of the Garden Suburb was learnt by the designers of the new towns of the 1950s. This is particularly evident in the low density achieved in comparison with Hampstead.

Barry Parker and Sir Raymond Unwin, with A. J. Penty and Charles Wade: the Club House, Hampstead Garden Suburb, NW11. (Destroyed.)

Paul Hoffmann: Mansion flats and shops, Gloucester Road, SW7.

Mansion Flats & Town Houses in London

Tall buildings in multiple occupation were no new thing in the Old Town of Edinburgh where land was scarce, and the idea had extended to Glasgow. In London, however, the chambers for lawyers in the Inns of Court and the rooms or chambers over shops, that were a feature of Regent Street when it was new, provided the only 'flatted' living accommodation until the middle of the nineteenth century. In other cities and towns no blocks of flats for people of ample means were built until after the Second World War.

At first considered somewhat Parisian and therefore, like cigarettes, slightly naughty and demi-mondaine, the first apartment houses were regarded with suspicion by respectable families in both London and New York. London's first blocks of 'mansion flats', as they were called, were built along the new Victoria Street from 1868. Until the advent of electricity made electrically-powered passenger lifts a practical reality, they were confined to the streets served by the mains of the London Hydraulic Power Company.

An early example of the tall building was Queen Anne's Mansions in Queen Anne's Gate, demolished in 1971. These were put up in 1874 without the benefit of architect by the speculator Henry Alers Hankey. Their fourteen storeys dwarfed the Greek Revival Guards Chapel in Wellington Barracks (tragically destroyed in the Second World War and now rebuilt) and presented such a grim silhouette to Buckingham Palace that the protests of Queen Victoria and the public hastened the London Building Act of 1874, restricting future buildings in London to a height of eighty feet with two additional storeys in a roof pitched no steeper than seventy-five degrees.

Many blocks along Victoria Street rivalled Queen Anne's Mansions in grimness. Although attention began to be paid to the planning and appearance of the new flats, they continued to rise, restricted only by the Building Act and the endeavours of adjoining owners to preserve a reasonable amount of daylight for themselves. In the piecemeal redevelopment that went on, the blank walls of mansion flats rising sheer from the property line became a familiar sight even in the best quarters of London. Norman Shaw's Albert Hall Mansions in Kensington Gore, for instance, the grandest and best-planned of the new luxury flats with a servants' wing in each, dwarfed the tall, moulded-brick chimney stacks and country-house-style roofs of Lowther Lodge, designed by Shaw only six years earlier.

28

Archer and Green were next to break the sober outline of Italianate mansions bordering Hyde Park with their château-style Hyde Park Court, completed in 1890 and converted into an hotel in 1900. They were also the architects of Whitehall Court, facing Victoria Embankment Gardens — a great picturesque range of gabled François Premier mansion flats which has enlivened the scenery of this part of the Thames for a century. Put up by Jabez Balfour of the Liberator Company, Whitehall Court was subsequently involved in the company's notorious financial crash.

The tradition of Archer and Green was continued by two of their assistants, Edward Boehmer and his brother-in-law Percy Gibbs; they designed Harley House, Marylebone Road, the great terrace of mansion flats in early French Renaissance style, built in the brown limestone Archer and Green had used at Cambridge Terrace, Regent's Park. Boehmer & Gibbs's blocks in Maida Vale (formerly Edgware Road) brought an almost Parisian atmosphere to this too-brief boulevard.

If the view from these serried and serrated ranks of flats here and in Kensington, with bay-windows angled to catch the daylight, was more often than not the view of another range of bay-windows on the opposite side of the street, the scenery within offered some relief with its medley of mantels, over-mantels, what-nots and knick-knacks, Japanese screens and silk fans of the Aesthetic period. By 1901, however, these over-furnished interiors by W. A. S. Benson or Mortimer Menpes were giving way to interiors of the Wren and early Georgian periods as reaction against the Arts and Crafts and Art Nouveau drove designers to seek security in period styles of decoration and furniture. Coleherne Court, in Redcliffe Gardens, and Old Brompton Road (1901–3), by Walter Cave was already in later English Renaissance with polite, carved swags on shallow bay-windows.

In St James's the design of bachelor chambers provided an opportunity for a more intimate and even exotic atmosphere as in Reginald Morphew's Marlborough Chambers (now Estate House), Bury Street, and 71–2 Jermyn Street.

Other Edwardian architects were to leave their mark on the changing skyline of London. Delissa Joseph, a redoubtable partisan of tall buildings, planned a whole street — FitzGeorge and Fitz-James Avenue — in West Kensington, while Edward Warren did a splendid if more sober block in St John's Wood High Street, NW1. Arnold Mitchell's houses and flats (part war-damaged) in Basil Street, SW3, intended to have glazed terracotta dressings but executed in brown limestone, were the best of their kind in a street of interesting buildings.

If the new century saw the return of simplicity, it also saw a disregard of scale, and what had been done by F. S. Chesterton and J. D. Coleridge to achieve a more intimate scale in Hornton Street,

Kensington, was disregarded when the same architects came to design Hornton Court in Kensington High Street. Frank Verity, on the other hand, maintained a just sense of scale and introduced the straight lines of the new classicism derived from his Paris training in so individual a way at Cleveland Row (St James's), Berkeley Square, Bayswater Road and, later, Marble Arch, that his buildings are immediately recognisable where not closely copied by others.

Mansion flats were just one aspect of the changing face of London in the late nineteenth and early twentieth centuries. In his *Remarks on Secular and Domestic Architecture* (1858), Sir Gilbert Scott had written:

> The fact that in most of our streets such as Cheapside, the Strand, Oxford Street, etc. each man has built his house as he liked and that the whole is cut into vertical strips, is the one thing which redeems them from that abject insipidity which we see in

G. Thrale Jell: Mansion flats and shops in Bury Street, SW1.

A London Fire Brigade Station and a terrace of flats in Basil Street, SW3. In the distance are flats by Arnold Mitchell (*q.v.*).

Below: **A doorway in the Basil Street Flats.**

Gower Street or Harley Street; but if every one of these vertical divisions had a beautiful design of its own, differing in height, in outline, and in treatment, and terminating in a good skyline, our streets would at once become as picturesque and pleasing as those of the great mediaeval cities ...

Made after a hundred years of sober classicism controlled by the great landlords through their surveyor-architects, Scott's statement reflected the contemporary mood. Here, then, was the licence to introduce into the sedate ranges of stock-brick house fronts on the ducal estates of Mayfair, Marylebone, Kensington and Chelsea, all the variety which the architects could contrive. Owned by the Portland, Grosvenor and Cadogan families since the time of Charles II, these estates were laid out according to the plans of their architects and, although built by individual speculators, the houses followed a prescribed pattern which Sir John Summerson describes in his *Georgian London*. When leases fell in on these estates and houses had to be returned to the ground landlord in good order before a new lease was granted, the opportunity to rebuild the front, or to rebuild entirely, was eagerly seized. On the Cadogan Estate the face of the area changed to terracotta and carved red brick when Cadogan Square and Pont Street were developed, and the architects prominent in the field were Ernest George and Harold Peto, building in the style irreverently dubbed 'Fire Station Holbein' or 'Pont Street Dutch'. That section of the Grosvenor Estate lying between New Bond Street and Park Lane underwent its first metamorphosis between 1885 and 1899. From then until 1910 individual works were entrusted to several

32 architects including M. C. Hulbert, A. H. Kersey,
31 Balfour and Turner, W. D. Caröe, Fairfax Wade, R. G. Hammond, and Read and Macdonald. After 1910 the architects most employed on the Mayfair portion of the Grosvenor Estate were Edmund Wimperis and his partners W. Begg Simpson and Flockhart's son-in-law L. Rome Guthrie, Wimperis having succeeded Eustace Balfour as architect to the Estate in 1910 after doing work on the Estate before that date.

A town house in Harley Street, W1. Before renewal of a lease, houses were either re-faced or entirely rebuilt.

If the Cadogan and Grosvenor Estates were not enough opportunity for the considerable skills in town house planning and façade building shown by London architects, the Portland (Howard de Walden) Estate provided further ground. Here the architects included W. H. White, Edward Boehmer, R. G. Hammond, Claude Ferrier, Sir Banister Fletcher, J. J. Joass and A. Beresford Pite.

119 Boehmer and Gibbs's façade on 80 Portland Place — based on the Louis XV style and carried out in stone — is of a type which appeared simultaneously in Paris, London and New York when cultural ties between the three cities were at their strongest.

In Bayswater, at 47 Palace Court, Leonard Stokes succeeded in combining the qualities found in Voysey's 14 and 16 Hans Road, Norman Shaw's 180 Queen's Gate (demolished) and the work of George and Peto, with a modernity that places it in advance of the period.

◁ Balfour and Turner: houses on the Grosvenor Estate in Upper Grosvenor Street, Mayfair, W1. The carving is by Laurence Turner.

31

A. H. Kersey: town houses in Park Street, Mayfair, W1.
The Flemish Renaissance style suited equally well town
mansions or mansion flats.

Country Houses

In the first half of the nineteenth century, A. W. N. Pugin and his contemporaries with their new mediaevalism had fanatically opposed the Roman, Graeco-Roman and neo-Greek styles fashionable in the early nineteen-hundreds. In their place they established a nostalgia for Gothic, particularly of the twelfth and thirteenth centuries. Indeed, some claimed that the Gothic style had never died. Others argued the same for the Renaissance style — introduced by Inigo Jones and carried on by Wren and his successors after the Restoration — for it was used by John Shaw junior in his Royal Naval School (now Goldsmith's College), Deptford, of 1843 and Wellington College, Berkshire, of 1856—9.

It was George Devey (1820—86), who had studied painting under John Sell Cotman, who did much to free domestic architecture from 'the smell of the lamp' and the discipline of the drawing board. Devey's cottages for Lord de l'Isle and additions to Penshurst Place, Kent, bear out the words of the architect and historian H. S. Goodhart-Rendel who said of him that 'he never wished either to sophisticate or to dramatise the forms that he re-used so lovingly'.

When Philip Webb, Norman Shaw and Eden Nesfield left the office of the neo-Gothic architect G. E. Street, each was to develop a style based on the stone, timbered and plastered houses of the sixteenth and seventeenth centuries. Webb chose to design from first principles, while Shaw and Nesfield adopted the gabled, half-timbered or tile-hung farmhouses of the Kent and Sussex Weald. But these old manor houses and farm houses which were their inspiration had received many additions. Beginning as timber-framed, wattle-and-daub panelled and thatched buildings, they had probably had their wattle-and-daub replaced by brick (plain or herring-bone patterned), or protected by tile-hanging, nor had their chimney stacks or leaded iron casements always been part of the original structure. Transformed and enlarged, they came to represent the vernacular style of those counties and became the basis of what was to be called the Vernacular Revival.

Although the 'Battle of the Styles' had been resolved and henceforward secular buildings were of any style but Gothic, it still remained to make a choice between the formal and the informal styles. In this Norman Shaw played a decisive part, choosing the formal style at 170 Queen's Gate, London, and at Bryanston House, Dorset, as well as in his additions to Chesters, Northumberland (all done between 1888 and 1891) and never returning to the informal.

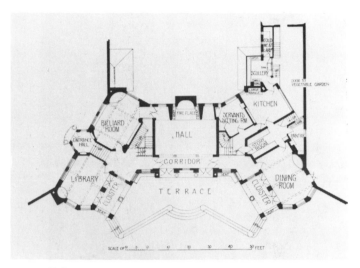

E. Schroder Prior: Home Place, Holt, Norfolk. *Above:* The Plan. *Below:* A wing. Materials were dug from the site.

W. H. Brierley: The Close, Brompton, Yorkshire.

Some, like Philip Webb, strove to establish an individual style based on first principles. Chief among them were the Arts and Crafts architects, Voysey, Edgar Wood, Baillie Scott, Prior, Lethaby, Ashbee and Mackmurdo, and James MacLaren and Charles Rennie Mackintosh in Scotland. Voysey was the most successful and his style of house with its white walls, large roof, wide eaves, tapered buttresses and chimney stacks and simple, open interiors, came to be known simply as 'Voysey'. Baillie Scott followed close with a cosier version of Voysey's long, low lines, with roofs derived from the re-tiled thatch cottage roof, while Mackintosh in his Scottish houses brought a new simplicity, building in stone, plaster and slate the lines found in the drawings of Cotman. Of his interiors Muthesius observed, 'his rooms are of a beauty too pure almost to live in'. George Walton and Mackmurdo built with an originality tending towards amateurism.

In their interiors these architects showed much invention, more if they were able to persuade their clients to let them design the furniture as well. Voysey was the most successful in this also until his style, debased by imitation, became the stock-in-trade of the house furnisher of the early twentieth century. Barry Parker, who had been apprenticed to an architect specialising in built-in fitments, designed interiors with the fixed furniture which is the fashion today and exhibited at the Royal Academy in 1896 a drawing of 'A room designed to fulfil in one all the functions of the ordinary Hall, Dining and Drawing Room'.

Through the pages of Charles Holme's *Studio* magazine, read as eagerly in Germany as *Deutsche Kunst und Dekoration* and *Innen-Dekoration*, the English style was propagated abroad. Mackintosh had a greater influence in Vienna, Munich and Turin than in Britain. He designed interiors and furniture so original that his style (called

'Mackintoshismus' in Germany) made a strong impact on the Vienna Secessionists whose ranks he was invited to join.

The essence of the new style of interiors was simplicity, for even Norman Shaw's endeavours to achieve that rare quality had been frustrated by his clients, who insisted on filling their galleried halls with tables and sofas, family portraits, trophies of the chase from home and abroad, and the screens found necessary to ward off the draughts from the tall windows towards the vast fireplaces. In the new interiors, if the architect succeeded in his ideas, the furniture and the fittings for the new electric lights would probably have been designed by Bainbridge-Reynolds, Heywood Sumner, or W. A. S. Benson, while the decorations were in early do-it-yourself style — light-coloured distemper, wood stains and stencilled patterns.

In direct line of succession to Norman Shaw came Edwin Lutyens. Well-schooled by the great gardener Gertrude Jekyll in West Surrey, Lutyens reintroduced into country buildings local stone, brick, tile and timber of a quality and texture which neither Shaw nor Webb had attained. And, with the simplicity which was Voysey's contribution, he adopted either an informal or a formal style as the site, the client and his own judgement indicated. Although his contemporaries sought to emulate him, few were to equal and none were to

H. E. Clifford: 37 Dalziel Drive, Glasgow.

Sir Edwin L. Lutyens, RA: Marsh Court, Stockbridge, Hampshire. Built of clunch.

surpass his superb skill. Lutyen's houses and Jekyll's gardens were illustrated in Edward Hudson's *Country Life* weekly and in Lawrence Weaver's *Houses and Gardens by E. L. Lutyens*, seldom in the architectural magazines, and thus were soon well known among the monied and landed classes.

Soon were the pioneer works of Mackintosh, Voysey and others almost forgotten. Voysey resorted to designing small objects. Mackintosh, disappointed, retired to Chelsea and Walberswick, Suffolk, to paint landscapes and draw flowers. Edgar Wood retired to Italy to paint and entertain fellow artists. A. J. Penty and Mackmurdo wrote on socio-economic subjects, Baillie Scott resorted to an even cosier style of thatch and half-timber, to 'stockbrokers' Tudor' and 'bankers' Georgian'. Ashbee, after rescuing the antiquities and improving the parks of Jerusalem, retired to Godden Green, Seale, Kent, where he altered his father-in-law's house to 'Georgian' and studied *Weltpolitik*. Barry Parker remained at Letchworth occupied on many housing schemes including the great Manchester suburb of Wythenshawe, and George Walton returned to his textile designs. By the time George V was on the throne most new houses designed by architects were, if not neo-Tudor, firmly neo-Georgian.

But the field was not left entirely to Lutyens.

272 Ernest Newton, who had been Norman Shaw's chief assistant, designed a large number of country houses in the home counties. Reginald Blomfield, faithful to Norman Shaw's last phase, designed in the English Palladian manner with French overtones, while Leonard Stokes designed strong and original four-square houses. Thomas
147 Collcutt continued his pleasant, easy-going style and Morley Horder successfully maintained the
34 vernacular tradition. W. H. Brierley around York,
123 the Batemans, W. H. Bidlake and Crouch and Butler around Birmingham, Arnold Mitchell and Mervyn Macartney in the home counties, all built comfortably, Belcher and Macartney's *Lesser Houses of the Renaissance in England* at their
162 elbow. Meanwhile Guy Dawber continued to design stone manor houses in the Cotswold tradition. Most of these architects were brother-upholders of the Art Workers' Guild. In Scotland, a relief from the extravagant houses and castles of wealthy
236 ship-owners was afforded by Robert Lorimer whose work had the clarity and simplicity of the best of Lutyens and of his master James MacLaren.

By a fortunate chance, thanks to the reputation it had earned abroad, domestic architecture in Britain between 1880 and 1904 had been well recorded and the work of architects who carried on into the reign of Edward VII described in detail. For this we have to thank Hermann Muthesius, attaché to the Imperial Prussian Board of Trade, who was sent to England between 1896 and 1904 specifically to study and report on recent architecture and

Sir Edwin L. Lutyens, RA, and Gertrude Jekyll: Hestercombe, Somerset. A garden gate.

Gardens

The culmination of the art of garden design and garden planting in Britain occurred between 1900 and 1910, and country houses in the reign of Edward VII owed much of their beauty and atmosphere to the making and maintaining of their gardens.

To the geometrical parterres and allées of the seventeenth century, the landscaping of the latter half of the eighteenth century and the rotation of bedding plants of the nineteenth century, were now added the planned herbaceous border and the further importation of new plants, shrubs and trees from far afield, already greatly assisted by Kingdon-Ward's simple discovery that plants could be safely transported if sealed in with their own moisture. By 1901 a further innovation, due largely to William Robinson (1838—1935), had widened the scope of garden-making — the introduction of the wild garden, nature's garden unadorned.

At the age of twenty-one Robinson had been foreman gardener on the estate of the Rev. Sir Hunt

the arts connected with building. His report, *Englische Baukunst der Gegenwart,* in which he described urban building and town houses, appeared in 1900. In a second work, *Das Englische Haus* (1904—5), he deals with country houses, their construction and equipment.

After his return to Berlin, Muthesius designed a house in the garden suburb of Zehlendorf in the style of Voysey for his chief von Seefeld and a house at Nicolasee in the style of Prior for Freudenberg. This house came in for some violent criticism, and after 1933 the Nazis kept his books in the 'poison cupboard' of the Berlin Technical High School. Muthesius wrote:

> In England, the good things in architecture are more hidden than elsewhere, chiefly by reason of the fact that urban life has been developed in a more haphazard way than on the Continent and, moreover, a good part of the best modern English architecture, the private dwelling house, lies scattered over the countryside.

But the inspiration which had descended on the disciples of William Morris now left their successors and drifted away to Europe where it visited the founders of the *Werkbund* in Germany and the *Werkstätte* in Austria. Muthesius's writings show how much continental exponents owed to English and Scottish pioneers.

Johnson-Walsh, Bart, of Ballykilcannan, Stradbally,
Ireland. A disagreement provoked him suddenly to
draw the fires and open the windows of his
employer's greenhouses and make for London
where he became head of the herbaceous section
of the Royal Botanical Gardens, Regent's Park
(now Queen Mary's Garden), and helped the
curator Robert Marnock on his collection of wild-
flowers from the London countryside. Robinson
was the author of numerous works on gardens, the
most famous of which was *The English Garden*
(1883). He also started *Gardening Illustrated* and
The Garden which he later installed in the fine
building in Kingsway designed for him by Edwin
Lutyens. Robinson bought Gravetye Manor,
Sussex, in 1884 and put his theories into practice
in the grounds, which he left to the nation. His
ideas were opposed in the contemporary press by
Reginald Blomfield, champion of the formal garden of the eighteenth century and author of a
book on the subject.

After Robinson, the other great influence on the
evolution of the English garden was Gertrude
Jekyll. Her meeting with Edwin Lutyens, from the
neighbouring village of Thursley in West Surrey,
began a collaboration between gardener and architect which resulted in a unique combination of the
best in architecture and gardening. Miss Jekyll's
methods, which owed much to Robinson, were in
contrast to those of the professional garden architects like the highly successful Thomas Mawson
who relied largely on a formal setting of walls,
clipped hedges and water tanks as represented by
the seductive drawings of C. E. Mallows. Her ideas
became known through the pages of *Country Life*
and her border of perennials for which she prepared her own special diagrams established this as an
important feature of the English garden.

The architect Harold Peto, after a period spent
studying and building gardens in Italy, returned to
England to make his own individual contribution
to the history of the English garden. His work can
be seen at Buscot Park, Farringdon, Berkshire, and
at his own home, Iford Manor, Bradford-on-Avon,
Wiltshire. His finest garden is at Garinish Island,
Bantry Bay, Eire.

Harry Inigo Triggs (q.v.) was another architect
whose search after better health led him from
architecture to gardening. He wrote several books
on garden design.

◁ Charles Francis Annesley Voysey: The Pastures, North
Luffenham, Rutland. A gateway.

Churches

By 1900, in the eighty years that had passed since
its inception, the Gothic Revival had undergone
three distinct phases. The 'Waterloo' church of St
Luke, Chelsea (1820—4), by James Savage (1779
—1852), is held to be the first example of the
Gothic Revival in which mediaeval construction
was seriously attempted. Here the Bath stone
ashlar is regular and smooth, reflecting the style of
line engraving then used to illustrate the mediaeval
and the Greek styles alike.

In the second phase, exhorted by Ruskin in
England and Viollet-le-Duc in France, architects
and the new Ecclesiologists put their faith in the
thirteenth-century style of Gothic which emphasised the construction. The thinness of early neo-
Gothic now gave way to the heavy stonework and
timberwork, coarse mouldings and grotesque carvings of High Victorian Gothic. Contemporary interest in illuminated manuscripts and especially in the
mediaeval sketches of Villars d'Honnecourt surviving in the Louvre influenced the style of draughtsmanship which was in turn reflected in the buildings of this period.

Frederick Wheeler: The Chapel, Mount Vernon Hospital, Northwood, Middlesex. Art Nouveau, rarely found in churches. *Below:* The west door.

It was George Frederick Bodley (1827—1907) who did most to bring neo-Gothic into its third phase and to give church architecture a new meaning. The church of the Holy Angels, Hoar Cross, near Burton-on-Trent, Staffordshire, built by the Meynell Ingram family in 1876, displays the full panoply of Bodley's ideas. He built in a style introduced after the Black Death in 1348 which the early Ecclesiologists considered inferior; classified as Late Decorated and Early Perpendicular by the first historians of Gothic, its virtue was the harmony achieved between masonry, fittings and glass.

By 1901, apart from Bodley and J. F. Bentley, all the great figures of the Gothic Revival were dead. A new generation of architects were designing churches; with some exceptions, they were carrying on the traditions their masters had revived.

Temple Moore was continuing the work of George Gilbert Scott junior, a more sympathetic artist than his famous father. Sir Charles Nicholson and Henry Wilson carried on the work of J. D. Sedding. Leonard Stokes, architect of numerous Catholic churches and seminaries, was the former pupil of G. E. Street, as was G. H. Fellowes Prynne. W. D. Caröe, with variations of his own, was continuing the traditions of J. L. Pearson's office, while Pearson's son Frank was completing his father's Truro Cathedral. Walter Tapper from Bodley's office, W. H. Bidlake in Birmingham, Burke Downing, Charles Spooner — a former pupil of

339

298

345

Basil Champneys: **St Mary Star of the Sea, Hastings, Sussex.** *Below:* Interior.

Sir Arthur Blomfield — and the dynasty of the Austins and Paleys of Lancaster were all contributing suburban churches in the prevailing style to cater for the growing populations of the cities and towns.

There had been and continued to be some notable exceptions to Bodleian Gothic. J. D. Sedding's Holy Trinity, Sloane Street, Chelsea, was completed by Henry Wilson with the support of fellow Art Workers and craftsmen. W. R. Lethaby's All Saints, Brockhampton-by-Ross, Herefordshire (1902), was concrete-vaulted. The following year its first cousin, the church of St Edward the Confessor and St Mary, appeared at Kempley, Gloucestershire, to the design of A. Randall Wells who had been clerk of works at Brockhampton. In the best church of the Arts and Crafts Movement, St Andrew, Roker, Sunderland (1906–7), E. S. Prior designed from first principles. With Arthur Grove, Prior added the nave and west front to St Osmond, Parkstone, Dorset, in a free manner of his own in 1913–14. Almost Art Nouveau is the Mount Vernon Hospital Chapel, Northwood, Middlesex by Frederick Wheeler.

Charles Harrison Townsend had designed a low,

43

381
382

296

297

38

Sir Robert Lorimer: St Peter, Falcon Avenue, Edinburgh.

was Reilly who contributed the only classical design in the competition for Liverpool Anglican Cathedral in 1903.

The revival of interest in Byzantium and its early Christian churches in the last decades of the nineteenth century led to some striking departures from the Gothic tradition. This interest was fostered by expeditions to measure, sketch and report on the architecture of the Near East. It bore fruit 101 in a curious way in the church of St Sophia, Lower Kingswood, Surrey, designed by Sidney Barnsley to incorporate fragments brought back from the area by Dr Edwin Freshfield. But the crowning achievement of this kind was the remarkable 41 Catholic Metropolitan Cathedral of Westminster. 109 Cardinal Vaughan had taken J. F. Bentley to St 111 Mark's, Venice, and to S. Vitale, Ravenna (cholera in Constantinople prevented their visit to Hagia Sophia), to persuade him that the Byzantine style of those churches was most appropriate for the new cathedral. The result, if not typical, was the most splendid of the Edwardian decade. The massive plain yellow stock brickwork of the interior and the concrete saucer domes it supported provided foundation for adornment with marble and mosaics, although many felt that the simple brick arches and piers were better left unadorned. Bentley died in 1902 and so did not see its completion. The influence of both Greece and Byzantium, this time mingled with Italian Mannerism, is evident in another London church building, 286 Beresford Pite's Christ Church, Brixton Road, Kennington.

Sir Giles Gilbert Scott: Liverpool Anglican Cathedral from the north east.

52 barrel-vaulted church, St Martin, Blackheath, 352 near Guildford, in 1892—5. In 1902—4 he built St Mary the Virgin, Great Warley, Essex — a casket for the remarkable metal furnishings of Sir William Reynolds-Stephens — covered by a vault decorated in aluminium leaf to a pattern of roses of Sharon, anticipating Art Deco.

Sir Ninian Comper, who over two generations fulfilled the role of the complete architect-designer-craftsman, applied his remarkable gifts to the 53 interior of St Cyprian, Clarence Gate, Regent's Park, illustrating his theory of 'unity by exclusion'. In St Mary, Wellingborough, Northamptonshire, in 1908—9 he illustrated his principle of 'unity by inclusion' by introducing fittings of various periods, including Renaissance.

Exceptions to Bodleian Gothic were not limited to churches of Arts and Crafts inspiration. J. D. Sedding had designed the Holy Redeemer, Clerkenwell, EC1, in simple North Italian Renaissance in 1888. In 1896 E. W. Mountford had designed the chancel and side chapels in the Greek revival church of St Anne, Wandsworth, SW18, in 303 'Wrenaissance' style. C. H. Reilly did the Mission Church of St Barnabas, Dalston, E8, and the east end of Holy Trinity, Wavertree, Liverpool, in classical Renaissance style (both in 1910—11) and it

J. F. Bentley: Westminster Cathedral from the south west.

40
42

In 1903 the winning design for Liverpool Anglican
Cathedral by Giles Gilbert Scott heralded a new
phase in church architecture and the end of
Bodleian Gothic, Byzantine and 'Wrennaissance' —
even though Bodley was assessor in the competition and later acted as consultant on the building.
After Bodley's death four years later Scott modified the design and — possibly encouraged by Sir
Charles Nicholson's paper on 'Modern Church
Design' read to the RIBA in 1907, which advocated simpler roof outlines — dispensed with the
gables over the aisle bays and introduced a central
tower and double transepts.

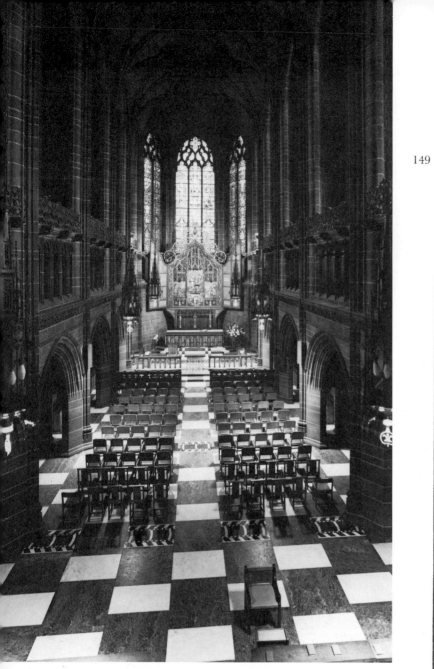

Sir Giles Gilbert Scott: Liverpool Cathedral, the Lady Chapel.

— the Society for Protection of Ancient Buildings— in 1877. In this field the Arts and Crafts made an enduring contribution, and hand in hand with the work of restoration went the beautiful church fittings and rood screens in which F. Bligh Bond of Bristol, C. E. Ponting of Marlborough, and Ninian Comper, Charles Spooner and W. D. Caröe of London, were so expert. To execute their designs they could call on the skills of excellent craftsmen like Harry Hems of Exeter and experienced church builders such as Cornish and Gaymer of North Walsham, Norfolk.

149

John F. Bentley: Westminster Cathedral during construction. An etching by Muirhead Bone.

Literary romanticism had led to the early plaster Gothic of a century before. Now it was pictorial romanticism as seen in the drawings of James Pryde and Frank Brangwyn which was the inspiration. Architects visited the cathedrals of southern France and northern Spain, including the fortresslike Albi Cathedral and the rich but sturdy Cathedral of Burgos, while in the architectural schools 'mass' was held to possess an inherent virtue independent of function. The young Giles Gilbert Scott was demonstrating this quality in his many churches and chapels while the choir of Liverpool Cathedral was slowly rising, leaving the Lady Chapel (consecrated in 1910) to commemorate his work with Bodley.

42

Of equal, if not greater importance in this period was the work done in the repair of churches on more sympathetic lines than had prevailed before William Morris established his 'Anti-Scrape Society'

W. R. Lethaby: All Saints, Brockhampton, Ross-on-Wye, Herefordshire. The roof is of concrete covered with thatch. *Below:* The interior.

The Art Workers' Guild and The Arts and Crafts Exhibition Society

The influence of the Art Workers' Guild upon architecture and the 'arts connected with building' in the first twenty years of its existence is clearly discernible. Its role in the origin of modern architecture is less easy to assess.

The Guild was founded on 11 March 1884 at a meeting held in the Board Room of the Charing Cross Hotel. It had grown out of the St George's Art Society, a club formed the year before by a group of Norman Shaw's pupils for the discussion of art and architecture — and named after the Bloomsbury church of St George near which they used to meet. The founder members were all young architects who were to be established names in the decade leading up to the First World War: Gerald Horsley, W. R. Lethaby, Ernest Newton, Mervyn Macartney and Edward S. Prior.

The Guild was open to all the arts and crafts and took its inspiration from the ideals of Morris and

Ruskin. Its motto, 'to use materials aright', was anticipated by the great French architect Eugène Viollet-le-Duc when he wrote:

> Amongst all these cheap splendours of false taste and false luxury we are delighted when we find a seat really well made, a good oak table thoroughly strong on its legs, woollen curtains which really look like wool, a comfortable and solid chair, a cupboard which opens and shuts well showing us inside and outside the wood it is made of and the object for which it is intended; let us hope for a return of those healthy ideas in the making of furniture as in everything else, that we may come to understand that true taste consists in appearing as one is and not as one would wish to be ...

In the north, where the influence of the Guild was also strong, the Liverpool Art Workers' Guild was founded in 1886, and in Manchester ten years later Walter Crane founded the Northern Art Workers' Guild (later the Red Rose Guild). The Women's Guild of Arts, initiated by William Morris's daughter May Morris and Mrs Thackeray Turner, wife of the architect, was founded in 1907.

Of the atmosphere and aspirations of the Guild's early days E. S. Prior wrote:

> Art and architects were drifting asunder. Was it possible to do anything to bring them together again?
> On the one hand was the Royal Academy, chartered for Architecture, Painting and Sculpture alike, but now giving its favour almost entirely to oil-painting, allowing to architects a membership of five out of a total of seventy ... On the other hand there was the Royal Institute of British Architects, whose theory of architecture had driven from its doors most of those architects whose art was acknowledged; which had forbidden to Artists a personal interest in their handicrafts and had opened its doors so widely to business, that Surveyors had become the largest element of its body ... There were many who were neither the oil-painters of the Academy nor the Surveyors of the Institute, but craftsmen in Architecture, Painting and Sculpture, and on the basis of a principle they could be brought together.

From these basic ideals, directly opposed to the separation of the arts, the Guild was gradually to enlarge its aims and, particularly in the field of architecture, to strive after a new and simpler style in keeping with the spirit of the Arts and Crafts Movement.

The Arts and Crafts Exhibition Society (today known as the Society of Designer Craftsmen), which held its first exhibition at the New Gallery, Regent Street, in 1888, sprang from the activities and discussions of the Guild, and membership to a large extent overlapped. The small displays of work at the Guild's hall at Barnard's Inn, Holborn, had been altogether inadequate. Now the exhibitions of the Arts and Crafts Exhibition Society, supported by the forward-looking *Studio* magazine founded by Charles Holme in 1893, did much in the closing decade of the century to enhance the reputation of British domestic architecture and crafts abroad. Ruskin had summed up the object of the Society when he wrote to William Morris in 1878:

> How much good might be done by the establishment of an exhibition, anywhere, in which the *right* doing, instead of the clever doing, of all that men knew how to do should be the test of acceptance ...

In their first aim, the Guild and the Exhibition Society succeeded fully. They gave to the crafts of carving, metalwork, mosaic work, stained glass, wall painting, needlework, and pottery the importance usually accorded to the three academic arts. Many of the best artists in each sphere were brother-upholders of the Guild. But the Guild was founded in a period when the function of the crafts was not altogether clear, complicated as it was by the advent of mechanisation. William Morris had greatly stressed the importance of individual design, the integrity of the workman, but his attitude to the role of the machine was less clear.

Artists, craftsmen and architects made a brave attempt to restore the arts to the position they had occupied before the Black Death, but they had yet to come to terms with the machines which had become essential if a population ten times that of the Middle Ages was to be supplied with even the necessities of life.

The position of the machine was confused even more by a new fashion sweeping Western Europe, the style called in England, France and Belgium Art Nouveau. Swirling freehand curves, impossible to reproduce mechanically, were characteristic of the style, which pervaded all the crafts and materials, as a style should. But in England Art Nouveau never reached the extremes it reached on the Continent. In twenty years it had burnt itself out, leaving in its place in England an even greater eagerness to return to the style of Queen Anne and the first two Georges, and by the end of another decade English architecture had assumed the forms which were to prevail in the reign of George V.

In the meantime the Art Workers, although faithful to the principles of their enthusiastic youth and endeavouring to preserve the integrity of the materials they used, still lacked the unifying influence of a new style for which they had so earnestly striven. Their labours, however, had not been entirely in vain, for Walter Crane was able to write:

> ... if they had not turned all craftsmen into artists nor all artists into craftsmen, they had

done not a little to expand and socialise the idea of art and (perhaps it is not too much to say) had made the tasteful house with its furniture and decorations a model for the civilised world.

Encyclopaedia Britannica

Perhaps the Art Workers had been seeking after a lost simplicity — the simplicity of the masons who, after the departure of the Romans, began again from simple stonework, and even when they had reached the heights of mediaeval construction, were transparently clear in their purposes. And there had been successes. Arts and Crafts ideals produced that Parthenon of the Movement, Bentley's Westminster Cathedral, Schultz Weir's Khartoum Cathedral, which demonstrates honesty of construction *in excelsis*, Lethaby's All Saints, Brockhampton, and Prior's St Andrew, Roker.

43
296
297

But the principle 'to use materials aright' had perhaps obscured the fact that in every age forms developed in one material are copied in another, and the craft, not the form, is adapted to the material used. So it was forgotten that mediaeval wood choir stalls were copies of external stone forms and, as in the seventeenth century, stone gatepiers, parapets and balustrades followed internal wood details, while for both stone and wood were borrowed designs from leatherwork.

Disregard of this fact in the Arts and Crafts Movement led to stylistic confusion and, in reaction, to a return of period styles in all the crafts. And yet the peak achievements of the Periclean Age of the Art Workers displayed the skills of many brilliant artists and craftsmen closely associated with the Movement. Bentley's Cathedral contains the work of Anning Bell, Eric Gill, and Ernest Gimson; Sedding's Holy Trinity had glasswork by Morris's company and works by F. M. Pomeroy, Christopher Whall and others; and the last of the line, Schultz Weir's Khartoum Cathedral, has fittings by Ernest Gimson.

106

In the years that followed, the best fruits of the Movement were reaped further afield, and perhaps Muthesius was justified in writing, rather in the manner of Tacitus: 'England often invents something and discards it without having drawn the full conclusions; this the English leave to less original peoples.'

There were other spheres in which the Art Workers' Guild made undeniable contributions to art and architecture. Many of its members belonged to the Society for Protection of Ancient Buildings in the days before the proliferation of protection societies. They concerned themselves with the preservation both of buildings and of amenities as in the modification of the building bye-laws related to party walls to enable roofs to run unbroken over a row of cottages — a relaxation which made possible the cottage architecture of the Garden City and the Garden Suburb. They took up the cudgels over issues like the threat to Waterloo Bridge in 1895, the threatened illumination of the St Paul's

25
26

Cathedral clockface, the attempt to 'restore' the west front of Peterborough Cathedral, the threat to the Tudor Gateway of Lincoln's Inn and the plans for drastic reconstruction in the city of Florence in 1898. Above all, they made a lasting contribution to the sympathetic repair of churches and old houses.

Oeil de boeuf and over door, Basil Street and Sloane Street, SW3.

∫culpture

At the time of the Great Exhibitions of 1851 and 1862 sculptors in Britain were still emulating the style and finish characteristic of the work of the Italian Antonio Canova (1757–1822), a dominant influence in both Europe and America over the preceding fifty years. The story is that the genius of Canova was first revealed in a lion which he modelled in butter while still a boy. Apocryphal or not, it expresses a certain truth since Canova's style relied much upon the importance he gave to the roundness and smoothness of his marble and bronze. In England the sculptured groups by Foley and others on the Albert Memorial in Kensington Gardens are representative of his style.

The low state to which the art had sunk, in both content and execution, prompted Francis Turner Palgrave, the poet, critic and sometime Assistant Secretary in the Education Office, to refer to sculpture, in the official guide to the Fine Art section of the 1862 Exhibition as 'the forlorn hope of modern art'.

The restoration of vitality to British sculpture was due primarily to events in France, and the force which revitalised French sculpture — then suffering the same malaise — was Jean Baptiste Carpeaux (1827–75). A former student of Jean Baptiste Rude, the creator of the group 'La Marseillaise' on

Thomas E. Collcutt: Lloyd's Registry of Shipping,
Fenchurch Street, EC3. Sculpture by Sir George
Frampton; painting by Gerald Moira.

the Arc de Triomphe, Carpeaux won the Prix de
Rome in 1854. Although he was fascinated by
Donatello, the greater influence on his work was
Michelangelo. Carpeaux made his reputation with
the group 'Ugolino and His Sons' which he had
sent from Rome to the Paris Salon. It was during
this period that Paris began to replace Rome as
the centre for the study of art, but owing to the
political disturbances there in 1870—1 many
Frenchmen, including Carpeaux, sought refuge in
England.

A pupil of Carpeaux was Aimé-Jules Dalou (1838—
1902) whose brief stay in England was to leave a
lasting mark. Having accepted the curatorship of
the Louvre from the 1870 Commune, Dalou was
obliged to leave France the following year. He
came to England where his friend of student days,
the painter and etcher Alphonse Légros (1837—
1911), had been settled since 1863.

For a brief period Dalou taught modelling at the
Lambeth School of Art and then at the South
Kensington Schools before returning to Paris in
1879, the year in which he did 'Charity' (actually
'Femme Paysanne laitante') near the Royal

Exchange, EC3. He was succeeded at the South
Kensington Schools by another political refugee,
Edouard Lantéri, who continued his teaching.
Meanwhile Légros had been appointed Slade
Professor of Drawing at University College,
London. At Dalou's suggestion he extended his
teaching to modelling and sculpture, and the ad-
vances made at the Slade, where he taught for
seventeen years, were in large measure due to him.

In the years that followed, the influence of the
Lambeth School of Art was felt increasingly in
many spheres. Established in 1854, it had initially
provided instruction for the apprentices of the
many workshops in Lambeth occupied in the arts
connected with building — chiefly Farmer and
Brindley's stonemasons' yards, Doulton and Company's Lambeth Pottery and Starkie Gardiner's
metal works. In 1878 it was taken under the wing
of the City and Guilds College. Many of its students went on to the South Kensington Schools
and the Royal Academy Schools where they figured among the winners of the Gold Medal and
Travelling Studentship. But since the prize was
awarded only every second year, competition was
great and many gifted students from Lambeth who
reached the Royal Academy Schools failed to get
the coveted award. Among these were C. J. Allen,
who became Professor of Sculpture at Liverpool,
W. A. Colton, RA, who became Professor of
Sculpture at the Royal Academy Schools, Henry
Poole, RA, John Tweed, F. Brook-Hitch, Wenlock
Rollins, F. Lynn-Jenkins, Abraham Broadbent and
Charles Hartwell. The Royal Academy subsequently imposed an age limit on entrants which reduced
the stream of mature students from Lambeth. In
his London School Report for 1898, the Principal
of Lambeth summed up developments in British
sculpture towards the end of the nineteenth century as follows:

> At that time emancipation of Sculpture from
> the conventional bonds and limitations that
> had hampered it had hardly taken place. The
> men of distinction now were students then.
> French technique had begun to press on the
> notice of these English sculptors the greater
> powers that deeper and more systematic
> study of the figure had endowed their
> neighbours.

In spite of the French influence so glowingly represented by Sparkes, the words used to describe
Sir Thomas Brock still applied in some degree to
many contemporary creators of public sculpture:
'the English representative of the more conservative aspects of French sculpture in the second half
of the nineteenth century' (DNB).

What also helped to liberate sculpture from stale
convention and unite the 'arts connected with
building' was the foundation of the Art Workers'
Guild in 1884. The first Master was a sculptor,
George Blackall Simonds, and many sculptors and
architects met in an endeavour to restore the harmony which had once united their arts and to en-

sure that architecture gave to sculpture that 'loving assistance and unobtrusive support' preached and practised by John Belcher.

The Art Workers' Guild also encouraged work in materials other than stone and marble. Some of the aura of the Pre-Raphaelite Brotherhood attached to the Guild, and artists were reminded that there were other materials besides statuary marble and polished bronze, that the 'heroic' was not the only scale to work in, that there were other ways of producing small pieces of sculpture than by mechanical reduction, and that the sculptor himself was the best person to interpret his own ideas. The introduction of colour, semi-precious stones, enamels and a variety of metals recalled the mediaeval, the mystical and the Florentine which the Pre-Raphaelites had loved.

High Victorian buildings had been on a colossal scale, and the sculpture proportionately large. The Albert Memorial is twice the height of the monument to the Scaglieri in Verona which it resembles. Working to a smaller scale, the artist now endeavoured to handle the work himself, to carve his own marble, to re-introduce the *cire-perdue* method of casting bronze and to beat out his own metalwork.

But a revival of the methods of the Florentine *botega* depended on apprentices, and without small orders of the kind the Florentine workshops had executed — such as carving, gilding and the making of marriage chests — the financial burdens could

Captain Adrian Jones: the Peace Quadriga for the Wellington Arch, Hyde Park Corner, after completion of the casting in Burton's Foundry, Thames Ditton, Surrey.

Sir George Frampton, RA: Peter Pan in Kensington Gardens. The model was Nina Boucicault.

be overwhelming. The combined pressures of being artist, estimator and contractor proved too great, and the difficult and risky work of bronze casting reverted to the foundries.

The brightest luminary of the sculptors of this minor renaissance was Alfred Gilbert. In spite of more than one eclipse in his stormy progress, he produced the finest works of his age — 'Eros' at Piccadilly Circus, 'Queen Victoria' at Winchester and the Clarence Tomb at Windsor. After him came George Frampton whose 'Peter Pan' in Kensington Gardens is a distant reminder of the Eros fountain. Captain Adrian Jones, more than twenty years a veterinary officer in the Royal Artillery, made the greatest quadriga of modern times — 'Peace' on the Wellington Arch at Hyde Park Corner.

Between 1901 and 1910 the embellishment of a great number of new public buildings kept sculptors busy. Most of these were in the neo-Baroque style where sculpture plays an important part, so that *The Builder* could say of William Young's New (now Old) War Office in Whitehall (1901): 'Mr Drury's groups go far to save the building'. But 'programme' sculpture had its problems. On the War Office Drury was required to represent 'The Fatherless Widow', 'The Winged Messenger of Peace', 'The Horrors of War', 'The Dignity of War', 'Truth' and 'Justice', 'Victory' and 'Fame'.

London Underground Railways: figure from Oxford Circus Station.

On the bridge connecting Scott's and Wyatt's Foreign and India Offices to the New Government Offices by J. McK. Brydon, Paul Montford had been asked by the Office of Works to base his sculpture on the fact that:

> the bridge leads to three departments of the Home Office as well as to the Education Board and Local Government Board ...
>
> Accordingly the allegorical figure on the right is represented as protecting and encouraging the youth who is taking up the burthen of life; she has the breast-plate and the helmet of Minerva or Britannia *[sic]*. The female figure on the left is represented maintaining and helping the aged worker who is now too old and weak to use the hammer on which he leans. She wears the civic crown, as her action is mostly civic or local, not national...

103   The building which stood out as a landmark in the evolution of neo-Baroque and established a model for the relationship between the architect and the sculptor was the Hall of the Incorporated Institute of Chartered Accountants in Moorgate Place, by Belcher and Joass (1890). The sculpture here was by Harry Bates (d. 1899) and Sir Hamo Thornycroft. Thomas Collcutt's building for Lloyd's Registry of Shipping in Fenchurch Street (1902) followed the ideas expressed by Belcher, incorporating external work by George Frampton and internal work by Lynn-Jenkins. But all eighteen sculptors engaged under Sir Aston Webb on the new Victoria and Albert Museum imparted to

that diverse building little of the quality their talents were capable separately of achieving.

After Belcher and Joass's Accountants building, the frieze of figures became a favourite motif in sculptured decoration. A noteworthy example is that by H. C. Binney on the best building of
327   Norman Shaw's retirement years, the Gaiety Restaurant, Aldwych and Strand. Binney's frieze endeavours to represent such diverse subjects as Canada, Australia, South Africa, Britannia, Comedy, Tragedy, Shakespeare's Portia, Beatrice and Cleopatra, Engineering, Mining, Weaving, Astronomy, Electricity, the Spirit of Progress, War, Peace, etc.

62   The cherubini on the Waldorf Hotel, the faience spandrils high above the Strand courtyard of the Savoy Hotel, the trophies on the Royal Automobile Club, are all of this decade. At the Cardiff
309   City Centre Henry Poole's and Paul Montford's groups reflect the Franco-Viennese élan of the Lanchester, Stewart and Rickards building. In contrast, the procession of worthies by Charles
211   Pibworth on Adams and Holden's Bristol Central Library — Cynwulf the Wandering Bard, Nennius the Historian, King Alfred, Wace the Norman Minstrel and others — convey a mood proper to the serious lines of the building, the first public library to break away from the neo-Baroque. A frieze in similar vein by Henry Wilson occurs on
387   All Saints' Convent (now the Pastoral Centre), London Colney, in Hertfordshire, by Leonard Stokes.

In 1925 came Ernest Gillick's 'Britannia' seated between figures representing 'Higher Mathematics'

Arthur Cooksey: Sir John Cass Institute, Jewry Street, EC3. A detail.

and 'Lower Mathematics' backed by 'Mercury' and 'Truth' and the 'Owl of Wisdom' in one corner — on the National Provincial (now National Westminster) Bank in Poultry and Princes Street, EC2 — terminating an age which, one might be forgiven for feeling, had produced more than its share of heroic sculpture.

Failing to invent a wholly original building in which sculpture could be given free reign, architects sometimes resorted to the Mannerist style of Michelangelo. This provided an opportunity for the sculptor in tune with that great master's style, as in the interpretations of Alfred Stevens. Belcher and his partner J. J. Joass provided such an opportunity to Alfred Drury and Bertram Mackennal on the Royal Insurance building at the corner of Piccadilly and St James's Street, while 82 Mortimer Street, W1, displays what amounts to a burlesque on the Medici Tombs in a setting by Beresford Pite. The design, by J. Attwood Slater, was carried out by Thomas Tyrell. Henry T. Hare's now demolished Ingram House, Strand, exhibited similar sculptures by Henry Poole, amputations from which are preserved on a terrace on the site.

The last and also the best exponent of Edwardian sculpture was Francis Derwent Wood who studied under Frampton and whose work showed something of the delicacy and seriousness of Donatello. Examples can be seen on the Glasgow buildings of Salmon, Son and Gillespie and on the pedestal 'Australia' at the Queen Victoria Memorial, Buckingham Palace, on which he assisted Sir Thomas Brock.

The time had come, however, for the English version of French and Italian sculpture, revitalised though it was, to be replaced by a new style. The inspiration came from Auguste Rodin through the medium of the young New York sculptor lately arrived in London from his studies in Paris, Jacob Epstein (q.v.), whose genius was soon recognised by a discerning few. His statues on the new British Medical Association building in the Strand and Agar Street, WC2, heralded the dawn of modern sculpture in England and prepared the way for its rise to the place it holds today.

Art Nouveau

While the origins of the art form which in England came to be called Art Nouveau can be traced to the 1880s, its influence on the decorative arts continued into the 1900s. In 1904 the London *Magazine of Art* asked thirty-six leading figures in the art world to comment on the movement, which by then had come of age. From the replies received it was clear that artists whose own work had Art Nouveau tendencies now preferred to ignore it.

Sir George Clausen, Professor of Painting at the Royal Academy, regarded the style as a continuation of the Baroque, and referred to Sir Alfred Gilbert's Shaftesbury Memorial Fountain at Piccadilly Circus as 'the antithesis of Art Nouveau'. Sir George Frampton thought the style was 'made to frighten naughty children — worse than the bogey man'. Walter Crane, who had helped, innocently perhaps, to foster it, said: 'Have I understood it rightly, or is it still a matter of the grave to which I must come before I understand?' C. F. A. Voysey saw in it 'no sign of reverence — but atheism, conceit and apish imitation'.

The most sensible observation came, surprisingly, from Reginald Blomfield, later Professor of Architecture at the Royal Academy, who said that Art Nouveau was no new art but had in fact been introduced by two young architects (meaning A. H. Mackmurdo and Herbert Horne) with an uncommon share of eccentric ability who for the first time revealed the numerous possibilities of the 'swirl' and the 'blob'. He added that, having been noticed in Germany and Austria, their work was returning to the country of its origin by way of France. *The Studio* magazine, after illustrating it for many years, was also prompted to ask in 1904 'What is meant by Art Nouveau?'

Among the several characteristics of the style was that noticed by Blomfield, the 'swirl' and the 'blob' — the whip-lash curve which Henri van der Velde was to call the 'line of force'. This curve can be found in sources as diverse as the decoration of Gaulish Samian Ware, fifteenth-century English Gothic foliage, a drawing by Albrecht Dürer, silverware, the stems of lilies and tulips and the work of William Blake and Edward Burne-Jones — even in the curve of Jane Morris's neck. Owen Jones's *Grammar of Ornament* reveals more sources, and the spandrils of the iron arches of I. K. Brunel's Paddington Station, decorated by Owen Jones (his colours have been obliterated), illustrate Jones's theory of the beauty of forms — 'born out of each other in gradual undulations'.

Christopher Dresser, author of *General Principles of Ornament*, wrote, perhaps a little unprecisely: 'The arc is the least interesting, an ellipse is the

W. S. Worley: A building in Soho Square, W1. Art Nouveau. A drawing by Charlotte Halliday.

more beautiful curve since it is traced from two centres, the curve following the shape of an egg is more subtle still since it is traced from three centres'.

The first new manifestation of this line — the swirl and blob referred to by Blomfield — was on the title page of Mackmurdo's *Wren's City Churches* of 1883. Further examples appear in his furniture and a large permanent example can be seen in the remaining cast-iron balconies of the Savoy Hotel (1889), probably also by him. His exhibition stand for the Century Guild was an early example of a style of furniture and shop fittings which was to become fashionable over the next twenty years. While in England these art forms were at first confined principally to graphic designs, bookbinding and textiles, in Europe they appeared in the solid in furniture and in interior and even exterior architecture.

In the eighties and nineties the urge to cast off nineteenth-century classic forms had spread throughout the arts, even finding expression in the dancing of the American Loie Fuller and the Austrian Cléo de Mérode. The same need to break with orthodox aesthetics was expressed in literature in the poems of Baudelaire, Mallarmé and Verlaine and in music by Debussy and the whole-tone scale.

In painting the movement led to the 'Nabis', to the work of Gauguin and Van Gogh and the drawings of Toulouse-Lautrec. Artists throughout England and the Continent contributed enough designs in the new fashion to constitute a style — Aubrey Beardsley in England, Victor Horta and Henri van der Velde in Belgium, Otto Wagner, Joseph Hoffmann and Maria Olbrich (founders of the Secession) in Vienna, Hermann Olbrist in Munich, Peter Behrens and Patrig Huber in Darmstadt, Hector Guimard and René Lalique in Paris, and Emile Gallé in Nancy. But its largest monuments, large enough to constitute a style in themselves, are to be found in the work of Antoni Gaudi in Barcelona where the church of La Sagrada Familia, an apartment house, a park and a school are in remarkable mosaic-encrusted forms. The influence of Art Nouveau reached as far as America. In New York Louis Comfort Tiffany (1898—1933), whose father had a branch in Regent Street and knew Ruskin and Morris, made glass and jewellery, while in Chicago Louis Sullivan (1856—1924) designed buildings of fundamental design decorated with plant forms deriving from *Gray's Botany*.

The new form of expression acquired a different name in each country and often, as with fashions in dress, a name foreign to that country — in Italy it was *Floreale* or *Stile Liberty* from Lazenby Liberty's shop in Regent Street; in Spain *Modernista*; in Germany *Jugendstil*, from the Munich magazine of that name. In England, the name Art Nouveau was adopted from the name of the shop in Paris opened in 1895 by Samuel (Siegfried) Bing of Hamburg. An importer of Japanese art work, Bing opened 'La Maison de l'Art Nouveau' in 22 Rue de

Provence, with an interior designed by Van der Velde painted by Albert Besnard. The exterior was covered with long paintings on canvas by Frank Brangwyn. Bing exhibited 'l'Art Nouveau Bing' at the Exposition Universelle des Arts Decoratifs in Paris in 1900.

The forms which had been given extreme expression in France and Belgium were used with caution

Saul and Hardy: this (former) dairy with flats over, in New Cavendish Street, W1, has Art Nouveau tendencies.

in England where the Arts and Crafts movement provided sounder reasons for an alternative escape from conventional imitations. And, after 1904, when both movements were on the wane, Hermann Muthesius could report that 'museums of Arts and Crafts which in 1900, the time of individualism, had bought works of modern decorative art in Paris, have since put them into a quiet corner in the basement'.

Decoration

At the turn of the century important buildings were expected to provide a setting for pictures in colour, both for decoration and to tell a story. But the choice of the medium and the style presented all kinds of difficulties which frequently inhibited further efforts in that direction. First, the fugitive nature of those materials which gave the best results, as in tempera painting; then the still limited life of more permanent materials, as in oil painting; and finally, the unsuitable nature for some situations and subjects of permanent materials like mosaic, whether vitreous, ceramic or marble.

Selecting a suitable medium was only the beginning. As with sculpture, the choice of subject, artist and style in harmony with the complex variety of architectural styles flourishing simultaneously in the 1900s presented further complications. Such harmony had been achieved for a brief period in the nineteenth century at the height of the Gothic Revival, not only in churches but conspicuously in Manchester Town Hall where Ford Madox Brown's paintings, the coloured tiles and painted glass, perfectly accord with the stern architecture of Alfred Waterhouse.

But the reintroduction of the Renaissance and Baroque styles for public buildings demanded new inspiration since the tradition of Renaissance heroic painting, like the sculpture of the 1860s, was in the doldrums. As with sculpture, the inspiration came from France, from the work of Pierre Puvis de Chavannes (1824—98).

At first rejected by the French Salon, Puvis de Chavannes had gone on to win public acclaim with his 'Peace' and 'War', now in the Museum of Amiens. In the 1870s he was asked to paint three panels for the Pantheon in Paris illustrating the life of St Geneviève, a work which occupied him intermittently until his death. In the meantime he decorated a staircase in the Lyons Museum and in Paris a hemicycle at the Sorbonne and a grand staircase and reception room at the rebuilt Hôtel

Charles Harrison Townsend: St Martin, Blackheath, Surrey. Painted by Mrs. Lea Merritt.

de Ville. Between 1895 and his death Puvis de Chavannes painted his remarkable nine large panels for the Boston Public Library. Sir Frank Brangwyn summed up the significance of his work as:

> ... a noble attempt to create a new logic of mural painting which would exclude any tricks of illusion, but would preserve the sense of the wall. To that end he simplified his drawing, distributed his points of interest by a landscape setting which fulfilled its function as a foil and background without 'making a hole in the wall'.
>
> *Encyclopaedia Britannica*

Brangwyn was himself a leading figure of the period with a feeling for the grand manner. He gave his age what it demanded, painting for city companies, the Royal Exchange, Lloyd's Registry, the Canadian Trunk Railways and Christ's Hospital, wall pictures which reflected their pride in history and commerce — although his etchings have stood the test of time more successfully. Gerald Moira also made a contribution to the field with works like his paintings in the New Sessions House, Old Bailey, alongside those of Sir William Richmond, RA. Another painter in this manner was George Murray.

The superiority of the colour and line and the translucency of the methods of wall paintings in use before the introduction of oils have always attracted painters, but to acquire permanency has always been a problem. Even the Pre-Raphaelite painters of the nineteenth century were at first not aware of the nature of tempera painting. When John Ruskin saw an early revivalist of tempera,

Lady Herringham, copying the 'Death of Procus' in the National Gallery, he asked her why she was copying in tempera colour what had been painted in oils. When told that not only this painting, but the greater part of the work in the Early Italian Room was in that medium, Ruskin is said to have done a round of the walls to verify this for himself.

The revival of interest in tempera painting dated from the translation of Cennino Cennini's work by Mrs Merriefield in 1844. One of its principal exponents in the early 1900s was John D. Batten who died in 1932. His 'Atlanta', for which his wife modelled, is now in the Victoria and Albert Museum. Henry A. Payne did a tempera painting in the Peers' Corridor of the House of Lords in 1910 and the same year paintings in the chapel of Madresfield Court, Worcestershire, while Charles Harrison Townsend provided a setting for Mrs Lea Merritt's wall paintings in St Martin's Church, Blackheath, Surrey, in the early 1890s. An unusual attempt to provide work of some permanence was made by Frederick Shields who between 1900 and 1910 executed paintings in the style of Puvis on slate riveted to the walls of the Chapel of the Ascension, Bayswater Road, W2 (destroyed).

The Society of Painters in Tempera was founded in 1901 by Lady Herringham who had written *The Book of the Art of Cennino Cennini* (1899). But tempera painters had to struggle to gain admission to the art circles of London. When a group of them tried to send their works to the New Gallery in Regent Street, the director, Sir Charles Halle, re-

268

52

plied that he could not see his way to such an arrangement — he feared 'the making of a new medium popular was only a trap for the unwary ... If a man cannot draw and paint in oil and water colour, he doesn't succeed in producing good work because he takes up tempera'. An exhibition of tempera paintings was, however, held by the Art Workers' Guild in 1914.

Dependent on the skill of the plasterer and the quality of the materials, and equally on the climate, artists in true tempera colour had a difficult time. The stronger colours of the post-impressionist, cubist and futurist painters did not require material as ephemeral in appearance, and the struggle was abandoned. Nowadays the ingenuity of the chemist in producing permanent paints has opened up new fields of applied permanent colour decoration.

Doyen of the Edwardian generation of painters was the American artist Edwin Austin Abbey who painted 'The Quest of the Holy Grail' for the Boston Public Library in his studio in the Cotswolds. Under his tutelage the artists Henry Payne, Denis Eden, Frank Cowper and Frank Salisbury did a series of paintings for a corridor of the House of Lords.

W. J. Neatby: The Winter Gardens, Blackpool, Lancashire. One of twenty-six painted tile panels.

In the field of interior decoration much was also achieved as a result of the work of Charles and Margaret Mackintosh and George Walton in Glasgow. Their work, inspired originally by William Morris and Burne-Jones, had its impact abroad and even to some degree altered the course of Art Nouveau.

But the cross-currents of style, now Byzantine, now Baroque, now Arts and Crafts, were weathered most successfully by the art of mosaics. An able exponent, in the direct line of William Morris and Burne-Jones, was Robert Anning Bell, whose work appears on the west porch of Westminster Cathedral and on the Horniman Museum, Forest Hill — in a perfect setting by C. Harrison Townsend. At St Paul's Cathedral, where Sir James Thornhill had painted the interior of the dome, the temporary nature even of oil paintings had encouraged the Dean and Chapter to order from Sir William Richmond mosaics for the diagonal apses and the central space to agree with the mosaic spandrils by Alfred Stevens.

106
107

A third and even more durable material for pictorial or pattern decoration was the glazed ceramic tile or moulded and glazed coloured terracotta (faience). In the nineteenth century, unglazed terracotta had been used on the exterior of the colleges and museums of South Kensington, while faience had been introduced for the interiors, notably in the Refreshment Room and on the Henry Cole staircase in what is now part of the Victoria and Albert Museum.

◁ Sir Ninian Comper: St Cyprian, Clarence Gate, NW1. The Rood Screen.

Greater beauty and variety were added to the art and craft of tile making by the ceramicist and writer William De Morgan. Although his factory

164 at Fulham closed before 1900, his stock of tiles continued to be used. They were distinguished by a rich glaze and patterns which resemble those of the Persian tiles which were their inspiration. At Doulton and Company's Lambeth works the great modeller and craftsman George Tinworth continued to make beautiful high-relief pictures in terracotta into the twentieth century. But possibly the most original and the most eccentric work in glazed ceramic and tile is that of W. J. Neatby who did the decoration of the Game and Fish Hall in

53 Harrods Store and a ballroom at Blackpool which still survives.

Almost daily the transformation or destruction of dairies and butchers' shops reduces the amount of appropriate gay decorative tilework which once enlivened the scene for customer and shopkeeper alike. Typical of such losses was the disappearance in 1964 of the tiled arcaded hall of a dairy in Heath Street, Hampstead, to form a standard 'supermarket'. But occasionally a gamedealer in Mayfair, a fishmonger in St James's, or a butcher in South Kensington or St Marylebone has the good sense to preserve his cool, clean and cheerful tilework.

London Theatres

Short leases, fires, street improvements, bankruptcies, reconstructions, orders for safety measures and other vicissitudes have for centuries embarrassed theatres to the point where each of them has a sizeable case history. Their various ups and downs have been well documented in two books by Raymond Mander and Joe Mitchenson, *The Theatres of London* and *The Lost Theatres of London*.

Towards the end of the nineteenth century the many serious theatre fires had led to drastic reforms in the regulations governing fire precautions. The architects Edwin Sachs, Ernest Runtz and Walter Emden, sharing a concern over two disastrous theatre fires, were among those who drew the attention of the authorities to the problem. The more recent disaster was the Iroquois Theatre fire in Chicago in 1903. Earlier and closer to home was the Paris Charity Bazaar fire of 1897 in which a number of society women lost their lives. Among them was Sophie, Duchesse d'Alençon, Princess Wittelsbach, whose gruesome death is mentioned by Queen Victoria in a letter to one of her daughters, 'the most awful catastrophe, only her head was found ...'

Two important structural changes brought about by the new regulations were the omission of the 'gods' or third tier from new theatres and the compulsory installation of the asbestos safety curtain across the proscenium. Few other changes were made to the horseshoe-shaped auditorium, orchestra pit, short apron stage and proscenium opening with the deep rectangular stage behind it. The richly moulded and gilt plaster decorations on swelling balcony fronts in renaissance taste provided sufficient acoustical correction.

Many London theatres were small and pitifully inadequate in accommodation for artists, retaining the atmosphere of the Restoration playhouse of Samuel Pepys's time. Most had been founded in the nineteenth century, some earlier, and the story of the Edwardian theatre is more one of reconstruction and removals than of new foundations. Music halls, theatres of variety, 'Palaces' and 'Hippodromes' multiplied until they were surpassed by the super-cinemas, which have in their turn been taken over for bingo, television or ten-pin bowling, or left empty or demolished.

The special requirements of the theatres called for architects, engineers and contractors with special experience. Often three architects were involved, the architect for the building, the theatre specialist and the interior designer. Difficult enough even with modern builders' plant, metal scaffolding and electric lighting, rapid building without these aids must have been a nightmare.

In the history of the English theatre this was an age of superlatives. For the comfort and convenience of their patrons the promoters of a new theatre would sometimes indulge in lavish and occasionally disastrous expenditure. When the

257 London Coliseum (afterwards the Coliseum) was built in 1904 for Oswald Stoll by Frank Matcham, it contained spacious tea rooms on every tier and between performances five o'clock teas were served by Fuller's. In each tea room was a ticket office and an information bureau where 'physicians and others expecting urgent telephone calls or telegrams should leave a notification of number of the seat they are occupying', and where telegrams could be despatched and postage stamps bought. A band in the Terrace Tea Room gave four performances daily, and to overcome a difficult crossover, the Royal Box was approached from the Royal Lift by means of a Royal Ante-Room on wheels which trundled across the public corridor.

After eighteen months the new theatre failed and was repurchased by Stoll who made extensive improvements, including a double revolving stage. The Coliseum, now the home of the English National Opera, has had its cheerful pink terracotta painted cream.

From 1890 to 1910 the 'King' of theatre, music hall and variety theatre architects, Frank Matcham, designed one hundred places of entertainment. Other busy theatre architects were the Veritys (father and son), C. J. Phipps, W. G. R. Sprague and Bertie Crewe.

After the Theatre Royal, Covent Garden, opened as the Royal Italian Opera in 1847, there was no new opera house until Richard D'Oyly Carte's unsuccessful experiment with the new English Opera House at the junction of the new Shaftesbury Avenue and Charing Cross Road in 1891. This became the Palace Theatre of Varieties in 1892. The London Opera House — the only other attempt in this field — was built on the new Kingsway in 1911 by Bertie Crewe for Oscar Hammerstein, the American impresario. This did not succeed either and was bought by Sir Oswald Stoll in 1917, became a cinema and then again served as a theatre until its demolition in 1957 when it was replaced by an office building and a new theatre.

The Imperial Theatre was reconstructed in 1901 from the Royal Aquarium, Tothill Street and Dartmouth Street, SW1. The old theatre was bought for Emily le Breton, Lily Langtry the 'Jersey Lily', and paid for by Leslie Cohen who had it practically rebuilt. According to the *Era*, 'it bore the stamp of the fair manageress's individuality'. But the site was bought in 1902 for the Wesleyan Central Hall and the theatre was demolished in 1906. The interior was designed by Frank T. Verity who also designed the Scala Theatre, Charlotte Street, for Distin Maddick, opened in 1905 and demolished in 1970. The interiors here were of similar design, more classical than the versions of French renaissance usual for theatres at that time. The Imperial surpassed the Scala in both design and finish since more money was available and *real* marble was used.

The opportunity for two new theatres on a new street came when Aldwych was constructed, partly on land belonging to the Duke of Bedford who had to approve the façades. The Aldwych and Waldorf Theatres, both designed by W. G. R. Sprague in 1905, were placed on each street corner flanking the new Waldorf Hotel.

57 The Aldwych was built for Seymour Hicks and the impresario Charles Frohman. While admitting its handsome and ornate features, the *Era* claimed 'the words that correctly describe the impression conveyed are "cosy and comfortable" ' (30 Dec-
57 ember 1905). The Waldorf, the last three-tier theatre to be built in London, was renamed the Strand in 1909 when the old Strand Theatre was pulled down to make way for Aldwych tube station. The name was changed to the Whitney in 1911 and back to the Strand in 1913. The two theatres have changed very little in appearance over the years.

57 The new Gaiety Theatre was built for George Edwardes in 1903 to replace the old Gaiety demolished for the Holborn-Strand improvements. The architects for the theatre and the adjoining restaurant of the same name were Ernest Runtz and George Ford, with Richard Norman Shaw as con-

sulting architect for the exterior. Threatened with demolition for the improvements of the approaches to Waterloo Bridge, the Gaiety was closed in 1939 and stripped of its fittings. The actor Lupino Lane made a brave attempt to refit it after serious damage in the Second World War but had to sell it at only the site value. It has since been replaced by an office building.

When Shaftesbury Avenue and Charing Cross Road were constructed by the Metropolitan Board of Works in 1886–7, the new sites were slow in being taken up and there was no official control over the architecture. Although the new streets hardly merited the term 'urban improvement', they brought an opportunity for the construction of new theatres to replace those lost in the Strand slum clearances. Their modest size and cosy character suited London theatre-goers who from Elizabethan times have associated the theatre with the noise, the bustle and even the discomfort of the fair-booth. The atmosphere was now heightened by the commissionaires' shrill silver whistles (suppressed during the First World War by the Defence of the Realm Act, never to return), the pink glow and flicker of the arc lights, the clip-clop of hansom cab horses, the chug of Napier taxis and the faint whine of the electric broughams.

Five new theatres were built in Shaftesbury Avenue, including the Apollo in 1901 and the Globe and the Queen's in 1906 and 1907, while in Charing Cross Road the Garrick had already risen in 1889 and Wyndhams in 1899. In St Martin's Lane arose the New (now the Albery).

The Apollo was designed by Lewen Sharp for Henry Lowenfeld who intended to call the theatre 'The Mascot'; he had placed a badge on the front of the dress circle representing a 'silver chain and buckle on which is a flying lizard supported dexter and sinister by lions rampant' — the original badge of the German gipsies connected with Lowenfeld's estate in Poland. For better acoustics the orchestra conceived by Lowenfeld was constructed in the form of a hollow oval with a hard polished surface over which was a wooden sounding board, while on this a three-tier rostrum stood on glass legs. The only change since it was built is a simplification of the decoration and the reseating of the 'gallery', renamed the 'balcony'. The adjoining Apollo Restaurant, a charming building in the Dutch style, also by Sharp, is now a wine shop.

The Globe was opened as the Hicks Theatre in 1906, after the actor Seymour Hicks, but was renamed the Globe three years later. This and the Queen's were part of a speculation by Jack Jacobus, the shoeshop proprietor who, with Sidney Marler, bought houses in Wardour Street on which to build the two theatres and enlarge his shop. The architect for the whole scheme was W. G. R. Sprague and the promoters were Seymour Hicks and Charles Frohman. The Globe and the Queen's were given similar elevations. Removal of the rear boxes, and improvements to the stage boxes and the gallery (renamed the balcony), are the only changes of consequence made since.

The Queen's Theatre, opened in 1907, was slightly larger than the Globe. The name first intended was the Central — 'as if it were a criminal court or a railway terminus' was Bernard Shaw's comment. There had been a Queen's theatre in Long Acre, closed in 1887 for the extension of Odhams Press. The front of the new Queen's and the back of the 'house' were heavily damaged by enemy action in 1940, and the rebuilding was carried out in modern style by Westwood, Sons and Partners in 1958. With the collaboration of Sir Hugh Casson, however, the auditorium has retained its original atmosphere.

The Playhouse, Northumberland Avenue, first opened in 1882 as the Royal Avenue Theatre, was bought by Sefton Parry, a speculator who acquired it in the hope that the London and South Eastern Railway would bid for the site. Parry had built the Globe, Newcastle Street, Strand, in 1868 as a similar speculation and together with the adjoining 'opéra comique' that scheme had earned the nickname of 'The Rickety Twins'.

Cyril Maude took over the management of the Royal Avenue in 1905 and started on reconstruction, retaining the architect of the original theatre, F. H. Fowler. The work was nearly completed when, on 5 December 1905, the end of the lattice truss carrying the roof of Charing Cross Station slid from its bearing and brought the high and immensely thick wall down on top of the auditorium. Six men were killed and twenty-six injured. Reconstruction began again under new architects, Detmar Blow and Fernand Billerey, with decorations by the Australian Mortimer Menpes. The theatre opened in 1907. In 1935 the name was changed to the Playhouse Theatre and in 1951 it became a BBC studio.

Among notable theatre reconstructions in the period was that of the Kingsway, Great Queen Street, WC2. This began life in 1882 as the Novelty Theatre and was in turn called Folies Dramatiques, Jodrell, New Queen's and Eden Palace of Varieties, reverting to the Novelty in 1894. In 1900 it was reconstructed by John Murray for the comedian W. S. Penley. The decoration was by Gerald Moira and F. Lynn-Jenkins. Five years later the construction of the new Kingsway, which fortunately just missed it, provided better access, and suggested its new name. The first play presented was *The Lost Legion*, by W. J. Locke, then the secretary of the Royal Institute of British Architects. In 1907 the interior was again extensively reconstructed by F. W. Foster, John Murray's partner, in the style of the Louis XV period. The theatre was closed in 1940 and was damaged in the Second World War. Attempts at revival failed and it was demolished in 1959 to make way for an extension of Newton Street and an office block.

The Empire Theatre, Leicester Square, on the site of Saville House, was originally the Royal London Panorama. After many name changes it was finally to be the Pandora Theatre and the architect commissioned was Thomas Verity. But the company failed and the building was bought by Daniel Nicol of the Café Royal and was finished by Thomas Verity, as the Empire Theatre. Even after a rousing send-off opera and a presentation of *Round the World in Eighty Days* with a chorus of four hundred and an elephant, the theatre declined. George Edwardes had it redecorated by Romaine-Walker in 1887 and Walter Emden designed the scenery for the first spectacle. The ballets under this management were equally enterprising — a female 'Marylebone Cricket Club Team' and 'Australian Eleven', 'Yachtsmen', 'Huntsmen in Pink', and 'Noble Sportsmen and Sportswomen', meaning, of course, boxers male and female. The variety entertainment included a performance of 'Massa's in de Cold, Cold Ground' on sleigh-bells.

One event before the closing of the theatre for improvements by order of the LCC in 1904 was a demonstration by reformers nicknamed 'Prudes on the Prowl' led by Mrs Ormiston Chant, who succeeded in inducing the LCC to insist on canvas screens between the auditorium and the famous, or notorious, 'Empire Promenade' — the patrons tore them down. Sir Winston Churchill's recollections of how he made his 'maiden speech' on that occasion is recorded by E. S. Turner in *Roads to Ruin*. The improvements of 1904 by Frank T. Verity resulted in the best fitted and decorated theatre of the decade. Among the many innovations were 540 lights in the centre electrolier. Moving pictures were shown there for the first time in November 1896; by 1928 the moving picture had taken over, and in 1961 the auditorium was reconstructed again for the wide-screen cinema, and a separate dance hall of two storeys was designed by George Coles.

The Theatre Royal, Haymarket, while retaining its John Nash exterior, was reconstructed internally in 1904 by Stanley Peach in the record time of five months. The whole of the 'house' in front of the curtains was rebuilt, including foundations, brickwork and steelwork. Feats of this kind, in spite of wooden scaffolding and poor lighting, were not uncommon, witness the achievements at the Savoy Hotel in 1910 and at Buckingham Palace in 1912.

The Holborn Empire, one of the Moss Empires, was rebuilt by Frank Matcham in 1906 on the site of the Royal Music Hall, the front of 1897 by Ernest Runtz being retained. It was closed as a result of war damage in May 1941 and demolished in 1960 for an extension to the Pearl Assurance Company.

The London Hippodrome, built in 1899 and 1900, and the most vulgar of the Frank Matcham theatres, is of pink stone in Flemish renaissance style with an open iron crown surmounted by a two-horse

The Holborn-Strand Improvements, WC2. *From left to right:* The *Morning Post*, Mewès and Davis. The Aldwych Theatre, W. G. R. Sprague. The Waldorf Hotel, A. Marshall Mackenzie. The Strand Theatre, W. G. R. Sprague. The Gaiety Theatre, behind it The Gaiety Hotel and Restaurant, Runtz and Ford, Consultant R. Norman Shaw, RA.

chariot flanked by gladiators. It exceeded in vulgarity even the exhibition buildings of the period and also accommodated shops and offices, a public house and, later, the entrance to the Leicester Square tube station. It even boasted a circus arena (abolished in 1909) — it had been Edward Moss's ambition to provide a circus show.

No theatre built between 1890 and 1910 was so fortunate in its architectural embellishment as Daly's, Cranbourne Street, Leicester Square, W1, originally to be called the Salisbury and built by George Edwardes to the design of Spencer Hardwick and C. J. Phipps in 1893, for it was decorated with the sculpture of Alfred Gilbert (*Daily Graphic*, 28 June 1893). The superiority of the external sculpture over contemporary theatre sculpture also indicated the hand of Gilbert. The theatre was demolished in 1937 to make way for the Warner Theatre Cinema.

The Palladium, now the London Palladium, Argyll Street, W1, was designed by Frank Matcham for Walter Gibbons, who was in competition with Oswald Stoll's London Coliseum, Edward Moss's London Hippodrome and Alfred Butt's Palace. The Palladium was built on the site of Hengler's Circus, founded in 1871 and rebuilt in 1884 by C. J. Phipps, then in 1895 turned into the National Skating Palace, which had real ice. The Palladium was opened on 26 December 1910. In the Palm Court, lined with Norwegian rose granite, 1,000 people could be served tea comfortably. By means of a box-to-box telephone it was possible for 'friends in one box, recognising friends in another box, to enter into conversation with them'. The provision of amenities such as these, even in those days of low wages and low taxation, put a great strain on the finances of the theatre proprietors, but they contributed to that atmosphere of comfort, entertainment and showmanship which enabled the public of the day to take their pleasures by no means sadly.

Hotels

Early in the nineteenth century, when the need for accommodation for visitors to London began to exceed the capacity of private town houses and coaching inns, many of the private hotels which opened in response to the growing demand were established by retired family butlers, who took great pains to maintain the select nature of their establishments, sometimes requiring the intending guest to produce a letter of introduction. The famous Claridge's Hotel in Brook Street, W1, which was rebuilt between 1894 and 1897 to the designs of C. W. Stevens with decoration of the principal rooms by Ernest George and Alfred Yeates, was started by a contract butler employed by Gunters, the caterers.

The second half of the century saw the rise of the great hotels in cities, inland spas and seaside watering places in Great Britain and Europe, in emulation of the large 'caravanserais' growing up in the cities of North America. Their style often followed the phases of French renaissance architecture introduced into America by Richard Morris Hunt, the first American architect to receive his training in Paris. A characteristic feature of these hotels was the large mansard roof, named after Louis XIV's great architect. Of two pitches, this was especially useful for hotels since it could accommodate additional storeys above the main cornice line for cheaper bedrooms for hotel staff and the servants of guests. But the bulky proportions of the mansard roof called for a correspondingly coarse treatment of the building, as in the Grosvenor Hotel at Victoria Station — one of the series of London hotels built adjacent to the main-line railway terminuses.

The last of these was the Great Central, opposite the St Marylebone terminus of the Great Central Railway which sent its line from Sheffield to London in 1899 — its Wharncliffe banqueting rooms were named after the Railway's chairman. The Great Central was owned by the chain of Gordon and Frederick Hotels started by Frederick Gordon. A chairman, Sir Blundell Maple, owned the furniture store which furnished the hotels. The architect was Sir Robert Edis, a keen advocate of terracotta, as is amply demonstrated by this great salmon-pink building, now in use as offices.

The construction of Northumberland Avenue on the site of Northumberland House, Charing Cross, WC2, provided sites for three mammoth hotels, all Gordon & Frederick Hotels: the Grand of 1880, the Metropole of 1885 and the Victoria of 1890, bought from the collapsed Jabez Balfour empire, all now offices. The Gordon and Frederick Company also owned hotels at Dieppe, Cannes and

Thomas E. Collcutt: The Savoy Hotel, WC2. A cross-section from the Strand to the Victoria Embankment. In 1910 Richard D'Oyly Carte's first Embankment building, *c.* 1888, was extended eight feet forward by hanging bathrooms over the columns of the restaurant.

Monte Carlo and along the south coast of England, especially at Brighton where 'a weekend at the Metropole' was not an expensive affair in 1902. Combined hotel and railway tickets were offered at £2 5s. 0d. a head and the sum included 'first-class railway fare by express trains both ways and two days' full board and lodging'. The Brighton Metropole, designed by Alfred Waterhouse, RA, unfortunately lost its top hamper in the Second World War.

In these mammoth hotels more attention was given to the grandeur of the public rooms and main staircases than to the sanitary accommodation and wardrobes, for there was seldom more than one bathroom to a floor and the bedroom furniture was not built in. Chambermaids carried a portable sitz bath and cans of hot water into the bedroom, and the slops were taken away in pails. These conditions prevailed until the great impresario Richard D'Oyly Carte returned from visits to North America determined to build a London hotel which not only avoided these defects but surpassed in comfort and convenience the American hotels he had stayed at.

The Savoy

Richard D'Oyly Carte's father Henry Carte was a famous flautist and a partner in the long established firm of Rudall, Carte and Company, the flute-makers and musical instrument dealers of Berners Street, then of Denman Street, W1. His mother was the daughter of the Rev. Thomas Jones, descendant of the D'Oyly family and chaplain at the Chapel Royal, Savoy, Strand. After a brief period in his father's business, D'Oyly Carte opened a theatrical agency, also organising lecture tours, including Oscar Wilde's American tour of 1882 on 'The English Renaissance' and 'The Practical Application of the Principles of the Aesthetic Theory to Exterior and Interior House Decoration with Observations upon Dress and Personal Ornaments'.

D'Oyly Carte's success in bringing together W. S. Gilbert and Arthur Sullivan to write their English *opéra bouffe* led to the building of the Savoy Theatre in 1881, to the designs of C. J. Phipps. It rose on part of the site of the mediaeval Savoy Palace, presented by Henry III in 1246 to Count Peter II of Savoy, Earl of Richmond, who had 'the fayrest mannor in Europe' built on it. In 1888 D'Oyly Carte was to be found on this site on the Victoria Embankment one of the most consistently revitalised great hotels of the world. The Savoy had more than 400 rooms. Innovations included its own artesian wells and electric light plant, hydrau-

58
59

lic lifts and fire-resisting construction, together with numerous bathrooms, some of them *en suite* with bedrooms — a great advance in those years. The hotel was entered from Savoy Hill through the pink granite arches which survive today.

60

The hotel itself was a large rectangular courtyard building of the size and proportions of an Italian palazzo, though devoid of its beauty. On the Embankment front and returns were balconies with striped awnings and painted and gilded columns; the pink granite columns to the restaurant veranda with their unusual variety of Corinthian capitals still exist. The cast-iron balcony fronts, some of which also remain, were moulded in the 'swirl and blob' design which was to be the signature of the Art Nouveau movement. Two of the remaining balconies are decorated with a reclining figure of the muse Calliope in a low-relief style typical of the period. These features were probably by that versatile designer and architect Arthur Heygate Mackmurdo, who was related to the D'Oyly Carte family and later married Richard D'Oyly Carte's youngest sister Eliza. The builder was George H. Holloway, and the architect who interpreted D'Oyly Carte's ideas was Collin Beatson Young.

Although busy presenting his Savoy Operas, D'Oyly Carte still found time to apply his ceaseless flow of ideas to the running of the hotel, and at the same time to build his New English Opera House on the new Shaftesbury Avenue and Charing Cross Road intersection. A contemporary cartoon by 'Spy' shows him dashing along with the plans of both buildings under his arm.

D'Oyly Carte took pains to acquire the finest staff in Europe for his hotel, including the great hotelier César Ritz and the chef Auguste Escoffier. When Ritz left to start his own hotels, D'Oyly Carte bought the Restaurant Marivaux in Paris in order to acquire Joseph with it, and the Berkeley Hotel, Piccadilly, in order to have the services of the great hotel manager, George Reeves-Smith.

D'Oyly Carte died in 1901 at the age of fifty-five, and there is a memorial window to him in the Savoy Chapel. He was succeeded by his son, Rupert, and George Reeves-Smith. Under their management, the Savoy entered the new century with renewed vigour. The hotel had so far been an Embankment building, with an entry to the Strand through Beaufort Buildings. Reeves-Smith and Rupert D'Oyly Carte now proceeded to turn it into a Strand hotel as well, surpassing its neighbour, the monster Hotel Cecil, erstwhile casualty of the Jabez Balfour and Liberator financial crash.

145
146

This time Thomas E. Collcutt was called in. He had done the architectural work on the new English Opera House and had already made additions to the original Savoy Hotel in 1896. Experienced, adaptable and a typical Edwardian, Collcutt was equal to the occasion. Beaufort Buildings were demolished and at the same time the Strand was widened. Savoy Court (first offices, then residential suites and now part of the hotel), was built to the east, while to the west were built the West Block offices. Between the Embankment block and the new buildings were the entrance hall, lounge and foyer; the new Grill Room was situated under the east block.

Internally the change in levels between the Strand and the Embankment, the vistas and contrast between intimate lounges and spacious public rooms were put to good use by the combined genius of Collcutt, his young partner Stanley Hamp, and the D'Oyly Carte family. Collcutt carried out his favourite striped marble interiors with delicate mouldings and for the exterior obtained a sympathetic treatment of Carrara ware from Doulton's pottery.

The famous Simpson's Restaurant, demolished during the Strand widening, was now incorporated in Savoy Court. A large terracotta faced arch, unhappily cased in sheet metal in the 1930s, spans the entrance court and supports Lynn-Jenkins's gilded figure of Count Peter of Savoy, in chain mail and bearing a lance-pennant. In the entrance hall is a plaster frieze by Bertram Pegram. A lighting pillar was modelled on Germain Pilon's 'Three Graces' in the Louvre. 400 bedrooms were added. Arnold Bennett's *Imperial Palace* took a great deal of its inspiration from these transformations — the first wonders of the Savoy had already suggested his *Grand Babylon Hotel* (1902). But the 1905 extension northwards showed up the deficiencies of the 1889 building,

Thomas E. Collcutt: The Savoy Hotel, WC2. The Strand Front in Coronation Year, 1911.

The Savoy Hotel, WC2. The Gondola Banquet in the courtyard of the Embankment Block.

particularly its shortage of bathrooms — although the Savoy had been the first hotel to increase their ratio. The Embankment block had, moreover, never been renowned for its external beauty. Indeed *The Builder* had declined to illustrate it, observing that its only claim to enhance the London scene was that by comparison it at least made Stephen Salter's neighbouring Examination Halls of the Physicians and Surgeons more acceptable.

A daring operation was now planned. In the shortest possible time and without disrupting the tall, polished granite columns of the restaurant below, the balconies were to be struck off the river front and the rooms extended outwards with bathrooms inserted between them. Everything was carefully planned beforehand, the steelwork and Doulton's blocks all made and numbered and all the materials laid out on a vacant site in the new Aldwych. The extended floors were to be suspended from lattice girders laid across the tops of the existing walls so that no weight should come down upon the existing columns of the restaurant veranda.

Operations began on 1 August 1910. Aided by arc lamps at night, teams worked round the clock on every floor. Heating, plumbing, electric light, mosaic, marble and plasterwork, all had to be fitted in and carpets and furniture renewed. Guests were received *just ten weeks later* on 7 October.

The rooms on the river front were decorated and furnished from the designs of René Sergent of Paris. Whether the elevation of the new river front was also suggested by Mackmurdo, or whether the exacting conditions of clothing the steel frame and containing the bathrooms modified Collcutt's light touch and Hamp's *brio*, it is now difficult to say for certain, but the design is very functional and recalls earlier designs by Mackmurdo. The beautiful metal shop fronts to the Savoy Tailors' Guild under the West Block are worthy of note and are possibly by A. N. Prentice who was interested in work of this kind and had been an assistant of Collcutt's.

The Savoy did not stop there. After brief requisitioning for war purposes during the First World War, the number of bathrooms was again greatly increased by Collcutt and Hamp. The decorations were also continually updated. In the 1920s Basil Ionides (1884–1950) did one of the famous supper rooms named after the Savoy Operas. In the 1930s Easton and Robertson changed many interiors to Art Deco styles. And in the 1950s Eric Janes added a modern concrete vaulted canopy to the Embankment entrance.

The Ritz: Paris in London

In the 1880s César Ritz, thirteenth child of a Swiss peasant family, had won himself a reputation among the patrons of the spas of France and Germany as an expert hotelier. In order to enjoy the benefit of his attentive skills, guests were known to follow him as he progressed from hotel to hotel.

D'Oyly Carte first met Ritz at Baden Baden and in 1889 he invited him to demonstrate his hotelier's skills at the Savoy. At first sceptical of the ability of any London hotel to meet his exacting standards of cuisine and comfort, Ritz was won over by the Savoy and agreed to manage the hotel, although he continued his associations with the Continent.

After eight years at the Savoy he received an offer from a syndicate to manage a new hotel in Paris, which was to be fitted out behind the façade of No. 15 in Jules Hardouin-Mansart's Place Vendôme. A new luxury and elegance was entering the ancient occupation of innkeeping, for while the Earl of Bristol had given his name to a series of European hotels by demanding the elegance, Ritz, who provided the luxuries, now gave his name to the first of several Ritz hotels. He was soon back in London advising on the new Carlton Hotel, Haymarket, designed by Isaacs and Florence and opened in 1899.

The success of the Paris Ritz prompted the syndicate to seek a site in London. Their choice fell on that occupied by Walsingham House — a block of service flats — and the Bath Hotel, between Arlington Street and Green Park, Piccadilly. Charles Mewès, the architect for the conversion

of the Paris Ritz who had built up an international practice, was called in again. He appointed the young Paris-trained English architect Arthur J. Davis as his London partner. The London Ritz was to be a larger version of the Paris Ritz and an entirely new building.

The demolition of the old Bath Hotel and Walsingham House gave the authorities a chance to widen Piccadilly. Their plans would have left little space for the new hotel and Lord Wimborne, when asked by Ritz if he was prepared to sell any of the grounds of the adjacent Wimborne House, replied asking a similar favour of Ritz. Fortunately the authorities allowed Ritz to build over the pavement on the lines of the Rue de Rivoli, Paris, thus preserving the narrow opening to the Green Park section of Piccadilly, so important to the urban scene, and allowing the end of the hotel to face down Piccadilly.

158 Mewès and Davis had an opportunity here to design a little of Paris in London, and the elegance associated with the Ritz hotels is to be found in the interiors, still preserved much as the architects created them. As in the Paris Ritz, the architects were employed to direct the design of the furnishing and equipment, right down to the cutlery. The exterior, in spite of the splendid pavement arcade of unpolished Norwegian granite (with the vaulting sadly lacking), is overpowered by a French feature typical of an earlier style — the great mansard roof and dormer windows necessary to large hotels where the height to the cornice was prescribed.

An important innovation in the construction of the Ritz was the steel frame, used for the first time on such a scale in London. (Even had the design called for it, thin external walls could not be used to express the steel frame at this stage since the regulations then required the external walls to carry their own weight.)

The Lyons hotels

J. Lyons & Co., the largest catering organisation in Britain, if not the world, were well launched on their programme for providing the Edwardians with 'luxury for the million' when they built their first hotel, the Strand Palace. Begun in 1907, the Strand opened the following year. It stood on the site of Exeter Hall (1830–1), designed by J. P. Gandy-Deering and intended as a rival to the Royal Exchange. The new owners did not incorporate Gandy-Deering's Greek Ionic portico into the building as at first intended, but sixty years later the hotel's metal and glass Art Deco entrance lobby by Oliver Bernard was presented to the Victoria and Albert Museum.

The Strand front was faced with Doulton's Carrara ware, the cream, glazed terracotta Collcutt had used on the Strand additions to the Savoy Hotel in 1905. The change of taste in the few intervening years was clearly evident in the Strand Hotel. Instead of Collcutt's lighter style, so appropriate to

terracotta, Lyons's architects, Ancell and Tanner, chose the heavier Champs Elysées style. Together with the heavily moulded ceilings, mahogany or walnut panelling, marble mosaic floors, bronze-gilt fittings and coloured glass domes and windows, this was to remain for many years Lyons's 'house style'.

Five years later, Lyons began building their Regent Palace Hotel on a site at the junction of Glasshouse Street and Sherwood Street near Piccadilly — ideally placed between theatreland and the West End shops. Ancell died before work began and his assistants, including the office junior, F. J. Wills, who twenty years later was architect to the extensive additions to both the Regent Palace and the Strand, carried on.

A full page in the *Illustrated London News* of 22 May 1915 announced the opening of the new hotel on 26 May and listed the charges:

> 1028 bedrooms
>   6*s* 6*d* per day Single
> 12*s* 6*d* per day Double
> 13*s*   per day Double (Two Bedsteads)
> including bath, full table d'hôte breakfast
> Telegrams:— 'Untippable'
> Music Morning Afternoon and Evening

Lyons's Cumberland Hotel on the corner of Great Cumberland Place and Oxford Street opposite

Marble Arch was opened in 1933; the architect was now F. J. Wills. The elevations, designed in one piece with the adjoining Regal Cinema (since demolished), are by Henry Tanner junior.

Other Edwardian hotels

The Piccadilly Hotel is an example of the Edwardian style at its grandest. Its inception was due to the nephew of Sir Polydore de Keyser, builder of the De Keyser Royal Hotel at Blackfriars, EC4. Designed by Norman Shaw for the site of the St James's Hall, it offered an impressive front to Piccadilly and also began the rebuilding of the Quadrant, Regent Street (*see under* The rebuilding of Regent Street *and* Shaw, Richard Norman). But so generous was the expenditure on these grand façades and equally grand interiors that the venture failed in eighteen months and was bought by R. E. Jones of Cardiff. It is now one of the Grand Metropolitan hotels. In spite of the fact that the east gable intended on the Piccadilly front was forestalled by another lessee, Shaw's modified design lost none of the effectiveness of the open colonnade fronting the terrace restaurant.

No less splendid than its more famous competitors, but smaller and with only one façade, is the Waldorf Hotel. This was designed by A. Marshall Mackenzie and his son A. G. R. Mackenzie who had studied in Paris under the decorator Réne Sergent. Built on the gently curving concave side of Aldwych on the Bedford Estate, the hotel is

R. Norman Shaw, RA
with William Woodward:
Above: A drawing by
C. W. English and A. C.
Fare (*q.v.*) of the
South (Piccadilly) front
of the Piccadilly Hotel.
Forestalled by
Denman House from
building the East
Gable, Shaw
introduced a clever
adaptation. *Right:*
This view of the Tea
Terrace shows Shaw's
'Bridal Suite' bow
windows.

flanked by the identical twin façades of the Strand and Aldwych Theatres, both opened before the hotel was begun. All three buildings were carried out by the Waring—White building company.

According to *The Builder* (29.12.06), the Waldorf was 'modelled on the latest American Hotels having numerous bathrooms en suite with bedrooms so that visitors may, if they desire, have the convenience of a private bathroom'. The fine sculptured Portland stone frieze of *putti* is by Emil Fuchs and the interiors are still maintained in pristine condition.

Another notable addition of the period was the Welbeck Court Hotel and adjacent flats, a splendid block of buildings in the Louis XV style on the corner of Welbeck Street and Wigmore Street. Its designers were Boehmer and Gibbs who had inherited the mantle of Archer and Green and, like them had specialised in the design of fine blocks of mansion flats. The brown limestone building, erected on the newly aligned Southampton Row and looking rather like an over-windowed Scottish castle, was built in 1906 to a design by J. Bradshaw Gass as the Tollard Royal Hotel for A. Butterworth of Bournemouth. It originally had offices incorporated into the ground and mezzanine floors and is now entirely offices.

Walter Thomas: *Left:* **The glorious profusion of the gate to the Philharmonic Hotel, Hope Street, Liverpool.** *Above:* **The Hotel.**

Tearooms and Coffee Houses

The temperance movement gave rise to a significant feature of the urban scene in the last quarter of the nineteenth century — the tea and coffee houses, to which the Edwardian era was to impart its own particular flavour.

Among the early arrivals was the remarkable Coffee Tavern designed by George and Peto in Newark-on-Trent in 1882 — the gift of Viscountess Ossington. In Glasgow, the tea rooms established by Miss Catherine Cranston became famous as the Willow Tea Rooms, named after the site of one in Sauchiehall (Willowhall) Street. Miss Cranston engaged some of the brightest talents among young Glasgow designers for her interiors, among them George Walton and Charles Rennie Mackintosh and his wife Margaret. In Bristol, Stephen Carwardine, the tea and coffee importers, were opening restaurants, while tea rooms were beginning to appear in Manchester and Liverpool. The interesting interior of Deller's Café in Exeter (destroyed in the Second World War) was a late example of the Art Nouveau style applied to such an establishment.

The first teashop proprietors to expand into a large organisation were the Aerated Bread Co. whose first teashop opened in 1884. This company concentrated on the City of London where it still has numerous branches. Callard, Stewart and Watt opened a tea room and restaurant at 57–59 Piccadilly and 44–46 Old Bond Street, the background to a popular print titled 'His Majesty the Baby', and rebuilt by Read and Macdonald in their picturesque manner in 1904. Unhappily, the original shopfronts have been removed and replaced by others in a totally inappropriate style. The building is now in mixed occupation.

Fuller's, the 'American Confectioners', contributed a chain of dainty teashop-restaurants. Their branch in an angle of the Army and Navy Stores in Victoria Street clung staunchly to its site for many years, just as Ridgway's tea shops, similarly placed, held out for several decades against two mammoth building enterprises — Waring & Gillow's in Oxford Street and the Piccadilly Hotel.

While the teashops maintained a discreet and genteel style of decoration, the coffee houses, perhaps influenced by the more exotic aroma of their beverage, indulged in decoration of a more Art Nouveau style and, like the cigar divans and tobacco kiosks, affected Turkish or Arabic names like Kardomah and Mecca.

But the company which did most towards the proliferation of these establishments was undoubtedly J. Lyons & Co. The firm was a partnership between the Whitechapel tobacco importers Salmon and Gluckstein and Joseph Lyons (1848–1917) who came to business late, at the age of thirty-eight, having trained as an artist. Montague Gluckstein wanted to do something to remedy the lack of facilities for refreshment for women and children shopping in London. The first opportunity to enter the catering field came when Salmon and Gluckstein secured the contract for catering at the Newcastle upon Tyne Exhibition of 1887 with the help of Lyons. Other contracts followed, for the catering at exhibitions held at Glasgow and Paris and then at the Olympia Exhibition Hall in Kensington which opened with a show called 'Paris Hippodrome'. Lyons catered for its subsequent exotic spectacles, 'Venice in London', 'Constantinople in London' and 'The Orient in London'.

With this behind them, Lyons were able to move from their headquarters in a basement in Olympia to Cadby Hall in Hammersmith Road, formerly the piano factory of a Charles Cadby. A series of impressive contracts followed, including catering for the troops drafted to London for the funeral of Queen Victoria in 1901, the Franco-British Exhibition at the White City in 1908, and culminating in 1924 in a record-breaking feat — the catering for the British Empire Exhibition at Wembley Park for its first year.

Lyons also catered on the old London Chatham and Dover Railway, while Spiers and Pond, owners of the Criterion Restaurant, undertook the same on the old London and South Western Railway.

A first step towards realising Montague Gluckstein's original aim came with the opening of the first Lyons Tea Shop in 1894 at 213 Piccadilly, since closed. The decor of this and the first sixteen teashops was more French than English, with richly moulded ceilings, walls lined with silk damask, marble-topped tables with ornate iron frames, and chairs with red plush seats. The waitresses wore grey uniforms and French pastries were sold at the counter. The white-painted shop front with its carved and gilt wooden letters on the fascia soon became as familiar to Londoners and visitors to London as the red omnibus of the London General Omnibus Company.

More durable materials and more practical furniture went into the seventeenth Lyons teashop opened in Oxford Street in 1898 — opal glass ceiling panels, marble wall linings and bentwood chairs. Eventually, there were more than 200 teashops in London and more than 50 in other cities and towns, all conforming to this pattern.

The company's next venture was in the field of the high-class restaurant. In 1894 they were able to acquire the Trocadero Theatre in Windmill Street, which had been transformed from the notorious Argyll (Subscription) Rooms (not to be confused with those in Argyll Street, Regent Street) run by Robert Bignell.

With W. J. Ancell as architect, Lyons reconstructed the old music hall into a restaurant, formed a new entrance on the newly completed Shaftesbury Avenue, and built a new frontage to the old Trocadero. In 1901 the company acquired Avenue Mansions, already built on the new street. Joseph Lyons, himself a member of the Royal Institute of Painters in Water-colours, and sparing no pains in the decoration of the new restaurant, held a competition for a decorative frieze for the entrance hall, won by the painter Gerald Moira and the sculptor F. Lynn-Jenkins. The 'Troc' continued its association with variety entertainment and between 1920 and 1946, apart from the war years, C. B. Cochran presented his Cabaret and his 'Young Ladies' there.

Lyons next showed their genius for providing 'luxury for the million' with the Lyons 'Popular Café', also by Ancell, a few doors from their first teashop in Piccadilly and opposite the famous St James's concert hall and restaurant, soon demolished to make way for the new Piccadilly Hotel. Until it was damaged in the Second World War, the Lyons 'Popular' retained its Edwardian plush and gilt richness. When it opened on 11 October 1904, the press announcement ran: 'Luxury for the Million ... Music by Day ... No Tips', and proclaimed:

Ladies shopping will enjoy the Afternoon Musical Teas served between 3 and 6.

Delicious new Pastries 2d

Tea, 3*d* per pot
no gratuities
Luncheons   Four Courses 1*s* 6*d*
                     Five Courses 2*s* 6*d*

The introduction of the Corner Houses and
Maisons Lyons between 1907 and 1933 was yet
another important contribution to the comfort
and convenience of visitors to London's West End.
They included the Coventry Street Corner House
(greatly enlarged in 1923); the Strand Corner
House; Maison Lyons, Shaftesbury Avenue; the
Blenheim Restaurant, New Bond Street; Maison
Riche, Regent Street (later Maison Lyons); Maison
Lyons, Oxford Street; the New Oxford Corner
House; Maison Lyons, Marble Arch; the Birkbeck
Café, High Holborn, WC1; and the Throgmorton
Restaurant, Throgmorton Street, EC2. These
establishments have been described by J. M.
Richards who says:

> A great feature of democratic London life
> in the Twenties [but which began in the
> 1900s] was the so-called 'Corner House'
> operated by Lyons at Marble Arch,
> Coventry Street and Tottenham Court Road:
> multi-storey cafés, open all night [Richards
> is referring to the ground floor at Coventry
> Street] ... and thronged all day by shoppers,
> office workers, day-trippers from the provin-
> ces, tourists and students ... that gave ordin-
> ary people a sense of being pampered, and
> an awareness of luxury, without making them
> feel self-consciously out of their proper
> habitat, as they might feel, for example in
> the interiors designed to please the rich,
> such as big hotels and luxury liners ...
>   *Listener*, 11.9.69, p. 340

Until 1925 the 'house style' which Lyons had
given to their first hotel, the Strand Palace, was
applied to the Corner Houses and the Maisons
Lyons. Of these the Strand Corner House, Maison
Lyons, Marble Arch, and the Throgmorton
Restaurant still flourish. The faience of Maison
Lyons, 360–366 Oxford Street (now Avon House),
designed by Lewis Solomon, can still be seen above
the plain brick front which now replaces the beautiful Mond-nickel shop front of Lyons.

Beside the great additions made in 1923, the first
of the Lyons Corner Houses, the small Corner
House at the junction of Rupert Street and
Coventry Street, looks almost coy. Designed by
W. J. Ancell, this was built on property known as
the Arundel Estate, which included the Challis
Hotel, run by Lyons until plans for the Corner
House were ready. It was situated in the heart of
theatreland and much patronised by stage people,
as Sir Noel Coward recalled in his autobiography
Present Indicative.

W. S. Worley: Sicilian House, Sicilian Avenue, WC1.
These could be shops built in to a surviving Roman
colonnaded street, but this splendid theatrical scenery
is all carried out in glazed faience.

London's Edwardian Shops and Stores

Tallis's *Views of London Streets*, published early
in the nineteenth century, give support to the
notion of the English as a 'nation of shopkeepers'.
They show the vast extent of London's shops,
stretching from the City to Bond Street and from
Westminster to St Marylebone. The opening of
Regent Street in 1825 brought new stimulus to the
West End as a shopping centre which soon expanded to take in Knightsbridge and Brompton Road,
while cheap railway fares encouraged growing
crowds of shoppers.

To cater for this expanding trade, shopkeepers
steadily enlarged their shops by buying up adjacent sites, so that Gordon Selfridge, on his first
visit from Chicago, was able to describe the prem-

ises of some of his future competitors as 'an agglomeration of small shops'. Having gained a first foothold, proprietors would perambulate the boundaries of the block, reckoning up the establishments they would need to buy out. Mr Hollingsworth, for instance, found that the premises Bourne & Hollingsworth would have to acquire were:

A public house	A brothel
A dairy	A private residence
A branch of Finch's wineshops	A wholesale lace merchant
A barber	A nest of Polish tailors
A coffee house	A sweet shop
A carpet layer	Doan's Backache Pills warehouse
A costume manufacturer	A cigarette factory
A wholesale milliner	A wholesale blouse maker
A retail milliner	A wine merchant
A music publisher	A soda manufacturer
A musical instrument shop (German)	A jeweller
A palmist	A baby linen manufacturer
A beauty parlour	A wallpaper merchant
The New Columbia Gramophone Company	Two solicitors
An estate agent	A chapel

Once established, Gordon Selfridge himself used each week to beat the bounds of a block containing among other things the Hotel Somerset, the Wigmore Hotel, the Grotrian Hall, a convent and a street of small houses, seeking opportunities to purchase.

The first English stores to combine several departments of drapery and clothing were Kendal Milne's of Manchester and Bainbridge's of Newcastle upon Tyne, while Fenwick's (also of Newcastle) were the first to treat window dressing as an art. The first store in London to provide a variety of goods was the Post Office Supply Association in Queen Victoria Street, established in 1864. This became the Civil Service Supply Association in 1866 and was soon able to open a branch in the Strand which is still in operation.

The Army and Navy Stores opened in the new Victoria Street in 1872, followed by the Civil Service Co-operative Association in the Haymarket, the Junior Army and Navy Stores in York House, Lower Regent Street, and the West Kensington Stores.

The first private department store to open in London was William Whiteley's of Westbourne Grove (1865). This was followed by Harrods of Brompton Road which expanded from grocery to general merchandise in 1883. Selfridge's opened on the corner of Duke Street and Oxford Street in 1909, the year of Harrods' jubilee.

Some of the great drapery establishments still bear Welsh names since, along with dairies and pharmacies, this class of trade attracted the Welsh to London. Dai Harris Evans, a farmer's son from Llanelli, came to London in 1877 and bought a small drapery business in Westminster Bridge Road specialising in lace goods. Only two years later he bought No. 320 Oxford Street from which the present emporium has grown. In 1909 John Murray designed a splendid drapery establishment for D. H. Evans. It was faced with solid blocks of Greek Pentelikos marble and adorned with Ionic columns of Greek Cippolino, all in the wide proportions typical of Edwardian Baroque. In the oak-panelled restaurant plaster panels, modelled by F. Brook Hitch, represented 'Harvest', 'Commerce', 'Industry', 'Science' and 'Trade'. But in 1936 John Murray's marble palace was demolished to make way for a 'moderne' style store designed by Louis Blanc.

51 St David's House, New Cavendish Street (formerly Great Marylebone Street) W1, was designed by Saul and Hardy for B. Davies & Son's Dairies (now part of United Dairies). The tall, gabled premises, with their beautiful Art Nouveau sculptured orange trees, serve as a reminder of the elegance which the small business could then afford when in an affluent quarter of the town. The building is now in other occupation.

Then, as now, commercial vulgarity was the enemy of 'good taste', as the following outburst from Louis N. Parker in a lecture at the Royal Society of Arts in 1909 eloquently demonstrates:

> You are suddenly confronted with the latest steel framed six or seven storeyed emporium, the base of which is all plate glass and gingerbread, covered with horrible advertisements of monstrous comestibles, quack nostrums, foods for the fat, pale pills for pink people [a parody on 'pink pills for pale people', a contemporary nostrum], all labelled with hideous outrages on the English language in the shape of new words — CLENOL for soap, QUICKLITE for matches, RITEFAST for ink.

Between the small shop and the rapidly expanding department store, London also had its bazaars and arcades. The idea of a covered walk bordered by shops was not new to the Edwardian age. The Burlington Arcade, 'that sublimate of superfluities' as George Augustus Sala called it, was designed in 1816 by Samuel Ware for Lord George Cavendish, reputedly to prevent oyster shells being thrown over the wall into his lordship's garden at Burlington House. The idea was repeated under Queen Victoria in 1880 with the Royal Arcade in High Victorian 'Grand Hotel' style, between Old Bond Street and Albemarle Street. The Edwardian era was splendidly represented by the Piccadilly Arcade (1909), designed by G. Thrale Jell. This was built on the site of the Brunswick Hotel, 52 and 53 Jermyn Street, and incorporated into Piccadilly House. The Jermyn Street end, over which there were bachelor chambers, was destroyed in the Second World War and clumsily rebuilt as

Stevens and Munt: Harrods, Old Brompton Road, SW7. This drawing by Fred Taylor shows new shop fronts of the 1930s. The dome has no structural or spatial significance below the flat roof.

offices. The keystones of the arcade and alternate window spandrils on the Piccadilly front carry a curious carved emblem — a piccadil, or kind of cravat, sold by a haberdasher in the former Portugal Street and supposedly the origin of the name of Piccadilly (one theory among others).

Other English cities had their own versions of the arcade built in this period: the arcade at Deansgate, Manchester, was designed by John Brooke; in Northampton the Emporium Arcade was by Morley and Scrivener; in Castle Street, Norwich, in 1900 George Skipper did the Royal Arcade and public house with Arts and Crafts coloured tile tracery, possibly by W. J. Neatby.

Harrods

Henry Charles Harrod, the first Harrod in the retail business, was first a miller in Clacton, Essex, and then a tea merchant in the City of London. He bought Burden's grocery shop in Middle Queen's Buildings, Brompton Road, in 1849. His son, Charles Digby Harrod, took over in 1861 and in spite of total loss by fire in 1883, expanded the trade to include other merchandise; he was the first to introduce cash desks for the customer's use. When he retired in 1891 he was succeeded by Richard Burbridge from the Army and Navy, Whiteley's and the West Kensington Stores. Burbridge disapproved of passenger lifts but intro-

duced the first escalator — an inclined belt — the year he took over.

By 1900 Harrods had grown to contain eighty departments amounting to a total area of thirty-six acres, and had acquired the whole site between Hans Crescent and Hans Road. With the architects Stevens and Munt, Harrods began rebuilding, erecting the now familiar pale terracotta façade and the purely symbolic dome which reflects no majestic interior rotunda but stands on steel girders spanning a flat roof.

Inside were elegant carved mahogany door-cases, rich rococo ceilings with plaster pendants, a ladies' club in Adam style with a retiring room lined in Brescia Sanguine and Pavonazzo marble and onyx, a gentlemen's club in Georgian style, a Grand Restaurant and a Banking Hall which was 'a recognized rendezvous'.

Far and away the most astonishing of this splendid galaxy of departments is the Fish and Game Department, still carefully preserved, decorated with hand-painted ceramic tiles by W. J. Neatby, from Burmantofts of Leeds and Doulton's of Lambeth.

Debenham and Freebody

Of the large establishments for the retailing of

ladies' wear of a high-class order, the most Edwardian was Debenham & Freebody of Wigmore Street, W1 (now in other use).

William Debenham, the first Debenham to reach London, came from near Bury St Edmunds in Suffolk. In 1813, after an apprenticeship with I. & R. Morley, the great wholesalers in the City, he became a partner with Thomas Clark of Flint and Clark, established at 44 Wigmore Street, Cavendish Square, in 1788. Clark retired in 1837 and Pooley and Smith of Cheltenham Spa acquired his interests, the firm becoming Debenham, Pooley and Smith. One spa leading to another, so to speak, they opened a branch at Harrogate, calling both houses Cavendish House. William Debenham senior died in 1863. He had taken into partnership his eldest son William, his brother-in-law Clement Freebody and his younger son Frank who began expanding the business until its interests spread across the world. In 1883 the Wigmore Street premises, including No. 42, underwent its first rebuilding.

189 By 1905 Debenham & Freebody had acquired the whole block between Wigmore Street and Welbeck Street. Their new building, designed by J. G. S. Gibson and William Wallace, was carried out with the splendour of an Edwardian public building, the only difference being the essential plate-glass shop windows. The result was a grand establishment in the current Belcher and Macartney 'Wrenaissance' style, translated into imperishable Doulton Carrara Ware — a material even more soot-resistant than the unglazed red, pink or buff terracotta of the 1880s which it superseded.

The full orchestra was called up — columns in Cippolino marble, bronzework by Singer, decorative plasterwork by Ernest Gimson and Gilbert Seale, metalwork by the Birmingham Guild, metal windows by Henry Hope, steel doors by Crittall, electric lifts by Otis, all put together by Trollope and Sons in association with Colls and Sons just before they amalgamated. The building was opened in sections, floor by floor, a waterproof layer of asphalt being laid over each storey as it was completed.

The opening was in 1907 and at the Franco-British Exhibition at the White City a model of Debenham's was exhibited. The souvenir programme of the opening of the shop, printed in English and French and illustrated with water-colours by Byam Shaw and Mortimer Menpes, was printed at the Menpes Press.

A feature of the shop was the luxuriously appointed retiring rooms adjoining the Ladies' Club Room where the sanitary ware was appropriately labelled 'The Cavendish'.

Waring and Gillow

69
94 'Wren's east wing of Hampton Court on stilts in the middle of Oxford Street' is how Professor Charles Reilly described Waring's in his 'London

Streets and their Recent Buildings' (*Country Life*, 1922). How the firm established itself in London was recounted none too modestly by Samuel James Waring junior himself for the 1905 edition of *Who's Who*. It tells how,

> an enthusiast on Decorative Art, he established the business of Waring and Sons in London in 1893 and arranged a fusion of interests [*sic*] with the historic house of Gillow by evolving a style combining classic purity with English practicability, and, through his firm's operations in France, Italy, Germany, Austria, Greece, Turkey, Egypt, South Africa, Australia, America, exerted a powerful influence in promoting British decorative art and general recognition of the 'New English Renaissance' [an ambiguous term which could mean all things to all customers].

Waring's father, also called Samuel James, had come from Northern Ireland and established

R. Frank Atkinson: the former Waring and Gillow's, Oxford Street, W1. A design closely resembling this is among the Norman Shaw drawings at the Royal Academy. Did Shaw suggest this to Atkinson? On the right is Belcher and Joass's Mappin House.

businesses in Manchester and Liverpool, where the young Samuel Waring was born in 1860. Waring extended his father's business to London by buying the firm of decorators, Collinson & Lock, of Fleet Street, who had already purchased Gillow & Co, the famous cabinet-makers established in Lancaster in the eighteenth century. Waring got a foothold in Oxford Street by buying W. G. & P. Phillips' China and Glass Emporium which T. E. Collcutt had built, together with Duveen's, the fine art dealers, at Nos. 175–181 on the south side of Oxford Street. Following the by now familiar pattern, Waring also bought Hampton & Sons of Pall Mall, Decorators and Furnishers, and Bonsor Carpets.

Thus established on the shady side of Oxford Street, Waring looked across to the sunny side and bought up a square site complete but for the south-west corner already occupied by Ridgway's Tea Rooms — which held out for a further thirty years. Waring asked a fellow Liverpudlian, Frank Atkinson, to design his great furniture and furnishing emporium for the new site. As chief assistant to the Liverpool architect Francis Doyle, Atkinson had collaborated with Norman Shaw on the Royal Insurance Company's building in Liverpool and it seems possible that Shaw may have provided the inspiration for Waring's new building; there is a design for the principal elevation among the Norman Shaw drawings at the Royal Academy of Arts.

Waring's building exhibits all the tricks of Wren's south and east fronts at Hampton Court and more. The centre of the store was originally in the form of a splendid rotunda (now floored in), the floors are of reinforced concrete on the Columban patent system, the cast rainwater heads by C. Wragge are 4 ft 6 in. high, and the ground floor is faced in Grey Kenny granite to which were attached bronze medallions (transferred to 188 Regent Street) commemorating awards won at international trade fairs. Above are Thomas Lawrence of Bracknell's 'red rubber' bricks, Poulton's 'thin reds' for the side elevation and green Westmorland slates in graduated courses for the mansard roof. There are eight acres of floor space. The building has since undergone drastic reconstruction, preserving the façades.

Waring erected his building and supplied most of the fittings through the Waring-White Building Co. which he had formed with J. G. White & Co. The new firm grew at an astonishing rate — it built the New War Office, the Ritz Hotel, the Waldorf Theatre and Hotel, the Royal Automobile Club, the Hamburg-Amerika offices and Oceanic House in Cockspur Street, the cliff-like Parkside flats in Knightsbridge, the tower of Birmingham University, the Liverpool Cotton Exchange, several town halls, the Ashton Memorial in Lancaster and Selfridge's.

Waring was prominent in many enterprises calculated to benefit the public and, incidentally, his com-

pany. Of these his offer to build, free of charge, a Peace Memorial in Hyde Park after the First World War was the boldest. Waring was created a baronet in 1919 and 1st Baron Waring in 1922 — his motto, *Nec vi nec astutia*. He lived to be eighty.

Selfridge's

The spread of shops and stores further west along Oxford Street was considered a risky speculation, but this did not deter Gordon Selfridge when he came to build his new store at the corner of Duke Street and Oxford Street in 1908–9.

Born at Ripon, Wisconsin, in 1858, Harry Gordon Selfridge left school at fourteen to work in a bank while waiting to be accepted for the navy. Rejected as under height, he entered the Chicago mail order firm of Field, Leiter & Co. (Marshall Field's) as a junior clerk in 1879 and by 1886 had risen to the post of manager of the retail department. In this capacity he travelled extensively in the USA and Europe, collecting ideas for the store. He was made a partner in 1890 and was able to leave fourteen years later with a considerable fortune which he used to buy businesses which he re-sold at a profit.

Still only in his mid-forties, Selfridge grew restless, finding, as he put it, 'travel, growing orchids, club life and reading, poor substitutes for hard work'. He turned his attention to London. On his visits there he had taken an objective look at shopkeeping traditions and found room for improvement. For instance, he disapproved of the convention which had the customer approached by a floor-walker asking 'What does Madam wish to see?' and then calling up an assistant — often by number. He preferred to think that in his new store the customer would be 'spending the day at Selfridge's' without harassment. Shop windows he saw, not as an excuse for the display of every conceivable sample of goods on sale, but as a place for artistically arranged exhibits. He would display no name on the fascia. And so Selfridge with his family pulled up his Chicago roots and began to put his ideas for the new store into practice. He bought up the square site in mixed occupation at the corner of Duke Street, always paying a fair price when he bought out a business.

Selfridge was determined that the new store would have no grand staircase on the lines of the Paris *grands magasins* but the maximum uninterrupted floor area. However, because of the regulation which required the building of fire-resisting cross walls and steel shutters at intervals of forty feet, he was only able to realise this fully twenty years later when the regulations were modified.

To put his ideas into practice, Selfridge consulted Daniel H. Burnham, the Chicago architect whose new classic style had won the day on the main buildings for the Chicago World's Fair in 1893. Selfridge's new building was to conform to this style, but only an echo of 'the great booming voice

Francis S. Swales, R. Frank Atkinson and Daniel
H. Burnham: *Above:* The gigantic scale of the frieze of
Selfridge's Oxford Street store. *Below:* The centre bay
was the last to be inserted on the Oxford Street front of
this colossal store. Macfarlane's cast-iron windows are
here obscured by Jubilee decorations. The enrichment of
the columns derives from Philibert de l'Orme.

of Burnham', as Sir Nikolaus Pevsner has aptly
called it, was heard in Oxford Street. Selfridge had
in his possession a sketch from another source
'which', he told his biographer Reginald Pound,
'I kept so constantly at hand and fingered so
frequently that it had become dog-eared in my
pocket'. The author of the sketch was Francis S.
Swales, a Canadian-born American over on a
studentship tour of Europe including, of course,
Paris. Swales's design as realised consists of a great
order of Ionic columns from first-floor level to
crowning entablature standing on piers and separ-
ated by great cast-iron fronts by Walter Macfarlane's
of Glasgow. The upper storey of the end bays of
these fronts is enriched by tabernacles with 'barley-
sugar' columns entwined with vine tendrils, all in
cast iron.

Swales took the Ionic order from the great French
architect Philibert de l'Orme's Palais des Tuileries
where this was left standing after the Palace was
burnt down in the 1870 Commune. Swales gave
the order angled volutes but kept the cabled flutes
enriched with the acanthus shoots of the original.
In the first section there were ten columns on
Oxford Street and eight on Duke Street. The carving was by W. B. Fagan.

Selfridge at one time had hopes of a merger with
Samuel Waring whose rapidly expanding Waring—
White building company won the contract for
Selfridge's. Waring's architect Frank Atkinson was
also engaged.

For the design of the steel frame, then an innovation, Swales had introduced Sven Bylander (1877—
1943), a Swedish engineer from New York whose
firm is still in operation as Bylander, Waddell. The
site architect was W. E. Duke. The store opened
with great *éclat* in 1909.

After the First World War Selfridge began building
again, aiming to acquire the whole of the property
enclosed in the rectangle bounded by Oxford
Street, Orchard Street, Duke Street and Wigmore
Street. Building began at the west end. The consul-
tants were now Sir John Burnet and his partner
Thomas Tait, the architect Albert D. Miller,
London representative of Graham, Anderson,
Probst and White, successors to Burnham, and the
builder, D. Huntingdon, formerly site agent for the
Waring—White Company.

When both ends of his store were complete,
Selfridge filled up the centre of the Oxford Street
front with a great recess enriched with relief panels and a giant metal French-style mantelpiece
clock by Gilbert Bayes, all gilt.

Selfridge's site had now grown to the proportions
of Harrods, but Gordon Selfridge had ideas more
ambitious than simply balancing a dome on girders
over the store front as Harrods had done. A square
tapered tower was to rise from the centre of the
block, to the design of Philip Tilden. (Tilden had
also prepared a design for a mediaeval-style
Hadrian's Villa for Selfridge, to be built facing the

Channel at Hengistbury Head, Hampshire.) But America furnished Gordon Selfridge with yet another idea for the completion of his store — this time for a dome on a drum with a peristyle, equal in height to the dome of St Paul's Cathedral, which would have made the eighty-foot store beneath look like a mere plinth in comparison with so grand a superstructure. Foundations and steel work sufficient to support this great edifice were actually put in the ground before the project was abandoned.

William Whiteley's, Queensway, W2

William Whiteley's, Ribbons and Fancy Goods, opened in 1863 in Westbourne Grove, W2, then nicknamed 'Bankrupt Avenue'. Over the next twenty years William Whiteley expanded into eighteen premises and an equivalent number of departments, changing the name of his store to the Universal Provider. His success so incited the envy of his neighbouring shopkeepers that he was burned in effigy by the family butchers of Bayswater. His store also frequently caught fire and a huge fire in 1887 prompted cab drivers to display on their cabs the notice 'Going to Whiteley's Fire'.

Whiteley himself was murdered in 1907 by a man who claimed to be his natural son. In 1911, when the site of the old Paddington Public Baths became available, the company obtained a grand design for the site from Belcher and Joass. In contrast to the giant Ionic columns of Selfridge's completed first section, Whiteley's design of Corinthian columns over Doric columns was more articulated. Consent was obtained for a *grand escalier* on the lines of the Paris *magasin* but here it is *back to front*.

At Whiteley's the central recess in the façade, anticipating Selfridge's by some years, is embellished by grand carving, Roman in scale, and 'The Seasons' in bronze by a French sculptor. The corner pavilions in the Belcher manner are also embellished by sculpture while the central feature above the cornice echoes the Joass manner.

Some Edwardian trades

Of all the many and varied trades that flourished under Edward VII few seem so particularly of the period as the makers of the Player Piano.

In the decade leading up to the First World War, every small town which boasted a piano shop enjoyed a periodic visit from the demonstrator of this amenable instrument, an occasion more social than commercial, and anticipated with pleasure. On a date made known in advance the shop would open its doors to an audience of townspeople of all ages, come to hear a rendition of the classics by the pianist of the day, transferred on to piano roll.

The special requirement of the manufacturer of 'Player-Pianos and Mechanical Attachments to the

C. Wakley: Willie Clarkson's Costumier et Perruquier, 41 Wardour Street, W1. Sir Beerbohm Tree laid the foundation stone, and Sarah Bernhardt the coping stone. The building is now in other use. A drawing by Charlotte Halliday.

Organ' was a concert hall which could be used for demonstrations on a rather grander scale. Walter Cave designed such a building for the Orchestrelle Company at the Aeolian Hall, 135—137 New Bond Street. And Sir Herbert Marshall's Angelus Player-Pianos 'incorporating the Melodant Expression Device, the Phrasing Lever and the Artistyle', were housed in Regent House, the first of the new buildings in Regent Street. Designed by G. D. Martin, the building still bears in the spandrils of its arches mosaics of the arms of London, Paris, New York, St Petersburg and, oddly, Murano, home of the Italian mosaic workers.

Edwardians in more formal mood were encapsulated for posterity by the Edwardian Court photographers of whom some forty had studios in London's West End in the decade before the First World War. There, among the fluted columns and potted palms, gentlemen, in uniforms often hired for the occasion from the military tailors of Savile Row, and ladies in court dresses were arranged for the camera in the appropriate stylised poses of the period. A typical studio was that designed by the architect C. H. B. Quennell at 157 New Bond Street for the Court Photographer F. W. Speaight. The interior resembled the first class companionway of an Atlantic liner, with a mahogany staircase leading to a foyer with a decorated ceiling and the full range of potted palms and Ionic columns. William Flockhart converted 108 and 110 Old Brompton Road (formerly 7 Gloucester Terrace), SW7, to similar purpose for the Court photographers Elliott and Fry in 1898. Eleven years later, Flockhart moved into the upper storeys of 180 New Bond Street with the same photographers and their large studio windows can still be seen there today. The building was designed by Frank Atkinson who also provided a showroom on the ground floor for Darracq Cars (later Talbot—Darracq).

The motor manufacturer came into his own under Edward VII and the architectural profession had its share of enthusiasts. Keynes Purchase, for instance, was a keen amateur motorist whose name is associated with motor showroom buildings and with the Royal Automobile Club (*see under* Davis, Arthur Joseph). He had a hand in 11 Great Marlborough Street, which Frank Atkinson designed as a motor garage for Samuel Waring, hence the tall pilasters running through two storeys. It was never used for this purpose, however, but occupied by the woollen cloth merchants Cobb and Jenkins who still trade there. The pleasant Louis XV style building between Pall Mall and St James's Square by the firm of Boehmer and Gibbs was for many years a showroom for the latest models of Renault cars from Paris.

Cars were not the only form of motorised transport familiar in the Edwardian scene. Tradesmen from bakers to milliners delivered to their customers by means of those motor-driven tricycles with the epicyclic gear which revolved *backwards* when the vehicle was stationary. Some went under the French-looking name of L'Acre, which actually derived from Long Acre, the original address of the firm which made them. From there they moved to a pretty building of Art Nouveau pretensions at 1—5 Poland Street, W1, with a garage at 7 Livonia Street in the same style designed by Bartlett and Ross. The corbels between the arches have a device of foliage with the initials ER and the date 1902. Although this building is in other use the firm still flourishes.

No account of the Edwardian shops of London, however brief, would be complete without a mention of those very special premises for dressmakers and milliners, built on narrow sites in Bond Street

354

72

161

266

and the surrounding streets. The remarkable ingenuity shown by the architects Treadwell and Martin in combining Art Nouveau, Tudor and Baroque elements on a frontage only twenty feet in width makes these buildings most characteristic of the Edwardian age.

The business of Costumier and Perruquier to the theatrical profession was also a special trade characteristic of the Edwardian era and the celebrated 'Willie' Clarkson's premises at 41 Wardour Street, W1, are also typical of the architecture of these small buildings. The building (now in other use) is

This vigorous Baroque façade is now Sotheby's in St George Street, W1. A drawing by Charlotte Halliday.

by Wakley and in 1905 Clarkson enlisted Sarah Bernhardt to lay the foundation stone and Sir Herbert Beerbohm Tree to lay the coping stone, ceremonies recorded on the building by a beaten copper inscription.

Electricity Generating Stations

The introduction of electricity as a means of distributing power and providing heat and light in 1880 also provided the motive power for lifts and pumps, and for mechanical traction in trains and tramcars, and made possible the commercial production of aluminium. The first recorded plant in England for the production and distribution of electric power was erected at Godalming, Surrey, in 1881, and was operated by water wheel.

The Electric Lighting Act of 1882 allowed the distribution of electricity but prohibited the interconnection of generating stations for bulk supply or supply to industry. The first generating station under the new Act was erected in 1886. A second Act of Parliament passed in 1888 allowed for municipal undertakings.

That year the Borough of Deptford was supplied by Ferranti and the London Electricity Corporation was formed. The City of London Power Company built its station at Blackfriars in 1892, while Manchester built its first power station at Dickinson Street in 1893. In 1897 the County of London Electricity Supply Company opened its first generating stations at City Road, EC2, and at Wandsworth.

In 1899 the Liverpool Corporation opened its Pumpsfield Station in the town centre, and in the following year Lister Drive Station on the outskirts (engineer A. H. Holmes, architect Thomas Shelmerdine). In 1903 Manchester built Stuart Power Station (engineers Kennedy and Jenkin, architects C. S. Alliott and Sons). In Scotland the Fall of Foyers Generating Station at Inverness had

been built in 1898 for aluminium production and the Port Dundas Station at Inverness was opened in 1900.

Although the large smoke-stacks needed for the coal-burning boilers of factories and mines were no new thing, they now threatened districts hitherto spared such an intrusion and architects were occasionally called in to make the boiler house and generator house more 'architectural'. One device was to build around the fireclay flue lining an external square stack conforming to the conventional idea of a monument, like that at the Central Electricity Supply Company's Station which stood at Lodge Road, St John's Wood, NW8, until 1972. The architects here were Stanley Peach and C. H. Reilly. There were to have been six large, square stacks, but only one was built and the foundations of a second laid. Advances in electrical engineering and changes in legislation fortunately spared the neighbourhood such a calamity.

280
302

An early exponent in the field of designing for electric power, Stanley Peach was frequently called in as consultant both at home and abroad. He is reputed to have negotiated the Davies Street convertor station on the Grosvenor Estate (for the London Electrical Power Co.) over a glass of port with the Duke of Westminster. To house the electrical plant the whole site was excavated to a depth of forty feet and the garden which the Duke had laid out on the site of some derelict buildings was reinstated at the top of the station and given domed pavilions and a paved parterre.

More usually, however, architects were called in

solely for the design of the exterior. This was the case for the buildings of Hove Power Station and those for the London United Tramways at Chiswick and for the Bristol Tramways designed by William Curtis Green.

199

74
75
The electricity generating station built at Greenwich by the London County Council provided power for their extensive tramways system. Designed in 1902 and opened three years later, it was one of the largest in the United Kingdom, producing 52,000 h.p. This station was of advanced design, the fuel bunkers being set above the boilers, while the exterior shows the modern outlook of the LCC architects under W. E. Riley.

The Tube Railways and District Railway in London were provided with power from Lot's Road, Chelsea, station where four cylindrical stacks and a plain unadorned power house at first caused some dismay but soon became a familiar part of the river scenery often painted by artists. The Metropolitan Railway was provided with power at Neasden, NW10.

But, as opposed to the Continent where the architectural appearance of power plants was seen as of importance from the outset, collaboration between engineer and architect on the design of power station buildings in Britain was rare, rarer in fact than it had been in the railway building age.

London County Council Tramways Power Station: only two stacks were built, and they have been beheaded.

As in the United States, the general practice was to give out the contract to a firm of consulting engineers who designed the entire plant in their offices, in some cases without any architectural assistance at all. The architectural extravagancies in Germany and Austria where the 'Schloss' style, or even the 'Moorish' style, was applied, did not appeal to power companies in Britain or America. Better, but in turn to be superseded, was the 'brick cathedral' style of power station prevalent in Britain between 1920 and 1940. This was abandoned when it was found that the 'hardware' of the power station, for much of which there was no longer standing room in the 'nave', did not need brickwork to house it and that the plant of the new generating stations, if carefully planned, could exist in its own right in a properly landscaped setting.

London Tube Railways

The world's first public passenger-carrying underground railway was London's Metropolitan Railway, the first 3¾ miles of which were opened on 10 January 1863, between Bishop's Road, Paddington, and Farringdon Street in the City. Steam locomotives supplied the traction and carried ten million passengers a year. Something of the Roman scale of the brick tunnels and retaining walls can still be guessed from the sections now restored.

The Metropolitan and District Railways combined to form the Inner Circle (now the Circle Line) in 1864, constructed on the 'cut and cover' system of shallow tunnels — the intended Outer Circle was never built. The line linked ten railway terminuses and was achieved with remarkably little demolition of property; where it cut through a terrace of houses, a dummy façade was built.

The tube railways were a response to the urgent and growing need for cross-town communication. The idea for an iron-lined tube cut through London clay originated with P. W. Barlow, resident engineer on the Lambeth Suspension Bridge in 1862 where vertical iron tubes were being used as piers. Working on the idea of the 'shield' (first used on the Thames Tunnel) Barlow suggested its application in the building of a passenger-carrying tube railway. The result was the world's first tunnel constructed for the purpose, the Tower Subway Co.'s tunnel from Great Tower Hill in the City to Vine Street in Southwark, opened in 1870. But the experiment was a failure since each car could only carry twelve passengers and the trains worked on a

S. R. J. (Tate Gallery) Smith: This surface building catered for the extension to Euston of the world's first tube railway.

gravity system. The tube tunnel still exists, carrying water and hydraulic power mains.

Once a feasible method of construction was devised, the tube railways still had to wait for electric traction to make them a practical reality. Engineers in a number of countries were concentrating on this problem, and just three years after Dr C. W. Siemens demonstrated in Berlin the first electric railway in the world, an Act of Parliament authorised the Charing Cross and Waterloo Electric Railway.

In 1884, J. H. Greathead, who had perfected the 'Greathead shield' in work on the unsuccessful Tower Subway tunnel, succeeded in getting the London Bridge to Elephant and Castle tube railway through Parliament for the promoters, the City of London and Southwark Subway Co. The line was to have been operated by cable as advocated by Greathead, but electric traction had already been demonstrated by Magnus Volk at Brighton in 1883 and in 1885 the success of the electrically operated Bessbrook and Newry Railway in Ireland tipped the scales.

Opened in 1890 by the Prince of Wales, the line was eventually extended north to Euston and south to Clapham Common and called the City and South London Railway. In the 1920s it was joined with the Hampstead, Highgate and Charing Cross line to make the present Northern Line. Apart from the station at Euston by S. R. J. (Tate Gallery) Smith (1858–1913), the surface buildings were designed by T. Phillips Figgis in unglazed terracotta of a *thé-au-lait* colour. These were one-storeyed, surmounted by a dome over the lift hall.

The Waterloo and City Railway owned and operated by the London and South Western Railway Company (now British Railways Southern Region) opened next in 1898. Two years later the first modern tube, the Central London Railway, joined

Shepherd's Bush to the Bank. It was called the Tuppenny Tube at first, but it did not remain at two pence for long. The engineers with Greathead were Sir John Fowler and Sir John Baker — engineers of the Forth (railway) Bridge. Greathead died soon after work began and was succeeded by Sir Basil Mott. The electric locomotives were supplied by the General Electric Co. of America and the power station was built on the site of Woodham Park — a fine house in Wood Lane, Shepherd's Bush — where soil from the tunnelling formed the foundation for the White City Exhibition. The designer of the surface station buildings for the Central London Line was H. B. Measures, but many of the superstructures, which were often hotels, were done by the architect Delissa Joseph. In 1908 the line was extended to Wood Lane for the Franco-British Exhibition at the White City.

The next tube railways to open were the Great Northern and City Railway and the three so-called 'Yerkes' tubes — the Baker Street and Waterloo Railway, the Euston and Hampstead Railway, and the Great Northern, Piccadilly and Brompton Railway (a merger of the Great Northern and Strand and the Piccadilly and Brompton Railways). In spite of opposition from the directors of the Great Northern Railway who were sponsoring it, the first of these was later called the 'Bakerloo' on the suggestion of *Evening Standard* columnist 'Quex'.

The plans for the new tube railways had been drawn up and Acts of Parliament passed, but money was needed and the history of how it was raised is closely connected with the career of Charles Tyson Yerkes (pronounced Yerkeys). The son of a Quaker banker from Philadelphia, Yerkes, determined on making his own way in the world, started out as a clerk. He soon rose to be one of Philadelphia's leading financiers, but the panic provoked by the great Chicago fire led to his financial collapse and subsequent imprisonment.

Pardoned after serving seven months of his sentence, he set out on a second career in railway

A SKETCH AT TRAFALGAR SQUARE STATION

Leslie Green: The sketch shows Trafalgar Square Station (now Charing Cross) on the Bakerloo line. The architectural finishes were coloured tiles and voussoired arches. The coaches had doors at the ends only.

stocks before moving to Chicago where he switched his interests to public traction or street car railways, changing the horse-drawn car lines to cable traction, then to electric traction. His intricate financial activities were dubbed the 'Chicago Traction Tangle'. Yerkes's critics described his methods as 'Buy up old junk, fix it up a little and unload it on other fellows', and his motto was said to be 'It's the strap-hangers who pay the dividends'.

When Yerkes 'fixed' politicians to pass laws to his advantage, the city threatened his 'friendly' councillors with guns and a symbolic noose. Yerkes left for New York and in 1900 for England with $15,000,000 salvaged to prove he could prosper in a land where there was no 'boodle'. He arrived at a propitious moment since the financial empire of Whitaker Wright (an Englishman also from Philadelphia) on which the Bakerloo line depended for capital collapsed in 1903. Wright took cyanide and two years later Yerkes died broken and bankrupt in New York, whither he had returned to attempt new triumphs. But he had saved the Bakerloo Line and accelerated its construction with an injection of American capital — as well as providing the University of Illinois with the Yerkes Observatory.

With his fellow financiers, Yerkes not only restarted the construction of the new tube railways, he electrified the Metropolitan and District Lines which had relied on steam engines for traction for nearly forty years. The result was release from a smoky inferno and the availability of 'blow hole' sites for building. The first escalator was introduced by the engineer Sir Basil Mott at the Embankment Station.

More than fifty of the surface stations of the Yerkes tubes were designed by Leslie Green, who also provided the designs for the 'decorative work to stations, tunnels, platforms and passages'. The strain of keeping up with the indefatigable Yerkes and doing fifty stations in five years proved too much for Leslie Green's health. He died at Mundesley, Norfolk, at the age of thirty-three.

Harry Wharton Ford (1875–1947), architect to the Underground Railways from 1899 to 1911, designed Embankment, Temple, Walham Green, Ealing Broadway and Aldgate stations. He also designed the red and blue sign of the Underground Railways.

The single-storey surface buildings were so designed that superstructures for offices, flats and hotels could be added later and a steel frame was provided for the purpose. They were faced with glazed faience blocks of a shade flatteringly called 'ruby-red'. The platforms and pedestrian tunnels, the simple rail tunnel marked by *voussoirs* opening into the large platform tunnel with its coloured tiles, the change of colours to mark the stations, all show evidence of more imagination than features in London's recent tube railways. The official name 'Tube' was placed in illuminated red glass letters over the station entrances, the word

'Underground' appearing in white on blue with the end letters in larger capitals.

Yerkes's place as Chairman was taken by Sir Edgar Speyer, who was succeeded in 1910 by Sir George Gibb when the tubes were renamed the London Electric Railway.

A great rejuvenation of the tube railways took place only sixteen years after their opening when the admirable combination of the Chairman Lord Ashfield, Frank Pick the General Manager, and Charles Holden the architect resulted in the building of new stations and the reconstruction of booking halls, e.g. Piccadilly Circus, now sadly lacking all that they gave it.

The rebuilding of Regent Street

Leading from Carlton House to 'Marybone Park' as it was then called, the Prince Regent's new Regent Street was conceived primarily as a kind of Via Triumvalis. But when it opened after his accession in 1825, it proved useful in several other ways. It provided the public with a much-needed north to south thoroughfare and shopkeepers with grand parades of new shops, while it placed a wide division between the slums of Soho and the squares of Mayfair, increasing the value of property in its wake.

By 1901 the gradual accretion of innovations and devices introduced by shopkeepers to attract custom had obscured John Nash's well-proportioned, stucco-faced buildings. New shop fronts had sprung up with plate glass windows crowned by a continually mounting level of lettered fascias, awnings, crested flower boxes and Royal Warrant Holders' coats of arms. Supporting cast-iron columns cased in mirrors created the illusion of a continuous display of goods in the windows, while gas lamps or electric arc lights illuminated them from outside. These contrivances so impaired the once elegant Regency façades, and some hundred coats of paint often hanging in folds from what began as bare Roman cement plaster so detracted from their appearance, that as the 99-year leases terminated and the house-breakers' picks went into action, there were few mourners. Indeed the *Illustrated London News* of 1905 considered the buildings of Nash's Quadrant 'beneath contempt', proving once again that the architectural style of a period is often appreciated only after some of its most important works have been destroyed.

Only when George IV's Regent Street had been carted away as rubbish did the public listen to

A. Trystan Edwards who, in his *Good and Bad Manners in Architecture* and *The Things Which are Seen*, pointed out the consistency and appropriateness of Regency architecture, from Nash's grand terraces to the workman's terraced cottage.

No comprehensive design had been prepared for the rebuilding of Regent Street and the authorities in charge — quaintly, the Commissioners of Woods and Forests — did not concern themselves beyond requiring that the new buildings should be of fire-resisting construction, faced with Portland stone, and of a uniform height of 60 ft to the cornice with two storeys in a roof of 75-degree pitch covered with green slates.

This increase in the height of the buildings without a proportionate increase in the width of the Street spoiled the balance, but this was not solely the fault of the Commissioners. Early portents of the new scale had already made their appearance. Decimus Burton's York House, which still stands, had received several additional storeys; the St James's Hall in Piccadilly appeared above the Quadrant; the Criterion Restaurant dwarfed Piccadilly Circus; and as early as 1866 Lewis and Allenby, the mercers, had built a tall Italian palazzo of a warehouse around the corner in Conduit Street (also still standing).

Early rebuilding in Regent Street at the turn of the century was on the east side from 172 to 206, between Tenison Court and Foubert's Place. These nondescript elevations were by William Woodward, formerly with Arthur Cates, the Surveyor to the Commissioners, who, like Sir George Gilbert Scott forty years earlier, was an advocate of a diversified skyline. Numbers 180–182 had been partially built by C. W. Stevens, the architect of Harrods, but, because they contravened the Building Act, they were demolished and rebuilt by Woodward.

On the west side of Regent Street, Regent House (No. 233), with its octagonal dome, was another early arrival, this time a prominent one, replacing C. R. Cockerell's Hanover Chapel which Nash had set at the point where Regent Street bends to enter Oxford Circus, in order, as the Prince Regent observed, 'to prevent the sensation of crossing Oxford Street'. The architect was G. D. Martin, who also did the rogue Marlborough Hotel (now the Charity Commissioners) in Bury Street, St James's.

Another determined effort to provide a satisfactory elevation for the rebuilt street was made by Frank Verity. The five bays of Ionic columns on the Polytechnic in Upper Regent Street and the three bays of St George's House over the Raoul Shoe Company at 195 Regent Street are evidence of Verity's Beaux Arts training. In each case the powerful columns and pilasters supporting a frieze deep enough to contain windows and the proportionately powerful mansard roof and dormers were suggested by Verity for the whole block. But after the First World War this was given an astylar

(column-less) centre and wings. Similar adjustments were made on the block south of this. The most overpowering of the pre-1914 blocks is the former Robinson & Cleaver's Linen Hall by George Crickmay which 'got away with' polished pink Norwegian granite on the lower storeys and a pair of corner turrets like those on the (Old) War Office in Whitehall.

Architects for many of the new buildings in Regent Street were Henry Tanner junior and his brother E. J. Tanner, joined by their father Sir Henry Tanner on his retirement from HM Office of Works. As a student, Henry Tanner junior had won the Gold Medal and Travelling Studentship at the Royal Academy Schools with a design for just the kind of building that was being called for in Regent Street. The inspiration came from the Paris boulevards (the first Regent Street had been the inspiration for the Haussmann boulevards). The notebooks Henry and his brother Ernest Tanner brought back from their Paris studies included such details as the tabernacle windows, balconies, cornices and dormer windows now featured on their Regent Street buildings. The Tanners won a limited competition for Oxford Circus which is the best of their work and later did the strongly stylised Dickens & Jones building.

Viewed from Nash's monument in the peristyle of his church, All Souls, Langham Place, the present Regent Street is, alas! no pleasantly proportioned, gracious street. The chief fault lies in the steep and elaborate French mansard roofs which, ironically, in Paris would have been low-pitched zinc roofs over balconied set-backs. Commenting caustically on the completed Regent Street, Hesketh Pearson and Hugh Kingsmill wrote:

> Regent Street was practically unaltered since the time of the Regent until the early 1920s [depredations in fact began much earlier] when all these five-storeyed erections were run up by a number of cads who computed success by money and turned what was primarily a work of art and secondarily a shopping centre into what is primarily a shopping centre and secondly nothing at all ...
>
> *Talking of Dick Whittington*, 1947

The rebuilding of the Quadrant was a story in itself. There had been little protest at the rebuilding of the straight parts of Regent Street, but the Quadrant was the centre of a battle, not because of the threat to Nash's parade, but over the proposed design.

No scheme had been prepared for this unique and important section of the Crown leases, and when a newly-formed hotel company took a lease of a site in the centre of the concave side which extended through to the area occupied by St James's Hall and Restaurant in Piccadilly, there was no time to be lost. Their architect William Woodward, although skilled at designing small premises in the St James's Street area, had produced a design for the hotel which was mean and small in scale. On the recommendation of John Belcher, Sir Aston Webb and Sir John Taylor of HM Office of Works, the Commissioner asked Norman Shaw, then in retirement, to act as consultant.

At his house in Ellerdale Road, Hampstead, Shaw, then already over seventy, prepared a splendid design illustrated by the perspectives of C. W. English and A. C. Fare. This is Shaw's late style at its best: rusticated arches recalling Piranesi's *Carceri D'Invenzione*, Ionic columns 'blocked' one third up, circular windows set in a square of rich Grinling Gibbons swags, a bold modillioned cornice, grand dormers, linked together in the executed design to provide a continuous run of windows, and crowned by an even grander roof out of which rise tall, robust, rusticated chimney stacks.

But there was trouble ahead. When they saw the first section of the new Quadrant, the shopkeepers declared they were not going to suffer from the loss of floor space and daylight and the expense of the new design. They were justified to the extent that the new design would have made their shops shallower and they could ill afford to sacrifice space to the great columns. Moreover, daylight was a far more important factor then than it is today. The Commissioners upheld their objections and agreed to modify the design which drew from Shaw a letter with the ring of Michelangelo's letter to Pope Julius II after the abandonment of his Tomb.

> Dear Mr Leveson Gower,
> I have pored over the design of the Quadrant till I am worn out and now am most reluctantly compelled to ask you to allow me to retire. The question lies in a nutshell.
> At one time the design might be said to be mine and of course I was prepared to stand by its merits and demerits. But now it is all changed; and to fully understand this it is necessary to go into some detail. Thus the arches on the ground floor are gone bodily. The filling in between the columns of the first, second and the third floors are gone and commonplace bays inserted in their place giving the whole front the aspect of a block of flats. Even the columns themselves have been mutilated by the omission of the blocks on the lower part so that it can no longer be said to be my design, of which all the odium would attach to me and none of the credit.
> I cannot say that I should like that, nor do I think that I should be justified in pursuing this course ...

In six months Shaw was dead. To discover how best to modify his design on the rest of the Quadrant, the Commissioner appointed Sir Aston Webb, Sir Reginald Blomfield, Ernest

Newton, William Woodward, John Murray and Sir Henry Tanner of HM Office of Works. Their answer is the present Quadrant, together with the County Fire Office and two corners of what remained of the former circus after the intrusion of the deplorable Shaftesbury Avenue into the north-east corner in 1888.

In the remainder of the Quadrant, some of the strong character of Shaw's building survives in the roof, the cornice, the dormers and the rustication of the ground floor and especially in the great window derived from Shaw's hotel — the saving grace of Blomfield's elevations — which marches around the salient angles just as Wren's great window marches around the upper storey of St Paul's Cathedral.

79   In Lower Regent Street, Carlton House by F. E. Williams replaced St Philip's Chapel by G. S. Repton in 1907. British Columbia House by Alfred Burr occupies the site of Warren's Hotel, while in Waterloo Place, Nash's buildings were replaced by a taller design by Sir William Emerson, typically

F. E. Williams: Carlton House, Lower Regent Street, SW1. Even this handsome building does not compensate for the loss of its smaller Regency predecessor.

Edwardian in character with its steeply pedimented tabernacle windows. Other architects, including Claude Ferrier (for No. 11), did the actual buildings.

The remaining buildings of Lower Regent Street (now Regent Street) were rebuilt between 1928 and 1956. Nash's own house and picture gallery, surprisingly, remained standing until 1928, while No. 17, York House by Decimus Burton, even more surprisingly, dating from 1839, still stands, with subsequent additions.

The County Fire Office, however, presents a noble picture, looking down towards Westminster from Piccadilly Circus and still echoing Nash's arcade — Nash's original building, carried out by Abrahams, had followed the Jones Gallery of Old Somerset House. The present building was rebuilt to the general design of Blomfield, executed by Ernest Newton. On 23 June, 1927 King George V and Queen Mary marked the completion of the rebuilding by driving in state through the length of the street.

The Holborn~Strand Improvements

Until the building of Regent Street, London had no street of any importance above London Bridge continuing northwards from the Thames bridgeheads. The links between Fleet Street and the Strand and Holborn were Shoe Lane, Fetter Lane, Chancery Lane, Drury Lane, and St Martin's Lane, all mean and hazardous and surrounded by slum rookeries. John Nash's Regent Street was the first major north—south link, cutting through the slums. In 1836 and 1838 proposals were made to form a north—south route through Lincoln's Inn Fields, but nothing came of them. Fifty years after Regent Street, the Metropolitan Board of Works made Shaftesbury Avenue and Charing Cross Road. Unfortunately, they allowed them to be dressed with an array of buildings so mean that they became the very opposite of urban improvements.

When the newly-founded progressive London County Council succeeded the Metropolitan Board of Works in 1889, they directed their attention to linking Holborn with the Strand, simultaneously removing the Clare Market, Wych Street and Holywell Street slums. The new road was to be called Kingsway.

The RIBA and the Art Workers' Guild had suggested a new Thames bridge down-river from Waterloo Bridge, and a crescent — at first called Strand Crescent — with its western arm leading to Waterloo Bridge and its eastern arm to the proposed new bridge. The crescent also provided space for either a building or a 'Place' at the foot of the new road, but the bridge was never built.

The question then arose of a comprehensive design for Aldwych, as the new crescent was finally called. Afraid of discouraging prospective lessees, the LCC hesitated to insist on a single design for the elevations. The alternative would have been for the LCC themselves to become prospectors, but this they were not empowered to do.

For the elevations of the new buildings it was clear from the start that Anglo-Classic, Franco-Classic or neo-Classic were to be the rule. As William Woodward put it to the Society of Architects in 1900:

> I need scarcely say that the 'Greenery Yallery' and the 'Grosvenor Gallery' and the 'Queen Anne' and the 'Mary Anne' will be tabooed and I trust the Council will put its foot down heavily on terracotta and permit only Portland stone on the fronts as also in the chimney stacks and returns when left to be viewed from the streets.

The absence of powers to control so important an urban feature as a new street was referred to by Aston Webb in his Presidential Address to the RIBA in November 1902:

> The Government is largely engaged upon the erection of public buildings, local authorities are busy with the erection of town halls, asylums, schools and technical institutions at almost an alarming rate. What I think, strikes most of us in all this activity exercised by public authorities over the details of these buildings, such little control is exercised over the laying out of our cities that, to a great extent, they seem to be left to lay out themselves.

In April 1900 the LCC invited eight architects to submit designs for the elevations of the new Aldwych — Reginald Blomfield, Mervyn Macartney, William Flockhart, E. W. Mountford, Ernest George, Ernest Runtz, Henry T. Hare and Leonard Stokes. Their competing designs were exhibited at the Royal Institute of Painters in Water-colours in October and November 1900.

Norman Shaw was invited to advise on the designs but declined a fee, declaring he was anxious to 'place his services at the disposal of a body engaged in the congenial occupation of beautifying the architecture of the city in which one dwells'. The design by H. T. Hare was declared the winner but was not adopted and the architectural weeklies protested strongly that the Council had paid £250 to each of the competitors for what amounted to no more than a catalogue of designs from which anyone could choose whichever he liked. Eventually the Council retained the right to call on Norman Shaw to modify any design which did not show

Sir Edwin L. Lutyens, RA: premises in the new
Kingsway for William Robinson's *The Garden*
magazine, with two mezzanine floors, a 'frieze' storey
and two attic storeys. Lutyens, in this Sanmichele style
building, achieved full height without the repetition of
windows.

sufficient merit. But Shaw was to be called in for
one site only.

57   The *Morning Post*, who had selected Mewès and
Davis as their architects, met the required standard with their Louis XV building, since (sadly)
raised upon, and A. Marshall Mackenzie designed
62   the splendid Waldorf Hotel, flanked on either side
by W. G. R. Sprague's two theatres. The buildings
at the corners of Kingsway, Shell Corner and
Adastral House, designed before but built after the
First World War, are by Thomas Tait when chief
assistant to Trehearne and Norman.

The next building along, by Gunton and Gunton,
was built after 1920, as was the small elevation to
the east designed by E. Fraser Tomlins who succeeded Tait at Trehearne and Norman. The convex
130   frontage of No. 99, the former General Accident
Insurance Company, by J. J. Burnet, is a masterly
design in his Glasgow manner. To the east of
General Buildings lay Carr's Restaurant, an early

but poor starter, now replaced by a good
building.

The island between Aldwych and the Strand had
an even more chequered history. The Gaiety
Theatre, replacing the Gaiety lost in the improvements, and the adjoining Gaiety Restaurant had
Shaw as consultant and the two buildings, joined
by the stage wall of the theatre, displayed the
vigour and sureness of his touch even in his
seventies. The free disposition of the openings of
the restaurant façade, the sculptured frieze and
the sharp mouldings can still be seen today, but
the green slate roof and splendid dormer windows
above the bold cornice, so typical of Shaw, have
been obliterated. Compared with the *Morning Post*
building, the theatre was so bold a design that the
two were called 'Beauty and the Beast' by Professor C. H. Reilly in 'London Streets and their
Recent Buildings' (*Country Life*, 1922).

The eastern point of the crescent was also a joint
enterprise. The Australian State of Victoria, first
in the field, put up a building displaying a coarse
version by Alfred Burr of the details of Shaw's
Piccadilly Hotel. Australia House by A. Marshall
Mackenzie and his son A. G. R. Mackenzie was
built after 1920 to pre-war designs, linking up
with the Victoria building.

The centre site has an odd history. An American
syndicate submitted proposals for a £2,000,000
project providing the amenities of a modern office
building, and a 'Palace of French Industry' was
also proposed, while a scheme suggested by Lord
Strathcona and designed by A. Randall Wells and
one by A. Marshall Mackenzie for the 'Dominion
of Canada' also proved abortive. The site was
used during the First World War for the YMCA's
'Eagle Hut' converted — for American Troops –
from a cinema and skating rink. Finally, in 1922,
the Bush Terminal Company of America commenced Bush House, designed by Helmle and
Corbett of New York. The western arm of the
crescent is completed by Sir Herbert Baker's India
House.

Kingsway fared even worse. The sites were slow to
be taken up. Two churches appeared — St Cecilia
and St Anselm, as a replacement by F. A. Walters,
and Holy Trinity, by Belcher and Joass, intended
to have a tower and a concrete dome. This church,
which Professor Reilly called 'a Scotch version of
the Viennese Secession', is in Joass's own style,
derived from his early Glasgow Burnet training and
from association with Belcher. Various suggestions
were put forward for the completion of Kingsway,
including one from the *Daily Express* for a 'Hall
of Heroes'. But the skyline was already ragged and
the only control was a limitation of height which
still allowed one third of a frontage to be extended
upwards as an 'architectural feature'.

81   The best of Kingsway before 1910 is the building
for William Robinson's magazine *The Garden*,
Edwin Lutyens's second London building. The
'façade game' can be seen in full play here — until

Bush House was built it was a point of honour that no street façade should show a repeat vertically of the same window type. Burnet's No. 99 Aldwych plays the same game, but with Scottish and French overtones.

129 Two buildings of note in Kingsway built before the First World War were the London Opera House by Bertie Crewe (demolished), and Kodak House, by Burnet. The latter was the first building to be given a simple exterior over the newly introduced steel frame (the attic storey is recent). Magnet House, designed by Frank Atkinson for the General Electric Company (1920), has also disappeared.

The principal features in the construction of Kingsway are below ground — the tram tunnel running the length of the street, entered from the Victoria Embankment under Waterloo Bridge and emerging at Theobald's Road, and on each side of it the subways for sewers and services. The tunnel was heightened later to take two-decker trams, then altered and curtailed in length and used for motor cars after the installation of mechanical ventilation.

At the opening of Kingsway on 18 October 1905 by King Edward VII, an electrical device was used in the ceremony, drawing the following report from *The Builder*:

> A couple of temporary decorative gates had been placed across Kingsway north of the

marquee; but when the psychological moment for declaring the street open arrived, instead of a progress to open the gates, a movable pillar with a gilt ball on the top of it, and connected by an electric wire with the gates, was brought up to the King, who seemed much amused at this little bit of jugglery ...

82 In addition to this and 'certain ugly rushes by roughs who had stationed themselves near the Gaiety Theatre' (reported in the *Illustrated London News*), there was a presentation of a petition by the Mayor of Poplar on behalf of the unemployed. *Punch* showed a cartoon by Bernard Partridge reflecting upon the contrast between Paris and London in the matter of street improvements (*Punch*, 18.10.05, p. 273).

Essential reading:

Sir John Summerson, 'British Contemporaries of Frank Lloyd Wright', *Studies in Western Art* vol IV (Acts of the 20th International Congress of the History of Art), Princeton University Press 1963

Susan Beattie, *The New Sculpture*, Yale University Press, New Haven and London 1983.

Susan Beattie, *A Revolution in London Housing: LCC housing architects and their work 1893-1914*, GLC and the Architectural Press 1980.

Cartoon by Bernard Partridge in *Punch*, October 18, 1905. The Municipal Council of Paris had been invited to attend the opening of Kingsway by Edward VII. The caption reads: *Madam London*: "You see I've taken a leaf out of your fashion book, my dear." *Madame Paris*: "You flatter me, chérie. The book is always at your service."

THE DICTIONARY

ABBEY, Edwin Austin, RA   1852—1911

E. A. Abbey was the eldest child of William Maxwell Abbey, a Philadelphia merchant; his mother was the grand-daughter of Joseph Kypel, a Bavarian farmer who emigrated to America.

Abbey went to Randolph School in Philadelphia in 1864 and then to Dr Gregory's School where he had drawing lessons from Isaac L. Williams. He studied penmanship at Richard S. Dickson's writing school and while there contributed picture puzzles to *Our Boys and Girls* under the pseudonym 'Yorick'. In 1869 Abbey entered the studio of the Philadelphia wood-engravers, Van Ingen and Snyder, where he did commercial and news illustration. He studied art under Professor Christian Schussel at the Pennsylvania Academy of Fine Arts and worked on historical compositions. Abbey was to excel in the presentation of historical scenes for which the original inspiration came from the books at Van Ingen and Snyder's, including works illustrated by Millais and Rossetti.

In 1871 Abbey went to New York and joined Harper Brothers, the publishers, for whom he was to work for twenty years. Refused an increase in pay, Abbey left Harper's in 1874 and free-lanced. He also worked for Scribner's, illustrating American history of the seventeenth and eighteenth centuries.

In 1876 Abbey returned to Harper's, and in 1878 they sent him to England to illustrate their edition of Robert Herrick's poems. His illustrations for these and for Harper's editions of Dickens, Goldsmith and Shakespeare were to make Abbey's reputation as a black-and-white illustrator, while he became equally proficient in water-colour and pastel. On the morning of his departure for England, Abbey was breakfasted at Delmonico's and driven to the gangway of his ship SS *Germanic* in a four-in-hand.

In 1881 Abbey decided to settle in England and took a studio at 56 Bedford Gardens, Campden Hill, Kensington, W8. In 1890 he married Mary Gertrude Mead, sister of William Rutherford Mead of McKim, Mead and White, architects of the American neo-classical revival. Abbey moved to Broadway in the North Cotswolds, where Henry James was a neighbour. Also in 1890, on recommendation from McKim, who had been appointed architect of the Boston Public Library, Abbey was asked to undertake the huge frieze, 180 ft long and 8 ft deep, surrounding the Delivery Room of the new library. The subject was to be 'The Quest of the Holy Grail'. The frieze, which took Abbey eleven years of unremitting labour, was set up in

1902, while the great French painter, Pierre Puvis de Chavannes, did nine panels for the library between 1895 and 1898 and the Anglo-American painter John Singer Sargent (1856—1925) did 'The History of Religion' for the Great Hall of the library.

In 1890 Abbey took Morgan Hall, Fairford, in the South Cotswolds, where he built a vast studio which he shared with Sargent, collected a wardrobe of historical costumes and organised a cricket team of artists. After his death, the studio was pulled down on the order of his widow.

Abbey took great pains to achieve accuracy. His angels were painted from small lay figures draped in old cambric handkerchieves and pigeons' wings. Sargent, no less thorough, visited Greece, Egypt and Palestine for background to his work for the Great Hall, known afterwards as Sargent Hall.

In 1895 a 90 ft length of the Boston frieze was exhibited in London at the Conduit Street Galleries, and the complete series was exhibited at the Guildhall in 1901.

Abbey's next commission (in 1902) was for the decoration of the House of Representatives, Senate Chamber and Dome of the Pennsylvania State Capitol at Harrisburg (architect Joseph Huston). In 1908 eight panels of the composition representing the Apotheosis of Pennsylvania were shown at the Imperial Institute in London. This immense task Abbey completed just before his death.

Abbey was called in to direct the work of a group of younger artists selected for the decoration of the Peers' Corridor in the House of Lords, Westminster. They were H. A. Payne, Denis Eden, Frank Cadogan Cowper, Frank O. Salisbury, Ernest Board and Byam Shaw. Their paintings were completed in 1910 and, like the work of Abbey himself, were predominantly Pre-Raphaelite.

The painter Frank Brangwyn found Abbey 'too much of an illustrator to solve the problems of mural painting satisfactorily' — not a surprising comment, given that Abbey was an illustrator of books for twenty-five years. What is surprising, perhaps, is his successful transition from such small-scale works to achievements so colossal.

Abbey was made Associate of the Royal Academy in London in 1896 and RA in 1898 (diploma work, 'A Lute-Player'). 322 of his works were exhibited at the Old Masters Exhibition at the Royal Academy in 1912. He remained an American citizen and was made a member of many American

Percy Adams and Charles Holden: an etching by Muirhead
Bone of the Belgrave Hospital for Children, Kennington,
London SW9.

societies including the National Academy of
Design, New York. He was also made Chevalier de
la Légion d'Honneur, and was elected to the
Societé Nationale des Beaux-Arts. In Paris he
painted the triptych reredos of G. E. Street's
American Cathedral.

Edwin Austin Abbey died in Chelsea and his ashes
were buried in the churchyard of Old Kingsbury
Church, Middlesex. A bust of Abbey was made by
Sir Thomas Brock for the British School in Rome
in 1917, a tablet by Alfred Parsons is in the crypt
of St Paul's Cathedral and a tablet by Albert
Hodge was placed in Chelsea Lodge in 1918.
Through his widow, the Abbey Memorial Fund
was instituted at the Royal Academy of Arts to
commission mural paintings for the decoration of
public buildings.

Lucas, E. V., *Edwin Austin Abbey,* 2 vols, London, 1921.
Obit. RIBAJ, 26.8.11, pp. 695—6 *ABJ,* 9.8.11, pp. 138,
157—8.

ADAMS, Henry Percy   1865—1930

Percy Adams came of a medical family — his grandfather, Webster Adams, had been a surgeon attached to Guy's and St Thomas's Hospitals and his
father (also called Webster) practised as a surgeon
in London and Ipswich. Percy Adams was educated
at Epsom College, Surrey, and articled to Bright-
wen Binyon of Ipswich. In 1888 he entered the
office of Stephen Salter (1825—96) who was
architect to the Royal College of Surgeons. Salter
had done the Joint Examination Hall for the Physicians and Surgeons on the Victoria Embankment
(1885), which Adams and his partner Charles
Holden skilfully adapted as the headquarters of
the Institution of Electrical Engineers in 1910.
(Forty years later the building was raised higher by
Adams, Holden and Pearson.)

Adams won the RIBA Drawings Prize in 1888,
entered the Royal Academy Schools in 1890 and
studied at the South Kensington Schools. He was a
Prizeman at both schools and also won the
Donaldson Medal and in 1897 the Godwin
Bursary. After Salter's death he practised as
Salter and Adams. Adams's hospital work included
the County Hospital, Bedford; the Dorking
Infirmary, Surrey; and the Homoeopathic
Hospital, Southport; all won in competition.
In 1898 he was joined by Charles Holden, an
assistant of exceptional talent who brought to

Adams's competent plans a new, simplified and imaginative style. Their collaboration soon resulted in some unusual and interesting buildings, notably the extension to the Incorporated Law Society, Chancery Lane, WC2 (1902–4; *Bldr.* 23.4.04), and the Headquarters of the British Medical Association, Strand and Agar Street (*see under* Holden, Dr Charles Henry).

Holden became a partner in 1907. His friend from Manchester, Lionel G. Pearson, who had joined the firm in 1903, via Woodhouse and Willoughby, William Flockhart and E. S. Prior, became a partner in 1913. Adams's son, Percy Webster Adams, became a partner in 1925 and the firm continues as Adams, Holden and Pearson.

Other works by Percy Adams and Adams and Holden completed between 1901 and 1910 were:

	1902	Royal Infirmary, Newcastle upon Tyne (with W. L. Newcombe). Majolica by Conrad Dressler
	1903	The English Hospital, Constantinople
		Oakley House, Bloomsbury Street, WC1 (destroyed)
84		The Belgrave Hospital for Children, Clapham Road, Kennington, SW9 (south wing added 1924, west wing, 1926 (*Bldr*, 9.5.03)
		Sutton Valence School, Kent
		Woburn Hospital, Bedfordshire
		Woburn Town Hall (extension)
		Birchmoor Lodge and houses for the Duke of Bedford at Woburn
	1904	Tunbridge Wells Hospital, Kent
		West Ham Hospital, E13
		The Heart Hospital, Richmond, Surrey
		Norwich House, 296 High Holborn, WC1
		Hospital for Women, Soho Square, W1
		Lodge, Apsley Heath, Bedfordshire.
210 211	1905	Central Library, Bristol (with C. F. W. Dening) (*Bldr*, 2.9.05 and 20.1.06)
121	1905-10	Edward VII wing of the Bristol Royal Infirmary
214	1906	King Edward VII Sanatorium, Midhurst, Sussex
		Children's Hospital, Paddington Green, W2
		Ipswich Infirmary, Suffolk
		Evelyn House, 54 Oxford Street, W1

Obit. RIBAJ, 26.4.30, p. 431 *Bldr*, 11.4.30, p. 702.

ADAMS, Maurice Bingham   1849–1933

Maurice B. Adams was the son of Thomas Adams of Burgess Hill, Sussex. He was articled to H. N. Goulty of Brighton, became assistant to William Emerson, and was architect to the Brighton Borough Council. In 1872 he joined the staff of *Building News* and became its editor the same year.

This periodical had been purchased in 1862 for a nominal sum by that remarkable social benefactor, J. Passmore Edwards. The son of a Cornish innkeeper and market gardener, Passmore Edwards made and lost more than one fortune in his lifetime and built numerous public libraries and institutes which bear his name. Several of these Maurice Adams was to design. Adams's earliest work in London included the first building for the London School of Economics (demolished) and the surviving Passmore Edwards Hall, Clare Market, WC2 (opened in 1902), the Camberwell Polytechnic (1896–8), Peckham Road, SE5, which later became the Camberwell School of Arts and Crafts and South London Art Gallery, and the Passmore Edwards Library, St Georges-in-the-East, E1. His works outside London in this period included the Passmore Edwards Homes at the Chalfonts, Buckinghamshire, and some cottages at Port Sunlight, Cheshire, for William Lever (Viscount Leverhulme).

In association with his work on *Building News*, Adams instituted the *Building News* Designing Club which for more than thirty years held architectural competitions within the scope of junior architectural assistants and apprentices. Notable young contestants were W. R. Lethaby, Edwin Lutyens and Charles Holden. In 1928, *Building News* amalgamated with *The Architect* to become *The Architect and Building News* (now published as *The Architect* again).

Maurice B. Adams: the Passmore Edwards Library, Wells Way, London SE5.

Adams was also for twenty-six years honorary secretary of the Royal Architectural Museum in Tufton Street, Westminster, which housed 'a galaxy of architectural bits and pieces'. These came from what Sir Gilbert Scott, one of its founders, called 'a cock-loft' in Cannon Row, Westminster. It was on Adams's suggestion that the Architectural Association moved from its first home in 56 Great Marlborough Street, W1, to the Architectural Museum, enlarged for the purpose in 1902 by Leonard Stokes.

Apart from his editorship, Adams is best remembered for the part he played in the creation of Bedford Park, Chiswick, W4, the artists' colony founded by Jonathan Carr in 1875. Here Adams, a 'resident architect' in both senses of the term, supervised the building of Norman Shaw's church of St Michael and All Angels, and himself designed the Church Hall, the Chapel of All Souls, the School of Art and many of the houses. Adams's homes in Bedford Park were Kirkcote, 14 Woodstock Road and Edenhurst, Marlborough Crescent, where he died.

Adams also did designs for many country houses, for a railway station and houses in New Jersey, USA, for houses in Sydney, New South Wales, designs for fireplaces in cast iron for the Coalbrookdale Company and for architectural features in terracotta and Burmantofts Faience

Maurice B. Adams: the public baths, Wells Way, London SE5.

for Wilcock & Co. of Leeds (1882). His published works include a paper on 'Architects from George IV to George V' (*RIBAJ*, July 1912) and *Modern Cottage Architecture* (Batsford, 1904).

In following the style introduced by Norman Shaw, but without Shaw's skill, Adams contributed to making this style more typical of the period than the earnest endeavours of the Arts and Crafts Movement. With their cockney jollity and easy-going style, his buildings had more in common with the terrace houses and villas of the contemporary speculating builder.

Adams's other works include:

	1899	Passmore Edwards Library, High Street, Acton, W3
		Passmore Edwards Library, Shepherds Bush, W12
		Public Library, Edmonton, N9
85 86	1902	Library and Baths, Wells Way, SE5
	1905	Carnegie Free Library, Bromley, Kent
		Carnegie Free Library, Public Buildings and Town Hall, Eltham, SE9
		Almshouses for the Chiswick Charity Trustees, W4

Bldr, 14.11.41, p. 435.

Obit. RIBAJ, 9.9.33, pp. 814–15 *Bldr*, 25.8.33, pp. 295–300 *ABN*, 25.8.33, pp. 207–8 and 8. 9, p. 266.

ADSHEAD, Professor Stanley Davenport
1868—1946

Stanley Adshead was born at Bowdon, near
Altrincham, Cheshire, the son of an artist. He
was articled in Manchester to Medland and Taylor
and spent one year with Salmon and Stendhal of
Manchester. In 1890 he came to London and
entered the office of George Sherrin where
E. A. Rickards was also an assistant. After two
years there Adshead worked in turn in the offices
of Guy Dawber, Ernest George and J. H. Ince
where he met Rickards again, working with him
on the ill-fated house for Alfred Gilbert (*q.v.*) at
16 Maida Vale, NW9. Adshead then spent four
years with William Flockhart, one year in his
office and three years as resident architect on
Rosehaugh House — a great house built for
A. D. Fletcher, a millionaire tea and rubber
merchant, and son of a local fisherman at Avoch,
Moray Firth. Whilst on the site Adshead shared a
fisherman's cottage with the clerk of works. At
Avoch he met the village schoolmistress who
became his wife.

In 1898 Adshead set up in practice. With Ernest
Willmott (Sloper) he did the Carnegie Library at
Hawick, Roxburghshire (RA 1903). He also did the
Technical School and Carnegie Library at Ramsgate,
Kent (*Bldr*, 21.5.04), where his Royal Victoria
Pavilion (1908) shows the influence of the Marie
Antoinette Theatre at Versailles, for, like many of
his contemporaries, Adshead was turning from the
English neo-Baroque to late eighteenth-century
models English and French. He also did the
Pavilion at Colwyn Bay, North Wales and the
Pier Pavilion at Worthing, Sussex (destroyed by
fire and rebuilt in 1937). In 1908 Adshead did
offices at 15 Tooley Street, Southwark, SE1, for
the Bennett Shipping Co. (founded in 1873 by
John Bennett of Goole, E. Riding). The building,
resembling a quayside warehouse of the late
seventeenth century, is surmounted by a low-
relief stone carving of a steamship (*Bldr*, 24.9.10).
Adshead also did a warehouse in Charles Street,
Manchester. In 1906 he submitted a design in
competition for the Palace of Peace at the Hague.

Adshead was in great demand as a perspective
artist. In 1909 he became Reader in Civic Design
at Liverpool University; in 1912, Leverhulme
Professor of Civic Design (the first in England);
and in 1914, Professor of Town Planning at the
University of London.

In 1911 Adshead joined in partnership with
Stanley C. Ramsey and together they were asked
to design the Duchy of Cornwall Estate,
Kennington, SE11, where they were the first
to appreciate those modest rows of yellow stock
brick, slate or pantile roofed artisans' houses since
they were built in the early years of the nineteenth
century. These simple, well-proportioned terraces
had suffered the tirades of Pugin and Ruskin soon
after they were built and had been maligned or

ignored until the 1920s when A. Trystan Edwards
(1885—1973) in his *Good and Bad Manners in
Architecture* called attention to their virtues.
After the First World War Adshead and Ramsey
built again in London stock brick and Welsh slate,
reviving those 'good manners' for so long ignored.

In addition to houses and flats in Kennington
(Courtenay Square, Newburn Street, Kennington
Lane), Adshead's other works included the church
of St Anselm, on the Duchy of Cornwall Estate,
and the restoration of John Wood the Younger's
Assembly Rooms at Bath (destroyed by fire in
1942 and again restored).

AJ 'Draughtsmen of Today' by Kineton Parkes, 3.8.27
Obit. RIBAJ, Apr. 1946, p.309   *Bldr,* 19.4.46, p.385.

Stanley Adshead, architect: the carving crowning the offices
of the Bennett Shipping Company in Tooley Street,
London SE1.

ALLEN, Professor Charles John   1862—1936

C. J. Allen became Liverpool's leading sculptor of
the Edwardian period. He was born at Greenford,
Middlesex, the son of a stockbroker, William Allen,
and was educated at Palace School, Enfield,
Middlesex. Allen was apprenticed to and then
worked for Farmer and Brindley between 1879
and 1889 when he executed the marble reredos
(destroyed in the Second World War) for St Paul's

C. J. Allen's figure crowning the memorial to Queen Victoria which houses the public convenience in Derby Square, Liverpool. Architect: F. M. Simpson.

Combining beauty with utility, the group forms a roof to an underground public lavatory and is surmounted by a dome lined in gold mosaic. (*Bldr*, 3.3.06).

Other Liverpool works by Allen include the reliefs on the base of the Samuel Smith Obelisk, Sefton Park; the choir stall canopies at Ullet Road Unitarian Chapel, Sefton Park (1896–1902), by Thomas and Percy Worthington; the sculptured frieze on the Royal Insurance Building, Dale Street, by J. Francis Doyle and R. Norman Shaw (1897–1903); and the sculpture on the Mersey Docks and Harbour Board Offices (1907) by Briggs, Wolstenholme and Thornely.

Allen did a frieze on Parr's Bank, Leicester (*Bldr*, 26.10.01); and for the churchyard of St Mary Aldermanbury, EC4, he did a bronze bust of William Shakespeare and bronze inscriptions in memory of John Heminge (*c.* 1556–1630) and Henrie Condell (*c.* 1550–1627) who collected and saved Shakespeare's manuscripts. In the National Portrait Gallery there is a bronze medallion by Allen of William Rathbone (1819–1902). He also designed the Hemans Medal for Lyrical Poetry (RA, 1900). Allen's 'Love and the Mermaid' is in the Walker Art Gallery, Liverpool and his 'The Woman Thou Gavest Me' in the Glasgow Art Gallery. Allen was a member of the Art Workers' Guild.

Cathedral. Like many of that firm's promising pupils, Allen studied at the Lambeth School of Art and went on to the Royal Academy Schools which he entered in 1887.

103 While assistant to Hamo Thornycroft, Allen worked on the Hall of the Institute of Chartered Accountants, Moorgate Place, EC2, for John Belcher. He also assisted George Frampton on Lloyd's Registry of Shipping for T. E. Collcutt.

In 1894 Allen was appointed teacher of sculpture at University College, Liverpool (now Liverpool University), and later became Professor and Vice-Principal of the Liverpool School of Art. He did the Florence Nightingale Memorial, Liverpool, and in 1894 with Thomas Stirling Lee and Conrad Dressler completed the marble relief panels in the screen walls of Harvey Lonsdale Elmes's St George's Hall and Assize Courts, Liverpool, from designs left by John Flaxman. From 1902 to 1906 Allen did the allegorical figures representing Education, Industry, Commerce and Agriculture, Justice, Charity,
88 Knowledge and Peace, on the Queen Victoria Memorial, Derby Square, Liverpool, in a setting by F. M. Simpson and Willink and Thicknesse.

ANCELL, William James   1852–1913

W. J. Ancell was born at Stony Stratford, Buckinghamshire, and was articled to Edward Middleton Barry, RA (1830–80), who had designed hotels at the Cannon Street and Charing Cross terminals of the London South Eastern and Chatham Railway. Ancell's own practice was to follow similar lines and with the railway's architect, A. C. Blomfield, he did the new ornate front to the London Chatham and Dover Railway's terminus at Victoria, SW1. (*Bldr*, 5.6.09). The sculpture is by H. C. Fehr.

Ancell entered the Royal Academy Schools in 1872 and was assistant to T. Chatfield Clarke and to Verity and Hunt. From 1896 until his death he was principally engaged in building hotels and restaurants for Joseph Lyons, Barnett Salmon and Montague Gluckstein and their sons. Among these was the conversion of the Trocadero Restaurant from the Trocadero Music Hall on the corner of Great Windmill Street and Shaftesbury Avenue in 1896, which he did with J. Hatchard Smith (1853–1936), and the Blenheim Restaurant, New Bond Street, now in other use.

Two of Ancell's earliest works were the Town Hall, Richmond, Surrey (1893) and the tobacco factory,

Silvertown, E16, for Salmon and Gluckstein. *His principal works include:*

1901	Additions to the Trocadero Restaurant for J. Lyons & Co. (1930 additions by F. J. Wills (1885—1938)).
1903	Lyons Popular Café, 201 Piccadilly (now offices).
1907	Coventry Street Corner House for Lyons (1921—3 additions by F. J. Wills).
1907-9	Strand Hotel (soon re-named Strand Palace Hotel), Strand, WC2, for Lyons, on the site of Exeter Hall, Haxell's Hotel, and offices of the *Globe*, later *Pall Mall Gazette*, then *Evening Standard* (extended in the 1930s by F. J. Wills).
	Strand Corner House, WC2.
1912-15	Regent Palace Hotel, Piccadilly, for Lyons. Continued after Ancell's death by Henry Tanner junior and F. J. Wills who carried out subsequent work for Lyons.

Obit. Bldr, 31.1.13, p. 161.

ANDERSON, John MacVicar   1835—1915

J. MacVicar Anderson was born in Glasgow and educated at the Collegiate School and Glasgow University. He was articled first to Clark and Bell, then to his uncle William Burn (1789—1870) whose partner he became, continuing the practice after his uncle's death.

Among his earliest works were alterations to Christie's Auction Rooms at 8 and 9 King Street, SW1 (1883), additions to David Brandon's Junior Carlton Club, Pall Mall (1885) and the Annexe to Brooks's Club, St James's Street, SW1 (1889). Also in 1889 he did St Columba's Church of Scotland in Downing Street, Cambridge. An early country house by Anderson was Barrington Park, Great Barrington, Gloucestershire (1870—3), and he did the alterations and additions to Addington Park, Kent, in 1894. In 1896 he did the Commercial Union Insurance offices in Cornhill, EC3 (rebuilt by Sir Aston Webb and Son after its collapse into the excavations for the new Lloyd's Bank in 1923).

After the turn of the century Anderson did the British Linen Bank (now the Bank of Scotland), 38 Threadneedle Street, EC2 (*Bldr*, 22.8.03 and 3.10.03) and Coutts's Bank, Strand and Chandos Street, WC2 (1903) on the site of Lowther Arcade — a stodgy Classic building which for three-quarters of a century interrupted John Nash's stucco terraces (now rebuilt inside the *partly* restored terraces by Sir Frederick Gibberd and his partners). In 1904 Anderson did St Columba's Church of Scotland, Pont Street, SW1, where he was an elder. This was destroyed in the Second World War and rebuilt by Sir Edward Maufe, RA.

Anderson was President of the RIBA from 1891 to 1894.

Other works by Anderson are:

1900	Ashurstwood House, Forest Row, Sussex.
1901-7	Sudeley Castle, Gloucestershire (minor improvements).
1902-4	Croxteth Hall, Liverpool (additions).
1904	Liverpool and London Globe Insurance Co., corner of Cornhill and Lombard Street, EC3 (*Bldr*, 25.6.04).
	St Mary-le-Strand, WC2 (restoration).
1907	National Bank of Scotland, Nicholas Lane, EC4.

BN Feb. 1890, p. 326

Obit. RIBAJ, 12.6.15, p. 403 and 26.6, p. 416 *Bldr*, 18.6.15, p. 564.

ANSELL, William Henry, CBE, MC, FSA 1873—1959

W. H. Ansell was born in Nottingham. He was articled to Naylor and Sale of Derby and went to London in 1897 where he commenced practice in 1900.

One of Ansell's London buildings was the National Deposit Friendly Society in Queen Square, WC1. In Kent he did the Convalescent Homes for the Zachary Merton Trust, St Margaret's Bay, and a hospital at Sevenoaks. Other works by Ansell included the Church of Humanity, Liverpool; the Butchers' Charitable Institution, Hounslow, Middlesex; Gresham's School, Holt, Norfolk; and houses in Exmouth, Devon and Farnham, Surrey.

Keenly interested in architectural education, Ansell was President of the RIBA from 1940 to 1943 and was a member of the Art Workers' Guild and a founder of the National Buildings Record.

Arthur Bailey, who joined him in 1934, continues the practice as Ansell and Bailey.

Obit. RIBAJ, March 1959, pp. 267—8 *Bldr*, 20.2.59, p. 373 and 27.2, p. 411.

ASHBEE, Charles Robert   1863—1942

C. R. Ashbee was born of 'Kentish Yeoman stock', to use his own phrase, at Isleworth, Middlesex, the only son of Henry S. Ashbee. His mother, whose maiden name was Lavy, was the daughter of a Jewish merchant from Hamburg. Ashbee was educated at Wellington and King's College, Cambridge, and studied at the Slade — then under Professor Frederick Brown. He was articled to the great church architect G. F. Bodley (1883—7) and lived at the first university slum settlement, Toynbee Hall. The example of Arnold Toynbee and the work of the Barnetts in Whitechapel was

C. R. Ashbee: 38 and 39 Cheyne Walk, Chelsea, London SW3.

to make a profound impression on Ashbee, as it did on many of his generation.

The energy Ashbee brought over a lifetime to an unending flow of ideas moved a fellow architect to write of him: 'He was on the side of the angels who, however, may often have found him a difficult and even exasperating ally' (W. H. Ansell, *DNB*).

In 1887 Ashbee established the Guild of Handicraft, a craft workshop and training school, in Commercial Street, E1, where he organised training in furniture-making, jewellery, metalwork, printing and bookbinding. In 1891 he moved his workshop and school to Essex House, 401 Mile End Road,

Bow, E3, but lack of funds forced the school to close in 1895.

Ashbee married Janet Elizabeth Forbes of Godden Green, Seal, Kent, in 1898. Four years later, after consulting his friend and supporter of the Guild, the banker Holland-Martin (then Mr Martin) of Overbury, Worcestershire, on the question of a suitable location, Ashbee led an exodus of 150 men, women and children to the ancient Cotswold town of Chipping Campden. Here Ashbee took the Old Silk Mill for the Guild, converted Woolstaplers Hall for his own residence, and in 1904 founded a school of arts and crafts. Inspired by John Ruskin and William Morris, whose work he helped to sustain, and like them acutely aware of the desperate position of the arts of manufacture (the very meaning of the word had changed), Ashbee made his own contribution to the revival of craftsmanship. To his generation this meant hand-craftsmanship, since the misuse of men and machines had engendered in Morris and his followers a distrust of power-driven machines.

Mindful of the health of his charges, Ashbee began their working day with physical exercises and encouraged the innovation of 'mixed' swimming in a pool he had constructed. Despite these attempts in the unsullied atmosphere of the countryside to promote *mens sana in corpore sano*, despite the uniformed brass band, the morris dancers, the Christmas mummers and performances of the plays of Dekker, Beaumont and Fletcher, Shakespeare and Sheridan, the members of the Guild and their families pined for London. After five years a great many of them drifted back to the East End. Ashbee himself, with a few faithful friends, continued at Chipping Campden until 1917. Some of his followers and their descendants still remain.

During the Guild's halcyon days pieces made by them were shown first at Conduit Street, then at 16a Brook Street, and finally at 67a New Bond Street and Dering Yard, W1. They were also shown at exhibitions at home and abroad, including those of the Arts and Crafts Exhibition Society, the success of whose exhibits in Ghent in 1911 and in Paris in 1914 led to the formation of the Exhibitions Branch of the Board of Trade. Among the Guild's patrons were Queen Alexandra and a grandson of Queen Victoria, Ernest Ludwig, the Grand Duke of Hesse-Darmstadt. The British architect M. H. Baillie Scott (*q.v.*) furnished two rooms in the Palace of Darmstadt for the Grand Duke with products of the Guild. At home architects ordered from the Guild joinery and furniture for their buildings and ecclesiastics ordered for their churches the silverwork which Ashbee's special genius produced.

In the midst of all these activities, and in addition to cottage and church restorations in the Cotswolds, Ashbee had been busy building in Chelsea where he set up in practice in 1890. He rebuilt the Magpie and Stump, 37 Cheyne Walk, SW3 (*Bldr*, 11.1.01)

for his mother and rebuilt some houses adjoining, including 38 and 39 (RA 1900); these came to be known as 'the Ashbee Group'. He also restored others, including No. 119, which had been the home of J. M. W. Turner, RA. Here Ashbee preserved Turner's roof balcony and did a studio for E. A. Walton where Epstein later carved the Oscar Wilde Memorial. Between 1912 and 1913 he did No. 71 for Mrs Trier.

90

91

In 1902 James McNeil Whistler took No. 74 where the front door of beaten copper and other embellishments drew from him the sort of remark which Oscar Wilde might well have claimed as his own — he called them 'a successful example of the disastrous effect of art upon the British middle classes'. Whistler complained that 'the designer Ashbee' had been 'designing enough first to let the house and then to start building operations next door' (No. 75). Advised that legal proceedings would be in vain, Whistler went to Holland to escape the noise. When he returned it was to No. 76, but the noise had not abated. He died there in the ground-floor front room on 17 July 1903.

Ashbee made 37 Cheyne Walk his home. 'The Ashbee Group' was in the style which, through the medium of the English *Studio* magazine and the German *Moderne Bauformen* and *Deutsche Kunst und Dekoration*, was receiving well-deserved attention. The designer Lewis F. Day in the *Art Journal* of 1900 referred to it as 'on the whole much cleaner and wholesomer than the art of the continental decadents'.

Ashbee's interests extended even further. We owe to him the inauguration in 1894 of the Committee for Historical Memorials of the County of London whose still continuing publication, *The Survey of London*, he edited from 1899 — a task in itself. Unhappily it did not lead to a reinstatement of his own war-damaged Chelsea houses (Nos. 74–76) or prevent further depredations upon them by speculating builders (the demolition of No. 37).

Like Morris, Mackmurdo, Herbert Horne and others, Ashbee felt the urge to set up a printing press and design type. He purchased Morris's two presses, set them up in Essex House in 1891 and engaged three of Morris's men, providing his own specially designed founts, of which one is the Endeavour. At the Essex Press he produced *King Edward VII's Prayer Book*, the *Essex House Song Book* and other works. After restoring the Norman Chapel at Broad Campden, Ashbee installed the Press there in 1907 for the Indian artist Dr A. K. Coomaraswamy and lived there himself from 1911 to 1917. (*Bldr*, 24.8.07).

Through the generosity of Josiah Fels of Philadelphia, who had read Ashbee's *Craftsmanship in Competitive Industry*, the Guild continued in another form which included the addition of a farm established at Broad Campden. Here Fels's ideas on agriculture were put into practice — he was an advocate of the 'back to the land movement' and his ideas were to attract Miss Annie Lawrence and her disciples at The Cloisters in Letchworth (*see under* Cowlishaw, William Harrison).

C. R. Ashbee: 72-75 Cheyne Walk, Chelsea, London SW3. The architect's own drawing.

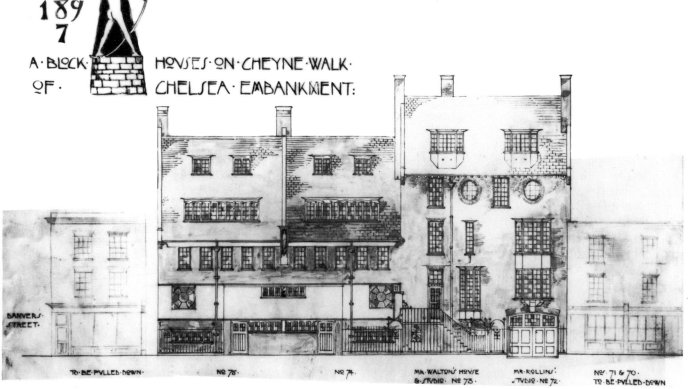

Ashbee was a member of the Society for the Protection of Ancient Buildings and built, restored and altered cottages and churches. He was made an honorary member of the Secessionists of Vienna and honorary corresponding member of the Deutsche Bildender Künstler. He was asked by the Hungarian government to prepare a report on the English-speaking universities and made several lecture tours in the USA where he met Frank Lloyd Wright. Ashbee was the first English architect to call attention to Wright through his introduction to the Wasmuth edition of Wright's work in 1911 (re-issued in English by the Frank Lloyd Wright Foundation, Horizon Press, New York, 1968).

Ashbee would have had major buildings to his credit if he had been able to realise his designs for a church at Springfield, Wolverhampton; a London Fraternity House at Shrewsbury Court, Chelsea; the development of the Dromenagh Estate at Iver Heath, Buckinghamshire (where he did a house); a garden suburb at Ruislip Manor Estate, Middlesex; or Danvers Towers, Chelsea — studio flats for Augustus John, John Singer Sargent, Edwin Austin Abbey, John Tweed, and other artists. For this last scheme the young Charles Holden prepared drawings in 1897 (RIBA, Drawings Collection). William Flockhart (q.v.) designed and built a similar scheme in Lansdowne Road, W11.

Ashbee's architectural works included model cottages in Beachfield, Dudley and Enfield Roads, Ellesmere Port, Cheshire (*Bldr*, 23.4.10) for Peter Jones and his Wolverhampton Corrugated Iron Co. He did restoration on Calne Church, Wiltshire, Seal Church, Kent, and Holcombe Rogus Poor Houses in Somerset. For Colonel Shaw-Hellier, Ashbee did the additions to Wombourne, Wodehouse, Staffordshire (already altered by G. F. Bodley in 1872–3), and for the same client designed the Old Manor House, Taormina, Sicily.

In 1915 Ashbee went to Cairo University as a lecturer in English Literature and at the end of the First World War he was asked by Sir Ronald Storrs to prepare a report upon the future planning of Jerusalem after its liberation by General Allenby in 1917. As a result he was appointed Civic Adviser, first Military, then Civil, to the Palestine Administration under Sir Herbert Samuel, and Secretary to the Pro-Jerusalem Society. With his wife and children he lived in Jerusalem, laid out a plan for the city's parks, rescued and restored ancient buildings, cleared and planted the City Fosse, recreated the encircling rampart walk, revived traditional Arab arts and crafts, rescued the ancient Suk-el-Qattanin, or Cotton Market, from use as a public latrine, and designed furniture for Government House.

In 1924 Ashbee and his family returned to England and settled in his wife's family house at Godden Green. He set to work to transform the 1897 French Gothic house into 1924 neo-Georgian, a style which he had previously decried as guilty of 'aristocratic bias and failure to get to the heart of the modern problem'. He improved the gardens, built a swimming pool, took an interest in local music and drama societies, worked for the cause of town planning, and saved parts of Sevenoaks from 'development'.

Ashbee joined the Art Workers' Guild in 1897 and was Master in 1929. His knowledge of French, German and English literature was wide; he discussed *Weltpolitik*, but not national politics, and never said how he voted — the angels had a good ally after all.

A prolific writer on social economics and art, Ashbee wrote, among many other works:

Transactions of the School of Handicraft (London, 1890)

Chapters on Workshop Reconstruction and Citizenship (London, 1894)

The Treatises of Benvenuto Cellini on Metalwork and Sculpture (Essex House Press, 1898 and 1909)

An Endeavour towards the Teaching of John Ruskin and William Morris (Essex House Press, 1901)

A Book of Cottages and Little Houses (limited edn London, 1906)

Craftsmanship in Competitive Industry: being a record of the Guild of Handicraft and Some Deductions from Twenty-one Years' Experience (Essex House Press, 1908)

Modern English Silverwork (London, Batsford, 1908)

The Building of Thelema (London, Dent, 1910)

Should We Stop Teaching Art? (London, Batsford, 1912)

The Hamptonshire Experiment in Education (London, Allen & Unwin, 1914)

Where the Great City Stands (London, Essex House Press and Batsford, 1917)

Lyrics of the Nile (London, Essex House Press, 1917).

A Palestine Notebook (1918–23) (London, Doubleday, Page & Heinemann, 1923)

Crawford, Alan, Index to the Ashbee Journals now at King's College, Cambridge. Leicester 1965
Deutsche Kunst und Dekoration, 1906–7, pp. 213–15
MacCarthy, Fiona, *The Simple Life: C. R. Ashbee in the Cotswolds*, (London, Lund Humphries, 1981)

Pearson, Hesketh, *The Man Whistler*, London, 1952
Posener, Julius, *Anfänge des Funktionalismus*, Berlin, 1964, pp. 95–6
Studio, May 1895

Victoria and Albert Museum library: 'The Ashbee Memoirs, 1884–1936' (typescript), 6 vols, and 'The Ashbee Collection' (photographs), 5 vols.

Cheltenham Art Gallery and Museum, *The Work of C. R. Ashbee*, exhibition catalogue, 1981

Obit. RIBAJ, June 1942, p. 134 *Bldr*, 29.5.42, p. 476
ABN 1942, pp. 123, 132 and 137

ASHBY, Dr Thomas, DLitt Oxon   1874–1931

Thomas Ashby was born at Staines, Middlesex, the only child of Thomas Ashby, a member of the Quaker family of bankers and brewers. He was at school at Winchester. When he was sixteen his father settled in Rome and became an explorer of the Campagna and an associate of the archaeologist

Rodolfo Lanciani (1846–1929). Thomas Ashby junior obtained a scholarship to Christ Church, Oxford, where he was a pupil of F. J. Haverfield and J. L. Myres. He obtained the DLitt in 1905.

In 1901 he was the first student at the British School at Rome, which began as a school of archaeology and was first housed in the Palazzo Odescalchi in the Corso. Ashby was made Assistant Director of the school in 1903 and Director in 1906. His scholarship was remarkable, as was his fluency in Italian. His knowledge of the architectural and artistic monuments of Rome and of the drawings and prints in Rome, Windsor Castle, Eton College and the Soane Museum was prodigious.

Ashby directed the excavation of the Romano-British town of Venta Silurium (Caerwent), near Chepstow, between 1899 and 1910, and the megalithic monuments of Malta and Gozo between 1908 and 1911.

In 1916, with the aid of funds from the proceeds of the Great Exhibition of 1851, the British School of Rome under Ashby expanded to include architecture, painting and sculpture, and moved to new premises on the new Viale delli Belli Arti in the Valle Giulia. Edwin Lutyens played an instrumental part in this development and had designed the British Pavilion for the Rome Exhibition of 1911, the façade of which was to resemble the upper order of the west front of St Paul's Cathedral, minus its bell tower and clock tower. As Lutyens explained in a letter to Herbert Baker, 'the condition to copy, *i.e.* adapt, the upper order of the west front of St Paul's was given me by the Board of Trade. They all thought it very like, but it wasn't a bit, which is where the fun came in for me'. The result pleased the Rome authorities who gave the site to the British School, and the building which had been of plaster was put into more permanent materials, but still finished in the superb Italian *stucco duro* to imitate travertine stone. This provided only a grand entrance hall and offices; the studios and residences were built at the rear.

In 1927 Ashby revised the second part of W. J. Anderson and R. Phené Spiers's *Architecture of Greece and Rome*, and he revised S. B. Platner's *Topographical Dictionary of Ancient Rome* (1929). Dr Ashby was made a member of the Accademia Pontifica in 1914, and of the Reale Società Romana di Storia Patria in 1923, a foreign member of the Reale Accademia di San Luca in 1925 and a Fellow of the British Academy in 1927. He made over eighty contributions to the *Encyclopaedia Britannica* on the cities of Italy and Sicily. During the First World War Ashby joined the Red Cross on the Italian Front and was mentioned in dispatches. He died in a tragic accident, falling from a train on the Southern Railway between Malden and Raynes Park. His portrait by George Clausen and a bronze head by David Evans are in the National Portrait Gallery.

Obit. RIBAJ, 6.6.31, p. 565 *Bldr*, 22.5.31, p. 920.

ASHLEY, Henry Victor 1872–1945

H. V. Ashley was the son of John Ashley of the Great Northern Railway. He was born at Edmonton, Middlesex, went to Merchant Taylors' School and was articled to William Dunn in 1889. He was assistant to F. T. Baggallay, John Belcher, Dunn and Watson, J. H. Ince and W. J. N. Millard. In 1896 Ashley commenced practice on his own account. F. Winton Newman, a chief assistant to Ernest Newton, joined him as a partner in 1907. The firm continues as Ashley and Newman.

Ashley, who lived in a pleasant house of his own design in Frognal Gardens, Hampstead, designed and presented the cloisters in the graveyard attached to the parish church of St John, Hampstead.

Ashley and Newman did the Greaves Pumping Station for the East London Waterworks (RA, 1904) and, in 1910, extensions to the Birmingham Council House (*Bldr*, 9.1.07), which they won in a competition assessed by Sir Aston Webb. They also designed East Weald, The Bishop's Avenue, Hampstead Heath, N2 (*AA*, 1910) — an early arrival in that depressing array of mansions. Ashley was a member of the Art Workers' Guild.

Obit. RIBAJ, Sept.,1945, p. 340 *Bldr*, 10.8.45, p. 113.

R. Frank Atkinson: medallions commemorating exhibition awards, from the former Waring & Gillow building, Oxford Street, London W1.

ATKINSON, Robert Frank 1871–1923

Frank Atkinson, the son of John F. H. Atkinson, was educated privately and travelled extensively in Europe and the USA. He was articled to the Liverpool architect J. Francis Doyle and continued in his office for six years. He was chief draughtsman when Doyle was doing the Royal Insurance

94

R. Frank Atkinson: a detail of the main front of the
former Waring & Gillow building, Oxford Street, London
W1, "Hampton Court Palace on stilts in the middle of
Oxford Street" (Prof. C. H. Reilly).

Building and the White Star (now Pacific Steam Navigation) Building with R. Norman Shaw as consultant. In 1897 Atkinson opened his own office in Liverpool and the following year did some residences at New Brighton, Cheshire and later Briar Dene there (RA, 1902).

In 1898 Samuel J. Waring, whose large Lancashire furnishing business had extended to London, bought Foot's Cray Place in Kent as his country seat, calling in Atkinson to remodel the interior and add a mezzanine floor and garden house (gardens by Thomas Mawson). The mansion was pulled down after a fire in 1950. In 1901 Waring called on Atkinson again to design a huge furniture emporium on the north side of Oxford Street — an undertaking which was to take five years (*Bldr*, 4.11.05 and 30.9.09) (*see under* London's Edwardian Shops and Stores).

93
94

Atkinson opened an office in London. He married Ada Everdene Towle, whose father, Sir Francis Towle, was chairman of the great chain of Midland Hotels and the opportunity to do a great hotel came in 1912 when he was asked to do the (Midland) Adelphi Hotel in Liverpool. In contrast to Waring's Oxford Street building, the external walls here are supported by steelwork. But the full scheme was never realised and after the First World War the hotel was completed to a modified plan by Stanley Hamp of Collcutt and Hamp.

In 1908 Frank Atkinson was one of the twenty-three architects invited to compete for the new London County Hall. The previous year he was invited by Gordon Selfridge to collaborate with his Chicago architect Daniel Burnham on the new Selfridge's Store in Oxford Street (RA, 1907; *Bldr*, 23.1.09, pp. 92–3 and 3.4.09; *see under* London's Edwardian Shops and Stores).

71
95

In 1912 Atkinson's plan was selected from those of six invited architects for William Whiteley's Village Homes at Burhill, Walton-on-Thames, Surrey. Atkinson did the entrance gates and lodges, a bridge and some cottages. Other well-known architects contributed cottages and community buildings (*ABN*, 10.4.69). Atkinson also did houses in the Liverpool area, including one at 78 Warren Road, Blundellsands. In the London area he did houses at Maidenhead, Wimbledon and Sanderstead, and an entrance lodge at Chislehurst, Kent.

Atkinson designed the interiors of the public rooms in the Cunard liner *Transylvania* in 1914 and the interior of the Pullman cars for the 'Southern Belle' (later the 'Brighton Belle') of the London, Brighton and South Coast Railway. His last work was Magnet House, Kingsway, WC2, for the General Electric Co. (1921), demolished in 1964 and replaced by a cylindrical building by Richard Seifert. Atkinson's practice was continued by his former assistants, Charles D. Carus Wilson and W. Boyd Scott.

Other major works by Atkinson include:

1905	Council offices and courts, Bromley, Kent (won in competition assessed by J. G. S. Gibson in a style called by Atkinson 'Free Georgian') (*Bldr*, 14.1.05)
	Cottage homes, Radlett, Hertfordshire, for the Furniture Trades Benevolent Association (*A*, 4.8.05)
1907-9	Olympia Exhibition Hall extension, Kensington, W14 (1930 additions by Joseph Emberton)
	Newton House, 151–153 Great Portland Street, W1 for Mme Newton, Costumier. (The name carved over the door survives.)
	Premises, Bolsover Street, W1
	Motor Car Showrooms, 11 Great Marlborough Street, W1, for Waring (never used as such and taken over by the woollen merchants Cobb and Jenkins) (*AA*, 1909)
	Motor Car Showrooms, 180 New Bond Street, W1, for the Darracq Motor Co.
	Council offices and fire station, Carshalton, Surrey

Obit. RIBA*J*, July, 1923, p. 566 *Bldr*, 20.7.23, p. 91.

R. Frank Atkinson: the Duke Street corner of the first section of Selfridge's Store, Oxford Street, London W1, the Chicago architect Daniel Burnham, as consultant, set the style.

ATKINSON, Thomas Dinham   1864—1948

T. D. Atkinson was educated at Rossall School, Lancashire, and at University College, Cambridge. He was articled to Sir Arthur Blomfield, ARA, in 1882, studied at University College, London, and at the British School at Athens, and set up in practice in Cambridge in 1889.

Atkinson is best known for his books on church architecture, *English Architecture* (1904) which went into eleven editions, and *Glossary of English Architecture* (1906) which went into its fifth edition in 1937. He also wrote extensively on Cambridge, Winchester, and the English and Welsh cathedrals. His last book was *Local Style in English Architecture* (1946).

Atkinson did a church at Maes y Groes, North Wales, and houses and churches in Cambridge and elsewhere. In 1911 he did the Solar Physics Laboratory in Cambridge in partnership with William M. Fawcett (1833—1909), whom he had joined in 1906. Atkinson was Surveyor to Ely and Winchester cathedrals.

Obit.   RIBAJ, Jan., 1949, p. 143   *Bldr*, 7.1.49, p. 18.

AUMONIER, William   1839—1914

The first of three generations of architectural carvers, William Aumonier was the son of J. H. C. Aumonier, a craftsman in gold of Huguenot descent. He was apprenticed to Colman and Davis of George Street, Portman Square, W1, where he worked with Alfred Stevens. At nineteen, Aumonier went to study in Paris and worked for Viollet-le-Duc on the restoration of Amiens Cathedral.

Among the many works of modelling and carving undertaken by Aumonier, on which he was later assisted by his son, were the terracotta enrichments for Birmingham Law Courts (1887—91) for Aston Webb and Ingress Bell (RA, 1889); carving at Bath Municipal Buildings for J. McK. Brydon; and carving at Oxford Town Hall for H. T. Hare. The
116   carving at the United Universities Club, Pall Mall East, SW1, for Reginald Blomfield was executed by Aumonier's son from models by Henry Pegram.

William Aumonier senior also did the carving for
115   Lady Margaret Hall, Oxford, again for Blomfield. For Percy Adams and Charles Holden he did
214   carvings at King Edward VII Sanatorium, Midhurst,
215   Sussex, the Hall of the Incorporated Law Society, Chancery Lane, WC2, and the Central Library, Bristol. For C. Harrison Townsend he did the carving at the Horniman Museum, Forest Hill, SE23. Aumonier did the sedilias and faldstools at St Paul's Cathedral and carving for many other architects of the period.

Three Aumoniers became members of the Art Workers' Guild — William Aumonier in 1885, his son William, who later went to New Zealand,

in 1914, and his grandson W. Whitworth Aumonier in 1932.

Obit.   RIBAJ, 14.2.14, p. 239   *Bldr*, 30.1.14, p. 143 (with list of works)

AYRTON, Ormrod Maxwell   1874—1960

Maxwell Ayrton was articled to Henry Beswick of Chester in 1891. He was assistant to W. A. Pite in 1897 and to Edwin Lutyens from 1897 to 1900. Most of Ayrton's work was done during his partnership with J. W. Simpson (*q.v.*) which began in 1905. Their best-known work, which won Simpson a knighthood, was for the British Empire Exhibition held at Wembley Park in 1924 and 1925. With Owen Williams, who was the civil engineer engaged on the exhibition buildings, Ayrton did the bridges for the new roads in the Scottish Highlands which harmonise so well with the landscape and are an excellent example of collaboration between engineer and architect. Ayrton also did the additions at Bedford College, Regent's Park, to earlier buildings by Champneys and S. R. J. Smith, and at the Royal Free Hospital Medical School, Hunter Street, WC1, to earlier buildings by J. McK. Brydon; a new concert hall to the Royal College of Music (by Sir Arthur Blomfield); and additions at the Medical Research Council's Mount Vernon, Hampstead. He married Eliza, eldest daughter of Sir Edwin Waterlow.

Other works with Simpson include:

1905-8	The Lodge and Form Rooms at Haileybury College, Hertfordshire
	Hall Ingle, Heath End, Checkendon, Oxfordshire (RA, 1902)
	Langtree Cottages, Checkendon (RA, 1906)
	Audley House, Margaret Street, W1
1907	Messrs Kay's premises, The Tything, Worcester
1911	Field's House, Gibbs' House and Masters' Tower, Lancing College, Sussex

Obit.   RIBAJ, May, 1960, p. 247   *Bldr*, 26.2.60, p. 402

BAGGALLAY, Frank Thomas   1855—1929

F. T. Baggallay was born in Wandsworth, London, and was articled to Thomas Henry Wyatt. He studied under Professor Roger Smith at King's College, London, where he won the RIBA Ashpitel Prize in 1877. He entered the Royal Academy Schools in 1876, winning the Gold Medal in 1879. Baggallay was a draughtsman on the staff of *The Builder*, worked in the office of Sir Arthur Blomfield, ARA, and commenced practice in 1880 with fellow-student Walter Millard. (For their work together, *see under* Millard, Walter John Nash.)

With George Gale, Baggallay won the competition for St Luke, Grange Road, Bermondsey, SE1 (1884), and with F. E. Bristowe he won the competition for the Royal Baths at Harrogate, W. Riding (1897, additions in 1937 by L. H. Clarke).

Among Baggallay's pupils were Dunbar Smith and Cecil Brewer.

Obit. RIBAJ, 12.4.30, pp. 379—80 *Bldr*, 14.3.30, p.520.

BAILEY, Thomas Jerram   1844—1910

Thomas Bailey was articled to R. J. Withers of Doughty Street, WC1, in 1859 and was assistant to Ewan Christian and S. S. Teulon. He entered the office of the London School Board in 1872, succeeding E. R. Robson (1836—1917) as chief architect in 1884 and continuing in the post, after the board was taken over by the London County Council in 1904, until his retirement in 1909.

With a staff of only a fraction of its present strength, Bailey carried through an extensive programme of school building, including many of those well-lit, well-ventilated buildings of the 'Hall' type which raise their copper-pennoned weather-vanes over stretches of blue slate roofs, recalling lines from James Thomson's 'Sunday in Hampstead':

> And the mighty city of London,
> Under the clouds and the light,
> Seems a low wet beach, half shingle,
> With a few sharp rocks upright.

Some of these were at Alexis Street, Southwark, SE16 (RA, 1902), Cassland Road, E9 (RA, 1904), Hortensia Road, SW7 *(Bldr*, 5.12.08) and Broomwood Road, SW11 *(Bldr*, 11.12.09).

Bldr, 22.6.01 *AR*, June, 1958, p. 393—8: 'Towers of Learning' by David Gregory Jones.
Obit. RIBAJ, Sept. 1910, p. 766 *Bldr*, 25.6.10, p. 735

BAKER, Sir Herbert, KCIE, DCL Oxon, RA 1862—1946

Herbert Baker was one of the ten children of Thomas H. Baker, JP, of Owletts, Cobham, Kent. He went to Tonbridge School and in 1881 was articled to his uncle A. H. Baker, a church architect of Upper Phillimore Place, Kensington, W8. Baker acted as clerk of works for his uncle on the church of St Padern, Llanberis, Caernarvon. The Bakers were made Honorary Architects to the Cambrian Academy of Arts for their measured drawings of Plas-y-Mawr, Conway. In 1886 Baker entered the office of George and Peto where he became chief assistant and where he met Edwin

Lutyens with whom he went sketching in the country. Baker entered the Royal Academy Schools in 1887 and in 1889 won the RIBA Ashpitel Prize.

When in 1891 Baker's brother Lionel went to the Cape of Good Hope (then Cape Colony) to start a fruit farm, Baker went out to advise on the situation. He soon met Cecil Rhodes who asked him to restore his home, Groote Schuur. This was completed in 1893 but destroyed by fire and rebuilt by Baker three years later *(Bldr*, 24.4.1900). Bequeathed to South Africa by Rhodes, it is now the Prime Minister's residence and with its furniture represents the prototype of the revival of the Cape Dutch style.

Sir Herbert Baker, RA: Groote Schurr. Cecil Rhodes's house in Pretoria, South Africa, in the "Cape Dutch" style.

Rhodes saw in Baker just the man to help him realise his dreams of a great and permanent culture for South Africa, and his choice was justified. In his early work in the Cape, with great patience and energy, Baker brought the building crafts of South Africa to a high standard.

Baker was appointed Diocesan Architect for Cape Town where his first churches were St Andrew (1894) and St Michael and All Angels (1898), both at Newlands, and the Mission Church of St Philip, District Six (1898). Baker also did the parish hall (1901) and chancel, sanctuary and Lady chapel (1904) at St Michael and All Angels. He was assisted by Francis E. Masey (1861—1912), from the office of Alfred Waterhouse, a fellow-student at the Royal Academy and winner of the Tite Prize, Soane Medallion and Owen Jones Medal. Masey became a partner in 1899 and together they did St George's Cathedral in Cape Town (1897—8, with glasswork by Christopher Whall) and St George's Grammar School (1904). In his South African churches Baker introduced a simple, round-arched style in which rough-hewn stone contrasted with white plaster — much as Brunelleschi had contrasted pietra serena with plaster in his quattrocento Florentine churches, but without his classical mouldings. St George's Cathedral was later altered by Franklin D. Kendall (1870—1948), from Sir Ernest George's office, who joined Baker in 1899.

Sir Herbert Baker, RA: Union Buildings, Pretoria.
Diploma work for the Royal Academy of Arts. The twin
towers recall Wren's Greenwich, the Hemicycle, the
London County Hall.

Also in Cape Town, Baker and Masey did the
Wilson and Miller Building; the Rhodes Building
for de Beers, the mining company founded by
Rhodes; the Marks Building (1905); and the
Mutual Life Association of Australia Ltd.
(1903–5). The partners did many fine houses in
the environs of Cape Town including The Retreat,
built in the grounds of Government House, which
they altered for the visit of the Duke and Duchess
of York in 1901; Welgelegen, Rhodes's gift to Sir
Donald Currie of the Union Castle Line; The
Woolsack, lent to Rudyard Kipling; Rust en Vrede
(1905), Rhodes's posthumous gift to Sir Abe
Bailey; and Baker's own house, Sandhills,
Muizenberg. Baker had earlier supervised the
building of the Union Castle Line Building and
the Mount Wilson Hotel, Cape Town, for Dunn
and Watson, Currie's Scottish architects.

Rhodes had visited Egypt, Greece, Italy and
Sicily with Dr Jameson in 1899 and in the following year sent Baker on the same tour. The trip had
generated in Rhodes ideas for a Lion House on
Table Mountain, based on the Temple of Poseidon
at Paestum, and similar architectural fantasies —
neo-Greek dreams which, however, were realised
only in his own memorial at Mowbray, Cape Town,
where Baker provided a setting for a bronze head
of Rhodes by J. W. Swan. A bronze cast of George

Frederick Watts's colossal 'Physical Energy' now
in Kensington Gardens was set up at Rhodes's
tomb in the Matopo Hills, Bulawayo. Baker also
did the memorial in Rhodesia to the Shangani tribe
for the Matabele War of 1897 and a monument to
the Honoured Dead at Kimberley, Cape Province
(1904–5).

After Baker's first patron, Cecil Rhodes, died in
1902, Lord Milner was entrusted with the task of
reconstruction in the Transvaal and Orange River
Colony after the Boer War. Baker, assisted by
Masey, was again engaged in the building of
government buildings, churches, houses and agricultural and mining settlements. The Cathedral of
St Alban in Pretoria was begun in 1905 but only
the sanctuary, chancels and side chapels were built.
It was completed in 1958 by E. N. Wilfrid Mallows,
son of C. E. Mallows (q.v.). Baker's other churches
included St John the Evangelist, Mafeking (1901);
St John the Divine, Randfontein, and St George,
Cullinan, for the Premier Diamond Mine (both in
1904); and St Michael and All Angels, Boksbury
(1911). Baker, Masey and Sloper designed
Government House, Pretoria (*Bldr*, 14.9.07), the
splendid Pretoria Railway Station (1908–9) —
where the style anticipates Baker's design for the
Pretoria Union Buildings (1910); Government
Offices, Bloemfontein, and the South African

292

Institute of Medical Research at Johannesburg, completed in 1912.

Masey left in 1909 to start up practice in Rhodesia and F. L. Hodgson Fleming (1875–1950), who had joined Baker in 1903, became a partner the following year. Together they did more than eighty churches in the Union. Baker had also been joined in 1903 by Ernest Willmott (Sloper) from Bodley's office in London and he became a partner the same year, but ill-health forced Willmott (*q.v.*) to return to England in 1907. Kendall became a partner in 1906.

The great South African mining boom was brief, but between 1902 and 1904 Baker did a great number of houses in the environs of Johannesburg which were well suited to the needs of the wealthy mine owners and the managers of mining companies. Left to speculators and less experienced hands, these houses could well have looked ostentatious and vulgar in the bright South African sunlight. Baker's many Transvaal houses include Villa Arcadia, Parktown, Johannesburg, for Sir Lionel Phillips, and Stonehouse (his own house) and the White House, for Lionel Curtis, both in Pretoria.

In 1910 General Botha, first Prime Minister of South Africa, asked Baker to report on a site for the Union Administrative Buildings at Pretoria, as the legislature was to remain in Cape Town. Baker reported favourably on Meintjes Kop and designed buildings with twin cupola towers, recalling those on Wren's Greenwich Hospital, linked by a concave hemicycle so that they did not dominate the low hill they crowned. Interior courts show the cool patios and columns which the South African writer Olive Schreiner had urged Baker to introduce into his houses. Union Buildings were Baker's crowning achievement in South Africa and a preparation for his next great task at New Delhi.

Baker had invited his friend Edwin Lutyens to the Transvaal, a visit which resulted in Lutyens designing the War Memorial and Art Gallery in Johannesburg. Lutyens recommended Baker to share with him the building of the great new government buildings at New Delhi where the government of India was being transferred. In 1913 Baker left his South African practice to Fleming and returned to England. Baker was now fifty-one and with a full career behind him, but he proved equal to the challenge of New Delhi. With Fleming, who had meanwhile moved to India, he designed the twin-domed Secretariat Building and the circular Legislature Building. Disagreement over the levelling of the central King's Way leading to Lutyens's Viceregal Lodge — in reality a palace the size of Versailles — led to a long estrangement, ended only in their later years. Lutyens's building was cold, masterly and dramatic, where Baker's were warm and comfortable. Baker had inclined more closely to the Mogul tradition while Lutyens had adapted it in his own brilliant way. In their disagreement, the two great architects attracted staunch partisans and no doubt will continue to do

so, since their buildings reflect dichotomies of a fundamental kind.

After twelve years' dedication to New Delhi, Baker turned his attention to buildings in England after the First World War. The list is formidable, ranging from the Bank of England in the City of London to Winchester College War Memorial Cloisters, which Baker saw as his best work of the period. Other works of these years were the Harrow School War Memorial; an apse to the School Chapel, Haileybury; Church House, Broad Sanctuary, SW1; the Ninth Church of Christ Scientist, Marsham Street, SW1; London House, Guilford Street, WC1; Cable (now Electra) House, Victoria Embankment; India House, Aldwych, WC2; the Royal Empire (now Commonwealth) Society, Northumberland Avenue, WC2; Glyn Mills and Martin's banks, Lombard Street, EC3; Rhodes House, Oxford; Chiswick Bridge, W4; and the war cemeteries at Neuve Chapelle and Delville Wood on the Somme. In 1927 Baker received the Royal Gold Medal for Architecture.

Baker was made ARA in 1922, RA in 1932 (diploma work, Government Buildings, Pretoria). He was a member of the Art Workers' Guild.

Baker, Sir Herbert, *Cecil Rhodes, by his Architect*, London, 1934

Baker, Sir Herbert, *Architecture and Personalities*, London, 1944

Greig, Doreen E., *Herbert Baker in South Africa*, London and Cape Town, 1970. (A complete account, including notes on his assistants and partners.)

RIBAJ, 10.12.27, pp. 63–77: 'The Government Buildings of Pretoria, New Delhi, Rhodesia and Kenya'

The Times, 8.6.62: (To mark the centenary of Baker's birth) 'Sir Herbert Baker, Architecture and Personalities'

Obit. *RIBAJ*, Mar., 1946, pp. 189–90 *Bldr*, 15.2.46, pp. 158–9

BALFOUR, Colonel Eustace James Anthony 1854–1911

Eustace Balfour was the fifth and youngest son of James Maitland Balfour of Whittinghame, East Lothian, and a brother of Arthur J. Balfour (Prime Minister, 1902–5). A sister, Eleanor Mildred Balfour (Mrs Sidgwick), became Principal of Newnham College, Cambridge. Eustace Balfour went to Harrow and to Trinity College, Cambridge. He was articled to Basil Champneys and set up in practice in 1879. He married Lady Frances Campbell, daughter of the 8th Duke of Argyll.

In 1890 Balfour was appointed surveyor to the Grosvenor Estates in Mayfair, Belgravia and Pimlico and took into partnership Thackeray Turner. Together they introduced into the estates the more fashionable red brick and stone houses and mansion flats which were superseding the Victorian and Georgian terraces. But the work of Balfour and Turner differed from the contemporary 'Wrenaissance' fashion in that Turner — a friend of William Lethaby — closely followed the principles that were the watchword of the Arts and Crafts Movement, while their buildings were embellished by the individual carvings of Turner's brother, Laurence A. Turner. For details of their work, *see under* Turner, Thackeray H.

31
356
358

Eustace Balfour was Colonel (1892—1904) of the London Scottish Corps of Volunteers and on his retirement was made ADC to King Edward VII. After his death, Thackeray Turner took into partnership A. R. Powys (1882—1936), expert on the preservation of ancient buildings, and continued the firm as Balfour and Turner.

Obit. RIBAJ, 18.2.11, p. 283 *Bldr*, 17.2.11, p. 222.

BALL, Joseph Lancaster   1852—1933

Joseph Ball was born at Maltby, W. Riding. He was articled to W. W. Pocock in London and set up in practice in Birmingham where, in partnership as Ball and Goddard, he designed Handsworth Methodist College (1880—1) and collaborated with W. R. Lethaby on the (former) Eagle Insurance Building, 122—124 Colmore Row (1900). Lethaby's influence is evident in St Gregory, Small Heath, which Ball did in 1902 and also in Winterbourne, Edgbaston Park Road, of the following year.

235

Ball was Director of the Birmingham School of Architecture (1909—16) and President of the Birmingham Architectural Association. A late work, the Blue Coat School, Harborne (1930, in association with H. W. Simister), is still markedly in the Arts and Crafts tradition.

Obit. RIBAJ, 24.2.34, pp. 418—19 *Bldr*, 22.12.33, p. 985.

BANKART, George Percy   1866—1929

George Bankart was born in Leicester, son of an insurance broker. He went to Wyggeston Grammar School and Leicester School of Art and Technical College. In 1883 he was articled to Leicester architect Isaac Barradale. A fellow-pupil there was Ernest Gimson who remained a lifelong friend. At Bankart's father's house they both met William Morris, and the meeting left a lasting impression on the two young craftsmen. To gain experience Bankart worked in various architects' offices in London and elsewhere. On the Fairfax-Cholmeley Estate in Yorkshire he made early experiments in moulded decorative plasterwork.

Bankart was instructor in plasterwork at his old art school in Leicester (1897—9). He was also in charge of the plasterwork at the Bromsgrove Guild of Handicraft, Worcestershire, where he was responsible for many important works including the ceilings for the Cardiff City Hall and Law Courts for Lanchester, Stewart and Rickards. When he left in 1908 to establish himself in London he was succeeded by Walter Gilbert.

At his workshop in Gray's Inn Road, WC1, Bankart continued his special style of plasterwork derived from his study of the work at Haddon Hall, Derbyshire. One of Bankart's first orders came from Guy Dawber for ceilings at Hartpury House, Ashleworth, Gloucestershire, now the Agricultural College.

The ceilings which Bankart prized most were done for the Glynde School of Lady Gardeners at Glynde, Sussex. The house, now called Ragged Lands, is described by the founder, Viscountess Wolseley, in *A Cottage Garden*. However, the birds and flowers Bankart modelled in plaster have since been removed. One of his ceilings is at Upton Grey, near Basingstoke, Hampshire, designed by Ernest Newton for Charles Holme of *The Studio*. For the Council Offices at Lewes, Sussex, Bankart did a relief of oxen ploughing. For this, his son Hugh Bankart recalled, Bankart sketched one of the last ox ploughs in Sussex on the downs above Lewes.

Bankart's largest contract was for all the decorative plasterwork at the Victoria and Albert Museum, South Kensington, for Aston Webb, a contract which involved Bankart in distressing litigation and financial loss. Most of the architects of the day specified Bankart's work, and he was also successful with cast lead work for rainwater heads and fountains, but after the First World War, fewer orders came his way. The Bankart moulds are preserved in the hands of George Jackson and Sons, who can still reproduce Bankart's work.

George Bankart was a member of the Art Workers' Guild, wrote *The Art of the Plasterer in England* (1908), towards the end of his life revised William Miller's *Plastering, Plain and Decorative* (1927) and with his son, G. E. Bankart, wrote *Modern Plasterwork Construction* and *Modern Plasterwork Design*, published by the Architectural Press in 1926 and 1927.

AJ, 12.10.27, pp. 470—2 and 26.10, pp.536—8. *Obit. Bldr*, 19.4.29, p. 719.

BARNSLEY, Ernest Arthur   1863—1926

Ernest Barnsley was born in Birmingham, the son of John Barnsley, the builder of Birmingham Town Hall. From 1886 to 1889 he was articled to J. D. Sedding, the church architect, with offices next door to William Morris's showroom in London. Barnsley started his architectural practice in Birmingham, married, and built himself a house at Four Oaks. Later he joined in partnership Ernest Gimson, a fellow-pupil at Sedding's. He joined

Gimson in a move to the Cotswolds, settling at
Ewen in 1893, and then moving to Pinbury, where
he began designing and making furniture.

Later, Barnsley moved to Sapperton where he
converted a cottage into Upper Dorvel House for
himself. He also did work on Coates Manor at
Sapperton, and designed the village hall in
collaboration with Norman Jewson (from the
office of another Sedding pupil, H. G. Ibberson),
who married his daughter Mary.

Although he largely gave up furniture-making, his
architectural work in the Cotswolds was extensive.
His largest work was Rodmarton Manor near
Cirencester, for the Hon. Claud Biddulph, on
which he was engaged from 1912 until his death.
The work was continued briefly by his brother
Sidney Barnsley (*q.v.*), who died the same year,
and finally completed by Norman Jewson.
Rodmarton Manor has been described as the last
great house built in England. It was furnished
mainly by Ernest Gimson and Sidney Barnsley,
Peter Waals and Alfred Wright (*Country Life*,
Vol. LXIX, p. 422).
Barnsley was a member of the Art Workers' Guild.
Jewson, Norman, *By Chance I Did Rove*, Kineton,
Warwickshire, *c.* 1950 and 1973.

Ernest and Sidney Barnsley: The Leasowes, Sapperton,
Glos. The cottage was originally thatched.

BARNSLEY, Sidney Howard   1865–1926

Sidney Barnsley was born in Birmingham, the
younger brother of Ernest Barnsley. He entered
the Royal Academy Schools in 1885 and the
following year was articled to R. Norman Shaw.

Barnsley's travels in Greece with Robert Schultz
Weir inspired a book on the church of St Daphne,
and he collaborated with Weir on *Byzantine
Architecture in Greece* for the Byzantine Research
and Publication Fund. The influence of the eastern
Mediterranean can be seen in the church of St
Sophia, Lower Kingswood, Surrey. Barnsley
designed the church in 1891 for Dr Edwin
Freshfield and Sir Cosmo Bonsor. It contains
fragments from the church of St John, Ephesus,
the Bogdan Serail, St Studion and the Church of
the Pantocrator in Constantinople, and from the
Blachernae Palace nearby.

Sidney Barnsley was one of the group of young
designers and craftsmen dedicated to the ideals
of William Morris who formed Kenton & Co.
between 1890 and 1892 (*see under* Blomfield,
Sir Reginald Theodore).

Daunted by the prospect of years of drudgery in
London architects' offices, Sidney Barnsley joined
his brother and Ernest Gimson in their exodus to
the healthier air of the Cotswolds, then relatively
unexplored architecturally. They settled at Ewen,
then at Pinbury, finally moving to Sapperton
where Sidney designed his own cottage. When his
children required schooling, he moved to Cirencester.

Sidney Barnsley: the east end of the church of St
Sophia, Lower Kingswood, Surrey.

While his brother concentrated on building, Sidney continued to make furniture, but after Gimson's death in 1919, he moved into architecture, superintending Gimson's buildings at Bedales School, Petersfield, Hampshire. On the death of his brother in 1926 he supervised the completion of Rodmarton Manor, near Cirencester, for a brief period before his own death. He did additions to Lodge Farm in Painswick, Gloucestershire, and the Gyde Almshouses in Painswick. His other works included a cottage for Sir Oliver Lodge at Andover, Hampshire, and Cotswold Farm for Lady Birchall.

Sidney Barnsley was a member of the Art Workers' Guild. His son Edward, who continued the work at Bedales after his father's death, designs and makes furniture at Froxfield, near Petersfield.

Jewson, Norman, *By Chance I Did Rove*, Kineton Press, Warwickshire, *c*. 1950 and 1973

BATEMAN, Charles Edward   1863—1947

C. E. Bateman was born at Castle Bromwich and went to St Marylebone Grammar School in London and to the Grange School, Eastbourne. He was articled in 1881 to his father John Jones Bateman (1818—1903) of Castle Bromwich, who founded the firm of Bateman and Bateman. His grandfather, Joseph Bateman, was also an architect. In 1885 Charles Bateman came to London as an improver with Verity and Hunt of London and Evesham and studied at the Architectural Association. In 1887 he returned to Birmingham and became a partner in his father's firm.

Houses by the firm, such as Redlands, Hartopp Road, Sutton Coldfield (*c*. 1900; *AR*, 1906) have a quality which set a high standard in the domestic architecture of the more comfortable suburbs of Birmingham. Other houses by Charles Bateman are Beechcroft, Barnt Green, with a cottage and stables; The Grey House, Barnt Green (*Bldr*, 1.6.01 and 23.11.01); The Homestead, Woodbourne Road, Edgbaston (*Bldr*, 2.3.01); Hawkesford, Bracebridge Road, and Bryn Teg, Sutton Coldfield (1905) and The Gable House, Kings Heath. The Batemans' work is mentioned by Muthesius in *Das Englische Haus*. Charles Bateman also did St Chad, Whitehouse Common, and the completion of the 1834—5 church of St James, Sutton Coldfield (1906—8). His training with Verity and Hunt equipped Bateman with a knowledge of Cotswold building and he carried out work at Honiley Hall, Warwickshire, at Asthall Manor, Oxfordshire, for Lord Redesdale, and at the Lygon Arms, Broadway, Worcestershire.

With Alfred Hale (d. 1948) Bateman won the competitions for High Wycombe Town Hall (*BN*, 14.10.04) and the Free Library at Northfield, Birmingham, both of 1905. Hale became a partner.

Obit. RIBAJ, Sept., 1947, p. 575 *Bldr*, 15.8.47, p. 175

BAYES, Gilbert   1872—1953

Gilbert Bayes was born in London, the son of A. W. Bayes, painter and etcher. He studied at the City and Guilds College and the Royal Academy Schools (1896—9), where he won the Gold Medal and Travelling Studentship in 1899. He exhibited works at the Paris Exhibition of 1900.

Bayes's preference was for romantic subjects taken from the classics and from Wagner's operas. His 'Siegfried', shown at the Royal Academy in 1910 and exhibited at the Tate Gallery, was bought by the Chantrey Bequest. (There is a replica in the Ashmolean, Oxford.) Bayes did the model for the bronze lions' heads on the embankment wall of

231   the London County Hall for the architect Ralph Knott. He also did the figures of the architects Sir William Chambers and Sir Charles Barry on the Cromwell Road façade of the Victoria and Albert Museum and the reliefs for the bronze doors of the New South Wales Art Gallery in Sydney.

71   Bayes's most familiar work is the gilt clock centrepiece at the Selfridge store, Oxford Street, W1 (1928), for the architects Sir John Burnet and Partners for whom he had done the seated stone figure of Joseph Priestley (1733—1804) at the Institute of Chemistry, Russell Square, WC1, in 1914. Bayes designed the Great Seal of King George V in 1911 and the First World War Memorial for the MCC at Lords and the memorial plaque to the architect Ralph Knott, at County Hall, SE1.

In 1926 he was Master of the Art Workers' Guild where there is a portrait bust by him of W. R. Lethaby (Master, 1911). A brother was Walter Bayes, painter, and a sister was Jessie Bayes, illuminator.

AJ, 1906, p. 30 and 1908, p. 103.
Obit. Bldr, 17.7.53, p. 111.

BEGG, John   1866—1937

John Begg, the third son of an ironmaster of Kinneil, was born at Bo'ness, W. Lothian. He was educated at the Edinburgh Academy, was articled to Hippolyte Blanc of Edinburgh and entered the Royal Academy Schools in London in 1890. He was assistant to Alfred Waterhouse, RA, and afterwards chief assistant to Sir Robert W. Edis. Begg won the RIBA Pugin Prize in 1890 and the Ashpitel Prize in 1891, and was second in the Soane Medallion competition in 1892. He set up in practice with R. Sheckleton Balfour.

In 1896 Begg went to the Cape of Good Hope where he became chief architect to the Real Estate Corporation of South Africa until 1899 and did the York and Penlar Building in Johannesburg. In 1901 he was made consulting architect to the Government of Bombay and succeeded James Ransome as consulting architect to the Government of India from 1908 to 1921. On his retirement from India Begg became for seven years head of the Architectural Section of the Edinburgh College of Art in 1922 and set up in practice in Edinburgh with A. Lorne Campbell.

Begg contributed to the fine tradition of British architecture in India with his General Post Office, Bombay (1903–9; *BN*, 1.1.09). Since there were no fire protection regulations here, brick and steel are both revealed. Begg did many other public buildings in India, including the Agricultural College, Poona (1902). His son, K. A. Begg, was chief architect to the Government of Uganda.

BN, 1.10.20, p. 161.
Obit. RIBAJ, 6.3.37, p. 466 and 20.3, p. 519 *Bldr*, 5.3.37, p. 534 *Times* 26.2.37.

BELCHER, John, RA   1841–1913

John Belcher was born in Southwark, London. His father, John Belcher (1816–1890), was an architect and surveyor well established in the City. Belcher was educated privately and at a school in Luxembourg. He was articled to his father and also worked in other London architects' offices. In 1862 Belcher went to France for two years, where, in preference to the ancient cathedrals which were then the principal objects of study, he chose contemporary French architecture.

In 1865 he became his father's partner and did his first building, the Royal Insurance building in Lombard Street, EC3 (demolished in 1913).

John Belcher, RA and A. Beresford Pite: the Hall of the Institute of Chartered Accountants, Moorgate Place, London EC2. The sculpture, by Sir Hamo Thornycroft, RA, Harry Bates, J. E. Taylerson, C. J. Allen and John Tweed, illustrates Belcher's thoughts on sculpture in relation to architecture.

Although this was in the French Renaissance style, the influence of William Burges was still strong enough for him to use the Gothic style for the familiar Mappin & Webb corner between Queen Victoria Street and Poultry in 1870.

Apart from their City practice the Belchers did considerable work in country houses. John Belcher senior retired in 1875 and his son took into partnership J. W. James. Many a young architect chose to enter the office as an improver, for Belcher, with the help of two remarkably talented young men, established a style of architecture which became representative of the Edwardian era — in fact, a press advertisement of the day once offered 'instruction in the Gothic, Renaissance, Classic and Belcher styles'.

Arthur Beresford Pite, also an architect's son, entered the office in 1882 and his arrival was to have a pronounced effect on secular English urban architecture for the next thirty years. Belcher was forty-one and Pite, who joined as an improver at twenty-one, had already won the RIBA Soane Medallion and the Grissell Medal and had been accepted for study at the Royal Academy Schools. The combination proved fortunate, for Pite had scholarship as well as energy and Belcher encouraged new ideas.

In 1890 their work culminated in a remarkable building which brought the following comment thirty years later from James Bone of *The Manchester Guardian*: 'Belcher, 'with him' (as the lawyers say) Beresford Pite, began the modern expression of the cavalier spirit in architecture in
103   that jewel of City buildings, the Hall of the Institute of Chartered Accountants'. The building is in Great Swan Alley and Moorgate Place, EC2. The sculpture, by Harry Bates (1850—99) and William Hamo Thornycroft, illustrates to good effect what Belcher meant in his talk to the RIBA on 'Sculpture and Sculptors' Methods in Relation to Architecture' when he said: 'when sculpture stands forward to illustrate a subject ... architecture should give it loving assistance and unobtrusive support, treating the work as a jewel whose beauty is to be enhanced by an appropriate setting'. The note struck by the Accountants' building was never repeated. T. E. Collcutt came close to it with Lloyd's Registry of Shipping in Fenchurch Street, but the mood had passed and even he did not succeed in recapturing it.

In 1897 Beresford Pite left Belcher's office to set up on his own. In the same year John James Joass entered the office from J. J. Burnet's office in Glasgow and Sir Rowand Anderson's office in Edinburgh. For the next few years Belcher's work was to look more like his own style, with a few details from Joass.

Electra House, Moorgate (1902—3), for the Eastern Telegraph Co. (*Bldr*, 26.5.1900 and 3.11.1900), the first of the prestige office buildings and now the City of London College, tends to grossness. Among the seven sculptors engaged in addition to

stone carvers were George Frampton, William Goscombe John, C. J. Allen, F. W. Pomeroy and Herbert Hampton. This was followed by Winchester House, Old Broad Street, EC2 (*Bldr*, 29.6.07).

Another building charged with the Belcher ebullience is Colchester Town Hall, won in competition in 1898 and completed in 1902 (*Bldr*, 17.5.02). Nicknamed 'Belchester', this building contains inside and bears outside a profusion of heraldic devices and symbolic sculpture. On the tower, the gift of James Paxman, JP, is a bronze figure of the Empress Helena, mother of Constantine I, attended at the four corners by four bronze ravens — the symbol of Colchester — possibly taken from the sketches of the famous bird artist and political cartoonist Sir Francis Carruthers Gould, MP (1844—1945). Allegorical sculptures represent Engineering, Fishery, Agriculture and Military Defence.

Between 1898 and 1900, with Mervyn Macartney, Belcher was engaged on *Later Renaissance Architecture in England* (Batsford, 1901). This went a long way towards saving buildings of the William and Mary, Queen Anne and early Georgian periods from destruction. To compile it Macartney had visited most of the buildings of those periods and the authors had the help of measured drawings by Horace Field and others.

105   The last building to stand out prominently as a
224   markedly Belcher building is the Ashton Memorial, Williamson Park, Lancaster (*Bldr*, 26.5.06). Williamson Park had been rough ground filled in as relief work during the cotton famine of the 1860s, and was laid out in 1878 as a park by Lord Ashton's father, Alderman James Williamson, the linoleum manufacturer. At the highest point in the park Lord Ashton built this memorial to his family. The domed monument with four corner cupolas is faced with Portland stone, has a staircase of Cornish granite from Penryn and is crowned by a copper dome. In the rotunda is a Temple of Fame, and paintings and sculpture represent Commerce, History, Science and Art.

223   Mappin & Webb's, Oxford Street, and the Royal
222   Insurance, St James's Street, in the last phase of Belcher's work with Joass (a partner since 1905), show more evidence of Joass's influence and it is interesting to contrast Joass's Glasgow-derived style with that of Beresford Pite (*see under* Joass, John James, *and* Pite, Arthur Beresford).

In 1908, with as yet no hint of the coming war to cloud the spirit of the *entente cordiale*, the Franco-British Exhibition was held at the White City, Shepherd's Bush (*AR*, 1908, pp. 32 and 110). Belcher and Joass were entrusted with the design of buildings for the British section where good use was made of the opportunity to display neo-Baroque at its most ebullient with the touch of fantasy appropriate to an exhibition.

John Belcher, RA: Edwardian profusion at the Ashton Memorial, Williamson Park, Lancaster. ▷

Had funds been available, Belcher would have completed the Catholic Apostolic Church, Gordon Square, WC1, begun by Raphael Brandon; his design for a second church at Maida Vale (*BA*, 10.5.1889) was supplanted by that of J. L. Pearson.

Belcher was a musician of considerable ability, a singer, conductor and cellist; he wrote a paper on musical requirements in church planning (*RIBA Trans.*, 1889), and a 'Report on the Position of Organs in Churches' (1892). In fact he was better known to the public as a musician than as an architect.

He was President of the RIBA from 1904 to 1906. In 1907 he received the Royal Gold Medal for Architecture and was made ARA in 1900, RA in 1909 (diploma work, 'The Ashton Memorial, Lancaster'). He was a founder member of the Art Workers' Guild, and wrote *Essentials in Architecture* (1907), widely read in its time.

The principal works of Belcher and Joass from 1901 to 1910 are:

	1902-	Birmingham Daily Post, 88 Fleet Street, EC4 (*Bldr*, 24.1.03)
		Guildown Grange, Guildford, Surrey
		Tapeley Park, North Devon (reconstruction)
	1902-3	Electra House, Moorgate, EC2 (*Bldr*, 2.1.04)
		Cornbury Park, Oxfordshire (additions) (*Bldr*, 16.5.03)
	1904-5	Royal London Friendly Society, Finsbury Square, EC2 (*Bldr*, 16.5.03)
		Winchester House, Old Broad Street, EC2 (*Bldr*, 29.6.07)
105 224	1906	Ashton Memorial, Williamson Park, Lancaster (*Bldr*, 6.4.07)
223	1906-8	Mappin & Webb's, Oxford Street, W1
		Base for Statue by Captain Adrian Jones of the Duke of Cambridge, Whitehall, SW1
222	1907-8	26 and 28 Margaret Street, W1
223	1907-9	Royal Insurance, St James's Street and Piccadilly, SW1
	1910	Holy Trinity, Kingsway, WC2 (tower not built)
15		Royal Society of Medicine, Henrietta Street, W1 (additional storey added in the 1950s)
		Headquarters of the Royal Zoological Society, Regent's Park, NW1
		Whiteley's, Queen's Road (Queensway), Bayswater, W2
		Tatmore Place, Hitchin, Hertfordshire

Obit. RIBAJ, Nov., 1913, pp. 50, 55 and 75 *Bldr*, 21.11.13, p. 560

BELL, Robert Anning, RA, Hon LLD Glasgow 1863—1933

Avoiding the influences of continental Art Nouveau — what Walter Crane called 'this strange decorative disease' — Anning Bell carried the spirit of Burne-Jones and Morris into the twentieth century.

Robert Anning Bell was born in Soho, London, the son of Robert George Bell, FGS. He was educated at University College School, Gower Street, and was articled to an architect, entering the Royal Academy Schools at the age of eighteen. He also studied at Westminster School of Art under Professor Frederick Brown and in Paris with Aimé Morot. In London he shared a studio with George Frampton.

106

Anning Bell did numerous designs for stained glass and mosaics, and designed fabrics for Morris & Co. and wallpapers for Essex & Co. He designed the mosaics in the tympanum of the main porch of Westminster Cathedral. The subject is Christ seated, with the Virgin and St Joseph on either side; kneeling are St Peter and Edward the Confessor, Saint and King, to whom the campanile is dedicated. The tympanum was designed by J. A. Marshall after the death of the Cathedral architect, J. F. Bentley, in 1902.

Anning Bell was Professor of Art at Liverpool from 1894, Professor of Decorative Art at Glasgow School of Art from 1911, and then Professor of

The mosaics by R. Anning Bell over the west door of Westminster Cathedral. Architect: J. F. Bentley.

Mosaics by R. Anning Bell on the Horniman Museum of Ethnology, London SE23. Architect: C. Harrison Townsend.

Design at the Royal College of Art, South Kensington (1918–24). He was a member of the Art Workers' Guild and Master in 1921, exhibiting with the Arts and Crafts Exhibition Society in London, Paris and Turin. He was made ARA in 1914 and RA in 1922 (diploma work, 'The Women going to the Sepulchre').

He worked in special sympathy with C. Harrison Townsend, the architect of the Horniman Museum, Forest Hill, SE23 (1902), where he did the mosaic on the main front. His largest work is on the north front of Birmingham University for Sir Aston Webb and Ingress Bell. In 1923 and 1924 in the central lobby of the House of Lords, Westminster, Anning Bell added the mosaics of St Andrew and St Patrick to Sir Edward Poynter's St George of 1870 and St David of 1898.

Anning Bell wrote 'Notes on the practice of pictorial mosaic' (*RIBAJ*, 23.11.01, pp. 25–38). He married Laura Richard-Troncy, a pupil of Alphonse Légros at the Slade School.

Cowan, Mrs Stewart Erskine, 'Robert Anning Bell', *Old Water Colour Society's Club*, Vol. XII (1935), p. 51
Fine Art Society, *Catalogue of memorial exhibition of the works of the late R. A. Bell*, London, 1934
Obit. RIBAJ, 29.12.33, pp. 201–2 *Bldr*, 1.12.33, p. 857 *Times*, 28.11.33

BENSON, William Arthur Smith, MA 1854–1924

W. A. S. Benson, one of the four sons of William Benson, JP, of Alresford, Hampshire, was born in London. A younger brother was Sir Frank Benson, the Shakespearean actor-manager. Benson went to Winchester and New College, Oxford. His sister, who had modelled for Sir Edward Burne-Jones, married the artist and craftsman George Heywood Sumner who had shared lodgings with Benson at Oxford. Benson was articled to the architect Basil Champneys until 1880 when William Morris encouraged him to set up a workshop for metal-work, which he did in a factory, still standing, near Chiswick Mall, W4.

In 1887 Benson opened showrooms at 82–83 New Bond Street, W1, where he displayed metal utensils of simple design and fittings made of a special copper alloy for the new electric lighting. Benson supplied light fittings for several colleges, including his own, and for many churches and cathedrals, including St Paul's, where they were designed by Somers Clarke, then the Cathedral Surveyor, and presented by the American banker John Pierpont Morgan in 1902. His skill in this craft earned Benson the nickname 'The Lamplighter'.

Benson also designed furniture for Morris's firm and for J. S. Henry & Co. He designed wallpapers for Morris and grates and fireplaces for Coalbrookdale, and for the Falkirk Iron Co. One of the founders of the Arts and Crafts Exhibition Society in 1888 and the Home Arts and Industries Association, Benson lectured on decorative design. A Benson lamp features in Aubrey Beardsley's drawing of J. McNeill Whistler and there is a similar one at the Victoria and Albert Museum.

In 1895 Benson exhibited his products at Samuel Bing's shop in Paris. He designed his own Benson Pavilion for the Glasgow Exhibition of 1901. A Benson product which the designer used wherever the opportunity occurred was his curious patent glazing, examples of which can still be seen in the houses he designed and in the bay window of 63 Bayswater Road, Lancaster Gate, W2.

Among Benson's few architectural works are the additions to Burne-Jones's house at Rottingdean, Sussex; his own house, Windleshaw, Withyham, Sussex, which still contains furniture designed by him; and a house (now a school) for the banker, A. H. Drummond, at Maltman's Green, Gerrards Cross, Buckinghamshire (referred to by Muthesius as Mallman's Green, Uxbridge).

Benson disposed of his business in 1920 and retired to Menorbier on the Pembrokeshire coast, where he had previously altered a house for himself and designed the village school. The building he had occupied in New Bond Street came down under the housebreaker's hammer in 1970, its lofty red brick and tile-hung gable bringing with it the rusting remnants of its metal pennons and halberds.

Benson wrote *Elements of Handicraft and Design* and *Drawing; its History and Uses* (Oxford University Press, 1925). He was a member of the Art Workers' Guild.

BENTLEY, John Francis   1839—1902

Bentley died 'in harness' a year after the death of Queen Victoria, but his greatest work, Westminster Cathedral, was not consecrated until 1910. This noble building, a cathedral of the Arts and Crafts Movement, embodies its aims and ideals.

John Bentley was the third of the seventeen children of Charles and Ann Bentley of Doncaster; he went to a private school. In boyhood Bentley showed an interest in buildings, making a model of St George's Church, Doncaster. When his beloved church was burnt down in 1853 and Sir George Gilbert Scott was called in to rebuild it, Bentley, who knew the building by heart, helped in the office of Cleverly, the clerk of works.

At the age of sixteen Bentley acted as clerk of works on Loversall Church near Doncaster and afterwards worked in the engineering works of Sharpe, Stewart & Co. of Manchester. Bentley was next apprenticed in London to the contractors Winsland & Holland, for his father wanted him to become a practical man.

The following year Bentley's father died and

Richard Holland, observing young Bentley's interest in architecture, got him accepted as an improver in the office of the church architect, Henry Clutton, a partner of the mediaevalist William Burges. Here he stayed until 1860 and worked upon the Chapel of the Sacred Heart, Farm Street, W1, which Clutton, a convert to Catholicism, was building for the Jesuits.

Clutton offered Bentley a partnership at the early age of twenty-one, but Bentley, wishing to be independent, when twenty-three set up an office at 14 Southampton Street, Strand, WC2, in 1862. In 1861 he had been received into the Church of Rome, taking the baptismal name of Francis.

Bentley continued his studies at the Architectural Museum, that 'strange galaxy of plaster bits and pieces' as Sir John Summerson describes it, 'lodged in the loft of a building standing in a creek of the Thames at Cannon Row, Westminster', which owed its origin to Ruskin, Pugin, Burges, Sir George Gilbert Scott and Cottingham.

Most of Bentley's early works were fittings for churches, among them a font for St Mary, Bridgetown, Barbados (a drinking fountain by Bentley 24 ft high was presented to that town by the Montefiores of Streatham in 1864) and the altar for St Francis, Pottery Lane, Notting Hill, W11, a Clutton church, where Bentley was baptised into the Catholic Faith by Cardinal Wiseman.

Early in his life Bentley came to certain conclusions. Firstly, that it is not architecture to copy old work however excellent the subject or the copy. Secondly, that old and tried methods are the most sound. Thirdly, that form and colour are inseparable. Bentley put George Edmund Street at the top of his list of church architects and William Butterfield second, until he saw his decoration at Winchester College, when Butterfield fell in his regard.

Two circumstances had increased the demand in England for new buildings for the Catholic religious houses, Catholic Emancipation in England, and in France withdrawal of support for the religious teaching orders. As a result Bentley received a number of commissions.

In 1866 Bentley altered Heron's Ghyll, a house near Uckfield, Sussex, for the poet Coventry Patmore, an association which encouraged Bentley to try his hand at verse. In 1868 Bentley moved his office to 13 John Street, Adelphi, WC2 (now John Adam Street). There followed a long line of churches, including additions and furnishings.

1869-87	St Mary of the Angels, Moorhouse Road, W2 (additions and furnishings)
1870	Presbytery, St Peter & St Edward, Palace Street, SW1
	Franciscan Convent, Portobello Road, W11
1873-6	St Charles, Ogle Street, W1 (furnishings)
1876-84	St Thomas's Seminary, Hammersmith Road, W6 (now Convent of the Sacred Heart)
1877-9	St Mary, Cadogan Street, Chelsea, SW3

Bentley's most important work completed before Westminster Cathedral is the Church of the Holy Rood, Watford, Hertfordshire, built between 1887 and 1889 through the generosity of S. Taprell Holland of the family of builders who had taken Bentley as a learner.

41 It was due largely to strong recommendation by Taprell Holland that (in 1894) a most important call reached Bentley. After years of negotiation and after several sites had been considered, a site was eventually chosen for a Catholic cathedral in London. Since the re-instalment of a Catholic Archbishop of Westminster in 1850, the first Archbishop, Cardinal Wiseman, had used St Mary, Moorfields, EC2, and his successor, Cardinal Manning, adopted Our Lady of Victories, South Kensington, as a pro-cathedral. Towards the end of his life Cardinal Manning acquired the present site in Ashley Gardens, SW1, in 1884. Its previous use had been for the Middlesex Penitentiary.

J. F. Bentley: the plan of the Byzantine styled Westminster Cathedral.

For the new cathedral Bentley's old master Henry Clutton had done a Gothic design and indeed Bentley too had Gothic in mind. But for Taprell Holland's confidence in Bentley, this preference for Gothic might have 'put off' the new Cardinal, Cardinal Vaughan, who wanted an early basilican type of building.

But the problems presented by the site — proximity to Westminster Abbey and the peculiar relationship between the two churches — made the choice of style a delicate one. If Gothic, proximity to Westminster Abbey would have been an embarrassment, the work would have been costly, and the serried and serrated ranks of tall mansion flats already surrounding the site would have mocked at a Gothic building. If the Roman style were chosen, there was already the Oratory Church, Brompton Road, SW7. One suggestion was to reproduce the old Basilica of St Peter's at Rome, demolished for the baroque St Peter's. In search of inspiration Cardinal Vaughan and Bentley set off for Italy. In Rome Bentley declared St Peter's the worst building he had ever seen, St Paul-beyond-the-Walls, Rome (similar to old St Peter's) and the Duomo Florence 'the most unreasonable buildings in the world', and Roman Renaissance 'dreadful and without the least Christian significance'. But Cardinal Vaughan guided Bentley's steps to the Byzantine churches of Ravenna and Torcello and St Mark's, Venice; Bentley's health and warnings of cholera prevented him from seeing Hagia Sophia, Istanbul. Bentley afterwards said — 'Personally I would have preferred a gothic church yet, on consideration, I am inclined to think the Cardinal was right'. And so Byzantine won the day. It avoided a clash of styles with the baroque St Paul's

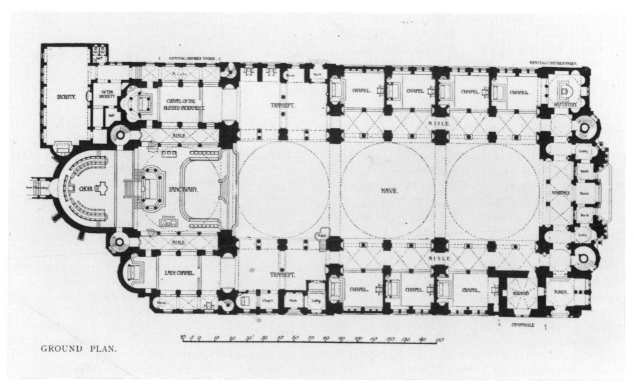

GROUND PLAN.

and the mediaeval Westminster Abbey, neither would it compete with the recently completed baroque Oratory Church in Kensington. It was cheap and quick; it could be built without a large number of skilled masons. The foundations over the old prison site could be massive and simple, the building could be decorated afterwards with marble, mosaic and painting as funds became available, and the tall campanile, appropriate to the style, could out-top more quickly, and at less cost, all buildings except St Paul's Cathedral. The Cardinal had wanted two towers, it is said.

Bentley succeeded in satisfying most requirements. In plan the Cathedral resembles Vignola's Renaissance Gesu Church in Rome, in section it resembles a vaulted Roman basilica or a smaller and longer Hagia Sophia, Istanbul; in scale it is near to St Mark's, Venice and St Front, Perigueux. When Bentley returned to England towards the end of March 1895 he pressed on with his design, so that the foundation stone was laid on 29 June. With the exception of a brief visit to New York in 1898 to advise upon a new Catholic cathedral for Brooklyn the rest of Bentley's life was spent upon the Westminster Cathedral. So great was the pressure of work that on the voyage to New York his wife and family, who accompanied him under the care of a major-domo, hardly saw him, for he was busy in his cabin at his drawing board.

The vast brick Cathedral of Westminster is 360 ft long, 156 ft wide and 117 ft high. The bricks Bentley selected carefully — Faversham Kentish stocks for the walls and piers, Bracknell Berkshire red facings, Fletton wirecuts for the interior of the large piers, Poole wirecuts for the interior of the small piers, and Blue Staffordshires for the outside facings of the vaults and for damp courses. Fourteen million bricks were used and the monotony of the work led to a strike of bricklayers. For the vaults Bentley designed saucer domes in concrete. Resisting all suggestions that rolled steel joists were necessary, he said 'I have broken the back of that terrible superstition that iron is necessary to large spans'.

When E. A. Rickards took Arnold Bennett to see the works, Bennett wrote in his journal: 'A work of great monumental art. Bentley the architect was wandering under the dome examining and enjoying his mighty production'. Bennett incorporated the scene in his novel, *The Roll Call*. In 1902, when the campanile had been raised to within 50 ft of the top, Bentley died suddenly. The added strain of the New York commission had proved too much. His chief assistant, J. A. Marshall, completed the fabric.

Over the period of sixty years since its consecration the Cathedral has been enriched by many artists and craftsmen. The decoration of the Chapel of St Gregory and St George is to Bentley's own designs. The mosaic over the west doors is by Robert Anning Bell *(q.v.)*. The Chapel of St

Andrew and the Saints of Scotland, the gift of the Marquess of Bute and completed in 1915, is by Robert Schultz Weir. Here the mosaics are also by Anning Bell, the carving is by Thomas Stirling Lee and the 'stalls are the finest work of Ernest Gimson and his craftsmen. The High Altar and Baldacchino, of 1907, is to Bentley's own design; the stalls in the sanctuary are by L. H. Shattock; the Stations of the Cross are by Eric Gill. Other mosaics are by Christian Symons and Gilbert Pownall; metal screens are to the designs of Bentley and Shattock. The Archbishop's House, the Clergy House and the Diocesan Hall are all to Bentley's design. The forms which Bentley used here are freer, showing an affinity with the work of Philip Webb and William Lethaby. Under the guidance of L. H. Shattock the work is being finished as Bentley intended.

Today, an intelligent rebuilding of the Victoria Street buildings by the architect Cecil Elsom has opened up a vista to the Cathedral never enjoyed before.

Bentley was a member of the Art Workers' Guild. He married Margaret Anne, a daughter of Henry J. Fleuss, a painter, of Düsseldorf. They had four sons and daughters (one daughter died in infancy). Bentley's third son, Osmond, succeeded to his practice with J. A. Marshall. Bentley's daughter Mrs Winifride de l'Hôpital has written the biography of her father.

Cut in the marble in the entrance hall of the Royal Institute of British Architects are these words:

> JOHN FRANCIS BENTLEY
> was nominated for the award of
> the Royal Gold Medal in 1902
> but died before the nomination
> could be confirmed

L'Hôpital, Winifride de [Bentley's daughter], *Westminster Cathedral and its Architect*, Introduction by W. R. Lethaby, London, 1919.

Obit. RIBAJ, 8.3.02, p. 219 and 26.7., pp. 437—41
Bldr, 8.3.02, pp. 228—9 and 243—4 and 15.3., p. 258

BIDLAKE, William Henry   1861—1938

W. H. Bidlake was the son of the church architect, George Bidlake, of Wolverhampton. He went to Tettenhall College, Wolverhampton, and to Christ's College, Cambridge, was articled to Sir Robert Edis and Bodley and Garner, and assistant to Sir Rowand Anderson, RSA. Bidlake entered the Royal Academy Schools in 1883 and won the RIBA Pugin Prize in 1885. In 1887 he joined another Pugin Prizeman, John Cotton, in partnership in Birmingham and carried out numerous churches in Birmingham and the West Midlands. Bidlake's earliest church work included St Thomas, Stourbridge, Worcester, where he did the apse and the chancel screen, St Oswald of Worcester, St Oswald Road, Bordesley (1892—9), and additions to St Stephen, Small Heath.

J. F. Bentley: Westminster Cathedral from the south west.
The domes are of mass concrete.

Bidlake also did many good houses in Birmingham and district, including, in 1898, Withens, 5 Barker Road, Sutton Coldfield, and Woodside and the Dene, in Bracebridge Road, Birmingham. He did a warehouse in Great Charles Street, Birmingham (RA, 1904).

Bidlake was an instructor at the Birmingham Central School of Art for ten years. He also did a

W. H. Bidlake: 37 Hartopp Road, Sutton Coldfield, Warwickshire

great deal towards the formation of the Birmingham College of Art School of Architecture of which he became a Director. Bidlake received the Gold Medal of the Birmingham Civic Society in 1923. He retired to Bestbeech, Wadhurst, Sussex, where he built Vespers (renamed Lorien), the house in which he died.

Bidlake's other works include:

1899-1901	St Patrick, Earlswood, Warwickshire (remodelling)	
	St Agatha, Stratford Road, Sparkbrook, Birmingham (furnishings later destroyed by fire; *Bldr*, 10.1.03)	
1900	Garth House, Edgbaston Park Road, Birmingham	
1901	St Leonard, Dordon, Warwickshire (south aisle to a church of 1867–8 by G. E. Street)	
	Emmanuel Church, Walford Road, Sparkbrook	
1903	St Mary, Wythall, Worcestershire (tower)	
	Bishop Latimer Memorial Church, Handsworth	
1904	Branch School of Art, Moseley	
1906	Woodgate, 37 Hartopp Road, Sutton Coldfield (his own house, mentioned by Muthesius)	
	A house at Winscombe, Somerset	
1907	St Andrew, Oxhill Road, Handsworth	
1908	St Matthew (formerly St Ann) Vicarage, Cato Street, Duddeston	
1909	Emmanuel Church, Wylde Green, Sutton Coldfield	

112

1910	St Stephen, Small Heath (additions to a church by R. C. Carpenter, since demolished)
	The Knole, Stoneygate, Leicester

Obit. RIBAJ, 10.1.38, p. 259 and 25.4., pp. 622–3, 669 and 720 *Bldr*, 15.4.38, p. 736 ·

BILLEREY, Fernand   1878—1951

Fernand Billerey was a student at the Ecole des Beaux-Arts and a friend of Auguste Rodin. He travelled in Italy and Greece. Emile Madeline and Henri Tastemain did English work through Billerey when he had established himself in England.

From 1906 to 1924 Billerey was in partnership with Detmar Blow and together they did the re-modelling of houses on the Grosvenor Estate, Billerey being mainly responsible for most of these. (For their work together, *see under* Blow, Detmar Jellings). The work at the Avenue Theatre, WC2, was largely Billerey's. On his own Billerey did the Egyptian Embassy, 75 South Audley Street (reconstructed internally in 1975—6), and made the master elevation for the north side of Grosvenor Square in 1933.

The following works were principally Billerey's:

1910-12	46 Grosvenor Street, W1, for Sir Edgar Speyer (remodelled 1922)
1910-11	Remodelling of 10 Carlton House Terrace, SW1
1910-12	10 Smith Square, SW1
	44-50 Park Street, W1
	9 Halkin Street, SW1

AR, 1923, p. 31 *RIBAJ*, 1937—8, pp. 273—80

BLOMFIELD, Charles James   1862—1932

C. J. Blomfield was the eldest son of Sir Arthur W. Blomfield, ARA (1829—99), and a cousin of Sir Reginald Blomfield (*q.v.*). His grandfather, Charles J. Blomfield (1786—1857), was Bishop of London for twenty-eight years. His brother was Arthur Conran Blomfield. Blomfield went to school at Charterhouse, entered the Royal Academy Schools in 1888, and was articled to his father. He was architect to the Dean and Chapter of St Saviour, Southwark, SE1. Originally the Priory Church of St Mary Overie, St Saviour became a cathedral in 1905. Its nave had been rebuilt by Blomfield's father to replace a mean design by Robert Wallace of 1836.

C. J. Blomfield also carried out restorations at St Cross, Winchester, and one of the many restorations of St Mary Redcliffe, Bristol. He made additions to many public schools, including Eton, Wellington (where he did the new dining room;

113

C. J. Blomfield: the dining hall at Wellington College, Berkshire.

AR, 1906), Malvern, Aldenham (Hertfordshire) and St Edmund, Canterbury. He did the rood screen in Aldenham Church and the memorial to the 1st Duke of Westminster in Chester Cathedral (the recumbent effigy of the Duke is by F. W. Pomeroy).

Blomfield was surveyor to the Eyre Estate, St John's Wood, his grandfather's name being perpetuated in Blomfield Road and Blomfield Villas on the adjoining Church Commissioners' estate.

Obit. RIBAJ, 24.12.32, p. 143

BLOMFIELD, Professor Sir Reginald Theodore, MA, Hon LittD Oxon, LittD Liverpool, RA 1856–1942

Reginald Blomfield was born at Bow Vicarage, near Exeter, where his father, the Rev. G. J. Blomfield, was curate. His mother was the daughter of C. J. Blomfield (1786–1857), Bishop of London from 1828, who did much to introduce legislation improving the condition of the London poor. Blomfield was brought up in Kent where his father became rector, first at Dartford in 1857 and then at Aldington in 1868. He went to Haileybury College, Hertfordshire, in 1869 and went on to Exeter College, Oxford. At Oxford he attended Ruskin's lectures but found that 'the atmosphere of rapt adoration with which Ruskin and all he said was received by the young ladies of Oxford was altogether too much for me ...'

Blomfield entered the Royal Academy Schools in 1881 when R. Phené Spiers was Master of the Architectural School and the 'Visitors' were Norman Shaw, Alfred Waterhouse, J. L. Pearson, G. F. Bodley and G. E. Street. He also entered the office of his uncle, Sir Arthur Blomfield, that year, after having toured the Continent as a tutor. He found his uncle's office typical of architects' offices of the day — 'run by a managing clerk, two or three assistants and half-a-dozen cheerful young pupils whose usual remark every morning was: "Any spice in the papers?" '. (The Norman Shaw papers in the Royal Academy include a sketch — slightly out of character, perhaps — of Shaw reading just such a paper).

After two years, Blomfield left his uncle's office (owing to a misunderstanding, he said) and set up in practice at 17 Southampton Street, Strand, WC2, where E. S. Prior had an office on the first floor. Through Prior, a former pupil of Shaw's, Blomfield met others of the great master's pupils and assistants, including Mervyn Macartney, Ernest Newton and Gerald Horsley. Although he never worked in Shaw's office himself, Blomfield was henceforth, like them, a great admirer of Shaw.

Blomfield had an exceptional gift for sketching and writing. Newton and Prior, who also sketched prolifically, nicknamed him 'the commercial sketcher' because he did illustrations for publication. When the 'Master of the Crumbling Line', the illustrator Herbert Railton (1858–1910), fell ill, Blomfield provided the illustrations for the Rev. W. J. Loftie's *Westminster Abbey*. He also wrote articles for *Portfolio* which later reappeared in his *History of Renaissance Architecture in England* (see below).

Blomfield was involved in the founding of the Art Workers' Guild and was made honorary secretary, but he attended infrequently and when admonished resigned in a huff. In retrospect, however, he paid tribute to these efforts to blaze a new trail: 'I think it is due to the young men of the eighties that the arts were rescued from the paralysing conventions of the Victorian era'. He little realised, of course, that the next generation in their turn were to be plunged into the conventions of the neo-Georgian style introduced by his own generation.

In 1886 Blomfield married the daughter of Henry Burra, of Rye, Sussex, where he designed several houses, including his own, the very informal Point Hill, Playden, where the family still lives. One he let to the American novelist Henry James. The same year Blomfield and the fine printer Cobden Sanderson (1840–1922) built for themselves a pair of pretty houses at 51 and 53 Frognal,

114

Sir Reginald Blomfield, RA: 51 and 53 Frognal, Hampstead, London NW3. One his own, the other for Cobden Sanderson, the fine printer.

Hampstead, NW3, looking across to the towering chimneys of Norman Shaw's own house, 6 Ellerdale Road; behind was Basil Champneys at Hall Oak and a few yards down the hill Kate Greenaway in her green-shuttered Norman Shaw cottage in which she died in 1901. No. 51 remained Blomfield's London home and he died there.

In 1890, with the idea of designing and making fine furniture, Blomfield, Gimson, Sidney Barnsley, Mervyn Macartney and William Lethaby joined forces to establish Kenton & Co., in a stable off Theobalds Road, taking the name of a street in the

area. They held an exhibition of their work at Barnards Inn (both sites have been demolished). Although the venture lasted only two years, some of their pieces still survive and one made from Gimson's designs is at the Victoria and Albert Museum.

Blomfield's first book, *Formal Gardens in England*, illustrated by F. Inigo Thomas, appeared in 1892. His views invoked the criticism of that great gardener and preacher of natural gardening, William Robinson, who kept up a wordy warfare with those architects who dared to meddle with gardens, especially Blomfield and Sedding. In 1897 Blomfield's first great historical work, *A History of Renaissance Architecture in England, 1500–1800* was published by George Bell and Sons. Hitherto the term 'English Renaissance' as applied to architecture referred to the rebirth in England of Roman architecture between 1525 and 1625. Blomfield extended the term to mean both rebirth and revival. The architecture of the Wren and Georgian periods now had its history book which, with the work of Belcher and Macartney, led not only to the preservation of many previously neglected buildings of those periods, but also to increased interest in the Georgian Revival or neo-Georgian style.

Encouraged by Edward VII as Prince of Wales and as King, social entertaining flourished at the turn of the century and country houses were enlarged and new ones built. Blomfield contributed commodious country houses in the later style of Norman Shaw whose last great houses, Chesters and Bryanston, he greatly admired. Nor were Blomfield's university and commercial buildings inferior and, as might be expected from his books and studies, these affected a mature Renaissance style with French overtones. In the meantime he was preparing his second great work, *A History of French Architecture, 1494 to 1661* and *1661 to 1774* (published 1911–21).

After 1920, however, the task of designing satisfactorily the really large-scale building proved too much for Blomfield as it had for many others. His 'Waterloo' was Menin Gate, the First World War Memorial at Ypres, and 4 Carlton Gardens, SW1. In the case of the latter, Blomfield fought hard to have the design extended the length of Carlton House Terrace. Had he succeeded it would have meant the destruction of George IV's great terrace.

Blomfield played a major part in the completion of the Quadrant in Regent Street when Norman Shaw withdrew from the project (*see under* The Rebuilding of Regent Street). He wrote a study of Shaw (Batsford, London, 1940) from Phené Spiers's notes, which scarcely does its subject justice. His other published works include:

Studies in Architecture (London, 1905)
The Mistress Art (London, 1908)
Architectural Drawing and Draughtsmen (London, 1912)

Sir Reginald Blomfield, RA: the Talbot Building at Lady Margaret Hall, Oxford.

The Touchstone of Architecture (Oxford, Clarendon Press, 1925)
Memoirs of an Architect (London, Macmillan, 1932)
Six Architects (London, Macmillan, 1925)

Blomfield was made ARA in 1905 and RA in 1914 (diploma work, New Buildings, Lady Margaret Hall, Oxford). He was Professor of Architecture at the Royal Academy (1907—11) and was awarded the Royal Gold Medal for Architecture in 1913. He was President of the RIBA from 1912 to 1914 and was knighted in 1919. A bronze bust by Sir William Reid Dick is in the National Portrait Gallery. Much of his architectural work was done in the latter part of his life so that the charming town house at 20 Buckingham Gate, SW1, with its stables in Catherine Place, done when Blomfield was already forty, is an early work. His last work, 4 Carlton Gardens, SW1, was done when he was seventy-six. Between these two extremes lies a

Sir Reginald Blomfield, RA: the United Universities Club, Pall Mall East, London SW1, with sculpture by Henry Pegram, RA and William Aumonier.

range of competent work, sedate, but charming. Highlights are:

1898	Wittington, Medmenham, Buckinghamshire
1898-1910	Broddesby Park, Lincolnshire (rebuilding)
	Heathfield Park, Sussex (rebuilding)
1899	Caythorpe Court, Lincolnshire
	St Mary's Church Institute, Portsea, Portsmouth
1900	Stansted House, Sussex (rebuilding)
	Army and Navy Stores warehouse, Greycoat Place, SW1 (since remodelled)
1901-2	Yockley, Frimley, Surrey
1902	Godinton, Ashford, Kent (additions and garden)
1902-26	Sherborne School for Girls, Dorset
1903	Oliver Whitby School, Chichester, Sussex (now a shop)
	Hatchlands, Surrey, music room
1904	The South African War Memorial, Haileybury College (*Bldr*,3.9.04)
	Apethorpe Hall, Northamptonshire (additions)
	Knowlton Court, Kent (additions)
1905	Barclays Bank, Chelmsford, Essex
1906	The Free Library, Lincoln (won in competition)

	1907-8	Goldsmiths' College, SE14 (additions; *Bldr*, 15.8.08)
116		United Universities Club, Pall Mall East, and Suffolk Street, SW1 (*Bldr*, 27.2.09). Sculpture by Henry Pegram and William Aumonier junior
		Garnons, Mansell Gamage, Herefordshire (interiors)
	1908-9	Moundsmere Manor, Nutley, Hampshire
116	1909	National Westminster Bank, 224 King's Road, Chelsea, SW3 (*Bldr,* 1.5.09)
	1909-12	Chequers, Buckinghamshire (reconstruction)
	1909-23	Sherborne School, Dorset (additions)
248	1910	Paul's Cross, St Paul's Churchyard, EC4 (with sculpture by Sir Bertram Mackennal). After destruction by lightning in 1382 this was first rebuilt in timber to the order of Thomas Kempe, Bishop of London 1448–9, and pulled down by order of Parliament in 1643. The foundations were discovered by F. C. Penrose, surveyor to St Paul's
		Water Tower, Lincoln
		Wyphurst, Cranleigh, Surrey (additions)
115	1910-15	Talbot and Toynbee Buildings, Lady Margaret Hall, Oxford (Blomfield did the Wordsworth Building in 1896)
	1911	Woodcote Manor, Bramdean, Hampshire (additions)
	1912	The Lordship, Much Hadham, Hertfordshire (additions)
		Wretham Hall, Norfolk (demolished)
	1912-13	John Barker's store, Kensington High Street, W8 (north side; now in other uses)
	1913	Waldershare Park, Kent (reconstruction)

Obit. RIBAJ, Jan., 1943, pp. 65–7 and Feb., pp. 88–9
Bldr, 8.1.43, pp. 39–40

Sir Reginald Blomfield, RA: the National Westminster Bank, King's Road, Chelsea, London SW3.

BLOW, Detmar Jellings   1867–1939

Detmar Blow: Happisburgh Manor, Norfolk.

Detmar Blow was born in London, the son of
Jellings Blow. He was educated at Hawtrey's and
articled to Wilson and Aldwinckle in 1883. After
studying at the South Kensington Schools (a contemporary of his friend Lutyens), he won the
Architectural Association Travelling Studentship
in 1888 and the following year accompanied John
Ruskin on a tour of Italy. On return he was
apprenticed to a builder at Newcastle upon Tyne,
and was engaged (1891–3) by Philip Webb on
East Knoyle Church, Wiltshire, for the Hon. Percy
Wyndham. Blow won the Pugin Prize in 1892 and
in 1893 was appointed architect to the estate of
Hugh Fairfax-Cholmeley at Gilling Castle, N.
Riding. Between 1899 and 1900 Blow laid the
stonework on two cottages for Ernest Gimson,
Stoneywell and Lea Cottages at Markfield,
Leicestershire. He also acted as clerk of works
at Brockhampton Park, Herefordshire, and in 1905
designed a cottage built for the Cheap Cottages
Exhibition at Letchworth. His careful reconstructions of Elizabethan and Jacobean country houses
included Heale House, Woodford, Wiltshire (1894)
and Lake House, Wilsford, Wiltshire (1898).

Up to this point Blow's career was that of an
artist-craftsman of the school of Morris and Webb—
he had been a member of the Art Workers' Guild
since 1892. But after 1906, when he was joined in
partnership by Fernand Billery from the Ecole
des Beaux-Arts, Paris, his practice increasingly
involved alterations and additions to country and
town houses, most of them of the eighteenth
century. Blow earned the confidence of the Duke
of Westminster when he designed his hunting

lodge, the Woolsack (demolished) at Mimizan,
Landes, France, in the Cape-Dutch style as revived
by Herbert Baker. When the houses of Mayfair
needed rebuilding, a number of them were undertaken by Blow and Billery, and Blow was a
member of the Grosvenor Estate Board of Management for seventeen years (1916–33). Noteworthy
in this period is 9 Halkin Street, SW1, a large,
mellow brick house, built for the Scottish millionaire Hugh Morrison who later gave it to the
Caledonian Club.

Of similar massive proportions and mellow brickwork is the addition to 34 Queen Anne's Gate,
SW1 (now the St Stephen's Club), for Lord
Glenconner (Sir Edward Tennant), for whom
Blow had designed Wilsford Manor near
Salisbury in 1904–6. Blow and Billery also did
44–50 Park Street and 3 Mansfield Street, W1,
for the builder William Willett (1912); alterations
to Wimborne House, 22 Arlington Street, SW1,
for Lord Wimborne (now offices); and offices at
103–109 Wardour Street, W1 (1912) and at 6 and
7 Queen Street, EC4. In collaboration with G. D.
Martin, who carried out office buildings and
hotels, Blow and Billery did Harewood House,
Hanover Square, W1 (1913), a large office
building faced with faience.

Blow designed Government House, Salisbury,
Rhodesia, but his setting for John Tweed's statue
of Cecil Rhodes there was not carried out. He was
a friend of Lord Kitchener and did alterations to
his country house, Broome Park, near Faversham,
Kent, in 1909. (Sixteen years later, with Sir
Mervyn Macartney, he did the Kitchener Memorial

in the Chapel of All Souls, St Paul's Cathedral.) For the actor-manager Cyril Maude, Blow and Billerey carried out the repair and reconstruction of the Avenue Theatre, Northumberland Avenue, WC2, after part of the roof and great wall of Charing Cross Station had collapsed into the auditorium in 1905.

Blow's understanding of the repair of churches is seen in St Michael, Onibury, Shropshire, where he introduced the coat of arms of King Edward VII and Commandment boards of 1902. In 1909 he enlarged the chapel at Stockfield Park, W. Riding (a house by James Paine), and did the wooden ceiling of the chapel at Hewell Grange, Tardebigge, Worcestershire.

Blow's domestic work included Fonthill House, Tisbury, Wiltshire originally Little Ridge, a large mansion for Hugh Morrison (1904), incorporating a carefully salvaged seventeenth century manor house from nearby (all demolished 1972). In 1906 he did Happisburgh Manor, Norfolk, a house resembling in plan and materials E. S. Prior's Kelling Place, Holt, Norfolk. With Alfred Powell, Blow did Mill Hill, Brandsby, N. Riding.

Other works of 1901–15 by Detmar Blow and Fernand Billerey include:

1901	Breckles Hall, Norfolk (additions)
1903	Leadenham Hall, Lincolnshire (interiors)
1906	Christ Church, Thorney Hill, Hampshire, in the Baroque style, for Lord Manners, with inscriptions by Eric Gill and murals by Phoebe Traquair
1907	Bramham Park, Yorkshire (reconstruction)
1908	Hatch House, Newtown, Wiltshire (additions)
	12 Carlton House Terrace, SW1 (interiors), for Viscount Ridley
1910	Woodcote House, Oxfordshire (alterations)
1911	Eaton Hall, Cheshire, gardens, for the Duke of Westminster
	King's College Chapel, Cambridge, reredos (since removed)
1911-12	Cheam School, Kingsclere, Hampshire
1911-14	Grimsthorpe Castle, Lincolnshire (interiors)
1912	Horwood House, Little Horwood, Buckinghamshire
1913	Stanway House, Gloucestershire (additions since demolished), for the Earl of Wemyss
	Gate Burton Hall, Lincolnshire (additions)
1914	Stannington, Northumberland, tomb of Viscount Ridley
	All Saints, Hundon, Suffolk (reconstruction)
1915	Wootton Place, Folkington, Sussex (additions)

Blow's later works included the Earl Grosvenor monument in Eccleston churchyard, Cheshire (sculpture by Emile Madeline); the Wyndham family tomb, Knoyle, Wiltshire; and the south aisle altar at Westminster Abbey (1929). Blow and Billerey did the interior of the Duke of Westminster's yacht in 1923. They converted three houses to form Sir Edgar Speyer's house, 46 Grosvenor Street, W1, in a fusion of Italian and French styles

which they again converted into the American Women's Club in 1922.

Detmar Blow's marriage to the daughter of the Hon. Hamilton Tollemache in 1910 entitled him to become the Lord of the Manor of Painswick in Gloucestershire, and in 1914 he designed Hilles House, Harescombe, near Painswick (a stone roof replaced the original thatch after a fire in 1951). In 1925 Blow added a new wing and a lodge to Halcombe House, Painswick. He gave one of his houses to a charity as a convalescent home. Detmar Blow was buried at Cud Hill, a spur of the Cotswolds overlooking the Severn estuary, on a piece of land specially blessed by the Suffragan Bishop of Gloucester.

Obit. RIBAJ, 3.4.39, p. 571 *Bldr*, 10.2.39, p. 305

BOEHMER (BOMER after 1915), Edward 1861–1940

Edward Boehmer was born in Philadelphia, of a Pennsylvania German family. Considering that the best education for her son was to be found in Germany, his mother put him to school in Stuttgart. From there Boehmer spent one year at a technical school in Hamburg, two years with a Hamburg architect, one year with an architect in Berlin, and finally two more years at the Hamburg school. In 1883 Boehmer came to London to the office of Archer and Green where he met Percy Gibbs, whose sister he married. The brothers-in-law set up in practice together in 1889.

Harley House, Boehmer and Gibbs's splendid range of brown limestone mansion flats in Marylebone Road, NW1, and works like Portland Court and their mansion flats in Edgware Road, all derive in some measure from the fanciful palaces of Whitehall Court and Hyde Park Court (now Hotel). This is not surprising, for these buildings were designed by Archer and Green in the 1880s, when Boehmer and Gibbs were the assistants, occupied on the drawings for Whitehall Court until it was completed in 1887, and on those for Hyde Park Court which opened in 1890.

Both these enterprises comprised high-class service flats and club premises, and Hyde Park Court, with its 200 private rooms served by 200 servants, was one of the sights of London. George Newnes, writing in *Around London* (1896), found it worth noting that 'in the summer months the residents of the Court are sometimes seen having tea on the balconies'. Together with the Hotel Cecil, the Birkbeck Bank and other speculations, these two ventures were involved in October 1892 in the notorious financial collapse of the Liberator Permanent Investment Society, whose chairman, Jabez Spencer Balfour (1843–1916), had accumulated debts of over £8 million.

With the collapse of their principal client, Archer

117

Edward Boehmer: 80 Portland Place, London W1.

and Green dissolved partnership and Arthur Green became a Crown Surveyor. By then Boehmer and Gibbs were already practising on their own account. Their first work was for mansion flats near that part of Edgware Road between Paddington and Kilburn which has been renamed Maida Vale. But before he had enjoyed a year of private practice, Percy Gibbs died suddenly of a brain tumour, leaving Boehmer to carry on the practice, which included showrooms for Renault motor cars, Pall Mall and St. James's Square, SW1, in Louis XV style (the building is now in other use), and shops in High Street, Kensington. Boehmer also did private houses at Stanmore, Middlesex, and (with Charles Rees) the German Lutheran Church in Brompton, SW5.

The practice continues as Bomer and Ransom.

The principal works of the firm of Boehmer and Gibbs are:

    Maida Vale

1890-1907   Vale Court; Blomfield Court; Aberdeen Court; Biddulph Mansions; Delaware Mansions; Sandringham Court

    St Marylebone

1904   Harley House, on the site of a house of that name, Marylebone Road, NW1 (additions by W. and E. Hunt (*q.v.*)

1904-12   Portland Court, 160—200 Great Portland Street, W1, and of equal length in Bolsover Street, in brown limestone with a high pavilion roof

1909   Welbeck Court Hotel (now Welbeck Court), Wigmore Street and Welbeck Street, W1, in Louis XV style

1907   11—14 Hobart Place, SW1. Three houses and an estate office (*Bldr*, 10.10.08)

1909   44 Harley Street, W1

           80 Portland Place, W1, with an elegant façade in the Anglo-French-American Classic style ignoring Robert Adam's façades but not so flagrantly as did the RIBA at 66 Portland Place

BOLTON, Arthur Thomas   1865—1945

Arthur Bolton was the son of a London solicitor, A. T. Bolton. He went to school at Eagle House, Wimbledon, SW19, and then to Haileybury College, Hertfordshire. Bolton studied architecture at University College, London, and at the Architectural Association. He was articled to Sir Robert Edis (1884—7) and for one year acted as clerk of works to Ewan Christian, remaining in his office until 1888 when he entered the office of R. Phené Spiers. He set up in practice in 1890, and won the Soane Medallion in 1893 and the RIBA Essay Prize in 1895. Bolton was the first Master of the Architectural Association Day School at Great Marlborough Street, W1, in 1901—3. He designed Ingram House, Stockwell Road, SW9, planned in the form of a St Andrew's cross and named after the Bishop of London. This opened in 1905 as a hostel for City clerks and is now a boys' hostel administered by the John Benn Hostels Association (*Bldr*, 12.9.03 and 10.2.06; *Country Life*, 6.3.20, pp. 315—16).

On the death of the architect, Henry Stock of Stock, Page and Stock, Bolton completed the Hamburg-Amerika Line building at 14—16 Cockspur Street, SW1 (*Bldr*, 23.3.07 and 11.4.08). After the First World War, the building was assigned to the P & O Steam Navigation Co. as part of war reparations, and the bronze 'Amerika' and 'Germania' panel by J. Wenlock Rollins (*Bldr*, 23.3.07 and 19.12.08) was remodelled to include the P & O rising sun and figures symbolical of their service to the Orient. Also at 14 Cockspur Street were offices for the Allen Line and for that Napoleon of the furniture trade, Samuel J. Waring, who housed his mushroom Waring-White Building Company there.

Bolton's houses included Hurtwood Edge (now Hurtwood) at Ewhurst, Surrey (1910), and Larkscliffe, Birchington, Kent, which he built for himself. He also did St Stephen's Schools in Westbourne Park, W2, and a factory and offices at Limehouse, E14 (*Bldr*, 22.5.09).

Bolton's chief concerns were scholarly and he was particularly interested in the work of the brothers Adam. He wrote *The Architecture of Robert and James Adam*, a two-volume work published by *Country Life* in 1922. His knowledge of their work brought him many commissions for alterations and restorations to houses of that period.

In 1917 Bolton was appointed Curator of the Sir John Soane Museum, 13 Lincoln's Inn Fields, WC2, in succession to Walter L. Spiers, brother of R. Phené Spiers. He wrote numerous papers on Sir John Soane and the contents of his remarkable museum, continuing in the post until his death, when he was succeeded by Sir John Summerson. His *Portrait of Sir John Soane* was published in 1927. With T. D. Henry, Bolton edited twenty volumes of the publications of the Wren Society (1923—45). It was Bolton who unearthed the large pinewood 'Great Model' of Wren's favourite design for St Paul's Cathedral, based on a Greek cross with a single giant order of columns within and without rather than the single internal order and false double external order of the executed design. Bolton's 'reconstructions' of French and Spanish castles are in the Victoria and Albert Museum Library.

Obit. RIBAJ, Feb., 1945, p. 115 *Bldr*, 26.1.45, p. 79

BOND, Frederick Bligh   1864—1945

Bligh Bond was the son of the Rev. Frederick Hookey Bond, headmaster of the Royal Free Grammar School (now the Grammar School), Marlborough, Wiltshire (1853—76). Bligh Bond went to Bath College and was articled to C. F. Hansom, architect of Clifton College, Bristol, and brother of J. A. Hansom, architect of Birmingham Town Hall and inventor of the hansom cab.

In 1885 Bligh Bond went to London and worked for eighteen months as an improver in the office of Sir Arthur Blomfield, ARA, returning to Bristol in 1886 to join C. F. Hansom as a partner. Together they did work for the British School Board. On the death of Hansom, Bligh Bond set up in practice on his own account, sharing some work with Edward Hansom (a son of J. A. Hansom) and his partner Archibald Matthias Dunn (later of Dunn and Fenwick).

Bligh Bond's work in Bristol included the Music School at Clifton College and the Handel Cossham Memorial Hospital, Kingswood, with which his former pupil W. H. Watkins was associated. Bond also did the Medical and Engineering Schools there. In 1897 he was appointed Honorary Architect to the Diocese of Bath and Wells and became an authority on church screens. He wrote *Roodscreens and Roodlofts* (Pitman, London, 1909) with the Rev. Dan Bede Camm, and did many rood screens throughout the country. One of his best was in All Saints, Clifton, a church by G. E. Street, destroyed by fire in the Second World War.

In later years Bligh Bond undertook the archaeological research and restorations at Glastonbury Abbey, where he was Director of Excavations from 1908. Bond became profoundly affected by the mystery surrounding Glastonbury and claimed that automatic writing directed him in his discoveries on the site.

Bond's church work included the remodelling of St. John, Chilcompton, North Somerset, in 1897. He also worked on Tavistock Grammar School in Devon.

His other works included:

c. 1900	Estate Office for King's Weston, now the Post Office Engineering School (*BJ*, 1905) and the Public Hall, both at Shirehampton, near Bristol
1909	St George, Hanham Abbots, Gloucestershire (restoration)
1910	St David, Moreton-in-Marsh, Gloucestershire (chancel screen)
1912	St Aidan, Small Heath, Birmingham (rood and screens, and re-siting of 15th-cent. font from St Stephen, Bristol)

Obit. Bldr, 16.3.45, p. 220

BONE, Sir Muirhead, Hon LLD St Andrews, Liverpool and Glasgow   1876—1953

The fourth of the eight children of a journalist, David Drummond Bone, Muirhead Bone was born in the Glasgow suburb of Partick. After attending the local school he studied at the Glasgow School of Art from the age of fourteen before being articled to an architect for three years. Bone then worked in a 'home crafts' shop which closed for the summer, enabling him to go on painting excursions, often in the company of the portrait etcher Francis

Dodd, whose sister, the writer Gertrude Helena Dodd, he was to marry.

After a few months as illustrator on the *Scots Pictorial* Bone was introduced to Lord Carlisle in London, who, impressed by Bone's etchings of architectural subjects, introduced him in turn to Alphonse Légros, Henry Tonks, J. P. Heseltine and the art dealer Dunthorne. In 1899 Bone produced a portfolio of etchings of Glasgow which were shown at the New English Art Club.

In 1900 Bone decided to settle in Ayr working as an art master. But his new 'Glasgow in 1901' etchings, published with a text by his brother James, brought such favourable comment from the Director of the East London Art Gallery, Charles Aitken (afterwards director of the Tate), and Campbell Dodgson, Keeper of the Prints at the British Museum, among others, that he was encouraged to return to London. Muirhead Bone and his brother stayed with their architect friend, Charles Holden, at Norbury, SW16, and with Charles Aitken in the Temple.

Holden immediately put Bone in the way of commissions and he did 'Belgrave Hospital' (RA, 1902) and later 'Bristol Royal Infirmary', while the *Architectural Review* published some of his drawings in 1902. His next commission came from Obach's (later Colnaghi and Obach) to do etchings of Southampton. In 1903 Bone found a stock of very special Japanese paper which lasted him four years and greatly improved his work.

In 1905 Bone did 'Ayr Prison' and 'The Demolition of St James's Hall' (Piccadilly), his first major work in a field he was to make his own. In 1908 his works were exhibited at the Franco-British Exhibition, London. His 'The Last of Newgate' emphasised the architectural loss London suffered with the demolition of George Dance the Younger's masterpiece (*see under* Mountford, Edward William). Bone's etching appeared as the frontispiece to Reginald Blomfield's *Studies in Architecture* (1905). His etching 'The Great Gantry' (1906) is a study of the Charing Cross Station disaster of 1905 when two main girders of the station roof and part of the gigantic side wall crashed down into what was then the Avenue Theatre.

During the First World War Muirhead Bone was commissioned as an artist and worked in France and in the Royal Navy. After the war, his etchings of new buildings under construction behind a screen of scaffolding — in those days, round wooden poles — were in demand on both sides of the Atlantic during the post-war building boom. The reason was, no doubt, best expressed by Whistler when he presented Richard D'Oyly Carte with his etching of the Savoy Hotel under construction in 1888, telling him 'the building will never look so nice again'.

Muirhead Bone was knighted in 1937 and was again official artist in the Second World War, this time on the home front. Four portraits of Bone

are in the National Portrait Gallery, three by Francis Dodd and one by Stanley Spencer. Bone was a member of the Art Workers' Guild.

An elder brother, Sir David William Bone, became Commodore of the Anchor Line and a writer on seafaring subjects. His nephew, Stephen Bone, artist and critic and son of James Bone, married Mary Adshead the mural painter and daughter of Professor S. D. Adshead (*q.v.*).

Obit. Times, 23.10.53.

**An etching by Muirhead Bone of the King Edward VII wing of Bristol Royal Infirmary.
Architects: Percy Adams and Charles Holden.**

BRANGWYN, Sir François (Frank) Guillaume, RA 1867—1956

Frank Brangwyn was born at 24 rue du Vieux Bourg, Bruges, where his father, William Curtis Brangwyn, designer of the church of S. André there, had set up a workshop for church embroideries. On the family's return to England, Brangwyn went to Westminster School and then studied at the South Kensington Museum where his work caught the attention of the painter and potter Harold Rathbone. The architect and designer A. H. Mackmurdo, always one to encourage young artists, noticed Brangwyn sketching in Oxford Street and brought him to Morris and Co.'s shop. William Morris put him to work making cartoons from the work of Burne-Jones for textiles and tapestries. Of this phase of his life Brangwyn recorded: 'Education — worked under William Morris, but, tiring of this, went to sea'.

Purchase by a shipowner of his picture, 'A bit on the Esk', shown at the Royal Academy, led to Brangwyn signing on as a cabin boy on a boat which took him to Tunis, Tripoli, Smyrna, Trebizond, Constantinople, Spain, Russia and South Africa. These voyages and the watercolours of Arthur Melville were strong influences in forming Brangwyn's style. Although he was to become a 'popular' artist, Brangwyn began as a painter and designer in the Arts and Crafts movement, with a leaning towards Art Nouveau.

In 1895 Brangwyn received a commission from the Paris antique and décor dealer Samuel Bing, to do a long painting for the front of his shop, 'La Maison de l'Art Nouveau'. Using a process invented by Keim of Munich, Brangwyn worked at a feverish pace to complete the work. It was afterwards purchased by a Monsieur Agache.

Brangwyn designed metalwork, furniture and whole interiors in a style in advance of Art Nouveau, anticipating the Secessionists of Vienna. He designed a billiard room for Thurstons of Leicester Square (destroyed) with the architects Wimperis and East, and found an early patron in the South African diamond merchant, Sir Edmund Davis, for whom the architect William Flockhart had combined 9 and 11 Lansdowne Road, W11, into a town house (now the Knights of Columba Club). Here Brangwyn decorated the Music Room with painted friezes, now badly deteriorated, and repoussé metalwork, radiator grilles and switch plates (*Studio*, 1900, p. 178). He also designed and painted a bedroom and its furniture, and did a frieze *en grisaille* of 'The Seasons'.

Although Brangwyn was then a member of the Secession, he is remembered more for his great wall paintings. These show a variety of influences and a mixture of qualities, making assessment difficult. However, Brangwyn undoubtedly performed for the legislators and businessmen of the day what the Florentine artists had done for their merchant princes, confirming them in the belief that theirs was a noble role in society. Much of Sir Frank Brangwyn's success and international reputation can be attributed to his skill in imbuing the territorial and commercial ambitions of his patrons with the romance and glamour associated with the early traders and navigators. Shipowners, trading companies and legislators were able to identify their efforts with those of Columbus, Vasco da Gama, Henry the Navigator and the great law-givers, while Brangwyn's style encouraged them to feel that their dreams were being represented in a vigorous, contemporary style of painting.

Brangwyn continued his designing for the domestic arts and in 1930 designed a dinner set in Royal Doulton. But the field he excelled in was that of his etchings, the best known of which is his famous series, 'The Bridge'. He also did 'Building the New Kensington Museum' and 'Breaking up the [SS] *Caledonia*'.

In 1916 Brangwyn did designs in mosaic of scenes from the life of St Aidan for the apse of St Aidan in Leeds. Brangwyn's last works included a wall panel for the Rockefeller Centre in New York (1930–4), to replace one by Diego Rivera found politically unacceptable. Between 1923 and 1935 Brangwyn did sixteen panels in the House of Lords as a memorial to peers who died in the First World War, the gift of Lord Iveagh. But the work was rejected and Lord Iveagh's heirs presented it to Swansea Town Hall.

In his article on Mural Painting in the *Encyclopaedia Britannica* Brangwyn modestly refrains from mentioning his own name or his considerable contribution to the art.

Brangwyn married Lucy Ray, who died many years before him, and he lived at Temple Lodge, Hammersmith, later moving to Ditchling, Sussex. Brangwyn was made ARA in 1904, RA in 1919 (diploma work, 'The Market Hall'); he was knighted in 1941. During his lifetime he received honours in eleven countries and was made an honorary member of twenty-eight societies. Brangwyn's works are shown in many art galleries of the world. There is a Brangwyn Museum at Bruges and a Brangwyn and Belleroche Museum at Orange, France, and a Brangwyn Gallery was to have been opened in Tokyo for Matsukata, a shipping magnate and collector of European art and furniture, but the valuable collection which Brangwyn assembled for him and stored in a London dock warehouse awaiting the end of the Second World War was destroyed by fire bombs. Three portraits of Brangwyn are in the National Portrait Gallery.

Sir Frank Brangwyn's principal wall paintings of the Edwardian period include:

1903	'Modern Commerce', in the Royal Exchange, EC3
1904-10	The Hall of the Skinners' Company, Dowgate Hill, EC4; ten panels of historical subjects and three allegorical groups (*Bldr*, 17.6.10 and 25.6.10)
1905	Venice International Exhibition; six panels now at Leeds Art Gallery
	Grand Trunk Railway of Canada, Cockspur Street, SW1; frieze depicting 'The Introduction of Civilisation into the Country of the Red Indian' (removed)
1906	Lloyd's Registry of Shipping, Fenchurch Street, EC3; panels in the committee room and lunch room
1913-15	Christ's Hospital, Horsham, Sussex; paintings in the chapel
	Paintings at the National Museum of Wales
	First World War memorial panel at Parliament House, Ottawa
	Paintings at the Court House, Cleveland, Ohio
	Paintings in the First Class Saloon of the Canadian Pacific Railway's *Empress of Britain*

Belleroche, William de, *Brangwyn Talks*, London, 1946.

Belleroche, William de, *Brangwyn's Pilgrimage. The Life Story of An Artist*, London, 1948.

Catalogue of the Collection of Works by Sir Frank Brangwyn, RA, formed by Count William de Belleroche, sold by Christie's, 1961

Macer-Wright, Philip, *Brangwyn. A Study of a Genius at Close Quarters*, London, 1940.

Sir Frank Brangwyn, Paintings at Lloyd's Register, Catalogue in the Library of the Victoria and Albert Museum, 1914

Battersby, Martin, *The World of Art Nouveau*, London, 1968.

Obit. Bldr, 22.6.56, p. 778.

BREWER, Cecil Claude   1871—1918

Cecil Brewer went to Clifton College, and was articled to F. T. Baggallay in 1890. He attended the Architectural Association School, and entered the Royal Academy Schools in 1893, winning the Gold Medal and Travelling Studentship. He won the RIBA Pugin Prize in 1896 and the Godwin Bursary in 1911, and was awarded the Donaldson Prize.

Brewer was assistant to Robert Schultz Weir and in 1895 entered into practice with Arnold Dunbar Smith whose training had taken a similar course. Together they did some noteworthy buildings (*see under* Smith, Arnold Dunbar). Both were members of the Art Workers' Guild.

RIBAJ, 6.4.35, pp. 629—47, and 27.4.35, p. 738

Obit. RIBAJ, Sept., 1918, pp. 246—7 *Bldr*, 16.8.18, p. 101 and 25.8., p. 260

BRIERLEY, Walter Henry   1862—1926

Walter Brierley was articled to his father in York and then to architects in Warrington and Liverpool. In 1885 he joined James Demaine whose practice, founded by John Carr of York (1723—1807), had passed to him through Peter Atkinson, father, Peter Atkinson, son, and William Atkinson, grandson.

Brierley was architect to the North Riding County Council (1901—23) and consulting architect to the Diocese of York (1908—21). In his secular work he was the leading exponent in the north-east of England of the prevailing 'Wrenaissance' style and his work is mentioned by Hermann Muthesius. In 1918 Brierley took J. H. Rutherford (1875—1946) into partnership.

Brierley's earliest church and church restoration work included All Saints', Rufforth, W. Riding (1894—5), and the church of the Blessed Virgin Mary, Goathland, N. Riding (1894—6). He also did restorations after fire to Welburn Hall, N. Riding, and built the outbuildings there in 1890 and a new wing later (*Bldr*, 18.5.01). In 1891 he did the Midland Bank at Whitby and in 1895 The Close, Brompton, Northallerton, N. Riding. In 1896 he designed Scarcroft Road School, the first of a series of excellent buildings for the York School Board.

Later works by Brierley include:

1892-1901	St Peter, Newton-le-Willows, Lancashire
1900	York City and County Bank, Bridlington Quay, E. Riding (*Bldr*, 23.6.1900)
1901	Grimston Court, E. Riding (*AA*, 1901; *Bldr*, 14.9.01)
1902	St Oswald, Sowerby, N. Riding (north aisle)
	St Luke, York
	St Philip, Buckingham Palace Road, SW1

W. H. Brierley: The Close, Brompton, Northallerton, Yorkshire.

		St Thomas, Kensal New Town, W10
		The Galtres, Easingwold, N. Riding (*Bldr*, 9.5.03)
	1903	The Vicarage, Huntington, N. Riding
		Heslington Hall (now York University), interiors
123	1904	The Close, Brompton, Northallerton, N. Riding (additions)
		Poppleton Road and Haxby Road Schools, York
	1904-6	County Hall, Northallerton, N. Riding (*RA*, 1904; *Bldr*, 24.9.04 and 1.12.06)
	1905	Brackencliffe, Scarborough (RA, 1905)
		Bishopsbarns, St George's Place, York
	1906	Burrough Court, Leicestershire (hunting lodge, stables and cottages; *Bldr*, 6.4.07)
	1907	The Garth, Bishopthorpe, W. Riding (*Bldr*, 13.12.09)
		Normanby Park, Lincolnshire, for Sir Berkeley Sheffield (additions)
		Whixley Hall, Whixley, W. Riding (restorations)
	1908	Howarth Art Gallery, Manchester Road, Accrington, Lancashire
		Crendle Court, Purse Caundle, Dorset, for the Hon. Mrs Alfred Kerr (*AR*, 1911)
		Thorpe Underwood Hall, W. Riding
	1910	Hackness Hall, N. Riding, for Lord Derwent (restoration after fire)
	1910-11	Dyke Nook, Whalley Road, Accrington, Lancashire
		Lynn Garth, Stockton-on-the-Forest, N. Riding
	1911	High Green, Ilkley, W. Riding
		Lumley Barracks, York
	1912-13	Sion Hill, Kirby Wiske, N. Riding
		Additions to Acklam Hall, Acklam, N. Riding

Obit. RIBAJ, 18.9.26, p. 575 *Bldr*, 3.9.26, p. 365.

BRIGGS, Robert Alexander   1858–1916

R. A. Briggs was articled to Gilbert R. Redgrave in 1867, won the Soane Medallion in 1883 and commenced practice in 1884, at first with C. G. Killmister when they did the West End Hospital, Welbeck Street, W1 (RA, 1887).

His publications — *Homes for the Country, The Essentials of a Country House, Country Cottages and Homes, Pompeian Decorations* — won Briggs a practice in houses, while his *Bungalows and Country Residences* earned him the nickname 'Bungalow' Briggs. His works included flats at 60 Brompton Road, SW3, and in Earl's Court Square, SW5, houses at Dormans Park, West Lingfield, Surrey, and Kenilworth Road, Leamington Spa, Warwickshire (*Bldr*, 9.6.1900) and additions to 54 Kensington Park Road, W11 (*Bldr*, 28.5.04) and to the Old Mill, Aldeburgh, Suffolk (*Bldr*, 10.9.04 and 3.12.04).

Obit. RIBAJ, 20.5.16, p. 246 *Bldr*, 26.5.16, p. 385 and 2.6., p. 409.

Carving by Abraham Broadbent in the style of Grinling Gibbons at Great Maytham Hall, Rolvenden, Kent. Architect: Sir Edwin Lutyens, RA.

BROADBENT, Abraham   d. 1919

Abraham Broadbent studied at the Lambeth School of Art and became the craftsman *par excellence* of the 'Wrenaissance'. He is best remembered for the fine quality of his carving in which he perpetuated the style of Wren's great carver, Grinling Gibbons. His work appears on all Lutyens's buildings, beginning with the *Country Life* building in Tavistock Street, WC2.

Broadbent's carving also appears on the Kings Road extension of the Chelsea Vestry Hall, for Leonard Stokes; on Bibsworth Manor, near Broadway, Worcestershire, and Nether Swell Manor, Stow-on-the-Wold, Gloucestershire, both for Guy Dawber; and at the Eton College Library and school hall, by L. K. Hall and S. K. Greenslade.

Broadbent was one of the galaxy of sculptors employed on the façades of the Victoria and Albert Museum (1899–1909), his contribution being the figures on the Exhibition Road façade of the clock-maker Thomas Tompion and the smith Huntingdon Shaw to whom Jean Tijou's wrought-iron screens at Hampton Court Palace and St Paul's Cathedral had been wrongly attributed.

Broadbent was a member of the Art Workers' Guild. His work was continued by his son, E. R. Broadbent.

BROCK, Sir Thomas, KCB, RA   1847–1922

Best known as the sculptor of the Queen Victoria Memorial in front of Buckingham Palace, Thomas Brock was born at Worcester, where he became a modeller in the Worcester China Works and studied at the Government School of Design there. In 1866 Brock entered the studio of J. H. Foley (1818–74), sculptor of the Prince Consort and 'Asia' on the Albert Memorial, Kensington Gardens, SW7. Brock entered the Royal Academy Schools in 1867 where he won the Gold Medal in 1869. After Foley's death, Brock completed many of his works, including 'Lord Canning' for Calcutta.

Among Brock's earlier works are Richard Baxter at the Bull Ring, Kidderminster (1875), Robert Raikes for Bristol, for Toronto and for Victoria Embankment Gardens, WC2 (1880), Sir Rowland Hill for Town Hall Square, Kidderminster (1882), the bust of Henry Longfellow in Westminster Abbey (1884), Sir Henry Edward Bartle Frere for Victoria Embankment Gardens (1888) and the monument to Richard Crosher in Emmanuel Church, Loughborough (1888). He also did the memorial to Bishop Philpott in Worcester Cathedral (1893), Granville Leweson Gower, at St James Titsey, Surrey (1897), Bishop Hervey for Wells Cathedral and Sir Richard Owen for the Natural History Museum, SW7.

In 1900 Thomas Brock was selected to carry out the Queen Victoria Memorial in front of Buckingham Palace before the competition for its architectural setting was won by Sir Aston Webb. When Brock told King Edward it would take ten years to execute, the King replied — 'Why, *we* shall all be in our graves by that time' — which in his case came true.

The monument is 82 ft high and 2,300 tons of gleaming Carrara marble went into it. The crown-

Sir Thomas Brock, RA:
the Queen Victoria Memorial
in front of Buckingham Palace.
Architect: Sir Aston Webb, RA.

ing bronze gilt figure of winged Victory and her globe are supported by bronze gilt figures of Courage and Constancy. On the east side of the central pier facing the Mall is the seated figure of Queen Victoria in marble holding the sceptre and the orb, her wedding ring on her right hand, German fashion, as the Prince Consort wished. On the side facing the Palace is the seated figure of Motherhood, with children; on the other sides are seated 'Truth' with mirror, and 'Justice' with sword, all in marble and 'heroic' in scale. Seated on curved pediments over fountains at the base are 'Science and Art' and 'Naval and Military Power'; on plinths set diagonally between water basins are 'Industry', 'Agriculture', 'War' and 'Peace', also 'heroic' in scale and each accompanied by a lion. The circular plinth behind the water basins is decorated with low reliefs in marble of naiads, boys and tritons with dolphins and conch shells. Two scallop-shell fountains have a bronze river god and a bronze river maiden.

The importance in its period of this national monument to Queen Victoria is scarcely equalled by the sculpture, for Brock was (in words of the *DNB*) 'the English representative of the more conservative aspects of French sculpture in the second half of the nineteenth century', and thus

echoed the spirit of the times (*AR*, June, 1911). Ten years' work on the memorial received recognition dramatically when, at the unveiling ceremony on 16 May, 1911, Brock received the accolade of knighthood from King George V.

Thomas Brock also did the tomb of Lord Leighton in St Dunstan's Chapel, St Paul's Cathedral, an effigy on a sarcophagus with 'Painting' at the head and 'Sculpture' at the foot holding a representation of Leighton's 'Sluggard' (1901). In 1902 he did the equestrian statue of Edward the Black Prince for City Square, Leeds. Brock did a bust of Lord Leighton for the Town Hall, Scarborough (1916), and Edwin Austin Abbey, RA, for the British School at Rome. His last work, 'Lord Lister' in Portland Place, W1, was unveiled posthumously in 1922.

Brock provided the design for the Royal Academy Schools Gold and Silver Medals for the reigns of Edward VII and George V. He was made ARA in 1883 and RA in 1891 (diploma work, 'Lord Leighton, PRA').

Other works by Brock are:

1902   William Ewart Gladstone for Westminster
         Abbey, Westminster Hall and St John's
         Gardens, Liverpool

1903	Queen Victoria supported by 'Shipbuilding' and 'Spinning', and Sir Edward Harland, for Belfast City Hall
	Queen Victoria, Hove, Sussex, and a copy for Birmingham which was given a new pedestal in 1951
1904	Brigadier General John Nicholson for Nicholson Gardens, Delhi
	Sir John Everett Millais, bronze, outside the Tate Gallery, SW1
	Lord Russell of Killowen, Lord Chief Justice, Royal Courts of Justice, Strand, WC2
	Colin Minton Campbell, London Road, Stoke-on-Trent, Staffordshire
1905	Sir Henry Tate, bronze bust, Library Garden, Acre Lane, SW2
1906	Thomas Gainsborough, Tate Gallery. (A copy (1939) was made for the staircase of the Royal Academy under the Leighton Fund.)
1910	Sir Henry Irving wearing a gown of a Doctor of Literature, north side, National Portrait Gallery, WC2
1911	'Navigation' and 'Gunnery', Admiralty Arch, SW1
1912	Lord Lister, portrait medallion, Westminster Abbey
1913	Royal Coat of Arms, new centre pediment, Buckingham Palace
1914	Captain James Cook, The Mall, SW1 (his foot resting un-nautically and dangerously on a coil of rope)
1915	Lord Sydenham, Bombay

Obit. RIBAJ, 23.9.22, pp. 609-10 *Bldr*, 8.9.22, p. 331.

BROWNE, Sir George Washington, RSA 1854—1939

Washington Browne was born in Glasgow and articled to J. J. Stevenson. He was the first Scot to win the RIBA Pugin Prize and in 1879 became chief assistant to Sir Rowand Anderson, RSA, in Edinburgh. He competed in the Glasgow Municipal Chambers Competition (1882), won by William Young, and was placed in the London County Hall Competition (1908). He came first in the competition for St Paul's Bridge, EC4 (not carried out). He was for a time in partnership with J. M. Dick Peddie.

Browne did the King Edward VII Memorial Gates at Holyrood, with sculpture by H. S. Gamley. His other Edinburgh works include the Hospital for Sick Children; the British Linen Bank in George Street; the YMCA, South Andrew Street; and the Edinburgh Carnegie Public Library (with Dick Peddie). In Glasgow he did Miss Cranston's Tea Room, 91 Buchanan Street (1896), now a branch of the Clydesdale Bank.

Washington Browne was made RSA in 1902, was President of the Scottish Academy in 1926 and was knighted the same year.

Obit. RIBAJ, 17.7.39, p. 904 *Bldr*, 23.6.39, p. 1187.

BRYAN, Henry Dare   1868—1909

H. Dare Bryan was born at Weston-super-Mare and started practice in 1890 at the early age of twenty-two. He did the Wesleyan Church at Westbury Park, Bristol, additions to the Deanery, Bristol, and the Queen Anne monument and other buildings at Minehead, Somerset. His best-known building is the Western College (Highbury Chapel), Bristol (*Bldr*, 9.9.05, p. 276). He also did the headquarters premises for Lennards, Queens Road, Bristol (destroyed 1940), and schools in Bristol including Merrywood Elementary School, Bedminster. After his early death his practice was continued by Silcock and Reay.

Obit. RIBAJ, 12.6.09, p. 562 *Bldr*, 19.6.09, pp. 736—7.

BRYDON, John McKean   1840—1901

J. McK. Brydon was born in Dunfermline, educated at the Commercial Academy of Dunfermline and articled to Douglas Hay in Liverpool. He travelled in Italy and was assistant to David Bryce in Edinburgh in 1866. He was chief assistant to Campbell Douglas (1828—1910) and J. J. Stevenson (1831—1908) in Glasgow, where B. J. Talbert, William Leiper (1839—1916) and William Wallace were also in the office.

On coming to London Brydon was assistant to Eden Nesfield and R. Norman Shaw for three years. In 1871 he joined William Wallace and Cottier in establishing Morris & Co. in Langham Place, W1, a decorating and art furnishing business with no connections with William Morris's firm of similar name in Oxford Street. After a few years Cottier switched to fine art dealing while Brydon and Wallace returned to architecture, setting up in practice together in 1880. In 1887, with James Cubitt, Brydon showed a design at the Royal Academy for a Congregational church in West Kensington.

Success in a limited competition in 1898 brought Brydon one of the most important public buildings of the Edwardian era, the new Government Offices, Great George Street and Parliament Street, Westminster (*Bldr*, 6.7.07 and 8.8.08), but Brydon died of a throat infection before building started. As in the case of William Young's War Office, the Government proposed taking over the working drawings and supervising the work, a move strongly opposed by the Royal Institute of British Architects and the professional papers, but the Government had its way and Sir Henry Tanner senior took over on behalf of HM Office of Works.

In contrast to the mammoth Government Offices, Brydon's earlier work was domestic and in keeping with his interest in interior decoration and furniture design. He had done a studio at Haverstock Hill, NW3, for the painter James Jacques Tissot

Dare Bryan: the Western Congregational College,
Cotham, Bristol.

(1836–1902) when he took refuge in England
after the Commune of 1871, and another at
Tissot's home, Château de Buillon, Besançon, after
the painter's return to France when he became
dévot and illustrated the Old Testament and the
Life of Christ with 700 water-colour drawings.

In 1886–7 Brydon did the splendid additions to
Chelsea Vestry Hall fronting on Chelsea Manor
Gardens, SW3 (additions by Leonard Stokes and
Public Baths by Wills and Anderson). In 1891–5
he did the Chelsea Polytechnic, Manresa Road.

Brydon's work at St Peter's Hospital, Henrietta
Street, Covent Garden, WC2 (1880–4) and the
School of Medicine for Women in Handel Street
and Hunter Street, WC1 (1896) and the Elizabeth
Garrett Anderson Hospital, Euston Road, NW1
(1889–94), show that he had absorbed much from
Shaw during his period in Shaw's office. His later
buildings, however, have the wide proportions
which became characteristic of the last years of
the Victorian and first years of the Edwardian
neo-Baroque style; this is evident in his Bath
Municipal Buildings, well tuned though they are
to the English Palladian manner of Baldwin's
Guildhall which he incorporated in the scheme
(begun 1891).

AR, July–December, 1905, 'Brydon at Bath'

Obit. RIBAJ, 8.6.01, pp. 381–2 *Bldr*, 1.6.01, pp. 540–
1 and 8.6., p. 569.

BUNNEY, Michael Frank Wharlton, MBE
1873–1926

Michael Bunney was born in Venice. His father,
John W. Bunney — a disciple of John Ruskin, for
whom he made water-colours of Florence, Verona
and Venice — was Venice correspondent of the
Society for the Protection of Ancient Buildings.
Michael Bunney went to Fettes School and studied
at the Architectural Association and at the Royal
Academy Schools from 1895 to 1900. He was
articled to Horace Field and became his chief
assistant, taking part in designs for the offices of
the North Eastern Railway in York (1902).

Bunney began practice on his own account in 1902
and from 1905 worked in partnership with Clifford
C. Makins, also from the Royal Academy Schools
and from Field's office. Bunney married Edith
Hewetson whose father had founded furniture
businesses where Heal's of Tottenham Court Road
and Selfridge's of Oxford Street now stand.
Bunney's principal works were houses of medium
size at Esher in Surrey, Gidea Park in Essex, and
above all in the Hampstead Garden Suburb. Here
he did ninety-two houses including his own — one
of a group of four in Meadway — and others in
Bigwood Road, Erskine Hill, Hampstead Way,
Willifield Way and elsewhere. All were built
between 1907 and 1914, the vintage years of the
Suburb, some modelled on the seventeenth-century
vernacular of Hertfordshire and its borders, others
modelled on the eighteenth-century doctors',
bankers' and brewers' houses of English country
towns. Sir Raymond Unwin commented on 'the good
example set by Michael Bunney in his work in the
Hampstead Garden Suburb', adding 'I regard him
as a great contributor to the merits of the estate'.

128

Michael Bunney: 7 to 13 Meadway, Hampstead Garden Suburb, London NW11.

Bunney collaborated with Horace Field on the compilation of *English Domestic Architecture of the XVIIth and XVIIIth Centuries*, published by George Bell and Sons in 1905 and again in 1928. To make sketches, photographs and measured drawings for this book, Bunney and his wife cycled all over England. This valuable work provided an exemplar when a fashion for close reproduction of the domestic buildings of those centuries was replacing the eclecticism of Free Renaissance. But, more important still, it drew attention to those buildings which had survived, encouraging their repair and intelligent use at a time when existing guidebooks, many of them written by clergymen, still classed as 'modern' buildings erected since the Commonwealth. The Cross Keys Temperance Inn, Cautley, near Sedbergh, W. Riding, is an example (1903) of Bunney's work of restoration and addition (illustrated in Pevsner, *W. Riding*, plate 1).

During the First World War, at the request of Raymond Unwin, who had become chief inspector to the Local Government Board seconded to the Ministry of Munitions, Michael Bunney, like C. M. Crickmer and others who had supported Parker and Unwin at Hampstead, was appointed to do the housing required near the munition factories. This was no temporary affair, but became a basis for post-war housing under Dr Christopher Addison.

Michael Bunney was awarded the MBE and after the war became deputy architect to the Ministry of Health. His son, Michael J. H. Bunney, and his son's wife, Charlotte Bunney, practise as architects at Kendal and at Ravenstonedale, Kirkby Stephen, Westmorland.

Obit. RIBAJ, 5.2.27, p. 255 *Bldr*, 11.2.27, p. 237.

BURNET, Sir John James, RA, RSA, Hon LLD, FRS Edinburgh   1857–1938

J. J. Burnet was the son of the Glasgow architect John Burnet (1814–1901) and entered his father's office at the age of fifteen. Two years later, following the example of the young painters of the Glasgow School, Burnet went to Paris where he studied under Jean-Louis Pascal (1837–1920) of the celebrated Atelier Blouet, Gilbert, Questel and Pascal, and entered the Ecole des Beaux-Arts. One of Burnet's fellow pupils was Henri-Paul Nénot (1853–1934) who nicknamed the ruddy-complexioned young Scot *confiture de groseilles*. Nénot's New Sorbonne in Paris was to help hasten the return of the new classicism to America and Britain, a development largely attributable to the teaching of Pascal (*Bldr*, 19.11.10, pp. 609–15.).

Burnet worked in the Paris office of François Rolland before returning to his father's firm, where he became a partner in 1879. The previous year, when Burnet was still only twenty-one, his Paris training had already borne fruit in a design placed first in the competition for the Glasgow Institute of Fine Arts in Sauchiehall Street (now demolished). This early work anticipated by many years the new classical revival in England.

Burnet continued in general practice, demonstrating his mature style in the 1903 Civil Service and Professional Supply Association building in George Street, Edinburgh. This carries the full panoply of his monumental manner applied to shop and business premises. Burnet's London contribution to this class of building is represented in 99 Aldwych, WC2, a 1909 building which gives free reign to the ploys of façade building, a field in which he, of all his contemporaries, was most adept. Indeed as late as 1922 the street façade was considered so important a part of architecture that the RIBA instituted its 'Street Architecture Award for the most meritorious example of a street façade as opposed to a church or public building'. This was the first instance of direct official recognition of merit in a specific building.

In the façade game *no* two storeys of a building could have identical windows; in fact the building was required to have the appearance of an Italian palazzo or a Paris *hôtel*, with ground floor, mezzanine, *piano nobile*, frieze and (in the classical sense) attic windows.

130 Known until recently as General Buildings, No. 99 was the first new building on the Aldwych section of the Holborn—Strand Improvements (1906—23) and was erected for the General Accident Fire and Life Assurance Corporation Limited. Burnet's Beaux-Arts training with Scottish overtones is easily discernible in his treatment of this gently convex frontage on a theme derived from his Glasgow and Edinburgh buildings.

The ground floor is recessed under a granite architrave supported on granite columns with black marble Greek Ionic capitals, and the main doorway is flanked by sculpture. The recess shelters a delicate Crestola marble screen surmounted by white-metal figures representing Strength, Prudence, Abundance and Prosperity. The devices for reaching the statutory main cornice line without a repeat come into play next — the windows of the first mezzanine are concealed under the recess and appear in the broken pediment of the doorways; the second mezzanine appears over the colonnade. Here the *piano nobile* of the Italians is extended to perform a double role: the architrave and entablature of its windows embrace the windows of two storeys masquerading as one — a device employed by the French who had already found the *piano nobile* too *nobile* for their purpose. With a height of five storeys reached without repetition, there are still two moves to come, rounding things off with a flourish — the 'frieze' windows beneath the main cornice, and the true 'attic', a set-back wooden pergola. Crowning all is a steep roof of green slates with ornamental cresting. The flanking chimney stacks protect each side from discordant neighbours, since the Aldwych scheme did not ensure uniformity. The sculpture, elegantly placed in five different situations, is by Albert Hodge (*q.v.*).

The first London building to abandon these rules and show a cliff of windows of identical pattern was Bush House, also on the Aldwych site (1922), built by the American architects, Helmle and Corbett, as a diminutive form of American skyscraper with base, shaft (of windows) and capital, like a column. Burnet himself made an important

129 exception to his façade-building game at Kodak House, Kingsway (1911), the only building in the new Kingsway to admit to its steel frame honestly. But this was a flash in the pan. In Kingsway architects continued after the First World War to give façades classical columns and cornices.

Sir John Burnet's *chef d'oeuvre*, for which he had been selected from among the leading British architects of his time, was the King Edward VII Galleries of the British Museum (1905—14) in Montague Place, WC1. Skilful in construction and detailing in stone and marble, Burnet revealed — even in this Classical building — his French-Scottish taste, mixing with the neo-Greek of the colonnade cambered arches and lions by Sir George Frampton. This is part only of a larger scheme for which Burnet prepared preliminary drawings.

The importance Burnet attached to working drawings encouraged his office to make important contributions in this field until the standard of working drawings in this country approached that of America. Burnet was made ARA in 1921 and

Sir John Burnet, RA: Kodak House, Kingsway, London WC2. One of the first buildings to declare its fire-resisting frame construction. The attic storey is recent.

RA in 1925 (diploma work, 'Section of the Staircase of the British Museum Extension'). He was
knighted, and in 1923 received the Royal Gold
Medal for Architecture. He was one of the principal
architects to the War Graves Commission after the
First World War. His firm, which has since made
many important contributions to architecture,
continues under Gordon Tait as Sir John Burnet,
Tait and Partners. Burnet was a member of the
Art Workers' Guild.

*Other important buildings by J. J. Burnet in the
Edwardian period are:*

1901	Elder Library, Govan, Glasgow
1905-6	McGeogh's, 28 West Campbell Street, Glasgow (demolished 1970)
1906-10	R. W. Forsyth's Shop, Princes Street, Edinburgh (additions, 1923–5)
1914	Institute of Chemistry, Russell Square, WC1

RIBAJ, 30.6.23, 'The Royal Gold Medal'
Obit. RIBAJ, July, 1938, pp. 893–6, 941 and 993
Bldr, 8.7.38, pp. 53, 59 and 104.

◁ **Sir John Burnet, RA: 99 Aldwych, London WC2,** with
sculpture by Albert Hodge, demonstrates Burnet's
Scottish and French training.

**Sir John Burnet, RA: the King Edward VII Galleries of
the British Museum.** *Right:* **His diploma work for The
Royal Academy of Arts shows Burnet's attention to
construction.** *Below:* **The north front. The lions are by
Sir George Frampton, RA.**

132

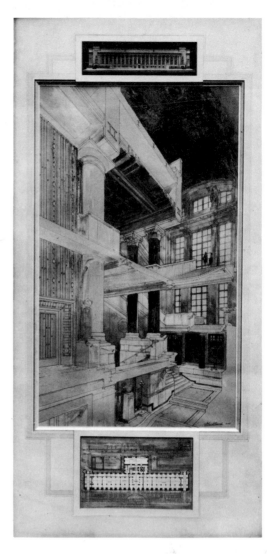

Sir John Burnet, RA: McGeogh's, 28 West Campbell Street, Glasgow (demolished), showed Burnet's highly sophisticated façade.

BURR, Alfred   1855–1952

Alfred Burr was born in London, educated at University College School and articled to T. Taylor. He set up in practice in 1877.

Burr did the new offices of the State of Victoria, Melbourne Place, WC2, at the western end of the eastern horn of the Strand—Aldwych improvements (*Bldr*, 22.5.09), where, after an abortive competition, R. Norman Shaw had been brought in to advise. Here the bronze 'Progress' was by F. W. Pomeroy. Burr did British Columbia House, (Lower) Regent Street, SW1, completed during the First World War (see page 79), and restored Dr Samuel Johnson's House, Gough Square, Fleet Street, EC4. He also did 50 Welbeck Street and 28 Queen Anne Street, W1 and 163a and b Sloane Street, SW1.

When Walsingham House, Piccadilly, came to be demolished to make way for the new Ritz Hotel, Burr was called in to advise the owners. He was succeeded in his practice by his son, Vincent Burr.

Obit. RIBAJ, Aug., 1952, p. 387 *Bldr*, 18.4.52, p. 584.

BUTLER, John Dixon   1861–1920

J. D. Butler was the son of John Butler, an architect in private practice who undertook the design of buildings for the Metropolitan Police, much of the work consisting of the conversion of existing buildings — in one case a vicarage — into police stations or section houses. After serving articles with his father and studying at University College, Butler began practice in 1883 in his father's office.

In 1895 Butler was appointed Architect and Surveyor to the department of the Metropolitan Police responsible for police buildings, since named the Receiver's Office. He served full-time in this capacity until his death. In the course of his service he was responsible for 150 police buildings in the Metropolitan area. He was succeeded by G. Mackenzie Trench.

Butler admired the work of R. Norman Shaw, whose New Scotland Yard building was finished in 1890, and collaborated with him on the southward extension of 1904–6. In the first year of Butler's appointment Shaw was asked for a design for the Police Station at Holmes Road, Kentish Town, NW5. Butler himself developed a distinctive style for many of his police stations, a crisp, austere version of the prevalent Free Classic or Anglo-Classic — the civic style doffing its regalia and donning a uniform. Most representative of the buildings in this vein is the Police Court and Station at Old Street, Shoreditch (1906; *Bldr*, 16.1.09) built on the site of the Porters' and Walters' Almshouses (provided with new premises at Wood Green, N22; see p. 157). A later example in the same style is the Hampstead Police Station and Court, Rosslyn Hill and Downshire Hill, NW3 (1912–13). Also noteworthy is the Fulham Police Station, Fulham Road, SW6.

Police station buildings built under Butler's direction from 1900 include:

1900	Muswell Hill, Claybury and Wimbledon
1901	East Ham and Waterloo Pier (River Police)
1902	Sidcup, Wallington and Barnes (River Police) Hyde Park (RA, 1902)
1903	Highbury Vale, Hackney, Bow, Lee High Road and East Molesey
1904	North Woolwich
1905	Wealdstone, Edmonton, Tottenham, West Ham and Hampton
1906	Old Street, Ilford, Barking and Tower Bridge
1907	Wood Green, Winchmore Hill and Woolwich
1908	Leytonstone, Erith, Cobham (Surrey), Erith (River Police) and Sutton (*Bldr*, 6.3.09)
1909	Banstead, Wapping, Beak Street Section House, W1 (mentioned in *Survey of London*)
1910	Northwood, Carter Street, SE17, Woolwich and Harlesden
1912	Plaistow, Deptford, Battersea, Harrow Road and Streatham
1913	Hampstead
1914	Barnet, Dalston, Earlsfield and Fulham
1916	Golders Green
1917	Bethnal Green and St John's Wood

Obit. Bldr, 5.11.20., p. 510.

133

CACKETT, James Thoburn   1860—1928

J. T. Cackett was articled to J. and L. R. Armour at Gateshead, commenced practice in 1884 and was in partnership with R. Burns-Dick (1869—1955) from 1896. In addition to a considerable general practice, the partners were engaged on the layout and installations for the Armstrong Shipyard at Walton-on-Tyne and shipbuilding yards for Vickers and Cammell Laird.

In Newcastle, the firm did Pilgrim House, Cross House, Westgate Road, and the Laing Art Gallery (1900). They also did police buildings there and the Northern Conservative and Unionist Club in Pilgrim Street (*AR*, November 1911), a splendid building which has since been demolished to make way for 'improvements'. The Primitive Methodist Church at Hexham and 'Spanish City', Whitley Bay, are also their work (*AR*, November, 1911).

The firm did the Police Courts at Berwick-on-Tweed, and business premises in Warrington, Lancashire. Their work after the First World War included the hangar for the airships R100 and R101 at Cardington, Bedfordshire, and the Flying Boat Works at Rochester, Kent, for Short Brothers. The practice continued as Cackett, Burns-Dick and Mackellar and later as R. N. Mackellar and Partners.

Obit.   RIBAJ, 14.4.28., p. 375.

J. A. Campbell: offices at 157 to 167 Hope Street, Glasgow.

J. Dixon Butler: Old Street Police Station and Court Room, Shoreditch, London E1, in the style introduced by Dixon Butler.

CAMPBELL, John Archibald   1859—1909

J. A. Campbell was apprenticed to J. Burnet and Son from 1877 to 1880 and, like J. J. Burnet, attended the Atelier Pascal in Paris until 1883. Campbell won the RIBA Tite Prize in 1885. He was a partner with Burnet and Son from 1886 to 1887 when he began practice in partnership with A. D. Hislop. Campbell's work included houses, one of them for himself at Bridge of Weir, Renfrew. He won the competition for the Edinburgh Exhibition of 1908 which he carried out.

After 1907 Campbell did work in Germany in collaboration with the German-American architect Pullich, which included Schlimmelpfeng, Zehlendorf, Berlin.

Campbell's Glasgow work included:

1902	157—167 Hope Street and 169—175 West George Street, 'a mighty commercial alcazar' (*Glasgow at a Glance*, Collins, 1971)
1904	United Kingdom Provident Building, 122—128 St Vincent Street
	50 Argyle Street. Offices
1908	Northern Assurance, 84—94 St Vincent Street, anticipating work of the 1930s

Obit.   Bldr, 31.7.09., pp. 136—7.

133

CAMPBELL-JONES, William   1862–1951

William Campbell-Jones was articled to E. H. Burnell from 1880 to 1884, and studied at the Architectural Association and at the Royal Academy Schools which he entered in 1883. He won the Donaldson Medal in 1882.

As Surveyor to the Skinners' Company, a post which he held for fifty years, he was architect for the Skinners' Almshouses at Palmers Green, N13, in 1891, the New Skinners' Commercial School, Tonbridge (1892), new buildings, including the Chapel, at Tonbridge School (1892–1909), the Skinners' Girls' Schools, Stamford Hill, N16 (1893) and St Olave's Girls' School, New Kent Road, SE1.

Campbell-Jones's practice consisted mainly of branch banks of which he did a great number, principally for the London and County Bank (now National Westminster Bank), and city offices. He was succeeded by his son, Lt-Col. Owen Campbell-Jones, R. M. Wakelin and F. K. Hewitt.

CARÖE, William Douglas   1857–1938

W. D. Caröe was born at Blundellsands, near Liverpool, the son of Anders Kruise Caröe, Danish Consul in Liverpool. He went to Ruabon Grammar School, and to Trinity College, Cambridge, in 1875. In 1879 Caröe was articled in Liverpool to Edmund B. Kirby. In 1881 he entered the London office of the great church architect J. L. Pearson, where he worked on the drawings for Truro Cathedral and became chief assistant. At the same time he did some work on his own account, mainly in Ireland. While with Pearson, Caröe dealt with the flank of the ancient Westminster Hall, left exposed by the demolition of the Old Law Courts in 1881 when these were moved to the Royal Courts of Justice in the Strand. To Caröe Pearson entrusted the architectural training of his son, Frank Loughborough Pearson (q.v.) who completed Truro Cathedral after his father's death. Frank Pearson in his turn directed Caröe's son Alban in his architectural studies.

The experience gained with Pearson led to Caröe's appointment in 1885 as an architect to the Ecclesiastical Commissioners — Pearson's brother-in-law Ewan Christian was then senior architect. Caröe became a partner of Ewan Christian's cousin, J. H. Christian, of J. H. Christian and Purday, who designed Mombasa Cathedral in 1904. Their work together included The Paddock, Leopardstown, Co. Dublin (1885) and Hanover Schools, Gilbert Street, Grosvenor Square, W1 (RA, 1889; demolished). Caröe continued his secular work with his chief assistant, Herbert Passmore, who became his partner in a separate practice in 1903.

After the death of Ewan Christian in 1895, Caröe became senior architect to the Church Commis-

sioners, an appointment he held for the rest of his life.

Caröe did his first church, Gustav Adolf Kyrka, the Scandinavian chapel in Liverpool, in 1886 (RA, 1884). In 1897 he won the competition for St David's Church, Exeter, with James Brooks (1825–1901) as assessor. With characteristic thoroughness and business sense, Caröe had submitted with his carefully detailed drawings a firm tender from a leading church builder — additional information of a kind which would disqualify a competitor today. Since the site was a narrow one, Caröe planned his church with 'passage' aisles as G. F. Bodley had done earlier at St Augustine, Pendlebury, Manchester. After St David's, Exeter, many new churches and additions to churches were entrusted to Caröe. Up to the turn of the century he did St John the Evangelist, Stansted Mountfitchet, Essex (1889–95); St Michael, Colehill, Dorset (1893–5); and St Stephen, Nottingham. The cathedrals, abbeys and priories to which Caröe was appointed included Canterbury, Durham, Southwell, Brecon, St David's, Malvern Priory, Romsey Abbey and Tewkesbury Abbey. He designed the Bishop's Palaces at Bristol (demolished) and at Southwell, restored Wolvesey Palace, Winchester, and designed numerous clergy houses; also dames' houses at Wycombe Abbey School, Buckinghamshire (RA, 1898).

W. D. Caröe: shops and flats at 75 to 83 Duke Street, London W1, have the "tumble home" to the turrets found in Merriott Church, Somerset, and used by Hare and Mackintosh.

Caröe repaired the central tower of Canterbury Cathedral, devising a means of supporting the tower temporarily on the walls of the nave and transepts. In London he repaired the steeple of St Bride, Fleet Street. He showed great skill in the design of choir stalls, rood screens, reredoses and organ cases and had a particular fondness for his woodwork for Winchester College Chapel (1908) and the organ case at Malvern Priory. Caröe did the Memorial Cloisters for the Boer War at Charterhouse School, Godalming; the commemorative floor tablet to J. L. Pearson in Westminster Abbey (*Bldr*, 8.11.02); the memorial to Archbishop Temple in Canterbury Cathedral; and that to Earl Stanhope at Chevening, Kent.

His secular work of this period included the Adelphi (now Martin's) Bank, Castle Street, Liverpool (1892) — a rich mixture inside and out, with bronze doors by Thomas Stirling Lee — and the Union of London and Smith's (now National Westminster) Bank in Cambridge (*BA*, 14.6.07). The largest of Caröe's secular works is the University of South Wales and Monmouthshire at Cathays Park, Cardiff, which he won in limited competition against Basil Champneys and John Belcher in 1903. The Great Hall of Caröe's winning design was never built, however, and later buildings have cluttered up the campus. Faced entirely in stone ashlar, Caröe's buildings lack the ebullience of his other secular work and the colour and texture of his brick and stone buildings (*Bldr*, 7.5.04 and 15.5.09).

At his own college of Trinity at Cambridge Caröe added bay windows to Anthony Salvin's Whewell's Court in 1908 and did the cloisters in King's Hall (1905–6). At Pembroke College he added a new range, linking it by an appropriate neo-Baroque screen to George Gilbert Scott junior's beautiful range of 1883. Caröe's restoration of Tom Tower, Christ Church, Oxford, in 1910 is recorded in an etching by Muirhead Bone.

134 After the Gilbert Street Schools (demolished) and the richly carved 55–73 Duke Street (1890–4), Caröe's next contribution to the London scene came with 75–83 Duke Street, W1 (1893–5). This outstanding block of shops and flats of warm red brick and a rich variety of windows has twin turrets with inward sloping walls recalling the 'tumble home', to use a nautical expression, on the tower of Merriott Church, Somerset, and anticipating a similar device on C. R. Mackintosh's Queen's Cross Church, Glasgow (1896–9) and on H. T. Hare's Westminster College, Cambridge (1897–9). Also in Mayfair Caröe did five elaborate houses bounded by (Upper) Grosvenor Street, Park Street and Culross Street. At 55–91 Knightsbridge, 135 also on the Grosvenor Estate, Caröe did the splendid range of shops for the carriage trade and mansion flats over. Inscribed ANNO EDW VII CORONATIONIS, they bear the heads of the Sovereign and Queen Alexandra in roundels and display a rich array of piers and pilasters, cornices

W. D. Caröe: shops and flats at 55 to 91 Knightsbridge, London SW1. Edwardian exuberance.

and chimney stacks. These flats enjoyed a view of Hyde Park until 1906 when Parkside, a tall, clumsy, long and narrow block of mansion flats by Alfred Hart and Leslie Waterhouse, rose opposite to block the view, occasioning an indignant outburst in the Press. With similar disregard for the view to, and from, the Park, the western end of this long, narrow site was rebuilt in 1969 to house the Household Cavalry.

136 More remarkable than either of these buildings by Caröe is his Offices of the Ecclesiastical Commissioners and Church Estates in Millbank, SW1 (1903), with its jovial scrolls and chimney stacks suggesting a Church jubilant. The rich variety Caröe brought to this building succeeds in achieving a balanced asymmetry (*Bldr*, 30.4.04). The same year Caröe designed the Working Men's College in Crowndale Road, NW1 (*Bldr*, 3.2.06) and he took an active interest in the work of the college. (The new building superseded the premises at 44–46 Great Ormond Street, WC1, which were needed for the extensions of the Children's Hospital there.)

23 In 1901 Caröe acted as assessor for the Millbank Housing Scheme for the London County Council, but the winning design (by Spalding and Cross) was not adopted — much to the relief of the Council's excellent architects who had already designed the first block. Caröe was also assessor in the competi-

tion for the Provincial Parliament Buildings in
Vancouver, British Columbia, and himself
competed, unsuccessfully, for the Lady Chapel
of St Patrick's Cathedral, New York, in 1902. He
was consulted on the proposed cathedral for
Washington, DC, and came down firmly on the
side of the classical style. He also advised on
Trondhjem Cathedral, Norway, where he was made
Antya Ridder, Order of St Olaf.

Caröe also did a number of country houses including North Foreland Lodge, Broadstairs, Kent; Fox
Rock, near Dublin, for Sir Horace Plunkett (*Bldr*,
23.9.05); and Meulenborg, Elsinore, Denmark
(with Tvede of Copenhagen, *Bldr*, 24.7.09). In
1908 he concluded extensive additions to his own
house, Vann, an old house at Chiddingfold, Surrey,
still in the family, which compares well with
contemporary work by Lutyens.

Caröe was a brother-upholder of the Art Workers'
Guild and author of a history of Sefton, Liverpool.
The letterer and sculptor Eric Gill was a pupil.

Caröe died at Kyrenia, Cyprus, in a house of his
own design, and was succeeded in his practice by

his partner Herbert Passmore and his son Alban
Caröe. The firm is now continued by Alban Caröe's
son A. D. R. Caröe and his partner D. S. Martin.

Other works by W. D. Caröe are:

1900-4	South Lytchett Manor, Lytchett Minster, Dorset (now a county secondary school) — an early 19th-cent. house 'revamped in Caröe's unrestrained neo-Baroque' (Pevsner). (RA, 1900; *Bldr*, 26.5.1900)
1901	St Michael, Edmonton, N9
1902	St Barnabas, Walthamstow, E17
	St Aldhelm, Silver Street, Edmonton, N18
	St Paul, Camberley, Surrey
	St Michael, Bassishaw, Lower Edmonton, N9
	St Andrew, Stoke Damerel, Devonport (Lady chapel of a new church, now a boys' club)
	St Michael and All Angels, Colehill, Wimborne, Dorset (*Bldr*, 14.3.03) — completion of his church of 1893-5
1903	St Luke, Finchley, N3
1904	St Bartholomew, Stamford Hill, N15 (*Bldr*. 7.4.06 and 19.12.08)

St Andrew and St Patrick, Elveden, Suffolk (additions; *Bldr*, 2.9.05)

1906	St Michael, South Beddington, Surrey
	Union of London and Smith's Bank, Cambridge
	St Edward's House, Great College Street, SW1
1907	St Mary of Bethany, Woking, Surrey (*Times*, 8.11.07)
1908	St Michael, Sutton Court, Chiswick, W4
	St David, Llanddewi Brefi, Cardiganshire (transepts)
1909	St Gabriel, Peverell Park, Plymouth (tower not built)
1910	St Peter le Poer, Friern Barnet, Middlesex
	St Sabinus, Woolacombe, North Devon
	Chapel at North Eastern School, Barnard Castle, Durham
1912	St John the Baptist, West Byfleet, Surrey (*Bldr*, 6.12.02)
	St Andrew, Oxshott, Surrey
	Memorial to Queen Victoria at Menton, Alpes Maritimes, France.

Obit. RIBAJ, 7.3.38, p. 459, 11.4, p. 558 and 9.5, p. 669 *Bldr*, 4.3.38, p. 435.

◁ **W. D. Caröe: the offices of the Ecclesiastical and Church Estates continue the exuberance characteristic of their decade.**

Walter Cave: houses on the Gunter Estate, London SW6.

CARTER, John Coates   1859–1927

Coates Carter was articled to J. B. Pearce of Norwich. In 1881 he came to London and entered the Royal Academy Schools. He became an improver with J. P. Seddon (1827–1906), who had been in partnership with John Prichard (1818–86) of Llandaff, and was a partner of Seddon from 1885 to 1904. Their work together included St Paul, Grangetown, Cardiff; All Saints, Penarth, Glamorgan; St Mary, Chepstow, Monmouthshire; and the first part of University College, Aberystwyth, Cardiganshire. Between 1888 and 1898 they did the main staircase and Sanctuary at Prinknash Park, Gloucestershire, for Thomas Dyer Edwardes who bought the house in 1888. (Prinknash is now a Benedictine monastery and the community has since carried out extensive building.)

On his own account Coates Carter did St John, Pontypool, Monmouthshire; St Luke, Abercarn, Monmouthshire; and St Terlo, Llandeloy, Pembrokeshire (reconstruction from a ruin). In 1907 he did the Abbey Gatehouse, Isle of Caldy, near Tenby, Pembrokeshire (RA, 1908; *BA*, 9.10.08), a religious house.

CAULFIELD, Sidney Burgoyne Kitchener 1877–1964

S. B. K. Caulfield was born in Holborn, WC1, was articled to J. L. Pearson and worked on the drawings of Truro Cathedral at the same time as Charles Spooner. They shared offices and both taught at the Central School of Arts and Crafts, Southampton Row, WC1, where Caulfield succeeded Halsey Ricardo as head of the Department of Architecture in 1910, and where he was assisted by F. Herbert Mansford, Basil Oliver and E. Fraser Tomlins. He did a factory at Bow, E3, for Lloyd and Sons (Lloyd Loom Furniture). Five houses in the Hampstead Garden Suburb, NW11, are by Caulfield — 1 and 3 Bigwood Road, 45 and 47 Meadway, and 16 Southway.

Obit. RIBAJ, Aug., 1964, p. 372   *Bldr*, 20.3.64, p. 611.

137

CAVE, Walter Frederick   1863–1939

Walter Cave was born at Clifton, Bristol, the third son of Sir Charles Daniel Cave, 1st Baronet of Sidbury Manor, Sidmouth, Devon, and a member of the Bristol banking family of that name. His mother, Lady Cave, was the daughter of the poet and critic, John Addington Symonds of Clifton. Cave went to Eton and to Bristol School of Art. He was articled to Sir Arthur W. Blomfield, ARA, and entered the Royal Academy Schools in 1885.

Cave set up in practice in 1889 and was appointed Surveyor to the Gunter Estate, Brompton, SW6, the property of the Gunter family of Mayfair caterers. He laid out their model housing estate at Tamworth Street, Fulham, SW6. He was also consulting architect to the Whiteley Cottage Homes, Burhill, Walton-on-Thames, Surrey, and did the first pair of cottages there in Chestnut Walk (1912).

Walter Cave's houses include Littlecourt, Farthingstone, Northamptonshire (*Bldr*, 16.3.07); Brick Walls, Headington, Oxford; Bengeo House, Hertford; and The Wharf, Sutton Courtenay, Berkshire (the home of Herbert Asquith, Prime Minister 1908–16). Two of Cave's Surrey houses —

Walter Cave: Burberry's, Haymarket, London SW1.

Belgaum, Woking, and Warren Mount (now Robin Hill), Oxshott – are mentioned by Hermann Muthesius. Cave also did the stables at The Coppice, Henley (RA, 1902), and Ewelme Down, Ewelme, both in Oxfordshire; Aldenham Grange, Hertfordshire; and the Church of the Nativity, Watlington, Oxfordshire.

138 Cave's best-known building is Burberry's, in the Haymarket, SW1 (1912), with its octagonal oak-panelled lift and staircase, still maintained in pristine condition. Less successful was his 1909 addition to T. E. Collcutt's Bechstein Hall (now Wigmore Hall), Wigmore Street, W1, where Cave's addition with its crude colour and coarse detailing emphasises the colour and delicacy of Collcutt's earlier 'Prince of Wales' style. Cave was a member of the Art Workers' Guild.

Walter Cave's other works include:

1901-3	Coleherne Court Mansion Flats, Old Brompton Road and Redcliffe Gardens, SW5, on the site of Coleherne House
	Studios, Bolton Gardens, SW5 (*Bldr*, 6.2.04)
1905	Reconstruction of 135 New Bond Street, W1, into the Aeolian Hall for the Orchestrelle Company, for the demonstration of their player piano
	Reconstruction of Chappell's Galleries, New Bond Street, W1 (destroyed by fire and rebuilt in the 1950s)
1907	Union Jack Hostel, Waterloo Road, SE1 (demolished and rebuilt)
1909	Somerville College, Oxford (additions)
	The Dock House, Beaulieu, and Rochecourt, Fareham, Hampshire

Obit. RIBAJ, Jan., 1939, pp. 362, 459, 558 and 669
Bldr, 13.1.39, p. 166.

CHALMERS, Peter Macgregor, LLD, FSA
1859–1922

P. M. Chalmers, who was a pupil of John Honeyman, did a number of churches in the Romanesque style. His rebuilding of the nave of Iona Cathedral, Mull, Argyllshire, was much criticised at the time as over-thorough. His most original building was the Neptune Building, Argyle Street, Anderston, Glasgow (1905; demolished 1966). Also in Glasgow, Chalmers did St Margaret's Church and Manse, Polmadie Road (1902), and Dennistoun Parish Church (1906).

Obit. RIBAJ, 20.5.22, p. 440 *Bldr*, 24.3.22, p. 436.

CHAMPNEYS, Basil   1842–1935

Basil Champneys was born in Whitechapel, the fourth son of the Rev. William W. Champneys, rector of St Mary's, Whitechapel, and afterwards vicar of St Pancras and Dean of Lichfield. Champneys was educated at Charterhouse and Trinity College, Cambridge. He served articles with John Prichard of Llandaff (1818–86), former partner of the church architect, J. P. Seddon, and began practice in 1867. He did an early London Board school at Harwood Road, SW6 in 1873 (now demolished).

140   Champneys's most outstanding work is the John Rylands Library, Manchester (1890–1905), an important nineteenth-century secular neo-Gothic building which he was invited to do after Mrs Rylands admired his work at Mansfield College, Oxford (1887–90).

Champneys was a surveyor to St Mary, Manchester (designated a cathedral in 1947), to which he added a west porch and vestries (1898) and a large south annexe (1902–3). The Manchester Church of the Holy Trinity in Blackley (1908) is also his work.

Champneys did a great deal of work in Oxford and Cambridge in schools, churches and colleges. Early works in Oxford were St Ebbe's School, Friar Street (demolished), and additions to the Infants' School in Paradise Square. He carried out the removal of St Peter-le-Bailey to a new site in the Castle grounds (1872–4) and he was engaged on the first extension to Lady Margaret Hall (1881–3). Champneys also did the Indian Institute at Oxford, combining Early English Renaissance with Indian detail (1883–96). His later college work there included the Rhodes Building at Oriel College (1908–11), the Library at Somerville College (1903), the St Albans Quadrangle of Merton College (1904–10) and the Warden's Lodging at Merton (now incorporated in the Science and Law Libraries).

At Cambridge Champneys did Newnham College, the work for which he is best known, begun with Old Hall in 1874–5, followed by the Pfeiffer Building in 1893, the Yates Thompson Building in 1897, the Kennedy Buildings in 1906 and Peile Hall in 1910. Earlier work had included the Divinity and Literary Schools (1879) and the Museum of Classical Archaeology (1883).

139   In London Champneys did the first buildings for Bedford College, Regents Park, when the college moved from Bedford to London in 1910. The later (1913) additions are by S. R. J. 'Tate Gallery' Smith (1858–1913) and those of 1927–31 by Maxwell Ayrton. With their warm red brick and white woodwork, an appropriate setting for tennis, croquet and tea on the lawn, Champneys's ladies' colleges recall lines from 'The Cathedral Close' by his friend Coventry Patmore:

> Red-brick and ashlar, long and low,
> With dormers and with oriels lit.
> Geranium, lychnis, rose array'd
> The windows, all wide open thrown;
> And someone in the Study play'd
> The Wedding-March of Mendelssohn.

Basil Champneys: the first buildings of Bedford College, Regents Park, London NW1. Additions by S. R. J. Smith.

Basil Champneys: the John Rylands Library, Manchester.

▽ Basil Champneys: Hall Oak, his own house off Frognal Lane, Hampstead, London NW3.

Champneys's first church was in his father's parish in London — St Luke's church and vicarage, Oseney Crescent, Kentish Town (1867–70). Later he did St Luke, Kidderpore Avenue, NW3 (1898) and the chapel at Mill Hill School (1896). Other Champneys churches include St John, the parish church of Havering-atte-Bower, Essex, where he did the rebuilding of 1878; the Sailors' Church of St Mary Star of the Sea, for Coventry Patmore, at Hastings in Sussex (1882); and St Chad, Slindon, Staffordshire (1894). A later church building by him was SS Andrew and Michael, Dreadnought Street, Tunnel Avenue, North Greenwich, SE10 (1900–2).

147

39

Champneys's domestic work is equally sunny and warm, in red carved brick, set off by white-painted woodwork with cheerful balconies and chimneys — like those of his own house, Hall Oak, in Frognal, Hampstead, NW3 (1881) with its cluster of four chimney stacks at the centre, each with *four* dwarf Ionic pilasters in brick. His houses included Haileybury, Branksome Park, Poole (Dorset), built as a boys' preparatory school in 1878 but

140

recently demolished. He did three houses in Surrey — Moxley, at Holmbury St Mary (1888; demolished), Clandon Regis, West Clandon (c. 1890), and Banacle Ridge, Witley (1893).

His schools included the Bedford High School for Girls (1878—82) and the King Edward VII Grammar School at King's Lynn, Norfolk (*Bldr*, 17.11.06). At Harrow, he did the Butler Museum (1886).

Champneys wrote poetry and also published *A Quiet Corner of England* (1875); *Henry Merritt: Art Criticism and Romance* (1879); and *Memoirs and Correspondence of Coventry Patmore* (1915). He wrote the introduction to *Poems of Coventry Patmore* (1915). Champneys was a member of the Art Workers' Guild and was awarded the Royal Gold Medal for Architecture in 1912. His son, Amian L. Champneys, was the architect of a charming bijou house, truly Edwardian in character, No. 102 Frognal, NW3, and some houses in Grange Road, Cambridge.

New International Year Book, 1935, p. 493

Obit. RIBAJ, 27.4.35, p. 737 *Bldr*, 12.4.35, p. 682.

CHANCELLOR, Frederick Wykeham 1865—1945

F. W. Chancellor went to Pembroke College, Oxford. He was articled to his father and in partnership with him (1893—1918). They did All Saints, Goodmayes, Essex, and parsonages and private houses in Essex and elsewhere. They were Diocesan Surveyors to the diocese of Chelmsford and repaired numerous churches, as well as Leigh Priory and Layer Marney Towers. They did schools at Burnham-on-Crouch, Braintree and Chelmsford, and Blundell's School Chapel, Tiverton, Devon. The firm continues as Chancellor, Simpson and Bragg at 19 Duke Street, Chelmsford.

Obit. RIBAJ, Feb., 1946, p. 143 *Bldr*, 4.1.46, p. 4.

CHARLES, Ethel Mary 1871—1932

Ethel Charles was the first woman Associate of the RIBA, elected in 1898. She was Institute Medallist in 1905, became a pupil of George and Peto in 1892 and also worked for Walter Cave in 1896. Ethel Charles did numerous houses, practising at Falmouth, London and Letchworth, where she did a cottage for the Cheap Cottages Exhibition of 1905. Her sister Bessie Charles was also an architect and was elected an associate in 1900. She worked in partnership with her sister on houses in Falmouth, and died in 1932.

CHARLEWOOD, Henry Clement 1856—1943

H. C. Charlewood was the son of the Rev. Thomas Charlewood. He was articled to J. S. Crowther of Manchester. He joined his brother-in-law, William Searle Hicks (1849—1902), Diocesan Surveyor to the Newcastle Diocese, becoming a partner in 1888. The practice was carried on by Hicks's son, Henry Leicester Hicks, from 1916, and by Charlewood's son, George Charlewood, from 1920.

Hicks and Charlewood were mainly engaged on churches in Yorkshire, among which were St Leonard, Welbury (1887); St Margaret, Brotton (1888—91); All Saints, Easington, N. Riding (1888—9); St Paul, Aldbrough, N. Riding (nave and chancel 1890—7); and St James, Dalton (1897—8).

Their other works included:

1899	St Helen, Carlin How, N. Riding
1901	All Saints, Deighton, N. Riding (restoration)
	St Oswald, West Hartlepool, Durham
	St Chad, Bensham, Gateshead, Durham
	St Aidan, Boosbeck, N. Riding
	St Matthew, Grangetown, N. Riding
1901-4	St Luke, Thornaby, N. Riding

Obit. RIBAJ, Nov., 1943, p. 17.

CHATWIN, Philip Boughton b. 1873

P. B. Chatwin was the son of Julius A. Chatwin (1830—1907), a Birmingham architect. He was articled to his father and to E. W. Mountford and joined his father in partnership in 1897. They were surveyors to St Philip's Cathedral, Birmingham, and did St Peter, Grove Lane and All Souls, Wenlock Road, Witton (both 1907). They also did the reconstruction of the nave and aisles of St Mary, Moseley (damaged 1940 and rebuilt 1952—4). The Chatwins' work included Lloyds Banks in High Street, Leicester (1903—6) and at Five Ways, Edgbaston (1908—9). The firm is continued by P. B. Chatwin's nephew, A. B. Chatwin.

CHESTERTON, Frank Sidney 1876—1916

Like the poet and writer G. K. Chesterton, Frank Chesterton was a member of the family of Kensington property owners and surveyors of that name. Frank Chesterton's work consisted of business premises, flats and houses in Kensington and on the Norbury Manor Estate, SW16 (RA, 1904). He carried out some joint work with John Duke Coleridge (1879—1934) of 10 Davies Street, W1, a former pupil of Walter Cave and Edwin Lutyens, and they did a terrace of houses on the east side of Hornton Street, W8 (RA, 1904; *AR*, 1905), which provided relief from 'the dreary South Kensington order'. Their Hornton Court in Kensington High Street, W8 (*Bldr*, 1.11.05 and 23.3.06; RA, 1906) was, on the other hand, much too large even for the High Street. It set the scale which was to turn this thoroughfare into a rival of Oxford Street. Much smaller was 13 Kensington High Street for Evans the butcher (*Bldr*, 2.7.10). Frank Chesterton also did Findon Place, Sussex, and Codicote Lodge, Hertfordshire. He died of wounds in the First World War.

Perks, Sydney, *Flats*, London, 1907

Sparrow, W. Shaw, *Flats, Urban Houses and Cottage Homes*, London, 1907

Obit. Bldr, 15.12.16, p. 375.

CLAPHAM, Frederick Dare   1873—1914

F. Dare Clapham was the son of Douglas Clapham of Broxbourne, Hertfordshire. After a 'trial' period with Norman Shaw, he became a pupil of E. J. May. He then joined E. W. Mountford as an assistant, becoming his chief assistant and then his partner in 1907, a year before Mountford's death. Clapham completed Mountford's buildings, adding the Court House, police headquarters, and fire brigade station to Mountford's Lancaster Town Hall (1909—10). He also completed the Northern Assurance Building, 1 Moorgate, EC2, and made additions to Battersea Polytechnic, SW11.

With Alfred Cox, Clapham designed the Public Library at Kingston-upon-Thames. He entered into partnership with B. H. B. Symons-Jeune, but died as a result of an accident when only forty-one.

CLARK, H. Fuller   *floruit c.* 1910

Examples of the work of H. Fuller Clark are rare and of special interest. Best known is his reconstruction of the ground floor of the Black Friar public house under the railway bridge at Blackfriars, EC4. This displays Art Nouveau tendencies, with Bavarian *Bierstein* overtones in the sculptures by Henry Poole. Other sculpture is by Charles Bradford.

Other works by Fuller Clark were done in conjunction with Percy Boulting of Boulting & Sons, the sanitary engineers, in the neighbourhood of the Middlesex Hospital, W1; these included 40 and 41a Foley Street, W1 (*Bldr*, 17.10.08), and Belmont House and Boulting & Sons' offices in Riding House Street (formerly Candover Street), W1, notable for the termination of the chimney stacks and parapets. The buildings are comparable in style to 10 Mortimer Street, W1, by W. T. Mynors Walker for Bratt Colbran.

Fuller Clark also did 75 Barry Street, Kingston, Jamaica, and Kildare, St Andrew, Jamaica (*ABJ*, 21.8.12).

143

CLARKE, John Daniel   1881—1947

J. D. Clarke received his architectural training in London in the office of the Crown Surveyor, Arthur Green, and in the Regent Street Polytechnic. With Septimus Warwick and Stanley C. Ramsey, he made early efforts to set up in private practice. A recorded work of this period is the flats illustrated by Sydney Perks (*Flats*, 1907). Poor health made Clarke leave for South Africa where he assisted Herbert Baker on Grey College and University, Bloemfontein. He returned to England in 1909, settled at Dann's Farm (later called Portsdown), Willingdon, Sussex, and began practice in Eastbourne with D. G. Tanner. He was principally engaged in designing new and restoring and enlarging old farms and cottages in Sussex and Kent, although his work occasionally took him further afield to the counties of Norfolk and Cornwall.

Like Ernest Willmott (Sloper), also back from Baker's office, John Clarke sometimes gave his English houses exotic reminders of South African days, such as an arcaded *stoep*, or a twin-arched window on a turned baluster mullion.

Although his health was far from strong, Clarke served in the Royal Naval Service in the First World War. His son David Clarke became a partner before the Second World War. The practice continues under David Clarke and Frederick Ernest Ford as John D. Clarke and Son.

J. D. Clarke's earliest houses were:

1910-12   Pytchley, Compton Place Road, Eastbourne

Thatched Cottage, Wannock, conversion of The Barn, Jevington, and Spotted Cow Farm, Buxted, all in Sussex

Obit. RIBAJ, Dec., 1947, p. 86   *Bldr*, 21.11.47, p. 578.

CLAUSEN, Sir George, RA   1852—1944

George Clausen was born in London, the second son of George Johnson Clausen, a Danish decorative artist. He went to St Mark's College, Chelsea, and in 1867 entered the drawing office of Messrs Trollope, the builders and decorators. He won a scholarship to the National Art Training School (later the Royal College of Art), South Kensington.

Clausen assisted the painter Edwin Long, RA, for whom he carried out historical research. His own particular interest lay in portraying the life of the agricultural labourer. Clausen studied in Paris under Bouguereau and Robert-Fleury, and Bastien-Lepage was an important influence on his work. Clausen was Professor of Painting at the Royal Academy Schools (1903–6), was made ARA in 1895 and RA in 1908 (diploma work, 'Interior of an Old Barn'). He was knighted in 1927; he was one of the 'Society of Twelve', and Master of the Art Workers' Guild in 1909.

H. Fuller Clark: premises in Riding House Street, London W1.

Apart from his easel painting, Clausen acquired considerable proficiency in the art of mural painting. He did lunettes at High Royd, Honley, W. Riding, and, when he was seventy-five, wall paintings in St Stephen's Hall in the House of Lords, Westminster.

A pen and ink self-portrait is in the National Portrait Gallery.

CLAY, Sir George Felix Neville, Bart, BA
1871–1941

Sir Felix Clay was the 5th Baronet, second son of Sir Arthur Temple Felix Clay, a barrister-at-law

and landscape and portrait painter. He went to Charterhouse and to Trinity College, Cambridge, was articled to Basil Champneys in 1893, and started practice in 1897. Clay was architect to the Board of Education (1904–27) and in 1928 became partner in the firm of Swan, Norman and Clay.

Clay wrote *Modern School Buildings* (Batsford, 1902, 1906 and 1929), *The Origin of the Sense of Beauty* (Smith, Elder, 1908), and an article on 'School Planning' in the *Teachers' Encyclopaedia* (1911), as well as numerous articles in the *Edinburgh Review* and other contemporary journals.

Obit. Bldr, 21.11.41, p. 469.

CLIFFORD, Henry Edward   d. 1932

Early in his career Henry Clifford was in partnership with William Landless. His church work is simple and sturdy, while his houses were considered worthy of inclusion in Muthesius's survey. The parish church of St James, Meiklerig Crescent, Pollokshields, was built by Clifford as Titwood Parish Church in 1893 and re-erected on its present site in 1953—4. Clifford won the competition for the Glasgow Royal Infirmary in 1901 (*Bldr*, 2.2.01), but the directors did not keep to the assessors' decision and gave the work to James Miller (*q.v.*). He designed the City Hall, Perth, in 1909.

Clifford's work in the Glasgow area includes:

1901	Stoneleigh House, Kelvinside	
	64—66 Cadogan Street, Blythswood	
1902	Newlands South Church (and hall in 1899)	
	St Michael's Parish Church, Carntyne	
	398 Albert Drive, Pollokshields	
	17—57 Fotheringhay Road, Crossmyloof	
1903	37 Dalziel Drive, Pollokshields	
1910	Education Offices, Bath Street, Blythswood	

H. E. Clifford: Newlands South Church, Glasgow.

COLLCUTT, Thomas Edward   1840—1924

T. E. Collcutt was born at Oxford, attended the Oxford Diocesan School at Cowley and then went to Mill Hill School. He was articled in London to R. W. Armstrong and worked in the office of Mills and Murgatroyd. Collcutt also worked for a time in the office of the great church architect, G. E. Street. In 1867 he entered the office of P. C. Lockwood, the Borough Engineer at Brighton, where he worked on the conversion of the Stables of the Royal Pavilion into the Assembly Rooms (now the Dome).

In 1872, while in partnership with H. Woodzell,

Collcutt won his first competition — the Public Library and Museum, Blackburn, Lancashire (enlarged in 1893). In 1877 he won the competition for the Town Hall in Wakefield. Street was the assessor and Collcutt wisely submitted a Gothic design, but the reaction against Gothic had set in and, in conformity with the change of taste, Collcutt changed his design to a free Tudor style leaning towards Early French Renaissance.

Collcutt firmly established his distinctive interpretation of this hybrid style when he won the limited competition for the Imperial Institute, South Kensington, SW7, in 1886. His competitors were Rowand Anderson, Arthur Blomfield, Thomas Graham Jackson and Aston Webb with Ingress Bell. The Prince of Wales suggested the building, to commemorate the Golden Jubilee of Queen Victoria, almost as if in response to the Poet Laureate Tennyson's exhortation to

> Raise a stately memorial
> Some Imperial Institute
> Rich in symbol and ornament
> Which may speak to the centuries
> 'On the Jubilee of Queen Victoria'

It was envisaged as a place where member countries of the British Empire could hold conferences and organise exhibitions of their produce and manufacture. But while costs rose, contributions from the Indian and colonial governments fell and, offended by the indifference of the home government, the Prince of Wales lost interest.

Collcutt is said to have refused to reduce the height of the principal tower to economise — a bold stand to take for which we have reason to be grateful today. But Collcutt's splendid building did not have long to 'speak to the centuries', for six years after the royal opening in 1893, part of it was taken over by the University of London and in 1946 the whole building passed to the Ministry of Education, which demolished it. But for public protest the Ministry would have demolished the tower as well. Now a solitary reminder of Tennyson's unfulfilled prophecy, Collcutt's beautiful tower continues to preside over South Kensington, flanked by the remaining pair of its four lodges and its pair of lions couchant, their rumps and tails now, incredibly, lying on the pavement.

Although Collcutt did not do another government building he had many opportunities to employ his genius at providing those comfortable and kindly buildings which to this day are associated with the spirit of that age. In 1890 he did the Bechstein Hall (now Wigmore Hall), 40 Wigmore Street, W1. His beautiful pale terracotta gabled front and Early French Renaissance detail reveal by contrast the deterioration in the colour and detailing of terracotta work by the time Walter Cave extended the frontage of the Hall to Nos 36 and 38 in 1909.

Also in 1890, on the gentle curve of the widened Ludgate Hill, EC4 (formerly Ludgate Street),

T. E. Collcutt: the Savoy Hotel, London WC2. The Strand
entrance. The style of the Plaza Hotel, New York, derived
from this. The figure of Count Peter of Savoy is by
Lynn-Jenkins. The steel casing of Collcutt's faience
arch is totally inappropriate.

Collcutt did 45 and 47, a branch of the City of London (later Joint City and Midland, now Midland) Bank. Its pale pink terracotta on a silver-grey granite base still provides, with St Martin's, Ludgate, a sympathetic foil to St Paul's Cathedral.

An earlier terracotta façade by Collcutt is at 175—181 Oxford Street, W1 (formerly 359, 358 and 357). It fronts a building formerly shared by Joseph Duveen, the fine art dealer, and W. P. and G. Phillips's China and Glass Emporium, later purchased by Samuel Waring as his first foothold in London. Only the eastern half of the building survives (No. 181) and that has been painted over — a fate shared by other terracotta buildings, including the once familiar pink Coliseum Theatre.

Collcutt designed the P & O Pavilion at the Exposition Universelle, Paris, 1900, and along the P & O route he did the Reina Christina Hotel, Algeciras, for Lord Faringdon's company, and the Galle Face Hotel, Colombo (both 1912). Collcutt's earliest ship interiors for the P & O company were music saloons on the *India* and *China* (1896), and on the *Egypt* and *Arabia* (1897).

Other works by him included extensions in Hanway Street to the Restaurant Frascati, 26 Oxford Street, W1 (1893; now in other use), and an additional storey to the Athenaeum Club, Waterloo Place, SW1 (1899, to an 1828 building by Decimus Burton). His domestic work included Oakdene, 105 Christchurch Road, East Sheen, Surrey (1884), Winchfield Lodge, Hampshire (1885), work at Warwick Castle for Lord Brooke, and houses at Goldhawk Road and Ravenscourt Park, West London, and East Grinstead in Sussex.

Collcutt designed the Wadia monument in Brookwood Cemetery, Surrey (*Bldr*, 6.7.01), based on an illustration in Perrot and Chipiez, *History of Persian Art.*

Collcutt's own office, 36 Bloomsbury Square, a gabled red-brick house which rudely interrupted the classical lines of the square, was demolished in the 1920s to make way for the Liverpool Victoria Building Society's building by Charles Long.

At the Imperial Institute only the small hall had been built, but Collcutt was given another opportunity to do a building of this kind when he added the King's Hall to the Holborn Restaurant in 1894. The Restaurant, together with its famous Long Bar by Archer and Green, was swept away with Collcutt's great hall in the 1950s to make way for an undistinguished office building.

Collcutt's association with Richard D'Oyly Carte began when he was asked to give architectural shape to a plan for a new English Opera House which the success of the Gilbert and Sullivan operas had encouraged D'Oyly Carte to build (1889—93). The venture failed and the theatre became the Palace Theatre of Varieties. D'Oyly Carte was building the first (Victoria Embankment) block of his Savoy Hotel at the same time and

145

T. E. Collcutt and Stanley Hamp: the River Front of the Savoy Hotel. This was extended forwards and raised in 1910. Remaining at the side are the original balconies of 1888, probably by A. H. Mackmurdo.

Collcutt was called in to make improvements soon after its completion. These were followed by the Savoy extension in the Strand, then the west block of the hotel (offices), both in 1905, and finally the extension to the Embankment block in 1910, on all of which Collcutt was engaged. (*Bldr*, 10.9.10. pp. 291—3; *and see under* Hotels.)

60
146

Collcutt's building for Lloyd's Registry of Shipping in Fenchurch Street (*Bldr*, 22.9.1900 and 31.8.01) echoes Belcher and Beresford Pite's Chartered Accountants' building of ten years earlier, but here the freshness of that unique example is not sustained — it was not Collcutt's true style. The sculpture is by Sir George Frampton and Frank Lynn Jenkins; paintings are by Sir Frank Brangwyn and Gerald Moira.

The relaxed manner of Collcutt's ship interiors is reflected both in his houses (*Bldr*, 5.10.07), including his own, The Croft, Totteridge, Hertfordshire, West Lodge and The Lynch House, Totteridge (1904), and in the additions and boarders' houses he designed for his old school, Mill Hill, and for Eton. At Eton he did Waynflete and Westbury (1899—1900), Wootton (1903) and Walpole (1906); at Mill Hill he did classrooms, the Murray Scriptorium, the library and tuck shop, Ridgeway House, and Collinson House. He also did a boarders' house at the South-Eastern Agricultural College, Wye, Kent.

147

147

In 1902 Collcutt was awarded the Royal Gold Medal for Architecture. His partner, Stanley Hinge Hamp, introduced a quite extraordinary exuberance into the firm's work, as can be seen at Thames House, Queen Street, EC4 (built in 1912). The firm of Collcutt and Hamp was continued under Stanley Hamp's son-in-law, Alexander P. Moira, the son of Professor Gerald Moira. The partners are now M. C. Holyer and M. J. O'Leary. Collcutt's younger son, Philip Martin Blake Collcutt, was killed in action in 1917. His nephew, Bertie H. Collcutt (d. 1938), practised as an architect in Buenos Aires. His daughter, Grace Marion Collcutt, a landscape painter, has works at the Brighton and Eastbourne Art Galleries.

Collcutt's other works include:

1901   Façade of Collinson & Lock (successors to Jackson & Graham), Fleet Street, EC4 (the firm of decorators which bought up Gillow's of Lancaster and was in turn bought up by S. J. Waring to form Waring & Gillow)

1902   Burlington Hotel, Boscombe, Hampshire (now flats)

1903   Parts of the P & O liners *Moldavia* and *Mongolia* (*Bldr*, 28.6.02) and public rooms on the *Marmora*

1904   Gloucester House, Piccadilly and Park Lane (flats and a motor showroom on the site of the house of the Duke of Gloucester where the Elgin marbles were first stored). Collcutt and Hamp's tall, gabled, green and white striped faience building disrupted the skyline around Hyde Park Corner

           John Lewis's Store, Oxford Street, W1 (destroyed in the Second World War and rebuilt to another design)

           Public rooms on the P & O liner *Macedonia*

T. E. Collcutt and Stanley Hamp: the library, tuck shop and Murray Scriptorium at Mill Hill School, London NW7. At the right is the chapel by Basil Champneys, at the left the music school by M. S. Briggs.

1908   Parts of the P & O liners *Morea* and *Salsette*

1910   The Moorings, Sunningdale, Berkshire

1911   Royal suite on board the SS *Medina* for the Delhi Durbar

1912   University Hotel, Endsleigh Gardens, WC1, later the Hospital and School for Tropical Diseases of the Seamen's Hospital Society (now the nurses' residence of University College Hospital)

Obit. RIBAJ, Nov., 1924, pp. 666–8 *Bldr*, 17.10.24, pp. 582, 587 and 594.

T. E. Collcutt: a house at Totteridge Green, Herts.

COLTON, William Robert, RA 1867–1921

W. R. Colton was born in Paris and came to England when he was three years old. He studied at Lambeth School of Art and the South Kensington Schools and entered the Royal Academy Schools in 1889. He was Professor of Sculpture at the Royal Academy (1907–11).

Public monuments by Colton include the Mermaid Fountain in the East Carriage Drive, Hyde Park, W1 1896); Edward VII at Basil Champneys's King Edward VII School, King's Lynn, Norfolk (*Bldr*, 24.11.06); and the Royal Artillery Memorial for the South African War in the Mall, St James's Park, SW1 (*Bldr*, 30.7.10). Colton received many commissions from abroad, including one for a portrait bust of the Maharajah of Mysore. He became ARA in 1903, RA in 1919 (diploma work, 'The Young Diana').

Obit. Bldr, 18.11.21, p. 668.

COMPER, Sir John Ninian 1864–1960

Ninian Comper was born in Aberdeen. His father, the Rev. John Comper, a High Churchman, was at that time rector of St John's, Crown Street, and from 1867 rector of St Margaret's, Gallowgate, Aberdeen, where Ninian Comper did his first work, the vaulted west chapel, in 1889; in the same year he did the chapel for the Community of St Margaret in the Spital. Comper was educated at Glenalmond Academy, Perthshire, and after drawing for a term at Ruskin's School at Oxford, he spent a year between the South Kensington Schools and the stained glass works of C. E. Kempe. He was articled to Bodley and Garner, the church architects, and like Bodley he developed a sceptical view of conventional architectural education and qualification by examination, and took an equally independent attitude with diocesan boards.

Comper's most notable early work is to be found at the village church at Cantley, near Doncaster, where he first attempted to re-create the typical English altar of pre-Reformation times (1893). Even Bodley designed the altar as a narrow shelf backed up by shelves for vases of flowers, but Comper now returned to the altar table or altar slab and designed from the altar outwards, declaring 'To the Altar every proportion and detail, every refraction of light, every embellishment [must be] subordinated'. The next year (1894) Comper did the 'English Altar' in the Lady Chapel at Downside Abbey, near Bath.

Comper's work falls into two periods and categories. At first he designed in the fourteenth-century style of Bodley, with every detail completely in period, which he called 'unity by exclusion'. After 1906 Comper included renaissance details in his church furnishings, as had been done after the fifteenth century; this he called 'unity by inclusion'.

Of his more important work before 1900 Comper did the crypt chapel of St Sepulchre at St Mary Magdalene's, Woodchester Street, W2 (1895); the College Chapel, Burgh, Lincolnshire (1895); the Workhouse Chapel, Oundle, Northamptonshire (1896); St Margaret, Braemar, Aberdeenshire, St Barnabas, Little Ilford, Essex, the Chapel of the Holy Name Convent, Malvern Link, Worcestershire, all in 1898; and the unfinished New Hinksey Church, Oxford, in 1899.

Comper's more important work from 1900 included:

1900	St George, Mexborough, W. Riding
	Chancel and Lady Chapel decorations, St Barnabas, St Barnabas Street, Pimlico, SW1
1902	Hearse and funeral trappings for *Requiem* for Queen Victoria at St Matthew, Great Peter Street, Westminster, and subsequently for Edward VII and Queen Alexandra at All Saints, Margaret Street, W1
1903	St Mary, Kirriemuir, Angus
149	St Cyprian, Glentworth Street, Clarence Gate, NW1
	Church at Yerendawana, near Poona, India
	Half-timber church of St Gilbert and St Hugh, Gosberton, Lincolnshire
1906	Chapel at St John's Hospital, Cowley St John, Oxford, for the All Saints' Sisters
	Additions to the nave of Holy Trinity Church, Southchurch, Essex
1907	Extensive restorations at East Meon Church, Petersfield, Hampshire
	Restorations, new screen and altar, etc., at Melton Church, Suffolk
1908	Font cover, St Alban, Brooke Street, Holborn, EC1

149 St Cyprian, Clarence Gate, the first church designed in every detail by Comper, has been described by the Rev. Canon Basil Clarke as 'the last development of a purely English Parish Church and an expression of the best in Anglo Catholicism in the reign of Edward VII'. At the consecration the floor was strewn with rushes.

In the furnishing of his beautiful church of St Mary, Wellingborough, Northamptonshire, designed in 1904 and not completed until forty years later, Comper introduced his 'unity by inclusion', a principle which guided him in his subsequent work. *Among Comper's other important works up to 1914 showing this tendency are:*

1907	Chapel for the Community of St Mary, Wantage, rebuilt at Horne, Surrey, in 1931
1910	Wimborne St Giles, Dorset. 18th-cent. church rebuilt after fire and refurnished
1911	St Mary, Rochdale, Lancashire, in which parts of the 18th-cent. church are incorporated
	St Michael, Newquay, Cornwall
	Panelling and glass in the Hall of Oriel College, Oxford; new altar and panelling at Merton College

Sir Ninian Comper: the interior of St. Cyprian, Clarence
Gate, London NW1.

	New chancel roof, organ loft and choir stalls at Mundford Church, Norfolk
	Chancel screen and organ loft in St Ethelburga, Bishopsgate, London
1912	New high altar, screen and Lady altar in the Grosvenor Chapel, Mayfair, London
1913	Sprotbrough Church, Doncaster, Yorkshire (complete restoration of eastern portion from surviving masonry in rectory garden)
	Altar screen in Wymondham Church, Norfolk (decorated in 1934)
	Chapel of St Helena's Home of the Wantage Sisters at Drayton Green, Ealing, W13
	The Heritage Craft Schools' Chapel, Chailey, Sussex
1914	Altar, rood-screen, font cover, and organ in Lound Church, near Lowestoft, Suffolk

One of the most splendid works of Comper is the unfinished chapel of 1927 at All Saints' Convent, London Colney, Hertfordshire (now the Pastoral Centre; *see under* Stokes, Leonard). An unexpectedly classical work was the Welsh National War Memorial (South African War) as part of the monumental civic centre at Cathays Park, Cardiff (1909); sculpture by Albert Toft (*q.v.*).

Comper's stained glass is at Downside Abbey, Somerset, and in the Chapel of St George (the Warriors' Chapel), Westminster Abbey and in Westminster Hall. He also did the windows in the north aisle, the altar frontals and vestments and the magnificent Royal Window at Canterbury Cathedral — designed in 1953 in his ninetieth year.

Comper was knighted in 1950. His *Of the Christian Altar and the Buildings which Contain It* was published the same year (SPCK). Comper's first partner was his brother-in-law William Bucknall, also a Bodley man, whose nephew Arthur Bucknall succeeded him as partner. Comper was succeeded by his own son, John Sebastian Comper.

AR, Feb.,1939, article by John Betjeman

Pax, the Benedictine Magazine, 1937 and 1950, articles on Comper by Peter F. Anson

Obit. RIBAJ, Feb., 1961, p. 145.

CONDER, Charles,   1868—1909

Charles Conder was born in London, the son of James Conder, a civil engineer and a direct descendant of the sculptor Roubiliac. His mother died early and he was taken to India as a small child, returning at the age of nine to attend Eastbourne College, Sussex. At the age of seventeen he went to Australia to join an uncle in the Lands Department in Sydney where he was engaged on a trigonometric survey, but, showing more aptitude for drawing than for surveying, he obtained a post on the *Illustrated Sydney News*. Two years later he moved to Melbourne and studied at the National Gallery while teaching painting under Arthur Stretton.

In 1890 Conder returned to Europe and studied in Paris at Julien's and Cormon's Ateliers and at the Louvre under Constant and Doucet. Conder's art was influenced by Toulouse-Lautrec, Daumier and Anquétin, and he was an admirer of Puvis de Chavannes. A joint exhibition of his work with William Rothenstein's was held at Galerie Thomas, 43 rue des Malherbes. But life in Paris took its toll of Conder and he went to live with the family of the Norwegian painter Fritz von Thaulow, at the Villa des Orchidées, Dieppe, where he was nursed back to health. Von Thaulow's introduction to Samuel Bing, dealer in Japanese works of art at his shop, 'La Maison de l'Art Nouveau' in Paris, led to Conder's exhibiting painted silk panels in London at the Grafton and Carfax galleries and at Bing's exhibition at the Paris Exposition of 1900. Conder was elected an Associate of the Societé National des Beaux-Arts and in 1891 became a member of the New English Art Club.

Back in England Conder continued to paint in water-colours on silk, usually in the form of decorative fans. In 1901 he married and settled in 91 Cheyne Walk, taking a studio at Glebe Place, Chelsea, SW3. In 1904 he joined the 'Society of Twelve' whose members included Muirhead Bone, George Clausen, Alphonse Légros, William Rothenstein, Charles Ricketts and Lucien Pissarro.

For Sir Edmund Davis, the South African diamond merchant, Conder decorated two rooms with painted silk panels at 9 and 11 Lansdowne Road, W11, converted from two houses by the architect William Flockhart. The panels are now lost and have been replaced by copies. Shortly before his death, Conder moved to Bramerton Street, SW3. Three portraits (one a self-portrait) are in the National Portrait Gallery.

AJ, Mar., 1909, article by J. Meiergraefe

Battersby, Martin, *The World of Art Nouveau*, London, 1968

Burlington Magazine, May 1909. Article by Charles Ricketts.

Studio, 1898, article by D. S. McColl

L'Art Français, Paris, 1896

Rothenstein, John, *The Life and Death of Charles Conder*, London, 1938

COOKSEY, Arthur William   1865—1922

A. W. Cooksey was born in London, the son of a hat manufacturer. He was educated at University College School and at University College, London, was articled to E. M. Whitaker in 1884 and was assistant, first to Henry Florence, then to E. W. Mountford.

In 1893 Cooksey commenced practice on his own account, at first in partnership with Alfred Cox at 19 Craven Street, Strand, WC2, until 1900, then alone at Adam Street, Adelphi, WC2. Cooksey won several competitions and in 1898 was invited

to take part in a limited competition for the Sir
48 John Cass Foundation Technical Institute, Jewry
151 Street, Aldgate, EC3, which he carried out in red
brick with stone dressings in a neo-Baroque style.
(The lead statue of Sir John Cass, by Roubiliac,
came from the old site.) Cooksey also did the
North East London Institute, Hackney Downs,
E8 (*BN*, 20.9.01), the Science Building at the
Northern Polytechnic, Holloway, N7, and the
Science Building at the Foundation Schools,
Whitechapel, E1.

In 1910 Cooksey did the Sir John Cass School,
Dukes Place and Mitre Street, EC3, in his favourite
'Wrenaissance' style; the Governors' Board Room
contains a moulded plaster ceiling, a chimney
piece and panelling painted with exotic tropical
scenes by R. Robinson (1696) from 32 Botolph
Lane, EC3. The carved oak staircase from the same
house was incorporated into a house in Essex
designed by Cooksey.

During the First World War Cooksey was the
London representative in the work of assisting
escape from German-occupied Belgium and was
awarded the Belgian Ordre de la Couronne, avec
Palmes. He designed the War Memorial at Leigh,
Tonbridge, Kent. Cooksey also carried out a number of houses in the Home Counties. His practice
has been continued by his son, R. A. Cooksey,
and his grandson, Arthur Cooksey, as Arthur
Cooksey and Associates.

Obit. RIBAJ, 17.6.22, p. 510 *Bldr*, 19.5.22, p. 725.

**Arthur Cooksey: the Sir John Cass Institute, Jewry Street,
London EC3.**

COOPER, C. J. Harold   1863—1909

C. J. Harold Cooper was the architect of three
houses in the Arts and Crafts style, 15 and 16
Stratton Street, W1 (*Bldr*, 19.4.02) were for a Capt.
H. A. Johnstone. Before the demolition of Devon-
shire House, Stratton Street was a quiet cul-de-sac
facing the garden wall of that mansion. Cooper
was a member of the Art Workers' Guild, and at 1a
Palace Gate, Kensington Road, W8 for W. A.
Johnstone, he enlisted all the arts connected with
building. Much of the work, preserved to this day,
provides an interesting record of the period.
Among those who contributed were Thomas
Stirling Lee, W. S. Frith, F. W. Pomeroy and
A. G. Walker.

Cooper also did the decoration and furnishing of
the steam yacht *Normania*, a bungalow at Selsey
Bill, Sussex, for S. H. Day, and the stud farm and
farm cottages at Shenley, Hertfordshire (*Bldr*,
26.12.03).

Survey of London, Vol. XXXVIII, pp. 39—41
Obit. Bldr, 27.3.09, p. 381.

COOPER, Sir Thomas Edwin, RA   1873—1942

Edwin Cooper came from Scarborough, the eldest
child of Samuel Cooper, a carriage proprietor. His
father died when he was a child. Aware of her son's
talent, his mother had him articled to an architect
in Yorkshire. After travelling abroad Cooper
became an assistant in the offices of several London
architects, including that of Goldie, Child and
Goldie.

Cooper was articled to and entered into partnership with J. Hall and Herbert Davis, winning the
competition for Scarborough Technical Schools
(*Bldr*, 8.6.01). Around the turn of the century
Cooper joined in partnership with Samuel
Bridgman Russell, who had already achieved
success in competitions jointly with his first
partner J. G. S. Gibson — partnerships were
rapidly formed and re-formed to combine talent
for the many competitions being held in the
period. When the new pair, Russell and Cooper,
entered the lists their victories were many. They
152 included the Guildhall and Law Courts, Hull (*Bldr*,
11.7.03 and 26.10.07; sculpture by Albert
Hodge), the Girls' Grammar School, Saltburn,
Yorkshire (also 1903), the Royal Grammar School,
Newcastle upon Tyne (1904; *Bldr*, 23.7.04) and
the Rochester Technical Institute (*Bldr*, 20.1.06).
1910 brought them three competition wins:
Middlesbrough Public Library; Burslem Public
Buildings, Staffordshire; and Watford Boys'
Grammar School, Hertfordshire. They also
reached the final stage of the London County Hall
competition. Such successes were never a guarantee
to a lasting partnership, however, and Russell left
in 1912.

Cooper carried on alone and his successes continued. His first win alone was St Marylebone Town Hall, Marylebone Road, NW1 (1911), which established him in London. His next competition win, the monumental headquarters of the Port of London Authority, Trinity Square, EC3, was not completed until after the First World War, when many more large commissions came to Cooper, principally in the London area. These included the Star and Garter Home, Richmond, Surrey (1921–4); the College of Nursing, Henrietta Street, W1, and the Port of London Buildings, Tilbury Dock (both 1922–6); the Banque Belge, Bishopsgate, EC2; and Lloyds Underwriters, Leadenhall Street, EC3.

As early as the 1900s Cooper had heralded the style of the reign of King George V — greater correctness with diminished vitality. But, as in the case of Vincent Harris, the power of his personal style compensated for the loss of vigour which characterised the period.

Cooper was knighted in 1923, made ARA in 1930, in 1931 received the Gold Medal for Architecture and was made RA in 1937 (diploma work 'The Head Buildings of the Port of London Authority, Trinity Square, EC3'). He was a member of the Art Workers' Guild.

Obit. RIBAJ, July, 1942, p. 154 *Bldr*, 3.7.42, p. 3.

Sir Edwin Cooper, RA: the Guildhall, Hull. The sculpture is by Albert Hodge.

Sir Edwin Cooper, RA: the main entrance to the Guildhall, Hull.

COWLISHAW, William Harrison   1869–1957

W. H. Cowlishaw was articled to Stockdale Harrison of Leicester and to Balfour and Turner in London. He had a craftsman's outlook and his approach to building was somewhat mystical. He married Lucy Garnett, sister of the scholar Edward Garnett, and his first work was a house for Garnett, The Cearne, Kent Hatch, Crockham Hill, Kent (1896). Edward Garnett's son David, in *The Golden Echo*, had this to say of Cowlishaw's work on the house:

> Harrison Cowlishaw ... was a disciple of William Morris with a love of the mediaeval. The first plan was for a great hall open to the roof, with a solar chamber on one side. There was to be a central open fire with louvres in the roof instead of a chimney ... my parents rejected this plan and a second plan was produced. It was to be on an L-shaped plan, the rooms of which were made smaller by the enormous thickness of the outside walls and by the gigantic stone fireplace partially screened by low oak beams and inglenooks from the rooms they were to warm. All the stone for the house was hewn out of the Chart Common and larger pieces for the fireplace were carved in the quarry by the master mason.

Cowlishaw was to become involved a second time in this idealistic way of building, on this occasion

153

for Miss Annie Lawrence, someone as dedicated to such ideas as himself. Miss Lawrence, whose remarkable family was descended from a Cornish journeyman joiner who, early in the nineteenth century, set out on foot from the village of St Agnes in Cornwall to seek his fortune, called in Cowlishaw on the building of her summer school, The Cloisters, at Letchworth Garden City. Cowlishaw gives an account of the building of The Cloisters in the *Architectural Review* of January 1908. Miss Lawrence was full of ideas: swimming lessons for children, who were rewarded with Blackbird fountain pens; the 'double day', short working hours which left enough time in the day for useful accomplishments; 'adventure' building, turrets and spiral stairs for children; open-air sleeping in hammocks; pedal-operated wash basins — all these and more were represented at The Cloisters. The building is still well-maintained, but it is now in other use and Miss Lawrence's special fittings have been removed. R. W. Sorensen (former MP for Leyton) describes how, as a theological student, he went to the 'remarkable institution called "The Cloisters" ... for a rest at the end of term, only to be yanked out of my bunk the first day at 6 a.m. and compelled to drill on the lawn, learn the arts of pottery and weaving and to gambol to the tune of the country dance "Rufty Tufty" ...'

Like many of his contemporaries who were inspired by William Morris, William Cowlishaw strove to be the complete artist and craftsman and ventured into many crafts, including church needlework (*Studio*, 1900, p. 49). He established

William Cowlishaw: The Cearne, Kent Hatch, Kent, the home of Edward and Constance Garnett.

the Iceni Pottery at Letchworth, and at The Cloisters modelled the small symbolical creatures cast on the lead rainwater heads and gutters. Cowlishaw was in the Ambulance Brigade in the First World War and afterwards was chief of the architectural staff of the Imperial War Graves Commission at Abbeville. The rest of his life he

William Cowlishaw: The Cearne, Kent Hatch, Kent, interior.

154

William Cowlishaw: The Cloisters, Letchworth, Herts, a summer college founded by Miss Annie Lawrence, now a Masonic Lodge.

spent quietly but independently in the service of other architects who were kindred spirits, among them Charles Holden. Cowlishaw called himself designer, craftsman and 'scribe', and introduced the small round handwriting which became fashionable for writing notes on architects' working drawings. One of his illuminated manuscripts is illustrated in *The Builder* (30.11.01).

Greenaway, R. L., unpublished thesis, Polytechnic of the South Bank, London

RIBA Drawings Collection, for his studies of French architecture

Obit. RIBAJ, July, 1957, pp. 293–4 *Bldr*, 22.3.57, p.560.

CRESWELL, Harry Bulkeley   1869–1960

H. B. Creswell's father was Secretary to the Post Office, Scotland. Creswell was educated at Bedford Grammar School and Trinity College, Dublin. He went to Lambeth School of Art, the Architectural Association, entered the Royal Academy Schools in 1892 and was articled to Sir Aston Webb in 1890. In 1895 he was a clerk of works and assistant architect in HM Office of Works under Sir Henry Tanner, until he set up in practice on his own account in 1899 in Rugby and London.

Creswell was Inspecting Engineer for the Crown Agents for the Colonies and for them prepared designs and working drawings for the Law Courts at Sierra Leone; the Public Library, Institute and School, Falkland Islands; and the Agricultural College, Mauritius. He did an interesting design for a boiler works for Willans & Robinson Ltd. Ferry Works, Queensferry, Flintshire (*Bldr*, 13.7.01 and 1.12.06), the form of which was suggested by the large roof span required and the nature of the ground. Piers carry the weight of the roof and travelling gantry, leaving the brick screen wall independent. Creswell also did large engineering works at Rugby and (1907–15) offices at Luton for the Vauxhall Motor Co. which had moved there from Vauxhall, London, in 1905 and started to make motor cars in 1907. Creswell also did St Philip, Wood Street, Rugby (1911–13).

Between 1896 and 1903 he wrote for the *Architectural Review* on subjects ranging from

155

Portuguese architecture to W. Eden Nesfield, Cartmel Priory and the arrangement of sculpture in galleries. Creswell is principally remembered for *The Honeywood File* and its sequel *The Honeywood Settlement*, published by the Architectural Press in 1930 (paperback by Faber, 1970). Here in an imaginary correspondence between client, architect, quantity surveyor and builder, Creswell describes the intricacies and warns of the pitfalls of architectural practice.

Obit. Bldr, 5.7.60, p. 108.

CREWE, Bertie   d. 1937

Bertie Crewe was born in Essex and educated at Merchant Taylors' School, was articled to Clement Dowling of Craven Street, Strand, WC2, and studied for three years at Atelier Laloux, Paris. He became chief assistant to the theatre architect Walter Emden (1847–1913), and after two years was chief assistant and then partner to W. G. R. Sprague, also the architect of a great number of theatres.

In 1895 Crewe commenced practice on his own account and in the course of a lifetime was responsible for more than 100 theatres and music halls and a large number of the early cinematograph theatres.

In 1904 Crewe carried out the fifth transformation of the interior of the Lyceum in Drury Lane (built by Samuel Beazley in 1834). In 1910 he designed the London Opera House on the new Kingsway for Oscar Hammerstein of New York (great-uncle of the American song writer, Oscar Hammerstein II). The venture did not succeed and the opera house became first a variety theatre and in 1917 a cinema. It has been demolished and rebuilt as an office building, incorporating within its compass the Royalty Theatre. In 1911 Crewe completed the New Prince's Theatre (now the Shaftesbury) in Shaftesbury Avenue, WC2, for Walter and Frederick Melville. The *Era* said of it:

> Externally an example of Modern Renaissance, internally the house is eclectical French in its decoration ... the saucer domed ceiling is ornamented with symbolic groups representing The Light of the World, Endeavour, Love, The Crowning Success and The Torch of Destiny.

In Paris Crewe did the Mogador Palace and the Alhambra in 1904, and in Brussels the Alhambra in 1907. More recent theatres by Crewe include the Phoenix, Denmark Street and Charing Cross Road, WC2, with Cecil Masey and with Sir Giles Gilbert Scott for the Charing Cross Road front, and the Piccadilly Theatre, with Edward A. Stone.

Bertie Crewe assisted at the birth of the cinematograph theatre by converting shop premises for the showing of films.

When he was about to rebuild the Tivoli Theatre of Varieties in the Strand, WC2 (1890, by Walter Emden, demolished in 1916), the First World War intervened, and, supposedly on Crewe's suggestion, the site was given over to the YMCA's 'Beaver Hut' for Canadian troops. Designed by Bertie Crewe,

H. B. Creswell: a factory at Queensferry, Flint.

with Gunton and Gunton, and built by Frederick Minter, the New Tivoli was opened in 1923 for Metro-Goldwyn-Meyer. It was the first 'super-cinema' with changeable lighting and a cinema organ, and was demolished in 1957.

Assistants of Bertie Crewe who in their turn became cinema architects were Cecil Masey and Robert Cromie. His practice was continued by Henry Kay who had joined him in 1916.

Other theatres by Crewe are:

1904   New Orient Theatre, Bedminster, Bristol
1909   The Hippodrome, Bedminster, Bristol
          The Pavilion, Glasgow
1910   The Golders Green Hippodrome, NW11
1913   The Palace of Varieties, Manchester
          The Coliseum, Dublin (burnt down by Sinn Feiners in 1918)

Obit. Bldr, 15.1.37, p. 156 and letter p. 252.

CRICKMAY, George Rackstraw   1830–1907

G. R. Crickmay was Diocesan Surveyor to the Archdeaconry of Dorset where he did many churches, schools and church restorations. In 1890 he opened an office in London. With his sons Harry William and George Lay Crickmay, he did Weymouth College Chapel (1894–6) and the Church of St Aldhelm, Lychett Heath, in 1898. The same year they did the Lytchett Minster Schools for Lord Eustace Cecil and in 1899 the Badger public house in Blandford Forum, Dorset.

In the Edwardian period Crickmay and Sons did the former Robinson & Cleaver building, 156–158 Regent Street, W1, (1903–4), a rather pretentious rebuilding of part of Regent Street, with corner turrets and cupolas similar to those on William Young's New (now Old) War Office. Between 1914 and 1917 they did All Saints', Portland, Dorset, built to occupy and train stonemasons during the First World War — as an exercise each stone was differently tooled. Thomas Hardy, the poet and novelist, was an assistant with Crickmay.

Other works by Crickmay and Sons were:

1901   St Nicholas, Broadway, Weymouth (extension to chancel)
1902   Greenhill Hospital, Weymouth
          Six Bells public house, Chelsea, SW3
          Buildings on the east side of Aldersgate Street, EC1 (destroyed) *(Bldr,* 5.4.02)
1903-4 The former New Zealand House, 415 Strand, WC2
1905   White Ensign Naval Club, Weymouth (demolished 1970)

Obit. Bldr, 16.11.07, p. 532 and 30.11, p. 591.

CRICKMER, Courtenay Melville   1879–1971

Courtenay Crickmer was born at St Pancras in London. He went to Highgate School and was articled to George Aitchison, RA (1825–1910), Professor of Architecture at the Royal Academy. Crickmer went to the Architectural Association School and was assistant to Aitchison, to Ambrose Poynter, to Pilkington and to Charles H. M. Mileham (1837–1913). He married Mileham's daughter and in 1904 took over his practice in Lincoln's Inn Fields. The First Garden City, founded at Letchworth in 1903, was then being built under the direction of Parker and Unwin. Crickmer moved to Letchworth in 1907 where he undertook, sometimes with Allen Foxley (a pupil of C. Hodgson Fowler of Durham), groups of houses, single houses, schools and churches.

From 1910 to 1914 Crickmer designed some seventy houses for the Hampstead Garden Suburb and housing was to be his principal concern for the whole of his career. Soon after the outbreak of the First World War, on the recommendation of Unwin who had been appointed Chief Planning Inspector of the Local Government Board and seconded to the Ministry of Munitions, Crickmer was made resident architect for housing at the new munitions town of Gretna, Dumfries. He also did schools and churches there.

After the First World War, Crickmer was for a brief period in the Ministry of Health, then the authority for post-war housing. He was deputy chief architect under Unwin when Dr Christopher Addison launched his famous housing programme, the results of which are still apparent today in towns and villages up and down the country — a large progeny, all with a family likeness, deriving from housing at Letchworth and Hampstead.

Back in private practice at Letchworth, Crickmer was consultant on many housing schemes, entered for some competitions, and was assessor for others. At Letchworth he added the Grange Estate, Pixmore Way and New Pasture Road.

When Ebenezer Howard transferred his interest to the founding of Welwyn Garden City there seemed a chance that Crickmer would contribute considerably to the planning of that new town. But policy had changed and it was decided that instead of Parker and Unwin's principle of variety within limits, a one-style town was preferred, and Louis de Soissons and A. W. Kenyon were appointed. Crickmer and Foxley did houses in Handside Lane in 1920, the first houses to be built in Welwyn.

After the First World War, again in the Hampstead Garden Suburb, Crickmer did houses to suit the changed conditions there; the founders had spread the boundaries further and suburban 'semis' had begun to spring up on the outer edges. After 1918 Crickmer did all the houses in Brunner Close, Cornwood Close and Howard Walk. In this period he also did Farringtons School and chapel, Chislehurst, Kent.

C. M. Crickmer: houses in Temple Fortune Hill, Hampstead Garden Suburb, London NW11. An Act of Parliament enabled the building line to be varied.

Crickmer did houses or advised on housing on the estates at Gidea Park, Essex; Oxford Garden Villages Ltd., New Eltham, Kent; Ruislip, Middlesex; East Grinstead, Sussex; Tunbridge Wells and Dartford, Kent; Hatfield and East Barnet, Hertfordshire; Epsom, Surrey; and Woodford, Essex.

His principal works before 1914 were:

1907-10   *At Letchworth Garden City*

Three first prizes in Urban Cottages Exhibition (1907)

St Michael (with E. H. Heazell, now replaced by a modern church)

Houses in Garth Road, Norton Road, and Baldock Road

South Place houses (with Allen Foxley)

Letchworth School

St Thomas à Becket, Bedford Road

Baptist Church, West View

Baptist Church, Grange Estate (with W. Knott)

Old People's Centre, Howard Green

Letchworth Library and Museum

Cottages for the Howard Society and the National Cottage Society

Shops and flats

1910-14   *At Hampstead Garden Suburb*

Erskine Hill (38 houses)

Willifield Way and Temple Fortune Hill (21 houses at this intersection)

1, 2, 3 and 4 Ruskin Close; 8 Linnell Close; 93, 95 and 97 Corringham Road; 17 Wellgarth Road

Letchworth Museum, a list of Crickmer's works prepared by his daughter, Mrs Cruse

Marriott, Charles, *Modern English Architecture*, London, 1924

Obit. Bldg, 5.2.71, pp. 6, 46.

CROSS, Alfred William Stephens   1858–1932

A. W. S. Cross was articled to his father's firm of Cross and Wells, of Hastings and London. In 1882 he moved to Weston-super-Mare and started practice on his own account. In Somerset he did the vicarage, Easton-in-Gordano (1885), Glendale, Clevedon (1887), and the remodelling of Stanton Drew Church (1881).

In 1889 Cross entered into partnership with Henry Spalding in London. They acquired a reputation for public baths, public libraries, laboratories and schools. Their work together included baths at Dulwich, SE21, Hoxton, N1, and Finchley Road, Hampstead, NW3.

Spalding and Cross also did the Technical College, Manchester, in 1890. They dissolved partnership in 1899 and Cross set up on his own. He did schools at Poplar, Finchley, Kentish Town and Gospel Oak in London. He also did additions to St John's College, Cambridge. With C. E. Mallows, Cross entered into competition for the Wesleyan Central Convocation Hall, Westminster (1905), and was selected for the final competition for the London County Hall (1908).

More recent baths by A. W. S. Cross and his son K. M. B. Cross (1889–1968), who became a partner in the firm, are at Marshall Street, W1 (1931) and (completed after Cross's death) at Seymour Place, Marylebone, W1.

With his son, Cross reproduced James Gibbs's *Book of Architecture*, a simplified Vitruvius, in an even more simplified form, putting the final nail into the coffin of the irregular Free Classic columns which architects had felt in honour bound to invent without the aid of pattern books.

Cross won more than twenty-six competitions and was assessor for twenty-three.

Other works by Cross include:

1900   Gosport Free Library, Hampshire

1904   Haggerston Public Baths, E8 (additions; *Bldr*, 18.4.03; RA, 1904)

The Porters' and Walters' Almshouses, 1–16 Nightingale Road, Wood Green, N22, for the Charity of St Leonard's, Shoreditch (RA, 1903; *Bldr*, 9.12.05) to replace those demolished for the Old Street Police Courts (*see under* Butler, John Dixon)

1905   Davis Memorial Laboratories, University College, Aberystwyth

1906   Restoration of Shoreditch Town Hall after fire

Obit. *Bldr*, 6.1.33, pp. 5 and 21   correction 13.1., p. 56.

CROUCH, Joseph   1859–1936

Joseph Crouch was born in Birmingham, the son of William Jeffs Crouch. He was educated at King Edward VI School, articled to David Smith and Son of Birmingham and attended Birmingham

School of Art. He was assistant in the offices of several London architects and studied at the South Kensington Schools.

Crouch commenced practice in Birmingham in 1882; Edmund Butler became a partner in 1886, Rupert Savage in 1911. Their works included the Birmingham Gaiety Concert Hall, premises for A. R. Dean, 155–157 Corporation Street, Birmingham (1896–8) and numerous schools, chapels, warehouses and private houses in Birmingham and district including Avon Croft, Edgbaston (1900) and The Anchorage, Handsworth Wood (1901). In 1906 they did the Public Library, Rawtenstall, Lancashire, part of a scheme won in competition, and the Public Library, Malvern (*Bldr*, 19.8.05). With Butler, Crouch wrote *The Apartments of the House: their furnishing and decoration* (London, Unicorn Press, 1900) and *Churches, Mission Halls and Schools for Nonconformists* (Birmingham, 1901).

Obit. Bldr, 10.4.36, p. 727.

Arthur Davis with the international architect, Charles Mewès: The Ritz Hotel, Piccadilly, London.

DAVIS, Arthur Joseph, RA   1878–1951

A. J. Davis was born in Bayswater, London. His family later moved to Brussels and he was educated in Brussels and Paris where he entered the Ecole des Beaux-Arts at the age of sixteen. He also studied at the ateliers of J. Godefroy and of Jean-Louis Pascal, who was then foremost in the teaching of the new classicism. Davis was a brilliant student and entered for twenty-six *concours*, completing twenty-three in fifteen months. He won the second-class prize in 1895 and the first-class in 1896.

On completing the course, Davis entered the office of Charles Mewès, also a student of Pascal, and assisted him on the competition designs for the Grand Palais and the Petit Palais at the Exposition Universelle of 1900 (which they did not win). Mewès had by then already designed the interiors of Europe's first Ritz Hotel, in Paris, for César Ritz. A subsequent chain of events led to Mewès and Davis introducing into London the classical style of the three Louis. Their first engagement there was to design the interiors of the Carlton Hotel, Haymarket, SW1, since destroyed to make way for the uncompromising tower of New Zealand House. Meanwhile César Ritz was preparing to build his own Ritz Hotel in London and this was the first of three major London works by Mewès and Davis (1906–9). It was also London's first steel-framed building.

Their next important work was Inveresk House, for the *Morning Post* on the newly constructed Aldwych in the Strand, WC2 (*Bldr*, 25.4.08). This has since been raised higher and its once elegant proportions lost. The third great building carried out by Mewès and Davis before the outbreak of the First World War was the Royal Automobile Club, Pall Mall, SW1 (1908–11). The site for this became available when the then new War Office had been completed in Whitehall, thus releasing the thirteen houses in Pall Mall it had previously occupied. Like the Ritz, this palatial clubhouse demonstrates Mewès and Davis's Beaux-Arts planning.

The sculpture in the pediment by Faivre shows a woman surrounded by four cherubs, one of whom holds the wheel of a motor car — 'Science inspiring the Allied Trades'. The anvil at the feet of Science is inscribed with the names of Mewès and Davis. The sculpture on the piers, by Rajon, represents the four elements, Earth, Air, Fire and Water. The keystones were carved by C. H. Mabey. The new Royal Automobile Club was to excel in magnificence every other Pall Mall and St James's Street Club and, like the hotels and transatlantic liners that Mewès and Davis were engaged on, was given period rooms, but within a discreet range. The Smoking Room perpetuates the Council Chamber of the Old War Office, the enriched plaster and painted ceiling of which was copied by Lenygon and Morant of Old Burlington Street, W1; the Great Gallery is in Louis XIV style by Boulanger

Arthur Davis with Charles Mewès: The Royal Automobile Club, Pall Mall, London SW1

of Paris; the Restaurant was decorated by Remon in the style of Louis XV. The Members' Dining Room, also by Lenygon and Morant, is in the style of Sir William Chambers. The annexe (originally the Card Room) is in the style of the brothers Adam, as are the Committee Room, Chess Room, the old Library (now the office), and the present Library. These were carried out by Jackson and Sons who still have the original Adam moulds. The present Card Room, by Thornton Smith and Russell, is in the Early Georgian style. The swimming pool is in Pompeian style in Sicilian marble and is reminiscent of the swimming pools on the Cunarders *Aquitania* and *Mauretania*. The engineering installation provided warmed and filtered air and an early form of panel-heating (*Bldr*, 28.4.11 and 5.5.11). Commenced in 1908, the Club was opened in 1911. The total cost was

£250,000 – equivalent to more than £6,000,000 in the 1980s.

Mewès and Davis remodelled Luton Hoo, Bedfordshire, for Sir Julius Wernher who had purchased the estate in 1903. Completed in 1907, Mewès and Davis's remodelling is indicative of the taste of the day – they transformed the interior into the style of Louis XV, substituting French casements for the sash windows of the mansion (originally designed by Robert Adam in 1767 for the 3rd Earl of Bute). In this period they did improvements to the Cavalry Club at 127 Piccadilly (1908) and to about forty town houses for some of the last residents of Mayfair, including 88 Brook Street, for the Hon. Mrs Henry Coventry (1913).

Charles Mewès had earlier designed interiors for

liners of the Hamburg-Amerika Line. With Davis he now did those on the liners *Aquitania*, *Franconia*, *Laconia*, *Servia*, *Valetta* and *Floriana* until Hamburg-Amerika protested and the work had to be divided between them.

Mewès died in 1914 at the age of fifty-four and Davis, after service in the First World War, took into partnership Charles H. Gage. In collaboration with B. W. Morris of Morris and O'Connor, architects of the Cunard Building in New York, and with Willink and Dod of Liverpool, Davis did the Cunard Building, Pier Head, Liverpool, for the Cunard and the Anchor and Dominion Lines. Difficult to analyse, half-Florentine, half-French, the building stands between the enormous and ugly Royal Liver Building and the be-domed Docks Offices. Davis also designed the Cunard War Memorial in front of the building and some of the rooms on the liner *Queen Mary* (others were done by Guy Grey Wornum in the style of the 1930s).

Before the First World War, Mewès and Davis had built branches of the London County and Westminster (now National Westminster) Bank at Antwerp, Brussels, Nantes and Valencia. After the war Davis did its head office in Lothbury, EC2, and the branch at 5 Threadneedle Street, EC2 — reminiscent of Peruzzi's Palazzo Massimi, Rome — which won him the London Street Architecture Medal in 1930. Davis continued in his favourite French styles well into the 1930s.

His post-war work also included Dormeuil-Frères, 25—29 Golden Square and Warwick Street, W1; 26—30 New Cavendish Street, W1; and the re-modelling of the Hyde Park Hotel Restaurant in 1925. Another notable later work was the Armenian Church of S. Sarkis at Iverna Gardens, W8 (1928), based on the church in the cloisters of Haghbat, Armenia, and built by Calouste Sarkis Gulbenkian in memory of his parents. Also in the twenties, Davis did Cunard House, Leadenhall Street, EC3; offices for the Hudson Bay Co. at 52 Bishopsgate, EC2, an 'hôtel de ville' design spanning St Helen's Place (and now in other use); the Leathersellers' Co., 9 St Helen's Place, EC3; and Morgan Grenfell's Bank, 23 Great Winchester Street, EC2 (1925).

Davis designed the street lighting standards for Piccadilly Circus — four round the Shaftesbury Memorial Fountain in bronze, the remainder in cast iron. At the West London Synagogue, in Seymour Place, W1, he designed the lecture hall, classrooms and offices, and with A. N. Prentice in 1926 he did the Auto Club in São Paulo, Brazil. He made an attempt to establish the Beaux-Arts system of architectural training in England, but without success.

Davis was a member of the Royal Fine Art Commission, and was made ARA in 1933 and RA in 1942 (diploma work, 'Westminster Bank, Threadneedle Street, EC2'). He was Chevalier de la Légion d'Honneur, and was decorated with the Belgian Ordre de la Couronne, avec Palmes. At an exhibition held in 1922 at the Salons des Artistes Françaises his old master, Godefroy, commented: 'We find the work of an old student of the Beaux-Arts School Mr. Arthur J. Davis — although an Englishman, he has so absorbed the spirit of our school that he really appears to be a living embodiment of the "Franco-British Union of Architects" [of which Davis was President in 1933]'. The firm of Mewès and Davis continues under D. G. Turner and E. N. Roberts.

Fleetwood-Hesketh, Peter, 'The Royal Automobile Club', *Country Life*, 14.10.71.
Anderson, Sir Colin, 'Ship interiors: when the breakthrough came', *AR*, June 1967, pp. 449—52.
Obit. RIBAJ, Nov., 1951, p. 35 *Bldr*, 27.7.51, p. 127.

DAVISON, Thomas Raffles 1853—1937

Raffles Davison was born at Stockton-on-Tees, Durham, son of a Congregational minister. He was trained as an architect but his amazing talent as a draughtsman and perspective artist meant that he was to spend his life doing 'Rambling Sketches' of which he did some 15,000, and perspective drawings of projected buildings for other architects.

Davison was able to put his talent for drawing to good use when he became Editor of the *British Architect*, a post he held for nearly forty years, for he illustrated the weekly magazine largely with his own pen drawings instead of by photo-lithography. He was thus able to encourage younger architects whose work became known through the pages of his magazine.

Raffles Davison's representation of Liverpool Anglican Cathedral is the best-known of his fine pen drawings.

DAWBER, Sir Edward Guy, RA 1861—1938

Guy Dawber was born at King's Lynn, Norfolk, the son of a merchant. He went to King's Lynn Grammar School and served articles with a local architect, William Adams. Dawber then worked in the Dublin office of Thomas Newenham Deane (1829—99) until 1882 when the murders of the Chief Secretary and Under Secretary for Ireland brought architectural work in Dublin to a standstill for a time. Dawber came to London and in 1882 entered the office of George and Peto, then engaged on country mansions and the rebuilding of town houses on the Cadogan Estate where Dawber was site assistant on a house in Cadogan Square for Sir Thomas de la Rue. He entered the Royal Academy Schools in 1883.

In 1887 trouble with his eyes led to Dawber's being sent as site assistant to Batsford Park at Bourton-on-the-Water in the Cotswolds, which

Sir E. Guy Dawber: Conkwell Grange, Bradford-on-Avon, Wiltshire. Additions by W. H. Watkins (*q.v.*).

George and Peto were building between 1888 and 1892. He spent his weekends walking, cycling and sketching in this architecturally unexplored county, expeditions on which he was sometimes joined by Herbert Baker, then chief assistant at George and Peto.

Encouraged by Freeman-Mitford, Dawber started on his own practice in 1890 at Bourton-on-the-Hill, renting a room at ninepence a week at the village institute. In 1891 he opened in London at 22 Buckingham Street, Strand, WC2, and gradually earned recognition as expert in the smaller country house in stone districts. Dawber's houses have been aptly described as of 'friendly gravity'. Not too clever, they neither display mannerisms nor proclaim a theory other than that of quiet accord with the countryside. They are included by Hermann Muthesius in *Das Englische Haus*.

Even so successful a country-house architect as Dawber hoped to build at least one building in a town street and his chance came in 1906 when he did the offices of the London and Lancashire Fire Insurance Co., 59–60 Pall Mall, SW1 (*Bldr*, 27.7.07). This was destroyed in the Second World War and rebuilt to a modified design by his partners. On the original neo-Baroque façade, 'Truth' and 'Justice' were by C. J. Hartwell, the stone carving was by Abraham Broadbent and the cast leadwork by George Bankart who also did most of Dawber's plasterwork.

Guy Dawber's early works included alterations to St David, Moreton-in-Marsh, Gloucestershire, the restoration of the Manor House, Bourton-on-the-Water (1890, further restoration in 1919), and the extensions to the Court House, Broadway, Worcestershire (1898). In this period he also did the Broadway Post Office, additions to Millbrook House, Broadwell, Stow-on-the-Wold and The White House, Moreton-in-Marsh, Gloucestershire (1898).

With Lord Crawford and Balcarres, Dawber was a founder of the Council for the Preservation of Rural England (now the Council for the Protection of Rural England). He married Mary Eccles of Roby, Liverpool, sister of the architect Thomas Edgar Eccles (1865–1946). He was a brother-upholder of the Art Workers' Guild, and made ARA in 1927 and RA in 1935 (diploma work, 'Ashley Chase, Dorset'). He was President of the RIBA from 1925 to 1927. In 1928 he received the Royal Gold Medal for Architecture and he was knighted in 1936. His published works include *Old Cottages and Farmhouses in Kent and Sussex* (1900), and *Old Cottages, Farmhouses and Other Stone Buildings in the Cotswolds* (1905). A portrait by Fred Roe is in the National Portrait Gallery.

**Sir E. Guy Dawber: Conkwell Grange, Bradford-on-Avon,
Wiltshire. Additions by W. H. Watkins (*q.v.*).**

Sir Guy Dawber's practice continues under the title
Sir Guy Dawber, Fox and Robinson; Albert
Robert Fox joined Sir Guy Dawber in 1910 and
Christopher Douglas Robinson became a partner
in 1955.

Dawber's other works include:

1900	The Old Stone House, Upper Oddington, Gloucestershire
	House at Cley, Norfolk (*Bldr*, 27.10.1900)
1901	Pittern Hill, Warwickshire
	Hartpury House, Hartpury, Gloucestershire (additions)
	Itton Court and village hall, Chepstow, Monmouthshire
1902	Westhope Manor, Shropshire (*Bldr*, 15.11.02)
1903-13	Nether Swell Manor, Stow-on-the-Wold, Gloucestershire, for Sir John Murray Scott, Bart. (now Hill Place School) (*Bldr*, 15.8.03 and 16.5.09)
1904	Bibsworth Manor, Broadway, Worcestershire (*Bldr*, 14.5.04)
	Coldicote, Warwickshire
	Park Down, Surrey
	Cottage, Great Warley Rectory, Essex (*Bldr*, 19.11.04)
1905	Solom's Court, Banstead, Surrey (*Bldr*, 15.7.05), and other houses in Banstead, Chipstead, Kingswood and Walton Heath, Surrey, and in Denbigh (*Bldr*, 3.6.05)

	1905-6	Dog and Doublet Inn and cottages, Sandon, Staffordshire (*Bldr*, 15.7.05)
		Village hall, Sandon, for the Earl of Harrowby (*Bldr*, 28.3.08)
		Donnington Hurst, Newbury, Berkshire
161 162	1907	Conkwell Grange, Wiltshire (additions 1952 by W. H. Watkins)
		Caldy Manor, Cheshire (alterations)
	1907-9	Wiveton Hall, Norfolk (major additions)
	1907-10	Houses at 38–48 Temple Fortune Lane, 20 and 36 Hampstead Way, 16 Linnell Drive, and 5 and 6 Ruskin Close, Hampstead Garden Suburb, NW11
	1910	Eyford Park, Upper Slaughter, Gloucestershire
		Wells Folly, Evenlode, Gloucestershire
	c. 1910	Golf Club House, Cassiobury Park, Watford, Hertfordshire
		Copseham, Esher, Surrey
		Baynards Park, Cranleigh, Surrey (alterations), for Sir Herbert Cook, Bart.
	1910-12	Hamptworth, Downton, Wiltshire
	1911	Tuesley Court (now Ladywell Convent), near Godalming, Surrey
		Burdocks, Fairford, Gloucestershire
		Heath Lodge, Headley, Surrey (*AR*, 1911)
	1912-13	Church Hall, New Brighton, Cheshire

Dawber's post-1918 career included several good
country houses still in Edwardian style, including
Stowell Hill, Templecombe, Somerset (*c.* 1923),

Bowling Green, Milborne Port, Somerset (1925) and Ashley Chase, Abbotsbury, Dorset (1925). He also designed the Foord Almshouses, Rochester (1926—31).

RIBAJ, 1928, pp. 543—54
A, 3.7.25 and 22.7.
Obit. RIBAJ, 9.5.38, pp. 631, 633, 666—8 and 23.5, p. 770 *Bldr*, 29.4.38, pp. 824 and 827.

DAWSON, Matthew James   1875—1943

Matthew Dawson went to Ardrossan Academy, Ayrshire, and to Sydney Grammar School and University, New South Wales. He received his architectural training at the Architectural Association and at the Central School of Arts and Crafts (then at Morley Hall, Regent Street, W1). He served articles (1900—1) with Ernest Weitsel and in 1902 received a consolation prize of the Soane Medallion (not awarded that year). Dawson also attended the Atelier Laloux in Paris. He began practice in 1907.

Dawson was head teacher in architectural design and drawing at the Camberwell School of Arts and Crafts (1907—12) and at both Camberwell and the Westminster Technical Institute (1918—23). He was principal of the LCC School of Building, Brixton, from 1927 to 1929 and senior lecturer at the Bartlett School of Architecture, London University, from 1929 to 1939. He was also a demonstrator in architecture at Cambridge University, and a member of the Art Workers' Guild.

Dawson's houses in Hampstead Garden Suburb, carried out between 1909 and 1914, show more individuality than was usually allowed to appear under the watchful eyes of Parker and Unwin. They included 87 and 89 Hampstead Way, 1 and

36—42 Meadway (one of which was his own). After 1920 he did 8, 62 and 64 Wildwood Road. Dawson also did renovations at The Park, Wrotham, Kent, and was invited to enter for the competition for the London County Hall. He assisted R. V. Brook-Greaves and Godfrey Allen on their great isometric drawing of St Paul's Cathedral (1923—8). In 1929 he did St Anne's Home at All Saints London Colney, adjoining Leonard Stokes's building there (now the Pastoral Centre).

Obit. RIBAJ, Feb., 1944, p. 94 *Bldr*, 28.1.44, p. 72.

DE MORGAN, William Frend   1839—1917

William Frend De Morgan was born in London at 69 Gower Street, the eldest son of Professor Augustus De Morgan (1806—71), the noted mathematician and scientist of London University. After attending University College School, De Morgan studied at the art school of Francis Cary and entered the Royal Academy Schools in 1859. He developed early an interest in designing stained glass and tiles and established a pottery at Fitzroy Square in 1869, but a fire destroyed the house. In 1871, after the death of his father, De Morgan moved with his mother and sister to Cheyne Walk, Chelsea, SW3, then to Orange House, Cheyne Row, where he re-established the kiln and 'practically re-discovered pottery from the beginning'. He invented most of the appliances for his pottery, introducing lustre ware and firing work to Doulton's. Edward Burne-Jones, D. G. Rossetti and William Morris were among his friends and in 1882 he joined Morris at his works at Merton Abbey, Surrey, for six years, then moved to Sands End Pottery, Townmead Road, Fulham, SW6.

De Morgan married the Pre-Raphaelite painter,

163

Matthew Dawson:
87 and 89 Hampstead Way, Hampstead Garden Suburb, London NW11.

William De Morgan: the fireplace tiles at Woodside, Graffham, Sussex. Architect: Halsey Ricardo (q.v.).

Evelyn Pickering, in 1887. They lived at The Vale, Chelsea, until 1909 when the house was bought by speculating builders. After what they called a 'house-cooling' party, the De Morgans moved to 125–127 Church Street (now Old Church Street), Chelsea.

After 1890, for reasons of health, De Morgan wintered in Florence. Here he employed Italian craftsmen to paint his tile designs on paper transfers which were then sent to Fulham to be transferred to clay tiles under the direction of his partners, the architect Halsey Ricardo, Frank Iles and Charles and Fred Passenger. De Morgan's pots, and especially his tiles, were in great demand. He had discovered how to reproduce the brilliant blue and green glazes of Persian pottery popularised by the paintings of Lord Leighton, RA, and Sir Laurence Alma-Tadema, RA. De Morgan's tiles can be seen *in situ* at Lord Leighton's 'Arab Hall', Holland Park Road, W7, and at 8 Addison Road, W8, the house Halsey Ricardo designed for the draper Sir Ernest Debenham. When De Morgan closed his pottery in 1904 there were still quantities of his tiles available, surplus from the decoration of six P & O liners under the direction of Thomas E. Collcutt, and from the Tsar of Russia's steam yacht *Livadia*.

De Morgan then turned to writing as a career and confessed, 'Charles Heath in *Alice for Short* portrays a good deal of myself'. During the First World War he applied his latent talents as an inventor to the problems of submarine and aerial warfare. He died from what was thought to be

trench fever contracted on a visit to the Western Front.

Single tiles, like De Morgan's pots, are now collectors' items and examples can be seen at Old Battersea House, SW11, at the Victoria and Albert Museum and at Water House, the William Morris Museum, Walthamstow, E17. The portrait of William De Morgan at the National Portrait Gallery and the bas-relief at Brookwood Cemetery, Surrey, are by Evelyn De Morgan (d. 1919), who completed her husband's two unfinished novels. There is a memorial tablet by Halsey Ricardo to De Morgan — 'Artist—Potter—Inventor—Novelist' — in the churchyard of Chelsea Old Church.

Clayton-Stamm, W. G. and M. D. E., *William De Morgan*, London, 1971

DENING, Charles Frederick William   1876–1952

C. F. W. Dening was born at Chard, Somerset, the son of an engineer. In 1896 he was articled in Bristol to Henry Dare Bryan. In 1902 he commenced in practice with a fellow pupil, Ernest George Rodway. Together they won the design for St Alban, Westbury Park, Bristol. Dening was resident architect on the Bristol Central Library for Adams and Holden. From 1918 he practised alone. Most of Dening's work consisted of houses of a high order of design in the neighbourhood of Bristol and he played an important role in Bristol's housing after the First World War. For more than twenty years Dening was Chairman of the Royal West of England Academy, Bristol. He wrote *The Eighteenth Century Architecture of Bristol* (1923) and *The Old Inns of Bristol* (1943) which he illustrated.

Obit. Bldr, 4.7.52, p. 25.

DETMAR, Lionel Gordon   1880–1910

Lionel Detmar was articled to W. Hilton Nash and later worked in turn in the offices of J. G. S. Gibson and John Belcher, subsequently joining Hilton Nash in partnership. He entered the Royal Academy Schools in 1900. When Nash retired in 1905, Detmar became a partner of Theodore Gregg. They were one of the three firms selected to participate in the design of the Franco-British Exhibition of 1908, held at the White City, Wood Lane, Shepherd's Bush, W12. Detmar did items as diverse as the Palace of French Applied Arts and Farrah's Toffee Pavilion (*Bldr*, 9.5.08, pp. 531–2).

Detmar did the (London City and) Midland Banks at Putney, SW15, Notting Hill, W11, and Willesden, NW10, and a skating rink at Maida Vale, W9. Detmar was killed when he was thrown from a horse.

Obit. RIBAJ, 23.4.10, p. 492   *Bldr*, 16.4.10, p. 444.

210

164

DICKIE, Professor Archibald Campbell
1868–1941

A. C. Dickie was born in Dundee and was a pupil of Carver and Symon of Forfar. He was one of the five original day-students at the Architectural Association, Great Marlborough Street, W1. Dickie was architect to the Palestine Exploration Fund between 1894 and 1897, a member of the executive committee (1906–41) and Secretary (1910–12). Among his discoveries was the *Temenos* of the Roman Temple at Damascus. On his return he joined the office of A. Beresford Pite at a time when Pite was changing from his Mannerist to his Greek style.

Dickie then joined Dunn, Watson and Curtis Green (they did the South Herts Golf Club House, Barnet; RA, 1903) and later became a partner with Claude Kelly while the latter was Master of Design at the Architectural Association (1906–11). Kelly and Dickie did the Mission Hospital, Hebron, Israel, for the United Free Church of Scotland (*Bldr*, 23.4.10).

Dickie became Director of the Manchester School of Architecture in 1912. He retired to Long Crendon, Buckinghamshire.

ABN, 14.7.33, pp. 29 and 30
Obit. RIBAJ, Nov., 1941, p. 10 *Bldr*, 12.9.41, p. 245.

DODGSHUN, Edward John   1854–1927

E. J. Dodgshun was articled to Thomas Ambler in Leeds and was in G. E. Street's office during the rebuilding of the Royal Courts of Justice. He later joined William Burges's office where he met W. F. Unsworth. When only twenty-one, Dodgshun, together with Unsworth, won the competition for the Shakespeare Memorial Theatre, Stratford-on-Avon. After the completion of the theatre the partnership was dissolved — Dodgshun went to Leeds, Unsworth to Sussex — and in 1898 Dodgshun was joined in partnership by G. Dale Oliver of Carlisle, a fellow student in Street's office. Together they did the Lancashire and Yorkshire Bank, the Commercial Union, and Holt & Co., East Parade (all in Leeds). They rebuilt Silcoates School, Wakefield, after it was destroyed by fire, and did a great deal of church work, including a new church and vicarage at Grayswood, Haselmere, Surrey (1900–2, with Axel Haig the etcher). They did a house in Surrey for Axel Haig, and with him designed a church in Örebro, Sweden.

Dodgshun designed a house for himself by the bridge at Boston Spa, W. Riding; a convent school at Clifford near Boston Spa; and (with Dale Oliver) the Crown and Mitre at Carlisle.

Obit. RIBAJ, 2.4.27, p. 377.

C. Fitzroy Doll: a drawing by Charlotte Halliday of premises in Gower Street and Torrington Place. Faced with terracotta.

DOLL, Charles Fitzroy   1850–1929

Fitzroy Doll's father was Page of the Presence to King William IV and Queen Victoria in succession for a period of fifty-two years. Doll received his architectural training at the Polyteknikum, Coblenz, under Dr Adolf Dronke. He was articled in London to Charles Gritten, a quantity surveyor, and was assistant to Sir Matthew Digby Wyatt (1820–77) in whose office he worked on the drawings for the India Office in Whitehall.

Much of Fitzroy Doll's architectural work derived from his appointment in 1885 as surveyor to the Bedford Estate in Bloomsbury and Covent Garden. His most remarkable building is the Hotel Russell, Russell Square, WC1 (1898). Frankly derived from the engravings of the Château de Madrid which once stood in the Bois de Boulogne (begun by

166

C. Fitzroy Doll: the Hotel Russell, Russell Square, London WC1, bears a resemblance to the short-lived Château de Madrid in the Bois de Boulogne, Paris. It is faced with the architect's favourite terracotta.

François I in 1528 and demolished by Louis XVI in 1785), the Russell Square version is higher and faced in the *thé-au-lait* terracotta. Sadly, the copper dome is now missing.

This venture tempted the Duke of Bedford or his advisers to have terracotta dressings added to the windows and doors of the plain, eighteenth-century houses of Russell Square, in a vain attempt to smarten up the yellow stock brick — the simple, unadorned Bloomsbury squares were not generally appreciated until the Danish architect, Steen Eiler Rasmussen, wrote his *London, the Unique City* (1934; English edition, London, 1937), and Sir John Summerson his *Georgian London* (1945).

167   In the Imperial Hotel, Fitzroy Doll went further, producing a design for an exterior that was little more than a façade of coloured terracotta turrets and flèches, with an impossibly steep roof of green Spanish tiles. All was demolished in the 1960s, the only relics being the stone Julius Caesar, Charlemagne and various kings and queens of England, some now standing in the new cortile.

A most intricate terracotta terrace of shops and flats by Fitzroy Doll stands at the corner of
165   Torrington Place and Gower Street, WC1 (1907), the base of which was even richer before it was damaged in the Second World War and repaired more simply. Other hotels by Doll were the Kingsley, Hart Street (now Bloomsbury Way), WC1, and the Bedford Hotel and Russell Mansions,

both in Southampton Row, WC1. He also did 191 Tottenham Court Road, W1 (since demolished), the former premises for the National Association for the Blind in Tottenham Court Road, W1 (RA, 1894) and the Memorial Plaque to A. W. N. Pugin, 107 Great Russell Street, WC1, in Kupron bronze, from a model by C. Langlois (*Bldr*, 26.10.07).

A scholar of German history, Fitzroy Doll undertook the German section of the 1893 edition of Fergusson's *History of Ancient and Mediaeval Architecture*, and wrote a history of the Teutonic Order.

His practice was continued by his son, C. C. T. Doll (1880–1955), who became his partner in 1910 and, a student of the British School at Athens, reconstructed the grand staircase of the Palace of King Minos at Knossos, Crete. C. C. T. Doll was Mayor of Holborn in 1950.

Obit. Bldr, 8.3.29, p. 478.

DOUGLAS, John   1829–1911

John Douglas, a pupil of E. G. Paley of Lancaster, set up in practice in Chester about 1855 and became the leading architect of that city, inspiring a whole 'school' of design, particularly in half-timber (*see under* Grayson, G. H. and Ould, E. A.). He was in partnership as Douglas and Fordham from 1885, as Douglas and Minshull from 1898. His major works included many estate buildings on the Duke of Westminster's Eaton Hall property, including model farms, cottages and houses for the Duke's agent and secretary. His churches, initally High Victorian Gothic, culminate in the bold timber framing of St Paul, Boughton, Chester (1876, enlarged 1902), St Michael, Altcar, Lancashire (1879) and St James, Haydock, Lancashire (1891–2). He designed cottages at Pool Baule and Wood Street, Port Sunlight and also the Post Office there (since demolished) and the school, now the Lyceum (1894–6); his style greatly influenced the other architects of Port Sunlight and also younger Arts and Crafts men such as Baillie Scott. In Chester he built St Werburgh Street (1895–9), close to the cathedral, as a speculation. His own substantial house, Walmoor Hill, Dee Banks, Chester (1896) is now the County Fire Brigade headquarters.

Douglas and Minshull's later works include:

1900-01	Swimming baths, Union Street, Chester
1901	Martin's Bank, Birkenhead, Cheshire
1902-3	St John the Evangelist, Sandiway, Cheshire (where he was Lord of the Manor)
	Buildings, in Bath Street, Chester
1903-4	The Bear's Paw, Frodsham, Cheshire (restoration)
1906	Congregational Church, Hoylake, Cheshire
1906-7	The Resurrection and All Saints, Caldy, Cheshire (chancel and tower)

C. Fitzroy Doll: the Imperial Hotel, Russell Square, London WC1. This fantasy in coloured faience has been sacrificed to a dull replacement.

DOWNING, Henry Philip Burke   1865—1947

Burke Downing was articled to A. Hessell Tiltman in 1882, worked for Henry Shaw and was chief assistant to Joseph Clarke (1819—88). He entered the Royal Academy Schools in 1884, studied at the Architectural Association, and set up in practice in 1888. Downing's 1908—14 works included the Boys' Grammar School in Hayes Lane, Bromley, Kent (the Hall was added in 1933), and schools at Bexhill, Sussex; Selhurst, SE25; Merton Abbey, Surrey; and Pelham Road, South Wimbledon, SW19. In this period he also did Lyndhurst, Streatham Park, SW16, and houses at Kingswood and Mitcham in Surrey.

Downing's churches include St Augustine, Tooting, SW17; St John the Evangelist, Waltham-stow, E17 *and:*

1911	Church of the Holy Spirit, Clapham Common, SW4
1913	St Mary, Beddington, Surrey (additions)
1914	St Barnabas, Mitcham, Surrey
	St Philip, Camberwell SE5 (redecoration of the chancel)

Obit. Bldr, 4.4.47, p. 315.

J. Francis Doyle: Martin's Bank, Edge Hill, Liverpool.

DOYLE, John Francis   1840—1913

168

Francis Doyle was born in Liverpool. In 1894—6 he collaborated with Richard Norman Shaw on the White Star Building (now the Pacific Steam Naviga-tion Building), James Street and the Strand, Liverpool, a first cousin of Shaw's New Scotland Yard, Westminster. The gable, damaged in the war, has been restored in simpler form. On the recom-mendation of Norman Shaw, Doyle was selected from among seven entrants for the important Royal Insurance Co. Building, Dale Street and North John Street, Liverpool (1897—1903). Shaw was assessor and also acted as advising architect. Full of characteristic Norman Shaw ideas but inclining towards the style of John Belcher or E. W. Mountford, the building is an example of the neo-Baroque which had already blossomed before the year of the Diamond Jubilee. The internal steel frame is bold, the stanchions inclining inwards from the ground floor to take arched girders supporting the floors and chimney stacks over. The base is of unpolished Aberdeen granite, the upper parts of Portland stone, and the sculpture is by C. J. Allen. Doyle's chief assistant when these two buildings were going up was R. Frank Atkinson (*q.v.*).

167

Also in the Liverpool area, Doyle did the David Lewis Hostel for Men, Great George Place (1902), Martin's Bank, Edge Hill (1905), and several

J. Francis Doyle: shipping office built for the White Star Company, Pier Head, Liverpool. Consultant architect: R. Norman Shaw.

churches, the earliest of which were: St Mary and St Helen, Neston, Cheshire, on which he did the rebuilding (1874—6); St Catherine, Tranmere, Birkenhead (1875—6); St Andrew, Maghull (1878—80); and St Ambrose, Widnes (1879—83), for which Doyle also did the vicarage in 1900.

Like other successful Liverpool architects, Doyle did houses in the more salubrious of Birkenhead's suburbs, including The Roscote, Wall Rake, which he altered and enlarged in 1893 for the banker and shipowner Thomas Brocklebank. He also rebuilt Haughton Hall, Spurstow, Cheshire (1891—2) for Brocklebank's brother Ralph.

Other works by Doyle include:
1898-1901 St Luke, Goodison Road, Walton, Liverpool
1900-14 St Barnabas, Mossley Hill, Liverpool
1908 St Olave, Marygate, York (and south chapel)
Obit. *Bldr*, 21.2.13, pp. 235, 253.

DRESSLER, Conrad   1856—1940

Conrad Dressler was born in London of German descent. He studied at South Kensington under Professor E. Lantéri and Sir Joseph Edgar Boehm and later in France. Dressler set up his own foundry in Chelsea, carrying out the *cire-perdue* casting process. He invented the tunnel kiln which revolutionised the manufacture of clay products.

Conrad Dressler did Dean Liddell at Christ Church, Oxford; 'Mary Magdalen' for Magdalen College, Oxford; and panels at St George's Hall, Liverpool, alongside those of C. J. Allen and Stirling Lee, from designs left by John Flaxman. He did majolica enrichment in the style of the Della Robbia family at the Royal Infirmary, Newcastle upon Tyne (1902) and 'Human and Divine Justice', 'The Lawgiver', 'Truth', 'Wisdom', 'Freedom', 'Knowledge', 'Mercy', 'Hope', 'Faith' and 'Charity' in majolica at the Law Society, Chancery Lane, WC2 (1902—4; *Bldr*, 23.4.04) for the architects Adams and Holden. The Tate Gallery has Dressler's terracotta busts of Ford Madox Brown, William Morris and John Ruskin, and a small bronze of John Ruskin by Dressler is at the National Portrait Gallery.

Conrad Dressler was a member of the Art Workers' Guild. He spent the latter part of his life in Paris and the USA.

DRURY, Edward Alfred Briscoe, RA 1856—1944

The son of Richard Drury, a tailor of London and Oxford, Alfred Drury went to New College, Oxford Choir School, and studied at the Oxford School of Art and at the South Kensington Schools under F. W. Moody and Aimé-Jules Dalou. When Dalou returned to France, Drury went to work for him there. He returned to London in 1886 to work for Sir Joseph Edgar Boehm, RA, Sculptor-in-Ordinary to Queen Victoria.

Drury shared with F. W. Pomeroy the task of modelling the colossal bronze figures standing in niches above the cutwaters of the piers of Vauxhall Bridge (opened in 1906). The bridge was designed by the London County Council to replace the first iron bridge across the Thames — the Prince Regent's bridge of 1816. There were protests from leaders of the architectural and engineering professions when it was learnt that the Council was going ahead with the design without calling in an independent architect or engineer, but the Council continued unperturbed. The piers up to the springing of the spans were designed in reinforced concrete cased in granite, while the spans were designed in steel. But the new Thames bridge was not so much a superb engineering design as an attempt at the monumental. Giant niches were formed in each pier by means of steel plates riveted together in a form that was closer to masonry than steel. Drury and Pomeroy were required to make colossal bronze symbolic figures to fill these niches and Drury's contributions were 'The Fine Arts' (with palette, statuette and brushes), 'Science' (contemplating a globe), 'Local Government' (with book), and 'Education' (with children). (*Bldr*, 5.10.07.) When the Council's chief engineer, Sir Alexander Binnie, retired and was succeeded by Maurice Fitzmaurice, it was found that the calculations for the bridge had to be redone. When all was completed the critics complained that since the river banks were in private tenure and the river steamers had ceased to run, the only way of seeing these giant symbols of civic pride in their steel-riveted embrasures was by hiring a boat. (*Bldr*, 23.5.03 and 26.9.09.)

In 1905 Drury did eight figures on the War Office in Whitehall, including 'The Fatherless Widow', 'The Winged Messenger of Peace', 'Truth', 'Justice' and 'Fame'. For Aston Webb on the Victoria and Albert Museum (1899—1909) he did the figures of Queen Victoria and Prince Albert, St Michael, St George, 'Inspiration' and 'Knowledge' at the main entrance, and stone reliefs on the main arch through which runs the motto, 'The excellence of every art must consist in the complete accomplishment of its purpose'.

Drury did figures of St George, St Andrew, St Patrick and St Michael for Harrow School Chapel and, in 1909, the putti and cartouche over the main door of the Royal Insurance Building, St James's Street and Piccadilly, following the style of Michelangelo. One of his last works was the statue of Sir Joshua Reynolds on a base by Sir Edwin Lutyens in the forecourt of Burlington House, Piccadilly (presented under the Leighton Fund in 1931).

Alfred Drury was made ARA in 1900 and RA in 1913 (diploma work, 'Lilith'). His 'Griselda' was bought by the Chantrey Bequest. He was a member of the Art Workers' Guild. Drury's son, Paul

169

Alfred Drury, RA: "South Africa" at the Buckingham Palace rond-point, London SW1.

Dalou Drury, has done a portrait drawing of his father which is in the British Museum. His grandson, Jolyon Drury, is an architect.

Alfred Drury's principal works include:

1898-1902	Decorative sculpture, and Joseph Priestley and Arthur Schuster, City Square, Leeds
1903	Queen Victoria at Bradford (setting by J. W. Simpson) and Portsmouth
	King Edward VII at Birmingham University, Aberdeen, Sheffield and Warrington
1904	Keystone, Royal London Friendly Society, Finsbury Square, EC2
	Bronze panel 'The Fine Arts'
	Queen Victoria Memorial, Wellington, New Zealand
	St George, Clifton College, Bristol
	Group, 'The Maritime Enterprises of the City of Hull', Hull Town Hall (for Russell and Cooper)
1907	Lieut. Col. William McCarthy O'Leary, and the South African War Memorial, Queen's Gardens, Warrington, Lancashire
1909	Richard Hooper, Cathedral Close, Exeter
	Memorial to Bishop Trelawny, Bristol Cathedral
	H.R.H. Princess of Wales, Cartwright Memorial Hall, Bradford, W. Riding
1911	On pedestals on perimeter of the Queen Victoria Memorial 'rond-point' in front of Buckingham Palace: West Africa — Leopard and Eagle; South Africa — Ostrich and Monkey; Canada — Wheat and Fruit and Seal •
1912	King Edward VII Memorial, Aberdeen
1915	Sir Robert Baden-Powell

DUNN, James Bow   1861–1930

J. B. Dunn was born at Pollokshields, Glasgow, in 1861, went to George Heriot's College, and was articled to James Campbell Walker in Edinburgh. He commenced practice in 1887 and won in competition the Library for the Society of Solicitors and the Dean and Charteris Memorial Churches, Edinburgh.

In partnership with J. L. Findlay from 1895 he did the offices of *The Scotsman*, North Bridge Street, Edinburgh (1902–4), a building with a floor area of 4 acres accommodating 12 shops and 200 office rooms. The sculpture is by F. E. E. Schenk. Dunn and Findlay also did the Adam Smith and Beveridge Halls, Kirkcaldy, Fife, and the reconstruction after fire of Norman Shaw's Haggerston Castle, Northumberland, c. 1913.

Obit. RIBAJ, 20.9.30, p. 711 *Bldr*, 29.8.30, p. 334.

DUNN, William Newton   1859–1934

William Dunn was assistant to William Flockhart and then to James MacLaren in whose offices he met his future partner, Robert Watson. MacLaren, who had developed an original style in London houses including two at Palace Court, W2 (1891), died in 1890 at the age of forty-seven and Dunn and Watson continued the practice. In 1900 they took into partnership William Curtis Green (*q.v.*).

William Dunn was a clear thinker on structural problems and one of the first exponents of reinforced concrete. With C. F. March, he wrote textbooks on the subject and was appointed adviser on reinforced concrete to HM Office of Works. He promulgated a 'theory of thin domes' (*RIBAJ*, 21.5.04).

Dunn and Watson's Inn at Fortingall, Perthshire (1891–2) is in the same simple vernacular style as MacLaren's designs for cottages and a farmstead there for Sir Donald Currie, chairman of the Union Castle Steamship Line. These were carried out by Dunn and Watson after MacLaren's death. The Scottish Provident Institution building of 1905 (extended in 1915 to accommodate the Scottish Widows' Fund), in Lombard Street, EC3, also maintained links with MacLaren, displaying the same preference for strange enrichment which he had shown in his remarkable pair of houses at 10 and 12 Palace Court, W2. In the Lombard Street building, the Corinthian capitals of the main colonnade are from *alternate* models. Together with the enrichment of the main doorways, the columns were carved by Laurence Turner (1864–1957). These and other details were possibly suggested by the restorations then beginning at Baalbek, which had roused new interest in the carving of the Eastern Roman Empire. (Dunn and Watson's assistant, A. C. Dickie, had recently returned from his Palestine Exploration Fund visits.)

Dunn and Watson also did the Scottish Provident
Institution's West End branch at 16 and 17 Pall
Mall, SW1. Here, following the fashion for Michelangelesque mannerisms adopted by A. Beresford
Pite and J. J. Joass, the balcony windows of the
façade's *piano nobile* are surrounded by tabernacles
which derive, with some modifications, from the
niches over the eight interior doorways of the
Capella Medici, or New Sacristy, of S. Lorenzo
in Florence. Other works by Dunn and Watson
included the Clerical, Medical and General Life
Assurance Society building in Carey Street, WC2,
and the same Society's branch in Duke Street, SW1.
Also in London, they did 46 Great Marlborough
Street, W1, in 1902, St John's Institute, Larcom
Street, Walworth, SE17 (*BA*, 7.9.1900), and the
British Bank of South America in Moorgate, EC2.
They also did some cottages at Abinger, Surrey. In
South Africa they did the Union Castle Line's
building in Atherley Street, Cape Town, and the
Mount Nelson Hotel, also in Cape Town. Herbert
Baker was resident architect on both these build-
ings.

William Dunn retired in 1919 to Kenya; he left a
bequest for the furtherance of research into tropical medicine.

Obit. RIBAJ, 24.2.34, p. 418 and 10.3, p. 475

**Dunn and Watson with Curtis Green and A. C. Dickie:
offices in Pall Mall, London SW1.**

F. C. Eden: cottages at Ardeley, Hertfordshire.

EDEN, Francis Charles   1864–1944

F. C. Eden was the son of a barrister, F. M. Eden,
Fellow of All Souls, Oxford, and agent to the Duke
of Buccleuch, who lent him as a home one wing of
Boughton House, Northamptonshire, where F. C.
Eden was brought up. Eden went to Wellington
and Keble College, Oxford, and was articled to
Bodley and Garner, the church architects. Here he
learned to be an expert in church architecture,
especially in furnishings and fittings, designs for
stained glass and heraldic devices.

Examples of his work can be seen at St Mary the
Virgin, Elham, Kent; St Protus and St Hyacinth,
Blisland, Cornwall; All Saints, North Cerney,
Gloucestershire; and St Lawrence at Ardeley,
Hertfordshire, where he also did the village hall
and thatched cottages round the village green.
Other works by Eden are St John, Harpenden,
Hertfordshire; St George, Newbury, Berkshire
(1933); fittings at St Melina, Mullion, Cornwall;
and he did the repair of the Treasury of Canterbury
Cathedral and St Paul's Vicarage, Observatory
Street, Oxford, in neo-Georgian style.

Obit. RIBAJ, Nov., 1944, p. 25   *Bldr,* 11.8.44, p. 144.

ELGOOD, Sir Frank Minshull, CBE   1865–1948

F. M. Elgood was articled to Alexander Payne and
was trained at the Architectural Association. He
was surveyor to the Hope-Edwards Estate and to
the Howard de Walden Estate in the Harley Street
area of St Marylebone, London, W1. Elgood rebuilt
or refaced many town houses in the area, including
49 Harley Street, 6, 8 and 10 Wigmore Street (*Bldr,*
5.4.02), 45 and 47 Wigmore Street (*Bldr,* 13.1.06),

and houses in Wimpole, Weymouth and Devonshire Streets. East of Portland Place, Elgood did 11 (Great) Castle Street, 7 Great Portland Street, 5 Margaret Street and houses in Bulstrode Street, W1. In Mayfair he did 7 Charles Street, W1. Elgood also did Dewar House, Haymarket, SW1 (*Bldr*, 2.7.10) for the whisky distillers and Northgate House, a large block of mansion flats in Prince Albert Road, NW1. In Woldingham, Surrey, Elgood did Cedar Lodge (now Tall Chimneys), Parkview Road.

In 1919 Elgood took Edward Hastie into partnership. The firm continues as Hastie, Winch and Kelly.

Elgood was a leading member of the Church Army; for his public work he received a knighthood in 1943 and had a block of municipal flats named after him.

Obit. Bldr, 28.5.48, p. 649.

EMERSON, Sir William   1843—1924

William Emerson, the son of a silk merchant, was born at Whetstone, Middlesex, and was educated at King's College, London. He wanted to be a painter, but was articled first to Habershon and Pite and then to William Burges. In 1864 Emerson went to India with Rudyard Kipling's father, John Lockwood Kipling, who had obtained a post at the Bombay School of Art and became Principal

Sir William Emerson: a model of the Queen Victoria memorial on the Maidan, Calcutta.

of the Mayo School of Art, Lahore. In India Emerson designed a number of buildings, including several churches and the covered markets of Bombay. He returned to England and continued designing buildings for India, including Allahabad Cathedral, Lucknow University, and a palace for the Maharajah Bhaun Bhaunagar.

In 1887 Emerson won the first abortive competition for a new Anglican cathedral at Liverpool on the site first selected, adjoining St George's Hall. (Not only was the site open to question but Emerson's design, a hybrid combining both Gothic and Renaissance elements, provoked much criticism.)

Emerson was asked to design the Queen Victoria Memorial for Calcutta, then the political and administrative capital of India, this time without competition (*Bldr*, 3.4.09). The idea of this enormous building, supporting *nine* turrets or domes and far exceeding in magnificence even the Belfast City Hall, was conceived by Lord Curzon, 1st Marquis of Kedleston, Viceroy of India (1899—1905). A contemporary guidebook describes the building as

> ... of Renaissance architecture with traces of Saracenic [*sic*] ... constructed under the supervision of V. J. Esch, CVO, at a cost of R.76,000,000 subscribed by the Peoples and Princes of India and opened by HRH The

172

Prince of Wales [Edward VIII] in 1921.
It is 339 feet long, 228 feet wide and 182
feet high ... The figure of Victory 16 feet
high and weighing 3 tons, revolving on a
globe, surmounts the dome ... At the lion-
guarded gate is a statue of Lord Curzon by
F. W. Pomeroy. The great Pro-consul stands
bareheaded facing his Sovereign and the
magnificent memorial he was instrumental
in raising to her Imperial memory. Surrounding his statue at the four corners are groups
of statuary representing 'Commerce',
'Famine Relief', 'Agriculture' and 'Peace'.
Proceeding up the drive we come to the
bronze statue of Queen Victoria by Sir
George Frampton RA (it was temporarily
set up on the Maidan awaiting its home).
Her Majesty is represented seated on a
throne wearing the robes of the Order of
the Star of India, on her head a Crown, in
her right hand the Sceptre, in her left hand
the Orb of State adorned with the figure
of St George.

Inside the Memorial is a large collection of monuments and relics including portraits of fifty-six
ladies of Queen Victoria's entourage, her favourite
desk and chair and a musical grandfather clock by
Whitehurst of Derby.

Emerson was President of the RIBA from 1899
to 1902 and was knighted in 1902. He died at
Shanklin, Isle of Wight. His works in England
included St Mary & St James, St James's Street,
Brighton (1877–9) and the Clarence Wing of St
Mary's Hospital, Paddington, W2 (1896).

Other works by Emerson are:

1898-1901	Hamilton House, Victoria Embankment, EC4, for the Employers' Liability Assurance Society
1902	Royal Caledonian Orphan School, Bushey, Hertfordshire
1910	Rebuilding of John Nash's Waterloo Place, SW1, a design for the Crown Commissioners. The buildings were carried out by A. E. Thompson (for Cox's Bank), Claude Ferrier (for Trafalgar House), Sachs and Hoffmann (for 3–7) and others

Obit. RIBAJ, 10.1.25, p. 155 and 24.1, p. 191 *Bldr*,
2.1.25, pp. 2 and 5.

173
174
215

EPSTEIN, Sir Jacob, KBE, HonLLD Oxon, LLD
Aberdeen   1880–1959

Determination combined with a measure of luck
enabled Jacob Epstein to put his work before the
public far in advance of general taste. For a sculptor, who has to find space not only in a gallery
but on a building if he is to place his works, this
was no mean achievement.

Jacob Epstein was born in New York, the son of
Polish-Jewish parents. As a child he showed an
aptitude for drawing which soon led to portrayals
of the scenery and racial types of New York's

Sir Jacob Epstein: the sculptor with one of his plaster
casts from which he carved the figures in situ on the
headquarters of the British Medical Association, Strand,
London WC2.

East Side. Epstein received his first training in art
at the Art Students' League in New York, where
his first teacher was George Grey Barnard, a pupil
of Cavalier in Paris. Barnard's group at the Capitol,
Harrisburg, Pennsylvania, 'The Two Natures' (now
in the Metropolitan Museum, New York), was an
early influence on Epstein. Determined to study
in Europe, Epstein paid for his passage by illustrating Hutchins Hapgood's *The Spirit of the Ghetto*.
He arrived in Paris in 1902 and entered the Ecole
des Beaux-Arts and the Académie Julien.

In 1905 Epstein came to London. Through the
critic James Bone, his brother, Muirhead Bone, and
Francis Dodd the painter, Epstein met the architect
Charles Holden whose design had won the competition for the Headquarters of the British Medical
Association in the Strand, WC2. Holden had designed a quasi-Mannerist, quasi-Secessionist building
and required stone figures in sympathy with a
style that was very new. In Epstein's studio in
Stanhope Street, Holden saw the statue, 'Girl with
a Dove', which led him to give Epstein a commission to do eighteen figures in Portland stone one
and a half times life-size. They were to stand
half-in and half-out of what were channels rather
than niches between the granite piers and stone
window imposts of Holden's highly original
building. The story of these sculptures was an
episode of major importance in Epstein's career,
and indeed in the history of sculpture in England.

Epstein immediately set to work drawing, model-

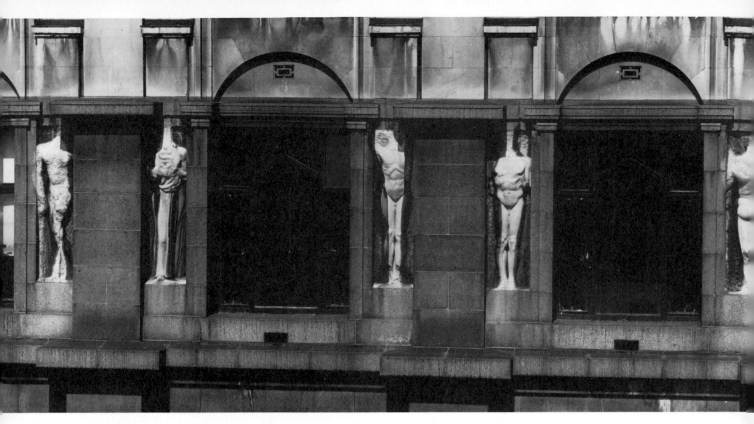

ling and casting the eighteen figures in plaster, ready to carve them on the spot himself. He had to work at great speed since the figures had to be executed *in situ* between completion of the stone-work and completion of the building. Of the eighteen casts he submitted, only one was rejected — 'Nature', a fleshy female figure which differed from his other ascetic figures. The eighteen figures were symbols of Birth, Youth, Life, Maternity, Age, Medicine and Chemistry. They were in a style reminiscent of the last unfinished works of Michelangelo and some of Rodin's works, while their situation recalled that of the central figures on Barthomé's Monument Aux Morts (1899) in the cemetery of Père Lachaise, Paris, which Epstein may have seen.

The resulting works were unlike anything previously seen in England. When the scaffolding was removed the storm broke — the first of many Epstein was to face throughout his life. Unluckily, the office of the National Vigilantes Society was right opposite and the full-size plaster cast for the 'Pregnant Mother' arrived on the scaffolding ahead of its first child; as a result it stood with bowed head contemplating, not its first child as intended, but its second pregnancy.

This was too much. Letters poured in to *The Times* and the *Evening Standard*, and the *St James's Gazette* referred to 'statuary which no careful father would wish his daughter or no discriminating young man his fiancée to see'. But the figures were declared decent by Dr Cosmo Lang, Bishop of Stepney and later Archbishop of Canterbury. In *The Times* they were defended by Sir Charles

Holmes, Director of the National Gallery, by the poet Laurence Binyon and, understandably, by the President of the British Medical Association which was paying for them.

The sculptor's profession requires him to be at once artist, estimator and contractor, and, not surprisingly, Epstein was out of pocket over the sculpture to the tune of £500, but the debt was paid by Mr Fels. The statues were allowed to remain and to be streaked by the sooty London rain. When the British Medical Association moved to the vacant Theosophists' building in Tavistock Square, WC1, in 1924, 419 Strand became the office of the High Commissioner of Southern Rhodesia who announced his intention to remove the statues. His excuse was that the figures, corroded by the acid-laden rainwater streaming down from the wall above, were dangerous, and part of one figure did come down after decorations for the coronation of King George VI were attached to it.

Walter Sickert, Kenneth Clark and others protested at the proposed removal and Charles Holden pointed out that the figures were an integral part of the building. The President of the Royal Academy, Sir William Llewellyn, declined to give his signature to the petition for their reprieve, while Sickert resigned from the Royal Academy over the issue. But the statues were saved, although their condition required some decapitations and amputations. A head, now owned by the Cochlan School for Girls, Bulawayo, Zimbabwe, was lent to the Edinburgh Festival exhibition of Epstein's works. Epstein commented on the fate of his work: '... Anyone passing along the Strand can now see, as on some antique building, the mutilated fragments of my decoration ...'

Epstein had just finished the Strand statues when he was asked to do the tomb of Oscar Wilde in the Cemetery of Père Lachaise, Paris. Epstein selected a twenty-ton block of Derbyshire Hopton Wood stone, the beautiful English semi-marble which he rescued from being cut up into wall slabs and which today he would find being burnt for lime. Holden was again the architect.

Epstein's design was a nude male angel with wings in a formalised Assyrian style, to which he gave a head-piece representing the Seven Deadly Sins. After the unveiling in 1912 at which Brancusi, Modigliani and Picasso were present, protestors succeeded in getting a bronze plate fixed to perform the function of the conventional fig-leaf, and supporters succeeded in removing it. Bernard Shaw and H. G. Wells tried unsuccessfully to get remission of customs duty on the work, and the tomb was covered by a tarpaulin until attention was distracted by the German invasion of 1914.

Epstein was, however, even better as a modeller than as a carver, and in his great bronzes he was not distracted from the steady course he set himself by excursions into Vorticism or the exotic forms of Mexico and Africa. Just as Balzac's features are now familiar through Rodin's representation of him, so Albert Einstein, George Bernard Shaw, Joseph Conrad and others are best remembered from Epstein's bronzes. The many bronze portrait heads and busts he did of sitters chosen simply for their outstanding features are also a part of his legacy. Many of Epstein's portrait bronzes are now in the Imperial War Museum.

Although consistent in his bronzes, Epstein continued to scandalise the public with his stone carvings. The unveiling in 1925 of his 'Rima', the W. H. Hudson memorial in Hyde Park (setting by Holden's partner L. G. Pearson), also unleashed a storm, and efforts were made to have it removed.

'Day' and 'Night' (1928 and 1929), the heavy and brooding figures on the Headquarters of the London Underground Railways, 55 Broadway, Westminster, SW1 — commissioned by Charles Holden once again — were equally misunderstood; while 'Genesis', shown at the Leicester Galleries (1931), was attacked by the majority of the press.

Epstein's 'Adam', an alabaster figure over 7 ft high, had a chequered career; the Leicester Galleries were reluctant to show it in 1938, it toured the country as a side-show, turned up in Louis Tussaud's Waxworks at Blackpool and visited the USA in 1940, before coming to rest at Harewood House, W. Riding.

Having passed through the Vorticist phase and the Mexican and African phases which so flabbergasted the contemporary public, Epstein entered his greatest period after the Second World War. Some of his greatest commissions and exhibitions of his works came after he had turned seventy, including the 'Madonna and Child' (1950–2) for

the Convent of the Holy Child Jesus, Cavendish Square, W1, which he considered his best sculpture, and 'St Michael and the Devil' in bronze (1956) for Coventry Cathedral.

Henry Moore wrote of Epstein:

> He took the brickbats, he took the insults, he faced the howls of derision with which artists since Rembrandt have learned to become familiar. And as far as sculpture in this century is concerned, he took them first.   (*Times* obituary)

Epstein recorded his views on sculpture in *The Sculptor Speaks* (1931) and *Let There be Sculpture* (1940). He was made a KBE in 1954.

Buckle, Richard, *Jacob Epstein, Sculptor*, London, 1963

Epstein, An Autobiography, London, 1955. (A revised edition of *Let There be Sculpture* by Epstein, 1940)
Obit. Bldr, 28.8.59, p. 102.

FAIRHURST, Harry Smith, senior   1868—1945

Harry Fairhurst was born in Blackburn, Lancashire, and articled to Maxwell and Tuke of Manchester in 1888. He travelled abroad for a time and then worked with William France, architect to Lord Bute in Cardiff. Fairhurst practised with J. H. France in Cardiff for a time, then in Blackburn from 1895 until 1901, when he moved to Manchester. He was joined by his son, Harry Fairhurst junior, and in 1929 by his grandson, P. Garland Fairhurst.

Fairhurst made important improvements in the method of handling cotton goods in and out of the great Manchester warehouses which he designed (*Bldr*, 1.9.06). They included India House, Lancaster House, Bridgewater House, Barclay's Warehouse, Reiss's Warehouse, Tootal Broadhurst Lee, Rylands and Sons' store, Blackfriars House, Arkwright House and York House.

Fairhurst was one of the architects employed by the manufacturer Richard Harding Watt to realise his ideas for a picturesque Knutsford, Cheshire (see title page).

After the First World War Fairhurst designed Ship Canal House in the new London style of Charles Holden's unrealised design for the Board of Trade building, Whitehall, SW1. Fairhurst's building was in Portland stone and thus inadvertently began to sound the death knell of the sandstone palazzo warehouses of Manchester's heyday. The Second World War and the Manchester population's understandable desire to escape from their sombre scenery hastened the destruction of the impressive picture once presented by this great city.

Obit. RIBAJ, May, 1945, p. 208 *Bldr*, 13.4.45, p. 287.

FALKNER, Harold   1876–1963

Harold Falkner was an orphan and was brought up by an aunt. He went to Farnham Grammar School, Surrey, where he came under the notice of W. H. Allen, the master of Farnham School of Art and the first to draw attention to the rich store of Farnham's eighteenth-century architecture. Falkner was articled to Reginald Blomfield. As architect to the landowner Ernest Borelli, Falkner contributed much to the preservation and embellishment of Farnham. He did many houses in and around the town and buildings by him range from the public swimming bath (1897) to the Town Hall (1930–4). In the same area he did The Chase, Churt, Ripley House, Liphook, and Tancred's Ford at Tilford. He contributed to the Cheap Cottages Exhibition, Letchworth, of 1905.

Falkner was a very able pencil draughtsman and many of his drawings appeared in the *Architectural Review*. Before Norman Shaw's Knights Bank, Farnham, was destroyed by its new owners, Lloyd's Bank, leaving only a chimney stack standing, Falkner made record drawings of it. Falkner was for a time in partnership with Niven and Wigglesworth, and later with Maxwell Aylwin.

From 1921 until his death Falkner built nine houses himself at Dippenhall with the help of two labourers. They are constructed from salvage from old timber buildings.

Obit. Bldr, 6.12.63, p. 1178 *AR,* Apr., 1964, p. 240.

FARE, Arthur C., RWA   1874–1958

A. C. Fare was born at Bath and went to Bath Forum School. He was articled to Silcock and Reay of Bath. When Fare was still quite young, Reay took him to see H. W. Brewer's 'Fifty years of Architecture' executed in 1892 for the jubilee of *The Builder*. Reay is reputed to have said, 'Now Fare, do you think you will one day be able to make a drawing like that?' The challenge was met by Fare fifty years later with a considerable feat of draughtsmanship in the drawing he did for the centenary of *The Builder*, representing the work of some seventy architects between 1892 and 1942.

Fare joined the office of C. W. English (1862–1931), then the leading perspective artist for coloured architectural drawings. Fare modelled his style on that of English until their work became almost indistinguishable.

In the rush of preparing designs for exhibitions, architects often relied, as they still do, on the perspective artist's ability to anticipate their ideas, as is reputed to have been the case with Frank Matcham's Coliseum — here the pink terracotta façade and dome on St Martin's Lane are said to have been worked out by Fare in his perspective. (The terracotta has since been painted over, alas!) The great drawing of the fine sweep of the Regent Street Quadrant as re-designed by Norman Shaw is also attributed to Fare. At the age of seventy-five he did drawings to illustrate the Bath Regional Plan by Mowbray Green.

Fare's memory for buildings was remarkable. A member of the Bristol 'Savages', he used to compete at their two-hour evening 'unseen' contests by illustrating the subject set with water-colour scenes of Bath or Bristol buildings and streets. None of his contemporaries had a better knowledge of Bath buildings.

After a period as partner with Frederick Cannon, Fare joined A. J. Taylor of Bath in partnership. The firm of Taylor and Fare was joined by A. J. Taylor's daughter, Mrs R. A. Gerrard, Taylor's son, A. Rowland Taylor, and A. W. Hind, and continues as Gerrard, Taylor and Partners.

Obit. Bldr, 17.10.58, pp. 659 and 698.

FARQUHARSON, Horace Cowley Nesham 1875–1966

Horace Farquharson was the son of Robert Nesham Farquharson, of the Bengal Civil Service. He went to Blundell's School and was articled to Gibson and Russell. He was an assistant to Edwin Lutyens for a year. Farquharson commenced practice in 1897 and, like Harold Falkner, did many houses around Farnham, an area rich in houses of the early Georgian period, which has received much attention from architects. Farquharson did Lodge Hill, Farnham (RA, 1902) with Norman Evill, also a Lutyens assistant, and in 1910 added a billiard room to Lutyens's Tigbourne Court, Witley, Surrey. He also did East Lymden, Wadhurst, Sussex and Hele Manor, Dulverton, Somerset and many restorations. In later years Farquharson joined in partnership with Donald H. McMorran.

Obit. Bldr, 29.4.66, p. 124.

A. C. Fare assisting C. W. English: a drawing of the design for the rebuilding of the Quadrant, Regent Street, London W1. Architect: R. Norman Shaw, RA.

FEHR, Henry Charles   1867–1940

H. C. Fehr was born at Forest Hill, SE23, the son of a wholesale merchant, Henry Fehr. He was educated at the City of London School, studied at the studios of Horace Montford and Thomas Brock and entered the Royal Academy Schools in 1885. His 'Perseus rescuing Andromeda' (RA, 1894) was purchased by the Chantrey Bequest.

Fehr's carved work is of a delicate order and his capitals sometimes have women's faces instead of the conventional acanthus flower. He did 'Astronomy', 'Architecture', 'Engineering', 'Literature' and 'Chemistry' on the Technical School at Scarborough (*Bldr*, 8.6.01); carvings on the Municipal Buildings in Walsall (*Bldr*, 28.10.05); sculpture on the School of Art, Hull; carving on the tower of the City Hall in Cardiff and the model for the Welsh Dragon surmounting the cupola there; Queen Victoria for Hull; and Doctor Cartwright for Bradford.

Fehr also did the over life-size bust of William Morris (RA, 1900) for the Art Workers' Guild and a copy for Water House, the William Morris Gallery, Walthamstow, E17. After the First World War Fehr did war memorials at Leeds, Colchester and Shepherd's Bush Green, W12. *His other works include:*

1900	J. Passmore Edwards, bronze bust
	Honor, Daughter of Fitzroy Doll, statue
1901	Honor, Daughter of Fitzroy Doll with dachshund puppies
1903	John Harrison and James Watt, City Square, Leeds
	Offices, Victoria Embankment, EC4
	Sculpture on Walsall Municipal Buildings (architects Wallace and Gibson)
1904	Figures on the Metropolitan Asylums Board's offices
1908	Modelling for bronze capitals to the internal marble columns at Debenham & Freebody (now in other use), Wigmore Street, W1
	Sculpture and carving on the London, Chatham and Dover Railway (now part of the Southern Region) Terminus at Victoria, SW1 (architects A. C. Blomfield and W. J. Ancell; *Bldr*, 5.6.09)
1912	John Hampden, Aylesbury, Buckinghamshire
1913	Figures and reliefs on the Middlesex Guildhall, Broad Sanctuary, SW1 (architects Gibson, Skipwith and Gordon)

FERRIER, Claude Waterlow   1879–1935

Claude Ferrier was born in St Marylebone, W1, the son of brain specialist Sir David Ferrier (1843–1928), who was attached to King's College, London. Ferrier went to Marlborough College, studied in Stuttgart from 1898 to 1901, under Professor Lauser and was articled to Sir Aston Webb. For Webb, Ferrier superintended construction in

Claude Ferrier: the headquarters of the Royal National Institute for the Blind, Great Portland Street, London W1. Had Ferrier's designs been adopted, a nobler rebuilding of Regent Street would have followed.

France from 1901 to 1902, when he commenced practice in London on his own account.

Claude Ferrier's work was principally connected with hospitals and houses for doctors in the Harley Street area; his hospital work included the Florence Nightingale Hospital for Gentlewomen, Lisson Grove, NW1, and the new consulting department at St Mary's Hospital, Paddington, W2.

Ferrier did houses at 58, 60, 65, 84, 87 and 119 Harley Street (No. 84; *AA*, 1910); others at 35 and 36 Cavendish Square, W1; and at 42, 43 and 44 Hertford Street, W1. He also did 81 New Bond Street, W1 and Seaford Court and Lexford Court in Great Portland Street, W1.

Ferrier did Trafalgar House, Waterloo Place, SW1, to the general design of Sir William Emerson, and the National Institute for the Blind for the British and Foreign Blind Association at 204, 206 and 224, 226 and 228 Great Portland Street (opened in 1914). These are especially noteworthy for their façades of clean-cut and well-detailed Portland stone which have a quality of expression achieved by few other buildings of the period.

From 1927 Major William B. Binnie was a partner. Claude Ferrier died in 1935 as the result of a road accident.

Obit. RIBAJ, 9.11.35, p. 37 *Bldr*, 12.7.35, p. 52.

Horace Field: Lloyd's Bank, Rosslyn Hill, London NW3, with red brick, Ham Hill stone and green slates, a splendid revival of the early XVIIIc manner by the co-author of a monumental volume on that period.

FIELD, Horace   1861–1948

Horace Field was the son of a London architect, Horace Field. He was articled to John Burnet senior in Glasgow and then to Sir Robert Edis (1839–1927) in London. Field entered the Royal Academy Schools in 1881, studied at the South Kensington Schools and commenced practice in 1881.

Although he made the best use of craftsmanship and traditional materials, Field's work is free of any hint of 'artiness', and least of all any trace of Art Nouveau. Field contributed measured drawings to Belcher and Macartney's *Later Renaissance Architecture* (1901) and some of his *new* work went into Mervyn Macartney's *Practical Exemplar of Architecture*.

178 Some early houses by Field are in Gainsborough Gardens, Hampstead, NW3. Field's Lloyd's Bank, Rosslyn Hill, Hampstead (1891) makes a perfect composition in the 'Wrenaissance' manner — the 'programme' can be read from the group constituted by the branch bank manager's house and adjoining houses, all in red brick with brown Ham Hill stone dressings and Westmorland slate.

178 While Lloyd's Bank at 112 Kensington High Street, W8, is an exercise in the Charles II manner, most of Field's work follows the 'Wrenaissance' style. The largest example of his work in this style is the

179 offices of the North Eastern Railway Co. (now British Railways Eastern Region) at York (RA, 1904). This was done in conjunction with the Railway's architect, William Bell. After this building, Field never managed to get the scale down, as

is evident from the company's London office in Cowley Street, Westminster (*Bldr*, 19.11.04). In 1903 Field did the adjacent offices of the *Church Times* and George Bell and Sons, 6 and 7 Portugal Street, WC2. In Westminster, Field also did 14 and 15 Great College Street (RA, 1906); 8 Barton Street (*AA*, 1910); and a house in Smith Square.

Stretching historicism further was the unrealised proposal put out to competition for demolishing the houses of Trevor Square, Knightsbridge, and replacing them with a miniature Place Royale (des Vosges), Paris. Field's design, in which he was joined by Cyril A. Farey, demonstrates how this might have been done successfully.

With Michael Bunney, his former pupil and chief assistant, Field compiled *English Domestic Architecture of the XVII and XVIII Centuries* (London, 1905). 'Field and Bunney' thereby contributed to the interest in and knowledge of houses of those centuries, and in so doing saved from destruction many which the guidebooks then ignored.

In 1906 Field took into partnership Evelyn Simmons and with him did 7 Palace Green, W8 (1913), houses in Elsworthy Road, NW8 (for William Willett), and houses at Letchworth Garden City and the Hampstead Garden Suburb. Here they did 80 and 82 Temple Fortune Lane (1908), 4 Wildwood Rise (1914), and Far End, Wyldes Close (1914). They also did South Hill, Hook Heath, Woking, Surrey; Thornhay, Great Missenden, Buckinghamshire; houses on an estate at Ripley, Surrey; Lloyd's Bank, Wealdstone, Middlesex (*Bldr*, 17.4.09); and Lloyd's Bank, Okehampton, Devon (*Bldr*, 26.2.10).

Horace Field was a member of the Art Workers' Guild. He retired to Stuttles, Military Road, Rye, Sussex.

Obit. Bldr, 25.6.48, p. 766.

Horace Field: a detail, this time from the XVIIc, in Field's characteristic larger-than-life style, for Lloyd's Bank, Kensington High Street, London W8.

Horace Field: offices at Toft Green, York, for the North
Eastern Railway Company in Field's over-life-size, early
XVIIIc manner.

FIGGIS, Thomas Phillips   1858–1948

After serving articles with Gresham A. Jones of
Dublin, Figgis was assistant in turn to A. E. Street
and to John Belcher. He entered the Royal
Academy Schools in 1883.

Figgis was responsible for the design of the surface
buildings for thirteen stations on the first succes-
ful Tube Railway in the world, the City and
Southwark Subway (afterwards called the City and
South London Railway and now part of the
Northern Line), first opened in 1890.

That year, with Henry Wilson of J. D. Sedding's
office, Figgis submitted in competition a highly
original design for the Free Public Library,
Ladbroke Grove, Notting Hill, W11 (RA, 1890),
showing a fusion of Tudor with the Art Nouveau
motifs then fashionable. Economies made in the
execution and the subsequent depredations of air

Horace Field: a detail of the Railway Offices, York. ▷

T. Phillips Figgis: the Radium Institute, now in other use, Riding House Street, London W1. Sponsorship by Edward VII and Sir Ernest Cassel and proximity to Queen's Hall and Foley House decided the first-class treatment of usually neglected side walls.

bombardment and weather on materials of poor quality have left a building in which the published Figgis and Wilson design (*A*, 20.6.1890) is scarcely recognisable.

Figgis worked in association in turn with Herbert Ibberson, A. Needham Wilson and Alan E. Munby (*q.v.*), articled to him in 1900. In 1909 Figgis and Munby won a competition for the Coopers' Company Schools, Bow, E3 (*Bldr*, 23.10.1909). Here the change in taste since the Ladbroke Grove Library is evident. The adventurous flights of Art Nouveau had given place to the historicism of the 'Wrenaissance' and to the full panoply of Wrotham red bricks, Portland stone, Buttermere (Westmorland) slates and carving (by E. Whitney Smith).

Also in 1909, Figgis and Munby did the Radium Institute, Riding House Street, W1 (now in other use). The idea for the Institute originated with King Edward VII who had seen the work of the original Institute in Paris. The building and equipment were the gift of Edward Cecil, 1st Viscount Guinness, and Swiss-born German financier and friend of King Edward VII, Sir Ernest Cassel.

Other works by Figgis and Munby included houses at Letchworth Garden City; a house at Wray Common, Reigate, Surrey and two at Bromley, Kent (RA, 1906; *Bldr*, 12.6.09); 12 Wellgarth Road, NW11 (1911); and an entrance lodge at Amersham, Buckinghamshire (*Bldr*, 19.11.04) for Cecil B. Cave-Brown-Cave.

Figgis was appointed architectural adviser to the Presbyterian Church of England. Figgis and Munby's church work included St Columba's Chapel, Oxford, St Ninian's Presbyterian Church and Hall, Golders Green, NW11, and St Aidan, West Ealing, W7. They did the Cassel Hospital for Nervous Disorders at Penshurst, Kent; the Home for Epileptic Children, Lingfield, Surrey; the Woolwich Polytechnic Institute, SE18; and the Borough Polytechnic Institute, SE1.

Obit. RIBAJ, June, 1948, p. 374 *Bldr*, 7.5.48, p. 564.

FLETCHER, Sir Banister Flight   1866—1953

Banister Flight Fletcher was the eldest son of Professor Banister Fletcher, author of *A History of Architecture on the Comparative Method for Students, Craftsmen and Amateurs* (first published by Batsford in 1896) — a work on which his son assisted him and succeeded him. Banister Fletcher senior had come from Newcastle upon Tyne and eventually became Professor of Architecture and Construction at King's College, Strand, WC2, in 1890.

Banister Flight Fletcher was born at Guilford Street, WC1, went to a private school in Barnet, then to the Norfolk County School at Bintree, and continued his general education at King's College and University College, London. He entered his father's office in 1884, attended the Architectural Association School, was a student at the Royal Academy Schools (1886—92) and entered the studio of Fasnacht in Paris.

Banister Flight Fletcher won the AA Medal for design, the Godwin Bursary, the Tite Medal of Merit and the RIBA Essay Medal. He was assistant to William Henman, Sir Robert Edis, and at the Metropolitan Board of Works under Thomas Blashill. In 1889 he entered into partnership with his father and his brother, Major H. Phillips Fletcher, DSO, who was killed in a flying accident in the First World War.

Like his father, Fletcher led an extraordinarily active life. He was honorary member, corresponding member or ordinary member of some fourteen professional or learned institutions at home and abroad; a barrister-at-law, he was senior sheriff of the City of London and was knighted in 1919; he was a member of many City of London committees, four City livery companies, seven masonic lodges and five golf clubs, and received decorations from France, Belgium, Italy, Rumania, Greece, Japan,

180

China and the Kingdom of the Serbs, Croats and Slovenes. He was President of the RIBA from 1929 to 1931.

Banister Flight Fletcher carried on his father's great *History*, and with the help of John Davidson, G. G. Woodward who made the drawings, and L. J. Flemen Gomme who did the distinctive lettering of the earlier plates, took the book through numerous editions until by 1928 the original edition had expanded to contain 3,500 subjects. The *History* is based upon a somewhat Darwinian view of architecture, similar to that expounded by James Fergusson, author of the first modern *History of Architecture* (1865). The view was welcomed in the second half of the century when a reaction had set in against copies of Greek temples, Italian palaces and French *châteaux*, made to perform a variety of functions in climates for which they were not evolved. Banister Fletcher's *History* is in a sense an *histoire à thèse*. It carries a message evident in its chapter headings, i.e. *Influences: Geographical, Geological, Climatic, Historical and Social, Religious.* The buildings described are clearly seen as the result of the

Sir Banister Fletcher: the tomb of Professor Banister Fletcher in Hampstead Cemetery, London NW6.

181

influences thus set out which provide a kind of moral check-list demanding observance of the 'Unities'.

Banister Flight Fletcher's principal works in London included St Aidan, Stratford, E15; St George's Hall and Schools, Old Kent Road, SE1; St Ann's Vestry Hall, Blackfriars, EC4; and the Roan School, Maze Hill, Greenwich, SE3. He did King's College School, Wimbledon Common, SW19 (1899), and the hospital and staff quarters of Morden College, Blackheath, are also his work. His Central London buildings include 30a and 30b Wimpole Street (1912), 46 Harley Street (*AA*, 1910; *Bldr*, 23.7.10), 20 Harley Street and 17 Kingly Street, W1. For Alfred Goslett & Co. Ltd. he did 127, 129 and 131 Charing Cross Road, WC2 (demolished), and other works by him are at 15 and 16 Garlick Hill, EC4, and 27 High Street, Kensington, W8. His Spence's building in St Paul's Churchyard, EC4, was destroyed.

Outside London Banister Fletcher did (National) Westminster Banks at Greenhill, Harrow (*Bldr*, 23.11.07), and at Hythe, Kent; The Dormers, Portishead, Somerset; Abbess Grange, Leckford, Hampshire (*A*, 25.8.05); and The Observatory, Canterbury Parade, Westgate-on-Sea, Kent. He also did the Banister Fletcher Mausoleum in Hampstead Cemetery, NW6 (*Bldr*, 23.11.01 and 23.11.07), where the bronze bust of Professor Banister Fletcher is by Nesfield Forsyth.

Sir Banister Fletcher wrote *Andrea Palladio, His Life and Works* (1902) and *The English Home* (with his brother), and revised his father's many textbooks. The most recent edition (1975) of his famous *History*, revised by James C. Palmes, is the eighteenth.

Smith, W. Hanneford, *The Architectural Work of Sir Banister Fletcher*, London, 1934.

Obit. RIBAJ, Sept., 1953, pp. 464—5 *ABN*, 1953, p. 238 *Bldr*, 28.8.53, p. 310 *Journal of the London Society*, 1954, pp. 18—26 *Times*, 19.8.53.

FLOCKHART, William   1854–1913

William Flockhart was born in Glasgow, went to Glasgow Academy and studied at Glasgow School of Art. He was apprenticed to Adamson and McLeod of Glasgow from 1870 to 1875 and, in common with other Glasgow students of his generation, studied in Paris. In 1878 Flockhart became assistant to Campbell Douglas and Sellars in Glasgow, but like many of his countrymen, he was drawn by Dr Johnson's 'fair prospect', and took the road to London. There he designed for manufacturers and studied at the South Kensington Schools.

In 1879 Flockhart joined another Campbell Douglas assistant, William Wallace, at 27a Old Bond Street, W1, first as assistant, then as partner. In 1880 Flockhart married Christina Jane

Lockhead. The following year he set up on his own account, undertaking business premises and town and country houses, while Wallace joined yet another former Campbell Douglas assistant, John McK. Brydon.

Flockhart's early works included the present Nos 2 and 4 Palace Court, Bayswater Road, W2 (RA, 1891), alongside a unique pair of houses by James MacLaren; 3 Hertford Street, W1 (RA, 1891), for Sir F. J. Mirrielees; and in 1893 Pasture Wood, Holmbury St Mary, Surrey, for the same client (additions in 1906 by Lutyens). He also did 108 and 110 Old Brompton Road, SW5 (formerly 7 Gloucester Terrace; *Bldr*, 9.10.1886), remodelling them in Early Renaissance style for Elliott and Fry, the Court photographers. Flockhart did a house and studio in Abbey Road, St John's Wood, NW8 (demolished) for the Edinburgh-born Royal Academician John McWhirter in 1894.

Flockhart was invited in 1900 to submit a design in limited competition for the elevations for the new Strand Crescent (Aldwych), part of the Holborn—Strand improvements (RA, 1901), but since the London County Council had no powers to impose a uniform design upon lessees the competition came to nothing (see pp. 80—2).

In 1905 Flockhart competed for the Wesleyan Central Convocation Hall, Westminster, and in 1908 was one of the twenty-three invited to compete for the new London County Hall in Lambeth.

At Nos 11 and 13 Lansdowne Road, W11 — two early stock brick and stucco Victorian villas which he joined together to form one house for the diamond merchant and art collector Sir Edmund Davis — Flockhart used brown limestone in the forthright manner of the time. The dining hall is in full 'Wrenaissance' oak panelling with nickel silver chandeliers by Osler. Other decorative work included oil paintings by Frank Brangwyn and painted silk panels by Charles Conder.

182 Lansdowne House, the craggy tower of flats and studios in the same road, was built for Sir Edmund Davis in 1904 to accommodate the inseparable artists Charles Shannon, RA, and Charles Ricketts, RA, and included adaptation of a pair of villas adjoining. James Pryde and Glyn Philpot occupied the studios when Shannon and Ricketts moved to Townshend House, St John's Wood, NW8, designed for them by Edward Warren (demolished).

At No. 180 New Bond Street, W1 — a building by R. Frank Atkinson for Darracq Cars — Flockhart set up his own office and also re-installed Elliott and Fry.

Worthy of a story to itself is Rosehaugh, Avoch, Ross and Cromarty, built for A. Douglas Fletcher, the fisherman's son who made his fortune in tea and rubber and returned to build himself a mansion near his birthplace. Including decoration and *objets d'art* of Duveen quality, the house cost £250,000 then, some £6,000,000 at present values.

William Flockhart: flats and studios in Lansdowne Road, London W11, built by an admirer for Charles Ricketts, RA and Charles Shannon, RA.

The resident architect was Stanley Adshead, then an assistant to Flockhart.

The practice was continued by Leonard Rome Guthrie (1880—1958), who married Flockhart's daughter. Guthrie was a pupil of William Leiper in Glasgow, an assistant at Campbell Douglas's office, and later a partner of Wimperis and Simpson.

Flockhart's other works include:

1903   The re-fronting of 12 Hill Street, Mayfair, W1, for Stuart Samuel, MP, in brick and terra-cotta, the models for which Flockhart did himself (since demolished)

Premises, Bond Street, W1, for Duveen Brothers, the fine art dealers

120 Long Acre, WC2

The Hall, Parkwood, Henley-on-Thames, Oxfordshire, for Sir Charles Henry (*AA*, 1903)

Technical Institute, Sydenham, SE26

1905	Presbyterian Church Hall and classrooms, (Upper) George Street, Marylebone, W1 (*AA*, 1905; *RA*, 1905)
	Alterations to 21 Kensington Palace Gardens, W8 (now the Lebanese Embassy), for Samuel Montagu (1st Lord Swaythling)
	Townhill Park, Swaythling, Hampshire, for the same client. Gardens by L. Rome Guthrie
1910	Royal State Rooms on SS *Balmoral Castle*, Union Castle Line, for the state visit of HRH The Duke of Connaught to Cape Town
	Work at Kinfauns Castle, Perthshire, for Sir Donald Currie, Chairman of the Union Castle Line

Obit. RIBAJ, 26.4.13, pp. 449–50 *Bldr* 18.4.13, p. 465 and 13.6, p. 681.

FRAMPTON, Sir George James, RA   1860–1928

G. J. Frampton was born in London. He started out in an architect's office and then became an outstanding pupil of W. S. Frith at Lambeth School of Art. In 1887 he won the Gold Medal and Travelling Studentship of the Royal Academy Schools which he entered in 1882. Frampton chose to go to Paris for his studentship, studying under Antonin Mercié. He exhibited 'Mysteriarch' at the Royal Academy in 1893, the year he married the painter Christabel A. Cockerell.

183

Frampton's best-known work is 'Peter Pan' in Kensington Gardens, erected in 1912. Sir James Barrie himself commissioned the statue and unofficially arranged with Leveson-Gower, First Commissioner of Works, to have it erected in the Gardens. A question was asked in Parliament, but the statue had quickly become so popular that it was allowed to remain. Frampton's model was Nina Boucicault, grand-daughter of the Irish-American actor and playwright, Dion Boucicault, and the first actress to play Peter Pan in the play based on Barrie's story, *The Little White Bird*.

Frampton taught modelling at the Slade School before the turn of the century and in 1894 was made director of the LCC Central School of Arts and Crafts, jointly with Professor W. R. Lethaby. Frampton was also Master of the Art Workers' Guild (1902). One of his earliest works (1883–6) was the terracotta decoration on the Constitutional Club, Northumberland Avenue, WC2 (architect Sir Robert Edis; demolished). On the Astor Estate Office, Victoria Embankment, WC2, Frampton did nine silver-gilt panels to the first floor centre door, of 'Ladies at the Court of King Arthur'. At the Savings Bank of Glasgow, 177 Ingram Street, Frampton did the sculpture on the additions by J. J. Burnet and Son and in 1898 he made a portrait of J. Passmore Edwards for Camberwell Museum and School of Art, SE5.

Frampton was made ARA in 1894, RA in 1902 (diploma work, 'The Marchioness of Granby'). He was knighted in 1908. After the First World War he did the memorial, near the National Gallery, to Edith Cavell, the nurse shot as a spy in that war; in Temple Gardens, WC2, the memorial (1920) to W. T. Stead, the journalist and editor drowned in the *Titanic* disaster of 1912; the silver statuette presented by the Royal Academy to King George V and Queen Mary on the twenty-fifth anniversary of their wedding, 6 July, 1918; and in the courtyard of the Pearl Insurance, High Holborn, WC1, St George and the Dragon, their memorial to the fallen in the First World War. A memorial to Frampton by Ernest Gillick is in St Paul's Cathedral and there is a self-portrait in the National Portrait Gallery.

Other works by Frampton include:

1900	External sculpture on the Glasgow Art Gallery and Museum (architects J. W. Simpson and E. M. Allen)
	Monument to Mrs Samuelson (d. 1898) at St John the Baptist, Kirby Wiske, N. Riding, with her children (white marble, attendant angels in bronze)
1901	The Coronation Medal of King Edward VII
	William Rathbone (1819–1902), St John's Gardens, Liverpool
	Queen Victoria for Woodhouse Moor, Leeds and at Newcastle upon Tyne
	Master's Badge, Art Workers' Guild
	Chaucer, the Guildhall, EC2
1902	'Sailing Ship' and 'Steamship', bronzes, Lloyd's Registry of Shipping, Fenchurch Street, EC3 (architect Thomas E. Collcutt)
	Figures for the entrance vestibule of Electra House, Moorgate, EC2 (now the City of London College), architect John Belcher
1904	Sir Arthur Bower Forwood (1836–98), shipowner, St John's Gardens, Liverpool.
	The 3rd Marquess of Salisbury (1830–1903) for the Oxford Union Society and for Hatfield House, Hertfordshire
	Monument to Georgina, Countess Howe, St Mary, Congerstone, Leicestershire

46

Sir George Frampton, RA: a detail from Peter Pan in Kensington Gardens, London W2. The character was derived from J. M. Barrie's story, "The Little White Bird"; the model was the Irish actress, Nina Boucicault.

Bronze bas-relief of Sir Walter Besant (d. 1901), Victoria Embankment, WC2, and in St Paul's Cathedral

Sir Alfred Jones, shipowner, Mersey Docks and Harbour Board, Pier Head, Liverpool

Archbishop Temple, Sherborne School, Dorset

John Feeney (d. 1899), plaque at St Peter and St Paul, Aston, Birmingham

War Memorial (South African War), Radley College, Oxfordshire

1906   Table Tomb (copper), Sir Bernhard Samuelson, Hatchford, Surrey (stolen in 1961)

Sir G. Williams (d. 1905), Crypt of St Paul's Cathedral

Quintin Hogg, Upper Regent Street, W1 (now in Portland Place). Bronze with two boys

Memorial to Dr Barnardo (d. 1905), Mossford Hall, Barkingstone, Essex

1907   Canon Thomas Major Lester (1829–1903) for St John's Gardens, Liverpool

1908   William Strong, RA, for the Art Workers' Guild, Queen Square, WC1

Monument to William Whiteley (d. 1907) for Whiteley Village, Walton-on-Thames, Surrey
Sculptured spandrels over the main entrance, Victoria and Albert Museum, SW7 (1899–1909; architect Sir Aston Webb)

Figures on the tower of St Mary, Oxford

Saints on the shrine of William of Wykeham, Winchester Cathedral

131   1909   Lions couchant flanking the entrance to King Edward VII Galleries, British Museum, Montague Place, WC1 (architect Sir J. J. Burnet)

1913   W. S. Gilbert (d. 1911), Victoria Embankment Wall, WC2. Bronze bas-relief with 'Tragedy and Comedy', inscribed 'His foe was folly and his weapon wit'.

FRERE, Eustace Corrie   1863–1944

Eustace Corrie Frere was born at Newlands House, Cape Town, the youngest son of George Frere, HM Commissioner of the Slave Trade in Cape Town and cousin of Sir Bartle Frere of India and South Africa. Eustace Frere went to Westminster School, was articled to F. Beeston and entered the Royal Academy Schools in 1886. He also attended the Atelier Pascal and entered the Ecole des Beaux-Arts in Paris, where he was awarded a silver medal.

Before setting up in practice Frere worked for a year as clerk of works for Reginald Blomfield. Frere did a number of medium-size houses in Shropshire, Hertfordshire, Essex and Surrey. His best-known work is the headquarters of the General Medical Council, Hallam Street, W1 (1915), with sculpture by Frederick Lessore (Royal Academy Schools, 1903–8) and his assistants, which the *Building News* (26.11.16) described as 'distinguished by delicacy and refinement in execution. The relief over the

entrance represents the cults of Asklepios and the pilasters support figures illustrating the functions of the Council'. The perspective drawings for this and other buildings by Frere, although signed by Frere, as was the usual practice, are by William Walcot — it was Frere who advised Walcot to take up painting. Additions made in the 1930s in the same style house the Medical Protection Society.

Among Frere's other works are St Oswald's Church House, Oswestry, Shropshire (*A*, 27.10.05); St John's House, Queen's Square, WC1 (sculpture by Lessore; *Bldr*, 3.8.07); rectories at Immingham and Fennyham, Suffolk (*AA*, 1908); and additions to All Saints' School and Mission Church and School, Boxhall Road, Leyton, E10 (*AA*, 1909 and 1911). Frere designed an eastward extension to the Royal College of Surgeons, Lincoln's Inn Fields (*Bldr*, 12.12.08; perspective by William Walcot).

FRITH, William S.   1850–1924

W. S. Frith entered the Lambeth School of Art in 1870. He became modelling master after Dalou's brief visit in 1880, the period when Lambeth was beginning to send out a stream of brilliant students who took half the Gold Medals at the Royal Academy Schools. (The age limit was finally lowered to give others a chance.)

Frith designed, modelled and supervised the execution of the ceilings, pediments and panels for the Victoria Law Courts in Birmingham, for the architects Aston Webb and Ingress Bell. He worked on Birmingham University for the same architects, and again for Webb did 'Grinling Gibbons' and 'John Bacon' on the Cromwell Road façade of the Victoria and Albert Museum (1899–1909).

Frith did the figures on the London School of Economics, Clare Market, WC2, for M. B. Adams (the building has been demolished), the figures in the spandrils of the arches of the screen connecting the new Government Buildings (where he carved the keystones) to the Foreign Office and India Office, in Parliament Street, SW1 for Sir Henry Tanner, and figures in the library and on the staircase of Cliveden, Buckinghamshire, for Lord Astor.

Earlier works included a marble chimney piece and bronze candelabra for the Astor Estate Office (now in other use), Victoria Embankment, EC4, for the architect J. L. Pearson (1895); and four statues over the doorway of the General Post Office, Leeds (1896), again for Sir Henry Tanner. Frith also did the stone obelisk with bronze figures of Liberty, Justice and children opposite the London Hospital, Mile End Road, presented by the Jewish residents of East London in memory of King Edward VII. Frith also carried out stone carving at 1a Palace Gate, W8, for C. J. Harold Cooper and did a bust of Selwyn Image (RA, 1902) for the Art Workers' Guild of which he was a member.

Obit. *Bldr*, 29.8.24, p. 310.

FULTON, Professor James Black   1876—1922

J. B. Fulton was articled to H. H. Wigglesworth and entered the Royal Academy Schools in 1898. He won the Tite Prize in 1899, the RIBA Drawings Prize in 1900, the Soane Medallion in 1902, and the Grissell Medal in 1903 (*Bldr*, 3.1.03 and 28.2.03).

His talents as a designer in the ebullient neo-Baroque of the Edwardian era were revealed in his designs for parts of the Franco-British Exhibition of 1908 where, in the words of an obituary, 'the opportunity of indulging in frisky French "patisserie" was seized upon by Fulton with avidity'. His work for the Exhibition included the Pavilion for Murati Mosaics (*Bldr*, 9.5.08, pp. 531—2). Fulton worked in the Architect's Department of the LCC and taught at the Brixton School of Building for nearly twelve years. In 1908 he was invited to compete for the London County Hall, and in 1914 for the Board of Trade Offices in Whitehall. His drawings of Santa Sophia, Constantinople, were a masterpiece.

Military service in the First World War left him in poor health and he died before he was able to take up the appointment of Director of Studies at the Glasgow School of Architecture.

Obit. *Bldr*, 12. 5. 22, p. 727.

GABRIEL, Edward   d. 1928

Edward Gabriel was the son of a Bristol architect, Samuel Burleigh Gabriel. The practice of Edmeston and Gabriel was founded by James Edmeston (1771—1867) who practised at Salvator House, City of London, where William Moffatt, of Scott and Moffatt, had been a pupil in 1830.

Edward Gabriel did Ashton Court Estate Almshouses, Bristol (RA and *AA*, 1904) and HMS *Formidable*, the nautical school at Portishead, Somerset (*AA*, 1904). On his London and Lancashire Fire Insurance Co. building in Bristol (*A*, 14.7.05) the sculpture was by Gilbert Seale. Gabriel also did the extensions to the South Western Bank, Leadenhall Street and Gracechurch Street, EC3 (*BN*, 1.1.09).

Obit. *RIBAJ*, 14.4.28, p. 375 *Bldr*, 2.3.28, p. 366.

GARBE, Louis Richard, RA   1876—1957

Richard Garbe was born at Dalston, London. After apprenticeship to his father, a manufacturer of tortoiseshell objects, he studied at the Central School of Arts and Crafts in its early days in (Upper) Regent Street, W1, and entered the Royal Academy Schools in 1901. In the same year, with Wenlock Rollins, he became instructor in sculpture at the Central School, remaining in the post until 1929 when he was appointed Professor of Sculpture at the Royal College of Art. On his retirement in 1946 he was succeeded by Frank Dobson, RA.

At the Baptist Church House, Southampton Row, WC1, for the architect Arthur Keen, Garbe did 'John Bunyan' and panels in the base of the dome representing 'Trees of the Bible'. Also for Arthur Keen he did the seated figures of King Edward I and King Edward VII — placed too high to be seen — on Kingsgate House, 114 High Holborn, WC1. At the National Museum of Wales in Cardiff (1910) Garbe did 'The Coal Age' and 'The Stone Age'. He was made ARA in 1928 and RA in 1936 (diploma work, 'Caprice', bronze); he was a member of the Art Workers' Guild.

Obit. *Bldr*, 2.8.57, p. 206.

GASS, John Bradshaw   1855—1939

Bradshaw Gass was the son of G. P. Gass of Annan, Dumfries, and was educated privately and at Bolton School of Art. Gass studied civil engineering at Owen's College, Manchester, entered the Royal Academy Schools in 1880 and was articled to his uncle, J. J. Bradshaw, in Bolton. He obtained the RIBA Godwin Bursary in 1885. After a period as assistant to Ernest George he entered into partnership with his uncle in 1880. They specialised in the design of cotton mills, dominating towns such as Oldham, and also designed many public buildings in Lancashire.

In 1903 Arthur John Hope (1876—1960), who joined Bradshaw and Gass in 1892 as an articled pupil, was made a partner, and the title of the firm became Bradshaw, Gass and Hope until 1913 when the present title of Bradshaw Gass and Hope was adopted. They won Manchester Stock Exchange, Norfolk Street and Pall Mall (opened 1906), in competition in 1904 (*Bldr*, 9.7.04 and 21.9.07). They also did the Co-operative Insurance Society, Corporation Street and Chesham Hill Road, Manchester, the Leysian Mission, City Road, EC1, in 1903, and the Tollard Royal Hotel, on the widened Southampton Row, WC1, in 1907 for A. Butterworth of Bournemouth. The lower floors provided offices for the Royal London Friendly Society (*BA*, 1.3.07). The building is now entirely occupied as offices.

Obit. *RIBAJ*, 14.8.39, pp. 952—3 *Bldr*, 7.7.39, p. 5.

GELDER, Sir William Alfred   1855—1941

'The maker of modern Hull', Sir Alfred Gelder was
five times Mayor of Kingston-upon-Hull and has a
street improvement named after him. He was the
son of William Gelder of Brough, E. Riding, and
was apprenticed for three years in a builder's
workshop, then articled to R. Clamp and W. H.
Harris of Leeds for 2½ years.

Gelder commenced practice in Hull in 1877 with
Llewellyn Kitchin and carried out the Covered
Market Hall and Corn Exchange (RA, 1902). This
was followed by mills, shops and warehouses,
offices and banks.

Gelder was Liberal MP for the Brigg Division of
Lincolnshire (1910—18).

Obit. RIBAJ, Sept., 1941, p. 186 *Bldr*, 5.9.41, p. 217.

GEORGE, Sir Ernest, RA   1839—1922

Ernest George was born in Southwark, SE1, the
son of John George who was in the wholesale iron
business. George was brought up in a house adjoining the yard and went to school at Clapham
Common, SW4, Brighton and Reading. He was
articled to Samuel Hewitt of Buckingham Street,
Strand, WC2, and entered the Royal Academy
Schools in 1857, where he won the Gold Medal
in 1859. On his return from abroad, when he was
still only twenty-two, George set up in practice in
partnership with a fellow student, Thomas
Vaughan, in Maddox Street, then moved to
11 Argyll Street in 1870, an area which, as George
was to say later, 'Norman Shaw had already made
classic ground'.

George and Vaughan's first major job was a country house for Sir Henry Peek at Rousdon, Devon ,
where they also did the church of St Pancras,
schools and farm buildings. But Vaughan died
young in 1871 and Harold Peto (*q.v.*) son of the
great railway builder, became a partner in 1876.

George and Peto designed many of the town
houses on the Cadogan Estate, Chelsea and
Kensington, and flats in Mount Street, W1, on
the Grosvenor Estate. Here George applied his
knowledge of the fifteenth- and sixteenth-century
architecture he had sedulously sketched, measured
and recorded in water-colours. George insisted on
a high standard of design and craftsmanship and
declined to delegate the design of interiors to
contractor-decorators, as was the general custom.
George and Peto were largely responsible for
transforming the 'dreary South Kensington
order' of the Cadogan Estate into various phases
of Flemish Renaissance with terracotta, red brick,
white woodwork, leaded casements and oak
panelling. Once known as 'Fire Station Holbein',
the style was more recently and with equal irrever-
ence called, by the cartoonist Sir Osbert

Lancaster, 'Pont Street Dutch'.

A pupil of George's, Darcy Braddell, dubbed the
practice 'the Eton of architects' offices' and
described how pupils 'were invited to cut their
initials in their bench and inlay them with red
sealing wax'. *The Times* called it 'that cradle of
the English Revival'. Pupils included Herbert
Baker, Edwin Lutyens, and Guy Dawber, each
of whom was to receive a knighthood. The
practice had meanwhile moved back to Maddox
Street and Ernest George continued to take a
personal interest in the design of large country
houses in Jacobean taste, which he illustrated
with his water-colour drawings. After a partnership of nineteen years, Harold Peto was constrain-
ed by poor health to live for a time in Italy, where
he made a special study of gardens. Alfred Yeates,
who had joined as a pupil and continued as an
assistant, was a partner from 1893 to 1919. In
1904 their contribution to the Louisiana World's
Fair was a British Pavilion designed as a double
version of the Kensington Palace Orangery (*Bldr*,
23.1.04).

George and Yeates's later country houses include:

1896	Shockerwick House, Bathford, Somerset, wings and lodge (stone, classical)
1899	Edgeworth Manor, Gloucestershire (major additions)
1900	Wayford Manor, Somerset (additions)
1900-4	Eynsham Park, Oxfordshire
1901-4	Welbeck Abbey, Nottinghamshire, recon- struction after fire for the Duke of Portland
1904	Ruckley Grange, Tong, Shropshire
1906	Busbridge Hall, Godalming, Surrey
1906-9	Crathorne Hall, N. Riding — large stone mansion in Edwardian Baroque for the Dugdale family
1907-9	Maristow, Devon (major additions)
c. 1908	Moor Place, Esher, Surrey, polygonal classical lodge
1911	Putteridge Bury, Lilley, Hertfordshire

The light, Flemish Early Renaissance style of
Edward Prince of Wales's age was indeed giving
way to the heavier, broader King Edward VII
Style. By 1907, when the firm did the Royal
Exchange Buildings, Cornhill, EC3, for the Union
Assurance Society (*Bldr*, 19.5.06 and 7.12.07),
the new style had set in, and by 1911 the Royal
Academy of Music, Marylebone Road, NW1, is
firmly of the Georgian Revival, as is Queen
Alexandra's Court for the Widows and Daughters
of Naval and Military Officers, Wimbledon, SW19
(1904, 1908 and 1912).

An exception to this trend is the crematorium at
Hoop Lane, Golders Green, NW11 (*Bldr*, 11.5.01),
opened in 1905, the second in the London area
(the first was at Woking, Surrey). Like the designers of churches and chapels, George and Peto were
experiencing the dilemma of style, and here chose
Lombardic brick Romanesque. The genius of the
place is, however, to be found in the gardens by
William Robinson who contrived to give to an area

Sir Ernest George, RA: the Royal Academy of Music, Marylebone Road, London NW1.

the size of a few suburban gardens the effect of spaciousness he achieved in his country gardens. George himself was cremated here, as was his famous pupil Sir Edwin Lutyens.

Unlike most of his contemporaries, George seldom entered for architectural competitions, but in 1900 he was invited to compete for the layout of the Mall and the rond-point at Buckingham Palace — a competition won by Sir Aston Webb. It was fitting that George should be invited to do the architectural trimmings of the new Southwark Bridge (completed in 1921) which leads to the Borough of Southwark and the site of the ironyard near where he was born.

In 1896 Sir Ernest George was awarded the Royal Gold Medal for Architecture, and he became ARA in 1910 and RA in 1917 (diploma work, 'Eynsham Hall'). He was knighted in 1911, was a member of the Art Workers' Guild, and was President of the RIBA from 1908 to 1910. His office was continued by Sir Guy Dawber and Dawber's partner, A. R. Fox, of Sir Guy Dawber, Fox and Robinson. Sir Ernest George published *Etchings on the Mosel, Etchings on the Loire, Etchings in Belgium* and *Etchings in Venice* (all published by Seeley & Co.).

Bradell, Darcy, 'Architectural Reminiscences ... Fugaces Anni', *Bldr,* 12.1.45.
Obit. RIBAJ, 23.12.22, pp. 106—7 *Bldr,* 15.12.22, pp. 900 and 903.

GIBBS, Edward Mitchel   1847—1935

E. M. Gibbs was educated at the Milk Street School, Sheffield, attended the Sheffield School of Art and was an assistant to Alfred Waterhouse, RA, in London, where he entered the Royal Academy Schools in 1871.

Gibbs started practice in Sheffield in 1872. In 1878 he became a partner with T. J. Flockton; they were joined in 1895 by C. B. Flockton under the style Flockton, Gibbs and Flockton. In 1902 the style of the firm was Gibbs, Flockton and Teather; in 1921, Gibbs, Flockton, Teather and Gibbs; and in 1923, Gibbs, Flockton and Gibbs. The firm, the largest in Sheffield, carried out many business premises, banks and factories. Their work there also included St John the Evangelist, Ranmoor Park Road (1887—8), the Mappin Art Gallery (RA, 1890), University College, (*AA*, 1903; *Bldr,* 9.5.03) and extensions to the Museum and Mappin Art Gallery (RA, 1904), Sheffield Public Baths, two branch libraries, and the Sheffield Telegraph Building. In London they did the Sheffield Telegraph Building, 181 Fetter Lane and Fleet Street, EC4 (1902).

Gibbs was instrumental in founding the Department of Architecture at Sheffield University.

Obit. Bldr, 3.1.36, p. 8.

J. G. S. Gibson: the Municipal Buildings, Walsall, Staffs. The sculptor, H. C. Fehr, has introduced women's faces into his foliage.

GIBSON, James Glen Sivewright   1861–1951

J. G. S. Gibson was articled to Ireland and Maclaren of Dundee, came to London in the early 1880s and worked in the office of T. E. Collcutt. After starting practice in 1889 he was joined in partnership the following year by S. B. Russell. They entered for competitions, succeeding with the LCC Hostel in Drury Lane in 1891, the West Riding County Offices, Wakefield, in 1894, the West Ham Technical College in 1895, the North Bridge Scheme Edinburgh (1896) and the Free Library, Hull. They were placed second in the competition for the Cardiff City Hall and Law Courts in 1897.

The Gibson-Russell partnership ended in 1900 and Russell joined Edwin Cooper. The same year
188 Gibson won the Walsall Municipal Buildings competition with William Wallace (*Bldr*, 13.10. 1900, 13.5.05 and 28.10.05) where the carving is by H. C. Fehr. In 1906–7, jointly with Wallace and Walter S. A. Gordon, Gibson did Debenham &
189 Freebody, 27 Wigmore Street, W1 (now in other occupation), a splendid ladies' department store for the 'carriage trade' in Edwardian neo-Baroque

(*Bldr*, 20.3.09; *see under* London's Edwardian Shops and Stores).

Gibson's best-known building is the former Middlesex Guildhall (now GLC), Broad Sanctuary, Westminster (*Bldr*, 3.3.11). Here the delicate late Gothic detail with tendencies towards Art Nouveau is by Frank Peyton Skipwith, then a partner, who was killed on active service in 1915. Here also the carving of a most delicate kind is by H. C. Fehr.

Other buildings by Gibson are Caxton House (alterations), Westminster (*Bldr*, 15.9.06), Mexborough House, 33 Dover Street, W1 (*Bldr*, 18.3.05 and 20.1.06), offices for the Scottish Equitable Assurance Society, 13 Cornhill, EC3, St James's Hospital, Balham, SW12, Arding & Hobbs's Store, Clapham Junction, SW11 (ground and mezzanine floors altered) and Parnall's Store (demolished), Wilton Road, SW1.

Gibson's practice was continued by W. S. A. Gordon, his partner since 1909.

Obit. RIBAJ, June, 1951, p. 332   *Bldr*, 11.6.51, p. 663.

▷ J. G. S. Gibson: a drawing by Charlotte Halliday of the tower of the former Debenham & Freebody store, Wigmore Street, London W1. The building is faced with faience, then popular as proof against the prevailing coal smoke.

J. G. S. Gibson: the Central Library, Walsall, Staffordshire.

GILBERT, Sir Alfred, MVO, RA, HRI, LLD
1854–1934

Throughout history, the important public commission has often meant great personal sacrifice for the artist so honoured. Michelangelo and the never to be completed tomb of Pope Julius II is the most famous example; Sir James Thornhill was held for nine years to an inadequate contract to complete the Painted Hall at Greenwich, while Alfred Stevens found he had undertaken to provide at his own expense full-size casts of the Wellington Monument for St Paul's Cathedral — a contract to which he was relentlessly held. For Alfred Gilbert, whose genius was to help raise English sculpture out of its slough, financial loss on the Shaftesbury Memorial Fountain led to a blighted career and voluntary exile from which he returned late in life to complete his last works.

Alfred Gilbert's parents, both graduates of the Royal Academy of Music, were teachers of music in Berners Street, W1. Gilbert went to a preparatory school at Southsea and hoped to join the Navy. When this idea was abandoned, he entered the Mercers' School, College Hill, Cannon Street, EC4, and finally Aldenham School in Hertfordshire, where his keen interest in modelling and

drawing developed; he hired a room in the village in which to practice.

Gilbert's father intended him to go to Oxford but Gilbert persuaded him to allow him to take the entrance examinations of the Royal College of Surgeons, which he passed in 1872. While waiting for a scholarship to the Medical School of Middlesex Hospital he attended Heatherley's, the nearby private school of art (still in existence). He failed to get the scholarship, but instead discovered his true vocation and continued at Heatherley's. He entered the Royal Academy Schools in 1874 while an improver to the Sculptor-in-Ordinary to the Queen, Sir Joseph Edgar Boehm, RA.

In 1875 Gilbert competed unsuccessfully for the biennial Royal Academy Schools' Gold Medal and Travelling Studentship, won by his fellow-student Thornycroft. On the advice of Boehm and Lantéri, Gilbert went to the Ecole des Beaux-Arts in Paris where he studied under P. J. Cavalier. The fear that the powerful influences of the Paris art world would overwhelm the individuality of his art prompted Gilbert to move on to Rome. His study of the fathers of the Italian Renaissance there confirmed his view that their work represented not so much a single style as the expression of the individuality of each master. Gilbert arrived in Rome in 1878 and stayed until 1884, sending works back from there to the Royal Academy and the Grosvenor Gallery. He had married his cousin, Alice Jane Gilbert, in 1875 and she accompanied him on his travels in France and Italy.

While Gilbert's preference was for the work of Florence and Venice, he did not undervalue the high standard of technical training offered in Rome and Paris. He was affected by the new influences at work towards the end of the century and in turn became a strong influence on his contemporaries and successors.

Monumental sculpture had reached its zenith — some would say its nadir — in the Albert Memorial of 1872, and a reaction followed. The whiteness, smoothness and roundness of statuary marble, a legacy from the Italian Antonio Canova, generated an opposite taste for the colour, texture and tenuous quality achieved by the combination of metals and coloured stones. The Pre-Raphaelite movement, and the subsequent taste for Japanese, Javanese and Art Nouveau objects, gave birth to a new style, one in which Gilbert excelled without indulging in its excesses.

The uncertainties of patronage, the hazards of contracts and his own inexorable standards restricted Gilbert's output to works of high quality which tended towards small-scale metalwork, jewellery and ceremonial regalia, but in moods of dissatisfaction Gilbert would destroy those of his works which did not come up to his demanding standards. His first important work in this field was the Preston mayoral chain, completed in 1888.

The 'Kiss of Victory' exhibited at the Royal Academy in 1882 and 'Perseus Arming' at the Grosvenor Gallery heralded Gilbert as the sculptor of the new Aesthetic style and his position was confirmed by 'Icarus', commissioned by Frederick (Lord) Leighton, PRA, and exhibited at the Royal Academy in 1884. In 1887 Gilbert completed the memorial to the blind Postmaster-General Henry Fawcett for Westminster Abbey and Queen Victoria for Winchester — the most outstanding memorial of its time. He did the memorials in St Paul's to Randolph Caldecott (d. 1886) and to the Earl of Lytton (d. 1891), and in 1890 did John Howard for Bedford. On the recommendation of Sir Edgar Boehm, Gilbert was commissioned for the memorial fountain in Piccadilly Circus to the 7th Earl of Shaftesbury (unveiled in 1893).

190

These works were followed by the tomb of Prince Albert Victor, Duke of Clarence, for the Wolsey Chapel at Windsor Castle, which Gilbert worked on between 1892 and 1898 but only completed in 1926. In this period he also did the monument to the 2nd Marchioness of Ailesbury, at Savernake, in Wiltshire, a statue full of beauty and mystery, veiled by a metal screen of rare design; the bronze grille in St Mildred, Whippingham — the church for Osborne House, Isle of Wight (a royal country home); Dr Thomas Arnold for Westminster Abbey; the High Altar in St Albans Cathedral; Lord Reay for Bombay; and the Lord Arthur Russell Memorial at St Michael, Chenies, Buckinghamshire, which has the finest collection of tombs in the country. Gilbert did Queen Victoria for Newcastle upon Tyne in 1900 and again in 1905 for Tynemouth.

Gilbert's portrait busts included among their subjects John Bright, George Frederick Watts, Sir Henry Tate, Sir George Birdwood, Sir Richard Owen, Sir George Grove, Cyril Flower and John R. Clayton — this last he destroyed. The Preston mayoral chain, the épergne for Queen Victoria, the figurine 'Victory' for the Winchester Queen Victoria, his 'St Michael and St George' for the Clarence Tomb, the presidential badge for the Royal Institute of Painters in Water-Colours, and his seals, keys and medals illustrate Gilbert's preference for working in the métier of Cellini, but with a style of his own — Auguste Rodin called him 'the English Cellini'.

Apart from monuments, memorials and insignia, Gilbert's only architectural and decorative sculpture was destroyed in 1938 when Daly's Theatre, Cranbourn Street, Leicester Square, W1, was pulled down quite unnecessarily to make way for the wholly insignificant Warner Theatre. The superiority of Gilbert's work can be seen in the photographs which survive and the interior was embellished by his inventiveness.

Self-criticism and depression left Gilbert ill-equipped to shoulder the triple responsibility of artist, estimator and contractor which is the sculptor's lot. His financial failure in 1901 was

Sir Alfred Gilbert, RA: the Shaftesbury Memorial, Piccadilly Circus, London W1.

precipitated by the building of his house at 16 Maida Vale, W9, opposite his parents' house, Woodlands, at No. 89, and designed for him by Howard Ince. The scale of the house and of his entertainment there (his guests included Queen Victoria) proved too much for Gilbert's resources.

King Edward VII offered Gilbert the opportunity of working at Windsor Castle to finish the Clarence Tomb, but, pressed by his creditors, Gilbert sought refuge in Bruges from 1903 to 1923 when he went to Rome. At the request of George V, Gilbert returned to England in 1926 to complete the tomb with statuettes of St Hubert, St Nicholas, St Catherine of Siena, St Etheldreda and St Catherine of Egypt. Replicas of the earlier statuettes, the Virgin and St Elizabeth of Hungary, are in the Kirk Sessions of Kippen Parish Church in Stirlingshire.

A new royal memorial followed, to Queen Alexandra, the Queen Mother and widow of King Edward VII (d. 1925). This, Gilbert's last work, which he modelled at Kensington Palace, is situated at Marlborough Gate, SW1. Executed in bronze, it is in the form of a wall fountain with a figure of Queen Alexandra seated on a canopied throne, a gem-like flow of water in a casket at her feet.

Gilbert also did in 1914 John Hunter (1728–93), Surgeon and Anatomist, St George's Hospital Medical School, Hyde Park Corner, SW1, moved from the Board Room to a gateway by Charles

Holden in Knightsbridge and then to the new hospital at Tooting, SW17.

190   The much loved fountain at Piccadilly Circus, by which Gilbert is most widely known, is a memorial to the great nineteenth-century social reformer Anthony Ashley Cooper, 7th Earl of Shaftesbury (1801–85). No gloomy monument with the conventional compassionate or protecting genii, Gilbert's work is a joyful fountain. The basin has some of the form and modelling of Art Nouveau, but free of its extravagances. The crowning figure of cast aluminium represents Eros, the Greek god, with bow and arrow. This was the first time Sir Humphrey Davy's new 'Aluminum' was put to such use in England. Its first use in art was seen at the Paris Exhibition of 1855.

But for Gilbert the memorial was fraught with disappointments and vexatious interference by the authorities. The water was not made to play as Gilbert intended, the basin was curtailed, and the site was an awkward one since it occupied one quadrant of the circus where, ironically, the hideous Avenue named after Shaftesbury debouched on the mutilated circus. The fountain cost Gilbert over £7,000, and he received less than £4,000. Worse was to come. The fountain was temporarily banished to Embankment Gardens during the reconstruction of the Tube station below and the flower girls who once sold roses and violets from their capacious baskets at its base never returned. Its future setting is still uncertain. There is a replica in Sefton Park, Liverpool.

No. 16 Maida Vale was subsequently occupied by two sculptors, first Herbert Hampton who died in 1929, and then Sir William Reid Dick, RA. It was demolished in 1969 for a block of flats which left 'not a wrack behind'.

Gilbert was elected ARA in 1887 and RA in 1892 (diploma work, 'Victory', silver). His wife died in 1916 and he remarried in 1921. He was Professor of Sculpture at the Royal Academy from 1901 until his resignation in 1908. He was re-elected in 1932, the year in which he received his knighthood. He was awarded the MVO in 1897 and the Gold Medal of the Royal Society of British Sculptors in 1926, and was a member of the Art Workers' Guild.

Sir Alfred Gilbert is buried in Westminster Abbey. He is also commemorated by a bronze tablet by Gilbert Ledward, RA, provided by the Leighton Fund, in the crypt of St Paul's (1937). The oval plaque bears a figure in low relief representing the Eros of the Shaftesbury Memorial. A chalk drawing (1887) by J. M. Hamilton is in the National Portrait Gallery.

AJ, 1903, Easter Art Supplement
Bury, Adrian, *Shadow of Eros*, London, 1952
Hatton, Joseph, *Alfred Gilbert RA*, London, 1903
McAlister, Isabel, *Alfred Gilbert*, London, 1929

GILBERT, Walter   1871–1946

Walter Gilbert was born at Rugby. He was instructor in metalwork at Rugby and Harrow Schools and joined the Bromsgrove Artificers' Guild where, with Louis Weingartner, he did the gates and screen at Buckingham Palace, part of the Queen Victoria Memorial in the Mall, SW1, and the altar rail and reredos for Liverpool (Anglican) Cathedral. He was a cousin of Sir Alfred Gilbert. His son, Donald Gilbert, became a sculptor.

Obit. Bldr, 1.2.46, p. 126.

Eric Gill: the inscription carved over the lychgate of St. Mary the Virgin, Great Warley, Essex.

GILL, Arthur Eric Rowton   1882–1940

Eric Gill was born at Brighton, a son of the Rev. A. T. Gill, a minister of the Countess of Huntingdon's Connection, and was articled to the church architect W. D. Caroë from 1899 to 1903. He soon took up designing and carving of inscriptions on wood and stone, and early commissions included the inscription on John Tweed's memorial to Sir George Ommaney Willes, GCB (1823–1901), in Holy Trinity, Sloane Street, SW1. He also did the inscription on the tie beam
191   of the lychgate to St Mary the Virgin, Great Warley, Essex (1903). Gill was a student of Edward Johnston at the Central School of Arts and Crafts and decided that the career of a busy architect like Caroë was not for him.

Eric Gill introduced the distinguished Roman lettering on the stationers' shops of W. H. Smith. Gill's first fascia for Smith's was in the rue de Rivoli, Paris (1903), and his Roman lettering continued to be used by Smith's until 1969. An early W. H. Smith shop front has recently been restored at Newtown, Montgomeryshire, and the restoration of others is to follow. But Gill is even better known for his 'Gill Sans' lettering. Gill was a convert to Catholicism and his greatest work is the Stations of the Cross for Westminster Cathedral (1912–13), done in a combination of line and low relief, anticipating a style which was to emerge in the 1930s. After the First World War Gill did many war memorials and turned to sculpture. His best-known work in this field is 'Prospero and Ariel' on Broadcasting House, Langham Place, W1. Earlier he did some of the 'Winds' on the Underground Headquarters, 55 Broadway, SW1, for Charles Holden.

Eric Gill was a member of the Art Workers' Guild and was made ARA in 1937. His brother, Macdonald Gill, designed maps in tapestry for South Africa House, Trafalgar Square, and tiles for Messrs Boots at Windsor, and painted the chancel ceiling at St Andrew, Roker, Sunderland, for Prior.

Attwater, David, *A Call of Good Living: the life, works and opinions of Eric Gill*, London, 1969
Gill, Eric, *Autobiography*, London, 1940
Gill, Evan R., *The Inscriptional Work of Eric Gill. An Inventory*, London, 1964
Obit. RIBAJ, 16.12.40, p. 20. *Bldr*, 22.11.40, p. 511.

GILLESPIE, John Gaff   1870–1926

Born in Glasgow, the son of a master baker, Gillespie was apprenticed to J. M. Munroe. A brilliant draughtsman, he won the Glasgow Institute of Architecture Prize in 1889, taking equal place with Charles Rennie Mackintosh. He entered the office of James Salmon and Son and in 1897 was made a partner. James Salmon junior (grandson of the founder of the firm) became a partner the following year. As their interesting and original work bears out, both young architects were in sympathy with the Glasgow school of painters and the work of the Glasgow School of Art. Their buildings gave full opportunity to sculptors like Derwent Wood, Albert Hodge and Johan Keller, the Dutch sculptor then working in Glasgow. (For their joint works, *see under* Salmon, James.)

The firm continues as Gillespie, Kidd and Coia.

Obit. Bldr, 23.7.26, p. 1142.

GILLICK, Ernest George, ARA   1874–1951

Ernest Gillick was born in Bradford and studied at the Royal College of Art. In 1908 he did 'J. M. W. Turner' and 'Richard Cosway' on the Cromwell Road façade of the Victoria and Albert Museum, SW7, and Sir Francis Sharp Powell, MP, Mesnes Park, Wigan, Lancashire (unveiled in 1910). Gillick

also did the memorials to Dr Shuckburgh (1909) and James Adam (1912) at Emmanuel College, Cambridge.

With his wife Mary (née Tutin), whom he married in 1905 and who died in 1965, he did many portrait reliefs and medals. Because of the curious history of the novelist 'Ouida', the memorial erected to her memory at Vinery Road, Bury St Edmunds, Suffolk, in 1909, was perhaps Gillick's most interesting commission. Ouida, whose real name was Maria Louise Ramé (or de la Ramée), was born at Bury St Edmunds in 1839 of an English mother and a French father believed to have died in the Commune risings of 1870–1. Ouida not only had a talent for writing melo-dramas set amid the glamour of society drawing rooms and the rigours of service in the Foreign Legion, but attempted to live out the extravagant life portrayed in her novels, the most famous of which was *Under Two Flags*. She settled in Florence in 1874 where her desperate efforts to hold sensationally large soirées led to her impover-ishment. She was buried at Bagni de Lucca where her tomb is by Giuseppe Norfini. When news came of her death, the *Daily Mirror* launched a memor-ial fund and sponsored a dramatised version of *Under Two Flags* at the Lyceum Theatre. Gillick's memorial to her is in the form of a drinking fountain with four troughs for horses and one for dogs, showing a bronze medallion of Ouida and allegorical figures — 'Courage' with a sword and 'Sympathy' with a dog in her arms. The inscription is by Lord Curzon of Kedleston, who was also interested in that other writer of extravagant tales, Elinor Glyn. Today Ouida's memorial stands isolated by unscrupulous road widenings and with a public telephone box for company.

After the First World War Gillick did one of the last of those allegorical groups typical of the Edwardian period, on the National Provincial (now National Westminster) Bank, Princes Street, EC2 — Britannia seated between the figures of 'Higher Mathematics' and 'Lower Mathematics', support-ed by 'Mercury' and 'Truth', with the 'Owl of Wisdom' in one corner. He also did 'Henry VII at Bosworth Field' (1918), the gift of Lord Rhondda to the City of Cardiff, and, later in his career, a figure for the Birmingham Hospitals Centre with the motto *Ex tenebris lux* (1935), and the memorial to Sir George Frampton, RA, in St Paul's Cathedral.

He was a member of the Art Workers' Guild and was made ARA in 1935 and Senior Associate of the Royal Academy in 1950.

Obit. Bldr, 5.10.51, p. 460.

Ernest Gimson: the Village Hall at Sapperton, Gloucestershire.

GIMSON, Ernest William   1864–1919

Ernest Gimson was born in Leicester. His father was Josiah Gimson, founder of the engineering firm of Gimson & Co. and a Secularist. Gimson was articled to the architect Isaac Barradale and attended Leicester School of Art. He met William Morris when the latter came to lecture at the Secular Hall, Leicester, in 1884. Morris recommended him to enter the office of J. D. Sedding, next door to his own Oxford Street showrooms. On completing articles, Gimson worked for Sedding from 1886 to 1888.

At Sedding's office he met Alfred Powell and Ernest Barnsley and for a time shared lodgings with Barnsley's brother Sidney who was at Norman Shaw's office. Through him he met others of Shaw's pupils including W. R. Lethaby and Robert Schultz Weir. United by their admiration for William Morris and Philip Webb, they used to accompany each other sketching and measuring at the South Kensington Museum and in the countryside.

In 1889 Gimson joined Morris's Society for the Protection of Ancient Buildings. Under Morris's inspiration and the technical guidance of Philip Webb, the Society was a remarkable training ground for practical building 'with all the whims which we usually call design left out', as Lethaby put it. On behalf of the Society, Gimson visited buildings threatened with demolition or bad restoration, giving practical advice.

Gimson exhibited his furniture at the Arts and Crafts Exhibition Society in 1890 and was one of the group, including Lethaby, which founded

Kenton & Co. that year (*see under* Blomfield, Sir Reginald Theodore).

To get away from what Alfred Powell described as 'the deathly dreariness of the respectable offices with framed perspectives on the walls and "clerks" (draughtsmen-assistants) slaving in the background', Gimson and the Barnsleys took an office next door to Philip Webb in Raymond Buildings, Gray's Inn. Here they installed oak furniture and a trestle table 'that at reasonable hours surrendered their drawing boards to a good English meal in which figured, at least on guest nights, a great stone jar of the best ale'. But this was only a compromise. After much scouring of the Gloucestershire countryside from a temporary base at Ewen, the three friends took a cottage at Pinbury, five miles from Cirencester, leased to them by Earl Bathurst. Gimson married the daughter of the Rev. Robert Thompson, vicar of Skipsea, E. Riding, in 1900.

At first Gimson and Ernest Barnsley set up a small workshop in the yard of the Fleece Inn, in Market Square, Cirencester. After a brief stay at Pinbury they moved to Sapperton where, with financial help from Earl Bathurst, whose family still owns the village, they built houses, completed in 1903. They also leased Daneway House from Earl Bathurst, using the stables as workshops and the old house for the display of furniture, metalwork and fabrics. Gimson learned decorative plasterwork from Whitcombe and Priestly, furniture-making from Philip Clisset of Bosbury, near Ledbury, and cabinet-making and smithying from William Bucknall and his son Alfred Bucknall, from Tunley. Sir William Rothenstein's contention, in his *Men and Memories*, that Gimson took over

Ernest Gimson: Lea Cottage, Markfield, Charnwood Forest, Leicestershire.

the village's craftsmen, is quite unfounded. The nucleus of the cabinet-makers came from London while local boys were apprenticed and trained. In charge was Peter (van der) Waals (1870–1937) who had come from the Hague in response to their advertisement for a chief cabinet-maker.

Gimson's work expresses the ideals of William Morris and the Arts and Crafts Movement — the materials, the right design for the materials, and the essential nobility of the craftsman and his work. But simple though it was, Gimson's work reached only a few. He had initially intended his furniture to be within the reach of many, but he came to regard aloofness from commercialism as 'our success, not our failure, as some think'. He wanted commercialism to leave handiwork and the arts alone and make use of its own wits and machinery. 'Let machinery be honest and make its own machine buildings and machine furniture; let it make its chairs and tables of stamped aluminium if it likes; why not?' Were it not for the Georgian and other period revivals, Gimson furniture and that of the Barnsleys, Peter Waals, Sir Ambrose Heal, Sir Gordon Russell, Henry Sellers and Charles Spooner might have sooner influenced manufacturers towards those simpler designs which only came into common use some thirty years later, and then by way of Scandinavia and as 'Utility' furniture, resulting from the work of Sir Gordon Russell during the Second World War.

Gimson's houses were derived from the vernacular styles of the fifteenth- and sixteenth-centuries. His early domestic work included a number of houses in Leicester: Inglewood, Ratcliffe Road (1892) for himself; The White House, North Avenue (1897) for Arthur Gimson; and (1899) Stoney-well Cottage and Lea Cottage at Markfield. He also

did alterations and additions to Pinbury Park, Gloucestershire, and two cottages at Kelmscott. In 1915 he did unrealised designs for the village hall at Kelmscott which was eventually erected in 1933 to the designs of A. R. Powys.

The stalls in St Andrew's Chapel, Westminster Cathedral, are Gimson's work, as are those for Khartoum Cathedral, also for Robert Schultz Weir. He also did the altar cross and altar candle-sticks — a memorial to Keith Debenham, killed in the First World War — at St Peter's, Vere Street, W1.

In 1911 Gimson submitted a design in competition for the Australian capital city of Canberra (won by Walter Burley Griffin of Chicago). After the First World War, Gimson designed the Hall at Bedales School at Steep, near Petersfield. (The first buildings were by Edward Warren.) This was followed by the War Memorial Library, designed by Gimson and built by Sidney Barnsley. The building is a perfect culmination to the work of Gimson, and his drawings for it are a model of what a craftsman-architect's drawings should be. His chairs for the Hall — the 'Bedales chair', originally known as the 'Mission chair' — were first used in a meeting hall by F. W. Troup at Wootton Fitzpaine, near Dorchester. After Gimson's death, the Library was carried on by

Ernest Gimson: the lectern at St. Andrew, Roker, Sunderland, a church of the Arts and Crafts Movement by E. S. Prior.

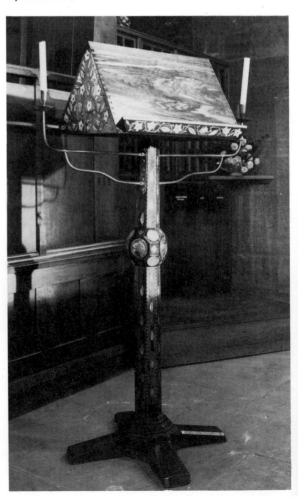

Sidney Barnsley, and after Barnsley's death, by his son Edward Barnsley. Gimson's decorative plasterwork closely resembled that of George Bankart, another Leicester architect turned craftsman, and both derived their plant forms from designs by William Morris.

In his contribution to the Catalogue of the Ernest Gimson Exhibition (Leicester, 1969), Sir George Trevelyan wrote:

> His genius was such that he could put himself completely into the understanding and experience of a craft, so that, as far as makes no matter, he *was* the craftsman in that skill ... Gimson cut right across the welter of Victorian design and lack of design by creating a woodworkers' tradition and reverting basically to the interest and delight in sheer honest construction in superlative woods used mostly in the solid.

Gimson died at Sapperton and was buried under the yews in Sapperton churchyard, his grave marked by a slab of Edgeworth stone with an inscription on a copper plate — a local tradition. Alongside are the graves of the Barnsleys and Sir Emery Walker, the fine printer. Gimson's work was continued by Peter Waals, the Barnsleys and by Norman Jewson (1884—1974) who came to Sapperton in 1907 from the Lincoln's Inn office of Herbert G. Ibberson.

Gimson was a member of the Art Workers' Guild.

Cheltenham Art Gallery, collected by D. W. Herdmann, (acquired by the Gallery in 1941), Working Drawings by Ernest Gimson

Jewson, Norman, *By Chance I Did Rove*, Kineton, Warwickshire, *c.* 1950 and 1973

Leicester Museum, Catalogue of exhibition of Gimson's work, 1969

Lethaby, W. R., Alfred H. Powell and Frank L. Griggs, *Ernest Gimson, His Life and Work*, 1924

Obit. Bldr, 22.8.19, p. 184 and 5.9, p. 230.

GLEICHEN, HSH Feodora Georgina Maud, Countess   1861—1922

Born in London, Countess Gleichen was the eldest daughter of Admiral Prince Victor of Hohenlohe-Langenburg, Count Gleichen, a son of Queen Victoria's half-sister Feodora. Her mother, Countess Gleichen, was the youngest daughter of Admiral of the Fleet Sir George Francis Seymour. After his retirement from the Royal Navy, Prince Victor took up sculpture and Queen Victoria gave him a studio in St James's Palace. Here he did King Alfred the Great, presented in 1877 by Sir Robert Loyd-Lindsay (later Baron Wantage) to Wantage, Berkshire, the birthplace of King Alfred.

Lady Feodora Gleichen studied at the Slade School under Alphonse Légros. Her sister Helena (d. 1947) was a painter and her brother, Major-General Count Edward Gleichen, was the author of *London's Open Air Statuary* (Longmans, London, 1928).

Lady Gleichen's earlier work included a monument to her father at Holy Trinity, Sunningdale, Berkshire (1891); the life-size group of Queen Victoria and her Children for the Children's Hospital, Montreal (1895); and Queen Victoria for Cheltenham Ladies' College, Gloucestershire (1895). In 1899 she did the Diana Fountain, commissioned by Sir Walter Palmer. This was first set up at Ascot in 1899 and presented to Hyde Park in 1906 by Lady Palmer.

Lady Gleichen lived in rooms in St James's Palace and was (posthumously) the first woman member of the Royal Society of British Sculptors. Among her last works were the Kitchener Memorial in Khartoum Cathedral (1920; architect Robert Schultz Weir), and the memorial to the dead of the 37th (British) Division (her brother's Division), at Monchy-le-Preux, France.

Lady Gleichen's other works include:

1900	Memorial to General Sir Henry Ponsonby, relief bronze (RA, 1900)
	Fountain in the garden of the Comtesse de Bearn, Paris
1901	Memorial to the Hon. Edward Lygon and the Hon. Richard Somerset, at St Mary, Madresfield, Worcestershire
	Florence Nightingale in front of the Royal Infirmary, Derby
1903	HM Queen Victoria bust, ivory (RA, 1903)
1904	HM Queen Victoria bust (RA, 1904)

GODDARD, Henry Langton   1866—1944

H. L. Goddard was articled to his father, Joseph Goddard of Leicester, and was assistant to Sir T. G. Jackson, RA (1887—8). On joining his father's office he won the competitions for the Leicester Cemetery and Crematorium, the Carnegie Library, Kettering (*Bldr*, 25.4.03) and the Alliance Assurance Co.'s offices in Birmingham and Sheffield.

Henry Goddard carried out many church restorations. He did the new church of St James, London Road, Leicester (1899—1914) — where the interior is in terracotta — and churches at Newbold Verdon and Ellistown. He also did many houses, including most of those at Horninghold, Leicestershire, for T. A. Hardcastle of Blaston Hall. Goddard was succeeded by his son Henry Gordon Goddard.

GODFREY, Walter Hindes   1881—1961

Walter Godfrey was born in London, educated at
Whitgift Grammar School and articled to James
Williams, the successor to George Devey. Godfrey
studied at the Central School of Arts and Crafts
and started practice in 1905 in partnership with
E. Livingstone Wratten who had been articled to
Devey. They continued the practice of James
Williams and were later joined by Godfrey's son
Emil. Wratten and Godfrey did the Eton College
War Memorial Chapel (First World War) and altera-
tions to Ascott, Buckinghamshire. They also
undertook the removal of Crosby Hall from
Bishopsgate, EC2, to its new home in Chelsea on
the site of Sir Thomas More's Garden (*AR*, 1910).
After the Second World War they did the restora-
tion of the Temple Church, WC2, and Chelsea
Old Church, SW3.

A member of the Committee for the 'Survey of
the Memorials of Greater London', started by
C. R. Ashbee in 1894, Godfrey was responsible
for several volumes of its publication (the first
appeared in 1899). He won the RIBA Essay Prize
with 'The Life of George Devey', which he rewrote
for the *AR* in 1908. He was also the author of a
three-volume *History of the Parish of Chelsea*,
Vol. 1 of which appeared in 1909. Godfrey was
also interested in gardens and produced a number
of books and articles on the subject in the course
of a lifetime's dedication to the nation's architectural heritage. His devotion to conservation,
preservation and sympathetic restoration shows
in his restoration of Herstmonceux Castle,
Sussex, for Sir Paul Latham in 1933, and in his
guardianship of the town of Lewes. He also
restored Horse-lunges Manor, Hellingly, Sussex,
in 1925. It was owing to Godfrey's foresight and
energy that the National Buildings Record was
built up so expeditiously during the Second
World War.

Obit. RIBAJ, Jan., 1962, pp. 17—8 *Bldr,* 22.9.61, p.534.

GOLDIE, Edward   1856—1921

Edward Goldie was born in Sheffield, went to
school at St Cuthbert's, Ushaw, County Durham,
and was articled to his father, George Goldie, in
1875. He subsequently became his father's assistant, and then in 1880 his partner.

George Goldie (1828—87) had established a
reputation among Roman Catholic communities
as an able designer of their churches, religious
houses and schools and his work had included the
great Jesuit Missionary College of St Joseph, Mill
Hill, NW7. Goldie senior had tried his hand at
competitions and been disappointed over those for
Lille Cathedral and the Brussels Hôtel de Ville.
But he won the award for St James, Spanish

Place, Marylebone, W1, in 1885, a success which
gave him particular satisfaction because it involved
replacing a chapel built by his grandfather, Joseph
Bonomi, ARA (1739—1808). The design was
reputedly largely the work of Edward Goldie and
C. E. Child (1843—1911), the chief assistant and
manager who had been with the firm since he was
a pupil.

George Goldie did not live to see the church
completed. Edward Goldie and Child became
partners for a short time, but when St James's
was finished in 1893, Child left and carried on a
small practice in Ealing. Edward Goldie took his
son Joseph (1882—1953) into partnership. He did
Ashorne Hill House, Newbold Pacey, Warwickshire (1895—7; *Bldr,* 1898).

Edward Goldie was buried in France where his
father was also buried, by the roadside at S. Jouan
des Guerets, St Servan, Ile-et-Vilaine.

*After 1900, the firm carried out the following
works:*

1900-1	St Alban, Larkhill, Blackburn, Lancashire
1901	Ss Peter and Paul, Wolverhampton (chapel, sacristy and guild room)
1901-2	Our Lady of Lourdes, Acton, W3
	Nazareth House, Oxford (new wing)
1902-3	St Mary, Middlesbrough (extension of transepts, chapel and baptistry)
	Hospital of St John and St Elizabeth, St John's Wood, NW8. (The Italianate chapel by George Goldie in Great Ormond Street, WC1, was rebuilt here.)
1904	St Paul, Wood Green, N22 (*Bldr,* 26.9.03)
	St Mary's Priory, Storrington, Sussex
1905-6	St George's Retreat, Burgess Hill, Sussex (sisters' wing and infirmary; *Bldr,* 28.4.06)
1905-7	Nazareth House, Middlesbrough
1906-7	Our Lady of Victories, Warwick Road, SW5 (demolished except for school buildings)

Obit. Bldr, 25.11.21, p. 706.

GOTCH, John Alfred   1852—1942

J. A. Gotch was born at Kettering, Northamptonshire, the son of T. H. Gotch. After attending
an elementary school at Ufford and Kettering
Grammar School, he went to Zurich University,
then to King's College, London and the
Architectural Association. Gotch was articled to
Robert Winter Johnson, of Melton Mowbray and
Kettering, where C. H. Saunders was a colleague.
On Johnson's death in 1879 Gotch and Saunders
acquired the practice, continuing in partnership
for fifty-five years.

In addition to a busy practice which included
many branches of the Midland Bank, J. A. Gotch
organised art classes in Kettering and became an
authority on Early Renaissance architecture,
particularly that of Northamptonshire. He wrote

numerous books, including *A Complete Account of the Buildings erected in Northamptonshire by Sir Thomas Tresham, 1575–1605* (Northampton, 1883). Batsford published his *Architecture of the Renaissance in England* (1894, with W. Talbot Brown); *Early Renaissance Architecture in England* (1901); *The Growth of the English House* (1909); and *The English Home from Charles I to George IV* (1918). He was President of the RIBA from 1923 to 1925, the first architect not practising from London to hold the office. His portrait there is by his brother, T. C. G. Gotch, RI.

In 1924 Gotch collaborated with Sir Edwin Lutyens on the head office of the Midland Bank, Poultry, EC2. His nephew, Laurence M. Gotch (1882–1964), was articled to him and became a partner, continuing the firm as Gotch, Saunders and Surridge. J. A. Gotch was a member of the Art Workers' Guild.

Obit. RIBAJ, Feb., 1942, pp. 66–7 *Bldr*, 23.1.42, p. 78.

GRAYSON, George Hastwell   1871–1951

G. H. Grayson went to Emmanuel College, Cambridge, and in 1892 was articled to Willink and Thicknesse of Liverpool. He was assistant (1894–6) to G. E. Grayson (1834–1912) and E. A. Ould (*q.v.*) and became a partner in 1897. Much of his work was in and around Liverpool, where he did a Lloyd's Bank in Victoria Street and another in Bold Street. He also did schools at Whitehaven, Carlisle and Bootle (1908–10) and his work is mentioned by Muthesius. Best known is his work at Cambridge where, with his partner Ould, he did the Hall at Selwyn College (*Bldr*, 30.11.07) and buildings at Westcott House and Trinity Hall (*Bldr*, 4.6.10). At Oxford, Grayson and Ould did 119 Banbury Road.

Grayson's partner between 1912 and 1933 was Leonard Barnish. Grayson retired to Great Milton, Oxfordshire.

Obit. Bldr, 30.11.51, p. 762.

G. H. Grayson and E. A. Ould: new buildings at Trinity Hall, Cambridge.

197

76
198

GREEN, Leslie William   1875—1908

Leslie Green went to Dover College, was articled to his father Arthur Green (d. 1904), a Crown Surveyor, formerly of Archer and Green. He studied at South Kensington, spent one year in Paris and two as an assistant in his father's office, where he worked on extensions to the Holborn Restaurant, WC1, the Pall Mall Safe Deposit, St Albans Street, Haymarket, W1 (demolished) and flats in Buckingham Palace Road, SW1. Green started practice on his own account in 1897.

Early commissions included the remodelling of 26 Kensington Palace Gardens, W8, and shops and chambers at 29 and 30 St James's Street, SW1 (RA, 1904; *Bldr*, 8.7.05), 26 and 27 Bury Street and 19 Haymarket.

Although his life was short — Green was thirty-three when he died — his work in one specialist field of architecture has provided the daily scenery for millions of travellers on London's tube railways.

Leslie Green: a platform at Piccadilly Circus Station, London Underground Railways.

Leslie Green: the surface buildings at Kilburn Park Station, London Underground Railways.

The opportunity which led Green to crowd so much into five years came in 1903 when he was appointed architect to the Underground Electric Railways Co. of London Ltd., in collaboration with Harry Wharton Ford (1875—1947) who was staff architect (1899—1911). Green's work consisted of 'the design of stations above ground and decorative work to Stations, Tunnels, Platforms and Passages' for the Baker Street and Waterloo Railway, the Great Northern, Piccadilly and Brompton Railway, and the Charing Cross, Euston and Hampstead Railway. Their construction had been in the balance after the financial crash of the London Globe Insurance Co. and the financial empire of Whitaker Wright, but the situation was saved by an injection of American capital (*see under* The London Tube Railways). Green did fifty stations in five years. He died at Mundesley-on-Sea, Norfolk.

Obit. RIBAJ, 26.9.08, p. 621 *Bldr*, 5.9.08, p. 264.

GREEN, Mowbray Aston   1865—1945

Mowbray Green was born in Surrey, articled in 1884 to Alfred S. Goodridge at Bath, went to the Architectural Association and attended the lectures of Professor Roger Smith at University College, London. He returned to Bath in 1890 where he carried on the practice of Elkington Gill. An authority on the City of Bath, he wrote *The Eighteenth Century Architecture of Bath* (Bath, 1902 and 1904). He restored the Assembly Rooms there (since destroyed and rebuilt) and compiled the list of buildings to be preserved under the Bath Act.

Obit. RIBAJ, Jan., 1946, p. 100 *Bldr*, 14.12.45, p. 484.

GREEN, William Curtis, RA   1875–1960

The son of a barrister, Frederick Green, William
Curtis Green was born at Alton, Hampshire, and
went to Newton College, Newton Abbot, Devon.
He studied engineering at West Bromwich
Technical School and architecture at Birmingham
School of Art under W. H. Bidlake. He was articled
to John Belcher, and entered the Royal Academy
Schools in 1895, where he won the Gold Medal
and Travelling Studentship. His skill in drawing
architectural subjects in pen and water-colour was
further developed on study tours in Italy and
Spain and resulted in his illustrations of both old
and new buildings for the architectural periodicals
of the time. He joined the staff of *The Builder* in
1897. The craftsman and furniture designer A.
Romney Green of Christchurch, Hampshire, was
a brother.

In 1898 Curtis Green set up in practice. He
provided the architectural shell of a number
of electricity generating stations which included
Chiswick Power Station, for the London United
Tramways; Bristol Tramways Power Station (RA,
1900) and Hove (Sussex) Power Station. He also
did Brislington Tram Depot, Bristol (RA, 1900;
Bldr, 3.3.1900) and factories at Hitchin, Hertfordshire, Chelmsford, Essex, and Hendon, NW4, for
Crompton & Co., the electrical engineers.

Curtis Green also acquired a reputation for houses
and cottages; these appear in his many lucid plates
in *The Builder* (particularly 18.9.09). There are
Curtis Green houses at Chislehurst, Kent (for
William Willett; *Bldr*, 1.8.03), Letchworth Garden
City, Hampstead Garden Suburb, and Great
Shelford, Cambridgeshire (with Archibald Dickie;
Bldr, 1.8.03). After the First World War he did
housing at Stanmore, near Winchester.

An opportunity to play a part in the construction
of new buildings in the City of London and the
West End came when he became a partner of
Dunn and Watson, who had continued the London
practice of James MacLaren. Curtis Green worked
on their largest London City building, the Scottish
Provident Institution (1905) in Lombard Street.
He was also concerned with the smaller, but still
significant, West End branch of the Institution at
17 Pall Mall, SW1. He was for a short time in
partnership with Archibald Dickie alone.

In 1921 Curtis Green did the showrooms for the
Wolseley Motor Co., 160 Piccadilly (now a
Barclay's Bank), awarded the first Street Architecture Medal in 1922 by the RIBA. The award was
made 'with a view to encouraging excellence of
design in STREET ARCHITECTURE', and the
conditions required that the building should
front to a street, road, square or court to which
the public had access, within a four-mile radius of
Charing Cross. Curtis Green's Wolseley House
(1921) and the Royal Insurance Building (1909)
alongside — by Curtis Green's first master, John
Belcher, and his partner Joass, and originally

W. Curtis Green, RA: the main power station of
Bristol Tramways.

intended to extend over the Wolseley House site
— clearly show how the neo-neo-Classic revival
from Paris via Chicago and New York had exting-
uished the adventurous spirit of the early 1900s.

Curtis Green's National Westminster Bank at 63
Piccadilly shows details derived from Peruzzi. His
Stratton House, Piccadilly, mildly follows Carrère
and Hastings's Devonshire House, while the
London Life Association building in King William
Street, EC3, continued in King George V idiom
his early work with Dunn and Watson in Lombard
Street. His office building at 25 Savile Row, W1,
and his Barclay's Bank at 29 Borough High Street,
SE1, displaying his liking for strange ornament,
show that the James MacLaren tradition was still
alive but working in another idiom.

Curtis Green successfully met the greatest
challenge of his career in a building typical of the
1930s and superior to most in that difficult era of
transition — the Dorchester Hotel. When
Dorchester House — built for R. S. Holford by
Lewis Vulliamy, with interiors by Alfred Stevens —
was sold, this great hotel was planned for the site
by the engineer Owen Williams. In reinforced
concrete, it has a slab three feet thick at first-floor
level spanning the principal public rooms, supporting over it the bedrooms and bathrooms with their
drains and services. The exterior design was considered too stark and Curtis Green was called in
to provide suggestions for clothing it outside and
beautifying it inside. Outside he covered the
concrete walls with terrazzo slabs. Internally he
selected 'Vanderbilt' Spanish, with ingredients
from the details of his favourite architect, Peruzzi.

W. Curtis Green with Dunn, Watson and A. C. Dickie: offices in Pall Mall, London SW1. The window motif is derived from Michelangelo's motif for the new sacristy, San Lorenzo, Florence. The ironwork is also Florentine.

After fifty years the hotel is still a credit to Sir Owen Williams and Curtis Green.

Curtis Green was a member of the Art Workers' Guild and was made an ARA in 1923, RA in 1933 (diploma work, 'The London Life Association'). In 1942 he received the Royal Gold Medal for Architecture. His son, Christopher Green, and son-in-law, W. A. S. Lloyd, Lloyd's son, and E. J. Armitage, son of the sculptor Edward Armitage, became partners. The title of the firm is now Green, Lloyd and Son.

Curtis Green's works include:

1904	South Herts Golf Clubhouse, Totteridge, N20 (*Bldr*, 19.9.03).
1906	The Institute, Bisley Street, Painswick, Gloucestershire (inscription by Eric Gill)
1907	135–141 Hampstead Way, NW11
1908	The Adult School Hall, Friends' Meeting House, Croydon, Surrey
1910	Chapel of the Good Shepherd, Dockenfield, Surrey
	All Saints, Shirley, Croydon

St George, Waddon, Surrey

St Francis, Stoke-on-Trent

Poultry Court, Painswick, Gloucestershire

20 Meadway, and 8 Hurst Close, Hampstead Garden Suburb, NW11

1913   Rystwood House, Forest Row, Sussex (*Country Life* 'Small Country Homes' Competition)

RIBA Heinz Gallery, catalogue of exhibition, Jan., 1978

Obit. RIBAJ, June, 1960, p. 307   *Bldr*, 1.4.60, p. 642 *Journal of the Architectural Association*, 1960, p. 229.

GREENAWAY, Francis Hugh   1869–1935

F. H. Greenaway went to King's College School, London, and was articled to Sir Aston Webb. He was first in partnership with J. E. Newberry (1862–1950). His first work was Southampton Isolation Hospital, won in competition.

His subsequent work included the churches of St Peter, South Wimbledon, SW19; St Andrew, Coulsdon, Surrey; St John, Belmont, Surrey; St James, Riddlesdown, Croydon, Surrey; St Paul, Furzedown, SW17; and the Church of the Epiphany, Stockwell, SW9. Greenaway also did the Godolphin and Latymer Girls' School, Iffley Road, W6.

In 1923 the partners won the RIBA London Architectural Medal with the Auctioneers' and Estate Agents' Institute, Lincoln's Inn Fields, WC2, which they had won in a competition assessed by Sir Reginald Blomfield. (A storey has been added since by C. W. Fowler.)

Other works by Greenaway include:

1905	Elementary Schools, West Ealing and South Ealing, W13
1908	St Hilda, Crofton Park, SE4
	St Nicholas, Plumstead, SE18 (large additions)
	All Saints, Hampton, Middlesex
1909-11	Kirkham Grammar School, Lancashire, for the Drapers' Company

Obit. RIBAJ, 27.4.35, p. 739.

GREENSLADE, Sydney Kyffin   1866–1955

Sydney Greenslade was articled to Edward Ashworth of Exeter in 1884, was Pugin Student in 1891, Grissell Medallist in 1897 and Godwin Bursar in 1900. He was a brilliant designer and had independent means. The architects he assisted included W. D. Caröe, T. E. Collcutt, and Henry Florence. In 1900 he assisted J. H. Eastwood on St Ann's Cathedral, Leeds, and in the following year assisted T. H. Lyon on St Peter's Cathedral in Adelaide, South Australia. His first exceptionally fine work was the South African War Memorial Library at Eton, with L. K. Hall (*AR*, 1911), won

in a competition held in 1904 with Reginald
Blomfield as assessor.

Greenslade's next architectural success was his win
in the competition for the National Library of
Wales at Aberystwyth, again assessed by Blomfield
(*Bldr*, 19.6.09). He entrusted the supervision of
the construction here to Adams and Holden,
whose design had been awarded second prize.
Both Greenslade's buildings show qualities in
common with those of E. A. Rickards, particularly in their strong, rectangular forms.

Greenslade's interests were divided between
architecture and designing for Martin ware, a
decorative pottery first produced at the Fulham
Pottery by the four Martin brothers whose pottery
works were at Havelock Road, Southall, from
1877 to 1923. (There is a collection of Martin
ware at Water House, Walthamstow, E17.)

After the Second World War Greenslade collaborated with E. Vincent Harris on the first buildings
for University College, Exeter (now part of the
University of the South West).

Obit. *RIBAJ*, June, 1955, p. 347   *Bldr*, 11.3.55, p. 428

S. K. Greenslade: the National Library of Wales,
Aberystwyth.

GRIGGS, Frederick Landseer Maur, RA
1876–1938

F. L. M. Griggs was born at Hitchin, Hertfordshire, and first trained as an architect with Walter
Millard, also of Hitchin, who taught him to draw
in the manner which was to become his distinctive
style.

Griggs was a Catholic and a mediaevalist, and a
member of the Royal Society of Painters, Etchers
and Engravers. He also belonged to the Art
Workers' Guild, the Council for the Preservation
of Rural England and the Society for the Protection of Ancient Buildings. His work on the
restoration of Cotswold buildings was as important as his work as a black and white artist and
etcher. His style of drawing was firm, strong and
detailed and his illustrations in Macmillan's
'Highways and Byways' series have done much to
stimulate interest in the beauties of the countryside and ancient villages.

Griggs did the First World War Memorial Cross at Biddenham, near Bedford, and that at Chipping Campden. With Norman Jewson he did Dover's Court, Chipping Campden, later bought by Sir Frank Brangwyn. Griggs advised the Archbishop of Westminster on the decorations for Westminster Cathedral. He also designed the Littleworth and Leysbourne printers' types. He was made ARA in 1922, RA in 1931 (diploma work, 'Lanterns of Sarras').

Colnaghi, P. & D., & Co. Ltd., catalogue of memorial exhibition, January 1939
Obit. *Bldr*, 10.6.38, p. 1127 *Times*, 8.6.38.

HALL, Edwin Thomas   1851–1923

E. T. Hall was the son of George Hall senior, an architect practising in the then new Victoria Street, Westminster. Hall spent two years at the South Kensington Schools and worked in the office of Joseph Fogerty. He started in practice in Moorgate Street, EC2, in 1875 and later moved to Bedford Square, where he remained until his death.

Hall's greatest work is the Manchester Royal Infirmary which, with John Brooke (d. 1914), a Manchester architect, he won in competition. The assessor was J. J. Burnet, and the competitors included Percy Adams. The design was on the pavilion plan which, given a large enough site, had been the accepted plan for every major hospital since 1871 when St Thomas's was completed in accordance with the precepts of Florence Nightingale. By 1908 there had been two notable exceptions — Alfred Waterhouse's University College Hospital, London, built on the cross plan, and the Royal Victoria Hospital, Belfast. The latter was unique among hospital buildings because the chairman of the Belfast shipbuilders, Harland and Wolff, had urged the fullest use of the Plenum system of ventilation then operating in ships (architects Henman and Cooper; *Bldr*, 21.12.01). The idea was supported by *The Builder*, whose editor, Heathcote Statham, suggested that Hall's return to the pavilion plan at Manchester was 'an extreme reaction from the great experiment made at the Royal Victoria Hospital ... where by the most skilful planning, a great array of single storey wards are connected by a main corridor, warmed and ventilated by the "Plenum System" '. The pavilion plan nevertheless prevailed at Manchester and again at King's College Hospital, London (won in competition by W. A. Pite in 1914), and many hospitals since.

Hall did the grotesque St Ermin's, Caxton Street, SW1, alternately a hotel and service flats and internally having the air of a transatlantic liner of the period. Edwin Hall also did many hospitals for local authorities and for the Metropolitan Asylums Board. During the First World War, Hall converted the Old HM Stationery Office, Stamford Street, SE1, into an emergency hospital.

Towards the end of his life Hall was engaged on the realisation of Captain Stewart Liberty's amazing dream of building a larger than life-size Elizabethan building behind Regent Street, W1, made out of the teak from three wooden ships. Liberty wanted this to be built in Regent Street itself where Nash's buildings were being replaced by Portland stone ones to no concerted design. But the Commissioners of Crown Lands refused permission and the space where the wooden building might have been Hall filled with a reminder in Portland stone of the Vittorio Emanuele Memorial in Rome — but with *stone people* looking over the stone parapet, above a stone frieze of elephants and camels bearing the riches of the East also carved in stone.

Edwin Hall's brother, G. A. Hall, was articled to him and then carried on his father's practice in Victoria Street. Edwin Hall was succeeded by his son Edwin Stanley Hall, with Murray Easton and Howard Robertson, both Royal Gold Medallists and both a decided influence on architecture and architectural education in the years between the two world wars. The practice continues as Easton, Robertson, Preston and Partners.

Hall also did:

1902	Public Library, Camberwell, SE5
	The South African War Memorial Library, Dulwich College, SE21 (Hall was a Governor of the College. *Bldr*, 27.12.02; RA, 1903)
1903	Frimley Sanatorium, Surrey (*Bldr*, 15.8.03)
1904	Council Offices, Camberwell, SE5 (RA, 1904)
	St Giles's Hospital, Peckham Road, SE5
	Metropolitan Asylums Board Offices, Victoria Embankment, EC4 (*Bldr*, 4.2.05)
1908	Homoeopathic Hospital, Queen Square, WC1 (a wing to W. A. Pite's hospital of 1893–5)

Obit. *RIBAJ*, 28.4.23, pp. 394–6 *Bldr*, 20.4.23, p. 633.

HALL, Herbert Austen   1881–1968

Austen Hall was the son of the Rev. Arthur Hall. He was articled to Philip Tree of St Leonards-on-Sea (1897) and worked for him as an assistant for one year. He then worked for Silcock and Reay at Bath (1901), Treadwell and Martin (1902), and Henry Tanner junior and the London County Council Architect's Department (1903). In 1905 Austen Hall opened an office at 26 Theobald's Road, WC1, in a partnership with Septimus Warwick which lasted until 1913 when Warwick went to Canada to undertake the Manitoba Parliament Buildings, Winnipeg, with F. W. Simon.

The eight-year association brought Warwick and Hall many successes in competitions. In 1905 they won Lambeth Town Hall against the usual competition winners. In 1906 they won the Holborn Town Hall in High Holborn (*Bldr*, 21.7.06), for a congested site on a street frontage, and in 1909 won the Berkshire County Offices and Shire Hall, Reading, in a competition assessed by Mervyn Macartney (*Bldr*, 18.9.09).

In 1922 Hall did Peter Robinson's on the corner of Oxford Street and Regent Street, W1, with T. P. and E. S. Clarkson (1866—1950). Hall had just returned from a RIBA Travelling Bursary trip to America to study retail stores, and the Oxford Street elevation derives from the Lord & Taylor Store, Fifth Avenue. But in common with other English buildings attempting to emulate their New York counterparts, the superstructure is scarcely taller than the base, in this case of granite.

In partnership with Whinney and Son (*q.v.*), Austen Hall carried out a number of bank buildings. Notable among them is the more recent Bankers' Clearing House, at 10 Lombard Street, EC3 (1920s and 1955).

The headquarters of the Metropolitan Water Board, Rosebery Avenue, EC1, and the headquarters of the Gas, Light and Coke Co., Church Street, Kensington, W8, are by Hall. He also did the headquarters of the Bristol Gas Co. in Bristol and of the Bristol Aeroplane Co. at Filton, Gloucestershire. With its robust, four-square quality, Hall's work recalls that of Vincent Harris and Edwin Cooper, but is more genial than either. The firm continues as the Whinney, Mackay-Lewis Partnership.

Obit. Bldg, 23.2.68, p. 75.

Austen Hall of Warwick and Hall: Lambeth Town Hall, the tower.

HAMMOND, Ralton Gardner   1867—1951

R. G. Hammond was articled to S. Fabian Russell in 1884. In 1887 he was assistant to C. W. Stevens, the architect of Harrods. He studied at the Architectural Association and commenced practice on his own account in 1895. This consisted principally of town houses in London, many on the Cadogan Estate, SW7, and the Grosvenor Estate, W1, where he designed for the builder John Garlick of Chelsea. Among them are houses in Hans Place, Cadogan Place (*Bldr*, 26.3.04), 117 Sloane Street (1899; RA, 1900) *and:*

1900	1 Berkeley Square (RA, 1901)
1901	30 Charles Street (RA, 1903)
	13 Charles Street (RA, 1902)
1904	43 Charles Street (RA, 1905)
1904-6	61—63 Grosvenor Street
1905	51 Upper Brook Street (RA, 1906)
	47 Upper Grosvenor Street (refronting)
1906	38 Grosvenor Street (RA, 1907; demolished)
1907	25 Upper Brook Street (RA, 1907)
	24 Charles Street (RA, 1909)
1908-9	39—42 North Audley Street

Obit. RIBAJ, Aug., 1951, p. 407 *Bldr*, 6.4.51, p. 480.

HAMPTON, Herbert   1862—1929

Herbert Hampton was born at Hoddesdon, Hertfordshire, the son of a builder, William Hampton. He went to Bishop Stortford College and studied at Lambeth School of Art, at the Slade and in Paris at Cormon's and Julian's. He was one of the sculptors employed on Electra House, Moorgate, EC2, for John Belcher (1902—3). Hampton also did the 7 ft bronze of Edward VII at the Hearts of Oak Building, Euston Road (architects Nicol and Nicol), now demolished.

Hampton occupied the house built for Alfred Gilbert (*q.v.*) at 16 Maida Vale, W9. *His other works include:*

1900	Lord Aberdare, Cardiff
	Fountain at Hewell Grange, Worcestershire, for Lord Windsor
1903	Luke Fildes RA, bust (RA, 1903)
1904	Hamo Thornycroft, bust (RA, 1904)
1907	Queen Victoria, Dalton Square, Lancaster, presented by Lord Ashton
	Queen Victoria, Ipswich, Suffolk (destroyed)
1910	The 8th Duke of Devonshire (d. 1908), Horse Guards Avenue, SW1

Obit. Bldr, 22.2.29, p. 370

HARE, Henry Thomas   1861—1921

H. T. Hare was born at Scarborough, Yorkshire, educated at Sheffield and Harrogate and articled to C. A. Bury, a Harrogate architect. Hare joined the London office of Z. King and R. H. Hill, and went to Paris to study at the Atelier Ginain. His fellow students there included A. N. Paterson of Glasgow and John M. Carrère, of Carrère and Hastings, who forty years later were the architects of Devonshire House, London's palatial service flats in Piccadilly (now offices).

The end of the nineteenth century saw the rise of a spate of public buildings, county halls, town halls, municipal offices, technical colleges, public baths and libraries, court houses, and police and fire brigade stations, their design often selected by competition. (Funds for the public libraries in most cases came from the Andrew Carnegie or J. Passmore Edwards trusts.) This was a field in which H. T. Hare had a great many successes, including the County Offices, Stafford (1892), the Municipal Buildings at Oxford (1897), and those at Southend-on-Sea and Henley-on-Thames (1898).

Hare's buildings at Stafford and Oxford are in the then prevalent Early Renaissance style, but he changed with the fashion to neo-Baroque, a style he managed well and which eventually became characteristic of his work, while the well-ordered plans of his libraries show the marks of his Paris training. His public library buildings include those for Wolverhampton (1902), Southend-on-Sea and

Henry T. Hare: the Carnegie Library, Harrogate, Yorkshire.

Henry T. Hare: the Strand, London WC2, offices of the United Kingdom Provident Institution, demolished

recently without mention or protest. Sculptors: Henry Poole, RA and F. E. E. Schenck.

Henry T. Hare: University College, Bangor.

Hammersmith (1903), and the Carnegie Library and Art Gallery at Harrogate (1904).

Apart from his public buildings, Hare did the Westminster (Presbyterian) College at Cambridge (1897–9; *Bldr*, 12.1.07; chapel 1921) and University College, Bangor, North Wales (1907–10; *Bldr*, 16.4.10), which he won in competition. These are in 'Collegiate Tudor', a style at which he was also adept. He did a range of buildings for Queens' College, Cambridge, in 1912.

Hare's few commercial buildings included premises in Carfax, Oxford (1908), in lively accord with his Oxford Municipal Buildings. In 1900 Hare was placed first among the eight selected to compete in the design for the Strand–Aldwych façades (*see under* The Holborn–Strand Improvements) but no design was carried out. Hare was also architect for Ingram House, 196 Strand, WC2 (*Bldr*, 10.8.07), built for the United Kingdom Provident Institution in 1906 and demolished in 1961. This once-familiar feature of the Strand was powerfully neo-Baroque and displayed an abundance of exterior sculpture and interior mosaic and painting. Its curved frontage provided an appropriate setting for Wren's Church of St Clement Danes and the visual arts were fully enlisted in the task of representing the benefits of wise insurance. Outside were sculptured female figures by Henry Poole (craning forward to allow light to enter the lunettes behind), representing Justice and Truth, Temperance, Providence, Security and Industry. Low-relief figures by F. E. E. Schenck between the second-floor windows added force to the message with personifications of Hope, Wisdom and Peace. Inside the story was continued with paintings by Gerald Moira depicting 'Providence protecting Childhood,

Henry T. Hare: offices of the United Kingdom Provident Institution, Strand, London WC2. The interior sculptures were by F. Lynn-Jenkins, the paintings by Gerald Moira.

Chastity and the Fruits of Abundance from the Evil Powers'. Other internal decorative works were a sculptured frieze in Pentelikos marble and a bronze by F. Lynn Jenkins, and a vaulted ceiling mosaic showing the signs of the zodiac. But the housebreaker's hammer came down on personifications of Good and Evil alike and the graceful curve of Ingram House has now been replaced by a square new building, where, on a terrace, can be found among other fragments the torso of Poole's 'Justice' with her scales *tilted on their side*.

Hare also did Beckbury Hall, near Bridgnorth, Shropshire, and a later work is the Frances Holland School, Park Road, NW1, opened in 1912. His chief assistant, Thomas Davidson, set up on his own account (he was the designer of Torquay Town Hall), and Hare's practice was carried on by A. Bertram Lisle. Hare was President of the RIBA from 1917 to 1919.

Other works by Hare (all won in competition) include:

1902	Municipal Buildings, Harrogate, Yorkshire (*Bldr*, 5.7.02)	
1903	Municipal Buildings, Pontypridd, Glamorgan (RA, 1904)	
	Municipal Buildings, Crewe, Cheshire (*Bldr*, 27.9.02; sculpture by Schenck)	
1904	Public Library, Shoreditch, E1 (*Bldr*, 23.7.04)	
206	1905	Central Library, Islington, N7 (*Bldr*, 1.2.08)
206	1908	Public Library, Fulham, SW6 (*Bldr*, 5.3.10)

Obit. RIBAJ, 22.1.21, pp. 173 and 180 and 5.2, p. 201. *Bldr*, 14.1.21, pp. 59 and 67 and 21.1, pp. 90 and 93–4.

Henry T. Hare: the Public Library, Fulham, London SW6.

Henry T. Hare: the Central Library, Islington, London N7.

HARRIS, Emanuel Vincent, OBE, RA 1879–1971

Vincent Harris, the son of Major Emanuel Harris, was born in Devonport. He went to Kingsbridge Grammar School and was articled to James Harvey of Plymouth. He was assistant in London to E. Keynes Purchase, Leonard Stokes and Sir William Emerson. Vincent Harris also worked in the Navy Loan Department where, under W. E. Riley, designs were prepared for civil and military buildings in colonial and other territories. He obtained an honourable mention for his entry for the Soane Medallion (*Bldr*, 19.4.02).
In 1900 Harris entered the Royal Academy Schools where he won the Gold Medal and Travelling Studentship in 1903. In 1901 Harris entered the Architect's Department of the London County Council, where Riley had succeeded Thomas Blashill as Chief Architect in 1899. At County Hall – then in Spring Gardens, SW1 – Vincent Harris took part in the preparation of plans for the electricity generating station for the new electric street tramways of the LCC at Greenwich, SE10. He also designed, as part of a road widening scheme, the monumental blind wall flanking Victoria Station along Buckingham Palace Road, SW1.

74
75

In 1904 Vincent Harris took chambers in Lincoln's Inn. T. A. Moodie (1875–1948), a Soane Medallist, was a colleague at the LCC and together they won the competition for the Glamorgan County Hall (*Bldr*, 6.2.09), part of that first of 'civic centres' at Cathays Park, Cardiff. Moodie subsequently left England for South Africa where he became chief architect to the South African Railways and designed the Central Station, Johannesburg.

At a time when Lanchester, Stewart and Rickards had astonished their contemporaries with their neo-Baroque City Hall and Law Courts at Cardiff; the more classic lines of Harris and Moodie's County Hall were a sign that the classic idiom from Paris and America had now arrived. In the execution of Glamorgan County Hall (sculpture by Albert Hodge), Vincent Harris made improvements and simplifications to the competition design and achieved the Roman scale he was to maintain in his work throughout his life. Also with Moodie, Vincent Harris did the Cardiff Fire Station in 1910.

Harris's first buildings in London were 2 and 3 Duke Street, and 1 King Street, St James's, SW1 — a building with brick and stone frontages on two streets but no corner, done in 1910 and Roman in scale.

Vincent Harris's design submitted in 1914 in competition for the Board of Trade building in Whitehall had to wait forty years to be realised, with two world wars intervening. During this interval Harris abandoned the steep pitched roof of his design and adopted the flat roofs and tabernacles which had figured in Charles Holden's more advanced design for the same competition.

Harris did a number of his principal works after the First World War. His public buildings in this period included the Central Library and extension to the Municipal Buildings in Manchester (1927–38); Sheffield City Hall (1932); the Civic Hall, Leeds (1933); and County Halls in Taunton (1932) and Nottingham (1925). His last work, the Central Library, Kensington, W8, was done when he was over eighty years old. Also by Harris are Braintree Town Hall, Essex, some of the buildings at Durham University (1947) and the first buildings at University College (now the University of the South West), Exeter (with S. K. Greenslade).

All Vincent Harris's buildings maintain the classic idiom, with two main exceptions — the Manchester Municipal offices which, since they stand alongside Waterhouse's Gothic Town Hall, are in an expurgated fifteenth-century Gothic; and the Carillon Tower of Atkinson's Scent Shop in Old Bond Street, W1 (now in other hands), in similar style, replacing a Gothic shop front by C. F. A. Voysey. Some of his buildings suggest the influence of Sir Edwin Lutyens, but all are bolder, balder, and less subtle or more frank, depending on one's point of view. Such is Harris's design for the Bristol

E. Vincent Harris: Glamorgan County Hall, Cardiff. The sculpture is by Albert Hodge.

Council House (1939). His smallest work is a brick wall in Carlos Place, Mayfair, W1, which once formed the back wall of a racquets court for Stephen Courtauld and contained in a niche a lead figure by Hardiman, now replaced by a shop window. He designed his own house, 10 Fitzroy Park, Highgate, N6.

Vincent Harris was made ARA in 1936, and RA in 1942 (diploma work, 'New County Hall, Nottinghamshire'). He was treasurer of the Royal Academy in 1942 and was awarded the CBE and in 1951 the Royal Gold Medal for Architecture. His office is now occupied by Donald Insall. Vincent Harris lies interred at St Michael and All Angels, Chaffcombe, near Chard, Somerset, where a monument by Arthur Bailey marks his grave.

Obit. RIBAJ, Feb., 1971, pp. 149–52, Apr., pp. 215–7 *Bldg*, 6.8.71, p. 66 *Times*, 2 and 13.8.71.

HART, Alfred Henry   1866–1953

A. H. Hart was educated privately, studied at the Architectural Association and entered the Royal Academy Schools in 1885, winning the Gold Medal and the Travelling Studentship in 1891. He was articled to James Edmeston and was an assistant in the office of Sir Ernest George. Hart set up in practice in 1893 in Staple Inn and then in Verulam Buildings, Gray's Inn, in partnership with Leslie Waterhouse (1864—1932), also from George and Peto's office.

Hart and Waterhouse did houses at Enfield, Middlesex (RA, 1905; *Bldr*, 13.5.05); Bushey, Hertfordshire; Henley-on-Thames, Oxfordshire; Winterslow, near Salisbury (*Bldr*, 19.9.03); and Tullylagan, Co. Tyrone, Northern Ireland (*Bldr*, 10.6.05). In 1902 Hart did offices for the Dominion of Canada Emigration Department, 9 Charing Cross, SW1 (*Bldr*, 4.6.04) and in 1904, 10 Park Place, St James's, SW1. In 1909 Hart and Waterhouse did Parkside, Albert Gate, SW1 (*Bldr*, 14.3.08 and 18.4.08; *AA*, 1909), a long, high wedge of building between Hyde Park and Knightsbridge. Clumsy by comparison with Caröe's rich terrace opposite, it turned Knightsbridge 'into a draughty corridor', to quote a contemporary critic. The same year the partners did the Messrs Willing Advertising building, 356 Gray's Inn Road, WC1 — a *petite* version of an *hôtel de ville* (now occupied by the London Borough of Camden), with carving by William Aumonier.

In 1938, as architect to the Royal Colonial Institute, South Kensington, Hart collaborated with Sir Herbert Baker on the Royal Empire Society Headquarters (now the Royal Commonwealth Society), in Northumberland Avenue, WC2. This was extensively damaged in the Second World War and repaired in a simpler form.

Other work includes:

1902	Trafalgar House, 11—15 Charing Cross, SW1
1903	10 and 11 Park Place, St James's, SW1 (*AA*, 1904 ; *Bldr*, 9.7.04)
1909	Cuddesden College, Oxford (additions)
	The Pryors, Hampstead, NW3, mansion flats intruding on the Heath (*Bldr*, 17.9.10)
	The Maternity Hospital, Clapham, SW4

Obit. *Bldr*, 8.5.53, p. 726.

HEATHCOTE, Charles Henry   1851—1938

Charles Heathcote was articled to Charles F. Hansom of Bristol. Most of his work was in Manchester and an early Heathcote building there was 107 Piccadilly. Outside Manchester, with his sons Ernest and Edgar Heathcote, he did the National Provincial (now National Westminster) Bank in Worcester (*Bldr*, 24.11.06); the station buildings in Altrincham, Cheshire; and the Magistrates' Courts, Horseferry Road, Westminster, SW1.

Heathcote's other Manchester works included:

| 1902-7 | Parr's (now National Westminster) Bank, Spring Gardens (*Bldr*, 14.6.02) |

	Scottish Amicable Life Assurance Society, Cross Street and Albert Square
	Hozle's warehouse, Piccadilly
1903	Eagle Insurance Co., Cross Street (*AR*, 1903; *Bldr*, 7.3.02)
1904	Union Cold Stores, and
1905	Eagle Insurance Co., King Street (both with his sons)
1908	The Metallurgy Building, Manchester University
	Higham's warehouse (with his sons)

Obit. *RIBAJ*, 21.2.38, p. 410 *Bldr*, 4.2.38, p. 263.

HELLICAR, Evelyn A.   1862—1929

E. A. Hellicar was the son of the vicar of Bromley, Kent. He was articled to T. G. Jackson, and studied at University College, London. Hellicar was Diocesan Architect for Rochester, and his churches included St Mark's, Bromley, and St John's, Welling, Kent.

Hellicar's country houses included Lufton Manor, Yeovil, Somerset (1897); the hall at Bingham's Melcombe, Dorset (1893—4); Backwell Down, near Bristol (*Bldr*, 7.11.08); Manor House, Raheen, Eire; and Woodlands, Caterham, Surrey. He also did South Hill Wood at Bromley, including a garden pavilion and stables (RA, 1902), and the Carnegie Library at Bromley (*Bldr*, 7.11.08). Among his pupils was Sir Albert Richardson, RA.

Obit. *RIBAJ*, 21.9.29, p. 772 *Bldr*, 30.8.29 p. 336.

HITCH, Nathaniel   1846—1938

Nathaniel Hitch was a carver and sculptor of Gothic Revival church work, and did more than 2,000 figures for the architect W. D. Caröe alone; under Caröe's master, J. L. Pearson, he had worked on the north transept of Westminster Abbey and on Truro Cathedral. He did the memorial to the 'Clapham Sect' of Evangelicals on the south wall of Clapham Parish Church, SW4 (architect H. P. Burke Downing, 1910).

His son, Frederick Brook Hitch, was trained at Lambeth School of Art. Among his works are the Submarine Memorial, a bronze panel on the wall of the Victoria Embankment (1922), the memorials to Ross Smith and to Captain Matthew Flinders in Adelaide, South Australia, and the bronze statue of Admiral Lord Nelson in Pembroke Gardens, Portsmouth, erected in 1951.

Obit. *Bldr*, 2.4.38, p. 263

Albert Hodge: sculpture at the Guildhall, Hull.
Architect: Sir Edwin Cooper, RA.

HOARE, Edward Barclay   1872–1943

E. B. Hoare went to Harrow and Magdalen
College, Oxford, and was articled to Edward
Warren in whose office he met his partner,
Montague Wheeler (1874–1937). They began
practice together in 1898 and did some good
town houses on the Howard de Walden Estate,
including 61 Harley Street; 19 New Cavendish
Street (RA, 1902; *AR*, 1903); 40a Devonshire
Street; 19 Charles Street (RA, 1902); and 47
Hertford Street, Park Lane (RA, 1902). They
also did the Church of the Holy Trinity, Newcastle
upon Tyne; St Saviour, Westcliff-on-Sea, Essex;
St Andrew, Higham Hill Road, and All Saints,
Higham Park, E17.

After the earthquake of 1907 Hoare and Wheeler
did the Colonial (later Barclay's) Bank in Kingston,
Jamaica (since demolished), an intricate design in
'Cape Dutch', a style which had come to represent
colonial architecture since Sir Herbert Baker's
renowned works in South Africa. Hoare and
Wheeler also did some buildings at Karachi,
Pakistan. They rebuilt Lees Court, near Faversham,
Kent, after destruction by fire in 1913 (*Building
Design*, 17.5.74, p. 12).

HODGE, Albert H.   1875–1917

Albert Hodge was born in Glasgow where he began
training as an architect. He did architectural
sculpture for Salmon, Son and Gillespie, and J. J.
Burnet, including the Clyde Trust Building, 16
Robertson Street and Broomielaw (1905–8), and
models for some of the plasterwork on the Glasgow
Exhibition of 1901 for James Miller.

In London for Burnet, Hodge did the sculpture on
the former General Buildings, No. 99 Aldwych,
in 1906, consisting of figures in white metal on a
marble screen representing Strength, Prudence,
Abundance and Prosperity, the figures 'Fire' and
'Life' in Portland stone above the ground-floor
columns, and 'Life' over the open pediment in the
centre. For Sir Aston Webb he did 'Thomas
Chippendale' and 'Josiah Wedgwood' on the
Exhibition Road façade of the Victoria and Albert
Museum (1899–1909). For Sir Ernest George and
Yeates, Hodge did the sculpture on Royal
Exchange Buildings, EC3, in 1907.

For Vincent Harris he did 'Navigation' and 'Mining'
on the Glamorgan County Hall, Cardiff (1910) and
a Druid and a Bard in the Guildhall, Hull.
The 'Daughters of Neptune' on the Guildhall, Hull
(*Bldr*, 26.10.07) are the work of Hodge (for
Russell and Cooper), and he did the reliefs on
the Robert Burns monument in Stirling.

Obit. Bldr, 18.1.18, p. 57.

130

207

152

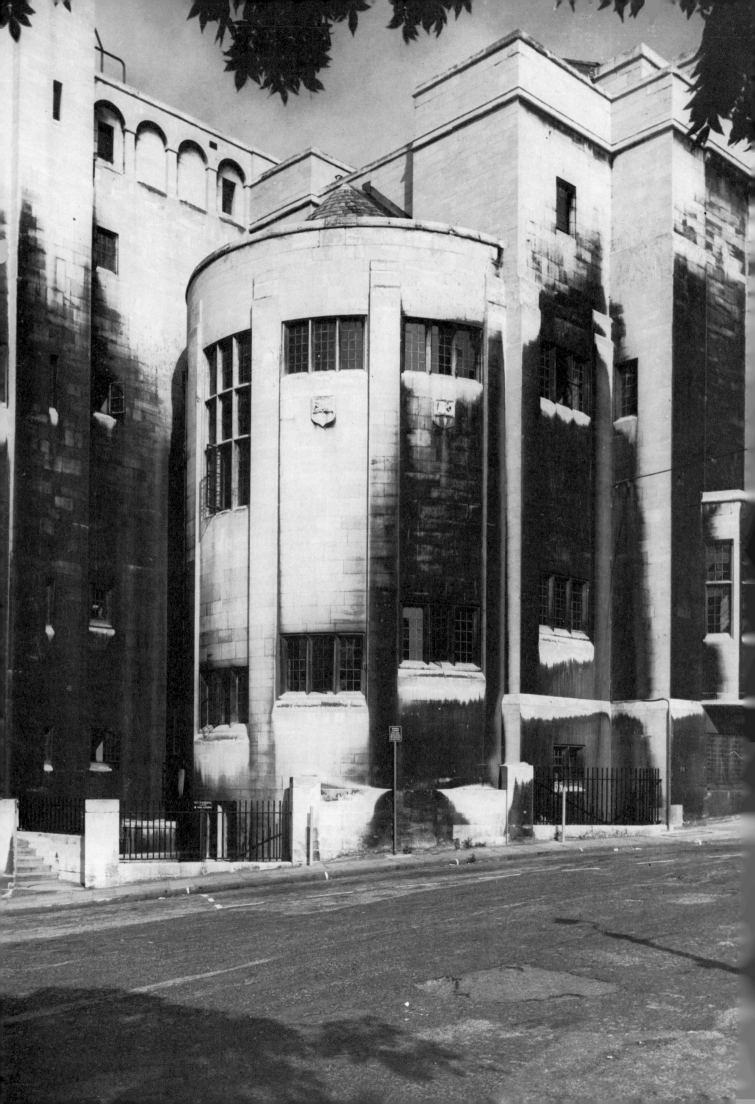

HOLDEN, Dr Charles Henry, DLitt London, LittD Manchester   1875—1960

Charles Holden was among that small number of architects who, in the early 1900s, continued to derive their inspiration from William Morris through the example of Philip Webb and William Lethaby, basing their work on first principles applied within the scope of traditional vernacular building. As a result Holden, escaping from the historicism of the neo-Wren and neo-Classical revivals, provided a link between the false dawn of modern architecture in Britain in the 1900s and the real dawn of the 1930s. That Holden was able to put his principles into practice on a succession of large buildings was due both to his good fortune in joining an established and busy practice, and to his shrewd good sense in expressing his ideas in a form consistent with the practical needs of his clients.

Holden was born at Bolton, Lancashire, the sixth child of a textile engineer who had established a drapery business in Bolton which failed. Holden's mother died while he was a child, and he was brought up by his sister. On leaving school, where he showed an aptitude for drawing, Holden entered the office of his brother-in-law, D. F. Green, in Bolton.

Holden was articled to F. W. Leeson in Manchester, where he attended the Technical College and School of Art and became an instructor. Here he met Francis Dodd, James and Muirhead Bone and Lionel G. Pearson, his future partner in architecture. With them he became one of the group of students calling themselves the Walt Whitman Society, studying the works of that philosopher poet and absorbing the ideas of Edward Carpenter.

In 1897 Holden came to London as assistant to C. R. Ashbee, whose work and writings he admired and with whose family he stayed. (Holden's drawings for Ashbee's unrealised Danvers Tower in Chelsea are in the RIBA Drawings Collection.) Two years later Holden entered the office of Percy Adams, a recognised planner of hospitals to whose skilful plans but conventional elevations Holden contributed new ideas in design. The combination brought success in competitions and commissions for other buildings. In the evenings Holden was studying at the Royal Academy Schools between 1900 and 1903. The first building to show the fruits of their collaboration was the new (1903) building at Kennington, SW9, for the Belgrave Hospital for Children. (The south wing was completed in 1924 and the west wing in 1926.) To illustrate this tall, gabled building, Holden commissioned an early sketch from his friend Muirhead Bone (*q.v.*).

With Holden, Adams won the competition for the Central Reference Library in Deanery Street,

◁ **Charles Holden with Percy Adams: the rear elevation of the Central Library, Bristol.**

Charles Holden with Percy Adams: the staircase of the Central Library, Bristol.

211
212

213

214

Bristol (1902; assessor E. W. Mountford). Here Holden brought a new solution to the design of public libraries then associated with the neo-Baroque of Henry T. Hare. He gave Charles Pibworth's external sculpture the 'loving assistance and unobtrusive support' advocated by Belcher, while to the interior he brought a cool quality, using blue-green mosaic and white marble. He was often to use this combination of materials and colours, as in the interior of the new Library for the Law Society (1902—4), next to Lewis Vulliamy's building of 1831 in Chancery Lane, WC2 (*Bldr*, 23.4.04). Here he expressed the plan and function externally by departing from the street frontage — a bold step when precedent usually required that a building should stand four-square on a street corner. Twenty-five years later Holden was to break this convention more dramatically with the Headquarters for the London Underground Railways at 55 Broadway, Westminster, which won him the London Architecture Medal for 1929. Symbolical figures at the Law Society are by Conrad Dressler.

In 1904, following another competition, Adams with Holden built the King Edward VII Sanatorium at Midhurst, Sussex, the gift of the millionaire banker and friend of Edward VII, Sir Ernest Cassel. Here for the first time the wards were stepped back, as was to become customary for Alpine sanatoria. The double chapels (a sight of members of the opposite sex at worship was considered to hinder recovery), gift of Sir John Brickwood of Portsmouth and recalling the work of

Charles Holden with Percy Adams: the Reading Room of the Central Library, Bristol.

Riemerschmid at Pasing, near Munich, have fittings by C. R. Ashbee's Guild of Handicraft; they originally had open sides (*Bldr*, 22.4.05). Heal's supplied the furniture for the sanatorium and the gardens were laid out by Gertrude Jekyll.

121 The following year they won the compeitition for the King Edward VII wings of the Bristol Royal Infirmary, largely the gift of Sir George White, founder of the Bristol Aeroplane Co. These twin wings, and tower, now engulfed by recent buildings, were many years ahead of their time and the most powerful of Holden's works. Again Muirhead Bone provided an etching.

215 The strongest impact Holden made on the contemporary scene was through the new headquarters of the British Medical Association in the Strand, completed in 1908 (*Bldr*, 8.12.06), on the site of C. R. Cockerell's London Westminster Insurance Co.'s office of 1832. Cockerell's building had been adorned with figure sculpture and Holden's strongly Mannerist design, which indeed verged on the Secessionist, required a style of sculpture modern and vigorous to fill the deep vertical channels provided between the piers and window architraves. For this, Holden selected the young New York sculptor Jacob Epstein, newly arrived from his studies in Paris.

In 1907, the year Holden became a partner, they prepared a design which represented the culmination of their ideas for a teaching hospital.

Charles Holden: design for the rebuilding of St George's Hospital, Hyde Park Corner, SW1. Drawing by C. W. English.

In 1913 Holden's friend L. G. Pearson became a
partner, and with him Holden extended and
rebuilt many voluntary hospitals. Percy Adams's
son, Percy Webster Adams, became a partner in
1925.

12   St George's Hospital was to rebuild on its site at
     Hyde Park Corner, to replace William Wilkins's
     building of 1829, and Percy Adams was asked for
     a design for the new building. The ideas he and
34   Holden had put into practice at the Belgrave
44   Hospital, at Midhurst, in Bristol and at the English
21   Hospital in Constantinople now found expression
     in this great imaginative design, unfortunately
     never executed.

Charles Holden with Percy Adams: the Library of the
Incorporated Law Society, Chancery Lane, London WC2.
The external sculpture is by Charles Pibworth, the
internal majolica by Conrad Dressler.

After the First World War Holden was made one
of the four principal architects of the Imperial
War Graves Commission. In 1923 Adams and
Holden were appointed consulting architects to
the London Underground Railways and Holden
introduced an idiom for the surface buildings
which, with the exception of the buildings for the
Miners' Welfare Association, were the first
examples of modern architecture in *public*
buildings in England.

In 1931 Holden was appointed architect to the

Charles Holden with Percy Adams: the King Edward VII Sanatorium, Midhurst, Sussex. The double chapel allowed men and women to participate in worship without seeing each other.

University of London, and in Senate House faced new problems, since this was then London's tallest building with the exception of St Paul's. Holden became a member of the Art Workers' Guild in 1917. In 1936 he was awarded the Royal Gold Medal for Architecture. In 1947 with William (later Lord) Holford he prepared a plan for the City of London. Holden wished 'to be excused from accepting a knighthood' (the expression he preferred to 'declined') because 'it would alienate me from ordinary people'. Two portraits by Francis Dodd are in the National Portrait Gallery. The firm of Adams, Holden and Pearson continues under the same title with the partners Martin Angus Charles Tarling and Keith Horton.

AR, Dec., 1975, pp. 349–56, article by Brian Hanson

Building Design, 11.4.75, pp. 12 and 13

Thesis on Charles Holden by Chris Arnold, Kingston Polytechnic

Obit. RIBAJ, Aug., 1960, pp. 383–4 *Bldr*, 6.5.60, p. 875.

Charles Holden with Percy Adams: the headquarters of ▷ the British Medical Association (now Zimbabwe House), Strand, London WC2. The figures carved in situ by Sir Jacob Epstein are in an advanced state of attrition due to wrong placing and failure to provide niches.

HORDER, Percy Richard Morley   1870–1944

Morley Horder was born at Torquay, the son of the Rev. William Garrett Horder, the Congregational hymnologist. He was educated at the City of London School and articled to George Devey, one of the architects instrumental in reintroducing the simple vernacular style of the sixteenth century into domestic architecture. Morley Horder's houses were simple and strictly in the vernacular tradition, as at Moonhill, Cuckfield, Sussex (RA, 1902; gardens by Thomas Mawson) and Greystock, near Warwick (RA, 1905).

Morley Horder set up in practice in 1890. Among his earliest works were 52 and 54 Brook Street, W1 (1896–7), much in the style of Voysey. His practice was to include a number of Congregational churches, including his father's at Ealing Green, W5 (1911) and those at Queen's Avenue, Muswell Hill, N10 (1900); Bushey, Hertfordshire (1904); and Penge, SE20, and Brondesbury Park, NW6 (both 1911). He also did Cheshunt (Congregational) College in Cambridge in 1913–14.

His domestic buildings included houses at Rosewalk, Purley, Surrey; Horncastle, East Grinstead, Sussex; and Little Court, Charminster, Dorset; and he did the remodelling of Waterston Manor in Dorset in 1911.

After the First World War, Morley Horder was a partner (1919—25) with Briant Poulter, MVO (1880—1972) and (1926—9) with Verner O. Rees (1886—1966), with whom he did the London School of Tropical Medicine in Gower and Keppel Streets, WC1, one of the most successful designs in Portland stone since Vanbrugh and Hawksmoor, here brought into a contemporary idiom.

After 1919 Horder did shops for Boots Cash Chemists at Bristol, Lincoln, Windsor, Brighton and Regent Street, W1. Through his friendship with Sir Jesse Boot (Lord Trent), benefactor of University College, Nottingham, Morley Horder did the College buildings of 1922—8. He also did a house for the Rt. Hon. David Lloyd George at Walton Heath, Surrey. Horder's other works in the post-war period were the National Institute of Agricultural Botany in Cambridge (1919—21), where there is a portrait of him by Clive Gardiner, and an extension to Westcott House, Theological College, Cambridge. He also did St Francis's College in Letchworth (the additions are by L. H. Shattock).

Morley Horder lived at the Court House, East Meon, Hampshire, which he restored. *His earlier works also include:*

1904	Village Hall, Pitsford, Northamptonshire
1905	110 New Bond Street, W1
1907	121—123 Hampstead Way, Hampstead Garden Suburb, NW11
1909	Gwynfa Hotel, Painswick, Gloucestershire (additions)
1910	Hengrove, St Leonards, Wendover, Buckinghamshire
1911	Munckmead, Pulborough, Sussex
	The Stonehouse, Hawes, N. Riding
	Two houses at Rodborough, Stroud, Gloucestershire
1913	The Gyde Orphanage, Painswick, Gloucestershire

Obit. RIBAJ, Oct., 1944, p. 320 and Nov., pp. 24—5
Bldr, 20.10.44. p. 317.

HORNBLOWER, George   1858—1940

George Hornblower was the son of an architect, Lewis Hornblower (1823—74), of Liverpool, and was articled to his father and his elder brother, F. W. Hornblower. In a brief partnership (1891—3) with the architect and designer A. H. Mackmurdo (1851—1942), Hornblower did a house and studio at 25 Cadogan Gardens, SW3, for Mortimer Menpes, the Australian Boer War artist, fine printer, interior designer and dealer in *japonaisene.* In the same period they did a house at 12 Hans Road, SW3, and St Mark's Rectory, Varley Road, Newton Heath, North Manchester.

On his own account Hornblower did the Linen and Woollen Drapers' Cottage Homes in Hammers Lane, Mill Hill, NW7 (1893—8), and St Swithin's church and residence, The Burroughs, Hendon, NW4. Hornblower's other works include: the electricity generating station for a works on the River Severn (*AA,* 1902; *Bldr,* 20.12.02); The Oaks, Frognal, Hampstead, NW3 (*AA,* 1902); The Croft, Etchingham, Sussex (*AA,* 1903); Branches Park, near Newmarket, Suffolk (RA, 1904); 352—354 Oxford Street, W1 (*AR,* 1905, p. 186); and the Village Institute, Robertsbridge, Sussex (*BA,* 15.1.09). From 1902 Hornblower was consulting architect to University College Hospital, Gower Street, WC1, where he did the new maternity wing and staff residences.

Obit. Bldr, 28.6.40, p. 745.

Gerald Horsley: Hatch End station on the London and North Western Railway, now British Rail.

HORSLEY, Gerald Callcott   1862—1917

Gerald Horsley was the second son of John Callcott Horsley, RA (1817—1903), the painter credited with designing the first Christmas card in 1843 (although the claim has also been made for Charles Dobson, RA). Gerald Horsley's brothers were the painter, Charles Horsley, and the surgeon, Sir Victor Horsley.

Horsley went to Kensington Grammar School, was articled to Norman Shaw in 1879 and was one of the group of Shaw's pupils who founded the Art Workers' Guild. (Shaw had designed the additions to John Horsley's house, Willesley, Cranbrook, Kent.) Gerald Horsley entered the Royal Academy Schools in 1881 and was the first winner of the RIBA Owen Jones Prize and Travelling Studentship. He illustrated E. S. Prior's *History of Gothic Art in England*.

A great part of Horsley's work was painted decoration which included that in the chancel of All Saints, Leek, Staffordshire. In 1899 he did a Music Room and other additions to Balcombe Place, Sussex (RA, 1900), a house by Henry Clutton, illustrated in Muthesius's survey. Horsley's principal work is the St Paul's School for Girls, on the site of the Grange, Brook Green, Hammersmith, W6, for the Mercers' Company, won in competition in 1897 and built in 1901—2, a building in robust 'Wrenaissance' style. Fagan and Murphy did the carving, the ceiling painting in the Dining Hall is by E. J. Lambert, and Henry Pegram did the sculpture in the gables (*Bldr*, 31.5.02 and 29.8.03; an annexe was added in 1913). The pretty station building, Hatch End (formerly Pinner and Hatch End), Middlesex, on the then London and

North Western Railway was done by Horsley in 1911, when he also did Harrow and Wealdstone station for the same railway, a skilful application of a Renaissance style to a difficult site.

Horsley's other works include:

1900	Church Schools, Arundel, Sussex (*Bldr*, 21.2.03)	
1903	St Chad, Longsdon, Leek, Staffordshire (RA, 1902; *Bldr*, 17.9.04 and 10.6.05)	
1904	Brantridge Forest, Balcombe, Sussex (RA, 1904)	
	Coombe Field, Frith Hill, Godalming, Surrey (*Bldr*, 28.5.04)	
1905	Framewood, Stoke Poges, Buckinghamshire (RA, 1905; *Bldr*, 18.6.04 and 13.5.05)	
1909	Coverwood, near Gomshall, Surrey, for Phillips of Phillips' Ink (*BA*, 21.8.08)	
	Reredos, St Peter, Hammersmith, W6 (*Bldr*, 27.2.09)	
1911-13	Baring's Bank, 10—12 Bishopsgate, EC2 (additions to Norman Shaw's building)	

Obit. RIBAJ, Nov., 1917, pp. 23, 231 and 240—1 *Bldr* 13.7.17, p. 23.

HORSNELL, Alick G.   d. 1916

Alick Horsnell was a casualty of the First World War, along with other young architects and architectural students whose names filled the obituary columns of the professional periodicals of the time. Horsnell was articled to Frederick Chancellor of Chelmsford, Essex. In 1906 he won the RIBA

Tite Prize with a design for a Shakespeare Memorial Theatre (*AR*, 1906), and he won the Soane Medallion in 1910. He was assistant to Ernest Newton, and also in great demand as a perspective artist. For Ralph Knott he did the perspective drawings showing the 1914 revisions to the competition design of 1908 for the London County Hall. Also in 1914 Horsnell was among those selected for the final competition for the Board of Trade building in Whitehall, won by E. Vincent Harris.

Obit. RIBAJ, 26.8.16, pp. 306 and 309.

HUBBARD, George   1858—1936

George Hubbard, a nephew of Sir John Evans, FRS (1823—1908), was born at Market Bosworth, Leicestershire, went to University College School, London, and was articled to Thomas Banks in 1879, later becoming his assistant and manager. He began practice on his own account in 1886 and later took into partnership Albert Walter Moore (1874—1965).

Hubbard's works include Heathfield and Cardiff House, Parkside, and houses in Parkside Gardens and Burghley Road, Wimbledon Common, SW19 (*Bldr*, 18.2.05); Hall Place, Godalming and Bunny Hill, Dorking, Surrey; schools at Roehampton and Wimbledon; Britwell, Berkhamsted (*Bldr*, 29.7.05), and Hazelwood, King's Langley, Hertfordshire (*Bldr*, 3.12.10; *AR*, 1911); the Ironmongers' Almshouses, Mottingham, Kent; and Villa Mauvanne, Cannes, France.

Hubbard also did Parkfield (now Witanhurst), West Hill, Highgate, N6, for the Warrington soap manufacturer Sir Arthur Crosfield. This enormous house in the 'Wrenaissance' style looks across from Highgate to Hampstead where the other great soap manufacturer from Warrington, Lord Leverhulme, had extended The Hill (now a hospital) to the designs of Leslie Mansfield.

In 1908, with Albert Moore, Hubbard designed houses in the Hampstead Garden Suburb for the Improved Industrial Dwellings Co. Ltd. at 17—75 (odd) Erskine Hill and 70—124 (even) Willifield Way. At Cambridge Hubbard did the Art School (1910) and Stuart House, the Extra-Mural Department (1925). He wrote 'Notes on the Cathedral Church of Cefalu' for *Archaeologia* (1898, p. 57).

Obit. RIBAJ, 4.4.36, p. 608 *Bldr,* 27.3.36, p. 624
Times, 27.3.36.

HULBERT, Maurice Charles   d. 1927

Hulbert was born at East Ilsley, Berkshire, the son of a solicitor. He was articled to J. A. Cossins in Birmingham. He came to London and was associated with the building firm of Matthews, Rogers & Co. who did work in the Earls Court area and on the Grosvenor Estate. Hulbert lived in Ealing where he contested the constituency in 1910.

On the Grosvenor Estate, W1, Hulbert did 2—8 Green Street in 1891—2 and:

1907-8	37 and 49—50 Upper Brook Street
1909-10	19 Upper Grosvenor Street
1910-12	80—84 Brook Street
	22—26 Gilbert Street

Obit. RIBAJ, 15.10.27, p. 698 *Bldr,* 26.8.27, p. 317.

HUNT, William   1854—1943

HUNT, Edward A.   1877—1963

Edward Hunt was articled to his father and became his partner. William and Edward Hunt maintained a practice in town houses and business premises in Mayfair and the Harley Street area, where they did 40 and 44 Old Bond Street, W1 (*Bldr*, 30.9.05), 35 Harley Street, W1 (1909), 43 Great Portland Street and 93 Mortimer Street (*AA*, 1910; *Bldr*, 15.10.10). They also did extensions to the Shoreditch Town Hall, EC1, in 1902 and did the Tooting Public Library and Redlands, Haslemere, Surrey (*RA*, 1906). After the First World War they did Brettenham House, Lancaster Place, WC2, and the Wandsworth Municipal Buildings, SW18, where William Hunt had been Mayor (1902—3). They also did an extension in totally different style to Boehmer and Gibbs's château-style Harley House, Marylebone Road, NW1, of 1904.

Obit. (William Hunt) *Bldr,* 22.1.43, p. 95

INCE, James Howard   d. 1920

J. H. Ince entered the Royal Academy Schools in 1876 where he won the Gold Medal and Travelling Studentship in 1881. In 1886 he showed a design at the Royal Academy for a monument to the historian John Richard Green to be erected in the Cemetery at Menton. He did the Ashburton Memorial overmantel at Charterhouse School in 1892 (*Bldr*, 29.6.01), and built a house for the sculptor Alfred Gilbert (*q.v.*) at 16 Maida Vale, NW9 — an undertaking which contributed towards Gilbert's financial failure and consequent long sojourn in Bruges. Howard Ince also left England and became a topographical artist in Italy and Sicily. He was a member of the Art Workers' Guild.

JACK, George Washington Henry   1855—1931

George Jack was born in Long Island, USA, of British parents. After his father's death his mother brought him to Glasgow where he was articled to Horatio K. Bromhead. In 1875 Jack came to London and, after one or two short-term jobs, joined the office of Philip Webb in 1880. On Webb's retirement in 1900 Jack continued the practice.

By 1880 George Jack had begun carving in wood and modelling in clay, helped by advice from Laurence Turner. From 1890 he was the chief furniture designer for Morris & Co., and under Lethaby taught at the Central School of Arts and Crafts, then in Regent Street, W1. From 1900 he taught carving at the Royal College of Art, also under Lethaby.

Between 1902 and 1907 Jack was in practice with T. Hamilton Crawford, while continuing and completing Philip Webb's work. His own included Four Winds, Ewhurst, Surrey; Shortenils Gorse, Chalfont St Giles, Buckinghamshire; additions to Great Tangley Manor near Guildford (RA, 1902); and a house at Compton, Winchester. He also did cottages and a village hall at East Rounton, North Riding, where Webb had built the main house (now demolished), and showed a design in the Royal Academy in 1903 for a house at Arisaig, Invernesshire.

Jack also designed the mosaics in the chapel of St Andrew and the Saints of Scotland (designed by R. Schultz Weir) in Westminster Cathedral. The mosaics, executed by Gaetano Meo, represent the six cities where relics of St Andrew came to rest. Jack was a member of the Art Workers' Guild. He wrote *Woodwork, Design and Workmanship* (1903) and contributed the article on woodcarving to the *Encyclopaedia Britannica*.

The Artist, Jan., 1899 'George Jack, Architect and Art Worker'
Obit. Bldr, 15.1.32, p. 133.

JACKSON, Sir Thomas Graham, Bart, Hon.LLD Cantab, Hon DCL Oxon, RA   1835—1924

T. G. Jackson was born at Hampstead in London, the son of a solicitor. He was educated at Brighton College and matriculated at Corpus Christi, Oxford. He won a scholarship to Wadham where he became a Fellow and later Hon. Fellow (1882). In 1858 he was articled to Sir George Gilbert Scott and four years later began practice in London.

Like other outstanding figures of the period, Jackson combined the roles of architect, artist and scholar. His work, most of which was carried out before 1900, consisted mainly of church additions and restorations and buildings at Oxford. In the absence of a New Architecture, Jackson offered a

220

solution to the dilemma between Gothic and Classic with his own version of the late sixteenth- and early seventeenth-century style which acquired the nicknames 'Jacksonbethan' and 'Anglo-Jackson'.

At Oxford Jackson did the New Examination Schools (1884—5), the Buildings in the Grove at Lincoln College, Trinity College New Buildings, the Corpus Christi Annexe, the Third Quadrangle at Brasenose and additions to Hertford and the Bridge of Sighs over New College Lane. He did the North Quadrangle and new Chapel at Hertford between 1903 and 1908 (*Bldr*, 23.5.03). Jackson also did restoration work to the Bodleian Library, the Radcliffe Science Library of the Electrical Laboratory (*Bldr*, 8.5.09), Parks and South Parks Road, and the Hall at Somerville. His later work at Oxford included the Lincoln Library (1906—7).

At Cambridge Jackson did the Squire Law Library and the Law School (1904—11) and, in the same period, the Museum of Archaeology and Ethnology (*Bldr*, 31.7.09 and 7.4.10) and the Sidgwick Museum of Geology, all in Downing Street.

Jackson's church work included restorations to the churches of St Mary and All Saints in Oxford (1907—8), the church of St Augustine, Wimbledon, SW19, where he also did 54 Ridgeway (*Bldr*, 2.5.08) and St Luke and St Augustine's Mission Church, Aldershot (*Bldr*, 11.5.07).

Jackson did buildings at several public schools, including the science block at Uppingham (1894—7), and the covered walk (1891), chapel (1895) and dining hall (1910) at Radley. At Giggleswick he did the chapel (1901), given by Walter Morrison, who insisted on a dome which Jackson made externally octagonal and internally a hemisphere, decorated with coloured marble and mosaics designed by George Murray (RA, 1906).

With the engineer, Sir Francis Fox, Jackson was consulted over the structural repairs to Winchester Cathedral, and acted for many other cathedrals and churches, including Bath Abbey, Great Malvern Priory Church, Christchurch Priory and the Hospital of St Cross, Winchester. He was also engaged on work at Longleat, Wiltshire, for the Marquis of Bath.

Jackson made a special study of the architecture of Ragusa, Dalmatia, Istria and the Adriatic coast and was asked to advise on the campanile at Zara (Zadar), Dalmatia, the restoration of which he completed in 1882.

Jackson was a member, and in 1896 master, of the Art Workers' Guild. He was made ARA in 1892 and RA in 1896 (diploma work, 'The New Schools, Oxford University'). In 1910 he received the Royal Gold Medal for Architecture, and was made a baronet in 1913. He was an Associate of the Académie Royale de Belgique. Jackson lived at

Sir Thomas Graham Jackson, RA: the covered walk at Radley College, Oxon.

Eagle House, Wimbledon Common, SW19, a fine Jacobean house which he had rescued and repaired in 1887.

Towards the end of his long life, Jackson's literary output was prodigious. One of his earliest works was *Modern Gothic Architecture* (1873). Later in his career he wrote *Byzantine and Romanesque Architecture* (Cambridge, 1913) and *Gothic Architecture in France, England and Italy* (3 vols, Cambridge, 1915). Between 1921 and 1923, when he was already in his late eighties, he published his three-volume work, *The Renaissance of Roman Architecture in Italy, England* and *France*, the last volume of which appeared the year before he died.

Jackson, Basil H., *Recollections of Thomas Graham Jackson Bart. RA* London, 1950

RIBAJ, 25.6.10, pp. 620–9, 'Presidential Address on the Presentation of the Royal Gold Medal' and 'Reply'.

Obit. RIBAJ, Nov., 1924, p. 49 *Bldr*, 14.11.24, pp. 748 and 753 and 12.12, p. 926.

JEKYLL, Gertrude 1843–1932

Gertrude Jekyll came of a long line of those whom she described as 'armigerous' gentlefolk. Her father was Edward Joseph Hill Jekyll (1804–76) of the Grenadier Guards; her mother, Julia Jekyll, was the daughter of Charles Hammersley of the Army Agency which became Cox's Bank. One of her three brothers, Herbert Jekyll, KCMG (1846–1932), was a Colonel in the Royal Engineers in the Ashanti War and Private Secretary to the Lord Lieutenant of Ireland. The family lived at the corner of Grafton Street and Hill Street, Mayfair, W1. In 1848 they also acquired Bramley House in Bramley, Surrey, where Gertrude Jekyll was to become interested in the surviving rural industries and crafts of West Surrey.

In 1861 Gertrude Jekyll entered the South Kensington Schools. In 1863 she accompanied Charles Newton — discoverer of the Mausoleum at Halicarnassos — and his wife on a visit to the Near East. On tour Gertrude Jekyll was constantly sketching and painting, mainly human subjects, and, but for her poor sight, she would probably have been a painter. In 1867 she attended Fiori's drawing classes in London, and in 1868 Gigi's Academy in the Via Margutta, Rome.

In the same year the family moved again, to Wargrave Hill, Berkshire. Here, the chalk soil did not suit Gertrude Jekyll's collection of oriental plants, and her dislike of the place was increased by the view of the chimneys of Huntley & Palmer's biscuit factory at Reading and by lack of a suitable boat. But she occupied her time with her studies at South Kensington and at the National Gallery and with embroidery, which she had taken up at the instigation of William Morris.

Gertrude Jekyll designed curtains and other furnishings for the Duke of Westminster at Eaton Hall, Cheshire, and did work for Kensington Palace, for Lord Ducie at 16 Portman Square, W1, and for Lord Stratford de Redcliffe at Frant, Sussex. She followed this with silver work (All Saints', Witley, Surrey, has a paten done by her in 1889), and quilts and a table-cloth for Lord Leighton and Sir Edward Burne-Jones.

Gertrude Jekyll numbered among her many friends Madame Bodichon (Barbara Leigh Smith), one of the founders of Girton College, Cambridge, and Bedford College, whose ladies' 'life class' led to the acceptance of women students at the Royal Academy Schools in 1861. At Scalands, Robertsbridge, Sussex, where Gertrude Jekyll planned a garden, Madame Bodichon introduced the genteel version of peasant life that so influenced Miss Jekyll and others who could afford it.

In January 1875 Gertrude Jekyll met William Robinson, an event which was to have a crucial influence on her subsequent career. She called on him at the office of *The Garden*, the paper Robinson founded in 1872 in which he preached

Gertrude Jekyll: a doorway in the gardens of Hestercombe, Somerset. Architect: Sir Edwin Lutyens, RA.

natural gardening and the 'wild garden' — his gospel fell on fruitful ground in Miss Jekyll's case.

After Captain Jekyll's death in 1876, Gertrude Jekyll and her mother moved to Munstead Heath, between Bramley and Godalming, Surrey, where they built a house designed by J. J. Stevenson. Here she developed a remarkable garden which Robinson and many other distinguished botanists came to see. In 1885 Gertrude Jekyll added photography to her numerous accomplishments, and in *Old West Surrey* recorded the old buildings, the farm implements and especially the local farm people, whose way of life was soon to disappear.

In 1894 at the age of fifty-one she began the first of her new homes, The Hut, which she built on land adjoining her mother's home. This was the first work in a long association with Edwin Lutyens from nearby Thursley, who was then twenty-five years old. They had met when he was building Crooksbury, near Farnham, for Arthur Chapman, a mutual friend. During their drives round the villages and farms in a dog-cart, Gertrude Jekyll imparted to Lutyens her knowledge of local country buildings.

When her mother died in 1895 the house passed to her brother Herbert Jekyll, who had a family. Gertrude Jekyll and Lutyens then embarked on the building of Munstead Wood, a house which was eventually to become the model for the Surrey farmhouse without a farm. Here Miss Jekyll cultivated her ground and furnished her house until the garden came to represent the 'Surrey school' of gardening, and the house the pattern for those Surrey and Sussex houses where

the domestic arts are nurtured with a precious and somewhat studied simplicity.

Miss Jekyll moved into Munstead Wood in 1897 and continued to play a part in Lutyens's success as an architect of country houses, teaching him the best use of natural stone, brick and timber, and how to plan house and garden together as a single work.

Munstead Wood brought her a long succession of commissions, for while her introduction of wild plants in a natural setting showed her to be a dedicated disciple of Robinson, she became, nevertheless, more adept than architectural gardeners like Thomas Mawson, Inigo Thomas and Reginald Blomfield at arranging the architectural features of the formal garden while giving first place to the plants. Of the three hundred or more gardens Gertrude Jekyll planned in her lifetime, more than forty were with Sir Edwin Lutyens. Others she did in collaboration with many of the leading architects of the period. With Sir Herbert Baker, Gertrude Jekyll did the South African First World War Memorial at Delville Wood, Northern France.

Miss Jekyll was also concerned with the introduction of new plants and new varieties, and her theories and practice were recorded in her many writings, amounting to some fifteen books and sixty articles, contributions and papers on gardening. Her collection of textiles went to the Victoria and Albert Museum.

Miss Jekyll's published works included *Wood and Garden* (London, 1898) and — published by

221
241
244

Country Life, 1901–27 — *Wall and Water Gardens*, with Lawrence Weaver, *Garden Ornament*, with Christopher Hussey, and *Gardens for Small Country Houses*, also with Weaver. Her portrait in the National Portrait Gallery is by Sir William Nicholson who also did a painting of her gardening boots. Her memorial by Lutyens is in Busbridge churchyard, where she is buried.

Jekyll, Francis, *Gertrude Jekyll, a Memoir*, with foreword by Sir Edwin Lutyens, London, 1934
Massingham, Betty, *Miss Jekyll*, London, 1966

JENKINS, Frank Lynn
see LYNN-JENKINS, Frank

J. J. Joass with John Belcher: offices at the corner of St. James's Street and Piccadilly, London SW1. A work of genius and a unique example of the style now called "Mannerist" and introduced by Michelangelo at the Laurentian Library, Florence. Sculpture by Alfred Drury and Sir Bertram Mackennal.

JOASS, John James   1868–1952

J. J. Joass was born at Dingwall on the Cromarty Firth in northern Scotland, where his father was an architect. After a short period in his father's office, he went as a junior to Burnet, Son and Campbell in Glasgow, leaving in 1889 to join the office of Sir Rowand Anderson, RSA, in Edinburgh where he also studied at the College of Art. Joass won the RIBA Pugin Prize and Travelling Studentship in 1892 and in 1893 went to London where he entered the office of Sir Ernest George. An excellent water-colourist, Joass was awarded the RIBA Owen Jones Prize in 1895. In 1896 he joined the office of John Belcher, shortly before Belcher's gifted chief assistant, Arthur Beresford Pite, left to set up on his own account. Joass was a partner with Belcher from 1905 until Belcher's death in 1913. The difference between the work of the Glasgow-trained northern Scot, accustomed to detailing for hard stone, and that of Belcher and Pite in Portland stone and red-brick, soon became apparent.

Electra House, Moorgate (1902–3), and Winchester House, Old Broad Street, EC2 (1904–5), had already shown signs of 'half-inch detailing' by Joass. Two remarkable buildings followed, which bore more of the mark of Joass than of Belcher, who was now encouraging Joass's ideas as he had Pite's. These were Mappin & Webb's Oxford Street, W1, branch (1906–8; *Bldr*, 12.3.10) and the Royal Insurance building at the corner of St James's Street and Piccadilly, SW1 (1907–9; *Bldr*, 20.2.09).

69
222
223

At Mappin & Webb's and at the St James's Street building, the Greek Mount Pentelikos marble, which has the warm whiteness of English alabaster, afforded an opportunity for the precision Joass liked; it provided him with a chance to express lightness in contrast to the heaviness of Waring & Gillow's next door in Oxford Street, and the solidity of the neighbouring Ritz Hotel in Piccadilly. But in the absence of a new idiom in which to formulate the clothing of the steel frame in a logical way, Joass expressed himself here in enigma and paradox, employing devices derived from very different sources.

In their two buildings, Belcher and Joass combined elements similar to those seen in Adams and Holden's extension to the Law Society in Chancery Lane (1902) and their British Medical Association Headquarters (1908). Like them, Belcher and Joass drew on Michelangelo's Mannerist style as displayed by the New Sacristy (Medici Chapel) and the Medici Library Staircase at S. Lorenzo in Florence; still other elements may derive from the Secessionist style as illustrated by Joseph Olbrich in his Secessionist building in Vienna (1898).

It was originally intended that the St James's Street building should extend over the whole block as far as Arlington Street, but the western half became the site of Wolseley House (now Barclay's Bank), designed in 1921 by W. Curtis Green and showing the reversion in taste which occurred in the intervening years. Even more than their Oxford Street building, the Belcher and (largely) Joass work in St James's Street reveals the freedom — not to say licence — which total use of the steel frame allowed in the absence of a new idiom. With its help, the Mannerist principle that 'form does not necessarily follow function' is here put into practice.

The coupled columns, taken from Michelangelo's library staircase walls where they *appear* to be doing no work, here appear to be doing *too much*. Above, the bay windows seem to usurp the function of the piers which are already weakened by niches, in their turn forsaken by Bertram Mackennal's putti. These, as *The Builder* pointed out at the time, appear to have climbed out of the niches to seek shelter under the cornice in a manner reminiscent of Michelangelo's caryatid *amorini* on the Sistine Chapel ceiling (*Bldr*, 29.8.08 and 20.2.09). The building exhibits in full measure the tensions it is now fashionable to detect in works of art, sustained even in the chimney stacks which could pass as the work of half a century later. As well, perhaps, that such stress was confined to half the intended length of the building. Over a whole block it might have been exhausting.

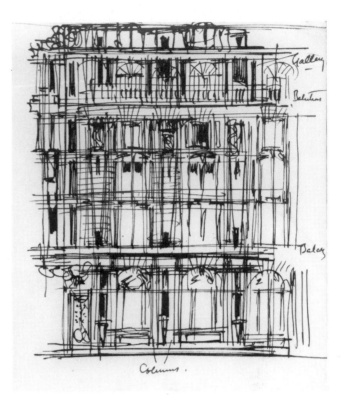

J. J. Joass with John Belcher: a unique sketch by Joass of a unique building, the St. James's Street offices on page 222.

These two buildings provided a host of imitators with a source of motives and devices to be used during the ensuing quarter-century on commercial buildings, seaside pavilions and amusement places. The square blocks and petrified swags with 'necropolitan' connotations — easy to dash off on the drawing board with the T-square and set-square which replaced the compasses and French curves of the previous quarter-century — produced results which at times verged on the ridiculous, for example, in the rusticated pilasters at the corner of Warwick Street and Brewer Street, W1 (by Metcalf and Greig) and on Minerva House, Chenies Street, WC1.

14

The later Joass manner can best be seen in the building for the Royal Society of Medicine, Henrietta Street, W1 (1910—12), altered by the later addition by Lesslie Watson of a copper-clad storey from designs left by Joass. The stone medallions and blank ribands, more appropriate to a military academy, are another Joass device often imitated. Two later Joass buildings, more sober still but in direct line, are Dorland House, Lower Regent Street, SW1 (1924), and the Commonwealth Bank of Australia, Old Jewry, EC4, one of the best City buildings of the 1930s. The last mainly Belcher building had been the extravagant Ashton Memorial (1907—9) in Williamson Park, Lancaster (*see under* Belcher, John), in which the Joass 'half-inch detailing' is still clearly discernible.

15

105
224

Between 1910 and 1912 the new store in Queen's Road (now Queensway), Bayswater, W2, for William Whiteley, the 'Universal Provider',

J. J. Joass with John Belcher: a detail of the former Mappin & Webb building, Oxford Street, London W1. Like the St. James's Street building, it is of Pentelikos marble.

J. J. Joass with John Belcher: the Ashton Memorial, Williamson Park, Lancaster. Joass had succeeded Beresford Pite as Belcher's chief assistant, as the contrast between the work of the two men shows.

replaced the collection of shops in Westbourne Grove into which his great emporium had initially expanded. The new building by Belcher and Joass, designed to be built in stages, avoided the difficulties of extending a continuous colonnade as at Selfridge's. Whiteley's is therefore a more articulated building than the great Oxford Street peristyle.

Two rogue buildings escaped the accustomed Joass discipline – Royal London House, Finsbury Square, EC2, a 1928 addition to an earlier Belcher and Joass building of 1904–5, and Abbey House, Baker Street, W1. The former could be an early Stalinist building, while the latter, suffering from the confusions of the 1930s, has a plain arched tower containing a carillon thrust through a steep, green Spanish-tiled roof.

Joass's only church was Holy Trinity, Kingsway, WC2 (see pages 80–2). Other Joass buildings make the Harley Street area and the 'garment district'

north of Oxford Street as interesting Joass country as it is Pite country; 26 and 28 Margaret Street, W1 (1907–8; *Bldr*, 12.12.08), has as 'busy' a façade as it is possible to achieve within such limits, and 31 Weymouth Street, W1, adds to the variety of the Harley Street area.

The headquarters of the Zoological Society, Outer Circle, Regent's Park, NW1, also belong to the pre-1914 period and are full of Joass dynamism. At Finnegan's (now Clarendon House), 17 New Bond Street, W1, and at the Lex Garage, Brewer Street, Soho, W1, Joass used the contemporary idiom of the late 1920s. In 1922 Joass was architect for the rebuilding of Swan & Edgar's shop, Regent Street and Piccadilly, W1, to the exterior designs of Sir Reginald Blomfield (*see under* The Rebuilding of Regent Street) and in the same year he did Mappin & Webb's, Regent Street, now in other use.

Joass continued in practice until 1952 when his work at Royal London House was continued by Harold Bramhill and his work at the Royal Society of Medicine by Lesslie K. Watson. A keen yachtsman, Joass converted for his own use Heathside, 355 Sandbanks Road, looking over Poole Harbour, Dorset (demolished).

AR, Nov. 1970.

Obit. RIBAJ, Aug., 1952, p. 386   *Bldr*, 16.5.52, p. 748.

JOHN, Sir William Goscombe, RA, Hon.LLD 1860–1952

Goscombe John was born in Cardiff, the son of a stone carver and sculptor. He studied with his father who was engaged on the works at Cardiff Castle for the Marquess of Bute, under the direction of William Burges. After studies at the Cardiff School of Art, John went to London in 1882 as assistant at Thomas Nicholls's Lambeth workshops, meanwhile studying at the Lambeth School of Art. He worked for Charles Bell Birch, ARA (1832–93), entered the Royal Academy Schools in 1884, winning the Gold Medal and Travelling Studentship in 1889. Between 1890 and 1891 John studied under Antonin Mercié in Paris where ten years later he was to win a Gold Medal in the Salon.

Goscombe John's work in the Edwardian period included some of the carving on Electra House in Moorgate for John Belcher (1902–3). In 1902 he did a bronze equestrian statue of King Edward VII for Liverpool and a colossal marble of the monarch for Cape Town. In 1903 John did the bronze of the composer Sir Arthur Seymour Sullivan (d. 1900) for St Paul's Cathedral and Victoria Embankment Gardens, WC2. The addition to the Embankment bust of the grief-stricken figure and her discarded mandolin, music score and mask of Pan, was a gift from the sculptor. The monument is inscribed 'Is Life a Boon?', Fairfax's song in *Yeomen of the Guard*. In the same year John did

225

a bust of Sir Aston Webb and the memorial in St Mary, Amport St Mary, Hampshire, to August John Henry Beaumont Paulet, 15th Marquess of Winchester, killed in action in South Africa in 1899.

Flanking the main portal of the Victoria and Albert Museum (1899–1909) are Goscombe John's statues of King Edward VII and Queen Alexandra. John's later works included John Brunner at Winnington Hall, Cheshire (1922) and, between 1925 and 1934, George V and Queen Mary at the entrance to the Mersey Tunnel; Caradog, conductor of Ycor Mawr (South Wales Choral Union), Victoria Square, Aberdare; and Lady Lever and Lord Leverhulme, for Christ Church, Port Sunlight, Cheshire.

Goscombe John was made ARA in 1899 and RA in 1909 (diploma work, 'Elf', bronze). He was knighted in 1911 and received the Gold Medal of the RBS in 1942. He was made Hon. LLD. (Wales), and was a member of the Art Workers' Guild.

Goscombe John gave 'Icarus' — considered Sir Alfred Gilbert's finest work — and many of his own works to the National Museum of Wales.

His other works include:

1902   The 7th Duke of Devonshire, Eastbourne, Sussex

Sir William Goscombe John, RA: the memorial to Sir Arthur Sullivan in Victoria Embankment Gardens, London WC2. The sculptor added gratis the mourner and her lute.

1903   The 3rd Marquess of Salisbury (Prime Minister 1885, 1886 and 1895), Westminster Abbey and Hatfield Church, Hertfordshire (monument designed by G. F. Bodley)
        The Rt. Hon. W. E. H. Lecky, Trinity College, Cambridge

1904   Prince Christian Victor of Schleswig-Holstein, Thames Street, Windsor (RA, 1903)
        King Edward VII for Cape Town (RA 1904)

1905   South African War Memorial, Royal Army Medical Corps, Aldershot (setting by R. W. Schultz Weir; *Bldr*, 10.6.05)
        South African War Memorial to the King's Liverpool Regiment (Britannia and soldiers), St John's Gardens, Liverpool
        Memorial to the Marquess of Winchester, Winchester Cathedral
        South African War Memorial to the Coldstream Guards, St Paul's Cathedral

1907   'Engine Room Heroes', Mersey Docks and Harbour Board Offices, Liverpool

1911   Medal commemorating the investiture of the Prince of Wales at Caernarvon
        Thomas Sutton, Charterhouse School, Surrey

1912   The Welsh Dragons on the posts of the forecourt, University of Wales Registry (architects Wills and Anderson)

1913   Alfred Lyttelton, St Margaret, Westminster, SW1, portrait in relief and four small seated figures

1914   Andrew Carnegie, bust, Palace of Peace, The Hague

1920   Field-Marshal Viscount Wolseley (d. 1913), Commander-in-Chief of the British Army, Horse Guards Parade, SW1. The statue cast from guns captured in Wolseley's campaigns.

JONES, Captain Adrian, MVO   1845–1938

The great 'Peace' Quadriga, surmounting the Wellington or Constitution Arch across Constitution Hill at Hyde Park Corner, SW1 — assuredly one of the greatest quadrigas of the world — was modelled by a man who had retired after an army career and served in three wars. He was Adrian Jones, born at Ludlow, Shropshire, the fourth son of James Brookholding Jones. Jones went to Ludlow Grammar School and entered the Royal Veterinary College where he passed the final examination at the age of twenty-one. In the same year he was gazetted to the Royal Horse Artillery stationed at Ahmadnagar, Bombay Province, and subsequently served in the 3rd Hussars, the Queen's Bays (with whom he spent ten years in Ireland), and the 2nd Life Guards. He served in the Abyssinian War (1868), the first Boer War (1881) and the Nile Expedition (1884), retiring as Captain in 1890.

Adrian Jones had learnt drawing under Henry Ziegler and his absorbing hobby was the representation of horses in water-colour and oils. C. B.

Birch, ARA (1832—93), who had modelled the Temple Bar Griffin and the Arab horses for Foley's equestrian statue of General Outram, suggested he should take up sculpture and gave him instruction in modelling. In 1884 Adrian Jones's 'One of the Right Sort' was accepted by the Royal Academy. This was followed the same year by a first-prize award from the Goldsmiths' Company for 'Gone Away' — a huntsman and two hounds. Returned from the Nile Expedition the same year, Jones did the 'Camel Corps Scout'. He sent 'Gone Away' to the Royal Academy in 1887. At the Grosvenor Gallery he showed 'The Lost Arrow', modelled from a Red Indian in Buffalo Bill's Wild West Show at the Earls Court Exhibition. After this, Sir Coutts Lindsay (1824—1913), the Crimean War soldier and painter who founded the Grosvenor Gallery, suggested that Adrian Jones should do a 'Quadriga driven by an Assyrian' for the centre of his gallery. But the famous 'Greenery-Yallery' Grosvenor Gallery closed before this group, called 'Triumph', was ready.

227 'Triumph' was the beginning of an achievement which was to be of great importance to the London scene. Adrian Jones changed 'Triumph' to 'Peace', shown alighting on the car from above, while the charioteer, his banner discarded, reined in the steeds of war. At the Royal Academy Exhibition of 1891 the group attracted the

Capt. Adrian Jones: the Peace Quadriga surmounting the Wellington Arch, Hyde Park Corner, London SW1, suggested by King Edward VII while Prince of Wales, was cast at Burton's Thames Ditton foundry. Here the sculptor holds a tea party in a plaster cast.

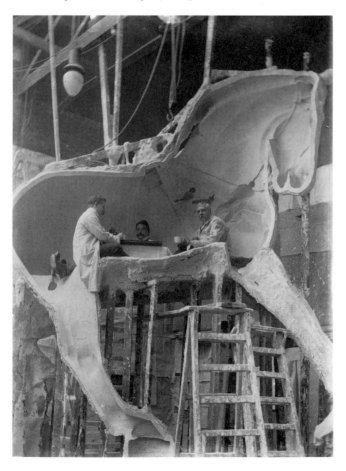

attention of the Prince of Wales who suggested that a quadriga such as this would look well on the top of the arch at Hyde Park Corner, then unoccupied. The arch was designed by Decimus Burton and built in 1828 as an entrance to the grounds of Buckingham Palace, directly opposite his Hyde Park Corner screen, and moved to its present position in 1883.

Built to support a quadriga, the arch was disfigured in Burton's eyes when, in 1846, it was made to serve as a pedestal for Matthew Cotes Wyatt's colossal statue of Wellington: so much so that Burton is said to have kept a clause in his will for many years, leaving £2,000 to the State for the removal of the figure (H. M. Colvin). The statue was eventually removed to Aldershot in 1885. In suggesting the quadriga for the arch the Prince of Wales was thus following Burton's original intention.

Hitherto, Adrian Jones's work had been statuette size. For so colossal a work he had now to face the structural problems of the armature, the handling of the clay and the casting of the plaster mould, and finally, the casting of the bronze group by the founders. The size of the group and its lofty situation also posed problems of scale, proportion and foreshortening, weight and, of course, wind-resistance.

While Adrian Jones was waiting for the idea of the quadriga to be taken up by the Government, his 'Duncan's Horses' was accepted by the Royal Academy in 1892, a work based on lines from *Macbeth*:

And Duncan's horses — a thing most strange and certain —
Beauteous and swift, the minions of their race,
Turn'd wild nature, broke their stalls, flung out,
Contending 'gainst obedience, as they would make
War with mankind.   (II, iv. 14—18)

This more than life-size group was an answer to a provocative remark by the President of the Royal Academy, Sir Frederick Leighton, who, when Jones told him he contemplated doing the quadriga, said 'we all think we can until we try'. Of 'Duncan's Horses' *Sporting Life* said it was 'a disgrace that among horse-breeding, horse-loving people there was no provision for the nation to acquire this work'. At the Royal Academy Summer Exhibition of 1893 *The Standard* declared that Jones's 'Maternal Care' should be the property of the nation. It was placed in the grounds of Washington Singer's house at Borman Court, near Salisbury. Of the 'Rape of the Sabines' (1894) *The Times* complained, 'it is relegated to a place [in the Royal Academy] where it cannot properly be seen'. This group was afterwards lent to the Alexandra Palace, N22, while 'Duncan's Horses', in polyester, stands in the grounds of the Royal Veterinary College, Hertfordshire.

Ever since the Prince of Wales had seen the quadriga, a drawing of Burton's arch with a photo-

Capt. Adrian Jones: it had always been intended by the architect, Decimus Burton, that a chariot with horses should crown the arch, but an enormous standing statue of Wellington occupied it, greatly to the Duke's annoyance, until the Prince of Wales saw Jones's miniature in the Royal Academy.

graph of the group on it had remained at the Office of Works awaiting funds. Each year Adrian Jones enquired about progress, until eventually the Comptroller of the Household, Lord Farquhar, called with a proposal. Only after the Comptroller, with the strictest economy in view, had extracted terms from him, did Jones learn that a wealthy banker, Herbert Stern, created Lord Michelham of Hellingly in 1905, was going to foot the bill.

The work started in 1907, and in the studio Jones had built for it in Chelsea the sculpture grew. Calculations were made of the weight, the armature and the reinforcement, and the figure of Peace in the car Jones lengthened so that it should appear in correct proportion when viewed from the ground. The size of the horses Jones demonstrated by entertaining his friends to tea inside the plaster mould of half of one of them.

The group, cast by Burton's at Thames Ditton, weighs 38 tons. On the way to the site the Chariot and lower half of Peace would not clear the railway arch at the foot of Kingston Hill and had to go round by way of Malden and Norbiton. The hooves of the bronze horses cleared the road by a few inches; the tips of their ears cleared the bridge by half an inch.

The final result — the leaping horses, the poised figure, the crouching charioteer, the silhouette carefully balanced by the discarded banner flung out of the car — remains unsurpassed in any capital city of the world. But the group, uncovered in 1912, was granted no official unveiling. Captain Adrian Jones had been awarded the MVO in 1907, but no membership of the Royal Academy followed; in this he was in good company with the great Alfred Stevens. His name did not appear on the arch for some years, and then only insignificantly (*Bldr*, 8.10.10).

The 'Peace' Quadriga was not Adrian Jones's only important work. The Duke of Cambridge, Whitehall (1907, on a base by John Belcher), he regarded as next in importance, and the amazing statuette group of artillery in action, 'Action Front' (RA, 1921), was his favourite piece.

In his eightieth year Jones did the Cavalry Memorial (First World War), at Stanhope Gate, Hyde Park, W1, in a setting by Sir John Burnet, with St

George on a charger, and the Dragon. Adrian Jones did other war memorials including that for the Royal Inniskillen Dragoons at York Barracks, those for Bridgwater, Somerset and Uxbridge, Middlesex, a great many statuettes and small groups of horses and dogs, and numerous paintings of horses, men and dogs. A portrait of Adrian Jones is in the possession of his grandson, Adrian Brookholding-Jones, and there is a bust by Roland Bevan at Aldershot. He was awarded the Gold Medal (RBS) in 1935. A few sketches by Adrian Jones are in the library of the Royal Academy.

Other major works by Captain Adrian Jones are:

1903	Royal Marines South African War Memorial, St James's Park (base by Sir Thomas Jackson, RA)
	Colonel Afsur Dowla, ADC to the Nizam of Hyderabad (statuette)
1904	Soldiers' National War Memorial (South African War), Adelaide, S. Australia
1905	Carabiniers' War Memorial (South African War), Chelsea Embankment, SW3
	'Persimmon', King Edward VII's Derby winner, portrayed as a stud horse, Sandringham, Norfolk
	General Redvers Buller, Exeter
1907	Field-Marshal HRH George, Duke of Cambridge (1819–1904). Bronze equestrian statue on a pedestal by John Belcher with bronze relief panels of a guardsman and a lancer, Whitehall, SW1

Jones, Captain Adrian, *Memoirs of a Soldier Artist*, London, 1933

Obit. Bldr, 28.1.38, p. 196

JONES, Ronald Potter   1875–1965

Ronald Jones was the son of the shipowner Charles W. Jones of Liverpool. He entered the Royal Academy Schools in 1901. In 1906 he did the chancel of the Essex Unitarian Church, Notting Hill Gate, W8 (demolished), named after the headquarters of the Unitarian Church, where the opus sextile work and some windows were by Henry Holiday (*Bldr*, 6.3.09). One window is in the Glass Museum at Ely.

Other Unitarian churches by Jones are at Cambridge and at West Kirby, Lancashire. He also restored the Old Meeting House, Alton, Lancashire and the pavilions for consolidated clubs, Magdalen College, Oxford (RA, 1904, *Bldr*, 20.2.04) and for Radley College, Berks.

In 1910 Jones did Lindsey Hall, The Mall, Kensington, W8 (*AR*, 1911, p. 344). He was a trustee of the Dr. Williams Trust, Gordon Square, WC1 and a brother upholder of the Art Workers' Guild. His cousins, John and Noel Brandon-Jones are architects.

JONES, William Campbell
see CAMPBELL-JONES, William

JOSEPH, Delissa   1859–1927

Delissa Joseph was the son of Solomon Joseph (of Joseph and Smithem), an architect of synagogues and industrial dwellings. Delissa Joseph's cousin, Ernest Joseph, was architect to Sir Marcus Samuel (Lord Bearsted) for the buildings for his Shell group of companies, and also for several synagogues. Delissa Joseph went to Durham House School and the Jews' College, and began practice in 1882. He married Lily Solomon, a painter and sister of the painter Solomon J. Solomon, RA.

Delissa Joseph did a number of works for the United Synagogue, including the Hammersmith and West Kensington Synagogue (1890, extended in 1896) and synagogues at Dennington Park Road, Hampstead, NW6 (1892), South Hackney (RA, 1897), Finsbury Park (1901), and Cardiff (RA, 1897), and the South East London Synagogue, New Cross. He also became expert in the provision of superstructures over the booking and lift halls of London Tube stations.

For the Great Northern and City Line (now part of the Northern Line), he did Moorgate Station Chambers. For the Central London Railway (now the Central Line), he did showrooms and offices (destroyed in the Second World War) at Post Office Station (the entrance has been moved and the station renamed St Paul's); chambers at Chancery Lane Station (the station has been moved); an hotel at Marble Arch Station, since demolished and replaced by the Cumberland Hotel; Coburg Court Hotel at Queens Road (now Queensway) Station, which was restored by Collcutt and Hamp in 1969. For the Baker Street and Waterloo Railway (now the Bakerloo Line), he did Oxford Circus House over Oxford Circus Station and the mezzanine floor at Piccadilly Circus. For the Great Northern Piccadilly and Brompton Railway (now Piccadilly Line), he did Hyde Park Corner Hotel (now in other use) over Hyde Park Corner Station.

Delissa Joseph was a persistent advocate of tall buildings for London where, up to 1945, the *occupied* part of buildings was restricted to a height of 100 ft. He created a complete street of mansion flats of intricate plan and varied skyline at Fitz George and Fitz James Avenues, North End Road, West Kensington, W14 (RA, 1902). He also did flats at Rutland Court and Rutland Gardens, Kensington Road, SW7 (demolished), where his name appeared in large letters in the gable, and at Chelsea Court and Chelsea Embankment Gardens, SW3, on the site of the Naval Exhibition of 1891.

Delissa Joseph was architect for the Rembrandt Hotel in Thurloe Place, SW7. His West End works included 37–39 and 299 Oxford Street, 43 and 44 Albemarle Street, 14 Hanover Street, and 169, 170, 219 and 225 Tottenham Court Road. In the City he did West India House, Leadenhall Street, Peninsular House in Monument Street, the Bond Court House in Bond Court, 5 Cheapside, 6 Old Jewry, 33 and 34 Bury Street, and 10, 11 and 31

Walbrook. His practice also extended to seaside houses, among them North Sea Lodge and Carmel Court in Birchington-on-Sea, and West Bay Lodge, Westgate-on-Sea, Kent. In 1923 Joseph did 62–64 Brook Street, W1.

Obit. Bldr, 14.1.27, p. 88.

KEEN, Arthur   1861–1938

Arthur Keen went to the City of London School, was articled to and later assistant to R. Norman Shaw, and entered the Royal Academy Schools in 1878. Keen was one of the group of young men in Shaw's office who started Kenton & Co. for craftsman-made furniture, textiles and the products of associated crafts. When he first set up in practice Keen shared offices with Ernest Newton.

Keen designed the Baptist Church House with Kingsway Chapel on the widened Southampton Row (*AA*, 1901; *Bldr*, 7.12.01). Here Richard Garbe did the statue of John Bunyan, Laurence Turner modelled the ceilings and Derwent Wood did the bronze of Dr Spurgeon. Doulton terracotta panels in the council room and visitors' room are by George Tinworth. Keen also did Kingsgate House, 114 High Holborn (*Bldr*, 21.5.04) and Ruskin House, Rochester Row, SW1, for Morris & Co. (*Bldr*, 14.1.05).

Keen's houses included Edgehill, Wildshaw (*Bldr*, 14.5.10), Headland Cottage (RA, 1900), Field House (*BA* 21.1.09), and other houses, all at Limpsfield, Surrey. He also did houses at Hampstead, NW3 (RA, 1902), at Shepherd's Hill, Highgate, N6 (1905), at Sanderstead, Surrey (*AR*, 1910) and five houses at Oakleigh Park, Whetstone, Barnet, including his own house, Littlecroft, which has a ceiling by Laurence Turner (*AR*, 1910). Keen also did the Cricklewood Baptist Church, NW2, and the interior decorations of the Royal Society, Chemical Society and Geological Society, Burlington House, W1 (*c.* 1905).

Arthur Keen's urban buildings derive from the neo-Baroque and bear traces of the influence of the Arts and Crafts Movement. He was a member of the Art Workers' Guild.

ABJ, 10.8.10, pp. 132-41

Obit. RIBAJ, 9.1.39, pp. 255–6 and 523 *Bldr,* 13.1.39, pp. 39 and 116.

KEITH, John Charles Malcolm   1858–1940

J. C. M. Keith was born at Nairn, Scotland, son of the Rev. Charles M. Keith. He was educated at Lincoln Grammar School and Clare Mount, Wallasey, Cheshire and articled to Alexander Ross of Inverness. In 1883 he came to London, worked in several offices, and in 1887 emigrated to California.

Two years later a competition was announced for the design of a new cathedral for Victoria, British Columbia, where the wooden cathedral of 1859 (rebuilt after fire in 1872) needed to be built in permanent materials. Keith moved to Seattle to qualify for entry in the competition, then moved to Victoria in 1891. The assessor was Sir Arthur Blomfield. Among the designs submitted from Britain were those of Henry Wilson (*RIBAJ*, 23.2.07) and A. R. Scott of Paisley. The entries were sent to London where it was arranged that Edmund Ferrey should select ten and submit them for Blomfield's adjudication (1892) – a procedure which would not be considered fair today. Keith's design was awarded first premium. In 1913 W. D. Caröe visited Victoria and advised a new site. The following year war interrupted Keith's new plans, and the foundation stone was not laid until 1926. The nave and baptistry were consecrated in 1929, and the western towers completed in 1954. Built in reinforced concrete and faced with stone, Christ Church Cathedral occupies a noble site facing the Pacific Ocean.

Obit. The Daily Colonist, Vancouver, 20.12.40.

KEPPIE, John   1863–1945

John Keppie was born in Glasgow, the son of a tobacco importer. He was educated in Glasgow and at Ayr Academy, then studied at Glasgow University and Glasgow School of Art and at the Atelier Pascal, Paris. He became chief draughtsman to Campbell Douglas and Sellars, to whom he had been articled before his Paris training. While with them he worked in the site office of the Glasgow Exhibition of 1888. When Sellars died in 1889 Keppie wound up the firm and joined John Honeyman. They did the *Glasgow Herald* building, 60–67 Mitchell Street (1893–5); the restoration of Brechin Cathedral; St Michael, Linlithgow, and many churches.

Charles Rennie Mackintosh (*q.v.*) already an assistant in the firm, became a partner with Keppie when Honeyman retired in 1900. Keppie's work owed much to Mackintosh, and if these two could have weathered together the storms of general practice, the great promise of the Glasgow School of Art Building might have been fulfilled. But the new art which had come in like a lion went out like a lamb. The influence of Paris, and particularly of the Atelier Pascal, directly or on the rebound from America, obliterated what remained of the originality based on first principles which had been the aim of the new architecture at the turn of the century.

In 1908 Keppie did the Parkhead Savings Bank, 1448–56 Gallowgate, Camlachie, which combines the influences of John Belcher and Mackintosh with a Scottish flavour. Mackintosh retired in 1913; A. Graham Henderson joined in the following year and Alexander Smellie in 1929. They were later joined by Joseph L. Gleave, who won the international Columbus Memorial competition, San Domingo. John Keppie retired in 1937. The firm continues as Keppie, Henderson and Partners.

Obit. *RIBAJ,* Sept., 1945, p. 340 *Bldr,* 11.6.45, p. 368.

Ralph Knott with E. Stone Collins: 21 Upper Grosvenor Street, London W1.

230

KNOTT, Ralph   1879–1929

Ralph Knott was born in Chelsea, educated at the City of London School and articled to Woodd and Ainslie in London. He was for eight years an assistant in Sir Aston Webb's office where he worked on the drawings for the Admiralty Arch. While with Webb, Knott entered for competitions in his spare time. He was second in the Bristol Central Library and Malvern Library competitions and in 1908 was selected to compete in the final round for the new London County Hall. This he won against the great guns of the competition world, including Belcher, Hare, Russell and Cooper, Warwick and Hall, and a brilliant newcomer to the field, Edwin Lutyens. The assessors were Norman Shaw and Sir Aston Webb. Although Knott was employed in the office of an assessor this was not then a disqualification, but it resulted in a new rule for subsequent contests (*Bldr,* 8.2.08).

231

Knott's great hemicycle on the *land* side was placed on the *river* front, as already suggested by C. H. Reilly in his entry for the competition (*Bldr,* 23.1.09 and 10.9.10). Delayed by difficulties with the foundations on the river bank, construction was further prolonged by the outbreak of the First World War. The London County Hall belongs to the period when neo-Baroque, tinged with Mannerist tendencies, was giving place to a neo-Classic revival with French overtones; and, perhaps because of the demolition of George Dance the Younger's Newgate Gaol, the etchings of Piranesi were being studied anew. It is the realisation to full scale and in three dimensions of an École des Beaux-Arts student's drawing. But here no ceremonial barge makes fast to the massive bronze mooring rings held by giant bronze lion heads; no doors on the river front open to receive visitors conveyed by water; and no 'antic' figures lurk in the gloom of the Piranesi-like arch leading from Westminster Bridge. There is a memorial plaque (1932) to Knott by Gilbert Bayes in the members' entrance in the courtyard. Additions to the building are by Sir Giles Gilbert Scott and, later, by the Council's architects.

Knott took into partnership a pupil of E. W. Mountford, Ernest Stone Collins (1874–1942), who had collaborated on the County Hall building while in the Architect's Department of the County Council and who continued the buildings after Knott's death. Together they also did 21 Upper Grosvenor Street, W1; 18 Upper Brook Street, W1; Mallord House, Chelsea, SW3; W. T. Henley's Cable Works, Gravesend, Kent; and additions to the Actors' Orphanage at Langley, Buckinghamshire.

230

Ralph Knott collaborated with Arnold Thornely on the design of the public offices and did the Speaker's House for the Northern Ireland Parliament Buildings at Stormont, Belfast.

Obit. *RIBAJ,* 9.2.29, p. 296 *Bldr,* 1.2.29, pp. 237 and 255.

Ralph Knott: the river frontage of the London County Hall, Knott's winning design had the hemicycle on the land side.

KNOWLES, William Henry   1858–1943

W. H. Knowles was articled to W. L. Newcombe at Newcastle upon Tyne, and was in practice from 1884 to 1922, for some time as Armstrong and Knowles, and later as Knowles, Oliver and Leeson. His principal works were Armstrong College (now King's College), Newcastle upon Tyne, including the west front, the Sir Lowthian Bell Tower and King's Hall, opened by King Edward VII in 1906

(*Bldr*, 14.7.06). He also did the College Gateway. Also in Newcastle, Knowles did the National Telephone Co. Exchange, School Board Offices (RA, 1901) and numerous banks and schools.

Knowles was an archaeologist and a great authority on Hadrian's Wall. He was honorary secretary for the excavations at Corstopitum (Corbridge), Northumberland (1907–14) and supervised excavations of Roman work at Bath and Gloucester.

Obit. *RIBAJ*, Feb., 1943, p. 90 *Bldr*, 29.1.43, p. 104.

KOCH, Alexander   1848–1911

Alexander Koch was born in Zurich, went to the architectural school in Eidgenöss (1867–70) and worked in the office of Gottfried Semper of Vienna, assisting on the competitions for the Town Hall and Imperial Museum, the Hofburg Theatre and the Bourse. In 1870–1 Koch studied at the architectural school in Berlin, then began practice with Heinrich Ernst in Zurich.

Koch came to live in London in 1885 and studied at the South Kensington Schools for a year and a half. Four years later he began publishing *Academy Architecture and Architectural Review*, a valuable record which continued until 1931. *British Competitions in Architecture*, another valuable reference work begun in 1905, was published for five years. Koch himself contributed a design to the competition for the Palace of Peace at The Hague in 1905.

Koch's two sons, who changed their names to Martin-Kaye during the First World War, were Neil Martin-Kaye, first Principal of the Southend School of Architecture, and Hugh Martin-Kaye, who continued *Academy Architecture* and founded *Architecture Illustrated*.

LAMBERT, Edwin J.   *floruit c.* 1905

E. J. Lambert was born in Australia. He did some of the paintings at Lloyd's Registry of Shipping, Fenchurch Street, EC3 (1900) and ceiling paintings at the St Paul's School for Girls, Brook Green, Hammersmith, W6 (1904–6). Lambert also provided some of the pen illustrations for *Garden Cities of Tomorrow* by his friend and neighbour Raymond Unwin (*q.v.*). His son was the sculptor Maurice Lambert, ARA.

LANCHESTER, Professor Henry Vaughan, Hon LittD Leeds   1863–1953

H. V. Lanchester was the son of H. J. Lanchester (1834–1914), an architect of London and Brighton. His brother, Frederick Lanchester, was the inventor and manufacturer of the Lanchester motor car. Lanchester was articled to his father and worked in the offices of F. J. Eadle, T. W. Cutler and George Sherrin. He entered the Royal Academy Schools in 1886 and began independent practice in 1887, winning the Aldwinckle Prize and Owen Jones Studentship in 1889. His first major work was Bovril's premises in Golden Lane and Old Street, EC1, using concrete. In 1896 he took into partnership James Stewart and E. A. Rickards whom he had met in George Sherrin's office, and the three tried their hand at architectural competitions. Stewart had won

the Gold Medal at the Royal Academy Schools in 1893 with a design for 'A Provincial Town Hall'.

In 1898 Lanchester, Stewart and Rickards entered the competition for the new City Hall and Law Courts, Cardiff, important because the buildings were to be the first of the new Civic Centre at Cathays Park donated by the Marquis of Bute. The first intentionally planned civic centre in Britain, this was a triumph but, regrettably, was the forerunner of a dismal line of successors. Many more competition successes followed. In 1904 James Stewart, who had contributed an important share to their success, died. Continuing with Rickards, Lanchester won other important competitions (*see under* Rickards, Edwin Alfred).

In 1912 Lanchester visited Delhi to report on a site for the new capital of India and prepared plans for Madras and other cities. He did a large palace for the Maharajah of Jodhpur, the Post Office at Lucknow, and the Birkmyre Hotel, Calcutta; he also did plans for Zanzibar and for towns in Burma.

Lanchester helped to found the Town Planning Institute in London in 1914. In 1919 he took into partnership Geoffry Lucas of London and Hitchin, and in 1923 Lucas's partner, T. A. Lodge. The title of the firm became Lanchester, Lucas and Lodge. Lucas soon retired from the practice which expanded to include universities, technical colleges and hospitals. The practice continues as Lanchester and Lodge.

Lanchester was Professor of Architecture at University College, London, and editor of *The Builder* (1910–12), succeeding Heathcote Statham. In 1924 he received the Royal Gold Medal for Architecture. He wrote *The Art of Town Planning, Talks on Town Planning, Town Planning in Madras & Zanzibar* and *Fischer von Erlach*.

ABN, 6.4.34, p. 384

Obit. RIBAJ, Feb., 1953, pp. 162–3   *Bldr,* 23.1.53, pp. 150, 154 and 204   *Times,* 17.1.53.

LANTERI, Professor Edouard   1848–1917

Edouard Lantéri was born at Auxerre, Burgundy, and studied at the Ecole des Beaux-Arts under Cavalier. Like Aimé-Jules Dalou he took refuge in England during the 1870 Commune and he succeeded Dalou as a teacher at the South Kensington Schools in 1880. Lantéri was assistant to Sir Joseph Edgar Boehm until Boehm's death in 1890. Works by Lantéri at the Tate Gallery include a bronze bust of Alfred Stevens, 'Paysan' in bronze and 'The Sacristan' in white marble. His other works included a portrait bust of Boehm and one of John Sparkes of the Royal College of Art (RA, 1899)

H. V. Lanchester with Stewart and Rickards: the City Hall and Law Courts, Cardiff. Sculpture by Henry Poole and F. W. Pomeroy

Lantéri was a member of the Art Workers' Guild. His other works include:

1903	King Edward VII bust for the French Hospital, London, WC2
1908	'Fame' surmounting the Imperial Crown on the Victoria and Albert Museum, SW7
1912	Ludwig Mond, founder of Imperial Chemical Industries, at Winnington Hall, Cheshire
1913	Sir Samuel Alexander Sadler (d. 1911), Victoria Square, Middlesbrough, E. Riding

LEE, Thomas Stirling   1857—1911

Stirling Lee was born in London and studied at the Royal Academy Schools (1876—80) where he won the Gold Medal in 1877. He went on to the Ecole des Beaux-Arts, studied at the Atelier Cavalier (1880—1) and was in Rome from 1881 to 1883. Like James Havard Thomas, a fellow student at Cavalier's, Stirling Lee carved his own works, a

practice which many busy and successful sculptors tended to neglect, passing their clay models over to others to cast in plaster and carve in marble or stone. Lee also helped Alfred Gilbert to revive the *cire-perdue* method of bronze-casting reintroduced by William Behnes.

For W. D. Caröe, Lee did the bronze doors of the Adelphi Bank, Castle Street, Liverpool (now the National Westminster), called the 'Brotherly Love door' (RA, 1893). His work includes some of the classical marble reliefs alongside those of Conrad Dressler and C. J. Allen, put up in 1894 to complete the screen walls between the piers of St George's Hall, Liverpool, and based on designs by John Flaxman. Lee also did low-relief carvings at Leeds Town Hall and in 1902 the carving on the highly original clock tower at Lindley, near Huddersfield, by the Manchester and Middleton architect Edgar Wood. In 1911 he did the bronze sculpture on the memorial to King Edward VII at Marienbad (now Marianske Lazne, Czechoslovakia) in a setting by W. R. Lethaby. In the Westminster Cathedral chapel of St Andrew and the Saints of Scotland, by Robert Schultz Weir, Stirling Lee did, in low relief, figures of St Ninian, St Margaret of Scotland, St Bride and St Columba.

233

He also did Bishop Gore in the churchyard of St Philip, Birmingham.

Stirling Lee was a founder member of the New English Art Club and a member of the Art Workers' Guild and Master in 1898, doing the portrait bust there of Mervyn Macartney (Master 1899). His own bust there is by A. G. Walker. His son, J. Stirling Lee, was an architect.

LETHABY, William Richard, DLitt Manchester
1857–1931

W. R. Lethaby was born at Barnstaple, Devon, the son of a carver and gilder, Richard Pyle Lethaby. Both parents were Bible Christians. Lethaby went to Barnstaple Grammar School and the local Literary and Scientific Society. In 1871 he was articled in Barnstaple to Alexander Lauder (d. 1920), an architect of Wesleyan chapels and schools and a Mayor of Barnstaple who founded the Devon Art Pottery and restored Queen Anne's Walk there. Lethaby continued as an assistant with Lauder until 1878 when he joined first the office of Richard Waite at Duffield, Derbyshire, then an office in Leicester. In 1879 Lethaby won the Soane Medallion and Travelling Scholarship and travelled in France where he measured and sketched in some thirty cathedrals. Norman Shaw noticed his drawings in *Building News* and engaged him in London. Lethaby entered the Royal Academy Schools in 1880, winning the Silver Medal the same year. He also won the RIBA Pugin Scholarship on which he did a tour of Somerset.

In 1879 Lethaby became chief assistant to Shaw, succeeding Ernest Newton. This was the period when Shaw's assistants used to meet in Newton's office at 14 Hart Street (now Bloomsbury Way) to discuss art and architecture, calling themselves the St George's Art Society, out of which grew the Art Workers' Guild. Lethaby was a founder member of the Guild and Master in 1911 (his portrait bust there is by Gilbert Bayes). Traces of Lethaby's influence in Shaw's office are discernible in buildings of that period which included the former New Scotland Yard building of the Metropolitan Police, now an annexe to the Houses of Parliament.

In 1889 Lethaby left Shaw's office, where he was succeeded by Percy N. Ginham, and took an office at 10 Hart Street to begin practice on his own account. That year he joined Reginald Blomfield, Mervyn Macartney, Ernest Gimson and Sidney Barnsley in the founding of Kenton & Co. with the intention of making furniture (*see under* Blomfield, Sir Reginald Theodore).

Lethaby augmented his small practice by designing for manufacturers — furniture for Marsh, Jones & Cribb of Leeds and John Pyghtle White of Bedford; fireplaces for Longden & Co., the Coalbrookdale Co., and Thomas Elsley; painted pottery designs

for Wedgwood; woodwork for Farmer & Brindley, the stone and wood carvers of Lambeth; and leadwork for Wenham & Waters. He also did designs for embroidery and 'ghosted' for friends with practices of their own, sometimes helping them with competitions. He moved his office to 2 Gray's Inn Place, WC1, then to Buckingham Street, Strand, and finally to 111 Inverness Terrace, W1, which he also made his home. In 1893 he visited Constantinople with Harold Swainson and collaborated with him on *Santa Sophia, Constantinople* (1894).

Lethaby's ideas on designing from first principles with great simplicity, much in the manner of Philip Webb, were illustrated at Avon Tyrell, Hampshire, for Lord Manners (1891); The Hurst, Four Oaks, Sutton Coldfield, Warwickshire (demolished); High Coxlease, Lyndhurst, Hampshire (1901); and at Melsetter House and Rysa Lodge, Isle of Hoy, Orkney (1898–1900). William Morris's daughter May Morris, writing in 1932, recalled Melsetter House as

> ... a sort of fairy palace on the edge of the great northern seas ... remotely and romantically situated, with its tapestries and its silken hangings and its carpets, which came from my father's workshop ... But it was a place full of homeliness and the spirit of welcome, a very lovable place ... (*RIBAJ*, 20.2.32).

235   Lethaby did one town building, an office in Colmore Row, Birmingham, for the Eagle Insurance Co. (now in other hands), in association with J. L. Ball — a building years ahead of its time. Another unique work by Lethaby, equally in advance of its time, is All Saints, Brockhampton, near Ross-on-Wye, Herefordshire (1901–2). The church is roofed with a pointed vault of concrete protected externally with reed thatch. The clerk of works at Brockhampton was the promising architect A. Randall Wells.

The greatness of Lethaby's work lay not just in his buildings but in his teaching and his ability to inspire others, enlisting their support in the furtherance of the aims and ideals of William Morris and Philip Webb. In the years that followed, any building designed from first principles was likely to owe much to inspiration derived from Webb through the interpretation of Lethaby. Lethaby's

356
358
31
10

friend Thackeray Turner, whose buildings on the Grosvenor estate were to show the Lethaby influence, was prominent among the Webb– Lethaby 'school', as were the architects of the recently formed London County Council.

Lethaby was given an opportunity to realise his ideas on the training of artists and craftsmen when he was appointed the first art adviser to the Technical Education Board of the new London County Council in 1892. He also helped to found the Central School of Arts and Crafts, Upper Regent Street, which moved to a new building in the newly-widened Southampton Row, WC1, in 1907

W. R. Lethaby with J. L. Ball: office building, Colmore Row, Birmingham.

and is today the Central School of Art and Design. With Lethaby were the sculptor, George Frampton, and Halsey Ricardo, the School's first teacher of architecture. Lethaby brought in well-known craftsmen and discovered new ones. He resigned in 1911 when his work increased at the South Kensington Royal College of Art, where he had become the first Professor of Design in 1900, a post he held until 1918.

When the competition for the new Anglican Cathedral at Liverpool was announced Lethaby collaborated in a design with a number of his colleagues at the Central School, Ricardo, Henry Wilson, who taught metalwork there, Christopher Whall, the glass designer, the sculptor Thomas Stirling Lee, and the architects Robert Schultz Weir and F. W. Troup — all brother-upholders of the Art Workers' Guild. But the resulting design, as might be expected with so many different talents at work, was clumsy. The new building for

the Central School of Arts and Crafts in Southampton Row, WC1, by the LCC architects was clumsier still, a broth spoilt by too many cooks.

In 1903 Lethaby and Ricardo submitted a plan in a limited competition for the First Garden City of Letchworth, but Parker and Unwin's plan was chosen. Lethaby was appointed surveyor to the fabric of Westminster Abbey in succession to J. H. Micklethwaite (1843–1906) in 1906, the year he wrote his book on the Abbey, *Westminster Abbey and the King's Craftsmen*. In 1911 Lethaby designed the setting for the memorial to King Edward VII at Marienbad (now Marianske Lazne, Czechoslovakia), where the bronze sculpture was by Stirling Lee.

Lethaby's written works included *Architecture, Mysticism and Myth* (1892); *Mediaeval Art* (1904, 1908); *Greek Buildings* (1908); *London Before the Conquest* (1911); *Architecture, an Introduction to the History and Theory of the Art of Building* (1912) and *National Architecture and Modernism* (1918–21).

Lethaby's influence on Norman Shaw's later work is notably evident in the introduction of colour and texture and greater simplicity. Lethaby's prophets were Ruskin, Morris and Philip Webb, of whom he said:

> The happy chance of close intimacy with Philip Webb at last satisfied my mind about that mysterious thing we call 'Architecture'. From him I learnt that what I was going to mean by 'Architecture' was not mere designs, forms and grandeurs, but *buildings*, honest and human, with hearts in them.

Lethaby married Edith Crosby of Boston, Massachusetts, in 1902. He died at Inverness Terrace and was buried at Hartley Wintney, Hampshire, where he had taken Albion Cottage near the Schultz Weirs' home in 1902. The epitaph he chose for himself was 'Love and Labour are all'. Lethaby had declined the Royal Gold Medal and he also declined burial at Westminster Abbey, but there is a memorial to him in the cloisters there. Lethaby was noted for his aphorisms. It was he who said: 'In looking back art loses its life', and 'The enemy is not science but vulgarity, a pretence of beauty at second hand'.

Architecture, Mysticism and Myth, a new edition with an introduction by Godfrey Rubens, London, 1975

'William Lethaby's Buildings' in *Edwardian Architecture and its Origins* (Ed. A. Service) London Architectural Press 1975

Rubens, Godfrey, *William Richard Lethaby, His Life and Work* (in preparation)

RIBAJ, 20.2.32, pp. 290 and 293–317: 'W. R. Lethaby, an Impression and a Tribute', by Sir Reginald Blomfield, RA, with contributions from many of his friends, and 'The Drawings of W. R. Lethaby', by Noel Rooke

Obit. RIBAJ, 8.8.31, pp. 696, 737, 19.9, p. 738, 17.10, p. 770 *Bldr*, 24.7.31, pp. 134, 138–9 and 179.

LORIMER, Sir Robert Stodart, KBE, RSA, ARA 1864–1929

Robert Lorimer was born in Edinburgh, the younger son of James Lorimer, Regius Professor of Public Law at Edinburgh University. His mother was the daughter of Robert Stodart, who was a pupil of John Broadwood and the maker of an early 'grand' pianoforte. The painter, John Henry Lorimer, was a brother.

Lorimer was educated at Edinburgh Academy and Edinburgh University. When his aptitude for architecture showed itself while his father was restoring Kellie Castle, Fife, he was articled to Sir Rowand Anderson, RSA, in 1885. In 1889 Lorimer went to London to the office of the church architect, G. F. Bodley, for eighteen months, followed by a year with James MacLaren, an architect of great originality who died while Lorimer was with him.

In 1893 Lorimer started in practice on his own account in Edinburgh. An early work was the restoration of Earlshall, Fife, in 1895, for R. W. Mackenzie, a friend of his father. Then followed work at Dunrobin Castle for the Duke of Sutherland, and at Briglands, Kinross-shire (mentioned by Hermann Muthesius). In England in the same period Lorimer did Whinfold (additions by Walter Tapper, 1903), and High Barn, Hascombe, near Godalming in Surrey (1901–3). In 1909 Lorimer did the Chapel of the Knights of the Thistle in St Giles's Cathedral, Edinburgh. Here the stonecarving is by Joseph Hayes, the woodwork by the brothers Clow, the windows by Louis Davis and the east window by Douglas Strachan.

Lorimer's greatest work is the Scottish National War Memorial Chapel (First World War) on Castle Rock, Edinburgh, a work of high seriousness in which Lorimer's Scottish fellow artists displayed their skills in stone, wood, metal and glass. He is best remembered, however, for his domestic architecture, from the sympathetic restoration of ancient castles to the building of cottages. Seen against the work of most of his contemporaries, the simple shapes and plain surfaces of Lorimer's work have the clarity of a winter landscape, and owe something, perhaps, to the influence of MacLaren.

Lorimer was made an Associate of the Royal Scottish Academy in 1892 and RSA in 1902. He was made Associate of the Royal Academy (London) in 1920, and was a member of the Art Workers' Guild.

RIBAJ, 21.2.31, pp. 239–49 and 292–5: 'The Work of Sir Robert Lorimer' by F. W. Deas

Obit. RIBAJ, 21.9.29, p. 771 *Bldr*, 20.9.29, pp. 458, 460 and 478.

Sir Robert Lorimer: St Peter, Edinburgh.

LOVEGROVE, Gilbert Henry   1878–1951

Gilbert Lovegrove was articled to Henry Lovegrove (d. 1927) and went to the Architectural Association and King's College, London. He did restoration work at Salisbury Cathedral and St George's Chapel, Windsor, and work at Eton, Repton, Shrewsbury and Oundle schools.

Other works by Lovegrove were the Mary Curzon Hospital for Women at King's Cross, N1; St John's Schools, New North Road, Hoxton, N1 (*Bldr*, 30.1.09); The Tiger public house, Tower Hill, EC3; and the Electric Theatre in Kettering. He also did the Wellgarth Nursery Training School (completed in 1915), Wellgarth Road, NW11, now a Youth Hostel. On this he was associated with Alfred Wyatt Papworth, the last of the line of architects of that name, who studied at the Royal Academy Schools (1902–5) and died on active service in 1915 (*Bldr*, 22.6.01).

Lovegrove's practice was continued by L. R. Foreman and E. C. Butler, followed by Leslie W. Lindars, under the title Lovegrove and Lindars.

Obit. Bldr, 28.9.51, p. 432.

LUCAS, Thomas Geoffry   1872–1947

Geoffry Lucas was born at Hitchin, Hertfordshire. He was articled to Walter Millard, also of Hitchin, and studied at the Architectural Association, University College, London, and Heatherley's. He won the RIBA Godwin Bursary and was assistant in turn to William Flockhart, Walter Millard, Frank Baggallay, Leonard Stokes, F. A. Walters, W. Curtis Green, R. Schultz Weir and A. Marshall Mackenzie. Millard and Lucas, themselves excellent draughtsmen, helped to encourage F. L. M. Griggs, another Hitchin man, to develop his exceptional talent for drawing.

Lucas began practice in 1895 in Hitchin where five years later, in collaboration with E. W. Mountford, he won the competition for the Town Hall (RA, 1900; *Bldr*, 30.3.01). In 1903, with Sydney Cranfield, Lucas prepared a plan for the First Garden City at Letchworth in competition with Lethaby and Ricardo, and Parker and Unwin whose plan was selected.

Lucas did small houses and cottages at Letchworth (RA and *AA*, 1905) and South Mimms, Hertfordshire (RA, 1906). He also did the Parish Nurse's Cottage at Heathfield, Sussex. He was one of the architects engaged on the Hampstead Garden Suburb under the direction of Parker and Unwin and did thirty-eight houses there — Lucas Square (named after him) at 60–82 Hampstead Way, 9–47 and 56 Willifield Way, 10 Southway, 42, 125 and 127 Hampstead Way and 16 Bigwood Road. Lucas won the Godwin Bursary in 1912. Lucas did Yewlands, Hoddesdon, and houses at Baldock and Broxbourne, Hertfordshire, a prize-winning house in Parkway, Gidea Park, Essex (*AR*, 1911), and a house at Ponders End, Middlesex. During the First World War, under the direction of Raymond Unwin, Lucas and other architects who had been working on the Garden Suburb helped to design the great munitions town of Gretna, Dumfries.

After the death of E. A. Rickards, Lucas became a partner of H. V. Lanchester in 1920. They were joined in 1923 by Lucas's former partner, T. A. Lodge. Lucas retired and Lodge remained with Lanchester, surviving them both. The firm continues as Lanchester and Lodge.

Obit. RIBAJ, Nov., 1947, p. 39.

LUCCHESI, Andrea Carlo   1860–1925

Lucchesi's father was a moulder from Tuscany living in London; his mother was English. He was educated at Euston College and went to the West London School of Art. Lucchesi first exhibited at the Royal Academy in 1881 and entered the Royal Academy Schools in 1887, remaining for five years. He was an assistant to H. H. Armstead, RA (1828–1905), and to Edward Onslow Ford, RA (1852–1901). Lucchesi also worked for two commercial silversmiths, Garrard's and Elkington's. His 'Destiny' won him a gold medal at Dresden in 1895.

In 1898 Lucchesi did a bronze bust of the explorer Sir John Franklin (d. 1847), now at the National Portrait Gallery, and a head of the actor C. Hayden Coffin (RA, 1899).

331 Lucchesi's best-known work is the memorial to Onslow Ford, erected in 1903, at the junction of Abbey Road with Grove End Road, NW8, incorporating a bronze replica of Ford's 'Muse' on the base of the Shelley Memorial, Oxford (1892), and a high-relief bronze medallion portrait of Onslow Ford by Lucchesi with the quotation 'to thine own self be true' and provided with a pair of bronze lamp standards. The monument was designed by Lucchesi in collaboration with the architect John W. Simpson (*q.v.*)

In 1906 Lucchesi did the bronze tablet to John Wareing Bardsley, Bishop of Carlisle, in Carlisle Cathedral. His 'Victory of Peace' (1901) was intended for Auckland, New Zealand.

He was a member of the Art Workers' Guild.

Sir Edwin Lutyens, RA: The Inn, Roseneath, Dunbarton.

LUTYENS, Sir Edwin Landseer, OM, KCIE, PRA
1869—1944

Edwin Lutyens was the eleventh of the fourteen children of Captain Charles H. A. Lutyens of the XX Foot (Lancashire Fusiliers). His mother Mary (née Gallwey) was an Irish Catholic turned Protestant and also came of a military family. The Lutyenses originated from Schleswig-Holstein. Lutyens was named after Edwin Landseer, the great academician, a friend of his father's.

As a rather frail child, Lutyens received most of his early education from family and friends. His mother took a part in his schooling, his brother Fred, six years his senior, gave him tuition in drawing and so did his father who, since his retirement from the army, had earned a reputation as a painter of fox-hunting subjects and landscapes. A neighbour, the poet and artist Randolph Caldecott, taught Lutyens to sketch the barns, farmhouses, cottages and scenery of the West Surrey countryside. Lutyens soon adopted a short cut to sketching using a picture frame and glass which he held up to the view. With a piece of soap he then traced on the glass the profiles and intersections of roofs, walls and chimney stacks — a practice which may account for the dominance these features were to have in his buildings. When he was in his early twenties, Lutyens met the great gardener, Gertrude Jekyll, who also helped to initiate him into the special qualities of the local landscape and architecture.

Although Lutyens did not make the large number of measured drawings and sketches of old work — usually churches — expected of students, he nevertheless prepared a portfolio of sketches, then the customary passport to an architect's office. Now in the RIBA Drawings Collection, his portfolio already indicates the direction his thoughts on design were to take.

In 1885 Lutyens entered the South Kensington Schools to study architecture. Before he had completed the course he obtained a place in that 'Eton of offices', George and Peto. Herbert Baker was then their chief assistant, and E. Guy Dawber was

an assistant. Baker quickly recognised Lutyens's promise and together they went on sketching trips in Surrey, Sussex and the Welsh Marches, Lutyens observing and committing to memory the traditional buildings which his artist friends in Surrey had already made familiar.

Soon after joining George and Peto, Lutyens was invited by Arthur Chapman to design his house, Crooksbury, near Farnham, Surrey (RA, 1890). This and other commissions encouraged Lutyens — with only six months' office experience behind him — to commence private practice. At the age of twenty he set up at 6 Gray's Inn Square, WC1. Lutyens added further to Crooksbury in 1898, 1899 and again in 1914. From these early works, as yet scarcely distinguishable from houses by the followers of Norman Shaw, came other commissions often hard won, cherished and cultivated by Lutyens who was spurred on by both a sense of destiny and, more immediately, the need to provide evidence of his financial prospects. This was required by the uncle of Lady Emily Lytton before Lutyens could formally ask for her hand. She was the daughter of the 1st Earl of Lytton, Governor-General (1875—7) and Viceroy (1877—80) of India, and the grand-daughter of the poet novelist Edward Bulwer Lytton, 1st Baron Lytton.

Even in these early years Lutyens's designs began to show improvements on the work of his contemporaries and, indeed, on that of his seniors. Simplifying, refining, using local materials in the right way and welding together the houses and their gardens (usually designed by Gertrude Jekyll), Lutyens devised for old problems new and brilliant solutions which he continued to improve upon throughout his life. This singular skill Lutyens soon applied to a house for Gertrude Jekyll herself, Munstead Wood, near Godalming, Surrey, where he benefited greatly from Miss Jekyll's unstinting advice and encouragement and where the gardens became the inspiration for a completely new approach to English gardening.

Connections with the Jekyll family and with the Court, where Lady Emily Lytton's mother was a Lady-in-Waiting, brought further commissions. For Princess Louise, Duchess of Argyll, the sculptress, Lutyens did The Inn, Roseneath, Dunbartonshire, in 1896; in 1898 he did Orchards, Godalming, for Sir William Chance.

238

After a romantic courtship during which they visited Lutyens's jobs on bicycles and exchanged amusingly illustrated letters, while Lutyens presented his fiancée with a miniature casket containing a plan of their ideal home, Lutyens and Lady Emily married in 1897. The same year they took over Norman Shaw's old office at 29 Bloomsbury Square, WC1, where they also made their home. Installed in No. 29, Lutyens drew around him a band of enthusiastic young assistants, among them S. H. Evans, Oswald Milne, George Alwyn, the Hon. Paul Phipps, Norman Evill and A. J. Thomas, who became his manager for many years, while from among craftsmen he selected Abraham Broadbent who worked in the style of Grinling Gibbons.

Sir Edwin Lutyens, RA: a detail from the offices of *Country Life*, Tavistock Street, London WC2.

Following the fashion of the times, Lutyens's houses are sometimes asymmetrical with gables and casement windows in the sixteenth-century vernacular; others are symmetrical (with hipped roofs and sash windows) and follow the formal style introduced in the seventeenth century, first by Inigo Jones and again by Wren. Houses by Lutyens were so superior that against those by his contemporaries they stood out with absolute clarity.

Through Sir Herbert Jekyll, Gertrude Jekyll's brother, Lutyens did the British Royal Pavilion at the Paris Exhibition of 1900, for which the Board of Trade wanted a replica of the Jacobean Kingston House, Bradford-on-Avon, Wiltshire, which allowed little scope beyond the Royal Suite. A grand piano with a case made from a design by Lutyens for Broadwood's was exhibited here (*Bldr*, 23.3.01). He also did the 'Shakespeare's England' Exhibition at Earls Court, SW5, in 1911.

It was the ambition of most architects to do a building in a London street, an achievement recognised by the RIBA in 1922 when they offered the 'London Street Architecture Medal'. Lutyens's opportunity came in 1904 when he designed his first town building with a street frontage — the offices of *Country Life*, 2–10 Tavistock Street, Covent Garden, WC2, for Edward Hudson for whom Lutyens had done Deanery Garden, Sonning, in 1901. Hudson was an admirer of Lutyens's work and was exclusive publisher of Lutyens's houses and gardens. Lutyens designed the *Country Life* offices in the Wren or William and Mary manner of Hampton Court Palace, completed, however, by a steep tiled roof and tall chimney stacks, more in the manner of Philip Webb. Here the tricks of façade building appear, and floors for identical use are disguised as 'mezzanine' and 'piano nobile'. Another clever London façade, again for a publisher, is 42 Kingsway, for William Robinson, the great gardener and proprietor of *The Garden* (now in other use). In 1905 Lutyens did the St John's Institute, Tufton Street, Westminster, SW1, with the simple treatment he was to use again for the Institute in Hampstead Garden Suburb.

240
242

Lutyens was now well launched into the 'High Game', as he called it in his letters to Baker, and victory seemed within his grasp when he was invited to compete in the competition for the new London County Hall in 1908. To satisfy his own fastidious requirements and those of the assessors, Norman Shaw and Aston Webb, Lutyens brought all his critical faculties to bear on the planning and refining of his design. But he lost to Ralph Knott who anticipated popular taste by designing a single large order of columns, and hinted cleverly at the newly fashionable French and Mannerist styles. After this disappointment, followed by the chagrin of seeing the adoption of Sir Aston Webb's design for the Queen Victoria Memorial *rond-point* at Buckingham Palace which to him appeared full of

**Sir Edwin Lutyens, RA: Marsh Court, Stockbridge,
Hampshire, is built of clunch. The gardens are by Gertrude
Jekyll.**

△ Sir Edwin Lutyens, RA: a sketch for a chimney stack for the *Country Life* offices, in a letter to Lady Emily Lutyens, in which he expresses his concern over comparison with Norman Shaw's great stacks.

Sir Edwin Lutyens, RA: a drawing by William ▷ Walcot reappearing on the Jubilee number of *Country Life*.

faults, Lutyens was encouraged by an invitation from Henrietta Barnett to collaborate with Raymond Unwin on the planning of the Hampstead Garden Suburb. Here Lutyens was to display 242 his remarkable invention in the centre with its two 243 churches and Institute and some of the surrounding houses of North Square and Erskine Hill.

Lutyens's work knew many phases which included the Lutyens of New Delhi, the Cenotaph, the War Cemeteries and the War Stone, the great prestige buildings in the City of London, and the Washington Embassy. Finally there was the Lutyens of the unrealised design for the Roman Catholic Cathedral of Christ the King in Liverpool. In all of these can be traced some development or culmination of the store of ideas Lutyens had formed and tested over the years — the light-admitting open-ended joists, 245 from Munstead Wood to Castle Drogo; arches with open spandrils, from Sonning to Ashby St Ledgers; the concave flight of steps meeting the convex flight, from Sonning to Liverpool Cathedral; the bolection moulding, Lutyens's trade mark, simplified until it appears in its ultimate refinement at the garden door of Middleton Park, Oxfordshire, which Lutyens did with his son Robert Lutyens.

◁ Sir Edwin Lutyens, RA: the rectory of St. Jude-on-the-Hill, Hampstead Garden Suburb, London NW11.

Sir Edwin Lutyens, RA: the nave and chancel of St. Jude-on-the-Hill, Hampstead Garden Suburb, London NW11.

Sir Edwin Lutyens, RA: Great Maytham Hall, Rolvenden, Kent.

For Lutyens the age of Edward VII concluded with his sketches for an Edward VII Memorial in the Green Park, which, fortunately, since the situation was not a propitious one, came to nothing. Lutyens had already emerged as the architect *par excellence* for the coming era of King George V. His buildings do not continue the brio and the panache of the neo-Baroque, for neither Bernini nor Borromini were his masters, but Bramante, Sangallo, Sanmichele, Peruzzi and Michelangelo. All Lutyens's ideas culminated in his design for the Roman Catholic Cathedral at Liverpool, unrealised except for the crypt. The drawings surrounded him on his death bed at 13 Mansfield Street, W1, where a blue plaque now commemorates his residence there.

Lutyens's heroes were Philip Webb and Norman Shaw, in that order. He had 'discovered' Webb when at South Kensington and had discussed the ideas and ideals of William Morris and Webb with fellow students like Detmar Blow, who had been a travelling companion of Ruskin. Years later Lutyens wrote:

> The freshness and originality which Webb maintained in all his work I, in my ignorance, attributed to youth. I did not recognise the eternal youth of genius though it was conjoined to another attribute of genius — thoroughness.

Sir Edwin Lutyens, RA: Heathcote, Ilkley, Yorkshire.
Left: **a fountain base at Heathcote, Ilkley.**

Of Norman Shaw, after seeing his additions to
Chesters, in 1901, Lutyens wrote to Herbert Baker:

> I believe Norman Shaw is a really great and
> capable designer, one of the first water.
> I put him with Wren — really ...

Standardising his mouldings at 54 degrees and 44
minutes (the golden mean), aware that Shaw could
be reticent (second Alliance Building, St James's)
or bold (Piccadilly Hotel), and tying his 'synco-
pated' windows to simple arithmetic at 68 Pall
Mall, SW1, aware that Shaw at the Gaiety and
Piccadilly Hotels had distributed his windows
freely, Lutyens, while never as free as Shaw nor
free of Shaw's presence, was the only one of his
generation with the ability to follow Shaw.
Lutyens was a member of the Art Workers' Guild
and was Master in 1933.

Lutyens was made ARA in 1913, RA in 1920
(diploma work, the 'Jaipur Column', New Delhi).
He was knighted in 1918; in 1921 he received the
Royal Gold Medal for Architecture and in 1924
the Gold Medal of the Institute of American
Architects. He was decorated with the KCIE in
1929 and made Hon. DCL (Oxon.) in 1934. In

1942 he was awarded the Order of Merit. Lutyens was President of the Royal Academy from 1938 until his death. The funeral service took place in Westminster Abbey.

There is a tablet to Lutyens's memory at the Crematorium, Golders Green, NW11, near that of its designer, his first master, Sir Ernest George, RA. Lutyens's ashes are interred in the crypt of St Paul's Cathedral, where he is commemorated by a tablet designed by William Curtis Green, the gift of the Leighton Fund. There is a bronze head of Lutyens by Sir William Reid Dick, RA, at the Royal Academy, and a cast at the RIBA. For many years a plaster head of 'Lut' smoking a pipe and wearing a topee shaped like his favourite Delhi cupolas — done by one of his Indian staff — stood behind the fanlight of the front door at 13 Mansfield Street, its back to the street. It is now in the RIBA Drawings Collection. In the National Portrait Gallery are a portrait by his son, Robert Lutyens, a chalk drawing by William Rothenstein, and a bronze cast from his death mask.

Two London buildings are named after Lutyens, one in Churchill Gardens, SW1 and his own great building in Finsbury Circus, EC1, built as 'Britannic House' for the Anglo-Persian (later Anglo-Iranian) Oil Co. and now 'Lutyens House', an office building.

Lutyens's principal domestic works include:

1899   Overstrand Hall, Norfolk, for Lord Hillingdon

Tigbourne Court, Witley, Surrey, for Edgar Horne. Gardens by Gertrude Jekyll

Goddards, Abinger, Surrey, for Sir Frederick Mirrielees, Gardens by Gertrude Jekyll

1900   Grey Walls, Gullane, East Lothian, for the Rt. Hon. Alfred Lyttelton, MP

1901   Deanery Garden (now The Deanery), Sonning, for Edward Hudson, proprietor of *Country Life*. Gardens by Gertrude Jekyll

241

Marsh Court, Stockbridge, Hampshire, for Herbert Johnson (now a school)

Homewood, Knebworth, Hertfordshire, for the Countess of Lytton

1902   Abbotswood, Stow-on-the-Wold, Gloucestershire (additions), for Mark Fenwick

Little Thakeham, Sussex, for Ernest Blackburn

Monkton House, Singleton, Sussex, for William James, one of Edward VII's circle. Gardens by Gertrude Jekyll

1903   Papillon Hall, Leicestershire for Frank Belville (demolished 1951)

Lindisfarne Castle, Holy Island, Northumberland (restoration), for Edward Hudson

Daneshill, Old Basing, Hampshire, for Walter Hoare

221   1904   The Gardens and Orangery, Hestercombe, near Taunton, Somerset, for the Hon. E. W. Portman, with Gertrude Jekyll

Ashby St Ledgers, near Rugby, for the Hon. Ivor Guest, MP (additions). Gardens by Gertrude Jekyll

1905   Lambay Castle, County Dublin, Ireland, for the Hon. Cecil Baring

Nashdom, Taplow, Buckinghamshire, for H. H. Princess Alexis Dolgorouki (now a Benedictine Abbey). Gardens (1909) by Gertrude Jekyll

244   1906   Heathcote, Ilkley, W. Riding, for Ernest Hemingway

Folly Farm, Sulhamstead, Berkshire, for H. Cochrane; additions (1913) for Mrs Z. Merton. Gardens by Gertrude Jekyll

Sir Edwin Lutyens, RA: Castle Drogo, Drewsteignton, Devon.

	1907	New Place, Shedfield, Hants., for A. S. Franklyn. Gardens by Gertrude Jekyll
	1908	Whalton Manor, Northumberland, for Mrs Eustace Smith
		Temple Dinsley, Hertfordshire (additions), for H. G. Fenwick. Gardens by Gertrude Jekyll
		Middlefield, Great Shelford, Cambridgeshire
243	1909	Great Maytham Hall, Rolvenden, Kent, for H. J. Tennant, MP
		Ashby St Ledgers (further additions)
	1910	Great Dixter, Northiam, Sussex (additions) for Nathaniel Lloyd, printer and author of *The History of English Brickwork*

Baker, David, Thesis for University of Newcastle upon Tyne, 1975, *Lutyens on Lindisfarne, 1906*

Butler, A. S. G., *The Architecture of Sir Edwin Lutyens*, London and New York, 1950

Hussey, Christopher, *The Life of Sir Edwin Lutyens*, London and New York, 1950

Lutyens, Lady Emily, *A Blessed Girl: Memoirs of a Victorian Girlhood Chronicled in Letters, 1887-96*

Lutyens, Mary, *Edwin Lutyens*, London, 1981

Lutyens, Robert, *An Appreciation in Perspective by his Son*

Lutyens, Robert, *Notes on Sir Edwin Lutyens for a Lecture to the Art Workers' Guild, 18 June, 1969*, London, 1970 in RIBA Library)

RIBAJ, March, 1945, pp. 123–31: 'The Work of the late Sir Edwin Lutyens, O.M.', by H. Goodhart-Rendel

Richardson, Margaret, *The Catalogue of the Drawings Collection of the Royal Institute of British Architects — Sir Edwin Lutyens, O.M.*, Farnborough, Hants, 1973

Weaver, Sir Lawrence, *Houses and Gardens by E.L. Lutyens*, London, 1913

Hayward Gallery Exhibition Catalogue 1981/82, London

Obit. RIBAJ, Jan., 1944, pp. 51–3 *Bldr*, 7.1.44, pp. 6–8, 31 and 53

LYNN-JENKINS, Frank   1870–1927

Frank Lynn-Jenkins was born at Torquay into a family of Torquay marble masons. A younger brother was the architect Gilbert H. Jenkins of Romaine-Walker and Jenkins. Lynn-Jenkins studied at Lambeth School of Art under W. S. Frith and at the Royal Academy Schools from 1893 to 1898.

In 1897 Lynn-Jenkins collaborated with Gerald Moira (*q.v.*), winning a competition for the decoration of the entrance hall of the Trocadero, the famous restaurant created by J. Lyons & Co. out of a 'shady' music hall. With Moira again, Lynn-Jenkins did a similar frieze in bronze, ivory and mother-of-pearl in Lloyd's Registry of Shipping, Fenchurch Street, EC3, in 1903 (RA, 1901). Also with Moira, Lynn-Jenkins carried out decorations at the Kingsway (formerly the Novelty) Theatre, Great Queen Street, WC2 in 1900.

At the Royal Academy in 1899 Lynn-Jenkins exhibited a marble group — 'St Georgius Puerorum Praeses' for St Matthew, Cockington, South Devon.

Other works were for the Rotherhithe Town Hall (destroyed), the Passmore Edwards Library, Shoreditch, E2, the Bechstein (now Wigmore) Hall, Wigmore Street, W1, the P & O Pavilion at the Paris Exhibition of 1900, and the Metropole Hotel, Folkestone.

On the Exhibition Road façade of the Victoria and Albert Museum (1899–1909) Lynn-Jenkins did the figures of St Dunstan (introducer of Church bells) and William Torel (goldsmith and bronze caster).

145   For the Savoy Hotel in the Strand (architect T. E. Collcutt) Lynn-Jenkins did a 9 ft figure of Peter II, 9th Count of Savoy (1203–68), in bronze gilt over the main carriage entrance. The arch on which he stands is no longer visible, having been encased in stainless steel in the nineteen-thirties — a period which saw the crack locomotive *Coronation Scot* similarly encased, its smoke-stack and steam dome peering through the casing much as Count Peter now protrudes from his concealed arch.

205   For the architect H. T. Hare, Lynn-Jenkins did a sculptured frieze in Pentelikos marble at Ingram House, 196 Strand, WC2 (demolished 1961).

For some years Lynn-Jenkins lived and worked in New York. He was a member of the Art Workers' Guild.

Obit. Bldr, 9.9.27, p. 406.

MACARTNEY, Sir Mervyn Edmund   1853–1932

Mervyn Macartney was the fourth son of Maxwell Macartney of Rosebrook, Co. Armagh, Northern Ireland. His brother, C. H. H. Macartney, was a painter. Macartney went to Lincoln College, Oxford (1873–7), then entered the office of Norman Shaw where among his fellow assistants were Ernest Newton, W. R. Lethaby, Gerald Horsley, E. S. Prior and Arthur Keen. Together they formed the group which eventually founded the Art Workers' Guild of which Macartney was Master in 1899. (His portrait bust there is by Thomas Stirling Lee.) Macartney was also one of those who started Kenton & Co. (*see under* Blomfield, Sir Reginald Theodore).

He began practice in 1882, showing a preference in his work for Shaw's later manner and for the style of the late seventeenth and eighteenth centuries. He competed for the Imperial Institute in 1886, and in 1891 under the motto 'English Tradition' he sent in a design for the Victoria and Albert Museum inspired by George Dance the Younger's Newgate Gaol, then already threatened with demolition.

Early domestic works by Macartney included Kent Hatch, White Cottage and additions to Mariners, Westerham, Kent, Court Hayes, Oxted, Surrey (RA, 1885), additions to Shanden Court, Tunbridge

Wells, Shalesbrooke, Forest Row, Sussex, and Sandhills, Bletchingley, Surrey (1893). Macartney also did the Guinness Trust flats at Vauxhall Square (now Vauxhall Walk), Lambeth, SE11 (1893, demolished) and at Marlborough Road (now Draycott Avenue), SW3.

In 1900 Macartney was among those invited to prepare a scheme of elevations for the new Strand Crescent (Aldwych) linking the Strand to the new Kingsway, but the competition came to nothing. In 1909 Macartney was himself assessor for the competition for the Berkshire County Offices and Shire Hall, Reading, won by Warwick and Hall.

Macartney's interest in buildings of the William and Mary, Queen Anne and George I and II periods sent him bicycling all over England seeking out surviving examples. He would challenge anyone to name any building of those periods he did not know, and between 1898 and 1901 he collaborated with John Belcher on the two-volume *Later Renaissance Architecture in England* published by Batsford. Measured drawings were contributed by many architects.

Macartney was also editor of the *Architectural Review* between 1906 and 1920 and the prominence that periodical gave to later Renaissance design was an indication of his preferences. Between 1908 and 1927 Macartney issued seven portfolios of *The Practical Exemplar of Architecture*, a series of plates of measured and also of contemporary work culled from the *Architectural Review* and *Architects' Journal*.

Macartney was surveyor to St Paul's Cathedral from 1906 to 1931, succeeding Somers Clarke. With Detmar Blow, Macartney did the Earl Kitchener of Khartoum Memorial Chapel in St Paul's after the First World War. His memorial is in the Crypt of St Paul's. Macartney was also consulting architect to Durham Cathedral. He married a daughter of Lord Ritchie of Dundee and received a knighthood in 1930. *His other works include:*

1900-1	Frithwood, Watford Road, Northwood, Middlesex (RA, 1900)
	Boarders' House, Bradfield College, Berkshire (RA, 1900)
	Welders, Chalfont St Peter, Buckinghamshire
1905	Kennet Orleigh, Woolhampton. Berkshire (his own house; RA, 1900)
1906-7	Bussock Wood, Winterbourne, Newbury Berkshire
1907	Minsted, Midhurst, Sussex
	Lombarden and the Red House, Limpsfield, Surrey
1908	The Hill Meadow, Baughurst, Hampshire
	The Court, Woolhampton
1916	Public Library, 115—117 Essex Road, Islington, N1 (opened in 1921). (The other two libraries in the borough were by H. T Hare and Beresford Pite.)

AR, 1908—11, special issues: 'Recent English Domestic Architecture', Vols I – IV, edited by Mervyn Macartney

222

Builders Journal and Architectural Engineer, 11.8.09, pp. 105 ff.

Obit. RIBAJ, 12.11.32, pp. 25—6 *Bldr*, 4.11.32, pp. 760 and 765 and 18.11, p. 846.

MACDONALD, Robert Falconer   1862—1913

R. F. Macdonald was articled (1882—5) to J. J. Stevenson, entered the Royal Academy Schools in 1884, and was assistant to George and Peto in 1886 and 1887 when they were carrying out their splendid town houses. Macdonald set up in practice on his own in Queen Anne Street, W1 in 1887. Four years later he joined Herbert Read in partnership; Read had been a fellow-assistant at George and Peto's and similar work soon came their way. (For their principal works together, *see under* Read, H.).

Obit. Bldr, 21.2.13, p. 253.

MACKENNAL, Sir Edgar Bertram, KCVO, RA 1863—1931

Bertram Mackennal was born in Melbourne, Australia, the son of a Scottish architectural sculptor, and studied first with his father, then at the National Gallery School in Melbourne. Mackennal came to London with the intention of studying the Elgin marbles and entered the Royal Academy Schools in 1883 but, dissatisfied with the routine, he left to study in Paris. His style was influenced by the French Academicians and then by the later works of Rodin.

Mackennal won the competition for the decoration of Government House, Melbourne, and left for Australia in 1889. He returned four years later and became head of the Department of Pottery at Coalport, Shropshire. Mackennal did the figures on the pediment of the New Government Buildings, Parliament Square, Westminster, by J. McK. Brydon (1902—8). Designs for both building and sculpture were won in competition. In 1909 he did the *putti* under the cornice of the Royal Insurance Building, St James's Street and Piccadilly, for Belcher and Joass. In characteristic Michelangelesque-Mannerist contradiction, these do not occupy the niches left empty beneath them, but shelter under the main cornice above.

Mackennal's post-war work included the tomb of King Edward VII and Queen Alexandra in St George's Chapel, Windsor (in association with Edwin Lutyens). He also did the bronze equestrian statue of King Edward at Waterloo Place, SW1, on a base by Lutyens, and designed the King George V carriage. His Thomas Gainsborough, RA stands in front of St Peter's church in Gainsborough's native town of Sudbury, Suffolk — a bronze standing figure with brush and palette and two bas-reliefs, one from a Gainsborough portrait painting and one of musical instruments. Mackennal also did the Curzon monument in G. F. Bodley's aisle of All Saints', Kedleston, and the figure of Lord Curzon (d. 1925) in Carlton Gardens, SW1, unveiled in 1931. The monument to the 15th Duke of Norfolk (d. 1917) in the Fitzalan Chapel in St Nicholas, Arundel, Sussex, is his work. With another Australian sculptor, Harold Parker, he did the sculpture on Australia House, Strand, WC2 (1913—18, architects A. Marshall Mackenzie and Son).

Mackennal was made ARA in 1909 and RA in 1922 (diploma work, 'The Dawn of a New Age', bronze). He was awarded the KCVO in 1921. *His other works include:*

	1905	Memorial to the Fallen, Boer War, Highbury Fields, Islington, N5. A bronze figure of Glory holding a 'Victory' and a wreath
248	1910	St Paul's Cross, St Paul's Churchyard, EC4. Bronze statue of St Paul standing on a Doric column and holding a cross. The base has four children supporting the column, two inscriptions on bronze panels and a bronze water basin. The architect was Reginald Blomfield, the donor, H. C. Richards, KC (*Bldr*, 12.11.10)

Obit. Bldr, 16.10.31, p. 620.

Sir Bertram Mackennal, RA: St. Pauls Cross, St. Pauls Churchyard, London EC4, in a setting by Sir Reginald Blomfield, RA.

MACKENZIE, Alexander Marshall, LLD, RSA
1847—1933

A. Marshall Mackenzie was born at Elgin, the son of the architect Thomas Mackenzie, a nephew of William Mackenzie, Town Architect of Perth. Thomas Mackenzie had been articled to his brother and was an assistant to Archibald Simpson who planned much of Aberdeen. Marshall Mackenzie's mother was the daughter of William Marshall (1748—1833), writer of reels and strathspeys and builder of roads and bridges.

Marshall Mackenzie was educated at Elgin Academy and at Aberdeen and Edinburgh. He was articled to his father's partner James Matthews, also from Simpson's office, and was assistant to the Edinburgh architect, David Bryce, RSA (1803—76). In 1870 he commenced practice on his own account in Elgin and in 1877 returned to James Matthews in Aberdeen as a partner.

Their principal works in Aberdeen were Greyfriars Church (*Bldr*, 18.1.02), the head office of the Northern Assurance Co., Aberdeen Art Gallery, the Harbour Office and Marischal College (RA, 1904; *Bldr*, 6.10.06), opened by King Edward VII and Queen Alexandra in 1906. Described in the contemporary press as 'perpendicular Gothic of the period of Henry VII', this is a lace-like, slender building, extremely delicate for granite, which keeps its silver-grey colour near the sea.

Their other works in Scotland included Mar Lodge for the Duke of Fife, Crathie Church and Elgin Town Hall, and they did work at Balmoral Castle for the Royal Family.

Marshall Mackenzie was one of that considerable band of Scotsmen whose success in their own country paved the way to further successes in London. He was joined by his son, A. G. R. Mackenzie (1879—1963), who was articled to him and became a partner in 1903 after studying in Paris with the interior decorator René Sergent. Their first work in London was the Waldorf Hotel (1906—7) on the new Aldwych, which bears a frieze of putti by Emil Fuchs, MVO, and is still maintained much as they completed it (*Bldr*, 29.12.06).

57
62
249

Following the success of the Waldorf, Marshall Mackenzie and his son were commissioned to design Australia House at the eastern tip of Aldwych. Part of the crescent had already been occupied by the State of Victoria in a building designed by Alfred Burr (*q.v.*). For Australia House Mackenzie and his son followed the main lines of Burr's building and heralded the Imperial Classic style which, interpreted by firms like Palmer and Turner, was to become the trademark of British commercial enterprise along the waterfronts and Bunds of Rangoon, Singapore, Hong Kong and Shanghai and in the Fort area of Colombo. The foundation stone of Australia House was laid by King George V in 1913; work continued through-

A. Marshall Mackenzie: the Waldorf Hotel, Aldwych, London WC2. The sculpture is by Emil Fuchs.

out the First World War and the building was declared open in 1918.

A sketch by the Mackenzies for offices for the Dominion of Canada to occupy the centre site in Aldwych now occupied by Bush House appears in the *Builder* of 17.8.07.

The Mackenzie family suffered badly in the First World War. The second son, Captain Gilbert Marshall Mackenzie, was killed in action and the eldest son suffered a long illness. In 1927 a former pupil, Herbert Hardy Wigglesworth (*q.v.*), joined A. G. R. Mackenzie in partnership.

Obit. *Bldr*, 12.5.33, p. 765.

MACKINTOSH, Charles Rennie   1868—1928

Charles Rennie Mackintosh's architectural work spanned little more than twelve years, the locale of his buildings was Glasgow and its environs, and *The Times* devoted only three and a half inches to his obituary, yet no other British architect of recent times has been more written and lectured about, or had his works exhibited more often.

Mackintosh was born at 70 Parson Street, Glasgow, the second son of a family of eleven. His father, who was of Highland descent and spelt his name McIntosh, was a police superintendent. Mackintosh went to Reid's School, then to Alan Glen's School, Glasgow. At sixteen he was articled to John

Hutchison and began attending evening classes at the Glasgow School of Art. In 1889 Mackintosh became an assistant with John Honeyman and John Keppie and the same year won the Alexander (Greek) Thomson Travelling Scholarship. This enabled him to visit France, Belgium and Italy where he made a prodigious number of notes and sketches. His chief interest was Italian Gothic. Mackintosh competed for the Soane Medallion in 1892 and again in 1893 when he submitted a remarkable design for 'A Railway Terminus'. This expansion into a grand design of a style generally associated with smaller buildings obtained a gold medal at South Kensington, although it did not win him the Soane.

In 1885 Francis H. Newbery, formerly art master at the Middle Class Corporation Schools in Cowper Street, City Road, EC1 and the Grocers' Company Schools at Hackney Downs, E8, became the new director of the Glasgow School of Art. Newbery and his wife were to have a profound influence on Mackintosh and his contemporaries — Newbery married Jessie Rowat, of Paisley, a student, designer and teacher of embroidery at the Glasgow School and the daughter of a manufacturer of Paisley shawls. New ideas were stirring in Glasgow in this period, the 'Glasgow School' of painters had made its appearance, and with a liberal-minded board of governors in charge, Newbery was able to encourage the more adventurous spirits among the students.

The Newberys noticed that four students in particular — Mackintosh, his office friend Herbert MacNair, and the sisters Margaret and Frances Macdonald — were doing similar design work independently. Under their guidance 'The Four' thereafter worked together and an exhibition of their work was held in London in 1896. It consisted mainly of designs for posters, book illustrations, leaded glass and repoussé metalwork in what came to be known as the Glasgow style. This differed from Continental, Belgian and French Art Nouveau in that it derived more from Japanese and Pre-Raphaelite sources, from Aubrey Beardsley and J. McN. Whistler, as well as spontaneously from natural forms. The same year, at an exhibition held by the Secession in Vienna, the work of 'The Four' was welcomed as a relief from the excesses of l'art nouveau. Exhibitions followed in Venice, Dresden, Munich, Budapest and Moscow.

Mackintosh was thus combining two careers, as a competent architect in a firm like Honeyman and Keppie, and as a leader in one of the most brilliant movements in decorative art in Western Europe. For Honeyman and Keppie, he designed the extension to the *Glasgow Herald* building (1893); the Queen Margaret's Medical College (1894); and the Martyr's Public School (1895). The tower of the Queen's Cross Church, carried out between 1897 and 1899, resembles the tower of All Saints, Merriott, Somerset, which Mackintosh had sketched.

C. R. Mackintosh:
the Scott Street façade of the
Glasgow School of Art.

The year 1897 brought Mackintosh what proved to be the opportunity of his life — the limited competition for a new building for the Glasgow School of Art. Mackintosh, still an assistant of Honeyman and Keppie, won the competition on behalf of his firm. Outstanding designs do not always win competitions, but the Glasgow School of Art was fortunate in the presence of not only the Newberys but the architect and scholar W. J. Anderson (1863—1900), director of the Department of Architecture, also an encourager of new ideas. Supported by Newbery, Mackintosh devoted most of his time and energy to the execution of this work, designing every detail at full size, sometimes on the spot, designing the furniture, light fittings and even the easels.

When the first section of the School of Art was completed, Mackintosh turned his attention to two other fields of architectural design, simple country houses, and Miss Cranston's Tearooms in Glasgow. The country houses followed from his own studies and from the simple lines of the work of James MacLaren. They include Windyhill, Kilmacolm,

Renfrewshire (1899—1901), illustrated by Muthesius in his survey on the English house; Hill House, Helensburgh, Dunbartonshire (1902—4), for the publisher Walter W. Blackie; and houses at Whistlefield, Argyllshire, and Nitshill and Killearn, Stirlingshire. With their extreme simplicity, they provided Mackintosh with an opportunity to display his sure 'line' which he could now draw with real stone and plaster against a background of hills and sky. The simple white interiors were in turn a background to the fine, tense line of his furniture, extended to the extreme limits of proportion and tone, either stumpy or greatly elongated and either black or white.

Mackintosh married his fellow student, Margaret Macdonald, in 1900. The following year he entered the competition for 'The House of an Art Connoisseur', organised by Alexander Koch. Mackintosh's design, together with one by M. H. Baillie Scott, caused a stir in the art circles of Germany and

C. R. Mackintosh: the Library of the Glasgow School of Art.

250 251 252

253

C. R. Mackintosh: a corridor *(right)*
and the Mackintosh Room *(below)*
at the Glasgow School of Art.

C. R. Mackintosh:
Hill House, Helensburgh,
Dunbarton.

beyond when it appeared in the *Meister der Innenkunst* series, published by Koch, in 1902. After the appearance of a room designed by the Mackintoshes for the Secessionist exhibition the students drew them through the streets of Vienna in a flower-decked carriage.

Between 1897 and 1910 the Mackintoshes and George Walton undertook various parts of the design and furnishing of Miss Cranston's group of Willow Tearooms. The Glasgow tearoom was a temperance restaurant, with billiard rooms and dining rooms for hire. There were branches in Argyle Street, Buchanan Street, Ingram Street and Sauchiehall Street.

In 1898 Mackintosh submitted a perspective design on behalf of Honeyman and Keppie for the Glasgow International Exhibition of 1901, won by James Miller; he also designed the Scottish Pavilion for the Turin Exhibition of 1902. That year Mackintosh entered a design in competition for the Liverpool Anglican Cathedral, a design more 'Gothic' than 'Mackintosh', since G. F. Bodley was joint assessor with Norman Shaw.

After John Honeyman retired in 1904 Mackintosh was made a full partner. Mackintosh's style had always been distinct from that of the other partners and he depended on clients who were both patient and tolerant and prepared to give him a free hand. Such clients being rare, there was less work for Mackintosh, who was increasingly relying on alcohol as a release from frustration and

anxiety. The exception was his crowning work, the library wing of the Glasgow School of Art, for which he had commenced revised plans in 1905. It anticipated ideas which did not appear again in Britain for another fifty years, and then only by way of Europe, America and Japan.

In 1913 Mackintosh resigned from Honeyman, Keppie and Mackintosh. He and his wife closed their Glasgow home and moved to Walberswick, Suffolk, where, in the countryside of painters like George Clausen and Arnesby Brown, Mackintosh did some powerful landscapes in water-colour. In 1915 they moved to Chelsea, and in 1916 Mackintosh designed the interior and furniture of 78 Derngate, Northampton, for the pioneer of true-to-scale model railways, W. J. Bassett-Lowke, and his wife, who were also patrons of modern architecture; they employed the Dutch architect Peter Behrens to remodel the façade.

In 1920 Mackintosh prepared designs for studios in Chelsea, only one of which was built. In 1923 the Mackintoshes moved to Port Vendres in the French Pyrenees where Mackintosh did delicate flower paintings and unusual water-colour landscapes. Mackintosh died in a London nursing home and Margaret Mackintosh died in Chelsea four years later.

Nearly half a century was to pass before a large building approaching the modernity of Mackintosh's Glasgow School of Art appeared in Britain. Hermann Muthesius said of him:

If one were to go through the lists of truly original artists, the creative minds of the modern movement, the name of Charles Rennie Mackintosh would certainly be included even amongst the few that one can count on the fingers of a single hand. (Introduction to *Meister der Innenkunst in Zeitschrift für Innendekoration*, Darmstadt, Koch, 1902).

And the modern French architect, Mallet-Stevens, said:

'If I were God I would design like Mackintosh'.

Edinburgh Festival Society/Scottish Arts Council, *Charles Rennie Mackintosh*, exhibition catalogue, 1968.

Howarth, Thomas, *Charles Rennie Mackintosh and the Modern Movement*, London, 1952

Macleod, Robert, *Charles Rennie Mackintosh*, London, 1968

Obit. RIBAJ, 12.1.29, p. 211 *Bldr*, 21.12.28, p. 1014

Architectural Association, London, C. R. Mackintosh, Drawings, Exhibition Catalogue, 1981

MALLOWS, Charles Edward   1864—1915

C. E. Mallows came of a Suffolk Huguenot family. His father, George Mallows, owned Kent & Gostick, an old-established boot and shoe shop in the High Street, Bedford. Mallows was educated privately, went to Bedford Art School and was articled to a local architect, T. Mercer, in 1879. In 1882 he joined the London office of Salamans and Wornum, entered the Royal Academy Schools the following year and subsequently worked in the offices of H. H. Bridgman, and Wallace and Flockhart. Mallows won the RIBA Pugin Prize in 1889.

In 1892 he commenced practice on his own account in Bedford where one of his early jobs was designing garden ornaments and pergolas for John Pyghtle White and his famous Pyghtle Joinery Works, for whom Lethaby and Baillie Scott were designing furniture.

C. E. Mallows: the courtyard of Tirley Garth, Tarporley, Cheshire.

C. E. Mallows: The Institute, Nettlebed, Oxon.

Between 1887 and 1891 Mallows made a series of pencil drawings for the 'Cathedrals of England' series of the *Century Magazine* and devoted six months of every year to travelling and sketching. In 1899 he married Sybil Lyndsey Peacock whose father, H. T. Peacock, a Biddenham farmer, was also of Huguenot descent.

Mallows, who had acquired great skill as a pencil draughtsman and perspective artist, was much in demand for the preparation of drawings for architectural competitions for public buildings, invitations for which were being announced with amazing frequency. Since competitions were a tempting way of achieving success overnight, much midnight oil was burned and many canvas 'strainers' of heavy linen-backed paper were covered with elaborately finished, 'blacked-in' plans, water-coloured elevations and those last-minute, brilliant perspectives at which Mallows was so adept. He prepared the perspective for the Wesleyan Central Hall in one night. Eager and willing, Mallows found himself being rushed into partnerships formed with the principal object of winning competitions, after which willing helpers like himself were sometimes jettisoned, even if the result was successful.

A survey of the major competitions alone gives some indication of the pressures under which Mallows worked. In 1898 he joined partnership with G. H. Grocock of Bedford, doing the (former) YMCA building at the corner of Silver and Harpur Streets, Bedford, and winning the competition for the Science and Art Schools at Newark-on-Trent (*AA*, 1898; now a secondary school). In 1900 Mallows and Grocock were joined in partnership by S. B. Russell who had just left partnership with J. G. S. Gibson after successes in several competitions. When the three had competed for the Science and Art Schools at Leamington Spa and won first premium for the Plumstead (now Woolwich, SE18) Municipal Buildings, Public Hall and Free Library, Russell veered off again and joined Edwin Cooper to win more competitions; the first was Hull Town Hall and Law Courts, and Mallows was 'borrowed' for the purpose. Although they won the competition as 'Russell, Cooper, (Herbert) Davis and Mallows' and the work did indeed proceed, Mallows did not remain with them. Nor did Russell stay with Cooper, although they had won many competitions together.

For the competition for the Wesleyan Central Convocation Hall on the important Royal Aquarium site in Westminster, Mallows joined with A. W. S. Cross of Spalding and Cross, but they came second, losing to Lanchester, Stewart and Rickards. With Brewill, Baily and Quick of Nottingham, Mallows entered for Coventry Municipal Buildings and Law Courts and won first place. With F. W. Lacey, Borough Engineer of Bournemouth, Mallows prepared a grandiose scheme for Bournemouth Municipal Buildings and Law Courts on the Horseshoe Common, Bournemouth, which came to nothing.

Mallows's last competition, the year before his sudden death of heart failure, was for the Board of Trade Offices on the site of Montagu House, Whitehall, won by E. Vincent Harris, but not completed until forty years and two world wars later.

In 1909, Mallows with customary willingness worked out a suggestion made by F. W. Speaight, the New Bond Street court photographer, for a scheme to lay out the Horse Guards Parade end of St. James's Park as *Jardins de plaisance* and parterres — a dubious 'improvement' — shown at the Royal Academy in 1911. He also illustrated a suggestion for an 'Embankment on the south bank of the Thames between Westminster and Waterloo Bridges', realised in part forty years later at the Festival of Britain Exhibition and still continuing in a half-hearted way.

Mallows also contributed drawings in the early years of the *Architectural Review* between 1895 and 1900, and was one of those who encouraged F. L. M. Griggs (*q.v.*), the black and white artist, etcher and architect from Hitchin. Griggs and Mallows both drew for *The Studio* magazine.

These multifarious activities did not deter Mallows from his natural bent, the designing of beautiful houses and gardens. His first were at Biddenham, his wife's village near Bedford, where (1899 –1900) he did Three Gables (now Clavering), 17 Biddenham Turn (*Country Life*, 29.1.10) for his father-in-law; Kings Corner (RA, 1899) for a member of the White family, who still live there (the garden front has been altered); and White Cottage, 34 Days Lane (now divided into two). Nearby are two houses by Baillie Scott who was practising at Bedford at that time, and, with the Whites, the Peacocks and the Mallows, was a kindred spirit. Mallows designed a row of four cottages at Brickendon, Hertfordshire (*Bldr*, 9.7.10).

Mallows's skill at presenting the designs of his houses and gardens using very soft 'Koh-i-Noor' pencils on handmade rag paper fascinated his clients. What Alfred Yockney in *The Studio* (September, 1915) called 'his silken pencil work, firm and expressive', encouraged the successful manufacturer and man of business to terrace his hillside with stone walls, flagged paths and yew hedges, to shape topiary work, to construct lily tanks and to turf parterres as a setting for sweeping roofs, tall stacks and welcoming loggias set between bland gables.

254   Mallows's houses and gardens occur at Tirley Garth, Tarporley, Cheshire (*AA*, 1907; *Bldr*, 28.11.08); Craig-y-Park, South Wales, for the coal magnate Sir Thomas Evans (*Studio*, 1913); Crocombe, Happisburgh, Norfolk; Bishops Stortford, Hertfordshire (a house for Cecil Rhodes); and Stapleford Park, Leicestershire. He did the Dutch Gardens at Eaton Hall, Cheshire, for the Duchess of Westminster (*Studio*, 1909, p. 128). Mallows also designed gardens for Canons, Edgware, Middlesex, for Sir Arthur Duclos, and for Eynsham Hall, Witney, Oxfordshire. His houses and gardens all reveal something of their generous-spirited and impulsive designer.

255   Mallows designed a superior village hall at Nettle-bed, Oxfordshire (Weaver, *Village Clubs and Halls*). His son is Professor E. W. Nassau Mallows, MA, retired head of the Department of Architecture at the University of Witwatersrand and now in private practice in Johannesburg.

The Studio, Sept., 1915
Obit. RIBAJ, 12.6.15, p. 403, 26.6, p. 407 and 31.7, p. 458 *Bldr*, 4.6.15, p. 528 *Country Life*, 18.3.1982

**Treadwell and Martin: 7 Hanover Street, London W1
A drawing by Charlotte Halliday.**

MARTIN, LEONARD   1869–1935

Leonard Martin and his partner H. J. Treadwell were authors of a remarkable series of buildings which provide an element of variety, even fantasy, among the façades of London's West End. (For a discussion of their joint work, *see under* Treadwell, Henry John.) Martin attended Lambeth School of Art, entered the Royal Academy Schools in 1887 and was articled to John Giles of Craven Street, Strand, WC2. In 1890 he set up in practice in London with his fellow pupil Treadwell, continuing until the latter's death in 1910. Martin then practised alone until 1929, when he entered into partnership with E. C. Davies.

On his own account Martin did houses in Ilchester Place, Kensington, W14; Burnt Stub, Chessington, Surrey, for Sir Francis Barker; housing schemes at Cobham, Oxshott and Molesey, Surrey; and almshouses and a lodge at Graffham, Sussex, for Lord Woolavington. He also designed St Paul's Church, Wad Medani, Sudan, and the Cathedral of Onitsha, Nigeria, since replaced by a striking building by Nickson and Boris.

With Davies, Martin did 7–9 Buckingham Palace Road, SW1; flats in Palace Gate, W8; extensions to Staines Hospital and to Christchurch, Fairways, Sussex; and a number of private houses.

Obit. RIBAJ, 7.3.36, p. 498

MATCHAM, Frank   1854–1920

The leading theatre and music-hall architect between 1880 and 1912, Frank Matcham designed or improved more than a hundred places of entertainment.

Frank Matcham was born at Newton Abbot, S. Devon. His father-in-law was T. Robinson, Architect and Surveyor to the Lord Chamberlain, and after his death during its construction Matcham completed the rebuilding of the Elephant and Castle Theatre after a fire in 1878 (now destroyed).

Matcham's best-known works are the London Coliseum (1904, now the Coliseum and home of the English National Opera), the London Hippodrome (1900), and the Palladium (1910, now The London Palladium). He also did the Empire and Grand Theatres, Birmingham, the Opera House, Blackpool (1889), the (old) Tivoli, Strand (1891), the Grand, Blackpool (1894), the Lyric, Hammersmith (1895), and the New Metropolitan, Edgware Road, NW1 (1897, demolished). The Arcade at Leeds is also by Matcham.

Frank Matcham: the Coliseum, St Martin's Lane, London WC2.

Matcham also did:

1901	Islington Empire, N1
	Theatre Royal, Newcastle upon Tyne
	Empire Theatre of Varieties, Leicester
	Empire, Hackney, E2
1902	Princes, Bristol (re-modelling)
	Olympia Theatre, Newcastle upon Tyne
1903	Theatre of Varieties, Glasgow
	Opera House, Buxton
	Marlborough Theatre, Holloway Road, N7

1904	Alterations to Drury Lane Theatre, WC2
1905	Olympia (later Locarno Ballroom), Liverpool
1906	His Majesty's, Aberdeen
	Holborn Empire, WC2 (alterations)
1907	King's Theatre, Southsea
1910	Finsbury Park Empire, N4
1911	Victoria Palace, SW1
	Winter Garden, Drury Lane, WC2 (demolished)
1912	Hippodrome, Bristol

Frank Matcham died at his home at Westcliff-on-Sea, Essex.

Theatre Notebook Quarterly, Spring, Summer and Autumn, 1971
Obit. Bldr, 28.5.20, p. 629   *AJ*, 26.5.20, p. 682.

MATEAR, Huon Arthur   1856—1945

H. A. Matear was articled to Francis Doyle in Liverpool and was his assistant (1876—82). He commenced practice with Doyle in 1887. Matear did a Pavilion for the caterers, Spiers & Pond, at the Liverpool Exhibition of 1886 and at the Paris Exhibition of 1888. For the same clients he did the London and Westminster Stores, Ludgate Circus, EC4 in 1889. He did Frimley Hall, Surrey (1895; *Bldr*, 16.3.01).

Matear won the competition for the Courts of Justice and the Police and Fire Stations at York in 1889, and in 1904, with F. W. Simon (*q.v.*), he won the competition for the Liverpool Cotton Exchange in Old Hall Street, completed in 1906 (*Bldr*, 9.7.04 and 29.1.10). Only the cast-iron side elevation of this splendid monumental design remains after demolition in 1967, a great loss to the city. Matear and Simon also did Holy Trinity, Southport (RA, 1897; *Bldr*, 21.12.04).

Obit. Bldr, 25.2.45, p. 159.

MAY, Edward John   1853—1941

E. J. May was Decimus Burton's last pupil and for more than fifty years, on the anniversary of his joining Burton, May used to visit the office in Spring Gardens, Charing Cross (demolished). Having served articles with Burton, May went to the office of Norman Shaw and Eden Nesfield. He entered the Royal Academy Schools in 1873 and won the RIBA Pugin Prize in 1876.

Between 1880 and 1885 May lived and worked at Bedford Park, Chiswick, the estate founded by Jonathan Carr in 1875 primarily as an artists' colony. There he did the Vicarage (RA, 1881) and several houses and developed his own practice in domestic architecture.

Matear and Simon: the remaining cast-iron side of the Liverpool Cotton Exchange.

258

May declined to take part in any of the numerous competitions for public buildings and his nearest approach to this class of work was the Children's Home at Pyrford near Woking, Surrey (*Bldr*, 14.5.10), now the Rowley Bristow Orthopaedic Hospital, which he did for the Waifs and Strays Society.

May's houses have a character at once generous and simple, avoiding the Arty and Crafty, and some are mentioned by Hermann Muthesius. His domestic work includes Swarland Hall, Northumberland (1884), Barnsdale, near Oakham, Rutland (1890), Kirklevington Grange, N. Riding (1892), Jardine Hall, Dumfriesshire (1894—8) and his own house, Lyneham, at Chislehurst, Kent (1892). He did The Homestead, Shepherd's Green, Throwleigh and Elmstead Spinney there, also The Croft, Hindhead (1895), and houses at Gainsborough Gardens, Hampstead, NW3.

May also did:

1900	4 South Side, Wimbledon Common, SW19 (*BA*, Jan., 1900)	
1900-5	Honeyhanger, St Hilders (now Branksome Hilders) and Ballindune, all at Haslemere, Surrey	158
	10 Palace Green, W8	
1908	The Three Firs, Hindhead, Surrey (*AR*, 1910)	
	Weblington, Somerset (*Bldr*, 5.9.08)	
1911	House at Tunbridge Wells (*AR*, 1911)	57
	House at Toddington, Gloucestershire	
	Gateway to James Brooks's Annunciation Church (of 1870), Chislehurst	159

Obit. RIBAJ, May, 1941, p. 124   *Bldr*, 28.3.41, p. 323.

MEWES, Charles   1860—1914

Although he was only a visitor to Great Britain, the part Charles Mewès played in three important London buildings in the first decade of the twentieth century entitles him to be considered a great Edwardian.

Mewès came of a Baltic family settled in Strasbourg. When he was eleven years old, his family fled to Paris to escape the German invasion of 1870. He studied at the Atelier Jean-Louis Pascal and at the Ecole des Beaux-Arts. His design for the Petit Palais for the Exposition Universelle de Paris (1900) was placed fourth and he was commissioned to erect the Palais des Congrès for the same exhibition, for which he was awarded the Légion d'Honneur.

Mewès's first building of note was his own house and office in the Boulevard des Invalides. Two remarkable houses were those built for his friend the actor Lucien Guitry, on the Champs de Mars, and for the banker Porgès at Contréxeville. These were in the style of Bélanger's 'Bagatelle' for the Comte d'Artois (1777). Mewès was next invited by César Ritz, former maître d'hôtel at D'Oyly Carte's

Savoy in London, to plan his hotel in the Place Vendôme, Paris, behind Jules Hardouin-Mansart's façade. Mewès by then had a large international practice run on French atelier lines where he was known as 'le Patron'. His representative in Paris was Templier; in Germany, A. Bischoff; in Spain, M. Landecho; in South America, Andrew N. Prentice (*q.v.*); and in London, A. J. Davis (*q.v.*), a former Ecole des Beaux-Arts student who had worked in Mewès's Paris office.

Shortly after the opening of the Ritz in Paris in 1900, Mewès was asked to London to design the interiors of the new Carlton Hotel, designed by Henry Florence (1841—1916) who, like Davis, was a former student of the Atelier Blouet, Gilbert, Questel and Pascal. With Sir Herbert Beerbohm Tree's Her Majesty's Theatre, the Carlton once formed a magnificent 'palais', rudely cut in half by New Zealand House when it took over the site in the 1950s.

The Mewès—Davis association bore splendid results. After the Carlton Hotel, they were asked to do the Ritz, in Piccadilly, on the site of the Bath Hotel and Walsingham House which had originally been built as a hotel but converted into service flats. The authorities gave permission for a pavement arcade similar to that of the rue de Rivoli, but unfortunately it remained unvaulted. The Ritz was followed by the building for the *Morning Post* at the corner of the new Aldwych, since spoilt by an additional storey. Then came the Royal Automobile Club in Pall Mall (*see under* Davis, Arthur Joseph) where the Pompeiian swimming bath is reminiscent of Mewès's work at Contréxeville. These three buildings were carried out in the style of Ange-Jacques Gabriel, with the greatest attention to detail. Mewès and Davis also remodelled the interior of Luton Hoo, Bedfordshire, in the same style.

Kaiser Wilhelm II had invited Mewès to control the interior planning and decoration of several of the Hamburg-Amerika Line ships. With Bischoff he did the *Imperator* (afterwards the *Berengaria*) and the *Kaiserin Augusta Victoria*. He also did houses in Cologne and Hamburg for bankers and shipowners — destroyed in the Second World War. Mewès began later to collaborate with Davis on interiors of the ships of the Cunard Line, but since Hamburg-Amerika took a poor view of this, James Miller did the *Lusitania* and Harold Peto the *Mauretania* until it was agreed that Mewès should design for the German line and Davis for the British.

Mewès had a château in Alsace and in London stayed with Davis at Inverness Terrace, W2.

AR, 6.67, pp. 449—52: 'Ship interiors: when the breakthrough came', by Sir Colin Anderson

Obit. RIBAJ, 29.8.14, pp. 652—3   *Bldr*, 14.8.14, p. 184.

MILLARD, Walter John Nash   1854–1936

Walter Millard went to Leeds School of Art, was articled to J. G. Gibbons and in 1876 entered the Royal Academy Schools where he gained a travelling studentship. He also won the RIBA Pugin Prize. He was assistant to William Burges, to N. Chevalier and to G. E. Street.

Millard and his partner Frank Baggallay (q.v.) were among those who tried to set up their own French-style ateliers in London. In a period when architectural education was dominated by the system of pupilage supported by tuition at the Royal Academy Schools, various efforts were made to explore other forms of training. The French system, though similar, in that it required attendance at the atelier of a *Monsieur le Patron* and his *sous-patrons* and involved a course of lectures and *concurrences* at the Ecole des Beaux-Arts, was more rigidly organised. Many British architects experienced it at first hand and carried away lasting influences, for Paris of *la belle époque*, bursting on the world with her Exposition Universelle of 1900, had her compelling attractions.

The idea of an atelier was originally suggested to Millard by Professor Roger Smith of University College, London, and with his fellow-student Baggallay, Millard set up at Heddon Street, Regent Street, W1. W. G. B. Lewis from William Burges's office, with red beard and long smock, acted as Maître de l'atelier, while Baggallay attended to the practice at 5 Bloomsbury Street. (The architect Fernand Billerey set up a similar atelier and another attempt to introduce the system was made in 1920 by Arthur J. Davis, himself a brilliant Beaux-Arts student, while Robert Atkinson introduced some of the methods and the jargon of the atelier into the Architectural Association of the 1920s).

When Millard's atelier closed, his collection of architectural plaster casts went to join those at the Architectural Association, then at Tufton Street, Westminster, and W. G. B. Lewis joined the Association as studio master. Meanwhile the expansion of architectural training in universities and colleges discouraged the Paris system, which had its serious faults and was finally abolished following the events of 1968.

Millard was an able draughtsman and watercolourist and also something of an archaeologist. He was one of the three architects (Mallows and Lucas were the others) who introduced F. L. M. Griggs (q.v.), the etcher, to architectural drawing.

The works of Millard and Baggallay included restoration of St Peter Mancroft, Norwich; the Parish Hall of St Mary, in Shortlands, Kent; and Northanger, Godalming, Surrey. They did the village church at Grambschütz Namyslov, Slask, Poland, for Count Henkel von Donnersmarck. Shenley Hill, Shenley, Hertfordshire, is also their work.

Millard's largest work, done in association with T. E. Pryce, was Thorney House, a block of mansion flats at the corner of Palace Gate and Kensington Road, W8 (1904–5). In 1972 this well-detailed building was pulled down and later replaced by a good building by John R. Harris.

Obit. *RIBAJ*, 5.12.36, pp. 152–3, 19.12, p. 194 and 9.1.37 p. 247 *Bldr*, 20.11.36, p. 982.

MILLER, James, RSA   1860–1947

James Miller was born at Auchtergaven on the Forteviot Estate in Perthshire and went to Perth Academy. He entered the office of Andrew Heiton of Perth in 1879. After working in several offices in Edinburgh, Miller was appointed in 1888 staff architect of the Caledonian Railway Co. for their buildings in the West of Scotland. In 1893 he set up in practice in Glasgow. Among his first works were Belmont Parish Church, Hillhead, Glasgow (1893); the little late-Gothic building resembling an oratory chapel in St Enoch's Square, Glasgow, for the Underground Railway (1896), for which he also did the Botanical Gardens Station; and Lancaster Crescent, Kelvindale (1898).

Miller's win in the 1898 competition for the Glasgow International Exhibition of 1901 (*Bldr*, 6.4.01) and his design for several of the exhibition buildings brought him further connections with the business community of Glasgow and resulted in his Caledonian Chambers, Union Street (1903) — the first of a series of business buildings which carried on into the 1930s.

Although the assessors had awarded the design of the new buildings for Glasgow Royal Infirmary to H. E. Clifford, the governors did not abide by the decision and Miller was appointed instead (*Bldr*, 18.5.07).

In 1908 Miller won the competition design for the Museum in Bombay and in 1912 the competition for the new building for the Institute of Civil Engineers, Great George Street, Westminster, SW1 (*Bldr*, 28.5.10), with a monumental neo-Classic design somewhat in the manner of a fellow Scot, J. J. Joass. Miller was thus yet another Scotsman to achieve a building in Westminster, where there already stood buildings by Shaw (from Edinburgh), Young (from Paisley), Brydon (from Dunfermline) and Gibson (from Dundee). The new Colonial Office, designed to be built on the old Westminster Hospital site by Sir J. J. Burnet and Thomas Tait, both of Glasgow, would have made a round half-dozen.

In 1912 Miller designed interiors for the ill-fated Cunard liner *Lusitania*. For the five-star hotel, Gleneagles, Auchterarder, Perthshire, he prepared

261

James Miller: Institute of Civil Engineers, Great George Street, London SW1

sketch plans for the hotel and staff houses carried out by the architectural staff of the Caledonian Railway in 1920. In 1925 he did the Union Bank, 110–120 Vincent Street, Glasgow, won in competition.

In *Architecture of Glasgow,* Andor Gomme and David Walker say of Miller: 'After the turn of the century he became the most persistent creator of massive mercantile monuments in the city, but his most attractive work is his houses of which Lowther Terrace is the nicest collection.' In the face of the threatened destruction by modern business expansion of the sober stone buildings of Glasgow, even Miller's mercantile monuments are to be preferred.

Miller's church work included a church at Jordanhill, and the Macgregor Memorial Church, Govan. Miller was made ARSA in 1901 and RSA in 1930.

Other works by James Miller include:

1904	St Andrew's East Church, 681 Alexandra Parade, Glasgow, won in competition
1907	Offices for the Anchor Line in Glasgow
	Glasgow Central Station and Hotel extensions, Hope Street
1908	Glasgow University Medical School and Natural Philosophy Building
	Princes Pier, Greenock, Renfrewshire
	Royal Infirmary, Perth
	Stirling Infirmary
	The Hydro, Peebles
	Turnberry Hotel, Turnberry Bay, Ayrshire
	Village Estate at Forteviot, Perthshire, for Lord Forteviot, Chairman of Dewar's
	Village Hall, Bournville, Birmingham, for Cadbury

Gomme, Andor and David Walker, *Architecture of Glasgow*, London, 1968

Obit. RIBAJ, Jan., 1948, p. 128 *Bldr*, 12.12.47, p. 682.

MITCHELL, Arnold Bidlake   1864–1944

Arnold Mitchell was articled to Robert Stark Wilkinson (1844–1936) of 14 Furnival's Inn, EC4, and was assistant to F. T. Baggallay and to George and Peto. He was clerk of works at St Luke, Bermondsey, SE1, for G. Gale and Baggallay and worked in the London School Board Office under T. J. Bailey. He was also assistant to Henry Spalding. Mitchell entered the Royal Academy Schools in 1884 and won the RIBA Silver Medal and Soane Medallion. He began practice in 1886 and was also London University extension lecturer in English architecture.

Mitchell's practice was principally in parish halls, houses and schools, one of the earliest recorded works being a house at Milford-on-Sea, Hampshire, for Siemens (1897), and Christ Church Hall, Harrow-on-the-Hill (1898). He also did Roxeth Schools at Harrow (RA, 1900); Dartford Schools, Kent (RA, 1900); St Felix School, Southwold, Suffolk (RA, 1902); Mattison Road Schools. Hornsey, N4 with Alfred Butler (*BA*, 15.5.03; *Bldr*, 27.12.02); and Orley Farm School, Harrow (*Bldr*, 27.12.02). University College School, Frognal, Hampstead, NW3 (*Bldr*, 28.1.05 and 28.9.07) is also a Mitchell work — a splendid, full-blown 'Wrenaissance' design won in competition in 1905, with Sir Aston Webb as assessor. 'King Edward VII' there is by Martyn of Cheltenham. At Cambridge Mitchell did the School

of Agriculture (1909–10; *Bldr*, 14.5.10) and the additions of 1913 and 1926.

His domestic work included houses at Barnet (Hertfordshire), Northolt (Middlesex) and Lewes (Sussex). He did a house at Bowden Green, Berkshire (*Bldr*, 20.4.01 and 9.11.01); one at Harrow Weald (RA, 1906); and one at Northwood, Middlesex (*A*, 28.7.05). For the Belgian King Leopold he did cottages at Ostend (RA, 1904) and the Royal Villa at Le Coq-sur-Mer (RA, 1902; *Bldr*, 28.3.03). Other domestic work by Mitchell included Port Jackson, Pangbourne, Berkshire (RA, 1901); The Willows, Northwood, Middlesex (RA, 1902); Barnett Hill, near Guildford, Surrey (RA, 1905); Toys Hill, Brasted, Kent (*Bldr*, 20.4.01); Maes y Crugian Manor, Carmarthenshire (*Bldr*, 5.12.03); and 1 Meadway Close and 34 and 36 Temple Fortune Lane, Hampstead Garden Suburb. He also did the Library at Tissington Hall, Derbyshire (*Bldr*, 18.5.01 and 16.4.04). Mitchell also remodelled the interior of Brook House, Park Lane, W1, for Sir Ernest Cassel (1905–6, demolished for the present Brook House by·Wimperis, Simpson and Guthrie). He also did 26 Upper Brook Street in 1908–9.

One of Mitchell's best designs was carried out in three houses in Basil Street, SW7, which survive today, but in a mutilated form, imperfectly restored after war damage. As illustrated in Shaw Sparrow, these were to have dressings of 'Doulton's Carrara Terra-Cotta with the maximum variety in its tints'. The Doulton's Carrara Ware was replaced during construction by beautifully detailed brown limestone, which today survives in only one of the houses (now flats).

Mitchell designed for the instructional toy, Lott's Bricks. Among his last works are Thomas Cook's offices in Berkeley Street, W1.

Mitchell retired to Lyme Regis, Dorset, where he built himself a house. At the age of seventy-five he submitted a competent design in competition for a new St George's Hospital, Hyde Park Corner, SW1. His son Edward Mitchell became an architect.

Flats, Urban Houses and Cottage Homes, Sparrow, W. Shaw, London, 1907

Obit. Bldr, 10.11.44, p. 375.

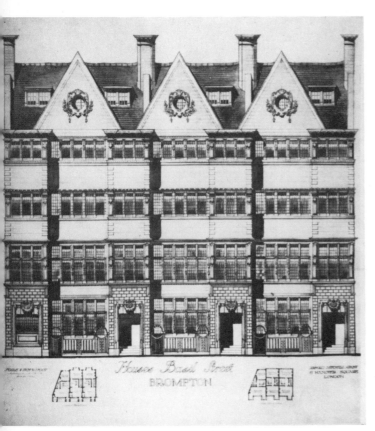

Arnold Mitchell: the best group of terrace houses of the decade — only one survives war damage but imperfectly restored. Basil Street, London SW7.

262

MOIRA, Professor Gerald   1867–1959

Gerald Moira was the son of Edouardo Lobo Moira (1817–87), a miniaturist, who originated from Beira Alta, Portugal. Gerald Moira was educated privately and in 1888 entered the Royal Academy Schools where he won the Armitage Prize. In 1896, in collaboration with F. Lynn-Jenkins, Moira won the competition held by Joseph Lyons for the decoration of the entrance hall of the Trocadero Restaurant in Shaftesbury Avenue. Their frieze, executed in coloured plaster relief, depicts scenes from Arthurian legend. Lyons's Throgmorton Restaurant, EC2, was decorated by Moira and Lynn-Jenkins in a similar manner.

46 In 1900 Moira decorated the Board Room of Lloyd's Registry at 71 Fenchurch Street, EC4, for the architect T. E. Collcutt. Also for him Moira did decorative paintings in the King's Hall of the Holborn Restaurant (demolished). Also in 1900, and with Lynn-Jenkins, Moira carried out decorations at the Novelty Theatre (later the Kingsway and demolished), Great Queen Street, WC2. Two years later he did 'Pursuit of Truth' for the Library and 'The Cardinal Virtues' for the Vestry of Ullet Road Unitarian Church, Sefton Park, Liverpool.

Moira also contributed to the rich range of decoration executed for the now demolished
205 Ingram House, head office of the United Kingdom Temperance and Provident Institution, in the Strand (1906), designed by Henry T. Hare. Moira did an oil painting with the appropriate theme of 'Providence protecting Childhood, Charity and the Fruits of Abundance from the Evil Powers' and designed a mosaic tympanum of 'St George and the
268 Dragon'. At E. W. Mountford's New Sessions House in the Old Bailey, Moira did 'Moses and the Tablets of the Law' and lunettes illustrating 'The Law', 'English Law' and 'Justice receiving the Homage of all Classes and Professions'.

Moira's works after the First World War included paintings at the Army and Navy Stores, Victoria Street (demolished), for the architect Maurice Webb; at the Foord Almshouses, Rochester, Kent for Guy Dawber; and miniature paintings for the Queen's Dolls' House (1924, now at Windsor Castle) for Sir Edwin Lutyens.

Moira also painted landscapes and still life. He was an exact contemporary of Frank Brangwyn and, like him, an admirer of the work of Puvis de Chavannes; both artists were influenced by the work of Paul Gauguin.

Professor Moira was Principal of Edinburgh College of Art (1924–31) and a member of the Art Workers' Guild. His son, R. E. Moira, is an architect in practice with his wife in Edinburgh as Moira and Moira; his son, Alexander Moira, also an architect, continues the practice of Collcutt and Hamp in London.

Obit. RIBAJ, Nov., 1959, p. 30 *Bldr*, 14.8.59, pp. 17–8.

MONTFORD, Paul Raphael   1868–1938

Paul Montford was born in Melbourne, Victoria, and studied under his father, Horace Montford (d. *c.* 1912), who became Curator of the Sculpture School at the Royal Academy in London in 1881.

Paul Montford: a group which echoes fully the flamboyant yet graceful spirit of Cardiff's City Hall. Architects: Lanchester, Stewart and Rickards.

Paul Montford was a student at Lambeth School of Art and entered the Royal Academy Schools in 1888, where he won the Gold Medal in 1891. In 1898 he became modelling master at the Chelsea Polytechnic.

Montford did the sculpture on the Battersea Town Hall and Polytechnic, SW8 (1892), and on the Northampton Institute, Clerkenwell, EC1 (1896), for E. W. Mountford. On Lanchester, Stewart and
263 Rickards's splendid Cardiff City Hall (1899), Montford did the groups of symbolic figures representing 'Welsh Commerce and Industry' and 'Welsh Poetry and Music' (other groups were by Henry Poole and Donald McGill). Montford also did 'Philosophy' and 'Inspiration' on Kelvin Bridge, Glasgow; and 'William Caxton, Printer', and 'George Heriot, Jeweller to James VI of Scotland and I of England', on the Exhibition Road façade of the Victoria and Albert Museum, South Kensington (1899–1909). In 1904 Montford did John Milton in front of St Giles, Cripplegate, EC2, and on the base by E. A. Rickards two bas-reliefs illustrating the 'Expulsion from Paradise' and a passage from *Comus*.

For his sculpture on the arched and columned screen between the Foreign Office in Whitehall and the architect J. McK. Brydon's New Govern-

Temple Moore: The Court House, now County Library, Helmsley, Yorkshire.

ment Offices, Montford was required to base his sculpture on the fact that the bridge connected three government departments — the Home Office, the Education Board and the Local Government Board (*Bldr*, 4.7.08).

Montford returned to Melbourne in 1922 and did the sculpture on the war memorial there. *His other works include:*

1908   Sir Henry Campbell-Bannerman, bronze bust in Westminster Abbey

           Sir William Randal Cremer (1838—1908) bronze bust, Geoffrye Museum, Kingsland Road, E2

1910   The mascarons on the School of Engineering and the busts of Julius Wernher and Otto Beit, School of Mines, South Kensington, SW7

Obit. Bldr, 28.1.38, p. 196.

MOORE, Temple Lushington   1856—1920

Temple Moore was the son of Major General G. F. Moore. He entered the Royal Academy Schools in 1877, was articled to George Gilbert Scott junior (1875—8) and was his assistant from 1878 until 1885 when Scott retired because of failing health. Temple Moore continued Scott's excellent work, but began to develop his own simpler style. The *DNB* says of his buildings: 'Although purely Gothic, [they] appear to have been designed with no constraint save that of his own vigilant good taste.'

Temple Moore's churches are an important link between the churches of the Bodley School and the final phase of Gothic revival as seen in the work of his own pupil, Giles Gilbert Scott, who won the competition for the new Liverpool Anglican Cathedral in 1903 for which Temple Moore also competed. The numerous churches which Temple Moore designed for expanding towns, particularly in the industrial areas of the north of England, include St Stephen, Redditch, Worcestershire (1893—4), where he did the chancel arch and chancel and the chapel arcades, and St Peter, Little Driffield, E. Riding (1889). At St Peter, Helperthorpe, E. Riding, in 1893 he added a north aisle to the original church by G. E. Street. The following year he did All Saints, Peterborough, St Peter, Barnsley, and St Augustine, Newland, Hull (additions). His secular work in this period included Holmwood, Redditch (1893), now the Council Offices.

Temple Moore was the designer of the Anglican Cathedral in Nairobi, Kenya, and of the Eleanor Cross, Sledmere — a copy of the Hardingstone (Northamptonshire) Eleanor Cross of 1291 made for Sir Tatton Sykes in 1895 and now serving as a First World War Memorial.

He did the alterations to Allerton Hall, near Leeds and to Bilborough Hall, W. Riding. His other domestic works included Kenwick Hall, Louth, Lincolnshire; Dian Close, Cookham Dene, Berkshire; and Grynfa, Painswick, Gloucestershire.

Temple Moore's son was drowned in the SS *Leinster*. His work was carried on by his niece's husband, Leslie T. Moore (1883–1957). *Temple Moore's other works include:*

1900	Gray's Court, St John's College, Oxford (restoration)
1900-2	St Cuthbert, Middlesbrough (RA, 1901)
	St James, Lealholm, N. Riding
	St Wilfrid, Lidget Green, Bradford
	St James, Nunburnholme, E. Riding (tower)
	St Columba, Middlesbrough (RA, 1902)
1901	Council Offices and Market Hall, Helmsley, N. Riding
1905-6	All Saints, Franciscan Road, Tooting, Graveney, SW17 (*Bldr*, 13.3.09)
1905-14	St Wilfrid, Harrogate (north and south transepts and Lady chapel by Leslie Moore 1935)
1906	St Luke, Eltham, SE9
	Rievaulx Abbey, N. Riding (restoration)
1908	St Andrew, Hexham, Northumberland (nave)
	All Saints, Eccleshall, Staffordshire (chancel and transepts)
	Priory of St Wilfrid, Springfield Mount, Leeds
1908-9	St Michael, Leeds (east end by George Pace, 1964)
1910-11	St Mary, St Giles, and All Saints, Canwell, Staffordshire
	Uplands Church, Stroud, Gloucestershire
	All Saints, Basingstoke, Hampshire
	St Augustine, Gillingham, Kent
	St Mary, Sledmere, E. Riding (RA, 1900)
	All Saints, Walesby, Lincolnshire
	St Anne, Royton, Lancashire (*Bldr*, 24.9.10)
	St Cyprian, Gorton, Manchester
	St Cuthbert, Preston, Lancashire
	St Luke, Walsall, Staffordshire
1913	St John, Hampstead Parish Church, NW3 (chapel)
	Hostel of the Resurrection, Leeds

Obit. RIBAJ, 31.7.20, p. 429 *Bldr*, 9.7.20, p. 37.

MORLEY HORDER, Percy Richard
see HORDER, Percy Richard Morley

MORPHEW, Reginald   1874–1971

Reginald Morphew was a middle child of a family of ten and the grandson of Edward Standen who had once shipped cattle to the Shetland Islands in exchange for Shetland knitwear — the first to be sold in London. (A cairn commemorates the spot where he was once saved from shipwreck). The knitwear was sold by Edward Standen's sister at 116 Jermyn Street, St James's, SW1. In 1901 Reginald Morphew designed a new building put up by his brother, Edward Standen Morphew, on the site of 111 and 112 Jermyn Street (RA, 1901; *Bldr*, 7.3.03). The building prompted E. V. Lucas to write in his *A Wanderer in London* (1906): 'London has everything — and she has Standen's in Jermyn Street which is a Florentine Palazzo'. Morphew was articled to A. J. Gale, went to the Architectural Association School, and was an improver to Ernest Runtz and assistant to Niven and Wigglesworth.

266
324

In 1902 Reginald Morphew designed Marlborough Chambers, service flats at 71 and 72 Jermyn Street (RA, 1902), now Estate House, on the corner of Bury Street, St James's, the site of a house once occupied by the 1st Duke of Marlborough (then Colonel Churchill). The fine sculpture is by Gilbert Seale whose name, together with Morphew's, is carved by the main entrance.

Morphew's two Jermyn Street buildings respond perfectly to the atmosphere of this unique quarter of London — Pall Mall and St James's, where the hatters', shirt-makers' and bootmakers' shops, art dealers, 'bachelor chambers' and Turkish baths still cater for the members of the St James's Street and Pall Mall clubs. Here each street is small in scale, terminating at a cross street and set obliquely to the cardinal points of the compass, and catching all the available sunlight, throws back the reflected light that enhances its charms.

Reginald Morphew's buildings, which retain something of the Art Nouveau flavour of 1900, also have a touch of the exotic about them. Nos 111–112 Jermyn Street, as the *Survey of London* points out, hint at the Davanzati Palace in Florence, while Marlborough Chambers recall the Austrian Tyrolean style (Morphew had designed a shop for Vienna). Both buildings anticipate the exoticism which was to become fashionable some twenty years later.

Morphew did a small building, very modern for its day, in High Holborn, WC1, destroyed in the Second World War, and in 1906 did Eyhurst, Kingswood, Surrey, later a training school for Lloyds Bank. (*See also* designs by Morphew in *Bldr*, 18.7.03).

After serving in the RNVR in the First World War Morphew was invalided out and went to live in Polperro, Cornwall, where he built some small houses and a larger one for himself. In France

during the German invasion of 1940, he remained there for the rest of his life, living in Cannes and Grasse.

MOUNTFORD, Edward William   1855—1908

E. W. Mountford was born at Shipston-on-Stour, Warwickshire, the son of John and Elizabeth Mountford. He went to school at Clevedon, Somerset, and in 1871 was articled to Habershon and Pite of Bloomsbury Square, WC1, for whom he acted as clerk of works at St Stephen's, Hounslow, Middlesex. In 1876 Mountford became principal assistant to Percy Elkington and Sons and in 1879 to Giles and Gough. The following year he set up in practice on his own account.

Mountford's early work was largely churches, church schools and rectories, many of them in Wandsworth, SW18. Some were done in association with H. D. Appleton (who changed his name to Searles-Wood in 1890). Among the works of this period were St Paul, Waldenshaw Road, Forest Hill, SE23 (1882—3; demolished) and St Andrew, Garratt Lane, SW18 (1889—91), the latter a red brick and brown limestone building in fourteenth-century Gothic to which two west bays and porches were added in 1902. Mountford was to build again in the same style and materials at St Michael, Wimbledon Park Road, SW19, in 1902 (the east front was added in 1905). In 1896 Mountford did a new chancel and chapels for St Anne, St Ann's Hill, SW18, a Greek Revival 'Waterloo' church by Sir Robert Smirke. Mountford's additions are firmly 'Wrenaissance' in style and make no reference to the Greek Revival. In 1901 he furnished the south chapel as a memorial to his wife.

In 1888 Mountford did his first public building, the Battersea Public Library, Lavender Hill, SW11, choosing the Early French Renaissance style introduced by T. E. Collcutt eleven years earlier in Wakefield Town Hall. Much of Mountford's subsequent work was in the field of town halls, municipal buildings, technical colleges and schools, many of them won in competitions. His first major success was Sheffield Town Hall (1890—4), again in Early French Renaissance. This was followed by Battersea Town Hall, Lavender Hill, in the same style.

In 1900, with the Hitchin architect Geoffry Lucas, Mountford won the competition for the small Hitchin Town Hall; in 1907, on quite a different scale, he won the splendid Lancaster Town Hall. The gift of the linoleum manufacturer, Lord Ashton, who had given Williamson Park to the town, this was a palace of splendid proportions, all correctly early Georgian and reviving the style of James Gibbs; the interior was equally grand and

the whole was built by the Waring-White Co., a subsidiary of Waring & Gillow of Lancaster and London (*Bldr*, 9.11.07).

Mountford's first technical institute was the 'Wrenaissance'-style Battersea Polytechnic, Battersea Park Road, SW11, built in 1891 on part of the site previously occupied by the Albert Palace — a second-hand iron building transferred to Battersea from the Dublin Exhibition of 1872 and opened as a concert hall and picture gallery by the speculator 'Baron' Grant. (The venture failed after a year, and the building was pulled down in 1894).

In 1896 Mountford won the competition for the Northampton Institute (now the City University) on the estate of the Earls of Northampton, St John Street, EC1. This is in a Free-Classic style, somewhat French in flavour. Mountford also designed the College of Technology and Museum Extension, Byrom Street, Liverpool, giving the façade paired columns, one square, one round, swathed in rustications and flanking wide pedimented niches which are surmounted by figures in Michelangelesque poses (*Bldr*, 11.1.02). The sculpture is by F. W. Pomeroy (*q.v.*).

Among his London buildings, the block of offices for Booth's distillery in Turnmill Street, Smithfield, EC1 (*Bldr*, 17.8.01) was of exceptional quality.

267

E. W. Mountford: Booth's Distillery, Smithfield, London EC1. This façade has been re-erected as part of a scheme of reconstruction.

◁ Reginald Morphew: Marlborough Chambers (now Estate House), 71 and 72 Jermyn Street, London SW1. Unhappily the sculpture by Gilbert Seale is now painted and in medieval primary colours.

E. W. Mountford: a drawing by Charlotte Halliday of the cupola of the typically Edwardian baroque New Sessions House at the Old Bailey which, after protest, replaced George Dance junior's unique Newgate Gaol. The crowning "Justice" is by F. W. Pomeroy.

Except for its northern-style roof and chimney-stacks it had the air of a small Italian palazzo. After standing derelict since the Second World War, the building has been demolished and the façade has been rebuilt into a scheme in Britton Street. Mountford chose 'Wrenaissance' again for St Olave's Grammar School, Tooley Street, SE1.

Mountford is best remembered for the New Sessions House at the corner of Newgate Street and Old Bailey (*Bldr*, 30.6.1900), EC4, won in competition in 1900. It stands on the site of George Dance the younger's Newgate Prison (1770—82), possibly the most remarkable design of its time in England and something of a *cause célèbre* when it was condemned. It had echoed in stone the etchings of the great Italian draughtsman Giovanni Battista Piranesi, whom Dance had met in Rome and whose *Carceri d'Invenzione* was published in 1750. These engravings idealised the powerful rusticated masonry of the external walls of the Forum of Nerva, rediscovered three hundred years earlier by Brunelleschi and Michelozzo and incorporated into the designs for their Florentine palaces.

Compensating for the loss of Dance's masterpiece was not the only responsibility that fell to the designer of the new Sessions House. Only two hundred yards away, St Paul's then reigned supreme over the surrounding steeples of some thirty Wren churches, none of them higher than the western towers of the Cathedral, while few buildings rose higher than the lower (Corinthian) order of the aisles. But today, among the crowd of tall, square buildings which press in on the dome of St Paul's, one cannot but be grateful for the company of Mountford's cupola, crowned by F. W. Pomeroy's gilt figure of Justice. Pomeroy also did the stone figures over the main entrance, while other artists who contributed statuary and painting to the new Sessions House included Alfred Turner, Gerald Moira, and Sir William Richmond who did the paintings in the domed ceiling of the central space representing 'The Golden Age Before Laws Became a Necessity'. When the building was opened by King Edward VII, Mountford, crippled by arthritis, was presented in a wheelchair.

Mountford was among those invited in 1900 to prepare a design for the elevational treatment of the new Strand Crescent. In 1908 he was also invited to compete for the new London County Hall, on which he was assisted by Cecil Pinsent.

In 1907 Mountford designed the Northern Assurance Co.'s building, 1 Moorgate, EC2, with frontages to Lothbury and Coleman Streets. (It now houses the Republic National Bank of Dallas.) This granite-faced building was done in collaboration with E. A. Grüning, a City architect who was managing director of the Gresham House Estate Co. (*Bldr*, 27.7.07). Mountford also designed a new States House for Guernsey, Channel Islands, which was not carried out.

In 1902 he built his own house at Munstead, near Godalming, Surrey, for which his famous neighbour, Gertrude Jekyll, designed the gardens (*Bldr*, 17.8.01). He had worked out every detail with his first wife, but she died in 1901 and Mountford did not live there until some years later, when he had married again. Two other houses at Munstead by Mountford are illustrated in *The Builder* (31.12.04).

In spite of visits to Egypt and elsewhere, Mountford's health deteriorated. He returned to live in London and died there while his best works were still being built. These were completed by his chief assistant, F. Dare Clapham (1873—1914), who carried on the practice and also designed the Fire Brigade Station in Lancaster in 1909. Wallis Mountford, a son by Mountford's first marriage, was articled to Walter Cave. Edward Mountford's

E. W. Mountford: the College of Technology at Liverpool illustrates the excessive blocking of columns, the excessive width and steepness of window pediments and the Michelangelesque poses of sculpture (by F. W. Pomeroy).

nephew, Richard Mountford Pigott, JP, after a period in his uncle's office, was articled to Beresford Pite and was assistant to William Pite and F. A. Walters. Pigott entered into partnership with his cousin, but Wallis Mountford died early and the practice is continued by R. M.

Pigott's son, Michael Mountford Pigott, and his partners.

Obit. RIBAJ, 22.2.08, pp. 274–5 *Bldr*, 15.2.08, pp. 175 and 190.

MUNBY, Alan Edward   1870–1938

Alan Munby was born in Manchester. His father, Frederick J. Munby, a solicitor, was Castellan of York and his grandfather was Recorder of York. Munby was educated at Repton School and at Heidelberg and Cambridge universities, where he studied natural science and was engaged in research and teaching.

At the age of thirty Munby took up architecture and entered the office of T. Phillips Figgis (*q.v.*). With his knowledge of laboratories Munby became a specialist in science buildings. In 1909 he collaborated with Figgis on the competition for the Coopers' Company School, Bow, E3, which they won and built. Munby built science buildings at the University College of North Wales, Bangor; Highgate School, N6; Clifton College, Bristol (1927); and Beaumont College. He wrote *Laboratories, their Planning and Fittings* (Bell, London, 1931).

Obit. RIBAJ, 7.2.38, pp. 361–2 and 21.2, p. 410.

269

A. E. Munby: the Coopers' School, London E3, is in a style generally adopted for school buildings since 1900.

MURRAY, John   1864–1940

John Murray studied at Blackheath School of Art and the South Kensington Schools, entered the Royal Academy Schools in 1886 and also studied at the Architectural Association. He was articled in 1880 to Edward Crosse in London and was his managing assistant for seven years.

Murray began practice on his own account in 1892 and was in partnership with Frederick Foster for seven years, during which time he did All Saints, Rotherhithe; Rotherhithe Town Hall (destroyed); 53 Queen Anne Street, W1; the Hotel Burlington, Dover; and Penley's Novelty Theatre, Great Queen Street, WC2 (demolished).

In 1904 Murray was appointed Crown Architect and Surveyor to HM Office of Woods and Forests (now merged with the Commissioners of Crown Lands) and was involved in the discussions over the rebuilding of Regent Street. Murray's official appointment allowed him to continue with his private practice and he carried out the Italian marble building for the drapery establishment of D. H. Evans at 308–322 Oxford Street (1909, demolished 1936; *Bldr*, 18.12.09).

John Murray's best-known work is the office of the Department of Woods and Forests in Whitehall, SW1 (now the Ministry of Agriculture; *Bldr*, 8.1.10), a building which exhibits, even more than William Young's War Office next door, the relaxed character of Edwardian classical design. Murray's other works included the old Westminster City Hall, Charing Cross Road, WC2; the Welsh Calvinistic Church, Willesden Lane, NW6; and the rebuilding of Cumberland Lodge, Windsor Great Park.

Murray presented the RIBA Library with a valuable album of photographs of Nash's Regent Street taken before its demolition in the 1920s. He was joined in partnership by his son, Charles Murray.

Obit. Bldr, 19.7.40, p. 58.

MURRAY, John C.T.   d. 1933

J. C. T. Murray was born in Glasgow where he served his pupillage. He was assistant to Sir Rowand Anderson on the Central Hotel, Glasgow.

Murray was appointed chief architect to the Admiralty in 1905. The Royal Naval Hospital, Chatham, Kent (*A*, 28.6.05), was designed under his direction, with the engineer-in-chief to the Admiralty, Colonel Sir Henry Pilkington, KG. Built on the pavilion plan, the Hospital had no less than four major accents on the centre line — the chapel, a domed octagon, a campanile and a combined water tower and stack. All in red brick with artificial stone dressings, it vied with the Army's Netley Hospital. It has now become a civil hospital and the dome and chapel have been demolished. Murray also designed the Royal Naval

Hospitals at Portsmouth and Gibraltar.

After leaving the Admiralty Murray did houses in the home counties and Presbyterian churches in Bromley, Kent, Dublin, Guernsey and Singapore.

Obit. RIBAJ, 11.2.33, p. 286.

NEATBY, W.J.   1860–1910

W. J. Neatby was articled to an architect in the north of England, worked in the offices of several architects and became a designer and painter of glazed ceramic building ware for the Burmantofts works of the Leeds Fireclay Co. In 1889 Neatby joined Doulton's of Lambeth and was in charge of their department of architectural decoration until 1900.

Three important examples of Neatby's work survive, the most remarkable being the façade of Edward Everard's printing works in Broad Street, Bristol (1901). The printery has gone but the façade has been incorporated into another building. It consists entirely of glazed terracotta painted by Neatby by a special process which ensured permanent colours. In the gable is a painted figure holding a lamp and mirror, symbolising Literature. In the left-hand spandrel of the arches below is Gutenberg at his press against a background of his alphabet; in the right-hand spandrel, William Morris at *his* press with *his* 'Golden Alphabet'; in the centre spandrel is a winged 'Spirit of Printing' reading a book. The architecture itself is a medley of neo-Baroque voussoirs, Gothic crenellations and Art Nouveau forms.

W. J. Neatby: one of twenty-eight panels in painted tiles in the Winter Gardens Ballroom, Blackpool.

271

W. J. Neatby: the surviving façade of Everard's Printery, Broad Street, Bristol, shows Gutenberg and William Morris each with his alphabet and the spirit of printing in the centre spandrel.

53
270 Another of Neatby's surviving works is in the Winter Gardens Ballroom, Blackpool, where in 1897 he did twenty-eight panels in painted tiles to fill ceramic wall arches; these depict girls in extravagant costumes which might be a parody of the style of the Pre-Raphaelites or of Walter Crane and seem to anticipate the drawings of Erté. Neatby's first wife Emily was the model for the panels, some of which have been destroyed. Those surviving deserve preservation.

The best-known of Neatby's works decorate the Poultry, Game and Fish Department at Harrods Store in Knightsbridge (opened 1902), a work Neatby completed in nine weeks. The painted tiles forming a decoration around the clerestory of this pillared, top-lit hall represent figures of 'The Chase' in roundels done in a nursery picture-book style, and fish underwater executed in a more delicate manner. The formalised pattern of game, fish and trees is remarkable for its fresh ingenuousness. The whole gives the impression that Neatby, well acquainted with the work of his contemporaries, had no desire to imitate them.

When he left Doulton's in 1900 Neatby set up independently at 15 Percy Street, W1, with the architect E. Hollyer Evans. As Neatby, Evans & Co. they undertook the design and manufacture of furniture, metalwork and stained glass.

Other work by Neatby, since destroyed, was at the Theatre Royal and at the Kings Smoking Café, Birmingham; on the balcony fronts at the Gaiety Theatre, Aldwych, London (1905); at the Restaurant Frascati, Oxford Street, W1, for Ernest Runtz and Ford; in Pagani's Restaurant, Great Portland Street, W1; the Redfern Gallery, Conduit Street, W1; and John Line's Showrooms, Tottenham Court Road, W1, and their pavilion at the Franco-British Exhibition at the White City (1907–8). The frieze in the directors' lunch room at the Norwich Union Life Assurance Society's Offices, Norwich (1902), was very probably done by Neatby.

Neatby was a member of the Royal Society of Miniaturists. His son, Edward Mosforth Neatby, was a painter.

Apollo, Mar., 1970: 'The Master of Harrods Meat Hall W. J. Neatby', by Julian Barnard

A, Sept., 1971: 'The Work of W. J. Neatby in Ceramics' by Julian Barnard

Studio, 1903: translation by Thomas Stevens of 'Keramischer Wandsmuck u. Dekorierte Möbel von W. J. Neatby', by P. G. Komody in *Kunst u. Kunsthandwerk*

Ernest Newton, RA: Steephill, Jersey. The architect's perspective drawing illustrates the calm, undramatic nature of his houses.

NEWTON, Ernest, CBE, RA   1856—1922

Ernest Newton was born in London, the fourth son of Henry Newton who was agent for the Sturt property, Hoxton, N1. Newton went to Uppingham School, Rutland, and was articled to Norman Shaw in 1873, remaining with him as an assistant. Newton acted as clerk of works on Shaw's great house, Flete, in South Devon and became his chief assistant until he left to set up in practice on his own account in 1879.

Newton opened an office at 14 Hart Street (now Bloomsbury Way), WC1, which in the evenings became a rallying point for his friends in Shaw's office. He developed the design of the smaller country house of his day — large by today's standards, but a welcome change from the grand houses hitherto the fashion. There was no Gothic gloom about Newton's houses, little of the romantic picturesque, or even of the Arty and Crafty. The cheerful exteriors with white barge-boards, white window frames and semicircular domed porches, the genial interiors with white-painted panelling and wide inglenooks containing sensible tiled fireplaces, suited those with less money and more taste. As further proof of the sound good sense of Newton's houses, their style was the preference of that excellent builder William Willett (proposer of Daylight Saving) and his sons.

The long list of Ernest Newton's houses is given in his books —A Book of Houses (1890), and A Book of Country Houses (1903) — and also in The Work of Ernest Newton (1925), by his son, W. G. Newton. Many of them were at Bickley, Kent (Bldr, 29.4.05), where he lived and did Little Orchard in 1902. Notable among his earlier works was Buller's Wood, Chislehurst, Kent, now a school; the drawing room ceiling by Morris & Co. was designed by Morris himself. Newton extended a cottage for himself at Hazeley Heath, and altered Banstead Hall, Surrey (1891—4 and 1905). Red Court (1894—5) is an important house at Haslemere, Surrey, which established the new standard of formal simplicity.

Between 1899 and 1914 Newton carried out works at Overbury, Bredon Hill, Worcestershire, for Sir Richard Holland-Martin of Martin's Bank. In 1904—6 he carried out Norman Shaw's design for the second Alliance Building, St James's Street, SW1, where the free distribution of windows on the façade is clearly a Shaw feature. The building completes a small 'piazza' with St James's Palace, buildings by Inigo Jones, Wren and Lutyens, and Shaw's earlier Alliance Building.

Before and after the First World War, Newton was one of the panel of architects, including Sir Aston Webb and Sir Reginald Blomfield, set up to devise a way of completing the rebuilding of Nash's Regent Street Quadrant, partially rebuilt to a design by Shaw. Newton undertook the County Fire Office, a building showing less departure from the original design (by Robert Abraham) than other new buildings in the street.

Newton was President of the RIBA from 1914 to 1917, during the First World War, when he organised employment for refugee Belgian architects. He was made ARA in 1911 and RA in 1919 (diploma work, 'House at Jouy-en-Josas, France'). In 1918 he received the Royal Gold Medal for Architecture.

His practice was continued by his son.

Ernest Newton's principal works included:

1899-1901 Steephill, Jersey (*Bldr*, 28.9.01)

1900 Martins Bank, Bromley, Kent (*Bldr*, 1.12. 1900; altered), and adjacent buildings

1901 The Leasowes, Four Oaks, Birmingham

Glebelands, Wokingham, Berkshire (*Bldr*, 14.9.01)

1902 House at Brockenhurst, Hampshire

Four Acre, West Green, Hartley Wintney, Hampshire (*Bldr*, 14.6.02)

1903 Shavington Hall, Shropshire (alterations to a house altered previously by Norman Shaw)

1904 Remodelling of Triscombe House, West Bagborough, Somerset

Clyffe Hall, Market Lavington, Wiltshire (alterations for the Rt. Hon. Lord Justice Warrington)

1905 St George, Bickley, Kent (spire and rebuilding of tower; *Bldr*, 11.11.05)

1906 Begbroke, Oxfordshire (addition and garden)

Ardenrun Place, Crowhurst, Sussex (burnt down in 1923 except for one pavilion; *Bldr*, 12.5.06)

1907 Ludwick Corner, near Welwyn, Hertfordshire (*Bldr*, 3.2.11)

Dawn House, Winchester (*Bldr*, 17.7.09)

Luckleys, Wokingham, Berkshire (*Bldr*, 12.9.08 and 17.7.09)

1907-9 House at Upton Grey, Hampshire (alterations and additions for Charles Holme of *The Studio*; *Bldr*, 11.2.09)

New wing to Moor Place, Much Hadham, Hertfordshire

1908 Scotsman's Field, Church Stretton, Shropshire

Feathercombe, Hambledon, Surrey

1910 The Greenway, Shurdington, Cheltenham, Gloucestershire, for Archdeacon Sinclair (additions and alterations)

House at Harefield, Middlesex

Additions to Oldcastle, Dallington, Sussex

Apsley Paddox, including the Chapel of St Gregory and St Augustine, between Woodstock Road and Banbury Road, North Oxford

1911 Lukyns, Ewhurst, Surrey

Brand Lodge, Colwall, Malvern, Herefordshire

1912 Great Burgh, Burgh Heath, Surrey

1912-13 Logmore, Westcott, near Dorking, Surrey

1913 House at Goring-on-Thames, Berkshire

House at Abbotsbury, Dorset

House at Jouy-en-Josas, near Versailles, France (half-finished when war broke out)

1914 Houses in East Avenue, Whiteley Village, Burhill, Surrey (in a layout by Frank Atkinson under the general direction of Walter Cave)

AR Special issues, 1908–11, 'Recent English Domestic Architecture', ed. Ernest Newton and W. G. Newton

Newton, Ernest, *Sketches for Country Residences etc.*, London, 1884

Newton, Ernest, *A Book of Houses*, London, 1890

Newton, Ernest, *A Book of Country Houses*, London, 1903

Newton, W. G., *The Work of Ernest Newton R.A.*, London, Architectural Press, 1925

NICHOLSON, Sir Charles, Bart   1867–1949

Charles Nicholson was the elder brother of Sir Sydney Hugo Nicholson, founder of the Royal School of Church Music, and Archibald Keighley Nicholson, a designer of stained glass and founder of the A. K. Studio in St John's Wood, NW8, where it still continues under Brian Thomas. Their father, Sir Charles Nicholson, Bart. (1808–1903), MD, Hon.DCL(Oxon.), Hon.LLD(Cantab.), Hon. LLD(Edinburgh), Speaker of the House of Assembly, New South Wales and Chancellor of the University of Sydney, graduated as a physician at Edinburgh, then emigrated to his uncle's property in New South Wales where he practised his profession and collected Etruscan, Roman, Greek and Egyptian antiquities which he later presented to the local university.

Charles Nicholson went to Rugby and New College, Oxford, was articled to J. D. Sedding and after Sedding's death continued the practice under the chief assistant, Henry Wilson (*q.v.*). In 1893 Nicholson left Wilson to set up in practice on his own, and in the same year won the RIBA Tite Prize. In 1895 H. C. Corlette from Sydney joined Nicholson in a partnership which lasted until 1916. Their first church was St Alban, Westcliff-on-Sea, Essex (1895–1908). In 1905 they submitted two designs in competition for the rebuilding of St Martin, Epsom, Surrey, one of which was successful, but only the new east end, crossing and transepts were built and completed in 1911 (*Bldr*, 1.12.06).

Nicholson was consulting architect to seven cathedrals — Belfast, Lincoln, Lichfield, Llandaff, Portsmouth, Sheffield and Wells, and Diocesan Architect to Chelmsford, Portsmouth, Wakefield and Winchester. Nicholson and his partner Corlette each separately submitted a design for the Liverpool Anglican Cathedral Competition in 1903, won by Giles Gilbert Scott. Nicholson and Corlette could both speak with authority on the design and furnishing of churches and each read a paper on the subject to the RIBA (18 February, 1907). *Modern Church Design* by Nicholson and *Modern Church Planning* by Corlette contain many pertinent observations which had considerable influence on later work in this field. Nicholson also compiled, with Charles Spooner, *Recent Ecclesiastical Architecture*, published by Technical Journals in 1912.

After the earthquake of 1907 in Kingston, Jamaica, Nicholson and Corlette designed what was probably the first extensive scheme of reinforced concrete buildings — the Government buildings and Government House, Kingston (*Bldr*, 24.9.10, pp. 341–3). Their work may well have influenced Leonard Stokes's bare concrete Catholic Cathedral in Georgetown, Guyana.

Charles Nicholson was a great draughtsman and water-colour artist and designed most of his work himself. His paper on 'The Churches of Northern France', read at the Birmingham Architectural

276

274

Sir Charles Nicholson: King's House, Kingston, Jamaica, West Indies. An early example of reinforced concrete in the reconstruction of government buildings after the earthquake of 1907.

Association (11 December, 1908, *RIBAJ*, Vol. XVII, 3), is illustrated by many of his sketches. He was a member of the Art Workers' Guild.

In 1927 Nicholson took into partnership his chief assistant, Thomas Johnson Rushton, who worked with him on the enlargement of St Thomas à Becket, Portsmouth, into a cathedral. Thomas Rushton's son, Henry Rushton, continues the practice.

Other works by Nicholson and Corlette include:

1900	The Grange, Totteridge, Hertfordshire (*Bldr*, 15.9.1900)
1901-2	St John the Baptist, Wonersh, Surrey (repairs and furnishings). The organ case is by J. F. Bentley and some (1914) glass by Nicholson
1904	Burton Manor, Wirral, Cheshire (RA, 1903; additions and remodelling for a son of W. E. Gladstone. The garden is by Mawson, the orangery by Beresford Pite
	The Vicarage, Burton
1905	The Choir School House, New College, Oxford
1906	The English Chapel at S. Raphael, Var, France (*Bldr*, 8.9.06)
1907-10	Clifton College, Bristol (remodelling of chapel)
	Winchester College (additions)

	Stileman's Copse, with stables and coachman's house, Munstead, Surrey (*AR*, 1910)
	St John, Curbridge, Oxfordshire
1909	St George, Minworth, Warwickshire
1910	St Augustine, Great Grimsby, Lincolnshire (except N. aisle)
	St Mary Magdalen, Plymouth (except W. bay)

Obit. *RIBAJ*, Apr., 1949, p. 290 *Bldr*, 11.3.49, p. 300.

NIVEN, David Barclay   1864–1942

David Niven went to Dundee High School and was articled to C. and L. Ower of Dundee (1880–4) where he was also assistant to J. Murray Robertson. He moved to London and was assistant (1889–91) to Aston Webb. In 1891 he went to Genoa to supervise the building of the Institute for Seamen and the Protestant Hospital, probably for Webb.

In 1893 Niven joined in partnership with Herbert Wigglesworth (*q.v.*). They did interiors of Castle Line ships for Donald Currie & Co. (RA, 1895, SS *Tantallan Castle*), and a house for Sir Donald Currie at New Brighton, Cheshire. They also did houses at Sevenoaks and Orpington, Kent, and at Byfleet and Walton-on-Thames, Surrey, including Hillington House, Station Avenue, Walton (1899) and Piper's Hill, Byfleet (1900). For houses in the Farnham area Niven and Wigglesworth worked in association with Harold Falkner, with whom they designed a cottage for the Cheap Cottages Exhibition in Letchworth Garden City in 1905. They also did a house in Deeside, Kincardineshire. In 1905 they did premises in Dundee for the *Dundee Courier and Advertiser* (*AA*, 1905) and in 1910 they did Ottershaw Park, Surrey, replacing a house by James Wyatt. In London they did 54 Harley Street, W1 (RA, 1905) and premises for the jewellers, Stewart Dawson & Co., at 19—21 Hatton Garden, EC1 (now in other use) — a Portland stone building correctly detailed in neo-Renaissance style (*Bldr*, 27.10.06 and 14.11.08). In 1925 they did Hambro's Bank, 41 Bishopsgate, EC2, in correct 'Georgian' taste.

Niven wrote *London of the Future* (T. Fisher Unwin, 1921). The partnership ended in 1926.

Obit. RIBAJ, Feb., 1942, p. 67 *Bldr*, 16.1.42, p. 62.

OULD, Edward Augustus Lyle   1853—1909

Edward Ould was the son of the Rector of Tattenhall, Cheshire. He was in partnership at Chester as Grayson and Ould, with G. E. Grayson and G. H. Grayson (*q.v.*). They had a large country house practice in styles derived from Norman Shaw and particularly in Cheshire half-timber. Grayson and Ould did Bidston Court, Cheshire (1898), for R. W. Hudson, Wightwick Manor House, Staffordshire, for S. J. Mander now owned by the National Trust and notable for its Arts and Crafts furnishings), and the new buildings at Trinity Hall, Cambridge. Also at Cambridge they did the hall of Selwyn College — a fourth side to Sir Arthur Blomfield's quadrangle — and additions to the Clergy Training School at Westcott House. Two of Ould's churches are St

E. A. L. Ould with G. H. Grayson: a beautifully executed range at Trinity Hall, Cambridge.

Barnabas, Rock Ferry, Cheshire, and St Faith, Waterloo, Liverpool. They also did buildings for Lever Brothers at Port Sunlight, Cheshire, and the Bank of Liverpool at Wrexham, Denbighshire.

Obit. Bldr, 6.2.09, p. 157.

OWEN, Segar   b. 1874

Segar Owen was the son of the architect William Owen (d. 1896) and entered the Royal Academy Schools in 1895. William Owen had a large general practice in Warrington and did churches in Lancashire and further afield.

William and Segar Owen: artisans' houses in Port Sunlight. An illustration from Hermann Muthesius's *Englische Baukunst der Gegenwart*.

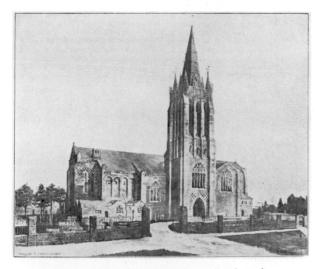

Nicholson and Corlette: design for St Martin, Epsom, Surrey.

275 The Owens did work for Lever Brothers at the model town of Port Sunlight in Cheshire, where the Lady Lever Art Gallery is Segar Owen's best-known building (1914–22). Lever Brothers' factory in Port Sunlight was built in 1888 and the first group of twenty-eight houses in 1889–90. The Owens did Gladstone Hall, Glendale Road (1891) and Victoria Bridge (1897, demolished). The Owens also did the Technical School, Palmyra Street, Warrington, and buildings for Lever Brothers at Durban, South Africa, and Sydney, Australia. After his father's death Segar Owen carried out further work at Port Sunlight, including Hulme Hall, Bolton Road, named after Lady Lever (1901) and Christ Church (1902–4), the gift of William Lever (Lord Leverhulme) (*Bldr*, 13.9.02).

PARKER, Richard Barry   1867–1947

Richard Barry Parker, the eldest son of a bank manager, Robert Parker, of Rotherham, Yorkshire, was born at Chesterfield, Derbyshire. The family had strong interests in social reform and in art, and Parker's brother, Stanley Parker, was a furniture designer. Barry Parker went to school at Ashover, Buxton, and attended a Wesleyan college. In 1886 he went to Simmonds Studios, Derby, and in 1887 attended the South Kensington Schools for three months. In that year he was articled to George Faulkner Armitage of Stamford, Altrincham, Cheshire, an architect and craftsman in domestic and church interiors who specialised in built-in fitments and painted decoration — he exhibited at the Manchester Arts and Crafts Exhibitions of 1891 and 1895. Parker's experience with Armitage, for whom he did some painted decoration, was to be a lasting influence.

After two years as clerk of works for Armitage on various buildings which included Brockhampton Court, Herefordshire, and a house at Caerleon, Monmouthshire, Parker opened an office in 1894 in Buxton, where his father had been transferred because of poor health.

In 1896 Raymond Unwin (*q.v.*), a cousin who had married Parker's sister, joined him at Buxton. Unwin had designed cottages for the Staveley Coal & Iron Co. and the brothers-in-law had a common interest in the designing of ideal village communities; Parker had had the experience of planning attractive homes for a number of discerning people who, freed from the conventions of the preceding era, had not yet acquired a taste for the neo-Georgian revival. The combination of talents was an ideal one — Unwin contributed a flair for inspiring reformers, and Parker a gift for designing original houses with original plans and decoration. 277 In 1901 they illustrated their ideas in *The Art of Building a Home*.

An opportunity to put their ideas into practice occurred when Joseph Rowntree asked Parker and 359 Unwin to lay out a garden village at New Earswick, near York. The first twenty-eight houses were built between 1902 and 1903. These were simpler than those already built by William Lever at Port Sunlight and George Cadbury at Bournville. Parker continued to work for the Joseph Rowntree Trust — the Rowntree Theatre, York, the Secondary School at New Earswick, and the Clifton Lodge Estate, York.

In 1903 Parker and Unwin were invited to compete for the layout of Ebenezer Howard's First Garden City at Letchworth, and when their plan was selected, the brothers-in-law moved first to Baldock 25 and then to Letchworth where they also designed simple houses and groups of houses.

No sooner had Letchworth got under way than their advice was sought by Henrietta Barnett. A disciple of Octavia Hill, Mrs Barnett had enlisted influential help to found the Hampstead Garden 27 Suburb, and Parker and Unwin now laid out a plan 282 for the whole estate. Parker continued to work from Letchworth and Unwin from Hampstead until the First World War; then in 1915 Unwin joined the Local Government Board, while Parker went to Oporto, Portugal, to design a civic centre (not carried out; RA, 1916; *BA*, June, 1916). Parker made a visit to São Paulo, Brazil (1917) to work on *Jardin America*, designed by Unwin.

All the best in the planning of residential estates came from the offices of Parker and Unwin and was achieved in *seven years* when extreme economy in roads, services and maintenance was the watchword. It is a sad fact that so much of this experience should have been lost and that the desolation of some of the new towns of the 1950s should have followed when, fifty years earlier England had given such a lead in this field.

After the end of the war, Barry Parker did housing schemes for Newark-on-Trent, Bolton, Wakefield, Bridport, St Neot's (Huntingdonshire) and Loughborough, while continuing to do single houses for private clients. Parker's largest commitment was the development of Manchester's new suburb of Wythenshawe, which occupied him from 1927 until 1941 when he was seventy-four.

Richard Barry Parker: "An Artisan's Living Room" from *The Art of Building a Home*.

In addition to his one hundred single houses, his town planning and work at Wythenshawe, Barry Parker was a member of more than twenty organisations and committees; his works, writings and lectures have appeared in more than 100 publications at home and abroad, and the Howard Medal for Services to the Garden City Movement was presented to him at Oxford in 1941. He was closely associated with the Northern Art Workers' Guild which he helped to found.

Barry Parker exhibited water-colours at the Royal Academy and was a member of the Letchworth meeting of the Society of Friends and a Justice of the Peace. He retired as consultant to Letchworth Garden City when he was seventy-seven years of age.

The work of Richard Barry Parker has been the subject of thorough documentation, now in the care of the Letchworth Museum. Part of his house, which was also his office, at 296 Norton Way South, is now a museum of his work and of the garden city movement. It has a portrait of Parker by Francis Dodd.

Works by Parker and Unwin from 1895 include:

1895-1903	Houses at Longford, Farringford, Moorlands, Strachur, and Buxton, for Robert Parker (his father) and for Miss Burgess and others
	Greenmoor, Buxton, for Mrs Bennett
	Houses at Marple, Cheshire, for Dr McNair, and at Chesterfield for Mr Woodhead
	Kildare Lodge, Townsend Road, Minehead, Somerset for Mr Corbett and Dr Gordon Henry

	Houses at Montreal, Canada for Dr Fred Walton, at Bradford, Yorkshire, for Dr Munro and at Church Stretton, Shropshire, for Dr Campbell Hyslop
	Carrig Bryne, Co. Wexford, for Colonel Harman
	The Vicarage, Thornthwaite, Keswick, Cumberland, for the Rev. William Unwin
	Houses at Harrogate and at Derby
1904-5	Rockside hydropathic establishment, Matlock, for Miss Goodwin, including all furniture
	House at Stone, Staffordshire, for Mr Bennett, and one at Hertford for William Graveson
1906-7	Whirriestone, Rochdale, Lancashire, including furniture and fittings, for Mrs Ashworth
	Oakdene Children's Home, Rotherfield, Sussex, for Miss Morton
	House at Repton, Derbyshire for Mr Macfarland
1907-9	The village hall and schoolhouse at Claydon, Buckinghamshire, for Sir Edmund Verney
	Hill Top, Caterham, Surrey, for William Steers
	Houses at Edinburgh for Mr Smith, at Bridgwater, Somerset, for William Thompson, and at Rosslare, Ireland, for Miss Goulding
	Furniture for the Headmaster's House, Campbell College, Belfast, for Mr Macfarland

Letchworth Museum, documentation of Parker's works compiled by Mrs Mabel Parker.
Obit. RIBAJ, Mar. 47, p. 286 *Bldr*, 7.3.47, p. 217.

PARR, Thomas Henry Nowell   1864–1933

Nowell Parr was born in Handsworth near Birmingham. He was trained as an engineer under Edward Case and as an architect under J. D. Dunn and F. W. Hipkiss, and was for a short time with W. H. Bidlake.

In 1892 Nowell Parr became assistant in the Borough Surveyor's department in Walsall. In 1894 he was appointed Engineer and Surveyor to Brentford (Middlesex) District Council. He was allowed to conduct a private practice as well. For the Council Nowell Parr designed the Clifden Road Baths (1896), the Fire Station in High Street (1898) and the Vestry Hall in Half Acre (1900; demolished). He also did the Carnegie Libraries in Brentford and Hounslow and the extension to the existing covered market and the new covered market (1905) and the Council House and Public Baths for Heston and Isleworth Council (1905).

Nowell Parr's private practice, in partnership with A. E. Kates, had grown and he resigned his post with Brentford Council in 1907. The growth in the practice had been due principally to Parr's appointment to two breweries, Fuller, Smith & Turner of Chiswick and the Royal Brewery, Brentford, for which Parr began to work about 1900.

As a result of taxation and the South African War, and the reaction against the Victorian 'gin palace' occasioned by the temperance movement, the public houses Parr designed were simpler than their elaborate predecessors of the boom years of 1886 to 1892 and 1896 to 1899.

Prominent among Nowell Parr's 'pubs' were the 'Northcote Arms', Northcote Avenue, Southall (1907), the 'Forester', Leighton Road, Ealing, W13, of 1909 and the 'Old Pack Horse', High Road, Chiswick, W4, of 1910. In these public houses Nowell Parr reduced the number of bar divisions and introduced plain wood panelling in place of the effusion of cut plate-glass screens of the Victorian 'pub'. Externally he favoured dark green or brown faience for the ground floor and red brick with stone dressings above.

His firm was continued by his son John Nowell Parr (d. 1975).

PATERSON, Alexander Nisbet, ARSA 1862–1947

A. N. Paterson studied at the University of Glasgow in 1883 and then (1883–6) attended the Ecole des Beaux-Arts and the Ateliers Jean-Louis Pascal and Galland. Paterson was assistant to Burnet, Son and Campbell (1886–9). Moving to London he entered first the office of Sir Robert Edis, and then that of Aston Webb and Ingress Bell, where he worked on the drawings for the

Victoria and Albert Museum competition. He was RIBA Godwin Bursar in 1896.

Paterson was a partner of Campbell Douglas (1828–1910) in Glasgow between 1904 and 1910 and was President of the RIAS in 1906, and an Associate of the Royal Scottish Academy in 1911. He lived at the Long Croft, Helensburgh, Dunbartonshire.

Paterson did many war memorials after the First World War. Notable among them is that at Helensburgh. A late work in Glasgow was his Muirend Savings Bank.

His Glasgow works include:

278

1906	The National Bank of Scotland, 22–24 St Enoch Square
	Printing Works, Anniesland, for Robert Maclehose
	Premises for Barr and Stroud
	Clyde Street Public School
1908-9	Liberal Club, St George's Place, 54 West Street and Buchanan Street (now part of the Royal Scottish Academy of Music)

His practice was continued by Watson, Salmond and Gray.

Obit. RIBAJ, Aug. 1947, p. 530 *Bldr*, 18.7.47, p. 75.

Alexander Paterson, ARSA: in this façade of the National Bank of Scotland, Enoch Square, Glasgow, formerly the National Bank, the influence of the architect's Ecole des Beaux-Arts training is evident.

Stanley Peach: a raised garden covers this electricity transformer station in Brown Hart Gardens, London W1, while at each end a pavilion provides on one side access for machinery and, on the other, a garden shelter.

PEACH, Charles Stanley   1858–1934

Stanley Peach came of a military family and was born at sea on the passage from India. He went to Marlborough and to University College, London, commenced training for the army and also began studying medicine, which poor health compelled him to abandon. As fresh air was prescribed, Peach then went to Texas, USA, and joined the Government Survey of Western States and Territories where he did geological and land surveys in the eastern Rockies in connection with the American railway route to the Pacific. He was also concerned with the erection of two suspension bridges over the Powder River, Wyoming, and his experiences were published in the *Graphic* of 1879.

A riding accident obliged Peach to follow a sedentary life, and he returned to London where in 1882 he entered the office of Hugh Roumieu Gough, staying for two years as an assistant and for a further year as a partner. In 1884 or 1885 Peach set up on his own account in Carlton Chambers, Regent Street, SW1, and then moved to the Adelphi, WC2.

Peach became associated with the design of the early electricity generating stations — he was a friend of Ferranti, Crompton and Kennedy, all pioneers in the generating and distribution of electrical power. Peach learnt from practical experience; he was one of the founders of the

Westminster Bush Terminal Co. Ltd., whose convertor station in Victoria Street, SW1, was a forerunner of the Westminster Electrical Supply Corporation in Eccleston Street, SW1.

As legislation governing the setting up of power stations progressed, Peach's advice was sought for other stations in London, including those at Marshall Street, W1; City Road, EC1; Wandsworth, SW18; Battersea, SW11; and Lodge Road and Grove Road, St John's Wood, NW8 (RA, 1902). The St John's Wood station was originally intended to have six smoke stacks identical to the one built. The solitary smoke stack erected nevertheless became a prominent landmark overlooking Lords Cricket Ground until its demolition in 1972 (*Bldr*, 10.1.03). For this work, especially for the elevation, Peach entered into partnership for a brief period with C. H. Reilly (*q.v.*).

A milestone in Peach's career was his paper 'Notes on the Design and Construction of Buildings connected with the Generation and Supply of Electricity', read to the RIBA in March 1904 and afterwards published in the *RIBA Journal* as 'Central Stations from the Architect's Point of View'. Peach's reputation extended to Europe, and he undertook more generating stations in Britain, including those at Oldham, Kirkcaldy, Kilmarnock, Ipswich (*Bldr*, 12.12.03), West Hartlepool and Weymouth. An interesting project which owed its inception and success to Peach was the Convertor Station, Brown Hart Gardens, Duke Street, W1, on the estate of the Duke of Westminster (*RA*, 1904; *Bldr*, 1.12.06). This still exists and is roofed by a paved garden with domed pavilions.

280
302

279

In spite of his slight frame and retiring nature, Peach earned a reputation for getting things done quickly which brought him a commission in another field — to complete the internal reconstruction of the Haymarket Theatre (1904–5) in the space of five months. Such energetic commitment to his work did not prevent Peach from pursuing for twenty-five years an absorbing personal interest — the 'reconstruction' of Solomon's Temple. He spent two years on research in Jerusalem and the perspective drawing coloured by Peach still hangs in his office.

The threat to the safety of St Paul's Cathedral in the 1920s fired Peach's imagination and, at the age of seventy, he made a large wooden model which could be stressed to indicate stresses on the fabric. Another work of dedication was his representation in water-colour of the symbolism of the cruciform plan of a Western Christian church.

Possibly his best-known contribution to the modern scene was the Centre Court for the Lawn Tennis Association at Wimbledon. This now familiar building received characteristically unstinting attention from Peach, who worked out by means of models the shadow which would be cast by the sun on the centre court during the two weeks of the tournament. His 'board-finish' reinforced concrete structure preceded by three years Sir Owen Williams's similarly finished Wembley Stadium. It was also Peach's idea to grow virginia creeper over the building.

The idea of using the difference between the levels of the Mediterranean and the Dead Sea to produce

Stanley Peach: Peach suggested six great smoke stacks as ultimately necessary at this St John's Wood, London NW8 power station, where this single monumental stack (*below*), now demolished, served for many years.

hydraulic power for electricity did not escape Peach's attention. His proposals were put before Dr Chaim Weizmann and Sir Alfred Mond, then the Commissioner of Works. Alongside all these varied activities Peach still found time to breed shire horses at his farm in Sussex.

Stanley Peach lost his only son in the First World War. His son-in-law, Major A. J. Harrington, and George Knight carried on the practice. They were recently succeeded by Messrs Allen, Mitchell and Preston, and George Knight's son, D. A. Knight, continuing as Stanley Peach and Partners.

RIBAJ, 2.4.04, pp. 230–318

Obit. *RIBAJ*, 11.8.34, p. 987 and 8.9, pp. 103–1 *Bldr*, 27.7.34, p. 158.

PEARSON, Frank Loughborough   1864–1947

F. L. Pearson was the son of John Loughborough Pearson (1817–97), the architect of Truro Cathedral and of many great churches. F. L. Pearson's grandfather was William Pearson of Durham, the water-colour painter and etcher. The architect Ewan Christian (1814–95) was an uncle. Pearson was educated at Winchester, articled to his father in 1882 and continued in his father's office, becoming a partner in 1890. J. L. Pearson entrusted his son's architectural education to W. D. Caröe (*q.v.*), his chief assistant, who became a leading church architect in his own right.

F. L. Pearson completed Truro Cathedral, adding the Choir School, Cloisters and Library (*Bldr*, 1.5.09), completed his father's church of St Stephen, Bournemouth, and between 1901 and 1910, in conjunction with Caröe, carried out his father's designs for the Cathedral of St John, Brisbane. The Bishop of Brisbane had been vicar of his father's famous church of St John, Red Lion Square, WC1 (destroyed). Pearson also completed his father's work at St Peter's Convent, Maybury, Woking (1898–1908), and at St Peter, Parkstone, Dorset (1900–1). His own churches included St Alban the Martyr, Middlesbrough, E. Riding (1902) and St Matthew, Auckland, New Zealand (RA, 1904).

Pearson's secular work included restoration and large additions at Hever Castle, Kent, for Lord Astor; Queen Anne Mansions on the corner of Wigmore and Wimpole Streets, W1 (RA, 1891), and 39 and 40 Margaret Street, W1 (RA, 1892). He did the South African War Memorial at Winchester College (*Bldr*, 13.3.09), and the Convent School of St Nicholas and St Helen's church in Abingdon, Berkshire (RA, 1904). (Pearson added a chapel at St Helen in 1922).

Pearson married Cecilia, daughter of Alfred Littleton, chairman of Novello the music publishers, whose former building in Wardour Street, W1 (recently restored), Pearson designed in 1906. It was originally intended to have large statues on the external piers but none were executed. The interior was richly panelled and plastered in 'Wrenaissance' style (*Bldr*, 25.1.08 and 30.4.10).

F. L. Pearson's other works include:

1901	Chancel and Aisle of St Ninian's Cathedral, Perth, W. Australia
1904	Wakefield Cathedral, W. Riding (chancel and retro-chapel)
1905	St Augustine, Rugeley, Staffordshire (chancel)
	St Patrick, Bordesley, Birmingham (chancel of a J. L. Pearson church of 1896)
1908	Farm Buildings, Hever Castle, Kent (*Bldr*, 5.12.08)
1910	Memorial Fountain, Children's Hospital, Great Ormond Street, WC1 (with sculpture by Nathaniel Hitch)

Obit. *RIBAJ*, Nov., 1947, p. 39.

PEDDIE, John More Dick   1853–1921

J. M. Dick Peddie was born in Edinburgh, the eldest son of John Dick Peddie, RSA (1824–91). He went to Edinburgh Academy, studied in Germany and became an assistant in the office of Sir George Gilbert Scott, RA, in London. He then joined his father's practice of C. G. H. Kinnear and Peddie, becoming a partner in 1879.

Frank L. Pearson: formerly the premises of Novello & Son, the music publishers, this Wardour Street, London W1 building has been likened by Sir Nikolaus Pevsner to a Hanseatic town hall.

The first public building designed by Dick Peddie was the Bank of Scotland Office, George Street, Edinburgh, a building which showed him to be a scholarly architect of great promise. His other buildings in Edinburgh include the Carnegie Library (with Sir George Washington Browne) and the head offices of the Scottish Provident Institution and of Standard Life Assurance.

Dick Peddie carried out branch banks throughout Scotland for the British Linen Bank and the Royal Bank of Scotland, and did many office buildings. He also did the parish churches in Renaissance style at Dalton, Dumfriesshire, Melrose, Roxburghshire, and Coldstream, Berwickshire (AR, 1909).

Country houses by Peddie include: Westerdunes, North Berwick, for Patrick Ford, MP; Coldstoun House, Haddington, East Lothian, for J. G. A. Baird; Blervie House, Forres, Morayshire, for Captain Galloway; Coldstones, Gullane, East Lothian, for the Hon. Percy M. Thesiger; Cheylesmore Lodge, North Berwick, for Lady Cheylesmore; and Poltalloch, Argyllshire, for Colonel Malcolm.

Dick Peddie was a director of several companies including the Edinburgh and District Tramways Co., the Scottish Equitable Life Assurance Society and the Scottish Investment Trust. His practice continues in Edinburgh as Dick Peddie and McKay.

Other works by Peddie are:

1900	National Bank of Scotland, 47 St Vincent Street, Glasgow
1905	North British and Mercantile Assurance Head Office, Princes Street, Edinburgh
1906	Scottish Provident Buildings, 17—29 St Vincent Place, Glasgow
1909	Edinburgh Life Assurance Co. building (AR, 1909)
	Caledonian Station Hotel
	Edinburgh College of Art
	United Free Church Assembly Hall and
	Church of the Holy Cross, Davidsons Mains, all in Edinburgh

Obit. Bldr, 18.3.21, p. 338.

PEGRAM, Henry Alfred, RA   1862—1937

Henry Pegram was born in London, entered the Royal Academy Schools in 1881 and was assistant (1887—91) to Hamo Thornycroft. Pegram did the pair of bronze candelabra in the nave of St Paul's Cathedral (1897—8) and the memorial to Sir John Stainer there (1903). His frieze for the Suffolk Street, W1, elevation of the United Universities Club was carved for Reginald Blomfield by William Aumonier and Son.

Pegram also had commissions from abroad, includ-

Barry Parker and Raymond Unwin: A. J. Penty was most probably the designer of these splendid buildings flanking a gateway to the Hampstead Garden Suburb, London NW11.

ing Sir John Campbell for Auckland, New Zealand (1908); the Cecil Rhodes memorial in Cape Town (1908); and Sir Robert Hart for Shanghai (1909). Pegram was made ARA in 1904 and RA in 1922 (diploma work, 'The Sculptor's Daughter Olive'). He was a member of the Art Workers' Guild where his relief of Heywood Sumner hangs.

Pegram's other works include:

1901	Relief over the Board Room fireplace, Lloyds' Registry of Shipping, EC3
1906	Sir Thomas Browne, Hay Hill Market Place, Norwich. Copy presented by the sculptor to University College, Gower Street, WC1
1906-9	Nine figures for the Great Hall of Birmingham University (architect, Aston Webb)
1909	'Hope' in Canterbury Cathedral
	'The Tree of Life' and 'The Tree of Knowledge' in tympana and 'Art' and 'Science' at St Paul's School for Girls, Brook Green, Hammersmith, W6, for the Mercers' Company. Architect: Gerald Horsley
	Rt. Hon. Cecil Rhodes, marble bust for the City of London (RA, 1903)

PENTY, Arthur Joseph   1875–1937

A. J. Penty was the elder of the two architect sons of Walter Green Penty of York, designer of the York Institute of Art, Science and Literature. While a pupil and assistant with his father, Penty absorbed the spirit of the Arts and Crafts Movement and the progressive movement in Glasgow. In York and its environs from 1896 to 1898 A. J. Penty did Aldersyde (his first important work), the Four Alls Inn, Malton Road, Dringhouses, York, and for the fish and game dealer Mark Relph Bullivant a shopfront in Feasgate. For the miller Sidney Leetham he did Elm Bank (now a hotel) and also furnished an office for him. The painted decoration and furnishings for Elm Bank were by George Walton of Glasgow, who had opened a branch in York in 1898. Penty also did the Coffee Tavern in Walmgate.

When Penty senior died in 1902 the York practice was continued by his other son, Frederick T. Penty (1879–1943), and Arthur Penty left for London, where he probably worked for other architects 'taking in washing'. He was in the meantime making a name for himself in the field of socio-economics

and his particular concern was Guild Socialism — the heading under which he figures in the *Encyclopaedia Britannica*. He was a member of the Fabian Society through which he met his Canadian born American wife, whom he married in 1910.

All architects who shared the enthusiasm and the ideals of the Arts and Crafts Movement felt they had fallen short if they did not turn their hand to designing and making furniture and other accessories of building, and Penty was no exception. In 1905 with Charles Spooner and Fred Rowntree he formed Elmdon & Co. with the aim of making fine furniture. (Their workshop still exists at 1 Ravenscourt Park, W6). An exhibition of their work was held at the Alpine Club in April of their first year. A dresser and pieces made in South Africa from the designs shown in the catalogue as Nos 4, 5 and 7 are at 59a Church Road, Old Isleworth, Penty's family home.

Penty was given an opportunity to combine his interests in social reform and architecture when he joined the staff of Parker and Unwin, the designers of the Hampstead Garden Suburb. Penty's contribution is believed to be the flats and shops, Arcade

282
283

283

House and Temple Fortune House, at the north-west gateway to the estate, and the Great Wall facing Hampstead Heath, possibly shared with Charles Paget Wade. Heath Close also carries the mark of Penty's work and he is known to have done Wyldesbottom, 3 and 5 Hampstead Way (1911—12), and the later, neo-Georgian Temple Fortune Court.

After his work in the unsophisticated sixteenth-century vernacular cottage style of Hertfordshire which was the model for the Hampstead Garden Suburb, Penty wrote *The Elements of Domestic Design*, a textbook of the vernacular style, first published in the *Architects' Journal* and then by the Architectural Press (1930). Penty wrote:

> The so-called Queen Anne movement took its stand on the validity of this [vernacular] tradition and it is important for us to realise that the movement which would have been called the 'Vernacular Revival' was the beginning of better things; for out of it has come everything that is vital in architecture at the present day — the Domestic Revival, the Arts and Crafts Movement and the Neo-Renaissance movement alike grew out of it.

Penty's book is in fact the Grammar of the Vernacular Revival, and houses which he did on his own account illustrate his text. Among them are Moonfleet (1912) at Haslemere, Surrey, and Kingsend, Ruislip, Middlesex. At Ditchling in Sussex he did Longridge and Hillway (1928), the latter for himself but never occupied by him. Penty's home at Isleworth, occupied by his family and identifiable from a now almost obliterated brass plate, is in Church Street, looking across the Thames to Kew Gardens.

In the field of guild socialism, Penty's best-known work is *The Restoration of the Guild System* (1906), but the system of social reconstruction that he elaborated with Edward Spencer and A. R. Orage, editor of *The New Age*, was never worked through because their views began to diverge. He also wrote *Old Worlds to New* and *Post Industrialism*.

Penty's architectural works also included:

1900   Terry's Almshouses, York
               Davy Hall Restaurant, Davygate, York (*AA* and RA, 1902), with a painting of King Arthur by G. Milburn of York, and light fittings by the Bromsgrove Guild

1901-2   The Creamery Restaurant, York
               Dunollie, Scarborough (damaged by bombardment from the sea in the First World War)

1903   Design for the Billiard Room at Burnholme, York (RA, 1903)

Lowman, Angela, *A. J. Penty*, thesis, Portsmouth Polytechnic.

Obit. RIBAJ, 6.3.37, pp. 466—7 *Bldr*, 29.1.37, p. 273.

PETO, Harold Ainsworth   1854—1933

Harold Peto was the fifth son of Sir Samuel Morton Peto (1809—89), the famous railway builder and contractor of Grissell & Peto, London and Lowestoft. Harold Peto was articled to a Lowestoft architect, J. Clements, in 1871, and was apprenticed to the local building firm of Lucas Brothers. He next joined Karslake & Mortimer of Great Queen Street, WC2, and Peto Brothers of Pimlico, who were then rebuilding or reconstructing many of the houses of the Cadogan Estate, replacing their stock brick façades by red brick and terracotta in the Flemish Renaissance style as interpreted by Ernest George. Peto joined George's office and became a partner in 1876, but poor health eventually caused him to leave England and he went to live in Italy.

The best of George and Peto houses in Kensington, Chelsea and Mayfair were put up during Peto's nineteen-year partnership. George and Peto paid as much attention to the interiors as to the exteriors of their houses, an exception at a time when much of the detailing of the rich panelling, plasterwork and metalwork called for was being left to contractor-decorators.

Peto studied and built Italian gardens abroad. On his return to England, his genius for garden design found expression in the Water Garden at Buscot Park, Berkshire, for Lord Faringdon, and especially in the gardens for Garinish Island, Glengariff, Co. Cork, for John Annan Bryce. Peto also did gardens at Bridge House, Weybridge, Surrey; Easton Lodge, Essex; Petwood, Lincolnshire; Hatham Park, Wiltshire; and Wayford Manor, Somerset; and Lord Allington's gardens in Dorset. Peto designed his own gardens at Iford Manor, Bradford-on-Avon, Wiltshire, where pieces of statuary and architectural objects collected on his travels are given a formal arrangement. Despite their formal setting, Peto's gardens won the approval of those 'natural' gardeners, William Robinson and Gertrude Jekyll, because they demonstrated his wide understanding of both plants and layout.

Harold Peto also designed some interiors for the Cunard liner *Mauretania* (1912). The panelling, by H. H. Martyn of Cheltenham, was among the effects auctioned when this winner of the Blue Riband of the Atlantic was sold to the shipbreakers in 1934. Some, reassembled by the architect W. H. Watkins (*q.v.*), can be seen at Avery's Wine Bars in Park Street, Bristol.

Obit. Bldr, 28.4.33, p. 704.

PIBWORTH, Charles James   1878—1958

C. J. Pibworth was born in Bristol. He studied at Bristol School of Art, and entered the Royal Academy Schools in 1899. As a sculptor in stone he carried out works for Charles Holden between 1900 and 1914 — relief panels of figures for the Central Library, Bristol, figures in the window recesses of the extension to the Law Society, Chancery Lane, WC1, and the relief 'Euterpe' on the façade of the Orchestral Association, Archer Street, W1.

A. Beresford Pite: if not all derived from Michelangelo's built work, the details of this scholarly invention at 44 Mortimer Street, London W1 can be found in Michelangelo's designs at his house in Florence.

PITE, Arthur Beresford   1861—1934

Beresford Pite was the younger of the two architect sons of A. R. Pite (1832—1911). He was educated at King's College School and at University College, London, and entered the South Kensington Schools of Design in 1876. The same year, he was articled to Habershon and Fawckner and then to his father in 1881, while his brother, W. A. Pite (*q.v.*), sensibly, was articled first to his father and then to Habershon and Fawckner.

Beresford Pite won the Donaldson Medal in 1879, the Grissell Medal in 1880, and the Soane Medallion in 1882 with a remarkable if absurd design for a 'West-End Clubhouse', an Albrecht Dürer-style Nürnberg castle drawn in pen and ink. The same year Pite entered the office of John Belcher as an improver and remained at Belcher's for fourteen years. Although Belcher made him 'managing clerk', he never made him a partner. This could have been by agreement since Pite carried out works on his own account as well as for his father and brother and was for a time staff artist on *The Builder*.

In spite of, or perhaps because of, their difference in age and temperament, the collaboration of Belcher and Pite produced a building which was to have a marked effect on the trend of secular architecture, not only in England and Scotland but also in Germany, principally in Berlin. This was the Hall of the Incorporated Chartered Accountants, Great Swan Alley and Moorgate Place, EC2 (*Bldr*, 12.1.1889), now discreetly modernised and extended by William Whitfield. The building not only illustrates Belcher's views on sculpture in relation to buildings but embodies the ingenious and sprightly detail of Pite — here Genoese in style. On the façades are three kinds of Baroque window pediment, while that on the angle bay hints at the pound (£) and dollar ($) signs mirrored. The sculpture is by Harry Bates, ARA, a fine artist who died too soon of overwork, and Hamo Thornycroft.

While still in Belcher's office, Pite carried out on his own account or for his father and brother the additions to the Endell Street Infirmary, WC2 (1884—5); the Dairy Supply Co.'s works at Stratford-le-Bow (1889); and the Marylebone Dispensary at 77 Welbeck Street, W1 (1892; demolished). In 1893 he did 82 Mortimer Street, W1, with sculpture modelled by J. Attwood Slater and carved by Thomas Tyrell; and 37 Harley Street, W1, where the sculpture is by F. E. E. Schenk. He also did 31 Old Bond Street (*Bldr*, 9.6.1900).

In 1897 Pite left Belcher's office, where he was succeeded by J. J. Joass, and set up entirely on his own account. It is interesting to compare the work of John Belcher's two lieutenants — Pite, a Londoner, designing for Portland stone and brick, and Joass, a northern Scot from J. J. Burnet's Glasgow office, accustomed to detailing for gritstone and granite. Whether Pite was genuinely seeking a new architecture or simply enjoying the successive phases, now eclectic, now exotic, of his own work, he was undoubtedly ahead of his time. While most of his contemporaries and even his seniors were still endeavouring to achieve the quality of the Accountants' Building, Pite was already passing on to new phases of style.

His next was Mannerist, a style close to Baroque in which form does *not* follow function. Pite found inspiration in Michelangelo's work at the New Sacristy and the Laurentian Library and its staircase at S. Lorenzo, Florence, and in the master's alternative sketches for these now at his own house, the Casa Buonarroti. But Michelangelo had designed for grey *pietra serena* and white Carrara marble, and the style did not lend itself so well to the Portland stone used by Pite as to the Greek marble used by Joass.

Such borrowing from Michelangelo was confined to London and was probably prompted by two things — the renewal of interest, principally due to

Hugh Stannus, in the work of the neglected artist Alfred Stevens who died in 1875, and the publication in 1893 of *The Life of Michelangelo Buonarroti*, by John Addington Symonds, the first work in English on the maestro. If indeed Pite took inspiration from this work, this would account for the difference between the details of his Welbeck Street building of 1892 which is *early* Italian Mannerist, and 82 Mortimer Street, done in the following year. Here the work, and particularly the sculpture, is directly derived from the New Sacristy, or rather is a parody of it.

Pite's next phases were Byzantine and Hellenic Greek, probably the result of his visit to the Near East to design a mission hospital for Jerusalem. He may also have been influenced by J. F. Bentley and Cardinal Vaughan's choice of Byzantine for Westminster Cathedral. Pite's most important work in the period was the Parish Hall and Church of Christ Church, North Brixton, SW2 (*AA*, 1901; RA, 1902 and 1905; *Bldr*, 5.12.03 and 9.9.05), where his wife's brother was the incumbent. The church is planned to give a large space at the crossing and the style is a restless mixture of Byzantine, Greek and Mannerist. The outside pulpit of 1907 is not by Pite. Pite also added the chancel, side chapel and vestries to the eighteenth-century church of the Holy Trinity, Clapham, in 1902 (*Bldr*, 30.8.02).

Like Robert Schultz Weir at Khartoum and Leonard Stokes at Georgetown, Guyana, Pite was able to build his ideas abroad. His largest church is the Anglican Cathedral at Kampala, Uganda. Pite also did a church at Entebbe, Uganda (*Bldr*, 22.10.04) and English churches in Safad, Israel, Bucharest and Warsaw. At home he did the chapel of Monkton Coombe School near Bath and a Wesleyan chapel at Lisburne Road, Gospel Oak, NW5 (*Bldr*, 24.8.07; demolished). He also did the Orangery at Burton Manor, Wirral, Cheshire, for a son of W. E. Gladstone.

Pite's third phase was his own scholarly adaptation of Greek. Ancient Roman architecture had been familiar to the English ever since the fashion for the Grand Tour began in the eighteenth century, but ignorance of original Greek architecture was such that before Stuart and Revett measured the remains of Greek temples, ancient Greek buildings were taken for Turkish architecture. There followed the first Greek revival, not only in architecture but in furniture and fashion, when in order to look like naiads, ladies risked pneumonia by wearing their gowns soaking wet and most architects learned to design in the Greek style.

After a gap of some seventy years Beresford Pite's building in Euston Square, NW1, for the Amalgamated Approved Societies (now in other hands; *Bldr*, 5.10.07 and 19.9.08) was the first and only scholarly building in London in the Greek style since the work of C. R. Cockerell. It is, however, more 'Pite' than Cockerell and more 'Cockerell' than Greek. The building makes use of the unusual

287

286

289

A. Beresford Pite: in Christ Church, London SW2, can be found elements of Greek, Byzantine and Mannerist styles, all revived in the 1900s.

A. Beresford Pite: at 82 Mortimer Street, London W1 is a witty comment on Michelangelo's work at S. Lorenzo, Florence; for here the architect and the sculptor (Thomas Tyrell) have awakened the Master's sleeping figures from their pedimented sarcophagi to perform the unenviable task of supporting another pediment.

Ionic Order from the interior of the Temple of Apollo Epicurius at Bassae, in Arcadia, and a collection of stonework details deriving from stele heads, sarcophagi and other sepulchral monuments. Next door, fronting a house converted into a Martin's Bank (now demolished) there once stood a wood portico of Pompeiian delicacy, also by Pite. In its place is a large extension to Pite's Insurance building by W. H. Gunton, completed in 1932.

Beresford Pite entered designs in several competitions, including those for the Anglican Cathedral and the Royal Insurance in Liverpool, the Cardiff Town Hall and Law Courts, and the Pearl Assurance Offices in Holborn, WC1.

288 Pite's other works included Pagani's Restaurant, Great Portland Street, W1, destroyed in the Second World War. This was a conversion of three plain houses over an existing ceramic front on the ground floor by C. Worley. The existing brick façades above were united by a large cove cornice and all was faced with glazed ceramic tiles to an unusual design with female figures incorporated into patterns anticipating the 'psychedelic' patterns of the 1960s (*Bldr*, 20.2.04 and 18.3.05).

A. Beresford Pite: the Thornhill Square Branch Library, London N1.

A. Beresford Pite: this coloured tile façade covering the three old houses of Pagani's Restaurant, Great Portland Street, London W1, carried an overall swirling pattern incorporating large female figures.

Between 1906 and 1908 Pite did the All Souls' Schools (*Bldr*, 17.10.08), New Cavendish Street and Foley Street, W1, in brickwork with interlacing arches, a favourite among brother-upholders of the Art Workers' Guild, of which Pite became
285 a member in 1884. He also did St Anne's House, Mortimer Street and Great Titchfield Street, W1 (*Bldr*, 14.10.05), a hostel. Other Pite works were 126 Great Portland Street, W1 (*Bldr*, 2.11.07), the Martin's Bank in Curtain Road, EC2, and the West
288 Islington Carnegie Public Library, Thornhill Square, N1 (*Bldr*, 16.1.09). He also did the First World War Memorial for the Royal Lancashire Regiment at Vendresse, France.

The Piccadilly entrance to the Burlington Arcade is also by Pite. He altered the original work by Samuel Ware (1781—1860) in two phases. First, in 1911, he very appropriately added above Ware's triple-arched entrance of 1816—18 an upper triple arcade on paired composite columns to which tile decoration was added in 1930. Later Pite was asked to sweep away Samuel Ware's arches and columns and provide one large opening, retaining his own upper arcade. Pite achieved this with a wide segmental arch, a broken pediment and *putti* flanked by a pair of terms, one male, one female, smiling cynically — Pite was never dull. (The north entrance of the Arcade was rebuilt in 1937 by W. G. Sinning.)

Beresford Pite's buildings were only a part of his work; he was a teacher throughout his career. He was Professor of Architecture at the Royal College of Art, South Kensington (1900—23) and Director from 1905 to 1928 of the London

County Council's Brixton School of Building. He was also a member of the Board of Architectural Studies at Cambridge.

Pite's practice was continued by a former pupil, F. E. P. Jackson, who became a junior partner in 1932, and, on Pite's death, a partner with Pite's son I. B. Pite.

RIBAJ, 7.12.35, pp. 117–31, article by H. S. Goodhart-Rendel
Obit. RIBAJ, 8.12.34, pp. 152 and 212, and 22.12, p. 277 *Bldr*, 30.11.34, p. 925 and 7.12 p. 969.

PITE, William Alfred   1860–1949

W. A. Pite was the elder brother of Arthur Beresford Pite (*q.v.*). He went to King's College School, Wimbledon, SW19, was articled to his father, then to Habershon and Fawckner, and was a junior assistant to J. Oldrid Scott. He won the Pugin Studentship in 1883 and began practice in 1884. R. Sheckleton Balfour was a partner (1901–6).

A. Beresford Pite: a neo-Greek Revival styled office building in Euston Square, London NW1.

Pite's church work included All Saints (Perceval Memorial Church) and Vicarage, Ealing, W5 (RA, 1904; *BJ*, 27.12.05); St James, Alperton, Middlesex; and the Presbyterian Church, Frognal, Hampstead, NW3, won in competition (*Bldr*, 1903). A domestic work of this period was Highcombe Edge, Hindhead, Surrey (1899). But Pite's practice was principally concerned with hospital design. An early example in this field is the infirmary wing added to St Giles's Workhouse, Short's Gardens, Holborn, WC2, which he did with his brother (*Bldr*, 1888). He also did the Royal Homoeopathic Hospital, Great Ormond Street, WC1 (1893–5; a wing was added by E. T. Hall in 1909); Bradford Royal Infirmary; Royal Victoria Hospital, Bournemouth, Hampshire; and the Boys' Garden City, Woodford Bridge, Essex, for Dr Barnardo's Homes (*BA*, 1909).

W. A. Pite's largest work is the new King's College Hospital and Medical School, Denmark Hill, SE5 (moved from the Strand), won in competition in 1905, built on the pavilion plan, and completed in 1914 (*Bldr*, 27.5.05).

W. A. Pite also did 16 and 17 Cavendish Square, W1 (*Bldr*, 1912; demolished), and St Peter's Church, Southfield Road, Acton, W4 (1914).

Obit. RIBAJ, Sept., 1949, p. 507 and Oct., p. 547 *Bldr*, 10.8.49, p. 225

POMEROY, Frederick William, RA
1856–1924

F. W. Pomeroy was born in London. Like many of the students of the Lambeth School of Art he went from there to the Royal Academy Schools, entering in 1881 and winning the Gold Medal and Travelling Studentship in 1885. Pomeroy studied in Paris under Frémiet and Antonin Mercié; he also studied in Rome. His early work showed an affinity with the Arts and Crafts Movement and he exhibited work at their exhibitions. Pomeroy did carving and statuary on many public buildings, especially on those by the architect E. W. Mountford, and monuments of many national figures and local worthies.

His work before the turn of the century included the capitals in the Holy Redeemer, Clerkenwell (1887–8); the chancel stalls and screen for Holy Trinity, Sloane Street, SW3 (1888–9); carving at Sheffield Town Hall (1890–4); the font at Carlisle Cathedral (1891); and some carving at Paisley Town Hall. His memorial work in this period included a recumbent effigy of Admiral Blake for Bridgwater, Somerset; Robert Burns for Paisley, Renfrewshire, and Sydney, New South Wales; and the First Duke of Westminster in Chester Cathedral.

Pomeroy did major statuary work for the Belfast City Hall and for Vauxhall Bridge. At Belfast his contributions are, in the central pediment, 'Hibernia' supported by 'Minerva', 'Industry', 'Labour' and 'Liberty', and symbolic figures of the branches of Commerce. He also did the bronze statue of the 1st Marquis of Dufferin and Ava, the supporting bronzes 'India' and 'Canada' and the figure of 'Fame' surmounting the canopy of this monument, designed in collaboration with the architect Sir Alfred Brumwell Thomas (*q.v.*). Pomeroy was assisted by the Belfast sculptor J. Edgar Winter on the statues of James Haslett and Sir Robert McMordie. On Vauxhall Bridge (opened in 1906), Pomeroy did the colossal bronze figures of 'Pottery', 'Engineering', 'Agriculture' and 'Architecture' standing in the steel-plated niches in four of the piers. (The figures in the remaining four are the work of Alfred Drury (*q.v.*).)

Pomeroy did the four small angels and a bronze female figure on the Kensington War Memorial (1922), a stone column at the junction of Church Street and High Street, W8 (architect Hubert Corlette).

Pomeroy was a brother-upholder of the Art Workers' Guild and Master in 1901. He taught at the Architectural Association School and was made ARA in 1906, RA in 1917 (diploma work 'Dione', relief).

His other works include:

1900	William Gladstone, Palace of Westminster, SW1
	Wood sculpture for the Orient liner *Ophir*
1900-7	'Justice', 'Law' and 'Truth' in the central pediment at the New Sessions House, Old Bailey, EC4, the bronze gilt figure of Justice surmounting the cupola and the plaster pendentives inside the dome
	Archbishop Temple for Canterbury and St Paul's Cathedral
	Oliver Cromwell for St Ives, Huntingdonshire
1901	Sculpture on Liverpool Museum and Technical Schools (architect E. W. Mountford)
	Memorial tablet to F. J. Horniman at the Horniman Museum, Forest Hill, SE23
	Dean Hook, City Square, Leeds
1902-3	At Electra House, Moorgate, EC2 (now the City of London College) carving and sculpture with many other artists from the Lambeth school
1903	Queen Victoria Memorial, Castle Square, Chester
	John Platt, Oldham, Lancashire
	Robert Ashcroft, MP for Alexandra Park, Oldham
	King Edward VII, pediment of Lancaster Town Hall
1905	Dean Hole for Rochester Cathedral
	Queen Victoria, Woolwich Town Hall, SE18
1906	Monsignor Nugent with a child, for his work for children, Liverpool
1907	Royal Fusiliers Memorial, Guildhall, EC2

F. W. Pomeroy: 'Pottery' on Vauxhall Bridge, London SW1, one of four giant figures modelled by Pomeroy.

1911	Michael Arthur Bass, MP, 1st Baron Burton for King Edward Place, Burton-on-Trent, Staffordshire
1912	Sir Francis Bacon for South Square, Gray's Inn, WC1

Obit. Bldr, 30.5.24, p. 862.

PONTING, Charles Edwin   1850—1932

C. E. Ponting was born at Collingbourne Ducis, Wiltshire, where his father was on the staff of the Savernake Estate. He began his career in architecture in 1864 in the office of Samuel Overton who was connected with the estate and in 1872 married Overton's daughter, who died in childbirth the following year. Ponting lived at Lockeridge from 1872 to 1896 and for eighteen years (1870—88) acted as agent for the Meux Estate at Overton.

In 1883 Ponting was made Diocesan Surveyor for the Wiltshire portion of the Salisbury Diocese. This expanded to take in a portion of the Bristol Diocese in 1887 and the Dorset half of the Salisbury Diocese in 1892, giving Ponting a district larger than that of any other diocesan surveyor in England. He resigned the Bristol portion in 1915 and the whole diocese in 1928. Ponting was also appointed surveyor to Marlborough College (1889—1921) where he carried out the gymnasium in 1908 (*Bldr*, 9.5.08).

Two hundred and thirty-seven churches came under Ponting's hand, the majority in Wiltshire and some hundred in Dorset. He acquired a special knowledge of the churches of the diocese and wrote a series of architectural descriptions of over a hundred Wiltshire churches for the *Wiltshire Archaeological Magazine*; he also acted as a guide to some of them. He was a churchwarden at Lockeridge and at St Mary, Marlborough. Examples of Ponting's church work occur in eight other counties in England and Wales.

From 1898 Ponting designed a wealth of furnishings at All Saints, Down Ampney, Gloucestershire, made for him by Harry Hems, of Exeter. According to a local obituary Ponting would have preferred to be judged for his restorations than for his new churches, but these too are praiseworthy. The earliest of his fifteen new churches was at West Overton and Ford, Wiltshire (RA, 1898). He also did the chapel of St Mary's School, Wantage, Berkshire (1898). Of his many works of restoration, that at the monastic church of the Blessed Virgin Mary, St Katherine and All Saints, at Edington, Wiltshire, was the most important and best illustrates his concern to preserve all the old work that could possibly be saved. He rescued the plaster ceilings of the nave, revealing much old painting and gilding, and preserved the Saxon windows, as he did at Avebury. In this way Ponting saved numerous churches from the dangers of 'restoration'. His advice was sought as far afield as Bucharest, Oporto and Australia.

His secular work included Marlborough Town Hall (RA, 1901; *Bldr*, 11.1.02), Dauntsey's Agricultural School at West Lavington, Wiltshire, and a house at Shillingstone, Dorset (RA, 1905).

Through his Meux Overton Estate connections, he was entrusted with the special task of re-erecting the stones of Wren's Temple Bar on the estate of Sir Hedworth Meux at Theobald's Park, Hertfordshire, in 1888, after its place at the boundary between the cities of London and Westminster had been taken by C. B. Birch's Griffin in 1880. He also restored the Cross at Waltham Cross, Middlesex.

Another unusual work by Ponting was the restoration of the mediaeval Bristol High Cross which now stands at Stourhead, Wiltshire. First erected in 1373, this had spent many years lying in pieces in the crypt of Bristol Cathedral until in 1780 it was presented to the banker, Henry Hoare, who had the pieces conveyed to Stourhead in six large wagons and re-erected.

After the turn of the century Ponting did church work in Wiltshire at St Thomas, Southwick (*Bldr*, 7.3.07), Christ Church, Shaw (*Bldr*, 22.1.10), Holt, and Stanton. From 1919 until his death he lived at Parkstone, Dorset, and he was buried at Cadley in Wiltshire. *Other post-1900 works by him are:*

1903	House, Tenantrees, Knighton, Dorset (*Bldr*, 7.3.03)
1906	St Quintin, Wiltshire (chancel)
1907	St Stephen, in the grounds of Kingston Lacy, Dorset (*Bldr*, 13.4.07)
	The Rectory, Donhead St Andrew (*Bldr*, 19.9.08)
1908	St Martin, Chickerell Road, Weymouth (now in other use, the aisles were never built)
1910-12	St Mary, West Fordington, Dorchester – 'Ponting's *magnum opus*' (Pevsner)
1914	Tidworth Garrison Church, Wiltshire

Obit. RIBAJ, 19.3.32, p. 406   *Bldr*, 5.2.32, p. 272.

C. E. Ponting: the Town Hall, at once Carolean and Edwardian, closes the eastern end of the High Street, Marlborough, Wiltshire.

A cast of Henry Poole's realisation of G. F. Watts's maquette is set up at the Cecil Rhodes Memorial in Zimbabwe. This is another cast set up in Kensington Gardens, London, where it is known as 'Physical Energy'.

POOLE, Henry, RA   1873–1928

Henry Poole was born in Westminster. His father, Samuel Poole, and grandfather were stonemasons and sculptors engaged on restoration at Westminster Abbey and other church work, principally for William Butterfield. Poole went to King's College, London, and entered the Lambeth School of Art in 1888 and the Royal Academy Schools in 1892.

He was apprenticed to Harry Bates, ARA, and then to the painter George Frederick Watts, RA (1817–1904). At Limnerslease, Compton, near Guildford, Surrey, Poole assisted Watts on his colossal equestrian work, 'Physical Energy'. Adapted from a work done for the Duke of Westminster at Eaton Hall to represent his ancestor Hugh Lupus, it was set up in the Matopo Hills, near Bulawayo, as a memorial tribute to Cecil Rhodes. In the words of those vainglorious days, 'Physical Energy' was intended to represent

292

> 'the embodiment of the restless energy of the present day and of the wonderful control which science has secured over the forces of nature, though it may be interpreted to symbolise the foresight and courage of an explorer who has ridden his horse to a lofty summit from which he has discovered a new country of which he is prepared to take possession...'

A cast of the colossal horse and its bareback rider stood for some time in the courtyard of Burlington House until the laying of wood paving provided the excuse for its removal and it was towed out by

steam-traction engine to its permanent home in Kensington Gardens, W2. The Scottish sculptor and poet J. Pittendrigh Macgillivray, RSA, tried unsuccessfully to get a cast made for the Scottish nation.

In 1897 Poole did the sculpture on the West Ham (Essex) Town Hall; the Town Hall, Rotherhithe, SE16 (destroyed); and Lanchester, Stewart and Rickards's Deptford Town Hall, SE14 (1903). Poole shared Rickards's love of Paris and thought along the same Baroque lines.

310
311
309 Poole won the competition for the sculptures on the Cardiff City Hall. His group at Cardiff represents 'Welsh Unity and Patriotism' balancing 'Welsh Commerce and Industry' and 'Welsh Poetry and Music' by Paul Montford, and 'Welsh Science and Education' by Donald McGill. Also at Cardiff City Hall Poole did the Mermaid panel, a large coloured relief in the ante-chamber, and the marble statue of Giraldus Cambrensis.

In 1902 Poole sent a relief panel, 'Hylas and the Water Nymphs', to the Royal Academy. This was set in the rose garden at St John's Lodge, Regent's Park (see p. 380). In 1906 Poole did the Michelangelesque figures on the pediments of H. T.
204
205 Hare's United Kingdom Temperance and General Provident Institution, 196 Strand, WC2. The building has been demolished and the fragments of the statuary lie on a terrace, poor Justice with her scales tipped sideways defying gravity. With Rickards, Poole won the competition for the
292 fountain in front of the Victoria Rooms, Clifton,

Henry Poole's King Edward VII at Victoria Rooms, Clifton, Bristol, crowns a modest system of fountains draped with giant bronze seaweed to a design by E. A. Rickards.

Henry Poole modelled the low-relief decoration for the Black Friar, London EC4, in an architectural setting by H. Fuller Clark.

Bristol (1907; *Bldr*, 13.1.11). (The memorial to King Edward VII was added in 1913.) Poole did the sculpture on the Wesleyan Convocation Hall, Westminster, for Lanchester and Rickards, for whom he also did the little porcelain figure on the façade of Colnaghi and Obach (now Frank Partridge), 144–146 New Bond Street, W1 (1913).

Henry Poole came close to the style of Art Nouveau in his sculptures at the Black Friar public house, Blackfriars, EC4, where the other sculpture is by Charles Bradford. In the chapel of St Michael and St George, St Paul's Cathedral, Poole did 'St George' on the reredos and the Baroque thrones for the King, the Prince of Wales and the Chancellor of the Order. Also at St Paul's he did the plaque to William Blake and the bust of Sir Anthony Van Dyck, and he renewed 'St Jude' and 'St Simon' on the west pediment. Poole did a monument to Lord Cowper (d. 1905) at St Mary, Hertingfordbury, Hertfordshire (1909) and the memorial in Nottingham to Captain Albert Ball, VC, of the Royal Flying Corps (1918, in a setting by Rickards).

Poole was made ARA in 1920 and RA in 1927 (diploma work, 'Young Pan'). In the National Portrait Gallery are bronze statuettes by Poole of G. F. Watts and Captain Ball. He was a trustee of the National Gallery, a member of the Art Workers' Guild and Master of the Sculpture School of the Royal Academy (1921–7).

Obit. Bldr, 24.8.28, pp. 288 and 290.

POWELL, Ernest Turner   1859–1937

Turner Powell was the son of James Turner Powell. He was educated privately, was articled (1876–80) to Sir Alexander Rosse Stenning of 157 Fenchurch Street, EC3, and became his assistant for three years. Powell then travelled abroad, studied in Paris, and on his return entered the firm of contractors Vernon & Ewens of London and Cheltenham.

Turner Powell commenced practice in 1885 doing houses, mainly in Surrey and Sussex. He did The Hermitage (rebuilding after fire), Shovelstrode Manor, Ardmillan (*Bldr*, 8.7.05), and Great House Court (*Bldr*, 1.4.05; RA, 1905 and 1906), all at East Grinstead. He also did Coolham and Shepherds Well, Ashdown Forest; Coldharbour Manor, Old End, and Priors Field, at Forest Row; The Old Barn, Shipley, Sussex; Greyfriars, Tilford, near Farnham (*c.* 1910); a house at Holmbury St Mary, Surrey; West Chart, Limpsfield, Surrey; New Place, Horsham, Sussex; Walstead House, Lindfield; Gerston, Storrington, Sussex; and Manor Grange, Tunbridge Wells. His style was traditional sixteenth-century vernacular, his medium appropriately warm brick, half-timber or tile hanging, with tile or Horsham stone roofs.

In the Hampstead Garden Suburb he did 1 Turner Drive, and in Russia he did a riding school for Countess N. Brobinskoy at Zakoziel near Grodno.

Obit. Bldr, 26.11.37, p. 986.

POYNTER, Sir Ambrose Macdonald, Bart.
1867—1923

Sir Ambrose Poynter's grandfather was a church architect, his father, Sir Edward Poynter, Bart., RA (1836—1919), was President of the Royal Academy (1896—1918). Ambrose Poynter was first cousin to Stanley Baldwin and Rudyard Kipling, connections which came through his mother, one of the five daughters of a Birmingham Wesleyan minister, the Rev. G. B. Macdonald.

Poynter went to Eton, studied at the South Kensington Schools and entered the Royal Academy Schools in 1889. He was articled to George Aitchison, RA, Professor of Architecture at the Royal Academy Schools (1887—1905). Poynter began practice in 1893. For a time he was a partner with Ernest Willmott (Sloper) who had been a partner of Herbert Baker in South Africa.

Poynter did the Greek Cippolino and Pentelikos marble balustrade around the Athenaeum Club, Waterloo Place and Pall Mall, SW1, in collaboration with Sir Laurence Alma-Tadema, OM, RA (1836—1912), and the decorations of 34 Queen Anne's Gate, SW1, for Lord Glenconner. He also did work at the Manor House, Mount Grace Priory, Northallerton, N. Riding (*Bldr*, 6.8.04) and additions and decorations to Polesden Lacey, Surrey, for the Scottish financier William McEwan (*Bldr*, 7.9.07). He was a member of the Art Workers' Guild.

Poynter's other work includes:

1903-5	95 Sloane Square, SW3 (*Bldr*, 30.9.05)
1906-8	Vernon House, Park Place, St James's, SW1 (alterations for Lord Hillingdon). Carving by William Aumonier and Sons (*Bldr*, 27.3.09); now the Overseas Club
1908	Pavilion of the Comptoir National d'Escompte de Paris at the Franco-British Exhibition at White City (*BA*, August, 1908)
1910	Village Hall, Ingleby Arncliffe, N. Riding

Obit. RIBAJ, 16.6.23, p. 504 *Bldr*, 8.6.23 p. 928.

PRENTICE, Andrew Noble   1866—1941

A. N. Prentice, the son of Thomas Prentice, was born at Greenock, Renfrewshire, studied at Glasgow University and was articled to William Leiper, RSA, until 1888 when he won the Soane Medallion and travelled in Italy, France and Spain. In 1890 Prentice entered T. E. Collcutt's office and after two years returned to Spain for four months. His studies there resulted in his book *Renaissance Architecture and Ornament in Spain* (Batsford, 1893), through which, according to a contemporary account, 'he rediscovered to his generation the special beauties of that phase of Spanish Renaissance design known as Plateresque'.

Prentice opened an office in 1891. His work consisted mainly of houses in the manner of

Ernest Newton, the largest of which was Cavenham Hall, Suffolk, where he also did the stables and coach house (*Bldr*, 18.5.01), and he did a house in Eglinton Drive, Glasgow (*Bldr*, 4.6.04).

His largest work is the Joint Examination Halls for the Physicians and Surgeons, Queen Square, WC1 (*Bldr*, 26.3.10), which he won in competition in 1909 with a design in correct 'Wrenaissance'. This took the place of Stephen Salter's Examination Halls on the Victoria Embankment, WC2, which were converted for the use of the Institution of Electrical Engineers by Adams and Holden.

Prentice designed interiors for ships of the Orient Line and for SS *Orviedo* and six other steamships of the Australian and South American Lines (*AR*, June, 1967). Prentice also did designs for metalwork and advocated its use for shop fronts.

He did additions to Buckland Manor, North Gloucestershire, and to Stringscot Manor and Witham Hall, Lincolnshire (*AA*, 1903; *Bldr*, 16.7.04). His domestic work included a house in de Pary's Avenue, Bedford (*Bldr*, 18.5.01; RA and *AA*, 1902); one on the Queensway Estate, Newmarket, Suffolk (*Bldr*, 25.11.05); houses at Broadway, Worcestershire; Fryerne, Caterham, Surrey (*BJ*, 26.6.01); The Retreat, Lakenheath Suffolk (*Bldr*, 4.10.02; RA, 1900); The Avenue, Pinner, Middlesex (*BN*, 24.8.01); Willersey House, Willersey, Gloucestershire (RA, 1907; *Bldr*, 15.6.07); and Chelwood Manor, Sussex (*Bldr*, 30.4.04; RA and *AA*, 1904). His design won the competition for the Lifford Memorial Hall, Broadway, Worcestershire.

In 1928 Prentice did the St Martin's Street, WC2 branch of the Westminster Public Libraries in the Louis XV manner.

AR, June 1967, pp. 449—52: 'Ship interiors, when the breakthrough came', by Sir Colin Anderson
Obit. Bldr, 2.1.42, p. 14.

PRIOR, Edward Schroder, ARA   1852—1932

E. S. Prior was born at Greenwich, the son of John Venn Prior, a barrister-at-law. He went to Harrow and Caius College, Cambridge, where he was later made a Fellow. Prior was articled to R. Norman Shaw in 1874 and was one of the group of Shaw's pupils and assistants who formed the St George's Art Society, forerunner of the Art Workers' Guild. Prior was a founder member of the Guild and Master in 1906. He was also secretary of the Arts and Crafts Exhibition Society (1902—17).

Prior's early domestic work includes High Grove, Harrow, 1881 (*BN*, 8.12.1882); Manor Lodge, Harrow (*Bldr*, 14.6.1884, *A*, 19.7.1889); and Carr Manor, Meanwood, Leeds, 1881 (*BN*, 21.7.1882; *A*, 2.5.1890). He did considerable work at Harrow School which included the laundry in 1887, the billiard room, to a highly

A. N. Prentice's Examination Halls, Queen Square, London WC1, creates, in an otherwise immaculate design, the illusion that the upper storeys are larger in scale than the lower, the ground storey being the meanest.

E. S. Prior: Home Place, Holt, Norfolk. The entrance front.

original design, in 1889, and the music room in 1890—2.

The Barn, Exmouth, Devon (1895) was the first of a series of X-shaped, symmetrical plans of which Lutyens's Papillon Hall, Leicestershire, was another example. Prior's building was originally thatched. The second of his X-plan houses was Voewood (now Home Place), Kelling, Holt, Norfolk (1904), which was supervised by Randall Wells. The house is built from materials excavated at the site but the money thus saved was less than that spent on restoring the grounds to order after excavations.

296

Among Prior's earliest works (1885; *Bldr*, 5.12.03) is Pier Terrace, West Bay, Bridport Dorset, a row of houses on an old deserted quay, known locally as 'Noah's Ark', with no obvious reason for their presence, unless for some vanished fishing or coasting industry. In this period Prior also did the Henry Martyn Hall, Market Street, Cambridge (1885—7), for the University Church Missionary Society, and High Grove, Hillingdon, Middlesex (1881).

297

Prior's early church work included Holy Trinity, Bothenhampton, Bridport, where the altar front in gesso is by W. R. Lethaby; the Mission Room, Barlow Street, Southwark, SE1, for Pembroke College, Cambridge, Mission (1892); and St Mary, Burton Bradstock, Dorset, where he did the south aisle in 1897. Prior patented a thick, hand-made 'Prior's glass' for church windows.

296
297

He did St Andrew, Roker, Monkwearmouth, Sunderland, in 1906—7 (*Bldr*, 12.10.07) — one of the best churches of the Arts and Crafts Movement, containing work by Burne-Jones, Louise Powell, Ernest Gimson and Macdonald Gill. Randall Wells was resident architect and carved the font.

Prior was Slade Professor of Architectural History (1912—32) at Cambridge where he voluntarily held classes that became the basis of the Cambridge University School of Architecture. He wrote on gardens (*Studio*, 1898), and published a *History of Gothic Art in England* (1900); *Mediaeval Figure Sculpture in England*, with Arthur Gardner (*AR*, 1902—4, published in book form, 1912); and *Cathedral Builders in England* (1905).

Prior was made ARA in 1914. He was the first architect to exhibit a model of a building (The Barn, Exmouth) at the Royal Academy. He married Louisa Maunsell, daughter of the Rev. F. W. Maunsell, in 1885. His chief associate was Arthur Grove (d. 1929).

Among Prior's other works are:

1901-2	Laboratories, Netley Hospital, Hampshire (*Bldr*, 21.9.01)
1901-4	The School of Medicine, Cambridge (now the Zoological Laboratory). The north front has been refaced
1903-4	Winchester College Music School
1905	St John the Divine, Richmond, Surrey (new chancel, chapel and vestries) in association with Arthur Grove (RA, 1905; RIBA Drawings Collection)
1908	Pembroke College Mission Church, Southwark, SE1
1911-12	Greystones, Highcliffe-on-Sea, Hampshire
1912	The Small House, Mid Lavant, Chichester, Sussex

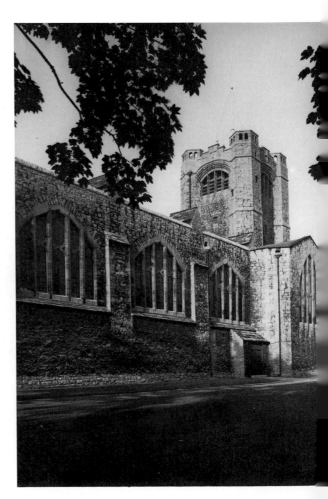

E. S. Prior: an unusual group of houses, much altered, at West Bay, Bridport, Dorset, by this scion of the arts and crafts movement.

1913-14   St Osmond, Parkstone, Dorset, in association with Arthur Grove (incorporating chancel by G. A. B. Livesay, 1904–5)

A, Nov., 1952, pp. 502–8, article by Christophe Grillet
Walker, Lynne, *Edward Schroder Prior* (in preparation)
Obit. RIBAJ, 10.9.32, p. 814 and 15.10, pp. 858 and 859 *Bldr*, 26.8.32, p. 328 *RIBAJ*, 21.9.29, p. 772 (Arthur Grove)

E. S. Prior: (left and above) St. Andrew, Roker, Northumberland, a church of the arts and crafts movement, containing work by Ernest Gimson.

PRYNNE, George Halford Fellowes   1853–1927

Fellowes Prynne was the son of the Rev. G. Rundle Prynne (d. 1903), whose church at Par, Cornwall, was the first church designed by G. E. Street. Fellowes Prynne's mother was the daughter of Admiral Sir Thomas Fellowes. His brother was Edward A. Fellowes Prynne, a painter of 'The Church Triumphant' and similar allegorical subjects.

Fellowes Prynne went to Chard College, Somerset, and Haileybury. In 1871 he went to Canada intending to take up farming, but, finding he preferred architecture, became a pupil of R. C. Windyer of Toronto. On his return to England Prynne entered Street's office and worked in the site office at the Royal Courts of Justice in the Strand. He entered the Royal Academy Schools in 1876. For a time he was chief assistant to R. J. Withers.

When Street died in 1881, Prynne completed Street's church of St Peter, Plymouth, where Prynne's father had been vicar. A succession of churches followed, among the earliest of which were St Peter, Leigham Court Road, SW16, where Prynne did additions and the baptistry (1886–7), and All Saints, Rosendale Road, West Dulwich, SE21 (1888–9). (The latter was damaged in the Second World War and restored in 1952.) Other Prynne church work of this period includes St Peter, Staines, Surrey (1894); St Paul, Westham, Weymouth, Dorset (1893–6), where he did the chancel and the chapel (1903); St Peter, Budleigh Salterton, South Devon (1893); Holy Trinity, Roehampton, SW15 (1896); and St Saviour, Ealing, W6 (1898), the church where he himself worshipped.

Fellowes Prynne did a number of his principal works overseas. He designed St John's Cathedral,

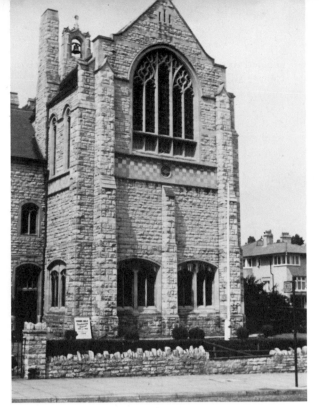

G. H. Fellowes Prynne: St Alban, Bournemouth, Dorset, by this former assistant of G. E. Street.

Umtata, Cape Province, S. Africa (1901–6; *Bldr*, 22.10.04), and St Mary's Cathedral and Hall, Johannesburg (*Bldr*, 8.9.06), but here only his Hall was built (1906); Sir Herbert Baker made designs for the Cathedral which were carried out by his partner Frank Fleming in 1926. In 1915 Prynne did a design for a new cathedral in Colombo, which the Rev. Basil Clarke has described as 'based upon a combination of Byzantine massiveness and proportions, emphasised with a recognition of Gothic detail and feeling for models and types of Eastern origin' (*Anglican Cathedrals Outside the British Isles*, SPCK, 1958). Fellowes Prynne lost two sons in the First World War. His son Harold practised as an architect in Madras.

Fellowes Prynne's churches from 1900 to 1913 include:

1900	All Saints, Elland, W. Riding
1901	Christ Church, Lower Sydenham, SE 26 (*Bldr*, 9.11.01; RA, 1901)
1902	St John, Sidcup, Kent (RA, 1902; *Bldr*, 13.9.02)
	St Peter, Ilfracombe, N. Devon
	St Peter, Whitstable, Kent
1903-11	St Martin, Worcester (*Bldr*, 21.10.05)
1905	Holy Trinity, Exmouth, Devon
1908	St Wilfrid, Bognor, Sussex (unfinished, *Bldr*, 7.5.10)
1908-9	St Alban, Bournemouth, Hampshire (*Bldr*, 31.10.08)
1909-10	St Mark, Peak Hill, Wallington, Surrey
	St Saviour's Church House and Schools, Ealing, W5 (*Bldr*, 7.5.10)
1911	St Peter, Bushey Heath, Hertfordshire (nave)
1913	St Peter, Harrow, Middlesex
	St Nicholas, Taplow, Buckinghamshire

Obit. RIBAJ, 21.5.27, pp. 494–5 *Bldr*, 20.5.27, p. 802.

298

PURCHASE, Edward Keynes   1862–1923

E. Keynes Purchase was born at Kington, Herefordshire, went to Brecon College, and was articled in 1879 to Thomas Nicholson, Diocesan Architect of Hereford. He was assistant to Jones and Parks of Newton, Monmouthshire (1883–4), and to Walter Emden, the London theatre and hotel architect, when Emden was engaged on Bedford Court Mansions and a number of business premises in the West End of London.

In 1884 Keynes Purchase joined G. D. Martin as a partner in a practice also principally involved in West End business premises. One of their first works together was Craven House and Admiralty House, Northumberland Avenue, WC2 (1885). Between 1886 and 1890 they did Albany Mansions, Cambridge Circus, WC2; Imperial Mansions, Charing Cross Road, WC2 (demolished in 1963 to make way for Centre Point); and Marlborough Mansions in Victoria Street, SW1. During the next five years their work included the George and Dragon, Shaftesbury Avenue, W1; the Pelican Club in Gerrard Street, W1; and 18, 19 and 20 Jermyn Street, SW1.

In 1895 the partnership with Martin was dissolved and, except for a brief partnership with Roland Welch, Purchase practised alone, doing shops and flats in South Molton Street and Oxford Street, W1. He did residential flats in South Street, Mayfair, W1 (*BN*, 1901), and the Palm Court of the Hotel Cecil on the Victoria Embankment, designed by Perry and Reed and demolished in 1930 to make way for Shell-Mex House (the earlier Strand block by Joseph Sawyer still remains). Purchase also did premises for the bankers Cox & Co. (now Lloyds Bank) at 80 Gracechurch Street, EC3. A pioneer motorist and aeronaut, Keynes Purchase, in association with Charles Mewès and A. J. Davis, advised on the new Royal Automobile Club in Pall Mall, SW1 (1909).

His other works include:

1895-1900	13, 14, 45, 46 and 126 New Bond Street, 55 Maddox Street
1900-6	55 Conduit Street
	71 Dean Street
	10 Great Marlborough Street
	14 New Burlington Street
	353 Oxford Street
	4 Prince's Street
	9 and 15–18 Rathbone Place
	1 Soho Square
	2 Woodstock Street, all in W1
1906 and after	11 Blenheim Street
	17 Conduit Street
	10 Golden Square
	24 and 45 Maddox Street
	39–42 and 105–106 New Bond Street
	40–44 Newman Street
	33, 64 and 66 Oxford Street

159

42 South Molton Street

16—19 Upper Rathbone Place all in W1

24—25 King William Street, EC3

1909-11 Aldine House, Bedford Street, Strand, WC2, in the 'Wrenaissance' style, for Dent's the publishers (now in other use)

Hay Green, Kingston Hill, Surrey, for D. Stoner Crowther

Obit. RIBAJ, 14.7.23 p. 567 *Bldr*, 18.5.23, p. 807.

QUENNELL, Charles Henry Bourne   1872—1935

C. H. B. Quennell was articled to Newman and Newman and worked in the offices of J. McK. Brydon and of J D. Sedding and Henry Wilson. He began practice in 1896, doing large detached suburban houses in the Hampstead Heath and Hampstead Garden Suburb area for his brother William Quennell and the West Heath Land Co. A drawing of Phyllis Court, Rosecroft Avenue, Hampstead, NW3 (*AR*, Mar., 1905) was shown in the Royal Academy in 1900. Quennell's houses in the Garden Suburb are 7, 9, 11, 15, 17, 10, 12 and 14 Hampstead Way, 6 Heathgate, 4 Turner Drive, 12 Turner Close, 3 Romney Close and 4, 5, 6 and 7 Morland Close.

In 1906 Quennell reconstructed the interior of the former Grosvenor Gallery at 157 New Bond Street, for F. W. Speaight, the Court photographer (the entrance gates were by Ingleson C. Goodison) and in the following year he did St John the Evangelist, Upper Edmonton, N9. In 1909 Quennell did two houses in Wells Road, Bickley, Kent — Linden Oak in Queen Anne style, and the informal Denbridge House for himself (Pevsner). Quennell did Four Beeches and other houses in Bickley, in St George's Road and Woodland Road, where Deerwood and Englefield were completed in 1912—13. The last house he built for himself is in Berkhamsted, Hertfordshire (*Bldr*, 21.4.1900). He designed garden furniture for J. Pyghtle White of Bedford, and did the mausoleum in St Mary's Cemetery, Kensal Green, NW10, and Mowden School, Brighton (*Modern Building Record*, 1912).

Quennell and his wife Marjorie (née Courtney) are remembered principally for their series of books on social life and history, illustrated by Mrs Quennell and published by Batsford. The series began with *A History of Everyday Things in England* and extended to the 'Everyday Life' series dealing with prehistoric and ancient times. Their son is the writer Peter Quennell.

Obit. RIBAJ, 21.12.35, p. 211.
Bldr, 13.12.35, pp. 1050, 1055 and 1097

RANSOME, James   1865—1944

James Ransome's work, divided between Britain and the East, while not extensive, was a significant contribution to the architecture of the day. He was articled to C. H. Driver and worked in the office of George and Peto. He was appointed consulting architect to the Government of India. A distinguished work by Ransome is Government Offices, Simla, Punjab (*Bldr*, 19.12.08; *RA*, 1908), built in steel and concrete after an earthquake there. He also did the Government Offices at Dacca (*Bldr*, 23.1.09) and Government House, Chittagong (both in Bangladesh); the agricultural college in Pusa and the Sanatorium at Puri, Orissa (both in India); and the Consulate at Ahwaz, Iran (*Bldr*, 23.1.09). He was succeeded in 1908 by John Begg. Ransome set out his views on contemporary architecture in India in his *Government of India Building Designs* and an article on 'European Architecture in India' (*RIBAJ*, Jan., 1905) as well as in his contributions to discussions on the capital, New Delhi (*RIBAJ*, November, 1913).

In England Ransome's domestic work included a house at Roehampton, SW15; 15 Lauriston Road, South Side (1891) and 13 Woodhayes Road, Wimbledon Common, SW19 (1894); a house at Leicester (*RA*, 1900; *BA*, 6.7.1900); one at Chobham, Surrey, for B. M. Caldicott (*AA*, 1902); Long Croft, Aldeburgh, Suffolk (*AR*, 1910); and Kingswear House, Beaconsfield, Buckinghamshire, for Basil H. Joy.

Obit. Bldr, 28.4.44 p. 345.

READ, Herbert   *c.* 1861—1950

Herbert Read was articled to George and Peto from 1878 to 1881, continuing as an assistant until 1888, with a break of one year at HM Office of Works. He entered the Royal Academy Schools in 1881, and began practice in 1888. His partnership with Robert Falconer Macdonald (*q.v.*), a contemporary at George and Peto's office, began in 1891. The work that came their way from the Cadogan and Grosvenor Estates shows the marks of the experience they had gained at that 'Eton of offices'. Sometimes romantic, sometimes sedately Georgian, their buildings reflected the age of Edward VII and perhaps even helped to give it its character, contrasting with the 'Pont Street Dutch' of George and Peto which they had begun to supersede.

Best known is the former Stewart's, the corner restaurant rebuilt in 1904 at 57—59 Piccadilly and 45—46 Old Bond Street for Callard, Stewart and Watt, a tea room popular with visitors to the Royal Academy. The ground floor shop fronts and their stone surrounds have been sadly obliterated, but the upper gables and tower with their variety of windows help to retain some of the flavour of Edwardian London, as its predecessor had for Victorian London. (Stewart's had figured in the popular lithograph, 'His Majesty the Baby'.)

Another corner bastion of Mayfair, in similar vein and for the same company, was 455 Oxford Street

300

Read and Macdonald: the former Stewart's Tea Rooms,
Piccadilly, London W1. The present occupants of this
delightful rococo version of Norman Shaw's baroque,
assuming that its elegant stone arches over the shop
fronts would inhibit the sale of air tickets, undeterred
by the City Authority, ordered their destruction.

and 22 North Audley Street (*Bldr*, 17.12.04).
Built in the same year as the Piccadilly branch but
in brick and tile with brown limestone dressings,
this romantic group (now demolished) has been
well illustrated by Shaw Sparrow. Read and
Macdonald's building in Long Acre, WC2, for
Stanford's, the map publishers (*BN*, 31.5.01),
with its wide gable and wide windows, retains its
freshness to this day. Their building for Bartholomew & Fletcher at 216—219 Tottenham Court
Road, W1, is typical of the neo-Georgian manner
which was superseding the 'free style' (*Bldr*,
17.12.04).

Also their work is 22 Grosvenor Square, the well-
mannered Portland stone faced town house at
the corner of North Audley Street and Upper
Brook Street, Grosvenor Square, which, perfectly
fulfilling its function as a rich and comfortable
Mayfair residence, could well serve as a setting for
the novels of Henry James. The large block of
shops and flats at the corner of Buckingham Palace
Road and Eccleston Street still survives, also eight
houses in Hans Crescent, SW7; the former Hans
Place Hotel and Cadogan Rooms (1895—6); 16—
26 Mount Street, W1 (*BN*, 31.5.01); Eaton
Mansions, Eaton Square, SW1; 13 South Molton
Street, W1; 4 and 6 Palace Green and Arundel
House, Kensington Palace Gardens, W8; and the
first buildings of the Children's Hospital, Vincent
Square, SW1 . 91—99 Oxford Street, W1 (*Bldr*,
5.11.04) has been demolished.

Outside London, Read and Macdonald did the
John Forest Library and five sets of rooms at
Lincoln College, Oxford (1905), and the Town
Hall at Lynton, North Devon, the gift of the
newspaper proprietor Sir George Newnes to mark
the coming of age of his son (Sir) Frank Newnes.
In Surrey they did Stoatly Hall, St George's Wood,
Bunch Cottage, Open Coombe and Marley Heights
(*AR*, 1911), all at Haslemere, and The Hostel at
Hindhead (*AR*, 1910).

REDFERN, Harry   1861—1950

Harry Redfern went to school at Abingdon,
Berkshire, was articled to Henry Woodyer, and
joined William Butterfield's office in 1877.
Commencing in private practice in 1896 he was
in partnership with John James Stevenson until
Stevenson's death in 1908.

At Cambridge Redfern did new buildings at
Christ's College and work at Magdalene College.
At Oxford he did the Chemical, Physical and
Biochemical Laboratories and work at Oriel and
St John's. With Stevenson Redfern did town
houses in Buckingham Palace Road, SW1 (1902),
and Queen's Gate, SW7, some houses for Cambridge
dons, and Helenstowe, Abingdon, Berkshire (*Bldr*,
24.8.01).

Redfern continued the interiors of Orient liners

Read and Macdonald: Stanford's, Long Acre, London
WC2. Narrow bricks enhance the Dutch character of this
beautiful, although strangely broad, composition.

which Stevenson had begun in 1891, doing SS
Ophir, and did the British Hospital, Port Said. He
was chief architect to the State Management
Districts (for the control of public houses) from
1915 to 1945 — this included much work at
Carlisle — and was a member of the Art Workers'
Guild.

Obit. RIBAJ, Apr., 1950, p. 245 *Bldr*, 19.5.50, p. 669.

REILLY, Professor Sir Charles Herbert, OBE, LLD
1874—1948

It can justly be said of Sir Charles Reilly that he
was a major force in helping the architectural
profession into the twentieth century. He made
his contribution not in London, facing Paris, but
in Liverpool, then the gateway to America.

Charles Herbert Reilly was the son of Charles

Charles H. Reilly: the most that can be said of this
building for the Students' Union, Liverpool,
is that it would have been done better
in the same style a century earlier.

Reilly (1845–1928), for forty years surveyor to
the Drapers' Company and the architect of
Throgmorton Avenue, EC2. Another son, Sir
Henry D'Arcy Cornelius Reilly, became Chief
Justice of Mysore. Reilly went to Merchant
Taylors' School and Queen's College, Cambridge.
On completing his university education he spent
two years in his father's office, followed by
pupillage with John Belcher during which he
attended King's College, Strand, WC2.

In 1900 Reilly entered into a brief association with
280   Stanley Peach (q.v.) – pioneer in the design of
302   electricity generating stations. In 1904 when
Reilly was lecturing at King's College, Professor
F. M. Simpson recommended him for the vacant
Roscoe Chair in Liverpool and he was appointed.
Reilly's was the one classical design for Liverpool
Anglican Cathedral in the competition of 1903,
favourably noticed by the assessors and perhaps
a factor in securing him the Chair.

As the gateway to North America, Liverpool was
a stimulating city in this period. When Sir William
Lever (1st Lord Leverhulme) proposed a Chair of
Civic Design for Liverpool University, Reilly was
instrumental in the appointment of Stanley
Adshead (q.v.), a friend from King's College and
Belcher days. Sir William also sent Reilly to the
USA where he met prominent American architects,
including Thomas Hastings, of Carrère and Hastings.

By this time the Chicago school's efforts to establish a rational architecture had been vanquished
by the neo-Classicism imported from France and,
in the wake of Professor Reilly's return, the new
style began to make its influence felt in Liverpool.
In spite of its cloak of classicism, the American
approach to building was a practical one and
Reilly's school produced a generation of able,
practical architects.

In the field of town planning Reilly made an
important contribution with his 'Reilly Plan', a
system of small, self-contained units within a
larger community.

302   He took an active interest in university and
Liverpool life, and designed the Students' Union
building (*Bldr*, 1.8.08) and Gilmour Hall (1908–
12) in neo-neo-Greek. (This was extended by
Reilly, Budden and Marshall in 1935, and by
Bridgwater, Shepheard and Epstein in 1961–3.)
Throughout his career Reilly kept in touch with
London and was for a time architectural editor
of *Country Life* and a reviewer on the *Architectural Review*, *The Builder's* (later *Architect's*)
Journal and *The Banker*. In black cloak and wide-
brimmed hat, Reilly was a familiar figure in both
cities at functions connected with the arts and was
an excellent critic of contemporary buildings. His
'London Streets and their Recent Buildings',
contributed to *Country Life* (1922–4), are
instructive, salutary and amusing. He also wrote
Representative British Architects of Today
(London, Batsford, 1931).

Charles H. Reilly: these two gables of the St John's Wood,
London NW8, Electricity Generating Station were to be
the first of twelve, and were the joint work of Reilly and Peach

Charles H. Reilly: St Barnabas, Shacklewell Lane, London E8. Interior.

Reilly's architectural work included cottages at Port Sunlight for Lever in 1905 and what he considered his best work, the simple classical interior of St Barnabas, Shacklewell Lane, Dalston, E8 (1910—11), for the Merchant Taylors' School Mission, and the east end of Holy Trinity, Wavertree, Liverpool, again in 1910—11 and in the same style.

In 1924 Reilly was instrumental in getting the New York architects Carrère and Hastings to design a block of luxury flats for the site of old Devonshire House, Piccadilly, for Cubitts. This was the first building in London where the plumbing services were put in *before* the partitions, a practice universal today. The building is now offices.

In 1943 Reilly received the Gold Medal for Architecture and he was knighted in 1944. There are three paintings of him in Liverpool. He figures in the 'New Testament Group' by Albert Lypinski, in the Faculty of Arts Common Room; the best portrait is by Augustus John, now in the School of Architecture, and the best likeness is by Marjorie Brooks (Lady Holford), in the University Club, Liverpool. His son is Lord Reilly, former director of the Council for Industrial Design.

RIBAJ, Nov., 1943, 'Presentation of the Royal Gold Medal'
Obit. RIBAJ, Feb., 1948, pp. 175, 212 and 228 *Bldr* 6.2.48, p. 161.

REYNOLDS, W. Bainbridge   1845—1935

Bainbridge Reynolds was articled for five years to J. P. Seddon and was assistant to G. E. Street during the building of the Royal Courts of Justice in the Strand. After a period as a draughtsman with the Royal Engineers he discovered his true bent, the designing and making of metalwork especially for church furniture and fittings, and set up a workshop at Old Town Works, Clapham, SW4.

Examples of the work of Bainbridge Reynolds occur at St Paul's Cathedral, Westminster Abbey, York Minster, Canterbury, Durham, Norwich and Llandaff cathedrals, at Christchurch Priory and in many churches, including St Cuthbert, Philbeach Gardens, Kensington, SW5, where his lectern is unique. Bainbridge Reynolds also made fittings for C. F. A. Voysey, and for Sir Giles Gilbert Scott for the Liverpool Anglican Cathedral. After 1900 he did a memorial to Canon T. T. Carter at St Andrew, Clewer, Windsor, and (1903—4) the screen, font cover, cross and vessels for the Church of the Ascension, Malvern Link, for the architect Walter Tapper. He was a member of the Art Workers' Guild.

Obit. RIBAJ, 11.5.35, p. 789.

REYNOLDS-STEPHENS, Sir William Ernest 1862—1943

Reynolds-Stephens was born in Detroit, USA, of British parents, educated in England and Germany, and trained as a painter and sculptor first at Heatherley's, then at the Royal Academy Schools which he entered in 1884. He worked in the manner of Alfred Gilbert, experimented with materials and, like Lynn-Jenkins, experimented with the electro-deposit process.

A beautiful work which early indicated his powers is the bronze grille to a bank (now National Westminster), High Street, Croydon (1889, architect William Campbell Jones).

His most interesting work is in the church of St Mary the Virgin, Great Warley, Essex (1901—5), for the architect Charles Harrison Townsend. Reynolds-Stephens did the whole of the interior fittings and decoration. The plaster reliefs of the arch ribs, representing the rose of Sharon and coated in aluminium leaf, anticipated Art Deco decoration by some twenty-five years. The dome of the apse is also covered in aluminium leaf. The rood screen, which bears a brass cross inlaid with marble and supported by angels, is constructed in brass in the form of pomegranate trees with mother-of-pearl flowers and ruby glass fruit. In each tree is an angel in oxidised silver. The organ front is of various metals; the altar rail, in dark Irish green marble, has the crown of thorns in brass in each panel.

Sir William Reynolds-Stephens: this brass cross (*above*), inlaid with marble, surmounts the rood-screen at St Mary the Virgin, Great Warley, Essex, designed by Harrison Townsend.

Part of this screen was shown at the Royal Academy in 1903 under the title 'The fruit of the spirit is love, joy, peace, long-suffering, gentleness, goodness, faith ...' (Galatians 5: 22, 23). The pulpit is of beaten copper inlaid with turquoise enamels and decorated with stylised brass trees. The same device of trees appears in the lectern; the chapel screen is of wood in Art Nouveau forms. But the glimpse of a new art ends here, for the war memorial of the First World War in statuary marble, also by Reynolds-Stephens, is in a classical idiom. The electroliers are of various metals, including galvanised iron, ornamented with glass and enamels.

Reynolds-Stephens did 'Archbishop Davidson' for the courtyard of Lambeth Palace, SE1; 'Fame' for Hong Kong; and in 1913 a monument to Sir William Orchardson in St Paul's Cathedral. He was knighted in 1931.

He was a member of the Art Workers' Guild.

'Art Nouveau in Essex' by John Malton in *The Anti-Rationalists*, Architectural Press, London, 1973
Obit. Bldr, 5.3.43, p. 225.

RHIND, William Birnie, RSA   1855—1933

W. B. Rhind was trained in the studio of his father, John Rhind, and attended Edinburgh School of Art and the Royal Scottish Academy School. His brother, John Massey Rhind, who trained under Gilbert and Brock, had a successful career as a sculptor in the USA. Birnie Rhind did sculpture for the central doorway of the Scottish Portrait Gallery, Edinburgh; the 'Mary Queen of Scots'

group, Edinburgh; sculptures for the Edinburgh offices of *The Scotsman*; the Black Watch memorial (South African War) on the Mound, Princes Street Gardens, Edinburgh; and the groups 'Sculpture' and 'Religion' on the Glasgow Art Gallery. Outside Scotland he did the crowning figures of 'The River Mersey' and 'The Ocean' on the Liverpool Cotton Exchange for Matear and Simon (which had other sculpture by E. O. Griffith of Liverpool and has been demolished), and sculpture for the Manitoba Parliament Building, Winnipeg, for the architect F. W. Simon (*q.v.*).

Obit. Bldr 21.7.33, p. 90.

RICARDO, Halsey Ralph   1854—1928

Halsey Ricardo was born at Bath, grandson of the Dutch-Jewish economist of Portuguese origin, David Ricardo (1772—1823), founder of the classical school of political economy. Halsey Ricardo's father, David Ricardo, had started training as an architect, but turned to business and banking. Halsey Ricardo was at Rugby when the school chapel was being built by William Butterfield. He was articled to a Cheltenham architect, John Middleton, and afterwards a pupil and assistant to Basil Champneys. After a year in Italy, Ricardo set up on his own account in London in 1878. He married Kathleen Rendel, daughter of the civil engineer Sir Alexander Meadows Rendel, of the firm of Rendel and Robertson, which is still in operation as Rendel, Palmer and Tritton.

One of Halsey Ricardo's first works was a small office building for Sir Alexander Rendel, at 8 Great George Street, Westminster, SW1. Domestic in appearance and with windows prettily varied and extended over four-fifths of the frontage, this was

△ Halsey Ricardo: Howrah Railway Station, Calcutta.

▽ Halsey Ricardo: gate and gateway to nos. 55 and 57 Melbury Road, London W14. The architect's name is incised in the stone balustrade.

one of those functional designs of the 1880s which tended to make the 'Wrenaissance' revival look like a retrograde step. Ricardo also did the porch at Hatchlands, near East Clandon, Surrey, in 1889.

The firm of Rendel and Robertson were builders of Indian railways and Halsey Ricardo designed Howrah Station, Calcutta, for the East Indian Bengal and Nagpur Railway (now the Central Indian Railway; *Bldr*, 11.5.01), an imaginative design with an exterior in brick and coloured tile. The architect and critic H. S. Goodhart-Rendel, who also carried out buildings in India, recalled:

> I remember his telling me of the large decorative grilles that he used there, instead of windows, in places where ventilation was of prime importance. If I remember right, they must be of metal ... I think he spoke of peacocks in outline, with blue and green glass for the eyes of their tails ... since peacocks, jewels, delicate and fanciful traceries, all in the intricate imagery of the East, were prominent in the rich furniture of his mind. (*RIBAJ*, 7.12.35).

In London, Halsey Ricardo did 55 and 57, Melbury Road, a pair of houses faced with brown salt-glazed bricks and with louvred shutters, in that once unique, but unfortunately now spoilt, street of houses designed by Royal Academicians for Royal Academicians in Kensington, W14.

Halsey Ricardo: 8 Addison Road, London W8. This
house for Sir Ernest Debenham is faced from ground to
chimney tops with green and blue glazed bricks with
lavish glazed faience dressings. Art Workers' Guild
brethren contributed to the interior decoration.

No. 55 was for his father-in-law, No. 57 for Sir Ernest Debenham. Ricardo proudly had his name cut in fine Roman letters in the wall of the forecourt. He also designed a house in Brooke Market, Hatton Garden, EC1; Fox Oak, Burhill, Surrey, for his brother, Arthur Ricardo; cottages at Whiteley Village — a group designed for retired staff of the retail stores in which many of his contemporaries also designed a part; and additions to Bishopsford, Mitcham, Surrey (*Bldr*, 22.3.02).

307
164   Halsey Ricardo designed his own home, Woodside, Graffham, near Petworth in Sussex, since occupied by his son, the engineer Sir Harry Ricardo. Also at Graffham, Ricardo made additions to a house for the painter Maresco Pearce, for whom he did 3 Old Church Street, SW3. Ernest Gimson, who made furniture for it, had prepared a design, but was baffled by such practical matters as dealing with district surveyors, drainage and party-walls. Pearce married Ricardo's daughter Anna; their son is the architect John Ricardo Pearce.

Halsey Ricardo was one of the team of Art Workers which submitted a design in the second competition for the Liverpool Anglican Cathedral. It included W. R. Lethaby, with whom Ricardo also submitted a design for the layout of the First Garden City at Letchworth in 1903.

306   Ricardo introduced the work of fellow Art Workers at the astonishing faience-faced 8 Addison Road for Sir Ernest Debenham (*AR*, 1905; RA, 1907) — William Aumonier's marble carvings, George Jack's balustrades, E. S. Prior's coloured glass, Ernest Gimson's modelled plasterwork, and

ironmongery (hardware), electric light switch plates and rainwater heads by the Birmingham Guild of Handicraft. The house also included a range of De Morgan tiles. The De Morgan Pottery at Chelsea and Fulham was one of Ricardo's absorbing interests and he was a partner of the founder, William Frend De Morgan, from 1888 to 1898. Ricardo's niece, the late Baroness Stocks, wrote in *My Commonplace Book* (Peter Davies, London, 1970):

> Under Ricardian influences Rendel households, our own included, became colourful with De Morgan tiles and pottery. To keep them company we all became patrons of Morris wallpapers, Morris cretonnes and Morris chairs ...

The Rendels and Ricardos used to spend their holidays at West Bay, Bridport, Dorset, where E. S. Prior's Pier Terrace may have been the inspiration when Ricardo was called upon to design the 'Home of Rest' — a children's convalescent home at Littlehampton, Sussex (RA, 1890). But his design was not adopted. Better than H. T. Hare's was Ricardo's unsuccessful design for the Municipal Buildings, Oxford (RA, 1892). Ricardo founded the Civic Art Association. Among his suggestions was the painting of street furniture in a distinctive colour for each London borough.

Although he enjoyed private means and never had to rely completely on his practice for a livelihood, Ricardo never employed an assistant or an office boy. After 1914, he did Bladen Valley Hamlet, Briantspuddle, Dorset, for Sir Ernest Debenham,

Halsey Ricardo's own house, Woodside, Graffham, Sussex. It has decorated tiles by William De Morgan.

with MacDonald Gill (Eric Gill did the war memorial there); the Eyot House, Sonning, Berkshire; and Norwood House, Charlwood, Surrey, where he had earlier done Ricketswood (1885).

Blunt, Reginald (ed.), *The Cheyne Book of Chelsea China and Pottery* (article on Halsey Ricardo), London, 1924
Country Life, 13.11.75, pp. 1290–3, and 20.11.75, pp. 1388–9: 'The Town Houses of Halsey Ricardo', by Madge Garland
RIBAJ, 7.12.35, pp. 117–31, article by H. S. Goodhart-Rendel
Obit. *RIBAJ*, 10.3.28, p. 312 *Bldr*, 24.2.28 p. 326.

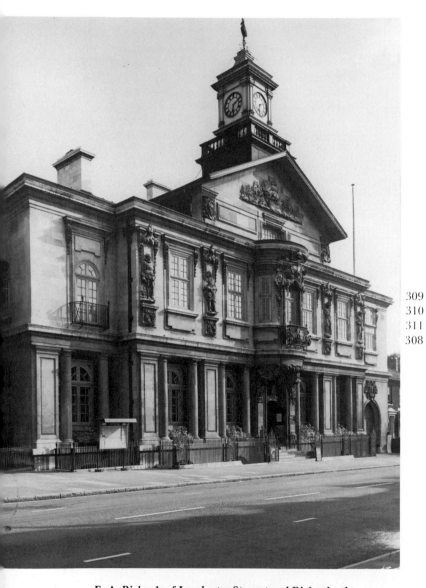

309
310
311
308

E. A. Rickards of Lanchester Stewart and Rickards: the Town Hall, Deptford, London SE8. Although far from the waterfront this building proclaims a maritime heritage, its form recalling a custom house and its sculpture, by H. C. Fehr and Paul Montford, the carved poops of ships.

(*Facing page*) E. A. Rickards: the profusion of architectural and sculptural forms produces an outline to the tower of Cardiff City Hall reminiscent of Indian work. The group, 'Unity and Patriotism', is by Henry Poole.

RICKARDS, Edwin Alfred   1872–1920

E. A. Rickards was born in Chelsea, SW3 and lived in the Fulham Road where for a short time he helped his mother in her drapery shop. At the age of fifteen he joined the office of Richard J. Lovell, and in the following year entered the Royal Academy Schools. At seventeen he went to Eadle and Myers and in the course of the next two years worked in turn for Dunn and Watson, Howard Ince, Leonard Stokes, George Sherrin and William Flockhart. At Sherrin's office Rickards assisted in the completion of the dome and lantern of the Oratory Church, Brompton Road, SW7, begun by Herbert Gribble. The lantern is probably Rickards's earliest executed work.

At twenty-one Rickards was working too hard and near collapse, and H. V. Lanchester, whom he had met in Sherrin's office, persuaded him to take a holiday in Italy. On his return, Lanchester, James Stewart and Rickards joined in a partnership which largely depended upon winning one of the many architectural competitions then being held for the design of public buildings.

Rickards's brilliant designing and draughtsmanship were balanced by the sound judgement and guiding hand of Lanchester so that Rickards was able to say towards the end of his short life, 'I never did any good until I met Lanchester'. The other partner in the firm, James Stewart, had won the Royal Academy Schools Gold Medal and Travelling Studentship in 1893 with a 'Design for a Provincial Town Hall'. Their first great competition win was for the Cardiff City Hall and Law Courts (1897). Other competition successes followed including, in 1899, the Godalming Town Hall (not built) and Deptford Town Hall, SE8 (1903) with its sculptures by Henry Poole, H. C. Fehr, Paul Montford and Donald McGill. Also in 1903 they won the competition for the Hull Art School (*Bldr*, 25.4.03).

In 1904 Rickards designed the base for Horace Montford's statue of John Milton in front of St Giles, Cripplegate, EC2 (destroyed) and the grand doorway of Bovril's premises in Golden Lane, EC1, is also by Rickards. Stewart died in 1904. In the following year Lanchester and Rickards won the major competition for the Wesleyan Central Convocation Hall, Westminster, which, like Cardiff, was considered a great prize because of the importance of the site, for the Central Hall was to be built on the site of the Royal Westminster Aquarium and the short-lived Imperial Theatre. Again, the great guns of the competition world competed (*Bldr*, 28.12.07).

With the pen or pencil as his baton, Rickards orchestrated the shapes which the building craftsmen translated into stone, marble, bronze, wood and plaster under the watchful eye of Lanchester. The inspiration had come from France, from Charles Garnier's Opera House and from visits to Vienna (*Bldr*, 28.5.10, 'The Art of the Monument').

E. A. Rickards: 144 to 147 New Bond Street, London W1, once Colnaghi and Obach's Gallery. The porcelain figure, by Henry Poole, together with the baroque central window, pulls this composition together.

Rickards designed several monuments himself: the fountain in front of the Victoria Rooms, Clifton, Bristol (sculptor, Henry Poole, 1907; *Bldr*, 13.1.11), with the Edward VII statue behind (1913); Captain Albert Ball, VC, at Nottingham (by Poole again, 1918).

Writing in 1920, James Bone, art critic of *The Manchester Guardian*, describes Rickards as carrying further the 'cavalier spirit in architecture' expressed in Belcher and Pite's Chartered Accountants' Hall in Moorgate, EC2, 'but his tragedy was that the Fates doomed him to express it chiefly through two religious buildings, the Wesleyan Central Hall and the Christian Science Church in Curzon Street'. Bone saw the Art Gallery of Colnaghi and Obach, 144—147 New Bond Street, as Rickards at his best, 'combining opulence and taste with a touch of refined swagger that perfectly express the Bond Street idea'. Completed in 1912, the building is now occupied by Frank Partridge.

Contemporary accounts are full of references to Rickards's personal brilliance which attracted many friends, including Arnold Bennett — Rickards drew one of the best-known caricatures of the novelist and illustrated his *Paris Nights* and *From the Log of the Vesta*. Bennett placed him

E. A. Rickards, architect, and Henry Poole, sculptor: the City Hall, Cardiff.

E. A. Rickards, architect, and Henry Poole, sculptor:
the principal front of Cardiff City Hall, with its dome,
recalls the Grand and Petit Palais of the Paris Exhibition
of 1900.

with H. G. Wells as one of 'the two most interesting,
provocative and stimulating men I have yet encoun-
tered'. Professor C. H. Reilly said of him: 'He was
the Augustus John of our profession, vigorous and
disturbing — he could out-Walcot Walcot — he
made the most delicate drawings of the Russian
Ballet to illustrate an article of Arnold Bennett's.'

Rickards took Bennett to see Westminster Cathedral in progress and they came across the architect,
J. F. Bentley, wandering under the dome, a scene
which Bennett put into his novel, *The Roll Call*,
in which the young architect George Cannon is
modelled on Rickards. Visits with Rickards and the
sculptor Henry Poole to the Paris of *la belle époque*
led Bennett to place episodes in his *Old Wives' Tale*
there.

In 1916 Rickards volunteered for military service
in the First World War. After three months in
France he was invalided home, but undertook the

supervision of the building of the Army Transport
Depot at Slough during a severe winter and in
1919 became seriously ill. Arnold Bennett noted
in his journal:

> Went down to Bournemouth to see Rickards.
> Glimpses through Rickards of a vast world
> of sickness and tragedy — a whole world
> complete in itself and looking angrily and
> resentfully and longingly at our world — all
> that he so extremely *savoured* rather than
> enjoyed.

Asked if there was anything he wanted, Rickards
replied, 'Yes, I want the world'.

*The Art of E. A. Rickards, comprising A Collection of
his Architectural Drawings, Paintings and Sketches with
a Personal Sketch by Arnold Bennett, etc.* London, 1920

Obit. RIBAJ 25.9.20, pp. 470—473 *Bldr*, 3.9.20, pp.
247—251 and 24.9, pp. 328–337.

The holding of the County Hall Competition and the task of commencing the difficult foundations on Lambeth Marsh came under Riley's direction until work was interrupted by the First World War. Riley retired in 1919, being succeeded by G. Topham Forrest, and set up in private practice with E. B. Glanfield.

Obit. RIBAJ, 24.1.38, p. 317 *Bldr,* 19.11.37, p. 917.

ROBSON, Philip Appleby 1871–1951

Philip Robson was the son of E. R. Robson (1836–1917), the first architect to the London School Board (1870). He was articled to J. L. Pearson, RA, the architect of Truro Cathedral. Robson worked in the office of his father and in the Home Office, the Scottish Office, and other government departments, before setting up in practice on his own account. He continued his father's interest in schools, doing the tall, well-windowed, red-brick Queen Anne style (Norman Shaw version) school buildings that are such a familiar part of the landscape seen from the heights of Hampstead,

W. E. Riley. *Above:* **Carrington House, Brookmill Road, SE8. One of the L.C.C. hostels carried out under Riley's direction.** *Right:* **Arnold Circus, Boundary Street, Shoreditch, E2, carried out under Riley to replace the infamous Nichol.**

RILEY, William Edward 1852–1937

W. E. Riley was born at Ossett, W. Riding, the son of a manufacturer of fireworks. He went to Batley Grammar School and was articled to William Crutchley of Wakefield in 1868. In 1872 he became assistant to Beck and Lee of Finsbury Circus, EC2. In 1877 Riley joined the staff of the director of architectural and engineering works at the Admiralty. In 1896 he was made an assistant director and put in charge of works at Devonport, Chatham and Portsmouth, Halifax, Nova Scotia, Bermuda, Malta and Colombo.

In 1899 Riley succeeded Thomas Blashill (1831–1905) as Architect to the London County Council and was in charge of the Council's first programme of slum clearance, Boundary Street, Shoreditch, E2 and Millbank, SW1, which set such a good example to other municipalities. The first of the Council's cottage estates were also commenced under Riley, who carried out a programme of building model lodging houses and provided the London Fire Brigade with a series of new fire stations. Also under Riley's direction the London School Board's programme, commenced by E. R. Robson and continued to T. J. Bailey, was taken over by the London County Council in 1904, and the new building for the Central School of Arts and Crafts was built on the widened Southampton Row (*Bldr,* 16.5.08).

312
313

10
313

W. E. Riley: London Fire Brigade Station, Old Court Place, Kensington, W8, carried out under Riley.

Highgate, Wimbledon, Sydenham and Blackheath (*see also under* Bailey, Thomas Jerram).

Philip Robson did the St George's Schools, South Street, W1 (1898—9); St Gabriel's College, Cormont Road, Camberwell, SE5 (1899—1903; *Bldr*, 18.11.05); and the Eastbourne School of Art and Technical College (1903—4; *Bldr*, 3.9.04). The latter consisted of the Free Library, Science and Art Schools, a fire station and electricity show-room, and was replaced by a new building after destruction in the Second World War. He also did the High School for Girls, Rotherham, W. Riding (*Bldr*, 14.5.10) and the church of St Andrew, Sandhurst Road, Catford, SE6 (1904; *Bldr*, 15 and 22.4.21).

AR, June, 1958, pp. 293–8: 'Towers of Learning', by David Gregory Jones

Obit. RIBAJ, Apr., 1952, p. 230.

ROMAINE-WALKER, William Henry
1854—1940

W. H. Romaine-Walker went to Lancing College and was articled to G. E. Street. He went into practice with Augustus W. Tanner, Street's

W. E. Riley: housing in Arnold Circus, Boundary Street, Shoreditch, E2, for the L.C.C.

manager, and together they undertook church restoration work and the additions to Wimborne Minster, Dorset. In 1887 they did the Pitt-Rivers Museum in Oxford, and on General Lane-Fox Pitt-Rivers's estate at Tollard Royal, Wiltshire, they did a jubilee room — built as a chapel — a village hall and the north gate of Rushmore Park.

After Tanner became a London District Surveyor, Romaine-Walker entered into partnership with Francis Besant in 1900. Their practice consisted of new town houses and alterations to many existing ones. Of the former, the most outstanding is Sunderland House in Curzon Street for which the French architect Alphonse Duchêne was consultant. Built for the Duke of Marlborough, the house is in a Louis XV style of gigantic proportions, crammed next to the small streets of Shepherd Market, Mayfair, W1. (The building is now offices.) In contrast, Stanhope House, 47 Park Lane (now a bank), built between 1899 and 1901 for the soap manufacturer, Hudson, in Forest of Dean stone, is in finely detailed fifteenth-century Gothic. Their other town houses were 1 and 2 Hamilton Place, and 2 Seamore (now Curzon) Place, W1.

At Chatsworth House, Derbyshire, for the Duke of Devonshire, Romaine-Walker and Besant did the hall staircase and galleries. They also did gardens for Sir Julius Wernher at Luton Hoo in Bedfordshire and a chapel for Luton parish church. Their church work was continued at St Michael, Brighton, where they did the reredos and decorations of the chancel, and at All Saints, Hastings, where they did decorations. Their best-known church additions are at the Jesuit Church of the Immaculate Conception, Farm Street, Mayfair, W1. Here the north aisle, the Calvary Chapel (1901—3) and the Chapel of the English Martyrs are their work. They also did the Pompeiian-style decorations in Beaumont College, Berkshire.

In 1905 Romaine-Walker and Besant did decorative panels to the additions by James Wyatt at the Old Town Hall (now the Mansion House) in Liverpool. In 1911 Romaine-Walker took into partnership Gilbert H. Jenkins, his chief assistant since 1901 and brother of the sculptor F. Lynn-Jenkins (q.v.). Between 1910 and 1914 they did the new banqueting hall and ballroom at Derby House, Stratford Place, W1; remodelled 34 and altered 46 Park Street, W1, and 19 Upper Brook Street (1903—4). They altered and extended Knowsley Hall, Lancashire; Holme Lacy, Herefordshire; Buckland, Berkshire; and Orozvar Castle in Hungary (completed during the First World War).

Romaine-Walker also designed two large houses, one at Nuneham Paddox, Warwickshire, for R. Emmett, the other Rhinefield Lodge, Lyndhurst, Hampshire (1889), a stone Tudor style mansion of great elaboration.

In 1928 Romaine-Walker and Jenkins did 68 Pall Mall, containing a branch of Lloyds Bank with offices and a penthouse over. The elevations, by Sir Edwin Lutyens, complete this little piazza which has buildings by Inigo Jones, Wren and Norman Shaw.

Romaine-Walker and Jenkins's best-known works are the extensions to the original building of the Tate Gallery, Millbank, SW1 (by S. R. J. Smith, 1897). Those of 1909 were the gift of Joseph Duveen senior, those of 1937, for which the American architect John Russell Pope (1874—1937) was consultant, were the gift of his son, Lord Duveen. They also designed Duveen's gift to the British Museum of a gallery to house the Elgin Marbles.

Obit. RIBAJ, 20.5.40, p. 181 (notice only) *Bldr*, 17.5.40, p. 582.

ROWNTREE, Fred   1860—1927

Rowntree was born at Scarborough and went to Bootham School, York. He was a member of the Society of Friends. Rowntree was articled in 1876 to C. A. Bury of Scarborough and was an assistant to Edward Burgess. After a short time in practice in Scarborough he became a partner of Malcolm Stark in Glasgow in 1890.

Rowntree designed a number of Meeting Houses and schools for the Society of Friends including additions to existing schools. In 1912 he won a competition for the design of the West China University at Chengtu, Szechuan, West China.

Rowntree joined with Charles Spooner and A. J. Penty in an enterprise employing Belgian refugees from the First World War in the pre-fabrication of buildings for re-erection in war-ravaged Belgium after the Armistice of 1918.

Rowntree also designed the Scottish Temperance Life Assurance building, Cheapside, EC2, and Newspaper House, Fleet Street, EC4.

In 1912 his sons, Douglas and Colin Rowntree, became partners.

Obit. Bldr, 14.1.27, p. 88   28.1, p. 150.

RUNTZ, Ernest Augustus   1859—1913

Ernest Runtz was articled in 1875 to Samuel Walker, an auctioneer, valuer and estate agent, and became his partner in 1883. At the age of thirty, Runtz took up the study of architecture, attending Professor Roger Smith's lectures at University College, Gower Street, where he won the Donaldson Silver Medal for Fine Art. After two years' further study under Frederick Farrow he qualified as an architect and began practice in 1897.

Runtz put in a scheme in the limited competition for the façades on Aldwych, the new crescent opened in 1905 to link the new Kingsway with the Strand. Although no comprehensive design was adopted, Runtz designed the Gaiety Theatre and the adjoining Gaiety Restaurant (*Bldr*, 25.4.08), Norman Shaw advising on the elevations. In 1907 Runtz did the Norwich Union Assurance building, Piccadilly, and 39 St James's Street, SW1. In spite of a wealth of Pentelikos and Cipollino marble and a bronze group by H. C. Binney, all wastefully employed, this garbled version of John Belcher's neo-Baroque is shown up by the Royal Insurance building opposite — Belcher and Joass's Mannerist *tour de force*. Runtz's office buildings at Storey's Gate, SW1 (1910) suffered a similar fate, from which the Gaiety Theatre and Restaurant were undoubtedly saved by Norman Shaw.

Runtz's partners were A. C. Bredan and George McLean Ford (d. 1921) from Edinburgh. His work before the turn of the century had included the Empire Palace of Varieties, Middlesbrough (1896–7), the Marine Palace of Varieties, Hastings, (1897–9), and the Crown Theatre, Peckham, SE15 (1898; RA, 1899), later called the Peckham Hippodrome, a remarkable building. With Otto Sachs and Walter Emden, Ernest Runtz was one of those who pressed for more fire precautions in theatres.

Ernest Runtz's other works include:

1901	Second rebuilding of the Adelphi Theatre, Strand, WC2 (rebuilt 1930 by E. Schaufelberg)
1904	Theatre Royal, New Street, Birmingham
	St Giles's Mission Church, Great Wild Street WC2 (RA 1904)
1905	Old Bank House, Lewes, Sussex (*AR*, 13.10.05)
1908	Premises in Berners Street, W1 (*Bldr*, 24.10.08)

Obit. RIBAJ, 8.11.13 p. 29.

RUSSELL, Samuel Bridgman   1864–1955

S. B. Russell was educated privately, was articled to H. Bridgman and entered the Royal Academy Schools in 1882. He worked in the offices of Chatfield Clarke and William Flockhart and joined J. G. S. Gibson (*q.v.*) in partnership *c.* 1889. They did the Passmore Edwards Libraries at Plaistow, Poplar and Bow, E3 (RA, 1904); the Bromley Cottage Hospital, Kent; Parker Street Hostel for the LCC (1893); and the W. Riding County Hall and Museum in Wakefield (1894–8), all resulting from competitions won jointly. They were second on Cardiff City Hall.

The partnership ended in 1900 and Russell went into partnership next with Mallows and Grocock

to compete for Plumstead (now Woolwich) Town Hall, SE18, and then with Edwin Cooper (*q.v.*). The association with Cooper brought still more wins — Hull Town Hall and Law Courts (with Davis and Mallows) (*Bldr*, 2.9.05); the Royal Grammar School, Newcastle upon Tyne; the Girls' Grammar School, Saltburn, N. Riding; Middlesbrough Public Library; Rochester Technical Institute, Kent; Burslem Public Buildings, Staffordshire; and Watford Boys' Grammar School, Hertfordshire. Russell, alone, did a social club at West Ham, E15 (*Bldr*, 24.8.01).

Although Russell and Cooper reached the final stage of the London County Hall Competition, even this combination of talent did not survive and the partnership ended in 1912. Each continued alone until Russell was joined by his son, R. T. Russell, CIE, DSO.

Russell later was Chief Architect at the Ministry of Health which he had joined during the First World War to work as one of the architects on the munitions town of Gretna. He retired in 1939. Russell took out patents for an internal combustion engine and a steam turbine and, said his son, would have made as good an engineer as he was an architect.

Obit. Bldr, 12.8.55, pp. 278 and 305.

SACHS, Edwin Otto   1870–1919

Otto Sachs was born in London and went to University College. He spent some time on the Continent studying architecture, and developed a keen interest in fire-fighting services and fire-prevention, particularly with regard to theatre construction and equipment, and was instrumental in introducing the safety curtain. Sachs commenced practice in London in 1892 and, with Ernest Woodrow, compiled *Modern Opera Houses and Theatres* (Batsford, 1896) — a monumental work in three folio volumes, illustrated by line drawings of every theatre and opera house of importance in Europe and England, with statistics of fires and details of safety apparatus.

Sachs joined in partnership with G. Spencer Hoffmann, a pupil of Sir Arthur Blomfield, with whom he did 3–7 Waterloo Place, SW1, to the external design of Sir William Emerson. However, Sachs's work consisted principally of alterations to existing theatres, often to meet new safety regulations. He was consulting architect to the Royal Opera House, Covent Garden, WC2, where in 1901, with great dispatch he improved the stage and proscenium.

The disastrous Paris Charity Bazaar fire of 1897 led Sachs to form the British Fire Prevention Committee, and after the terrible Iroquois Theatre fire in Chicago in 1903, Sachs, Walter Emden and Ernest Runtz (*q.v.*) put forward proposals which helped the LCC in drawing up new safety regulations for theatres. Before that latest disaster Sachs had already organised an International Fire Exhibition where a monument was unveiled to James Braidwood of the London Fire Brigade, killed in the great Tooley Street fire of 1861, in Southwark, SE1.

Sachs designed the Building Trades' gift of Almshouses for Discharged Soldiers, Bisley, Surrey (*Bldr*, 10.2.09); factories in Dalston, E8 (RA, 1902 and 1903); and the British Uralite Factory, Higham, Kent. (Uralite, an asbestos product — the invention of a Russian artillery officer, Colonel Imchenetsky — is a component in the construction of theatre safety curtains.)

Obit. *Bldr,* 12.9.19, pp. 260 and 286.

SALISBURY, Frank Owen, CVO, LlD 1874—1962

Frank Salisbury was born at Harpenden, Hertfordshire, the son of H. Salisbury. He was educated at home and for three years studied painting under his brother, H. J. Salisbury, who did some stained-glass work at St Albans Abbey. Salisbury then attended Heatherley's School and the Royal Academy Schools, which he entered in 1893 and where he won the Landseer Prize. He visited Italy in 1896, and in 1899 exhibited at the Royal Academy a portrait of Alice Maud Greenwood, whom he married in 1901. It seems likely that he studied heroic historical painting under Edwin Austin Abbey.

Salisbury did 'The Nativity' at Harpenden Church and 'Great Artists of Chelsea' in Chelsea Vestry Hall, SW3. He moved to Sarum Chase, which he had built in West Heath Road, Hampstead, NW3, and published his memoirs under the title *Portrait and Pageant.*

Other works by Salisbury include:

1907	'The Passing of Queen Eleanor' (RA, 1908) presented to St Albans Abbey in 1918
1910	'The Trial of Catherine of Aragon' (for a corridor of the House of Lords, under the direction of Edwin Austin Abbey)
	Painting in the Council Chamber, Glamorgan County Hall, for E. Vincent Harris and Thomas Moodie
1912	'Alfred the Great' and others in the Royal Exchange, EC3
	Paintings in Liverpool Town Hall
	Twelve paintings in the Queen Victoria Memorial, Calcutta, depicting the main events in the life of the Queen

Salisbury, Frank O., *Portrait and Pageant, Kings, Presidents and People*, London, 1944
Salisbury, Frank O., *Sarum Chase*, London, 1953

SALMON, James   1873—1924

James Salmon was the son of W. Forrest Salmon (1843—1911) and the grandson of James Salmon who founded the firm (*c.* 1825). He was articled to his grandfather's firm in 1888 and to William Leiper in 1890, studied at the Glasgow School of Art and entered what was now his father's firm in 1898. The previous year, J. G. Gillespie, an assistant and an able designer, had become a partner.

James Salmon: Lion Chambers, 170—2 Hope Street, Glasgow. An early example of the free treatment of reinforced concrete by Gustav Mouchel, using the Hennebique system.

James Salmon: the Savings Bank of Glasgow, 752—6
Argyle Street. Sculpture by Albert Hodge.

At the turn of the century, Glasgow led the way
in the design and construction of city buildings.
Although the local grey stone provoked some hard
thinking, it led occasionally to some playful
solutions. James Salmon's most interesting buildings in Glasgow are 142—144 St Vincent Street,
nicknamed 'The Hatrack' (the finial has been
removed), and Anderston Savings Bank, 752—
756 Argyle Street, both done in 1899. The former
offers a clever solution to a narrow frontage, while
the latter displays some delicate sculpture with
Art Nouveau tendencies by Albert Hodge.

Salmon's other pre-1900 buildings in Glasgow
included the remodelling of the interior of 22
Park Circus (1897); Mercantile Chambers,
39—69 Bothwell Street, Blythswood; St Andrew's
East Church Hall, 685 Alexandra Parade (the
church was done by James Miller in 1904); the
British Linen Bank (now Bank of Scotland), 162
Gorbals Street (1899); and 816—818 Govan Road,
where the carving is by Derwent Wood (q.v.) and
the Dutch sculptor Johan Keller. Outside Glasgow
in this period he did the Marine Hotel in Troon,
Ayrshire (1897) and Rowanhill, Kilmacolm,
Renfrew, for his father (1898).

Salmon, Son and Gillespie entered designs for a
great many competitions, including the first round
of the London County Hall Competition in 1907,
but their only successful design, that for Stirling
Municipal Buildings in the same year, was not
built.

James Salmon: 142 and 144 St Vincent Street, Glasgow.
Nicknamed 'The Hatrack'. A narrow building expressing
the lively character of Glasgow commercial work of the 1900s.

James Salmon's later works included:

In Glasgow

1893-1905	Scottish Temperance League Building, 106–108 Hope Street (*AA*, 1894)	
1899-1900	12 University Gardens	
317		Glasgow Savings Bank, Anderston Branch (*Bldr*, 21.3.03)
1902	Lloyd Morris Memorial Congregational Church, Rutherglen Road, Hutchesontown (demolished 1972)	
1903-4	79 West Regent Street (remodelling of façade)	
316 1906	Lion Chambers, 170–172 Hope Street (reinforced concrete structure by Gustav Mouchel)	
	Catholic Apostolic Church, 340–362 McAslin Street, Townhead (north aisle and narthex)	
1914	Dalmarnoch Congregational Church and Hall 231 Dalmarnoch Road	

Outside Glasgow

1904	Lanfine Cottage Hospital, Broomhill, Kirkintilloch, Dunbartonshire
1905	Mirjanoshta (now the Roman Catholic Bishop's House), Kilmacolm, Renfrewshire
1906	North Lodge, Edzell, Forfarshire
1906-8	School at Cartsburn, Greenock (destroyed in the Second World War)
1907	Nether Knockbuckle, Dilkusha and Den-o-'Gryffe, Kilmacolm

Obit. Bldr, 2.5.24, p. 741.

SCHENCK, Frederick E. E. *floruit c.* 1900

Frederick Schenck received his training at Edinburgh and at Hanley Schools of Art and was a National Scholar from 1873 until 1875, when he was appointed art master at Hanley. During the 1880s Schenck worked for several potteries including those of George Jones, Wedgwood and Brown Westhead Moore. About 1888 Schenck moved from Basford, Stoke-on-Trent to London and from 1889 showed models for architectural relief sculpture at the Arts and Crafts Exhibition Society.

Schenck worked mainly for architects. In 1898 he did the sculpture and carving on 37 Harley Street for Beresford Pite (*q.v.*) and for H. T. Hare (*q.v.*) he did the carving on Stafford County Offices in 1896, on Oxford Municipal Buildings in 1897, on Shoreditch Public Library and Baths and Hammersmith Public Library in 1904 and on Islington Central Library in 1905.

204
205 Schenck's best known London work, until it was demolished in 1961, was the low-relief figures, personifying Hope, Wisdom and Peace, on Ingram House, 196 Strand, W.C.2. for the United Kingdom Provident Institution, done in 1906.

SCHULTZ, Robert Weir, *see* WEIR, Robert Weir Schultz

SCOTT, Charles Marriott Oldrid 1880–1952

C. M. Oldrid Scott was the seventh son of J. Oldrid Scott (1842–1913), and was a grandson of Sir George Gilbert Scott and a cousin of Sir Giles Gilbert Scott, RA. He was articled to Sir Reginald Blomfield, and afterwards did many church restorations, including Hillesden Church, Buckinghamshire, where his grandfather had dedicated himself to architecture.

With his father, Oldrid Scott did All Saints, Newborough, Staffordshire (1901), Milton Church, Portsmouth, and the Rectory, Oxted, Surrey (*Bldr*, 24.12.04). With C. T. Miles of Bournemouth, they designed St Andrew, Boscombe (1907) and All Saints, Southbourne (1913). They restored St Mary's Cathedral, Edinburgh, and the south transept of Selby Abbey, W. Riding, where they rebuilt the central tower after the fire of 1906.

Obit. RIBAJ, May, 1952, p. 271 *Bldr*, 21.3.52, p. 453.

SCOTT, Sir Giles Gilbert, OM, RA, DCL, Hon.LLD Cantab, Liverpool and Trinity College, Toronto, Knight of the Norwegian Order of St Olaf 1880–1960

Giles Gilbert Scott was born at Hampstead, into a family of architects, the second son of George Gilbert Scott junior (1839–97), grandson of Sir George Gilbert Scott, RA (1811–78), nephew of John Oldrid Scott (1841–1913), brother of Adrian Gilbert Scott (1883–1963), and cousin of Charles Marriott Oldrid Scott. The progenitor of this long line of architects was Thomas Scott (1747–1821), the Bible commentator, whose son (the father of Sir George Gilbert Scott), was rector of Gawcott, near Buckingham, and an amateur builder.

319 Giles Gilbert Scott went to Beaumont College, Old Windsor, and was articled to Temple Lushington Moore, his father's pupil and assistant, who had continued his father's work. Pupillage with Temple Moore ended in 1903 when Scott's design was selected in the competition for the new Anglican Cathedral for Liverpool which had become a separate diocese in 1880. A competition had been held in 1887 for a cathedral on a site next to St George's Hall (with Ewan Christian as assessor). Not only was the choice of site unwise, but so was the design selected — that by William Emerson in a style close to Romanesque — and building did not proceed. A better site was found on St James's Mount and, as a result of protest, the condition that the building should be Gothic (and 1220–1320 Gothic at that) was withdrawn. One hundred and three applications in the form of portfolios of work were received: from these, five finalists were selected — Austin

Sir Giles Gilbert Scott: Liverpool Anglican Cathedral from the north-east. Scott's competition design had one transept but two towers.

and Paley of Lancaster, Charles Nicholson, Malcolm Stark, Walter Tapper and Giles Gilbert Scott.

The assessors were G. F. Bodley and R. Norman Shaw. When Scott was announced the winner, Shaw proposed that because of his youth he should have the benefit of Bodley's collaboration. But Scott and Bodley did not get on well together and after four years Scott sent in his resignation, but just before it was officially tendered to the Building Committee, Bodley died and Scott considerably modified his original design, abandoning the twin transept towers and the cross gables of the nave (*Bldr*, 30.5.03, 7.1.05 and 20.10.06) and introducing double transepts and a central tower at the crossing. The Lady chapel, which Scott had also modified in execution, was consecrated in 1910 (*Bldr*, 9.7.10), the foundation stone having been laid by King Edward VII in 1904. The corner stone of the Chapter House was laid by the Duke of Connaught in 1906. The cathedral was consecrated in 1924 when the choir and eastern transepts were complete. Scott continued to work for the cathedral until his death.

In those years Scott's brother, Adrian Gilbert Scott (1883–1963), also a pupil of Temple Moore, joined his brother in practice. He afterwards did the Anglican Cathedral in Cairo and many churches. Two early domestic examples of their joint work are Greystanes, Marsh Lane, Mill Hill, NW7 (1907) and 129 Grosvenor Road, Pimlico, SW1 (1913–15).

The experience which Scott was acquiring at Liverpool served him well at St Joseph, Lower Sheringham, Norfolk (1909–12); St Maughold and Presbytery, Ramsey, Isle of Man (1909–12); the Chapel of the Visitation Convent, Harrow (1905–6); the Church of the Annunciation, Bournemouth (1905–6); Our Lady of the Assumption, Northfleet, Kent (1913–16); St Paul, Derby Lane, Stonycroft, Liverpool (1913–16); and Charterhouse School War Memorial Chapel, near Godalming, Surrey (1922–7). Changing from the Woolton stone of Liverpool to brick as at Northfleet, Kent, Scott evolved a grammar of brick detailing using as few 'specials' as possible. This he employed to advantage in he building of those 'Cathedrals of Power', the generating stations for the Central Electricity Board, foremost among which is his Battersea Power Station of 1932.

Scott's fondness for powerful masses also found expression in his other buildings, notably in the Cambridge University Library of 1929; and his love of soaring towers is also revealed in his William Booth memorial building for the Salvation Army, Denmark Hill, SE5, of 1928.

Scott's long career continued into the 1950s and his acknowledged ability, coupled with his great earnestness and sincerity, made him very much in demand for causes requiring an aura of sanctity. Such a cause in more recent days was the Bankside Power Station of 1954, which required such support if politicians were to overcome the objections of the Dean and Chapter of St Paul's Cathedral to the site — immediately opposite the Cathedral. To demonstrate how little the power station would affect St Paul's, Sir Giles's drawing displayed cypress trees and lawns such as indeed might enhance a crematorium. 'Perhaps,' commented the *Evening Standard*, 'St Paul's might spoil the view of the Power Station.'

Throughout his long career Scott was to shape the face of contemporary architecture in many ways. At Cropthorne Court, Maida Vale, W9, in 1934, he introduced a new era in the design of mansion flats. Of the Thames bridges constructed in the twentieth century, none has had more appeal than the new Waterloo Bridge, completed in 1939. In spite of its ugly cutwaters and the contradictory *vertical* joints of its Portland stone facing, Scott's shapely bridge stands in no need of the groups of statuary for which distinguished sculptors submitted designs never executed.

For his own Chester House, Clarendon Place, Hyde Park, W2, a characteristically broad version of neo-Georgian, Scott was awarded the London Street Architecture medal in 1926. The jury could not know that they had in principle given the seal of approval to a succession of two-storey brick houses which in the ensuing fifty years would intrude upon the environs of the Royal Parks and that *urbs in rure*, St John's Wood, NW8.

In the 1920s Scott was entrusted with the task of designing street furniture — telephone boxes and traffic signs. His signs were in cast iron and highly 'architectural'. The 'No Entry' signs were cast iron boxes on tapered, fluted and decorated columns, surmounted by tapered, zig-zag patterned lanterns. These have all been replaced, but the telephone boxes still survive. Also architectural, with 'golden mean' proportioned glazing and shallow-domed lantern, these came in two sizes, often placed side by side like husband and wife. In Oxford, they were painted a discreet stone colour instead of red, and in Whitehall, grey. They were later crudely imitated in concrete.

Scott added a new wing to Basil Champneys's and Sir Reginald Blomfield's Lady Margaret Hall, Oxford, in 1931–6. He also did Memorial Court, Clare College, Cambridge (1924–5) and Whitelands College, Putney, SW15 (1930). His extension to the City of London Guildhall and the New Bodleian Library in Oxford (1937–41) show his endeavour to meet modern requirements by stretching the traditional lintel and arch to their limit.

After seventy years, the last in the Gothic tradition, Sir Giles's great Cathedral at Liverpool is complete. All but the roof trusses and the gantry for the bells are in the traditional materials put together

42

321

Giles and Adrian Gilbert Scott: Greystanes, Marsh Lane, Mill Hill, NW7. A house suggesting the influence upon these two young architects of T. E. Collcutt's work.

by the traditional crafts of the stonemason working on the 'banker', shaping the stone on the site, and by the joiner, metalworker and carver. Sir Giles was one of the assessors of the competition for the first modern English cathedral, at Coventry, won by Sir Basil Spence, RA, in 1951.

Scott was made ARA in 1918, and RA in 1922 (diploma work, 'Liverpool Cathedral, interior view of East End, from the South Choir Aisle'). He was knighted in 1924 after the consecration of the Cathedral and in 1925 received the Royal Gold Medal for Architecture. He was President of the RIBA from 1933 to 1935 and received the Order of Merit in 1944.

Country Life, 14.10.76, pp. 1022–4: 'The Last Gothic Cathedral', by Keith Spence

Fisher, Geoffrey, and Gavin Stamp, *Catalogue of the Drawings Collection of the Royal Institute of British Architects: The Scott Family,* Farnborough, Hants, 1976

Obit. RIBAJ, Mar., 1960, p. 149 *Bldr,* 19.2.60 pp. 345–6 and 360.

SCOTT, Mackay Hugh Baillie   1865–1945

Baillie Scott was born at Beard's Hill, St Peter's, Ramsgate, Kent, eldest of the fourteen children of Mackay Hugh Baillie Scott and his wife Martha. His father had considerable means derived from sheep farming in Australia. Baillie Scott went to school at Worthing and on to the Royal Agricultural College at Cirencester in 1883; his father intended him to manage the Australian farms, but Baillie Scott preferred architecture. From 1886 to 1889 he was articled to the City Architect of Bath, Major Charles E. Davis, whose father had been a pupil of Sir John Soane. Baillie Scott worked on Davis's construction of the Queen's Bath over the Roman remains, which was much criticised at the time.

In 1889 Baillie Scott married Florence Kate Nash, whose family claimed connections with 'Beau' Nash of Bath. They made their first home in Douglas, Isle of Man. Here Scott joined the office of Fred Sanderson, a surveyor and land agent, and was asked to design houses, a village hall and a police station, while his experience in the design of mosaics at Bath brought a commission to do the mosaic pavements for J. L. Pearson, RA, at St Matthew, Douglas (*Studio,* July, 1945; *V & A Catalogue of Victorian and Edwardian Decorative Art,* 1952).

321

Among Scott's principal works at Douglas, Isle of Man, were Oakley, Glencrutchery Road, and his own house, Red House, Victoria Road (*Dekorative Kunst* 5, 1900), both 1892—3. He also did Ivydene, Little Switzerland (1893—4, *Kunst und Kunsthandwerk* 4, 1901); Laurel Bank and Holly Bank, Victoria Road (1895—6); the interiors of 4 Albert Terrace (1895; since destroyed); terrace houses at Falcon Cliff (1897—8); the dining room and drawing room of Glencrutchery House (1898, *Dekorative Kunst* 5, 1900; the house has since been altered); the interiors of Glen Falcon, Broadway (*Bldr*, 12.5.1900; destroyed), and the fittings there with L. L. Corkhill on Onchan. In Onchan he did the Mansion, King Edward Road (1893), which has been altered and is now the Majestic Hotel; Leafield and Braeside, King Edward Road (*AA*, II, 1897; *Kunst und Kunsthandwerk* 4, 1901); and the village hall (*Kunst und Kunsthandwerk* 4, 1901).

Seeking good schools for their children, the Baillie Scotts moved in 1901 to Bedford, home of John Pyghtle White's joinery works for which Scott was doing designs. Baillie Scott by now held a special place in the so-called English Domestic Revival which was attracting attention from foreign journals and from Hermann Muthesius in his survey of English architecture. Scott took full advantage of such publicity with his pretty water-colour perspective sketches of houses, their interiors and gardens, which looked like real commissions but were often imaginary.

In 1896, Queen Victoria's grandson, Ernest Ludwig, Grand Duke of Hesse, asked Baillie Scott to decorate two rooms in his palace at Darmstadt in the new style (RA, 1898). C. R. Ashbee's Guild of Handicraft made the furniture and metalwork. In 1900 Scott did interiors for Carl Reiss at 12 Block E7, Mannheim (destroyed). The following year he took part in the competition held by *Zeitschrift für Innendekoration,* of Darmstadt, for 'The House of an Art Connoisseur'. Although none of the entries earned more than a consolation prize, one of these went to Scott and his design was among those illustrated in the *Meister der Innendekoration* series published by Alexander Koch.

Influenced by changes in public taste and perhaps also in their own, Baillie Scott and contemporaries like Barry Parker, Harrison Townsend and Frank Brangwyn began to abandon their original designing from first principles and to adopt the historical styles. Scott's name gradually came to be used as an adjective — like 'Lutyens' or 'Voysey' — to describe a particular style of house, not because his continued to be adventurous, but because he was now designing the kind of country retreat that was being called for. Some of the best brother-upholders of the Art Workers' Guild found themselves obliged to do likewise.

But in spite of competition and changes in taste,

Baillie Scott achieved some notable results. Outstanding among his early works were Blackwell, Bowness-on-Windermere, Westmorland (RA, 1899; *Bldr*, 24.2.1900; now Blackwell School) for Sir Edward Holt, and his largest single work, Waterlow Court, Hampstead Garden Suburb, NW11 (*Bldr*, 10.7.09), furnished by J. P. White and Heal. His largest house of the Tudor Revival, for the oil magnate Sir Boverton Redwood, was The Cloisters, Avenue Road, NW8 (1912—13). Based on a design prepared some years earlier, this was demolished in the 1930s and replaced by a block of flats by Stanley Hall, Easton and Robertson. Baillie Scott's other houses included Bexton Croft, Toft Road, Knutsford, Cheshire (1894—6; *Studio*, January, 1895); Le Nid, Sinaia, Rumania, for the Crown Princess Marie of Rumania (*Studio*, July, 1901; a house in the trees, since destroyed); the White Lodge, Wantage, Berkshire (1898—9). In 1909—11 he did Waldbuhl, Uzwil, Switzerland, and in 1912—13 a house at Laskowicze in Poland.

In 1905 A. E. Beresford joined Scott at Bedford as an assistant, becoming a partner in 1919. In 1911 Scott's office was destroyed by fire and he reopened again at St John Street, Bedford. The following year Scott and his family moved to a flat in Kensington Palace Hotel which was owned by the Scott family and in 1919 he opened an office in Gray's Inn Square. He moved to Bedford Row, WC1, in 1930, remaining until the Second World War, when the office was again destroyed by fire. After the death of his wife, Scott moved about in Devon and in Cornwall. He died at his home, Oakhams, Edenbridge, Kent, where his epitaph in the churchyard, adapted from Landor, reads: 'Nature he loved, and, next to Nature, Art'.

Some other works by Baillie Scott are:

1899-1900	White House, 5 Upper Colquhoun Street, Helensburgh, Dunbartonshire (RA, 1900)
	The Garth, Miles Lane, Cobham, Surrey (RA, 1900)
1899-1902	Winscombe, Beacon Road, Crowborough, Sussex (RA, 1900; interior altered)
1900	Police Station, Castle Rushen, Castletown, Isle of Man
1900-4	Deutsche Werkstätten interiors, furniture and crafts (see Muthesius, *Das Englische Haus*)
1901-2	The Manor, Cardington Road, Fenlake, Bedford (remodelling, for his own use, of two cottages, gutted by fire in 1911 and restored)
1902	Sandford Lodge, Wormit, Fife (now a hotel)
1904	Bregnehueset (now The Crow's Nest), Duddleswell, Ashdown Forest, Sussex
	House at Tyringham, Massachusetts, for Mrs Tyfus
1904-5	Elmwood Cottages, 7 and 7a Norton Way, Letchworth, Hertfordshire
1904-6	Heather Cottage, Coval Court, Cross Road and Greenways, Devenish Road, Sunningdale, Berkshire
1905-8	Springwood, Spring Road, Tanglewood, 17 Sollershott West, and Corrie Wood, Hitchin Road, Letchworth, Hertfordshire

1906-7	Bill House, Grafton Road, Selsey-on-Sea, Sussex (now a children's holiday home)
1907	Kirkstead, Church Lane, Godstone, Surrey
	Additions and gardener's cottage at Rake Manor, Milford, Surrey (earlier additions by Lutyens, 1897)
1907-8	Heritage Crafts School, Chailey, Sussex
1907-9	King's Close, Church Lane, and White Cottage, 17 Church End, Biddenham, Bedford
1908	White Cottage, Sudbury Hill, Harrow, Middlesex
	6, 8 and 10 Meadway, and 22 Hampstead Way, a group of four houses in Hampstead Garden Suburb, NW11
1908-9	Burton Court, and Stone Cottage, Long Burton, Sherborne, Dorset
	29, 30, 48, 54 and 56 Storey's Way, Cambridge
	Rosewall, Calonne Road, Wimbledon, SW19
	Undershaw (now flats), Garden Court, and Monks Path, Warwicks Bench, Guildford, Surrey
1909	Manderville, Yewlands Road, Hoddesdon, Hertfordshire
	Home Orchard (now Windmill House), Hillside Road, Sidmouth, Devon
	House at Seal Hollow, Sevenoaks, Kent (now part of a housing estate)
1910	Lower Mead, Templewood Lane, Stoke Poges, Buckinghamshire, for his brother Roderick
	Home Close, Sibford Ferris, Oxfordshire
1910-11	36 and 38 Reed Pond Walk, Gidea Park, Romford, Essex, furnished by Heal's tapestries and other fittings from the Deutsche Werkstätten to Scott's designs
1911	Cottage at Fox Hill, Haverhill Road, Stapleford, near Cambridge, for Sir Harry Anderson, Master of Caius
c. 1911	48 Storey's Way, Cambridge
1912	Michaels (now Havisham House), Palmers Cross Hill, Harbledown, Canterbury, Kent
1912-13	14 Western Drive, Short Hills, New Jersey, USA

Country Life, 22.1.76, pp. 198—9, piano designs

Kornwolf, James D., *M. H. Baillie Scott and the Arts and Crafts Movement,* Baltimore and London, 1972

Obit. RIBAJ, Mar., 1945, p. 143 *Bldr,* 16.2.45, pp. 136 and 159.

Mackay Hugh Baillie Scott: King's Close, Biddenham, Bedford.

Gilbert Seale: the entrance to Marlborough Chambers, Jermyn Street, SW1, by Reginald Morphew. This beautiful fairylike work has been painted in primary *oil* colours, a deplorable modern tendency.

SEALE, Gilbert *floruit c.* 1900

Gilbert Seale was a member of one of those families of craftsmen, marble workers, carvers and sculptors who carried on as nearly as possible the life of the craftsman before the industrial age, combining all levels of skill under one roof — one way of allaying the financial risks attendant upon the sculptor. In the late 1880s he carved reredoses and other church work for J. D. Sedding.

Seale's work is distinguished by a lightness of touch and modelling most appropriate to buildings with affinities with Art Nouveau which might justifiably be called *fin-de-siècle*. Seale did the angels flanking the doorway of Reginald Morphew's Marlborough Chambers (now Estate House), 96 Jermyn Street, SW1, and the carving at Lancaster Town Hall for E. W. Mountford in 1907. His son Barney Seale (d. 1957) concentrated on salon sculpture.

266
324

SEDDING, Edmund Harold d. 1921

Edmund Sedding was the nephew of John Dando Sedding (1838—91), an important architect of the Gothic Revival. His father, also Edmund (1836—68), was a very talented architect and musician (see *DNB*) who, like his brother, was a pupil of G. E. Street. He entered the Royal Academy Schools in 1884. Sedding did many church restorations, chancel screens and church fittings in Cornwall, Devon, Somerset, Essex and Suffolk. He won in competition St Mary, Highweek, Newton Abbot, Devon (*AA*, 1905; *AR*, 1908).

In 1906 he was invited to prepare a design for the Cathedral, Dunedin, New Zealand. It was erected in an altered form (1914—19) under the direction of Basil V. Hooper of Dunedin and Auckland.

In 1911 Sedding took into partnership Reginald F. Wheatley. Wheatley resigned in 1914 and Basil Stallybrass carried on. Edmund Sedding wrote *Norman Architecture in Cornwall* (1909).

Obit. Bldr, 4.3.21, p. 287.

SELLERS, James Henry 1861—1954

J. H. Sellers was born at Oldham, Lancashire, the son of a mill worker. From elementary school he entered the office of a local architect as an office boy, then worked in architects' offices in Liverpool, Birmingham, and London; in York he worked for Walter Green Penty. Sellers next obtained the post of Assistant County Architect at Carlisle, under George Dale Oliver (*see under* Dodgshun, Edward John). In 1899 he returned to Oldham and set up in practice.

A few years later, Sellers joined in practice, though not strictly in partnership, with Edgar Wood (*q.v.*) also of Oldham. They set up office at 78 Cross Street, Manchester. Each admired the other's work and both were interested in using reinforced concrete. Of the two, Sellers showed more taste for Classical designs, and Elm Street School, Middleton (1909—10) shows his influence. But it was also he who was first to build a design of outstanding modernity — his offices for Dronsfield Brothers, in King Street, Oldham (1906—7). The style and the materials, granite and green-glazed brick, are remarkable for the period.

325

Sellers also developed a talent for furniture design which equalled, and sometimes excelled, the work of his contemporaries Gimson, Waals, the Barnsleys, Spooner, Heal and Russell. This is evident from his pieces in the collection of the City of Manchester Art Galleries and those held by the Sellers family.

AR, March, 1976, pp. 128—9

Manchester City Art Galleries, *Partnership in Style: Edgar Wood and J. Henry Sellers*, exhibition catalogue 1975.

SETH-SMITH, William Howard 1852—1928

W. H. Seth-Smith, whose grandfather had built parts of Eaton Square, SW1, was articled to Habershon and Pite in 1876 and studied at the South Kensington Schools. He commenced practice in London in 1879. In 1896 he did the Greshambury Institute, Chilworth, near Shalford, Surrey (now the church of St Thomas) — 'an exceptional building' (Pevsner). He also did St Luke, Maidstone (*Bldr*, 7.4.1900), which contains works by Aumonier, Seale, Laurence Turner and Bainbridge Reynolds. Seth-Smith and Monro did the Grafton Hotel, Tottenham Court Road, W1 (now staff residences for University College Hospital); the Church Missionary House, Salisbury Square, EC4; Hyde House, Bulstrode Street, W1 (*Bldr*, 8.9.06); the Unity House Homes for Working Boys and Girls; and houses at Witney, Oxfordshire and Godalming, Surrey.

Obit. Bldr, 7.9.28, p. 394.

James Henry Sellers: solicitors' offices in King Street, Oldham, of granite and green-glazed brick, remarkably modern for the period.

SHAW, Richard Norman, RA   1831–1912

When Shaw heard that R. Phené Spiers and Herbert Batsford were planning to write a book about him, he is reputed to have said: 'They will be saying, what are all these old fogeys up to?' Spiers abandoned the idea, but forty years later, in 1940, Sir Reginald Blomfield collected the material together with Spiers' notes and published a short personal account of Shaw with Batsford which hardly did the subject justice. Shaw's life and works have, however, since received the degree of serious study they deserve in a new biography by Andrew Saint.

Richard Norman Shaw was born in Edinburgh in 1831, the youngest of six children. His mother was Scottish, his father an Irish Protestant 'of Huguenot strain' who died two years after Shaw was born. Shaw went to school at Hill Street Academy, Edinburgh, and then at Newcastle upon Tyne, where his master predicted that he 'would make an artist but not a scholar'.

When Shaw was fourteen the family moved to London. In 1846 Shaw entered the London office of the Scotsman William Burn (1789–1870), who had a large practice, principally in country mansions. Shaw remained with Burn for seven years, while studying under Professor C. R. Cockerell, RA, at the Royal Academy Schools which he entered in 1849, winning the Silver Medal in 1852 and the following year the Gold Medal. In Burn's office Shaw met Eden Nesfield (1835–88), son of William Nesfield, the landscape gardener. Both young assistants spent their spare time measuring Pugin's work at the new Houses of Parliament and their holidays measuring French and English cathedrals. In 1856 Shaw followed Nesfield into the office of Nesfield's uncle, Anthony Salvin (1799–1881). Shaw's sketches in France, Italy and Germany, were published in 1858 as *Architectural Sketches from the Continent*. The title page was designed with John Clayton, founder of Clayton & Bell, the stained glass makers.

After Shaw left Salvin's office it was some time before he found the office which suited him — that of G. E. Street, one of the great architects of the Gothic Revival. In 1859 Shaw was appointed chief

Richard Norman Shaw: 6 Ellerdale Road, Hampstead, NW3. His own house. The young Lutyens was worried lest his first London stacks (*Country Life* office) would compare unfavourably with Shaw's. In the chimney corner here, Shaw drew his last great works.

assistant to Street in succession to Philip Webb, an experience which was to prove the high point of his training.

In 1863 Shaw and Nesfield set up in practice at 30 Argyll Street, Oxford Street, W1. They were both modest and unassuming men, and work came at first through Nesfield's family connections. Shaw had an early client in the painter J. C. Horsley, RA, for whom he modernised Willesley, Cranbrook, Kent. Horsley's son Gerald was later articled to Shaw. Shaw's first large domestic works were Leyswood and Glen Andred, both in Sussex near Groombridge, Kent, and both in the late 1860s.

Although they shared the same office, Shaw and Nesfield never did a work together. Nesfield set up a separate office, while Shaw, now free of the influence of Street and Nesfield, developed on individual lines. In 1870 followed Cragside, Rothbury, Northumberland, for Lord Armstrong of Armstrong Whitworth, the armaments firm, and Grimsdyke, Pinner, Middlesex, for Frederick Goodall, RA, later the home of W. S. Gilbert. Then came Preen Manor, Shropshire, Wispers, Midhurst, Sussex, and Merrist Wood, Worplesdon, Surrey. Shaw was a great draughtsman, and his perspective style, in pen and ink, was imitated by his staff, including W. R. Lethaby, his chief assistant for eleven years. R. Blomfield said of Shaw: 'He was the only one of the "Visitors" to the Royal Academy Schools to whom we attended seriously'. In 1876 he moved his office to 29 Bloomsbury Square, WC1 — later the home and office of Sir Edwin Lutyens.

Shaw was more of an individualist than an idealist and his frankness earned him the complete trust of his clients; so much so that he was able to build

for his brother's firm, Shaw Savill, a red-brick, tile-hung, leaded-bay-windowed and pargetted shipping office building — New Zealand Chambers — in Leadenhall Street, EC3 (1871–3; since destroyed); put a plain red brick 'Queen Anne' front to their bank at 8 Bishopsgate for Baring Brothers (1881); and build Lowther Lodge (1873–5), a 'country house' with steep roofs and tall chimneys beside the taller stuccoed terraces of Princes Gate, Hyde Park, SW7, for the Hon. William Lowther. (With an added lecture hall, this is now the home of the Royal Geographical Society.)

Shaw's works of this period include 196 Queen's Gate, SW7 (1875), 180 Queen's Gate (1883) and Adcote (1876–9) in Shropshire. In 1876 he did Swan House and Cheyne House, Chelsea, SW3, and 8 Melbury Road, Kensington, W8, for Sir Luke Fildes, RA; Flete, Devon, followed in 1878; Albert Hall Mansions, Kensington, SW7, and The Clock House, Chelsea, SW3, in 1879. Shaw was made ARA in 1872, RA in 1877. His diploma work was 'View of Adcote'.

In 1882 Shaw's great Dawpool, Cheshire, was built for Thomas Henry Ismay of the White Star Line, and in 1888 when he was asked to do 170 Queen's Gate, on the corner of Imperial Institute Road, SW7, in the style of Wren, Shaw designed a house in this 'Wrenaissance' style which has never been equalled since (*Bldr*, 1.1.10).

Shaw acknowledged his debt to Philip Webb, but said of him 'a very able man indeed, but with a strong liking for the ugly'. Where Webb's houses reveal their designer's earnestness, Shaw's display his brilliance.

Although he protested in a letter to J. D. Sedding in 1886, 'You know I am not a "church" man but a "house" man, and soil pipes are my speciality', Shaw's churches were often low, wide and light in character. He was among the first to break with the tradition that new churches should be lofty, gloomy and of stone.

His church work before 1900 includes Holy Trinity, Bingley, W. Riding (1866–8; demolished 1974); St Matthew, Meerbrook, Staffordshire (1869–73); St Michael, Bournemouth (1874–6, with a 1901 tower by John Oldrid Scott); St Margaret, Ilkley, W. Riding (1878–9); St Mark, Coburg Road, SE5 (1880; now closed); All Saints, Leek, Staffordshire (1885–7); Holy Trinity, Harrow School Mission, Latimer (now Freston) Road, W10 (1887–9; since converted to a games hall); and All Saints, Swanscombe, Kent (1894–5). Shaw also did St Michael and All Angels at Chiswick, W4, the church for Bedford Park, a small picturesque suburb for which Shaw provided designs for houses for Jonathan Carr in 1875.

Before his retirement, Shaw completed two great houses, both begun in 1890 — additions to Chesters, Northumberland, and the rebuilding for Lord Portman of Bryanston House, near

Blandford Forum, Dorset, to replace a house of 1778 by James Wyatt. More classical than his former romantic work, these houses had a strong and immediate influence on younger architects, including Blomfield and Lutyens.

In 1888–90 Shaw did the former New Scotland Yard, Victoria Embankment, SW1 (*Bldr*, 20.7.07), a building which astonished London and received a mixed reception. Some called it a 'jam factory' after the turreted Crosse & Blackwell Pickle Factory in Charing Cross Road, W1, designed by Banister Fletcher senior, one turret of which still looms above a sad, remodelled façade. The smaller extension to the south of New Scotland Yard was added in 1904–6. The wrought-iron gates spanning between them were designed by Reginald Blomfield as a window exhibit for Thomas Elsley's, the craftsmen in iron and lead.

326 When Shaw closed his last office in Hart Street in 1896 and retired to the house he had built for himself in 1875 at 6 Ellerdale Road, Hampstead, NW3, he did not pack away his drawing board; he was still the authority when it came to the design of an important building, and was frequently consulted. Since New Scotland Yard, Bryanston and Chesters, Shaw was an acknowledged master of the neo-Baroque or Anglo-Classic, although he had been anticipated in that style by John Belcher and Beresford Pite. Shaw brought to this style freedom without chaos, and a fine sense of proportion, devoting as much care to the proportions of the wall *between* his windows as to those of the windows themselves.

Shaw was consultant to J. Francis Doyle for the Royal Insurance Co. building, North John Street, Liverpool (RA, 1897), for which he had been assessor, and on the White Star Line Offices (now the Pacific Steam Navigation Co.), James Street, Liverpool. From 1897 to 1900 Shaw advised Willink and Thicknesse on the design of Parr's Bank (now the National Westminster), Castle Street, Liverpool (RA, 1900). Shaw also designed the public rooms on the White Star Liner RMSS *Oceanic*. In Bradford, Shaw was consultant in 1905 to the City Architect, F. E. P. Edwards, on the extensions to Lockwood and Mawson's Town Hall of 1873. In 1906 he provided an elevation which was probably the basis of Frank Atkinson's design for Waring & Gillow's furniture emporium in Oxford Street, W1 (Royal Academy Collection).

Two important works on which Shaw was consulted were the design of the buildings which were to line the new Aldwych as part of the Holborn–Strand improvements (*q.v.*), and the design of the new buildings of the Regent Street Quadrant. The Holborn–Strand scheme had become involved in the kind of wrangle to which local government is especially prone. Although disappointing to all concerned, it resulted in two of Shaw's best façades — those of the Gaiety Theatre and the 57 adjoining Gaiety Restaurant, both in collaboration with Ernest Runtz. The theatre has disappeared,

the restaurant subsequently became Marconi's Wireless Telegraphy and is now a bank. Although in the 1960s its fine roof and dormer windows were masked by a stone attic storey, Shaw's skill in disposing windows freely over the facade and other strong characteristics of his style are still evident. The rebuilding of the Regent Street Quadrant, a still sadder story told elsewhere in this book (see pp. 77–80), involved Shaw's swan song — the Piccadilly Hotel (*Bldr*, 5.5.06 and 9.6.06).

176
63
328
329

In 1903 Shaw, with his former chief assistant Ernest Newton, designed the second Alliance Insurance building at the foot of St James's Street, SW1 (*Bldr*, 19.5.06). His first had been the splendid Dutch gabled corner opposite of 1882. Although many have claimed to see in Shaw's late works signs of decline or a lapse into grandeur, in fact none of Shaw's last buildings give any indication of failing powers. Shaw's touch, even in his seventies, was sure. One has only to compare the mouldings on his first Alliance Insurance building and his last, those on the Piccadilly Hotel and the Gaiety Restaurant, with those by others on the

Richard Norman Shaw, with Ernest Runtz: the former Gaiety Hotel and Restaurant, Strand, WC2. At much expense and for little gain the beautiful green-slated mansard roof has been hidden, and the great cornice deprived of its meaning. The lower windows, however, still demonstrate Shaw's skill at seventy-five years of age.

Richard Norman Shaw, with William Woodward: The
Piccadilly Hotel, Shaw's last great design. The 'transept'
gable and bay was introduced by Shaw to compensate
for the loss of the east gable. The colonnade enabled
Shaw to build higher further back.

Richard Norman Shaw, with William Woodward: The Piccadilly Hotel. Shaw overcame the loss of the east gable by filling in the last bay of his colonnade.

neighbouring Swan & Edgar building and the State of Victoria building, Aldwych. Shaw's secret was always to send out full-scale profiles of mouldings — even from his chimney corner in Ellerdale Road.

Shaw understood the nature of Portland stone, what mouldings suit it and how it is sharpened by weather, as is evident from the great scrolls of the Piccadilly gable. (The base of the flagstaff which is the culmination of the gable has been incorrectly renewed after war damage.) Shaw's boldness shows in his distribution of windows — in the continuous dormer windows of New Zealand Chambers and on the Piccadilly Hotel, where he improved on the original design. The spectacle of his great colonnade moving across the balconied windows of the hotel, his improvisation of 'stopping' the colonnade when the second gable could not be built because Denman House (*Bldr*, 2.12.05) had already snapped up the lease — these are the strokes of genius.

Norman Shaw was a tall, handsome Scot, apparently irresistible in his dealings with clients, but his often mischievous humour went hand in hand with a high opinion of the status and independence of the architect. When a number of his former assistants met to inaugurate the Art Workers' Guild, they called on Shaw for advice, and he took a leading part in the controversy, 'Architecture — a Profession or an Art'. Shaw held that 'if you elect to be an architect, you choose one of

the noblest as well as one of the most delightful pursuits — always supposing you follow it nobly and as an art ...' When officials asked to examine the final building accounts of his only Government building, Shaw was astonished that his final certificate was not accepted without question.

Even near contemporaries like Ernest George felt they were following in the steps of a master. Reginald Blomfield wrote of him:

Norman Shaw was unquestionably the most dominant architectural personality of the latter half of the nineteenth century. Living through the period of the Gothic Revival, he survived to witness its ultimate downfall and, late in life, by sheer strength of character, himself achieved something of the monumental manner.

Hermann Muthesius paid him, as it turned out, a premature tribute in his *Englische Baukunst der Gegenwart* (Berlin/Leipzig 1900):

It is only now after a lifetime of rich activity that R. Norman Shaw, the man who pointed the way, is laying down his pencil, the pencil with which he raised up English architecture to the forefront...

Saint, Andrew, *Richard Norman Shaw*, London 1976

Obit. RIBAJ, 23.11.12, pp. 55—6 *Bldr*, 22.11.12, pp. 598—601, 627 8, 29.11, pp. 35—6, 643—4 and 20.12. p. 745.

George Sherrin: the electrification of the Metropolitan Line enabled offices to be built over the stations. A happy example of 'Free' or 'Anglo' Classic at Moorgate Station.

	1901-3	St Mary's Church and Presbytery, Eldon Street, Moorfields, EC2 (*Bldr*, 31.8.07 and 5.10.07), after removal from Liverpool Street
330	1902-3	Chambers over Moorgate Station (Metropolitan Line) after electrification
	1907	St Mary-at-Hill House, Eastcheap, EC3 (*Bldr*, 2.11.07) after electrification of the District Railway
		Spencer House, South Place, Finsbury, EC2 (*Bldr*, 31.8.07)
	1909	The elevations of the (former) Ponting's store adjoining Kensington High Street Station, including the station arcade, W8

SIMMONS, Charles Evelyn   1879—1952

C. E. Simmons went to University College School, Gower Street, where his father was headmaster of the Junior School. He was articled to E. O. Sachs, the theatre and fire prevention expert, and attended the Architectural Association School. Simmons was assistant (from 1901) and partner (1906—15) to Horace Field. During the First World War, Field and Simmons did churches at Eastriggs and Gretna, Dumfriesshire, for the munitions town constructed under the aegis of Raymond Unwin. (For Simmons's houses in the Hampstead Garden Suburb, *see under* Field, Horace.)

SHERRIN, George Campbell   d. 1909

George Sherrin was articled to H. E. Kennedy junior, was assistant to Wilson and Whipple and for ten years was managing clerk to Fred Chancellor. For a short time he worked under Sir John Taylor in HM Office of Works. After the death of the architect Herbert Gribble (1847—94), Sherrin completed the dome and lantern of the Oratory Church in Brompton Road, SW7. E. A. Rickards (*q.v.*) assisted on this.

Sherrin's son Frank was associated with him. Sherrin did the Spitalfields Market, E1 and Tower Mansions, Tite Street, Chelsea Embankment, SW3. He also did flats at 2, 3 and 4 Church Row, Hampstead, NW3 (1897—8). Norman Shaw made a sketch for these (now in the library of the Royal Academy of Arts), suggesting a building less hurtful to Church Row.

In conjunction with John Clarke, Sherrin did the Kursaal — a tower, circus, arcade, ninety shops and fifty-three houses — at Southend-on-Sea in 1898. His domestic works include Wynnstowe, Limpsfield, Surrey; Norato, Beccles, Suffolk; Alexandra Hotel and houses at Dovercourt, Essex (*BA*, 18.12.03).

Other works by George Sherrin are:

1899-1900   84 Piccadilly, W1, for the Imperial Service Club

SIMON, Frank Worthington   1863—1933

Frank Simon was educated at King Edward's Grammar School, Birmingham, and in Paris at the Ecole des Beaux-Arts and the Atelier of Jean-Louis Pascal. He was articled to John Cotton, FRIBA, of Birmingham, and won the RIBA Tite Prize in 1887.

In the early 1890s Simon became a partner with Sir Rowand Anderson, RSA, in Edinburgh, as Anderson, Simon and Crawford. His next partnership was with Tweedie Crawford and next he joined Huon A. Matear (*q.v.*) who had done the Courts of Justice in York in 1890—2. Together they won in competition the Liverpool Cotton Exchange (1905—6), unhappily demolished in 1967 with the exception of the side elevation of cast iron. The main front was a splendid example of the neo-Baroque, which had by then become a recognisable Edwardian style. The internal columns were of blue Norwegian marble and the sculpture was by W. Birnie Rhind of Edinburgh and E. O. Griffith of Liverpool. Between 1903 and 1913 Matear and Simon did Holy Trinity Church, Manchester Road, Southport, the gift of the Elder family of shipowners and the cotton manufacturers Joseph Mallineaux and Joseph Dewhurst.

A restless genius, Simon then went in for competitions alone and won the Manitoba Parliament

Building, Winnipeg, which he and Septimus Warwick saw through on the spot to its completion in 1920.

Simon also taught at the Edinburgh School of Applied Arts, and in Liverpool assisted Briggs, Wolstenholme and Thornely on extensions to the University. He died at Menton, Alpes Maritimes, France.

Obit. RIBAJ, 17.6.33, p. 641 *Bldr*, 16.6.33, p. 954.

SIMPSON, Professor Frederick More
1855—1928

F. M. Simpson entered the Royal Academy Schools in 1880 and was articled to G. F. Bodley. After a time in the office of Charles Ferguson of Carlisle he was made Professor of Architecture at the University of Liverpool in 1894. When he was given the chair of architecture at London University which he held from 1903 to 1919, he was succeeded at Liverpool by C. H. Reilly (*q.v.*).

With Willink and Thicknesse, Professor Simpson designed the Queen Victoria Monument, Derby Square, Liverpool (1902—6), with supporting sculpture by C. J. Allen, whose statue of Queen Victoria shelters under a dome lined in gold mosaic, while beneath is a public lavatory of fittingly *magistrale* proportions.

In London, Simpson designed the Institute of Physiology and other departments of University College, Gower Street, WC1.

He wrote *A History of Architectural Development* and in 1922 was appointed Knight, First Class, of the Order of St Olav of Norway.

Obit. RIBAJ 23.6.28, p. 571 *Bldr*, 22.6.28, p. 1062 and 29.6, p. 1102.

SIMPSON, Sir John William, KBE   1858—1933

John W. Simpson was the son of Thomas Simpson, a Brighton architect. He entered the Royal Academy Schools in 1879. Most of his work before 1900 was in the vicinity of Brighton, where he did Roedean, the famous red brick and terracotta girls' school standing starkly on the bare cliff, founded in London by the Misses Lawrence as a preparatory school for Newnham College, Cambridge. Simpson added the chapel in 1906, the junior school and sanatorium in 1908 and the Art School and library in 1911. More recent additions have been made by Sir Hubert Worthington. The Elm Grove and Stanford Road schools in Brighton are also by Simpson (RA, 1903).

In 1893 Simpson, in partnership with E. Milner J. Allen, had won the competition for the Glasgow Art Gallery and Museum (1893), a permanent building which was incorporated in the Glasgow Exhibition of 1901. Between 1900 and 1903

Simpson and Allen built the Cartwright Memorial Art Gallery and Museum at Bradford (*Bldr*, 5 and 26.11.04).

331

In 1902 Simpson designed the memorial to Edward Onslow Ford, RA (1852—1901), at Grove End Road, NW8, which incorporates a bronze by Ford with a bronze relief of Ford by Andrea Lucchesi (*q.v.*). In the same year Simpson designed the memorial in Hampstead Cemetery, NW2, to Margaret Sophie Waterlow (d. 1899), wife of Sir Ernest Waterlow, RA.

At Glasgow and at Hampstead the sculptor was Sir George Frampton.

In 1905 Maxwell O. Ayrton (*q.v.*) became a partner. Their first work together was the lodge and form rooms at Haileybury College, Hertfordshire — designed by William Wilkins in 1806 as the East India Company's College. Later they did the New Hall there. In 1923 Simpson and Ayrton received their most important commission — to design the layout and permanent buildings at Wembley Park, Middlesex, for the British Empire Exhibition, held in 1924 and 1925. The first building of this large group, the Stadium, was opened in 1923. Except for the buildings contributed by Commonwealth participants, the group was constructed in mass concrete with a reeded finish and unplastered. Simpson and the structural engineer, Owen Williams, were knighted for their work there. Altered and adapted for every kind of minor industry, the park — once with a golf course and a lake — and its once resplendent buildings present a sorry sight today. But the Stadium still serves its original purpose.

Simpson was a member of the Art Workers' Guild and President of the RIBA from 1919 to 1921. For other works, *see under* Ayrton.

Obit. RIBAJ, 29.4.33, pp. 514—5 and 13.5, p. 557.

Sir John William Simpson: memorial to Edward Onslow Ford, RA, Grove End Road, NW8, with a bronze by Ford and a bronze relief by A. C. Lucchesi.

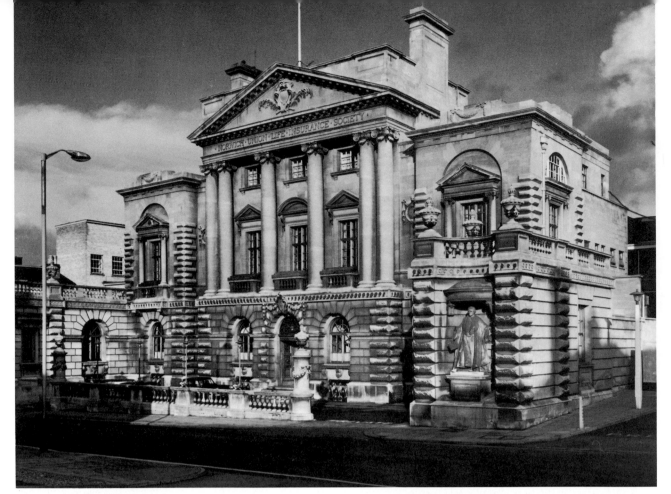

George John Skipper: offices of the Norwich Union Life Insurance Society, 30 St Andrew Street, Norwich. This building, like the Burlington-Kent Chiswick House, looks larger than it in fact is. The sculptor is Chavalliaud.

SKIPPER, George John   1854–1948

George Skipper is best remembered for the head office building of the Norwich Union Life Insurance Society at 30 St Andrew Street, Norwich (RA, 1904; *Bldr*, 7.7.06), won in limited competition in 1901. This building represents the high-water mark of Edwardian sumptuousness without vulgarity.

Like Lord Burlington's villa at Chiswick, London, it looks larger than it is, the parts being in perfect proportion and the detail correct in scale. Externally it is built in Clipsham stone. The niches contain statues by Chavalliaud, a French sculptor working for Farmer and Brindley — a figure of Bishop Talbot of Oxford who established the Amicable Life Insurance Office, granted a charter by Queen Anne, and one of Sir Samuel Bignold, who founded the Norwich Union. Internally the columns are of single blocks of Cipollino and Verde Antico with capitals and bases in white statuary marble. The entablature is alabaster, the wall lining in skyros, red-veined and grey-veined, with panels of porphyry-coloured Rosso Antico and cornices in alabaster. The two bronzes in the vestibule, figures representing Solace and Protection, are by A. Stanley Young. The walls of the staircase are in Cipollino opened up, the handrail in Pavonazzo, the pedestals, columns and bases in Brescia. George Murray painted the ceilings over the staircase and in the Board Room. The warm air heating operates through an opening in the centre, dispersed by a canopy surmounted

by a figure by H. C. Fehr which was cast by Singer's of Frome, Somerset. The frieze in the directors' lunch room is probably by W. J. Neatby (*q.v.*). Skipper also did the Norwich Union's branch office in St Andrew's Street, Cambridge (1909; recently demolished).

Skipper also did the Town Halls at Lowestoft, Cromer and Hunstanton, the Norwich and London Accident Insurance Association, Norwich (*Bldr*, 25.2.05) and the Royal Norfolk and Suffolk Yacht Club, Lowestoft (*Bldr*, 18.7.03). He also did the University Arms Hotel, Cambridge (1903, extended in 1926); the frontage of Telephone House, 43 and 49 Giles Street, Norwich (1906); the Royal Arcade and Public House, Castle Street, Norwich, in coloured tile tracery; and after the First World War, cottages for King George V at Sandringham. His practice is continued by his son as Edward Skipper and Associates.

AR, Mar., 1976, p. 129

Obit. *RIBAJ*, Sept., 1948, p. 519

SKIPWORTH, Arthur Henry   d. 1907

A. H. Skipworth was articled to G. F. Bodley. He did St Etheldreda's, Fulham, SW6, and prepared an imaginative design for the chapel for the Community of the Resurrection, Mirfield, Yorkshire

(*Bldr*, 16.6.06 and 27.4.07), which was abandoned in favour of one by Walter Tapper. He also did the Rectory, Ingrave, Essex (*Bldr*, 26.5.06). After his death Skipworth's work was carried on by William Curtis Green with Reginald Hallward, who had been with Skipworth for more than twenty years. Skipworth was a member of the Art Workers' Guild.

Obit. Bldr, 20.4.07, pp. 469, 483–4 27.4, pp. 509–10 and 515 and 15.6, pp. 731–2.

SLATER, John   d. 1924

John Slater was articled first to W. J. T. Newman, and then to Professor Roger Smith to whom he was assistant. He studied at University College, London, and commenced practice in 1871. Slater was architect to the London electricity generating stations at Kensington, Notting Hill and Wood Lane and in 1891 was appointed surveyor to the Berners Estate, W1.

Slater took into partnership J. Melville Keith, then in 1910 his son, J. Alan Slater (1885–1963). They did the Berners Hotel, Berners Street, WC1; factories for Caley's, Chenies Street, EC1; Schweppes mineral water factory, Hendon, NW4; and after 1920, the rebuilding of the Bourne & Hollingsworth store, Oxford Street, W1. J. A. Slater and Arthur Moberly were architects for the Peter Jones store, Sloane Square, SW3, in 1936, where William Crabtree, a student of Reilly's at Liverpool, was architect for the elevations and interiors, with C. H. Reilly acting as 'impresario'.

Obit. Bldr, 5.12.24 pp. 887 and 888 and 26.12 pp. 1006 and 1007.

SLOPER, Ernest Willmott, *see* WILLMOTT, Ernest

SMITH, Arnold Dunbar   1866–1933

Dunbar Smith was born in Islington, N1. He was articled to J. G. Gibbons of Brighton, studied at Brighton School of Art and the Architectural Association, attended the 'Atelier Millard et Baggallay' in London, and entered the Royal Academy Schools in 1890. He was also assistant to Millard and Baggallay and an RIBA Godwin Bursar. In 1895 he entered into partnership with Cecil Brewer (*q.v.*) who had followed the same course of training.

333 An early success was their win in the competition for the Passmore Edwards Settlement, Tavistock Place, WC1 (1896), now called the Mary Ward Centre after the novelist Mrs Humphrey Ward. The competition, intended for another site, was assessed by R. Norman Shaw. On this building Smith seized the opportunity for violent contrast

in styles often offered by a porch, here done in the style of Rudolf Steiner's first Goethenaeum, in Switzerland. A recent example is the porch to the Hampstead Public Baths by Sir Basil Spence, RA. In 1899 Smith and Brewer did Little Barley End, Tring, Hertfordshire, for Thomas Humphrey Ward. For the Albemarle Club at Ely House, 37 Dover Street, W1, they designed an interior corridor and staircase fully worthy of this beautiful town house. (Originally built for Bishop Keene of Ely by Robert Taylor in 1772, the building is now occupied by the Oxford University Press.) The elevation in brick to Berkeley Street is also interesting.

334 Smith and Brewer's finest work is the National Museum of Wales (1910) which forms part of the group of national, municipal and county buildings at Cathays Park, Cardiff, on the site presented by the Marquis of Bute. Their design was simpler and more classical than the neo-Baroque designs of the preceding decade and played a part in establishing the American version of the Ecole des Beaux-Arts style in England (*Bldr*, 2.4.10).

The partners' best-known work is the shop in

Arnold Dunbar Smith and Cecil Brewer: the porch of the Mary Ward Centre, Tavistock Place, WC1. A complete contrast to the building it serves.

Tottenham Court Road, W1, for Heal's, the long-established makers of fine furniture (1916). Smith and Brewer put many refinements coupled with original ideas into this work, but they had no new medium in which they could express these except pilasters and entablatures in a simplified form. Considerable additions were made in 1937 by Sir Edward Maufe, RA.

After the death of Brewer in 1918, Dunbar Smith did many houses, including work at Green Harp, Snape, Suffolk, and Rushymead, Coleshill, Buckinghamshire (1924). Between 1924 and 1933 he did additions to the Fitzwilliam Museum, Cambridge, lecture rooms at Mill Lane, Cambridge, the East Anglian Sanatorium, Nayland, Colchester and the Library of Armstrong College, Newcastle upon Tyne.

Other works by Smith and Brewer were:

1901	Nower Hill House, Pinner, Middlesex, for Ambrose Heal
	The Fives Court, Pinner, for Ambrose Heal junior
1902-9	The Malting House, Newnham High Street, Cambridge
1906	Sheldonian Theatre, Oxford (alterations)
1907	Ditton Place, Balcombe, Sussex (*Country Life*, 1.7.11, pp. 18–25)
after 1910	A house in The Bishop's Avenue, N2
	The Hostel at All Saints, London Colney, Hertfordshire (main building by Leonard Stokes), now the Pastoral Centre

Obit. RIBAJ, 23.12.33 pp. 200–1.

SNELL, Alfred Walter Saxon   1860–1949

A. W. Saxon Snell was the son of Henry Saxon Snell (1832–1904), and was articled to him in 1877. Their work consisted mainly of hospitals and Poor Law Institutions. Their grand-pavilioned St Marylebone Institution, Marylebone, NW1 (1900), was demolished in 1966 to provide a site for the new buildings of the London Polytechnic.

Obit. RIBAJ, Sept., 1949, p. 507   *Bldr*, 15.7.49, p. 80.

SPIERS, Richard Phené, FSA   1838–1916

Richard Phené Spiers, the well-loved teacher and mentor of generations of architectural students at the Royal Academy Schools, was born at Oxford, son of R. J. Spiers, Mayor of Oxford in 1854. A brother, Walter Spiers, was curator of the Soane Museum. Phené Spiers was educated at King's College School and at the engineering school of King's College, Strand, WC2. He attended the Atelier Questel and the Ecole des Beaux-Arts between 1858 and 1861.

Phené Spiers joined the office of Sir Matthew Digby Wyatt and worked on the interior of the India Office. He entered the Royal Academy

Schools in 1862, winning the Gold Medal in 1863. He also won the Soane Medallion and with C. J. Phipps, the theatre architect, competed in the design for the Church of the Sacred Heart in Paris (RA, 1875).

In 1870 Phené Spiers was appointed Master of the Architecture School of the Royal Academy and continued his classical studies there until he was succeeded in 1906 by Charles de Gruchy. His investigations at Baalbek resulted in the 'restoration' of the Circular Temple at the site (*Bldr*, 1.7.05). Between 1862 and 1904 Spiers exhibited more than 100 drawings at the Royal Academy.

Phené Spiers was held in high esteem by pupils and associates in England and abroad. In 1904 a collection of his essays, *Architecture East and West*, was published by Batsford as 'a testament to the author from his former students', and on 28 February 1905 a dinner was given him where he was presented with a testimonial signed by 600 of his students and admirers. Phené Spiers contributed many articles on architectural history to the *RIBA Journal* and the *Architectural Review* and with W. J. Anderson and Thomas Ashley wrote *The Architecture of Greece and Rome* (London, Batsford, 1902). He edited the third (1893) edition of Fergusson's *History of Architecture in All Countries* (London, John Murray).

Obit. RIBAJ, 21.10.16, pp. 334–5, *Bldr* 13.10.16, pp. 222–4.

SPOONER, Charles Sidney   1862–1938

Charles Spooner came from a family of ecclesiastics and was a cousin of the Rev. Dr. William Archibald Spooner of New College, Oxford, whose name is immortalised, erroneously, in the term 'spoonerism'. Charles Spooner was articled in 1881 to Sir Arthur Blomfield, ARA, and continued as his assistant. He entered the Royal Academy Schools in 1886 and studied at the Architectural Association, winning the travelling studentship. He also assisted in the office of J. Dixon Butler, the Metropolitan Police Architect (*q.v.*).

In 1892 Spooner set up office at 50 Queen Anne's Gate, SW1, and became an expert on small churches. His churches include St Gabriel, Aldersbrook, Wanstead, Essex, and the Row Chapel, Hadleigh, Suffolk (both 1892); St Bartholomew's Church and vicarage, Ipswich, Suffolk (1893); and St Michael and All Angels, Little Ilford, Essex (1897). He also did restorations at St George the Martyr, Queen Square, WC1; St Luke, Old Street, EC1; and Holy Trinity, Halstead, Essex. With Sir Charles Nicholson, Spooner compiled *Recent Ecclesiastical Architecture*, published by Technical Journals in 1912.

Spooner did a house at Steeple Claydon, Buckinghamshire, for the playwright, Henry Arthur Jones; the Dial House, village hall and cottages at Westhill,

Hertfordshire; the Vicarage, Aldershot, Hampshire; a library at Farnham Castle, Surrey for a cousin, Dr Randall Davidson, then Bishop of Winchester, and later Archbishop of Canterbury; and screens in the Parish Church at Farnham and in St John the Baptist and St Anselm, Pinner, Middlesex.

Spooner married Minnie Dibden Davison, a miniature painter, and he is best known for his stained glass and his furniture, on which his wife collaborated. He taught furniture design at the Central School of Arts and Crafts under W. R. Lethaby, and with A. J. Penty and Fred Rowntree started a furniture workshop (still standing) at 1 Ravenscourt Park, W6. They called their enterprise Elmdon & Co., after the eighteenth-century home of the Spooners, Elmdon Hall, Warwickshire, which stood near the present Birmingham Airport. Also with Rowntree, Spooner established workshops in Hammersmith called the Hampshire House Club. Here, during the First World War, with the help of Belgian refugees, they made pre-fabricated wooden 'knock-down' churches which were shipped to war-ravaged Belgium after the Armistice. Spooner's furniture has a professional look, for he avoided the temptation to wainwright's work which was apt to afflict the Cotswold workshops. He was a member of the Art Workers' Guild.

Other works by Spooner are:

1902-4	St Christopher, Haslemere, Surrey (RA, 1904; *Bldr*, 10.12.04; cast lead figure by Mrs M. D. Spooner, north chapel, 1935)
	Roman Catholic Church, Letchworth, Hertfordshire (now the church hall)
	St Paul, East Ham, E6
1912	Church of the Holy Spirit, Rye Harbour, Sussex (restorations)

Obit. RIBAJ, 23.1.39, pp. 311–2 *Bldr*, 6.1.39, p. 21.

SPRAGUE, W. G. R.   1865–1933

W. G. R. Sprague specialised in theatres, designing more than thirty during his career. In London's West End were Wyndham's (1899) in Charing Cross Road and the New Theatre (now the Albery Theatre) in St Martin's Lane, WC2, both for Sir Charles Wyndham; the Strand Theatre (built as the Waldorf) and the Aldwych Theatre, both built in Aldwych in 1905; the Globe Theatre (1906) and the Queen's (1908), both in Shaftesbury Avenue; the Ambassadors' (1913) and the St Martin's (1916), both in West Street, WC2. He took into partnership Charles Burton.

Outside London's West End Sprague did the Camberwell Empire (1894, with Bertie Crewe); the Shakespeare Theatre and Opera House, Lavender Hill, Battersea, SW11 (1896); the Broadway, New Cross, SE14, and the Grand, Fulham, SW6 (both 1897); the Kennington Theatre, SE11, and the Coronet, Notting Hill, W11 (both 1898); the Rotherhithe Hippodrome,

57
336

W. G. R. Sprague: the Aldwych Theatre, Aldwych, WC2. This theatre, the Strand Theatre and the Waldorf Hotel form the only sensible group on the Holborn-Strand Improvements, where the L.C.C. had no powers to insist upon the elevations. Fortunately they are on the Duke of Bedford's estate.

SE16 and the Balham Hippodrome, SW12 (both 1899); the Camden Theatre, Camden Town, NW1 (1901) and the King's Theatre, Hammersmith, W6 (1902). Sprague also designed the Edward VII Theatre in Paris.

Sprague's version of Renaissance, both rich and delicate, was ideal for the theatres of his age and a style well understood by the joiners, carvers, plaster-modellers, painters, gilders and upholsterers who had to work at top speed to finish new work or to convert old under poor conditions of lighting and scaffolding.

Obit. Bldr, 22.12.33, p. 985.

STATHAM, H. Heathcote   1839–1924

Born at Everton near Liverpool, the son of a solicitor, educated at Liverpool Collegiate Institution and articled to the Liverpool architect George Williams, Heathcote Statham was for twenty-five years the redoubtable editor and controller of *The Builder* (now *Building*). He practised as an architect in Liverpool for a time, meanwhile sending regular contributions to *The Builder*. On the advice of the then editor, George Godwin, Statham came to London and devoted his time to writing, showing a considerable flair for journalism. He succeeded Godwin as editor in 1884, and not only wrote criticisms for *The Builder* but contributed articles on musical and literary subjects to the *Fortnightly Review*, the *Nineteenth Century* and other contemporary journals, and was for many years music critic of the *Edinburgh Review*.

Statham was also a musician and an exponent of Bach on the organ. He gave organ recitals at the Albert Hall and was honorary organist at Canon Barnett's church of St Jude, Whitechapel, E1 (demolished and commemorated by St Jude-on-the-Hill, Hampstead Garden Suburb). Statham contributed to *Groves's Dictionary of Music* and wrote *The Organ and its Position in Musical Arts* (1909).

Under Statham *The Builder* provided a remarkable service to building and the associated arts. His criticisms on the Annual (Summer) Exhibition at the Royal Academy were lively and frank. Typical of his style was his observation on Robert Schultz Weir's Khartoum Cathedral: 'an interesting piece of work, but we cannot describe it as anything other than an eccentric one, even for Mr Schultz Weir'. The news reporting and commentaries covered a wide field. When a tram ran out of control down Highgate Hill, a horse cab went down the Duke of York Steps in a fog, or a ship collided with a jetty, *The Builder* was always ready to offer a caution and suggest a remedy, and Statham added to the Vauxhall Bridge controversy with a suggestion of his own (RA, 1901). Under Statham a number of young men were employed as artists who later became well known architects — notably A. Beresford Pite and W. Curtis Green (*q.v.*).

Because of road widening, Statham gave *The Builder* office and its neighbours in Catherine Street, WC2, a new front in 1903 (RA, 1904; *Bldr*, 1.11.02 and 19.5.06). He also did a lodge at Golders Hill Park, NW11, for Sir Spencer Wells, Royal Physician. The house, designed by E. F. C. Clarke in 1875, was destroyed in the Second World War and the grounds are now a public park.

After his long editorship of *The Builder*, Statham was succeeded (1910–12) by H. V. Lanchester (*q.v.*) and (1912–13) by Arthur Stratton (*q.v.*).

Obit. Bldr, 6.6.24, pp. 902–3.

Leonard Aloysius Scott Stokes: the Telephone Exchange, Highburgh Road, Glasgow. One of the twenty exchanges designed by Stokes for the National Telephone Company before its nationalisation in 1911.

STOKES, Leonard Aloysius Scott 1858—1925

By the end of the nineteenth century some half a dozen architects had evolved an architectural style which was founded firmly on tradition but enhanced by considerable innovation. Among them were J. F. Bentley, W. D. Caröe, Basil Champneys, E. S. Prior, C. F. A. Voysey and Leonard Stokes.

Stokes was born at Southport, Lancashire, the son of Scott Nasmyth Stokes, a barrister-at-law and chief inspector of schools. Stokes's eldest brother was the painter Adrian Stokes, RA; his youngest brother was the engineer Sir Wilfrid Stokes, who invented the Stokes gun. The family moved to London where Leonard Stokes was articled (1871—4) to the church architect S. J. Nicholl of Kentish Town.

To gain a knowledge of building quantities, Stokes then entered the office of James Gandy, G. E. Street's quantity surveyor. Stokes worked in Street's office for a time and acted as clerk of works for him on the restoration of Christ Church Cathedral, Dublin. He also worked in T. E. Collcutt's office and for G. F. Bodley and Thomas Garner. In 1878 Stokes entered the Royal Academy Schools, and won the Pugin Prize in 1880, travelling in Germany and Italy (with Walter Millard) in 1881—2. The ten years thus profitably spent provided Stokes with a sound basis for his personal architectural style in which traces of Street, Collcutt and Bodley can all be detected,

but which gives clear signs of modernity.

On his return from his studentship tour Stokes set up in practice and soon embarked on a series of Roman Catholic churches, chapels, presbyteries, convents, training colleges and schools. His first commissions — for a chapel and schools at St Patrick, Portsmouth Road, Woolston, in Hampshire (1883, demolished 1969) and the Church of the Sacred Heart, South Street, Exeter (with C. E. Ware; RA, 1883) — did not yet show promise of the more imaginative designs to come. And St Joseph, Cookham Road, Maidenhead, begun in 1884, was not built to Stokes's first design.

In 1886 Stokes submitted a design in competition for St James, Spanish Place, W1, won by Goldie, Child and Goldie. In the twenty years that followed Stokes was to do a great many churches all over the country. Those completed before the turn of the century included Our Lady and St Helen, Milton Road, Westcliff-on-Sea, Essex; the Church of the Sacred Heart and St Michael's Convent and Girls' School, Waterlooville, Hampshire (1888—95); St Clare's Church and Presbytery, Sefton Park, Liverpool (1888—9); Our Lady Help of Christians, Guildhall Street, Folkestone, Kent (1889); St Augustine, Sudbury, Suffolk (1893—4); All Souls and Presbytery, Park Road, Peterborough (1896); St Joseph's Church and School, Bugle Street, Southampton (1896—7) where he did the

337

completion of the nave and the decorations; St Philip, Begbroke, near Oxford (1896); Church of the Holy Ghost (unfinished) and schools, Nightingale Square, Balham, SW12 (1896); and the school chapel at Our Lady with St Anne, South View Road, Caversham, Berkshire (1899).

Stokes's church work of the Edwardian period included St Joseph's church and church hall at Potter Hill, Pickering, N. Riding (1907–11), where the font is by Eric Gill. In 1910 Stokes did St Wilfrid's Hall at Brompton Oratory in South Kensington, which provides an appropriate background for the statue of Cardinal Newman by Chavalliaud in a setting by Bodley and Garner. The building was designed to take another storey (*Bldr*, 10.12.10).

Most prominent among Stokes's churches is St Clare, Sefton Park, Liverpool, which represents a great step forward in the church architecture of the period. The interior, with its deep internal buttresses pierced to form passage aisles was intended to be faced in stone but for economy is plastered. The church is mentioned by Muthesius in *Die Neue Kirchlichen Baukunst in England* (1901). Had it been built, Stokes's church at Miles Platting, Manchester, for which he submitted designs in 1892, would have been another great advance.

For the Sisters of Nazareth, Stokes designed a wing of Nazareth House, Hammersmith Road, W6 (1888–9), and Nazareth House in Bexhill, Sussex

Above and right: **Leonard Aloysius Scott Stokes: All Saints, London Colney, Hertfordshire. The courtyard. Stokes was a master at balancing the vertical and the horizontal. The sculpture is by Henry Wilson.**

(1893–4). (He did the chapel for the Bexhill House in 1905). In 1895 Stokes produced a design for Nazareth House in Johannesburg. The Order's house at Lawrence Road, Southsea, Hampshire, was not executed according to Stokes's design of 1887.

338
339
The most outstanding of Stokes's convent buildings is All Saints, London Colney, in Hertfordshire. Built between 1899 and 1903 for the Anglican Sisterhood from All Saints, Margaret Street, London (*Bldr*, 3.2.1900), it is now a Pastoral Centre for the Roman Catholic See of Westminster. The building displays Stokes's favourite motifs — the many horizontal stone and brick bands tying in the window heads and sills, balancing the vertical mullions of the Tudoresque windows, the cleft parapets, the small *oeil de boeuf* openings, and the wide, low arches with hollowed archivolts
387
of the cloister court. The splendid band of figures on the entrance tower is the work of Henry Wilson. Subsequent buildings are by Smith and Brewer and Ernest Willmott and the chapel is by Ninian Comper.

Stokes did many school buildings, most, but not all, Roman Catholic. Before 1900 these included the Roman Catholic Schools at Lymington, Hampshire (1885); St George's Schools, Westminster Bridge Road, Southwark, SE1; schools in Northampton Place, Walworth, SE17 (1890); the

Guardian Angel Primary School, Mile End, SE1
(1894); and additions to St Mary's Training
College, 49 Brook Green, Hammersmith, W6
(1895—7).

39 In 1910 Leonard Stokes made an important
addition to Emmanuel College, Cambridge, where
he had already built a lecture room block the

previous year, enlarged into a library by George
Drysdale in 1930. Stokes's additions, completed
in 1914, consist of a hostel range on two sides and
a cloister on the the third. Here Stokes combined
his favourite and original versions of Tudor and
Renaissance motifs. Central corridors give access
to the students' rooms — a departure from the
traditional pairs of rooms off staircases.

After his church work, Stokes's houses also make
an impressive list. Muthesius mentions Yew Tree
Lodge in West Drive, Streatham, SW16 (1898—9)
and Stokes's own house, Littleshaw, Woldingham,
Surrey (1902—4). His earlier domestic work in-
cluded the west wing of Boxwood Court, Dilwyn,
Herefordshire, for Colonel Cox (1890—1; now
demolished); alterations to Nymans, Crawley,
Sussex (1891); a house near Dumshanbo and
Insfall, Lough Allen, Co. Leitrim (1895); and
Shooters Hill House and a cottage for his
in-laws at Pangbourne, Berkshire (1896—7).
He also did The Temple, Goring-on-Thames,
Oxfordshire (1895—6); Sootpray Farm,
Worplesdon, Surrey (1898—9); and Thirtover
House, Cold Ash, near Newbury, Berkshire
(1898; since altered).

Stokes did two London town houses, No. 10
Kensington Palace Gardens (1897) and 47 Palace
Court, Bayswater, W2, for Wilfrid and Alice
Meynell, a house rich in literary associations. The
gabled street front is remarkable for the sense of
breadth Stokes gave it, an easing of the vertical
stress usually found in the gabled 'Pont Street
Dutch' houses which preceded it.

At Pangbourne, Stokes also did the village hall and
shops and offices in Whitchurch Road, sponsored

**Leonard Aloysius Scott Stokes: Emmanuel College,
Cambridge, the North Court.**

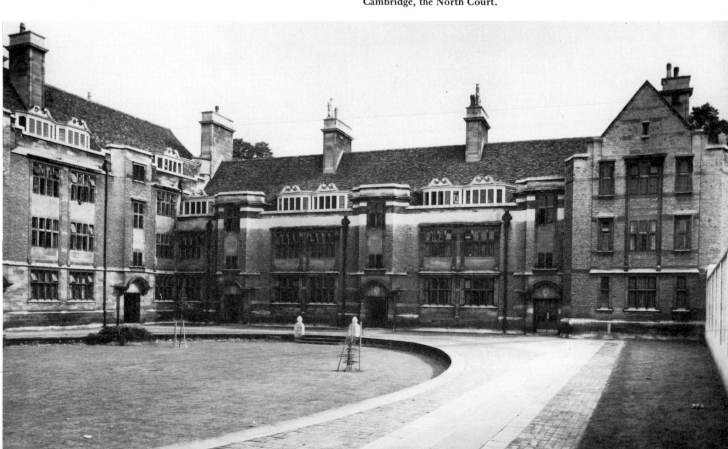

Leonard Aloysius Scott Stokes: Gerrard Street, W1.
Telephone Exchange. Demolished by the Office of
Works in 1930.

by Mr Evans, the Oxford Street draper. At Evans's
house Stokes met Edith Gaine, whom he married
in 1898. Miss Gaine was the daughter of the
General Manager of the National Telephone Co.
and between 1898 and 1908 Stokes did twenty
telephone exchanges for them. In 1911 a legal
judgement ruled that the transmission of telephone
conversations was the equivalent of telegraphic
messages and consequently was the prerogative of
the Post Office. As a result the whole of the
Company's installation, with the exception of the
service in Hull, was handed over to the Post Office
for a sum of £12,000,000.

340   The best-known of Stokes's telephone exchanges
was that at Gerrard Street and Lisle Street, in Soho,
W1 (*Bldr*, 11.1.08), demolished in 1930 and replaced by a building designed by Llewellyn of
HM Office of Works. The original building adopted
Stokes's favourite arches, splayed archivolts,
vertical mullions and horizontal bands — his
'balanced line'. The Southampton Exchange at
1 Ogle Road (1900) was equally interesting, but
the attic storeys have been drastically altered.
Stokes also did the Edinburgh Exchange building
at 149 Rose Street (1900), and exchanges for
337   Glasgow (the Western at 24 Highburgh Road),1),
Manchester (1906—7), Cambridge (1907—8),

Reading (1908) and Aberdeen (1908—9).

As early as 1887 Stokes had put forward a scheme
for the re-planning of the north side of Piccadilly
Circus, severely mauled by the intrusion of
Shaftesbury Avenue in 1886, and now, after
ninety years, in an even sorrier condition. His
ability in civic design was given recognition when
in 1900 he was one of the six architects invited to
prepare a design for the façades fronting on the
new Aldwych and the widened Strand (*see under*
The Holborn—Strand improvements).

Stokes's only muncipal building is the King's Road
SW3 extension to the Chelsea Vestry Hall (1908).
(The previous, south, extension was done by
J. McK. Brydon in 1887.) Stokes's building is in
well-proportioned 'Wrenaissance' with carving by
Abraham Broadbent in the style of Grinling
Gibbons. The jolly belfry perched on the parapet
now lacks its parish bell (*Bldr*, 13.11.09).

341   Stokes's only office building is not far from his
original Soho telephone exchange building and a
worthy match for it. Built for A. Gagnière & Co.
and prominent on the north side of Golden
Square, it displays Stokes's wide arches and
archivolts, his mullioned windows and carved
air inlets (also by Broadbent) — a feature of the
office buildings of this period. But the attic
storeys have been altered, the glazing bars are
missing and the beautiful sign has been replaced
by an illuminated glass box, in the last quarter of
the twentieth century a common feature. The
original owners are now installed in Warwick Street
nearby.

Leonard Stokes put a tremendous amount of
work into the improvement of the Architectural
Association School of Architecture, extending the
old Architectural Museum in Tufton Street, SW1,
so that the school could move there from its
address in Great Marlborough Street, W1, in 1902.

Stokes was a member of the Art Workers' Guild
and President of the RIBA from 1910 to 1912. In
1919 he received the Royal Gold Medal for
Architecture. His portrait by Sir William Orpen
is at 66 Portland Place. In the last ten years of his
life Stokes was seriously afflicted by paralysis.
His work was continued by George Drysdale
(1881—1949). His son David Stokes is a practising
architect, and his son Adrian Stokes and grandson
Peter Stokes are designers and manufacturers of
architectural metalwork.

Leonard Stokes's other works include:

1899-1901   Central School for Boys, Gloucester Green,
Oxford (now part of a bus station; *Bldr*,
25.1.02)

School for Girls and Pupil Teachers' Centre,
New Inn Hall Street, Oxford (*Bldr*, 18.5.01)

1901   East Oxford School, Union Street, Oxford

Church of England School, Arundel, Sussex

Westfield Secondary School, Brickfield
Road, Wellingborough, Northamptonshire

Brompton Oratory Schools, SW7

1901-2	Hill End House, near Wendover, Buckinghamshire (*Bldr,* 6.9.02)
1901-3	Ascot Priory, Berkshire (south wing; *Bldr,* 27.9.02)
	House at Ascot Heath (*Bldr,* 12.10.01)
1903	Lincoln Grammar School (*Bldr,* 3.2.06)
	Cottages and Lodge, Oakfield, Mortimer, Berkshire
	A house at Sunningdale (*AA*,1904)
1903-5	Minterne House, Minterne Magna, near Cerne Abbas, Dorset, for Lord Digby

Above and right: Leonard Aloysius Scott Stokes: the former A. Gagnière building, Golden Square, W1. This beautiful cartouche and grille, *above*, are by Abraham Broadbent. The building's façade, *right*, is sadly altered.

Below: Leonard Aloysius Scott Stokes: additions to Downside College, Radstock, Somerset. Features characteristic of Stokes appear here also.

RIBAJ, 8.1.27: 'The Work of Leonard Stokes', by George Drysdale

Obit. *RIBAJ*, 9.1.26, pp. 148–50 · *Bldr*, 1.1.26, p. 7.

STRATTON, Arthur J. 1872–1955

Arthur Stratton was a pupil of A. E. Street, the son of G. E. Street. He entered the Royal Academy Schools in 1894 and also studied at the Architectural Association. Between 1892 and 1895 he was assistant in turn to Leonard Stokes, Walter Millard, R. A. Briggs and J. J. Stevenson, and in 1896 commenced practice on his own account in Liverpool. Stratton was a demonstrator and assistant lecturer at the Liverpool School of Architecture.

With the painter Robert Anning Bell and the sculptor C. J. Allen, Stratton did the interior of the Philharmonic Hotel in Liverpool (1897–1900). In 1901 he moved to London and taught at King's College and University College. For his Banister Fletcher Bursary, Stratton made a study of Lord Burlington's Westminster School Dormitory (*Bldr*, 7.6.02).

Stratton wrote or edited many books on architecture and was editor of *The Builder* (1912–13). He wrote *The Life, Work and Influence of Sir Christopher Wren* (1897) and edited the 4th edition of W. J. Anderson's *Architecture of the Renaissance in Italy* (1901–9). With Thomas Garner he wrote *The Domestic Architecture of England during the Tudor Period* (1908–12) and his post-war works included *The English Interior* (1920) and *Elements of Form and Design in Classic Architecture* (1925).

His architectural works included the restoration of Chantmarle, Frome St Quintin, Dorset (1906–9), where the gardens are by Inigo Thomas. (The building is now the Police Training Centre.) Later additions (1919) were by E. P. Warren. Stratton also did the Science Building, King's College School, Wimbledon, SW19.

Obit. *Bldr*, 6.5.55, p. 761.

SUMNER, George Heywood Maunoir 1853–1940

Heywood Sumner was born at Alresford, Hampshire, the eldest son of B. H. Sumner, Jowett Fellow and Tutor of Balliol College, Oxford, and a grandson of the Bishop of Winchester. Sumner was educated at Eton and Christchurch, Oxford, and married his cousin, a model to Sir Edward Burne-Jones and sister of the architect and designer W. A. S. Benson.

In 1882, with A. H. Mackmurdo and Herbert Horne, Heywood Sumner was one of the group which formed the Century Guild for the designing and making of furniture, a venture which survived for six years. He also did wallpaper designs for Jeffrey & Co. of 31 Mortimer Street, W1. In 1884 he became a member of the Art Workers' Guild where his pastoral manner earned him the nickname of 'The Shepherd'. He was Master in 1894 and his bronze relief there is by Henry Pegram.

Sumner did the sgraffito decorations in All Saints, Ennismore Gardens, Kensington, SW7 (where the west front was re-modelled by C. Harrison Townsend in 1892), and the sgraffito murals at St Agatha, Portsmouth and other churches. In 1895 Heywood Sumner did a monument to his grandfather in the church of St Mark, Hale, between Farnham and Aldershot, Surrey. In his later years he studied archaeology, particularly that of the New Forest area, on which he published books illustrated by himself. He designed his own house.

George Lister Sutcliffe: houses in Temple Fortune Hill, Hampstead Garden Suburb, NW11.

SUTCLIFFE, George Lister c. 1863–1915

G. L. Sutcliffe was articled to his father, John Sutcliffe, of Todmorden, W. Riding, in 1880 and became his partner in 1895 in a general practice based in Todmorden and Hebden Bridge. In 1902 Sutcliffe opened a branch office in London and four years later went into practice on his own account.

Sutcliffe was appointed architect to the Co-partnership Tenants, a company formed to

Francis S. Swales: Selfridge's, Oxford Street, W1. Although the design of this store was by R. Frank Atkinson, with Daniel Burnham as consultant, Swales provided a sketch which gave Selfridge the idea.

develop non-profit-making estates all round the country. One of the earliest of these was Brentham, a 66-acre estate at Ealing, West London. It was considered a sister estate to the Hampstead Garden Suburb which overtook it during its great years between 1907 and 1914, where Sutcliffe contributed the Creswick Walk and Oakwood Road houses. As further areas of the Hampstead Garden Suburb came to be developed, Sutcliffe acted as architect to more companies there and elsewhere. His largest single work is Meadway Court in the Garden Suburb, in place of a design by M. H. Baillie Scott which was not carried out. Sutcliffe also amended and carried out Lutyens's design for half of North Square, Erskine Hill and Heathgate there. Ten years after Sutcliffe's death a close was named after him in the Garden Suburb where his work was continued by J. C. S. Soutar (1881–1957) and C. G. Butler.

Sutcliffe also designed Blackwood House, Byfleet, Surrey (*Bldr*, 24.9.04), The Dover, Poling, near Arundel (Shaw Sparrow, *Our Homes*), a house at Cowden in Kent (RA, 1910) and other houses in the Home Counties. Shortly before his death, he began supervising the construction of the Liverpool Garden Suburb, won in competition by J. N. Dixon.

Obit. RIBAJ, 25.9.15, p. 507 *Bldr*, 16.9.15, p. 206.

SWALES, Francis S.   *floruit c.* 1905

Francis Swales was born in Canada and studied architecture at the Rochester (NY) Athenaeum, and the Atelier Masqueray, New York. He also attended the Washington University, St Louis, where he won a travelling studentship which enabled him to study in Paris at the Atelier Jean-Louis Pascal and the Ecole des Beaux-Arts.

On his return to the United States, after working in the offices of George T. Otis, Mason and Wood, and Eames and Young, Swales was appointed chief of design for the Louisiana Purchase Centenary Exposition of 1904 at St Louis. He also practised for a time with J. M. Wood of Detroit.

Swales travelled frequently to France and England; he was European correspondent of *The American Architect* and Paris and New York correspondent of the London *Architectural Review*. He also designed buildings at Le Touquet, Paris Plage and Boulogne, and in 1906 started a practice at Bedford Park, Chiswick, where he lived for a time. He did a hotel at Sandwich, Kent, and the 'His Master's Voice' Pavilion for the Gramophone Co. and Maynards (confectionery) Pavilion at the Franco-British Exhibition at the White City (1908).

158
159
343

Swales played a notable part in three important buildings in London's West End. The steel frames of the Royal Automobile Club, Pall Mall, the Ritz Hotel, Piccadilly, and Selfridge's Store, Oxford Street — among the first in London — were all designed by Sven Bylander, a Swedish engineer from New York, introduced by Swales. (The firm of Bylander, Waddell still flourishes in London.) The mammoth columns of Selfridge's derive from a sketch Swales did for Gordon Selfridge and show the marks of his Paris studies.

Swales returned to the United States, but never developed a large architectural practice.

Sir Henry Tanner: Post Office Parcels Office, Waterloo Street and West Campbell Street, Glasgow. Tanner favoured the use of reinforced concrete for the structure.

TANNER, Sir Henry   1849—1935

Henry Tanner was born in London, the son of a builder, and was articled to Anthony Salvin (1799—1881). He entered HM Office of Works, then under Robert Richardson, in 1871 and won the RIBA Tite Prize in 1878. Tanner became a Principal Architect (1884), then Chief Architect (1898) in the Office of Works, and promoted the use of reinforced concrete by the Department.

The building for which he is best known is the King Edward VII building of the General Post Office, King Edward Street, EC1 (1907—10), constructed on the Hennebique System of reinforced concrete to the design of L. G. Mouchel and Partners. The general contractors were Holloway Brothers. The General Post Office, Leeds (1896), is also by Tanner and he did the Public Trustee Office (now in other use) on the new Kingsway, WC2, the west block addition to the Royal Courts of Justice in the Strand, and, after the National Telephone Co. was acquired by the Post Office, a large number of telephone exchanges.

On his retirement from public office in 1913, Sir Henry Tanner joined his son's firm which was chiefly engaged on much of the rebuilding of John Nash's Regent Street during the years 1905 to 1925 (see below).

Obit. RIBAJ, 12.10.35, p. 1160 *Bldr*, 6.9.35, p. 394.

TANNER, Henry, junior   1876—1947

Henry Tanner was the son of Sir Henry Tanner (q.v.) of HM Office of Works. He studied at the Architectural Association and entered the Royal Academy Schools in 1897 where he won the Silver Medal and Travelling Studentship with a 'Design for a Street Front' for a block of buildings such as would be required for Regent Street, where rebuilding was beginning as leases fell in (*Bldr*, 29.12.1900). Tanner was entrusted with the design of many of these buildings, on which he was helped by his architect brother, E. J. Tanner (1887—1939). Together they won the competition for the rebuilding of Oxford Circus. They also competed for the Quadrant, for which no award was made (see pp. 77—80).

Henry Tanner was joint architect with W. J. Ancell for the Strand Palace Hotel in 1907, and after Ancell's death, for the Regent Palace Hotel in 1912, both for Joseph Lyons & Co.

Tanner did Craven House in the new Kingsway in 1906 (RA, 1904); the Bank of New Zealand, Moorgate, EC2; 18 and 19 Pall Mall, SW1; and Oceanic House (1906) at the junction of Cockspur Street and Pall Mall East, SW1, for the International Shipping Co. which included the Red Star, White Star and other lines. The site belongs to the Crown, and the cornice line of Sir Robert Smirke's Union Club and Royal College of Physicians of 1824—7 had to be continued around the block. As the new building had to be taller, the two attic storeys thrust up through the vestigial Greek Revival entablature as if they were breaking out of an eggshell, parts of which still clung. Oceanic House is now a Barclays Bank; the College and the Club are now Canada House and the intervening building carrying several 'attic' storeys is by Septimus Warwick. With F. Dare Clapham of E. W. Mountford's office, Tanner competed for the Queen's University, Belfast, and was placed second (*BA*, 18.11.10). For Sir Edgar Horne, Tanner did Hall Place, Shackleford, near Godalming (now Aldro School), Surrey (RA, 1904).

In 1931 Tanner did the whole range of façades facing Marble Arch — the Regal Cinema (now rebuilt by Sir Thomas Bennett and Son as the Odeon); the Cumberland Hotel for Joseph Lyons & Co. (architect F. J. Wills); and Cumberland Court residential flats.

Tanner illustrated with his measured drawings *English Interior Woodwork of the XVI, XVII and XVIII Centuries* (London, 1903) and *Old English Doorways from the Late Tudor Period to the XVIII century* (London, 1903).

Tanner was joined by his father when he retired in 1913. Another brother, W. Hugh Tanner, a surveyor in the Colonial Service, joined him in the late 1920s to manage his City office. Their West End office is continued by E. T. Dowling and H. F. Morley.

Obit. RIBAJ, Mar., 1947, p. 286 *Bldr*, 31.1.47, p. 131.

TAPPER, Sir Walter John, KCVO, RA 1861–1935

Walter Tapper was born at Bovey Tracey, Devon. He was articled to Rowell and Sons of Newton Abbot, Devon, and at the age of twenty-one entered the office of Basil Champneys in London. Tapper then joined the office of the great church architects G. F. Bodley and Thomas Garner, where he remained to become chief assistant and manager.

At the age of twenty-four Tapper married Catherine Lydia Totcham, of Watts & Co., the church furnishers of Baker Street, W1 (now in Tufton Street, Westminster), of which Bodley was one of the founders. (There never was a Watts — 'What's in a name?' asked Bodley, seeking a title for the firm.)

In 1893 Walter Tapper opened an office at 1 Raymond Buildings, Gray's Inn, WC1, in partnership with J. L. Davenport, but he did not leave Bodley until 1901 when Bodley was seventy-four. Tapper was then forty, and very experienced in church work, which he continued with the same care and attention to detail which had characterised Bodley's work. Less money was now being spent on churches and Tapper's were mainly of brick, which he managed very well indeed, the church of the Annunciation, Old Quebec Street, W1 (1913), being a good example. Here the Baroque interior decoration is by John de Mars. Tapper's own favourite was St Mark, Whiteley Village, Burhill, Walton-on-Thames, Surrey (1919), where the master plan was by Frank Atkinson.

Walter Tapper did a considerable amount of restoration work and additions to a number of large houses, including Turville Grange, Buckinghamshire, and Chandos House, Queen Anne Street, W1 (1904–14). Other alterations by him were at Hengrave Hall, Suffolk (1902; *Bldr*, 3.6.05); Kenfield Hall, near Petham, Kent (1904); Bicton Hall, Devon (1908–9); and Penshurst Place, Kent (1918).

Tapper was appointed Surveyor to York Minster and after the retirement of W. R. Lethaby in 1928 was made Surveyor to Westminster Abbey where he became involved in the long, contentious debate on the siting of extra accommodation for the Abbey.

In 1924 he was appointed consulting architect to the Gas Light and Coke Company, which supplied London's town gas north of the Thames. For them he advised on design, from gas fires to the first waterless gas-holder. Tapper had by then already turned to classical design, as is evident from the First World War Screen at Christchurch Priory, Hampshire. He also designed the Loughborough (Leicestershire) Memorial Carillon Tower (1921).

Tapper was a member of the Art Workers' Guild. He was made ARA in 1926 and RA in 1935 (diploma work, 'Church of the Annunciation, Old Quebec Street, W1'), and was President of the

Sir Walter John Tapper: St Erkenwald, Southend-on-Sea, Essex. Recently redundant, this church appeared on the list of interesting buildings for disposal, issued by the Ministry of the Environment.

RIBA from 1927 to 1929. He received the KCVO in 1935. His portrait by Sir William Orpen is at 66 Portland Place. He lies interred in the West Cloister of Westminster Abbey. His practice was continued by his son, Michael Tapper, MC (d. 1963), who became a partner in 1920.

Walter Tapper's churches include:

1903	Church of the Ascension, Memorial Church to Archdeacon Livingstone, Malvern Link, Worcestershire (RA, 1904; *Bldr*, 10.12.04)
1904	St Mary, Harrogate, W. Riding
1905-10	St Erkenwald, Southend-on-Sea Essex, and Vicarage (tower not executed; *Bldr*, 3.6.05); plasterwork by Laurence Turner and electric fittings by Bainbridge Reynolds
1908	Community of the Resurrection, Mirfield, near Dewsbury, W. Riding, chapel (*Bldr*, 2.10.09; an earlier design by A. H. Skipworth, was not executed)
1910-11	St Oswald, Lythe, Whitby, N. Riding
1912-14	School Chapel, Guildford Grammar School, Perth, Western Australia
1913	St Michael, Little Coates, near Grimsby, Lincolnshire

Obit. RIBAJ, 12.10.35, pp. 1158–60 *Bldr*, 27.9.35, pp. 526 and 532.

TATCHELL, Sydney Joseph 1877–1965

Sydney Tatchell was born in London, the son of Joseph Veale Tatchell. He was educated privately, studied at the Architectural Association, and

345

studied modelling under F. W. Pomeroy. He commenced practice in 1905.

Tatchell's work before 1914 consisted principally of town houses in the Harley Street area, country houses including Western Acres, Woodmansterne, Surrey (1910), and suburban houses at Silver Lane and Rosewalk, Purley, Surrey. His houses in the Harley Street area included the Portland stone 90 and 90a Harley Street and 12 Devonshire Street. This has a remarkable façade of Portland stone in the French style of Louis XVI with urn-topped pilasters. Also in this area is Wyndham Court, Hallam Street, W1.

As Surveyor to the Worshipful Company of Ironmongers, Tatchell designed Ironmongers' Hall, Aldersgate Street, EC1 (1922—5), which survived the great fires resulting from bombing in 1940 by reason of the 'sprinklers' installed on the external walls on Tatchell's advice.

After association with Bouchier and Galsworthy, Tatchell took into partnership Geoffrey Wilson in 1920. His son Rodney F. Tatchell was made a partner and the firm which became Sydney Tatchell and Son in 1940 is now Tatchell and Learner.

THICKNESSE, Philip Coldwell   1860—1920

P. C. Thicknesse was the third son of the Bishop of Peterborough whose family had occupied the same manor house near Crewe for five hundred years. He was educated at Marlborough, articled to Norman Shaw and entered the Royal Academy Schools in 1880. Thicknesse went to Liverpool to supervise work for Shaw and in 1884 went into partnership with W. E. Willink. (For their joint work, *see under* Willink, William Edward.)

Obit. RIBAJ, 6.3.20, p. 211 *Bldr*, 5.3.20, p. 283.

THOMAS, Sir Alfred Brumwell   1868—1948

Alfred Thomas was the son of Edward Thomas, surveyor to the district of Rotherhithe (now part of Southwark). He was articled to W. Seckham and studied for three years under Farrow at the Architectural Association, Tufton Street, SW1. He commenced practice in 1894 adding the name of Brumwell.

In 1898 Thomas won the competition for the colossal Belfast City Hall (RA, 1899; *Bldr*, 18.8.06). The assessors were Alfred Waterhouse, RA, and J. C. Bretland, the City Surveyor. This huge building was paid for from the profits made by the Belfast Corporation on the sale of town gas (much as St Paul's Cathedral was paid for by a tax on sea coal). It was opened by Lord Aberdeen in 1906 and Brumwell Thomas was knighted the same year.

The arrangement of a central dome supported by four corner towers resembling the western towers of St Paul's was a favourite one at the time. But with or without this quincuncial device, the placing of a dome and drum on a podium too large for it has never been successful, from St Peter's on; and when, as in Brumwell Thomas's City Hall, the central dome is not central but discovered to be on one side of a courtyard encroached on by back annexes, the impurity of the whole idea is revealed. This could not be said of the treatment of the interiors, which Thomas made very noble in the English Baroque style, with generous space devoted to the grand staircase, as in William Young's Glasgow City Chambers of 1889. The interiors of Belfast are resplendent with Pavonazzo, Brescia and Carrara marbles and the exterior with the sculpture of F. W. Pomeroy. A statue of Queen Victoria by Sir Thomas Brock stands on a pedestal in front of the porte cochère — a domed pavilion marks the centre portico and may have encouraged Vincent Harris to put a similar construction in front of the Council House

Sir Alfred Brumwell Thomas: Belfast City Hall. The grand staircase. Grander, even, than William Young's at Glasgow.

◁ **Sir Alfred Brumwell Thomas: the dome of Belfast City Hall. Reconciliation between a cupola and the excessive size of the building it represents is seldom satisfactorily brought about. Neither is it here.**

46
47
48

DONECALL
SQUARE
WEST

Sir Alfred Brumwell Thomas: Belfast City Hall. *Above:* a study of the two façades seen here reveals many devices used in Baroque-Classic design. *Below:* the interior of the Rotunda. Several marbles were used.

in Bristol where it has been nicknamed the 'Elephant House'.

Sir Brumwell Thomas continued to win competitions for town halls and to carry them out successfully. Stockport Town Hall, Cheshire (*Bldr*, 19.12.03), won in a competition assessed by Thomas Collcutt in 1903 and completed in 1908, is a design which would seem to derive from the Palais des Beaux-Arts at Lille (1892 by Bérard and Delmas). This also seems to have influenced Thomas in his next success, Plumstead (now called Woolwich) Town Hall, won in a competition also assessed by Collcutt. He also did Clacton Town Hall, Essex, East Ham Town Hall, E6, and Deptford Central Library, SE14.

Sir Brumwell Thomas's other works are few. He did the Eye Hospital, Exeter; additions to the Elizabeth Garrett Anderson Hospital, NW1; and to the Addey and Stanhope Schools, SE8. He later prepared a design for the Hammersmith Town Hall, Brook Green, W6, which was not carried out. The Town Hall was built on another site in 1938—9 to a design by E. Berry Webber.

Obit. RIBAJ, Apr., 1948, pp. 271 and 272 *Bldr*, 30.1.48 p. 134.

THOMAS, James Havard   1854—1921

Havard Thomas was born in Bristol and studied
at the Bristol School of Art, in London where he
was a national scholar at South Kensington
(1875—81), and at the Ecole des Beaux-Arts under
Cavalier, where he did 'A Slave Girl', bought by
Richard D'Oyly Carte. Back in England, Havard
Thomas did Samuel Morley (d. 1886), MP for
Bristol and Nottingham (a plaster cast of a
statuette (c. 1885) is in the National Portrait
Gallery); and William Edward Forster for Forster
Square, Leeds, and for Bradford. With Thomas
Stirling Lee, Thomas revived the correct practice
of carving his own marble and stone, long
neglected by busy sculptors often to the detriment
of the finished work. Havard Thomas taught at
the Slade School. His other works include a
portrait in relief of H. O. Arnold-Forster at St
Margaret's, Westminster, SW1 (1909), and
Edmund Burke for Bradford and Bristol. His
portrait by T. Kerr Lawson is in the National
Portrait Gallery.

THORNYCROFT, Sir William Hamo, RA
1850—1925

William Hamo Thornycroft was the son of the
sculptor Thomas Thornycroft (1815—85) who had
worked in the studio of the portrait sculptor John

Above: **Sir Alfred Brumwell Thomas: Plumstead
(Woolwich) Town Hall, SE18. Baroque features, such as
a nest of pediments, abound.**

Below: **Sir Alfred Brumwell Thomas: Stockport Town
Hall, Cheshire. The cluster of columns recalls the Palais
des Beaux-Arts, Lille, France.**

Francis and married his daughter Mary Francis (1824–1906), also a sculptor. Their other son, John Isaac Thornycroft, builder of high-speed motor-boats, founder of Thornycroft's, the marine engineers, and member of the Royal Society, was also to receive a knighthood.

Thornycroft went to Macclesfield Grammar School and University College School, London. He received his training in sculpture in his father's studio and assisted him on the group 'Commerce' for the Albert Memorial and the figures of 'Comedy' and 'Fame' for the 'Poet's Fountain' in Park Lane — provided in 1875 from the estate of a woman who died intestate but whose wishes for such a fountain were respected. Happily this poor work was removed in recent years. Thornycroft entered the Royal Academy Schools in 1869, winning the Gold Medal in 1875. His Gold Medal entry was purchased by the Art Union of London.

In 1892 Thornycroft helped to put British sculpture on a new footing when, with Harry Bates, ARA, he took a major part in the sculptural
103 frieze on John Belcher's Hall of the Institute of Chartered Accountants in Moorgate Place, EC2. Thornycroft was assisted here by John Tweed and C. J. Allen.

Thornycroft's many commissions before the turn of the century included 'Artemis' for the Duke of Westminster at Eaton Hall, Cheshire (1879); 'The Sower' (1886) set up in Kew Gardens, Surrey in 1927, under the Leighton Fund, on a base by Sir Edwin Lutyens; General Charles George Gordon for Trafalgar Square (now on the Victoria Embankment) and a cast of General Gordon for Melbourne, Australia (1888); and John Bright, Town Hall Square (now in Broadfield Park), Rochdale, Lancashire.

Thornycroft did 'Benjamin Disraeli, Earl of Beaconsfield' for the Peers' Lobby of the House of Lords and the statue of Oliver Cromwell for Old Palace Yard, Westminster. 'Tipped off' by the editor of *The Times* that he would be publishing a letter the following morning from a well-known peer, protesting that Cromwell was about to be placed in front of the Parliament he had used so badly, Thornycroft acted swiftly and before *The Times* appeared the next morning Cromwell was on his pedestal. A vote of £5,000 for the statue was strongly opposed by the Irish Nationalist Party, and the Prime Minister, Lord Rosebery, paid for it out of his own pocket. It was unveiled in 1899.

350 In 1902 Thornycroft did the setting up at Westminster Bridge, SW1, of 'Boadicea, Queen of the Iceni and her Daughters', from a model which his father had made some fifty years earlier from the design of J. C. Jackson, intended for a group on the Decimus Burton screen at Hyde Park Corner. The work was presented to the nation by Thornycroft's brother, Sir John Thornycroft.

Hamo Thornycroft was made ARA in 1881 and RA in 1888 (diploma work, 'The Mirror', relief).

Sir William Hamo Thornycroft: Boadicea (Boudicaa), Queen of the Iceni, and her daughters. Westminster Bridge, SW1. Thornycroft set this up from a model made by his father from the design of J. C. Jackson intended for Hyde Park Corner.

Sir William Hamo Thornycroft: William Ewart Gladstone in the robes of Chancellor of the Exchequer. At the base 'Brotherhood', 'Education', 'Aspiration' and 'Courage'. The base by John Lee. Strand, WC2.

He was knighted in 1917 and received the Gold Medal (RIBA) in 1923. He was a founder member of the Art Workers' Guild in 1883. Sir Hamo Thornycroft's studio and house, still standing, were designed by John Belcher. Portraits by T. Blake Wirgman and by 'Spy' (Sir Leslie Ward) are in the National Portrait Gallery.

Other works by Thornycroft include:

1901	King Alfred the Great, Winchester, and a miniature for the Mayor
1902	John Colet, Dean of St Paul's (1467–1519), supported by two kneeling scholars, at St Paul's School, Hammersmith (now with the school at Barnes) under a gothic bronze canopy supporting angels, the Virgin Mary and the Infant Christ
	Archbishop Thomson, York Cathedral
	Bishop Godwin, Carlisle Cathedral
	South African War Memorial, Manchester
1905	William Ewart Gladstone in robes of the Chancellor of the Exchequer, for a new site created by the junction of the new Aldwych and the widened Strand but not set up according to the wishes of Thornycroft, who disagreed with the alignment. At the base the bronzes 'Brotherhood', 'Education', 'Aspiration' and 'Courage' by Thornycroft. The plinth by John Lee
	Bishop Creighton, bronze statue for St Paul's Cathedral
1906	William George, 1st Baron Armstrong (1810–1900), Barras Bridge, Newcastle upon Tyne, Northumberland
1909	Alfred, Lord Tennyson, Trinity College Chapel, Cambridge
	Sir G. Stokes, (d. 1903) portrait medallion, north aisle, Westminster Abbey
1912	George Nathaniel, 1st Marquess Curzon of Kedleston (1859–1925), Viceroy of India, for Calcutta
1914	Richard Norman Shaw roundel, designed by W. R. Lethaby, on (old) New Scotland Yard, Victoria Embankment, SW1
1915	King Edward VII, Karachi, Pakistan
	Thomas Gray, Pembroke College, Cambridge

TOFT, Albert   1869–1949

Albert Toft was born in Birmingham, the son of a designer and modeller, Charles Toft. His brother Alphonso Toft was a painter. Toft was educated at Stoke-on-Trent and apprenticed at Wedgwood's Pottery, then studied at the South Kensington Schools under Professor Lantéri.

Toft did a number of war memorials including the South African War Memorials at Ipswich (1905) and Cannon Hill Park, Birmingham (1906), the latter on a red granite base with bronze figures personifying Courage and Endurance (*Bldr*, 25.8.06; RA, 1906). In 1909 he did 'Warfare' and 'Grief' on the Welsh National War Memorial (South African War), Cardiff, for the architect Sir Ninian Comper (*q.v.*). A later work in this field was the War Memorial to the Royal Fusiliers at Holborn Bars, London, EC1 (1922). Toft was a member of the Art Workers' Guild. *His other works include:*

1900	Robert Owen, New Lanark
1902	Sir Charles Palmer, Jarrow
1906	Queen Victoria Memorial Nottingham
1909	Queen Victoria, Leamington Spa
1910	Monument to Alastair Mackenzie, St James's, Abinger, Surrey
1913	King Edward VII, Victoria Square (now Highgate Park), Birmingham, and at Leamington Spa

TOWNSEND, Charles Harrison   1851–1928

Harrison Townsend was born at Birkenhead, one of a family of eleven. His father, Jackson Townsend, was a solicitor, his mother the daughter of the Polish violinist Felix Janiewicz. Townsend went to Birkenhead School and was articled to a local architect, Walter Scott. The family moved to London in 1880 and Townsend joined the office of Thomas Lewis Banks, becoming a partner in 1884. With Banks, Townsend did a large house at West Hartlepool (RA, 1884); Upton Congregational Church, Forest Gate, E7 (*Bldr*, 5.4.1884); and a mission room at Lampleigh, Kirkland, Cumberland (*Bldr*, 25.12.1886).

Townsend set up on his own account *c.* 1888. In 1892 he did a new west front for All Saints, Ennismore Gardens, SW7 (an 1846–9 church by Lewis Vulliamy, now Russian Orthodox, to a design deriving from San Zeno Maggiore, Verona, which Townsend had visited in 1886). He designed the entrance gates and railings to Vauxhall Park, Lambeth, SW8.

Harrison Townsend is best known for three London buildings which are in a class by themselves: the Bishopsgate Institute, EC2 (RA, 1895), the East London Art Gallery, Whitechapel, E1, and the Horniman Museum, Forest Hill, SE23. The latter in particular shows the effects of the interest Townsend and his journalist brother Horace took in the work of the American architect Henry Hobson Richardson (1838–86) who did Lululand, Bushey, Hertfordshire, for the painter, Hubert von Herkomer, in 1885. Horace Townsend's article on Richardson appeared in the *Magazine of Art* (1894).

The East London Gallery was started in three school rooms by the rector of St Jude's, Whitechapel, Canon S. H. Barnett, and his wife Henrietta Barnett. Townsend's sister was a friend of the Barnetts and a trustee of the Gallery. The first design, exhibited in the Royal Academy in 1896, showed a symmetrical front; the design actually built was asymmetrical, but the upper part was destroyed in the Second World War. The Gallery was opened by Lord Rosebery in 1901.

The Horniman Museum (*Bldr*, 8.2.02) was founded by F. J. Horniman, a Quaker tea merchant and

Charles Harrison Townsend: the Horniman Museum of Ethnology, Forest Hill, SE23. The approach.

Liberal MP for Falmouth and Penryn, to house his collection of ethnographical and zoological objects. The collection was first housed in his home, Surrey Mount, behind the museum site, which he enlarged for the purpose. The present Museum was begun in 1897 and opened four months after the Whitechapel Art Gallery. The building is of Doulting 107 stone and the front bears a large mosaic by Anning 353 Bell, 32 ft long and 10 ft high, representing aspects of human life. It would be difficult to find a building of the modern period where mosaic and architecture combine more harmoniously. There is also a memorial tablet by F. W. Pomeroy, and a bronze fountain by J. Wenlock Rollins given by Horniman's son who presented the Museum and grounds to the LCC in 1912 and built the lecture hall and theatre there, at Forest Hill, SE23.

Townsend's collaboration with other artists again 304 bore splendid results in the interior of St Mary the 352 Virgin, Great Warley, Essex, designed to replace an earlier church to the south, and built by Evelyn Heseltine in memory of his brother Arnold. The church was consecrated in 1904. It is in simple late Gothic, but the interior, the greatest single work of Sir William Reynolds-Stephens (1862–1943; *q.v.*), is a complete example of metal church fittings and decorations in English Art Nouveau. The modelled plaster barrel vault could, however, be taken for a work of several decades later. The glass, largely destroyed in 1940, was the work of Heywood Sumner. The gardener's cottage here is

Left and above: **Charles Harrison Townsend: St Mary the Virgin, Great Warley, Essex. The rood screen and decorations to the arches are by Sir William Reynolds-Stevens. A memorial to Arnold Heseltine.**

Charles Harrison Townsend: The Horniman Museum of
Ethnology, Forest Hill, SE23. The mosaic on this
exceptionally original work is by Robert Anning Bell.

353

Henry John Treadwell and Leonard Martin: 7 Dering Street, W1. How a narrow frontage, previously occupied by a plain building, could be 'developed' in the early 1900s by these imaginative architects. A drawing by Charlotte Halliday.

not by Townsend but by Guy Dawber (*Bldr*, 19.11.04). The inscription on the tie-beam of the lychgate is by Eric Gill (1882–1940).

In his houses Townsend inclined more to the style which had been developed by George Devey and Eden Nesfield, with only faint reference to the powerful Romantic style of Richardson. A colony of Townsend houses can be seen at Blackheath, Chilworth, Surrey, where Sir William Roberts-Austen and Henry Prescott transformed a dull village into one of those Surrey retreats for town dwellers. Here Blatchfield, Rosemary Hill, Blatchcombe, and Townsend's own house, Cobbins, are among those surviving. The church of St Martin, designed by Townsend in 1892, is low and barrel-vaulted, in contrast to the tall churches of the Gothic Revival, and is decorated by the paintings of Mrs Lea Merritt, executed by a process of fresco painting invented by Keim of Munich. Townsend's Congregational chapel of 1893 and his village hall of 1897 also have low, wide roofs. Townsend designed the Village Cross, West Meon, Hampshire (RA, 1903; *Bldr*, 3.10.03) and the village hall, Panshanger, Hertfordshire (*Bldr*, 4.6.10).

Townsend went to Turin with Walter Crane and Anning Bell to arrange the hanging of the English section of the Exhibition of 1902. He was very much part of the Arts and Crafts Movement and, like the architects inspired by William Morris, practised craft-metalwork and leadwork. A fireplace designed by him and carved by George Frampton was exhibited at the Arts and Crafts Exhibition of 1896. Townsend was Master of the Art Workers' Guild in 1903. His portrait bronze there is by Derwent Wood. He was buried with his sister in Northwood Cemetery, Middlesex, in a grave marked by a stone of his own design.

'Art Nouveau' in Essex Architectural Press, by John Malton in *The Anti-Rationalists*, London, 1973

Obit. *RIBAJ*, 12.1.29, p. 211 *Bldr*, 4.1.29, p. 30.

TREADWELL, Henry John   1861–1910

Like many a famous music-hall double act, the names Treadwell and Martin (Leonard Martin, *q.v.*), are inseparably linked on the Edwardian architectural stage — their 'turn' was a very distinctive type of Edwardian building. Both were pupils and assistants of John Giles of Giles, Gough and Trollope of Craven Street, Strand. In 1890 they set up in practice together. Their work at first consisted of fever hospitals for the Metropolitan Asylums Board — the Southern Hospital in Carshalton, Surrey, and the Joyce Green Hospital in Dartford, Kent. But like most young partners of those years, they made determined efforts to win big competitions. They reached the final round for the Glasgow Art Gallery (1891) and the Birmingham Municipal Buildings (1907), and were placed second for the Hull Town Hall

Henry John Treadwell and
Leonard Martin: 78 to 81 Fetter
Lane, EC1. Formerly offices for James
Buchanan. A drawing by Charlotte Halliday.

extension (1903), but they never achieved a large
building of this kind.

Instead, Treadwell and Martin left a trail of
remarkable little buildings across London's West
End. They became expert in 'developing', to use
the modern term, small, narrow-fronted sites in
New Bond Street, Jermyn Street and the surrounding streets, providing shops for court dressmakers,
milliners, *parfumiers* and shirtmakers, with
workrooms and flats over. These they distinguished
by frontages in a cocktail of Tudor, Baroque and
Art Nouveau, a delightful mixture which
sometimes (as at 7 Dering Street, W1) frothed over
at the apex of a gable into a Baroque pedimented
tabernacle high over the roof line — had the
building been a church, this would have contained
a bell. These little buildings can be found at 23

354   Woodstock Street, 7 Dering Street, 7 Hanover
256   Street, 74 New Bond Street, 20 Conduit Street
(1906), 78 Wigmore Street (1906), 106 Jermyn
Street, 60 St James's Street (once offices for Lord

355   Furness, 1907–10) and 78–81 Fetter Lane, EC1;
and others can be discovered.

A larger building on this theme, originally the
well-known Scott's Oyster Bars and Supper Rooms

355   at 18–20 Coventry Street (1892–4), is now
part of a large complex. James Buchanan's, of 76
High Holborn (1909), was destroyed in the Second
World War, except for a gable surviving in Fetter
Lane, but the Rising Sun public house at 46
Tottenham Court Road (1897), though painted,
still stands. It is more visible today owing to the
setting back of the frontage next to it which
enables it to look *down* the street — an important
and necessary arrangement in any urban context.
Unfortunately, it may be doomed, since the

intention is to continue the road widening to include the demolition of this jolly building.

St John's Hospital in Lisle Street, Leicester Square (RA, 1904), has a Scottish (perhaps Dutch) corbie — or crow-step gable. Russell's shop, also by Treadwell and Martin, stood nearby on the site now occupied by the Swiss Centre. Whitehall House (1904) and the Old Shades public house in Charing Cross (1898) are also their work.

Treadwell and Martin did a number of public houses and breweries, including the Old Dover Castle, Westminster Bridge Road, SE1; the White Hart at Windsor — a grand hostelry; Edinburgh House, Kilburn, NW6; Shelley's Hotel, Albemarle Street, W1; and the Black Swan, Carter Lane, EC4.

The church buildings of Treadwell and Martin include the Presbyterian Church, West Norwood (*Bldr*, 6.2.97); Holy Trinity Mission Church, Tulse Hill, SW2 (RA, 1904); and St John's Church, Herne Hill (1910). They also did Sandroyd School, Cobham, Surrey (1905—6; *Bldr*, 23.7.10), and 5—17 Westbourne Grove, W2.

Bldr, 29.1.43, p. 106: 'Some early modernists', by H. V. Molesworth Roberts

Obit. Bldr 5.11.10 p. 559.

TRIGGS, Harry Inigo 1876—1923

Inigo Triggs was born in Chiswick and was descended colaterally from Inigo Jones. He went to Godolphin School, was articled to Peter Dollar, and attended Chiswick School of Art and the Carpenters' Company classes under Professor Banister Fletcher. He entered the Royal Academy Schools in 1897 and was RIBA Godwin Bursar in 1906.

Triggs worked in turn for Leonard Stokes, H. T. Hare, Sir Henry Tanner, the firm of Woolfall and Eccles of Liverpool, and W. F. Unsworth. Ill-health compelled him to spend much time in Switzerland, but he found compensation in the designing of gardens, on which he became an authority. Triggs did the layout of the gardens of Whiteley Village, Esher, Surrey. He became a partner of W. F. Unsworth and together they did many country houses, including those in the Petersfield district of Hampshire. They were later joined by Gerald Unsworth and did Ashford Chace, Petersfield. Triggs designed the Villa Guardamunt (*Bldr*, 18.6.04) and a house at Chasellas (*Bldr*, 4.8.06), both near St Moritz, Switzerland. He died at Taormina, Sicily, where he had just built the Anglo-American Church.

Triggs's published works include: *Formal Gardens in England and Scotland* (1902); *The Art of Garden Design in Italy* (1906); *Town Planning Past and Present* (1909); and *Garden Craft in Europe* (1913).

Obit. RIBAJ, 12.5.23, pp. 431 and 432 *Bldr*, 27.4.23 p. 690.

Thackeray H. Turner of Balfour and Turner: a house on the Grosvenor Estate in Upper Brook Street, W1. The carving is by Laurence A. Turner.

TROUP, Francis William 1859—1941

F. W. Troup was born at Huntly, Aberdeenshire, went to school at the Gymnasium, Old Aberdeen, and was articled to Campbell Douglas and Sellars of Glasgow (1877—82). He was assistant in turn to Sir Rowand Anderson, RSA, in Edinburgh, and to J. J. Stevenson, George Lethbridge, J. McK. Brydon and William Young in London. He attended the Royal Academy Schools (1884—6), began private practice at 9 Hart Street, WC1 in 1891 and later moved to Gray's Inn Square.

Troup did Farnley Almshouses, Leeds (1896); Mansfield House University Settlement, Barking Road, E16 (*RA*, 1898); and Sandhouse (now Kingswood), Witley, Surrey (1900). He also did a number of village halls, including one at Wootton Fitzpaine, Dorset, in 1906 (Weaver, *Village Clubs and Halls*). This was the gift of Mrs

A. E. Pass for whom Troup did Thistlegate House, Charmouth, Devon, in 1911.

Troup's 20 Old Queen Street, Westminster, SW1, for H. G. Spicer is a small Arts and Crafts town house worth a visit. His offices for Spicer Brothers in New Bridge Street, EC4 (1913) is one of the first steel-framed buildings in which the facing material frankly indicates dependence on the steel skeleton underneath. Troup also did the factory for W. H. Smith & Son at Letchworth Garden City (1910) and the Memorial Hall at Whitefield's Tabernacle, Tottenham Court Road, W1 (1909, destroyed).

Between 1910 and 1912 Troup assisted Schultz Weir in the design of the seaside convalescent home at Canford Cliffs, Dorset, for the Holloway Sanatorium, Egham, Surrey, where he did their staff houses. He also designed Rampton Hospital, Nottinghamshire.

Robert Schultz Weir, also from Sir Rowand Anderson's office, was a lifelong friend and had an office on the same landing in Gray's Inn Square. Like Schultz Weir, Troup was a brother-upholder of the Art Workers' Guild; he did the Guild's hall in Queen Square, WC1, in 1914 and was Master in 1923. Troup also taught leadwork at the Westminster Technical Institute (*Bldr*, 17.8.01). His name survives in the firm of Troup Steele and Scott, who have done the massive extensions to King's College, Strand, WC2.

Obit. RIBAJ, May 1941, p. 124 *Bldr*, 11.4.41, pp. 367, 382 and 404.

TURNER, Alfred, RA   1874–1940

Alfred Turner was born in London, the son of the sculptor C. E. Turner. He trained in the studio of Harry Bates, ARA, and studied at Lambeth School of Art. In 1895 he entered the Royal Academy Schools where he won the Gold Medal and Travelling Studentship in 1897 and for a time studied in Paris.

Turner taught at the Central School of Arts and Crafts, WC1. His work included the 'Fisherman' and 'Fisherwoman' — figures of heroic proportions — for the staircase of the Fishmongers' Hall, London Bridge, EC4 (RA, 1901). Since damage in the Second World War and reconstruction of the Hall by Austen Hall, the figures have stood on the river terrace. Turner also did 'Justice' for the Queen Victoria Memorial, Delhi (RA, 1903); 'Labour' and 'Maternity' for the Queen Victoria Memorial, Sheffield (1931); the memorial to John Constable, RA, in St Paul's Cathedral; Owen Glyndwr at Cardiff City Hall for Lanchester, Stewart and Rickards; Queen Victoria for Sheffield; and King Edward VII for Lyallpur, Punjab, Pakistan. Turner was made ARA in 1922 and RA in 1931 (diploma work, 'Dreams of Youth', in bronze).

TURNER, Laurence A.   1864–1957

The seventh son of the Rev. J. R. Turner, rector of Wroughton, Wiltshire, and brother of the architect Thackeray Turner (*q.v.*). Laurence Turner was educated at Marlborough and then at Oxford. He was apprenticed to John McCulloch.

The beauty and quality of his woodcarvings won Turner a reputation with G. F. Bodley, F. C. Eden, Walter Tapper, Robert Schultz Weir and other church architects of the time. His carvings were not in the usual line of Renaissance work but inclined more to the carved decoration of the Eastern Roman Empire, like that at Baalbek. This is evident in the work he did for Dunn, Watson and Curtis Green on the Scottish Provident Institution building (1905) and Scottish Widows' Fund (1915), in Lombard Street, EC3. It is equally clear in the work he did for his brother, Thackeray Turner, on the houses of the Grosvenor Estate in Mayfair and Belgravia. Laurence Turner also did work for Henry T. Hare at University College, Bangor, North Wales, and for Edward Warren on the Bodley Memorial, Holy Trinity, Prince Consort Road, SW7. He carved William Morris's tomb at Kelmscott designed by Philip Webb, and Norman Shaw's tomb at Hampstead designed by Ernest Newton.

Turner taught by his drawings and held exacting standards, preferring to lose money rather than economise in the work.

TURNER, Thackeray H.   1853–1937

Thackeray Turner was one of the seven sons of the Rev. J. R. Turner, rector of Wroughton, Wiltshire. One of his brothers was Hawes Turner, Keeper, Secretary and later Director of the National Gallery, and another the sculptor Laurence A. Turner (*q.v.*). Thackeray Turner was articled to Sir George Gilbert Scott and was assistant to John Oldrid Scott and George Gilbert Scott junior. In 1890 he became a partner of Eustace Balfour (*q.v.*) who was architect to the Grosvenor Estate in Mayfair, W1, and Belgravia and Pimlico, SW1. Thackeray Turner's work there is recognisable from the rough tooled stonework and the carving by his brother Laurence.

Balfour and Turner did Balfour Place, Balfour Mews and surrounding buildings in Mount Street and Aldford Street, Mayfair; and in Belgravia, Lygon Place, Edinburgh House, Eaton Gate, and the refacing of Wilton Crescent. In Davies Street, Mayfair, they did St Anselm (demolished), which replaced C. R. Cockerell's Hanover Chapel in Regent Street. Their other work together included the Scottish Church, Crown Court, Russell Street, Drury Lane, WC2 (1909); Aldford House (1895–7), Park Lane, W1, for Sir Alfred Beit (demolished); Campden House Chambers in Sheffield Terrace,

356

31
356
358

W8, where granite columns carry the superstructure; and York Street Ladies' Chambers, W1 (1890).

Thackeray Turner was a disciple of Philip Webb and a friend of W. R. Lethaby. Wycliffe Buildings, Portsmouth Road, Guildford — an 1894 range of flats on a steep site — is another interesting example of Turner's design in the Lethaby manner. Much of Turner's activities centred on the town of Godalming in Surrey, where he lived at Westbrook, a house of his own design (*Bldr*, 1.11.02), and where he founded the West Surrey Society. At the Godalming church of St Peter and St Paul he did the Phillips Memorial Cloister, in memory of the heroic wireless operator who went down with the *Titanic* in 1912.

Thackeray Turner was a brother-upholder of the Art Workers' Guild and first secretary of the Society for the Protection of Ancient Buildings. His wife, Mary Elizabeth Turner (1854–1907), was one of the founders of the Women's Guild of Arts.

Thackeray Turner's other works included Charlewood, East Grinstead, Sussex; Ampton Hall, Bury St Edmunds, Suffolk; Goodwyn's Place, Dorking, Surrey (*Bldr*, 11.10.02 and 1.11.02); and The Court (1902) — a group of fifteen houses in Buryfields, Guildford, near his Mead Cottage of 1895.

Obit. RIBAJ, 10.1.38 p. 258.

Balfour and Turner: houses in Lygon Place, SW1, on the Grosvenor Estate.

TWEED, John   1869–1933

John Tweed was one of the four children of a Glasgow publisher and was educated at Hutcheson's Boys' Grammar School, Glasgow. He showed an aptitude for art, but his father's early death obliged him to leave school prematurely and go into the family publishing business. Meanwhile he studied at Glasgow School of Art and worked for the sculptors G. A. Lawson, J. A. Ewing and J. Pittendrigh MacGillivray. In 1888 he took a studio for himself in Glasgow and submitted a sketch model for 'Lord Angus' for the Cameronian Regiment Memorial, but lost to Thomas Brock.

When he was twenty-one, Tweed sold the publishing business and left for London. Hoping to be accepted for a teaching appointment at the Crystal Palace, SE19, he took a room nearby, but failing to obtain the post he entered the studio of Sir Hamo Thornycroft, assisting him on the sculpture on the Hall of the Institute of Chartered Accountants, Moorgate Place, EC2. He also attended the Lambeth School of Art.

In 1893 Tweed visited Paris and met Rodin, beginning a friendship which continued until Rodin's death in 1917. Tweed studied at the Ecole des Beaux-Arts and under Jean-Alexandre-Joseph Falguière.

Towards the end of 1893 Tweed returned to London to do the 'Landing of Van Riebeck' (RA, 1894) and other sculptures for Cecil Rhodes for Cape Colony. In 1899 he did a full length Van Riebeck for Cape Town.

In 1912 John Tweed was entrusted with the difficult task of completing Alfred Stevens's Wellington Monument in St Paul's Cathedral where it still stood in the crypt, lacking the crowning equestrian statue of the Duke. The plaster model done by Stevens in 1856 had been treasured devotedly by his disciple, Hugh Stannus, against the day when the long and acrimonious discussions concerning its final position should be satisfactorily concluded. Objections had to be overcome to the idea of a horse in the cathedral looking at the High Altar, its rump turned to the congregation, and equally, to the weight of the monument. To the appeal by D. S. McColl, inspired by Légros, and to Stannus's persistent pleadings, we owe the splendid and complete Stevens memorial in the nave arcade. Tweed was in turn instrumental in persuading Alfred Gilbert (*q.v.*) to return to England to complete the Clarence Tomb at Windsor, and later to do the Queen Alexandra Memorial, Marlborough Gate, St James's, SW1.

Tweed's connections with Rodin helped to bring

about Rodin's visit to London in 1902 when enthusiastic students of the Slade and South Kensington schools hauled his carriage from the Café Royal to the Arts Club, with John Singer Sargent on the box. It was also apparently on Tweed's recommendation that the Rodin sculptures exhibited at Grosvenor House in 1913 were kept in England during the First World War, so that Rodin bequeathed them to the British nation. Tweed was instrumental in obtaining Rodin's 'St John the Baptist' for the nation, and he financed the Requiem for Rodin at St Margaret's, Westminster. He also did a relief of Rodin, now in the Victoria and Albert Museum.

Among Tweed's later works are Earl Kitchener, Horse Guards Parade (1926), Admiral Lord Beresford in the crypt of St Paul's (1919) and a medallion to Lord Clive in Westminster Abbey. Tweed was a member of the Art Workers' Guild.

Other works by Tweed are:

1902	Completion of Harry Bates's marble Reredos for Holy Trinity, Sloane Square, SW1
	Queen Victoria for Aden
	Cecil Rhodes for Bulawayo
	Death mask of Rhodes
1904	Lieut.-Col. George Elliott Benison (d. 1901) Hexham, Northumberland
1906	Joseph Cowan, newspaper proprietor and MP (1831–1900), Westgate Road and Grainger Street, Newcastle upon Tyne
1907	Bishop Wilberforce, Chichester Cathedral
1910	Charles Compton William Cavendish, 3rd Baron Chesham, KC, Bt., Market Square, Aylesbury, Buckinghamshire
1912	Captain James Cook, Whitby, N. Riding
	Robert, 1st Baron Clive of Bengal, Gwydyr House, Whitehall (moved to King Charles Street, Westminster, 1917). The bas-reliefs show Clive at Plassey, at the Siege of Arcot and reading the 'Grant of Bengal, Orissa and Behar'

Joseph Chamberlain, bust, Westminster Abbey
Field Marshal Sir George Stuart White, VC (d. 1912), Portland Place, W1

UNWIN, Sir Raymond   1863–1940

Raymond Unwin was born at Whiston, near Rotherham, W. Riding, the younger son of William Unwin, a tutor at Balliol College, Oxford. Unwin went to Magdalen College School, Oxford, trained as an engineer and joined the Staveley Coal & Iron Co. near Chesterfield, where in the early 1890s he designed pithead baths, miners' cottages and the church of St Andrew, Barrow Hill.

Unwin entered into partnership with his cousin Barry Parker, an architect trained in the design of domestic interiors who was to do much to simplify house design. Unwin married Parker's sister and went to live at The-Lodge-by-the-Beech, Chapel-en-le-Frith, Derbyshire. Both men were disciples of William Morris, Edward Carpenter and Patrick Geddes, and took a serious interest in such aspects of domestic architecture·as the public ownership of land, seen as a solution to particular social problems of the day. For their works together, *see under* Parker, Richard Barry.

In 1901 Joseph and Seebohm Rowntree, of the Quaker family of cocoa refiners, called in Parker and Unwin to design the garden village of New Earswick, near York. In 1903 work began on the layout of roads and model cottages which were not the animated stage set of some ideal village but followed the lines of the traditional English village in a practical way.

25
359

Barry Parker and Sir Raymond Unwin: houses in Chestnut Grove, New Earswick, for Rowntrees of York.

The work of Parker and Unwin attracted the attention of Ebenezer Howard whose conception of the ideal community, based on the writings of Thomas Davidson, Edward Bellamy and Henry George, was about to be put into practice at Letchworth in Hertfordshire. The brothers-in-law were asked to submit a plan to be considered along with plans invited from two other pairs of architects, W. R. Lethaby and Halsey Ricardo of London, and Geoffry Lucas and Sydney Cranfield of Hitchin. Parker and Unwin's plan was preferred and they came to live first at Baldock, then at Letchworth where work started in 1904. Among their first assistants were Robert Bennett who founded the firm of Bennett and Bidwell and Samuel Pointon Taylor, who became chief architect to the Ministry of Works.

Like most pioneers, Parker and Unwin worked rapidly and were soon in a position to take on a new commission. Shortly after work began at Letchworth, Parker and Unwin were invited by Henrietta Barnett to help on the Hampstead Garden Suburb which she had been instrumental in founding. Edwin Lutyens was appointed consultant, and in the brief period of seven years (1907–14) the best of Hampstead Garden Suburb was designed and built under their direction.

26
27
282

Soon after the outbreak of the First World War, Unwin was appointed Chief Planning Inspector of the Local Government Board which in 1919 merged into the Ministry of Health and became responsible for housing. Unwin was seconded to the Ministry of Munitions to carry out in permanent materials the large housing schemes required for munitions workers. He enlisted the services of the architects who had helped him at Hampstead, including Michael Bunney, C. M. Crickmer and Geoffry Lucas, who all went to the largest munitions centre, that at Gretna, Dumfries.

After the war, as chief architect to the Ministry of Health under Dr Christopher Addison, Unwin established the principles on which the new housing schemes were to be based. 'Addison' housing schemes are now recognisable all over the country from their resemblance to the cottage area of the Hampstead Garden Suburb, except for the use of the different local materials, rightly insisted on by Addison and Unwin, for in those days there were no 'pre-fabs', either in the munitions towns or on the post-war estates.

Unwin's reputation as a lecturer on town planning grew, especially in the USA where he was Professor of Town Planning at Columbia University. In this capacity he constantly warned against the danger of street congestion which he predicted would result if office buildings in the cities continued to become taller and more closely spaced. His advice was sought by Franklin D. Roosevelt when he elaborated the plans for his New Deal (1933–6).

Unwin was President of the RIBA from 1931 to 1933. He was knighted in 1932 and in 1937 received the Royal Gold Medal for Architecture. He died at Old Lyme, Connecticut, at the home of his daughter. His son Edward (1896–1936), named after Edward Carpenter, was also an architect and designed the TUC Memorial Cottages to the Tolpuddle Martyrs, Tolpuddle, Dorset.

Sir Raymond Unwin's many books, pamphlets and articles included *The Art of Building a Home* (1901); *Cottage Plans and Commonsense* (1902); and *Town Planning in Practice* (1909).

RIBAJ, Sept., 1963, pp. 355–7: 'Sir Raymond Unwin, 1863–1940', by T. Findlay Lyon
Obit. RIBAJ, 15.7.40, pp. 208–10 *Bldr*, 5.7.40, p. 4.

VERITY, Francis (Frank) Thomas   1867–1937

Frank Verity was the son of the architect Thomas Verity (1837–91) whose best-known but sadly mutilated building is the Criterion Restaurant and Theatre, Piccadilly, W1, built in 1873 for the caterers, Spiers & Pond, on the site of the White Bear Inn. Frank Verity went to Cranleigh School, Surrey, studied in the studio of A. F. Brophy, art teacher at the South Kensington Schools, and in 1883 was articled to his father. He also studied at University College, London, and at the Architectural Association.

In 1887 he entered the Royal Academy Schools where the architecture master was R. Phené Spiers. From there Verity went to the Atelier Blouet, Gilbert, Questel and Pascal, then under Jean-Louis Pascal whose name had become associated with the revival of the neo-classical style — an antidote to more romantic and less practical revivals. Verity was impressed by the work of one of Pascal's pupils, Henri-Paul Nénot, whose designs for the new Sorbonne in Paris were attracting a great deal of attention.

On his return to London, Verity won the Tite Prize in 1889 and in the same year became a partner in his father's practice, which was largely concerned with theatres (Thomas Verity was Surveyor of Theatres to the Lord Chamberlain from 1878 until his death). With his father Verity worked on the French Hospital, Shaftesbury Avenue, WC2; Hill's Bakery premises in Westminster, Kensington and Hampstead (the families were related); the Pavilion at Lord's Cricket Ground for the Marylebone Cricket Club; flats in North Audley Street, W1, for the Grosvenor Estate; extensions to the Civil Service Co-operative Society Store, Haymarket, SW1; and Elkington's of Cheapside, EC2 (demolished). Of Frank Verity's own design for 96 and 97 Piccadilly (1896; RA, 1892), built in brown limestone, for the New Travellers' Club, the architect and critic H. S. Goodhart-Rendel said,

Francis (Frank) Thomas Verity: Cleveland House, SW1.
Luxury flats in Verity's Champs Elysées manner.

'I do not think that anything has come into
Piccadilly of a higher class of merit in the last
forty years'.

In the early 1900s Verity designed two theatres —
the Imperial, Westminster, a reconstruction of the
old Aquarium Theatre for Lily Langtry, completed in three and a half months; and the Scala
Theatre and Restaurant, Charlotte Street, W1
(replacing the Prince of Wales Theatre), for Distin
Maddick, opened in 1905 and demolished in
1970 (*Bldr*, 17.12.04 and 2.12.05). In these two
theatre buildings Verity introduced a more classical style, using real marbles, bronze and French
'stuc' (plaster jointed to imitate stone). Frank
Verity's other theatres included the Theatre Royal,
Windsor, and the Theatre Royal, Bath.

When, after his accession, King Edward VII made
changes in the interior and furnishings of
Buckingham Palace, Verity was called in to re-
decorate the State Apartments. But his most
distinctive contribution to the London scene is
his apartment houses. With the exception of 11a
and 11b Portland Place, W1 (1908), which has
fluted Ionic pilasters, they are astylar, a London
version of the *appartements* of the Champs
Elysées. Of all borrowings from Paris, including
E. A. Rickards's Baroque and the literal translation
of A. J. Davis, these are the most successful.

The best of Verity's blocks is in Cleveland Row,
opposite St James's Palace, SW1 (*Bldr*, 30.6.06), a
1905 group of three mansions and apartments
which included the rehousing of the London
Fencing Club, formerly on the site. (The building
is now offices.) Verity's concern for detail is
instanced in the cornice which has *paired*
modillions to keep it in scale with both of its
neighbours, the modest Palace opposite and the
Italianate Bridgwater House by Sir Charles Barry.
Other apartment houses by Verity are at 12 Hyde
Park Place, Marble Arch, W2 (*Bldr*, 25.7.08), and
25 and 26 Berkeley Square, W1 (*Bldr*, 11.8.06;
the top storey is of later date). These apartment
houses by Verity set a style which prevailed until
the lean 1930s and was imitated by others,
including his former assistants Albert Richardson
and Lovett Gill, and by H. W. Wills and William
Kaula. The planning of the flats and the embellishment of their entrance halls and staircases by
French 'stuc' and scrolled wrought-iron balustrades
enriched by *repoussé* work all combined to bring
a touch of Paris to London.

Verity's effort to introduce a more dignified style
into the rebuilding of Regent Street resulted in his
façade for the Regent Street Polytechnic and a
similar façade at St George's House for the Raoul
Shoe Co. (*Bldr*, 16.6.11); this was to have been the
style for the whole block between Conduit Street
and New Burlington Street. (The stone carving is
by Charles Bradford.) To restore some semblance

361

of symmetry in this block, St George's House was repeated and astylar wings added by T. S. Darbyshire.

Verity was awarded the London Architecture Medal in 1924 for his Shepherds Bush Pavilion, W12, an early 'super-cinema'. He also did the Plaza Cinema, Lower Regent Street, SW1, since remodelled by his successors. Frank Verity was joined in partnership by Samuel Beverley. They became European advisers to the Paramount Cinematograph Company, an appointment which resulted in their doing the Paramount cinema theatres in Tottenham Court Road, W1, Birmingham, Manchester, Newcastle upon Tyne and Glasgow, and in Paris.

The practice continues as Verity and Beverley, under the direction of Beverley's son-in-law, Sir Anthony Denny, Bt., and his partner D. A. Butcher.

AJ, 7.1.25, pp. 36—59: 'The work of Frank T. Verity, by A. Trystan Edwards
Daily Telegraph, 17.6.65.
RIBAJ, Feb., 1963, p. 88.
Obit. RIBAJ, 11.9.37 p. 1008, 16.10, p. 1071 *Bldr*, 20.8.37, p. 312.

VOYSEY, Charles Francis Annesley
1857—1941

Charles Voysey was born near Hull, the elder son in a family of eight. His father, Vicar of Healaugh, Yorkshire, was expelled from the Church of England for his radical views and founded the Theistic Church, Swallow Street, W1. When Voysey was fourteen, his family settled near Dulwich School where it was intended the boys should be educated, but he failed to settle down at school and had a private tutor. The resulting close association with his father laid the foundation of many of his later views.

In 1874 the young Voysey was articled to the church architect J. P. Seddon, worked for him for a year as assistant and in 1879 was assistant to Henry Saxon Snell. In 1880 he joined the office of George Devey, an architect who had managed to recapture some of the lost, simpler elements of country buildings in his houses, cottages and gardens. One of Voysey's early opportunities to extend his experience in this field came when Devey asked him to superintend the building of some cottages in Northamptonshire, acting as agent, engaging workmen and buying materials.

Voysey had met Ruskin and was an admirer of Pugin. From contemporaries like A. H. Mackmurdo he learned to give the closest attention to the smallest details of domestic architecture and furniture design. Although not a rugged individualist, Voysey was a meticulous one. He is quoted as

saying: 'To be true to your material, true to your conditions, true to your highest instincts, is the surest and only way to true art'. Faithful to the Gothic ideal, Voysey disapproved of Shaw's defection to the Renaissance and its later continuation by Lutyens. Following the traditional use of building materials, but detaching himself from the traditional forms in which they were used, Voysey designed from first principles, and fitness for purpose was his watchword.

Voysey began practice on his own account in 1882 in Broadway Chambers, Westminster, SW1, and started with small jobs and surveys.

When Voysey married schoolteacher Mary Maria Evans in 1885 he gave up his office in Westminster and practised from his home, first at Bedford Park, W4, then at Streatham Hill, SW2, and later at 11 Melina Place and 6 Carlton Hill, St John's Wood, NW8. Although the Voyseys did not manage to build their own house for a time, the published designs were seen by Sir Michael Lakin who asked Voysey to design his house, The Cottage, at Bishops Itchington, Warwickshire. The Voyseys eventually built The Orchard, Chorley Wood, Hertfordshire, for themselves. Voysey took an office at 23 York Place, Baker Street, W1, which he occupied until 1913 when it was demolished.

Simplicity was characteristic of Voysey's houses with their long ranges of windows with square (not moulded) mullions and leaded lights, with their high-waisted, ledged-and-braced doors with Norfolk latches and cross-garnet hinges. Inside were simple fireplaces with low, log-burning andirons or coal-saving grates surrounded by glazed, oblong tiles *set vertically*. The staircase balustrades were simple slats, often reaching to the ceiling and forming a screen to the staircase. Easy to live in, his houses were a welcome antidote to the over-ornamented houses of the period which, despite their architects' search for simplicity, were usually over-furnished by their owners. This would probably have been the fate of Voysey's houses too, had he not been able to persuade his clients to furnish to his designs. Similar to that designed by George Walton, Voysey's furniture avoids the extremes of Charles Rennie Mackintosh's.

Even before his houses had become known and in demand, Voysey had found an outlet for his talent for designing from first principles. Mackmurdo had helped him to master the technique of designing wallpapers and fabrics and he did designs for Jeffrey & Co., the Essex Wallpaper Co., Arthur Sanderson & Sons, the Anaglypta Co. and Lincrusta Walton. Inspired, perhaps, by his furniture were the cabinets for the Gramophone Company whose famous 'His Master's Voice' trademark some say was suggested by Voysey. Photographs of the interiors of the offices of the Essex and Suffolk Equitable Insurance Co.'s office, 54—60 Old Broad Street, EC2 (1906, 1907 and 1910) show Voysey's planning and

365

Charles Francis Annesley Voysey: Spade House,
Sandgate, Kent. A watercolour by the architect for a
house for H. G. Wells, much altered.

equipment to have been well ahead of his time
(*Bldr*, 30.10.09).

Voysey's first country house was Walnut Tree
Farm, Castlemorton, Worcestershire (1890).
Voysey also did a house at 14 South Parade,
Bedford Park, W4. In 1896 at Studland, Dorset, he
did Hill Close for the playwright Alfred Sutro and
one of his best houses, at Greyfriars, near Putten-
ham, Surrey, for Julian Sturgis. His only town
houses are 15 and 16 Hans Road, SW3 (1891), for
Archibald Grove. There were to have been three
here but No. 12 was done by A. H. Mackmurdo

and Herbert Horne. By 1926 Voysey had done
some 120 private houses. His design for a house at
Tyringham, Massachusetts, USA, was not built.

Voysey had competed in 1884 for the Admiralty
buildings, Horse Guards Parade, but was unsuccessful. He competed, again unsuccessfully, for the
Ottawa Parliament Buildings, Lincoln Grammar
School, the Masonic Peace Memorial and Croydon
Town Hall. His scent shop for Atkinson's, 24 Old
Bond Street, W1 (1911; *AJ*, 24.12.24), disappeared
when the present building by Vincent Harris was
built, but the warrant holders' Royal Coat of Arms

designed by Voysey was preserved there in the basement. Voysey designed the marble medallion (carved by B. Creswick) on Thomas Carlyle's house, 24 Cheyne Row, Chelsea, SW3.

Voysey worked with George Walton for the Liquor Control Board (Carlisle) from 1915 to 1919. He was Master of the Art Workers' Guild in 1924 and in 1940 was awarded the Royal Gold Medal for Architecture.

While admiring Philip Webb and William Morris, Voysey disagreed with Morris's opinions on religious and social questions. An individualist and idealist, Voysey was not much in favour of collaborative work; he considered the Hampstead Garden Suburb 'a colony of flannelled faddists all prying into each other's gardens' (*AR*, July 1919). This did not deter him from preparing a design for No. 16 Bigwood Road, which, however, was not built (*BA*, 19 and 26.11.09).

Voysey was the author of a pamphlet, *Reason as a Basis of Art*, and expounded his principles in *Individuality* (Chapman and Hall, London, 1915). In his last years he lived in a flat in St James's Street, SW1, and spent his days at the Arts Club. His portrait by Meredith Frampton is at the Art Workers' Guild, one by W. Lee Hankey is at the Arts Club, and one by Harold Speed at the National Portrait Gallery.

Voysey's principal works after 1900 include:

364

1901   The Pastures, North Luffenham, Rutland (and alterations and additions, 1909)

Lodge Cottages, Madresfield Court, Worcestershire, for Earl Beauchamp

1902   Wallpaper Factory at Barley Mow Passage, Chiswick, W4, for Arthur Sanderson & Sons (partially destroyed; the remainder now in other use)

Vodin, Pyrford Common, near Woking, Surrey, for F. Walters (stables 1904)

1903   White Cottage, Lyford Road, Wandsworth, SW18

Upton Cottage (now Chimneys), Ockham, Surrey

Tilehurst, Bushey Grange Road, Bushey, Hertfordshire

1904   House at Highams Park, Woodford, Essex, for Lady Henry Somerset (in V&A and RIBA collections)

Myholme, Merry Hill Lane, Bushey, Hertfordshire (alterations 1911), a convalescent home for children

Housing and Institute, Whitwood Colliery, Normanton, W. Riding

1905   White Horse Inn, Stetchworth, Newmarket, Cambridgeshire, for the Earl of Ellesmere

House, Assouan, Egypt, for Dr Leigh Canney

1906   Hollymount, Knotty Green, Beaconsfield, Buckinghamshire, for C. T. Buck

The Homestead, Frinton-on-Sea, Essex

1907   Littleholme, Upper Guildown Road, Guildford, Surrey, for G. Muntzer

601 and 602 Finchley Road, NW3 (destroyed in the Second World War and replaced by houses by R. Seifert)

363   1908   Spade House, Sandgate, Kent, for H. G. Wells

1908-9   Littleholme, 3 Sedbergh Road, Kendal, Westmorland

1909   St Winifred's Quarry (now Lodge Style), Combe Down, Bath, for T. S. Cotterell, in Gothic style

House at Henley-in-Arden, Warwickshire, for Miss Knight

Charles Francis Annesley Voysey: *Left:* The Pastures, North Luffenham, Rutland. *Right:* The Orchard, Chorley Wood, Hertfordshire. The architect's own house.

AR, Sept. 1931: 'Charles Annesley Voysey', by John Betjeman

AR, Sept., 1931, '1874 and After', by C. F. A. Voysey

Batsford Gallery, London, catalogue of an exhibition of the works of Voysey, 1931

Brandon-Jones, John, *C. F. A. Voysey, a Memoir* with a chronological index of events and designs, London, 1957

Brandon-Jones, John, 'C. F. A. Voysey', in *Victorian Architecture*, ed. Peter Ferriday, London, 1963

Brandon-Jones, John and others, *C. F. A. Voysey: architect and designer 1857–1941*, London, 1978

RIBA, Catalogue of the Drawings Collection: 'C. F. A. Voysey', by Mrs. Joanna Heseltine (née Symonds)

Obit. RIBAJ, 17.3.41, p. 88 *Bldr*, 21.2.41, p. 197.

WADE (after 1900 WADE-PALMER), Fairfax Blomfield   1851–1919

Fairfax Wade was one of the fourteen children of the Rev. Nugent Wade, a canon of Bristol Cathedral and for fifty years rector of St Anne's, Soho. Wade's youngest brother was the sculptor George Edward Wade, and one of his eight sisters was Louisa Wade, first Lady Superintendent of the Royal School of Art Needlework for which Wade designed a new building (demolished 1962). In 1877 Wade married the elder daughter and co-heir of Robert Ruthven Pym, a partner in Coutts & Co., the bankers. When his wife inherited Holme Park and the Manor House, in Sonning, Berkshire, Wade adopted the name of Wade-Palmer.

Like his sculptor brother, Wade began his main career after he had tried a different profession, banking, and he became an assistant to Sir Arthur Blomfield, ARA. An early work was the restoration of Condover Church in Shropshire (1878) and he designed St Mary-without-the-Walls in Handbridge, Chester, for the Duke of Westminster in 1885–7.

Wade's practice consisted largely of work for the nobility and gentry at their country seats or London houses, ranging from iron lamp standards at Eaton Hall, Cheshire, for the Duke of Westminster (1884), to the town house at 54 Mount Street, W1, for Lord Windsor (1896–9). His earlier houses were Jacobean in style, the later ones were 'Wrenaissance', perhaps under the influence of his assistant, J. Leonard Williams — after a fall in the early 1890s, Wade was confined to a wheelchair. Compton House, Vicarage Lane, Denton, Northamptonshire (1893) is Jacobean, while Sherfield Manor (now North Foreland Lodge), Sherfield-on-Loddon, near Basingstoke (1898), is Classical. The latter, together with Arborfield Court, Swallowfield, and Highcockett, Hare Hatch, both in Berkshire, are illustrated by Mervyn Macartney in 'Recent English Domestic Architecture' (*AR*, 1910–14). Wade's other houses in Berkshire include two in Henley Road, Maidenhead, additions to a farmhouse at Burchett's Green, and restoration work at Ockwells Manor. He also did Angrove House, near Crowborough, Sussex.

Nos 63 and 64 Sloane Street, SW1, are an exceptional pair of town houses by Wade, the first being for his sculptor brother. At No. 53, Wade did a house for himself, while No. 3 Hans Crescent (*Bldr*, 27.2.1897 and 29.1.1898) is also his work.

Wade's best-known building, unhappily a victim of the relentless advance of the buildings of the Imperial College of Science, was the Royal School of Art Needlework, Imperial Institute Road, SW7 (*Bldr*, 2.5.03). Wade had prepared a Jacobean style design in 1893, but building did not begin until 1898 when a new design was adopted, highly Edwardian in its slack proportions and perhaps the work of Leonard Williams. The building was completed in 1903. Stone carving was by Henry McCarthy.

Obit. Bldr, 31.1.19, p. 104.

Fairfax Blomfield Wade (Wade-Palmer): the Royal School of Art Needlework, Imperial Institute Road, SW7 (demolished in 1962).

WADE, George Edward   1853—1933

George Wade was the youngest brother of the architect Fairfax Wade. Showing exceptional promise in his studies when a boy, he was sent at an early age to Dr Jessop, headmaster of Norwich Grammar School, to study for the Civil Service examinations which it was hoped he would pass in one year instead of the usual three. Not surprisingly, his health broke down and his father sent him to Switzerland to recuperate. On his return Wade began studying for the Bar but a chance event dramatically changed the course of his life.

During a visit to Rome, Wade was invited to meet Sir Coutts Lindsay (1824—1913), the Crimean War soldier and artist, founder of the Grosvenor Gallery and encourager of many young artists. While waiting in Sir Coutts's rooms for his host to appear, Wade made a sketch on some paper temptingly stretched on an easel. The result so delighted Sir Coutts that he advised Wade to take up painting. Thus encouraged Wade soon discovered a natural aptitude for modelling sculpture, and his bust of Lieutenant-Colonel Myles Sandys, MP, was accepted for the Royal Academy in 1889.

In the following year his bust of his father attracted the attention of Sir Joseph Edgar Boehm, Sculptor-in-Ordinary to Queen Victoria, who at first took it to be the work of a Frenchman — all the more surprising in view of the fact that Wade had had no formal training in his art. Boehm met Wade and told him he proposed passing any further commissions he was unable to undertake to a younger man and would recommend Wade.

The following December Boehm died suddenly while at work in his studio. He had been true to his word. A flow of commissions for public commemorative sculpture and portrait busts began to come to Wade. From Buckingham Palace and Windsor Castle came commands for bronze statues of royalty — two colossal statues of Queen Victoria, one for Colombo and one for Allahabad, the latter surmounted by a marble canopy, and Wade was also asked to do a statue of the Duke of Connaught for Hong Kong (RA, 1892). During the Japanese Occupation of 1942—5 this was removed to make way for a tennis court (they forgot he was royal). Wade also did statuettes of the Duke of Connaught, one for Windsor and one presented by Queen Victoria to the German Emperor.

Edward VII, declaring that Wade's was the most dignified representation of his mother he had seen, consented to four statues of himself, for Reading, Bootle, Madras and Hong Kong (1904). Wade's next commission was for two statues of Queen Alexandra, one for Hong Kong and one for the London Hospital in East London (1904) where the Queen is represented holding a Finsen lamp — a Danish invention introduced in 1900 for the treatment of the skin. A bas-relief in the base represents the King and Queen inspecting that department of the hospital. Wade then did statues of King George V for Bombay and King George V and Queen Mary for Hong Kong.

Among the many public statues cast in bronze from Wade's models are those of Sir John Alexander Macdonald (d. 1891), first Premier of Canada (1867), for Hamilton, Kingston and Montreal (RA, 1893); Lord Sandhurst and Mr Acworth for Bombay; Muthusami Iyer, first Indian High Court Judge of Madras, a seated figure of which a plaster copy was made for India House in Aldwych; and Chandra Shamshere Yung, Maharajah of Nepal, depicted reining in an arab horse, described as 'perhaps [Wade's] most delightful equestrian statue'.

Wade did some forty statuettes and portrait busts. The subjects included the composer-pianist and Prime Minister of Poland, Jan Paderewski, François Faure, the French Premier, Lord Strathcona, and the artist's daughter, Elmira Wade. His memorial work included the Gurkha Memorial, Dehra Dun, India, those to the St George's Rifles at their headquarters in Davies Street, W1, and the Cameron Highlanders in Inverness, and the War Memorial at Pietermaritzburg in Natal.

Wade's Children's Fountain in Victoria Embankment Gardens, WC2, erected in 1897 to commemorate Women's Temperance organisations and their supporter, Lady Henry Somerset (d. 1896), was largely the gift of the children of the Loyal Temperance Legion. Unfortunately it has been stolen.

Wade's memorial in St Thomas Becket, Hampsthwaite, W. Riding, to Mrs Amy Woodforde-Finden (d. 1919), composer of the 'Indian Love Lyrics', shows a recumbent figure of the composer in white marble and bas-reliefs representing Indian scenes. The general design is said to be by an Italian, Judini (Pevsner).

Late in his career Wade did sculptures of General Booth and Mrs Booth for the Salvation Army College, Denmark Hill, SE5 (1932). His last work was an equestrian statue of Earl Haig for the Castle Rock, Edinburgh.

WALCOT, William   1874—1943

William Walcot's life and work invite comparison with Whistler's. Both spent part of their youth in St Petersburg and Paris, both liked to live in the manner expected of a successful artist, and both employed the means of representing light and colour introduced by the Impressionist painters.

Walcot was born at Lustdorf, near Odessa, went to school in Amiens and Paris, and at seventeen began studies at St Petersburg Imperial Academy of Art under Louis Benois. In Paris he studied at the Ecole des Beaux-Arts and at the Atelier Redon.

Walcot first set up as an architect in Moscow, went to Rome and then settled in London where he worked for a time for C. W. English, the perspective artist. Walcot's etchings and paintings of architectural scenes and 'reconstructions' encouraged the Fine Art Society to send him to Venice and they exhibited his work in 1909.

Walcot's work falls into three categories: imaginative historical reconstruction, particularly of Egyptian and early Greek and Etruscan temples; etchings of buildings; and architectural perspectives of projected buildings. With unrivalled skill and imagination he combined the technique of watercolour and gouache with that of the tube and palette knife. A particularly successful example of his style is his series representing Sir Edwin Lutyens's Viceregal Lodge, New Delhi. The Walcot style was followed closely by others, especially P. D. Hepworth (1890–1963) and H. L. G. Pilkington. Walcot at the time of his death was working on Abercrombie's County of London Plan. He designed 61 St James's Street, SW1.

Obit. RIBAJ, July, 1943, p. 202 18.6.43, pp. 533 and 561.

WALKER, Arthur George, RA 1861–1939

A. G. Walker was born in Hackney, E8, the son of a shipping merchant. He entered the Royal Academy Schools in 1883.

Walker did the symbols at the top and at the base of the tower of the Four Evangelists at the Church of the Agapemonites (1895; later the Cathedral Church of the Good Shepherd of the Ancient Catholics) in Rookwood Road, Hackney, and the mosaics in the Greek Orthodox Church of Santa Sophia in Moscow Road, Bayswater, W2. For Aston Webb's Victoria and Albert Museum in South Kensington (1899–1909), Walker did 'Roger Payne, Bookbinder' and 'William Morris, Designer, Poet and Reformer' in stone on the Exhibition Road façade. Other works by Walker include the South African War Memorial to the men of Suffolk (bronze), in the Butter Market, Bury St Edmunds; the black marble bust of Orlando Gibbons, organist, in the north aisle of Westminster Abbey; Florence Nightingale in St Paul's Cathedral and Thomas Stirling Lee for the Art Workers' Guild, of which he was a member.

Walker did many war memorials after the First World War and the statue of Christ at St Anne, Limehouse, E14 (1921). Towards the end of his career he did Mrs Emmeline Pankhurst in bronze in Victoria Tower Gardens, Westminster (1930). (The bronze plaques, 'Dame Christabel Pankhurst' and 'To the Women's Social and Political Union', on the flanking pedestals were added later.)

Of the same period are his bronze equestrian figure of John Wesley for the courtyard of Wesley's 'New Room' — his first chapel — in Broadmead, Bristol,

and 'Charles Wesley' preaching, also in bronze, in the Horsefair courtyard of the chapel; and 'Dame Louisa Aldrich Blake', twin busts set back to back on a pedestal by Lutyens in Tavistock Square, WC1.

Walker was made ARA in 1925 and RA in 1936 (diploma work, 'Grief', marble). *Other works by him are:*

1904	Memorial to the Marchioness of Lothian, Blickling Church, Norfolk (*Bldr*, 17.6.05)
1905	Triptych Pièta, bas-relief in marble and silver, at the church of the Holy Angels, Parkstone, Dorset
1915	'Florence Nightingale' in Waterloo Place, SW1, on a granite pedestal and four bas reliefs representing 'A Conference of Nurses' 'The Visiting of a Hospital', 'The Transportation of Wounded Soldiers', and 'An Inter view with Military Authorities'
	Lady Mount Temple, at Torquay, S. Devon Sir Corbet Woodall (d. 1916), at Beckton Gas Works, E6

WALKER, William Henry Romaine, *see* ROMAINE-WALKER, William Henry

WALTERS, Frederick Arthur 1850–1932

F. A. Walters was a pupil of George Goldie and entered the Royal Academy Schools in 1871. He designed over forty of the many Roman Catholic churches and seminaries established in England during the latter half of the nineteenth century and the beginning of the twentieth. One of his finest is the Church of the Sacred Heart, Edge Hill, Wimbledon, SW19. Other churches and buildings for religious orders designed by Walters before 1900 included Our Lady of the Reparation, Wellesley Road, Croydon, Surrey (1883); the enlargement of the chapel of Douai Abbey and St Mary's College, Woolhampton, Berkshire, St Joseph, Falkland Grove, Dorking, Surrey, and St Peter, Winchester (all 1893–5); Greyfriars Monastery, Blackheath and St John's Seminary, Wonersh (both in Surrey and 1895); the Church of the Sacred Heart, Petworth, Sussex and St Thomas of Canterbury, Sevenoaks, Kent (both 1896); and Our Lady and St Peter, East Grinstead, Sussex (1898).

Walters's largest and best-known work is the design for the gradual rebuilding of the ancient Abbey at Buckfast, South Devon, originally founded by French Benedictines and refounded by Cistercians in 1137. The original Saxon abbey was destroyed at the Dissolution of 1539 and the new buildings, which are still being built by the monks themselves, were designed by Walters on a French Cistercian plan. The style is Norman and Early English (*Bldr*, 22.5.09).

Walters also did the church of St Anselm and St Cecilia, Kingsway, WC2, in 1909, to replace the old Sardinian Chapel lost in the slum clearances of 1900.

When the west front was rebuilt (1951–4) after war damage, a south aisle was added by S. C. Kerr Bate. His son, E. J. Walters (1880–1947; *Obit. Bldr*, 4.7.47, p. 17) continued his father's practice.

Other post-1900 churches by Walters are:

1900-3	St Anne, Kennington Lane, SE11 (tower 1906–7)
1901-2	Our Lady of Ransom, Eastbourne, Sussex
1902	St Joseph, Brighton, Sussex (temporary west front)
1903	St Elizabeth, Richmond, Surrey (chancel and presbytery)
	St Gertrude, Purley Road, Croydon, Surrey
1904-5	St John, Heron's Ghyll, Maresfield, Sussex
	Our Lady of Lourdes, Harpenden, Hertfordshire
	St Mary, Egremont, Cumberland (*Bldr*, 2.12.05)
1905-6	Les Oiseaux Convent, Canterbury Road, Westgate-on-Sea, Kent (chapel 1909–10 by his son E. J. Walters)
	St Winifride, South Wimbledon (*Bldr*, 2.12.05)
1906	St Edmund, Croft Road, Godalming, Surrey
1907	St Edmund's College, Old Hall Green, Hertfordshire (completed by his son)

Obit. RIBAJ, 6.2.32, p. 277.

WALTON, George   1868–1933

George Walton was born in Glasgow, the son of Jackson Walton, a once-wealthy Scottish painter reduced to poverty by misfortune and a large family. While a junior clerk in the British Linen Bank, Walton attended evening classes at Glasgow School of Art. At twenty-one he set up as a designer and decorator at 152 Wellington Street, Glasgow, as 'George Walton & Company, Ecclesiastical and House Decorators'. These were the days of the 'Glasgow Boys' when a group of young artists, including Walton's brother, E. A. Walton, was earning a reputation for new ideas in painting, exhibiting in London, Munich and Budapest.

George Walton decorated Miss Cranston's famous Willow Tea Rooms in Glasgow for which Charles Rennie Mackintosh and his wife Margaret were also designers.

Walton opened a shop in London in 1897 and in the following year one in York, where he decorated Elm Bank (1900), a house designed for Sidney Leetham by W. G. Penty and his sons. In 1903 Walton decorated the dining room of C. F. A. Voysey's home, The Orchard, Chorleywood, Hertfordshire (Art Workers' Guild Archives).

Through George Davison, the representative of Eastman's Kodak in England, Walton did the interiors of the Kodak offices at Clerkenwell Road, EC1, and five Kodak shops, including those in the Strand, WC2, Regent Street, W1, and Brompton Road, SW3. He also did Kodak shops in Brussels, Milan, Vienna and Glasgow, and a stand at the Glasgow Exhibition of 1901. Characteristic of these stands and shop fittings were the tall, slender tapering supports crowned by flat square caps with shallow ogee soffites — a style derived from A. H. Mackmurdo which, in a debased form and in yellow oak, became popular for men's outfitting shops.

Walton also did the shop fronts and interiors for Wellington & Ward, another supplier of photographic materials (*BA*, 5.6.03), and the offices of Walter Judd, Advertising Agents, 5 Queen Victoria Street, EC4.

Walton also did The Leys, Elstree, Hertfordshire (1901; now an old people's home), which is illustrated in Muthesius's survey. Most of the interior furniture, fittings and light fittings were lost after occupation by the military in the Second World War. Also at Elstree, Walton did the decorations in the chancel of St Nicholas's Church.

With C. F. A. Voysey Walton was architect to the Central Liquor Traffic Control Board (1916–21). He designed Morton-Sundour Fabrics (1926–30) for Alexander Morton and he laid out the garden of the old Bank of England before its demolition in 1928.

Other works by Walton are:

1903	The Log Hut, Bourne End, Buckinghamshire
1905	Finnart House, Weybridge, Surrey
1907-10	Wern Faur, Harlech, Merioneth, North Wales for George Davison (now a hotel)
1908	The White House, Shiplake-on-Thames, Oxfordshire, for Mrs Davison
1910-11	St David's Hotel, Harlech

RIBAJ, 3.4.39, pp. 537–48: 'George Walton, His Life and Work', by (Sir) Nikolaus Pevsner
Obit. Bldr, 22.12.33, p. 985.

WARD, William Henry   1865–1924

W. H. Ward was born at Iver, Buckinghamshire, the son of the vicar of Iver. He is best remembered for his two books, *Sixteenth Century French Châteaux and Gardens* (1909) and *The Architecture of the Renaissance in France* (1911). Ward was educated at Repton and Clare College, Cambridge, articled to Sir Arthur Blomfield (1890–2) and worked as an improver with George and Peto (1892–3). A period with Dan Gibson of Windermere, Westmorland, followed before he became assistant (1894–8) to Edwin Lutyens. Ward won the RIBA Silver Medal Essay Prize and first set up in practice in Charlotte Street, W1.

Ward did Woodside, a 'close' of twelve houses, but not built according to the published plan, in Erskine Hill, Hampstead Garden Suburb, in the vernacular

371

Edward Prioleau Warren: Hanover Lodge, St John's Wood High Street, NW8. The epitome of Edwardian comfort in high-class flats.

revival style of Parker and Unwin (RA, 1909; *Bldr*, 12.3.10). His other work included the Rectory at Marston, Leicestershire (*BA*, 25.5.01); the parish church at Fazakerley, Liverpool, with W. G. Cogswell (1908); a boys' preparatory school at Weston-super-Mare, Somerset; a boathouse at Derwentwater (RA, 1902); The Steep, Keswick, Cumberland (RA, 1900); and the gardens at High Moss, also in Keswick (RA, 1900).

Ward also did designs for furniture for the Church Craft League and a design for a Mission School in Lucknow, India. His death was precipitated by war service — he enlisted by greatly understating his age and returned to the front after being invalided home.

Obit. Bldr, 14.3.24, pp. 407 and 414 and 28.3, p. 488.

WARREN, Edward Prioleau   1856—1937

Edward Warren was the fifth son of A. W. Warren, JP. He went to Clifton College and was articled to G. F. Bodley. He later wrote a biography of Bodley and designed his memorial at Holy Trinity, Prince Consort Road, SW7.

Like many of his contemporaries, Edward Warren was an all-round architect, turning his hand with equal ability to churches, colleges, mansion flats and houses. His churches include St John the Evangelist, Caversham, Oxfordshire; St Mary, Bishopstoke, and St Michael and All Angels, Bassett, both in Hampshire; St Columba, Wanstead, Essex; St Martin, Bryanston, Dorset (RA, 1899; *Bldr*, 10.2.1900); and St Clement, Bradford, Yorkshire. He also did the addition of a new chancel and vestries to St Peter, Lowestoft, Suffolk (RA, 1903; *AR*, 1905; *Bldr*, 12.12.03); the centre of the reredos is by R. Anning Bell, the wings by Dacres Adams. A later Warren church is the Church of the Good Shepherd, Preston, Brighton (1922).

Edward Warren did additions to Magdalen College, Oxford, where his brother, Sir Herbert Warren, became President. Warren did the Warren Building at Balliol (1906; *Bldr*, 19.9.08) and the Junior Common Room there (1913). He also did additions to Merton and to St John's and to the Radcliffe Infirmary (1902—13). The William Dunn School of Pathology is a later work (1925—7). In the High Street, Oxford, he did the Eastgate Hotel (*Bldr*, 10.2.1900) and adjacent shops and houses (RA, 1899), and he did a house in King Street. The fountain and clock at St Clement's at the east end of Magdalen Bridge are also his work (RA, 1899).

At Cambridge he did work at Trinity and the hall oriel, gallery and panelling at Gonville and Caius

(1909–10). His other college work includes additions to Westminster School, Clifton College and Rugby School.

370 Warren's Hanover Lodge, St John's Wood High Street, NW8 (1903–4) — the best-looking block of mansion flats in an era of mansion flats — represents the height of comfort in that age of comfort for the well-to-do. Other domestic work by Warren includes 5 Palace Green and Estcourt House, Kensington Palace Gardens, W8 (RA, 1904); Townshend House, Prince Albert Road, NW8, for Charles Ricketts and Charles Shannon (demolished); Shelley House, Chelsea Embankment, SW3 (1912); 1 Campden Hill, W8; houses on the Magdalen College Estate, Wandsworth, SW18; and the Fishermen's Institute, Newlyn, Cornwall, the gift of Miss Bolitho (*Bldr*, 9.6.11).

Like that of many of his fellow brother-upholders of the Art Workers' Guild (Warren joined in 1892 and was Master in 1913), Warren's work is in a later seventeenth- or early eighteenth-century style, accepted as equally valid interpretations of the motto 'To use materials aright'. Warren's Eastgate Hotel, Oxford, in the vernacular style is a notable exception. So too are his buildings for Bedales School at Steep, near Petersfield, Hampshire, where the school moved from its original foundation at Bedales, N. Riding. Warren's first

Edward Prioleau Warren: the Warren Building, Balliol College, Oxford. A detail.

imaginative design for the new buildings (RA, 1901; *Bldr*, 7.9.01) was modified in execution. The Hall and Library were added later to designs by Ernest Gimson.

Among Warren's country houses are Maesruddud, Blackwood, Monmouthshire; Gorse Hill, Woking, Surrey (*Bldr*, 9.6.11); and his own house, Beech House, Cholsey, Berkshire (1906). He did alterations to Great Milton Manor, Oxfordshire, and to West Lavington Manor, Wiltshire (1905), for Thomas Holloway of Holloway Brothers, the building contractors. In the First World War Warren was seconded to the Serbian Army. He did the war cemetery at Basra, Iraq, and the setting for the memorial to General Maude in Baghdad. His son, Peter Warren, continued the practice.

Obit. RIBAJ, 20.12.37, pp. 203–4 *Bldr,* 26.11.37, p. 965.

WARWICK, Septimus   1881–1953

Septimus Warwick was articled (1895–8) to Arthur Vernon and was assistant in turn to H. Cowell Boyes, Charles Waymouth, W. A. Pite, R. S. Balfour and R. Frank Atkinson. In 1905 he set up in practice in partnership with Herbert Austen Hall (*q.v.*). In the same year they won the competition for Lambeth Town Hall, SW2 (1906–8; *Bldr*, 20.5.05). The Assembly Hall and attic storey are additions of 1937–8. Their next success was Holborn Town Hall, WC1, in 1906. In 1909 they won the competition for Berkshire County Offices and Shire Hall, Reading, where the assessor was Mervyn Macartney.

Warwick and Hall dissolved partnership in 1913 and Warwick went to Canada where he worked on the Manitoba Parliament Building, Winnipeg, won in competition by the architect F. W. Simon and completed in 1920, when Warwick returned to London. He extended the old Union Club (designed by Sir Robert Smirke), Trafalgar Square, SW1, to form Canada House, the offices of the Canadian High Commissioner and offices for the Sun Life of Canada Assurance Co.

Septimus Warwick's later work also included the Wellcome Research Institute, Euston Road, WC1 (1931); mansion flats, Albion Gate, Bayswater Road, W2 (1935); and Radnor Place, W2 — neo-Georgian houses misplaced in stately Bayswater but encouraged by the RIBA in 1932 when they awarded the London Street Architecture Medal to Sir Giles Gilbert Scott for Chester House, Clarendon Place, W2.

Obit. Bldr, 6.11.53, p. 701.

WATERHOUSE, Paul W.   1861–1924

Paul Waterhouse, the son of Alfred Waterhouse, RA, was born in Manchester, educated at Eton and Balliol, and articled to his father in 1880, becoming a partner in 1891. He won the RIBA Essay Prize in 1886.

Waterhouse continued his father's practice, completing University College Hospital, Gower Street, WC1, to which he added the Medical School and Nurses' Home (*Bldr*, 17.6.05). That year he completed also Mount Melville, St Andrews, Fife — one of the last of those sumptuous mansions which finally gave way to simpler houses. Here the interiors display a wealth of marbles, panelling, plasterwork and metalwork.

Waterhouse was a member of the Art Workers' Guild, and President of the RIBA from 1921 to 1923. An excellent draughtsman, he illustrated William Sanday's *Sacred Sites of the Gospels* (1903). Waterhouse died at the Waterhouse family home, Yattendon, Berkshire. He was succeeded in his practice by his son, Michael Waterhouse, MC (1889–1968), who in turn was succeeded by *his* son, David Waterhouse.

Other works by Paul Waterhouse are:

1902	Whitworth Hall, Manchester University
	Maurice Hostel, Hoxton, N1
1904	Prudential Assurance Building, Liverpool (additions)
1905	The London Salvage Corps, Watling Street, EC4 (*Bldr*, 3.6.05 and 23.11.07)
1906	Refuge Assurance building, Manchester (tower and additional wing; *Bldr*, 10.7.09)
1907	New Buildings, College Road, University of Leeds (*Bldr*, 18.7.08)
1908	Headquarters of the National Pensions Fund for Nurses, Buckingham Street, Strand, WC2 (*Bldr*, 29.5.09; demolished)
	New building for the Prudential Assurance, Aberdeen (*Bldr*, 29.5.09)
	The Schools of Chemistry, Oxford

Obit. RIBAJ, 10.1.25, p. 141 and 24.1.pp. 141–3.

WATERHOUSE, Percy Leslie   1864–1932

Percy Leslie Waterhouse was born in Hobart, Tasmania. He went to Christ's College, Cambridge (1883–7), was articled to George and Peto in 1887 and was assistant (1889–92) to J. Osborne Smith. He commenced practice in Staple Inn in 1894 and entered into partnership with A. H. Hart in 1902. (For their work, *see under* Hart, Alfred Henry.)

WATKINS, William Henry   1878–1964

W. H. Watkins was born in Bristol and was articled to Frederick Bligh Bond with whom he carried out the Handel Cossham Memorial Hospital, Kingswood, Bristol. He set up in practice in 1903. Soon afterwards Watkins designed the United Counties Bank, Clare Street, the Capital and Counties Bank, St Stephen's Avenue (demolished), and premises for the Bristol Tramways and Carriage Company.

After the 1914–18 War Watkins designed cottages and flats for the war-torn town of Béthune, Northern France, the gift of the City of Bristol.

In addition to conducting a general practice, designing houses and commercial premises, W. H. Watkins was one of the pioneers in the design of the early cinematograph theatres or 'picture palaces' and when that class of enterprise grew after the First World War into a major industry he carried out many of the 'super-cinemas' of the 1920s and 1930s at Plymouth, Exeter, Barnstaple, Bristol, Bath, Coventry, Truro and Chippenham. The Regent, Bristol, and the Gaumont Palaces at Plymouth and Coventry were destroyed by enemy action. Entering into a third phase, Watkins with his partners carried out hospitals on a large scale in England and abroad. The practice continues as Watkins, Gray, International.

William Henry Watkins: a taxicab garage at Westbury, Bristol, for the Bristol Tramways and Carriage Company.

WATSON, Robert   1865–1916

Robert Watson went to school at Edinburgh Institution and was articled in turn to Alexander Nisbet Paterson, Hippolyte Blanc, Hew Wardrop and Sir Rowand Anderson. He became assistant to James MacLaren, where he met William Dunn. On MacLaren's death in 1890 Dunn and Watson carried on his practice. (For their work together, *see under* Dunn, William Newton.)

Obit. RIBAJ, 19.2.1916, pp. 142–144.

WATT, Richard Harding   1842–1913

Although Watt, a Manchester glove merchant, employed the professional architects W. Longworth, Walter Aston, John Brooke, Harry Fairhurst and J. H. France to carry out his ideas, he provided the inspiration, form and style of the buildings for the embellishment of Knutsford, Cheshire. Watt had qualified as a teacher of drawing and in his extensive travels he sketched profusely all types of building which attracted him, mostly Italian and Islamic. He obtained architectural features from the housebreakers and insisted that his architects followed his instructions which he communicated, not by drawings, but by means

Richard Harding Watt: the Old Laundry and cottages,
Knutsford, Cheshire.

Richard Harding Watt: a villa in Legh Road, Knutsford, Cheshire.

of clay models. The Gaskell Memorial Tower of 1907–8 commemorates the Unitarian novelist Mrs Gaskell who was brought up in Knutsford and based her novel *Cranford* on the town. Quotations from her works are cut in surprisingly modern lettering into the stonework of the tower. Next to it is the King's Coffee House where Watt sought to attract the working-class population by installing an enormous bake-oven to provide freshly baked cakes (*see* title page).

Other buildings include The Old Croft, Watt's own house, by Brooke (1895) with a 1907 tower by W. Longworth; Moorgarth, by Fairhurst (1898); and the Ruskin Rooms and Cottages (1899–1902). After the turn of the century Swinton Square was added (1902) and the pairs of cottages in Drury Lane, houses in Legh Road and the laundry in Knutsford Mere (1904).

374
373

While the domestic buildings tend to be Italianate in style, the memorial tower still looks modern today.

AR, Oct., 1940, pp. 109–12.

WEBB, Sir Aston, GCVO, CB, RA, Hon.LLD Cantab. 1849–1930

Aston Webb was born in Clapham, SW4, the son of Edward Webb, an engraver and water-colour artist. In his time, Aston Webb had the largest practice in the United Kingdom, principally concerned with the design of public buildings. He went to school at Brighton, was articled to Banks and Barry, and commenced practice in 1873, winning the RIBA Pugin Prize the same year. Later he took into partnership Edward Ingress Bell.

In 1885 Webb and Bell won the competition for the Victoria Law Courts, Birmingham, which they carried out. In 1888 they did 23 Austin Friars, EC2; and in 1890–3, 13–15 Moorgate (Street), EC2, for the Metropolitan Assurance Society, in rich fifteenth-century Gothic.

Webb and Bell did the Gothic French Protestant Church (1891–3) in Soho Square, W1, and the church schools in Noel Street, W1, now in other use. They added the Royal United Services Institution (1893–5) to the south end of Inigo Jones's Banqueting House of 1619, then occupied by the Imperial War Museum and now restored to its original function. In 1894 Aston Webb and Ingress Bell won the competition for the new buildings at Horsham, Sussex, for Christ's Hospital, Newgate Street, EC1. These were constructed on land purchased from the Aylesbury Dairy Co. The chapel is decorated with five panels by Frank Brangwyn (*Bldr,* 3.1.03).

Sir Aston Webb, RA: *Above:* the Victoria and Albert Museum, South Kensington, SW7. The competition perspective drawing. *Below:* Gonville and Caius College, Cambridge. St Michael's Court.

Aston Webb did the Royal Naval College, Dartmouth, Devon (1899—1904), and the Imperial College of Science, South Kensington, SW7 (1900 —6; *Bldr*, 2.1.04), followed by the Royal School of 375 Mines (1901—13). At Cambridge he did St 376 Michael's Court, Gonville and Caius (*AR*, 1904). From 1906 to 1909 Webb was also building the University of Birmingham on land at Bournbrook 376 given by Lord Calthorpe. In red brick with terra- 377 cotta front, Webb's building has paintings by R. Anning Bell and nine life-size figures in the Great Hall by Henry Pegram (*Bldr*, 3.5.02, 18.5.07 and 13.7.07).

375 In 1891 Aston Webb and Ingress Bell won the competition for the extensions to the South Kensington Museums, renamed the Victoria and Albert Museum on completion. The collections had begun in 1852 as the Museum of Ornamental Art in Marlborough House, had moved into temporary courts in South Kensington in 1857 and into permanent buildings in 1865, part of a grand scheme designed by Captain Fowke under the guidance of the Prince Consort, Sir Henry Cole, and (to some extent) the Prince's adviser, Gottfried Semper. The foundation stone of Sir Aston Webb's design was laid in 1899 by Queen Victoria and the new buildings were opened by King Edward VII and Queen Alexandra in 1909. The buildings combine an astonishing variety of stylistic traditions, from an open mediaeval-style stone crown to a Venetian-style campanile, while the masonry looks as if it were from models made

for terracotta, an illusion heightened by the prominent jointing. An extensive array of sculpture contributed by eighteen Academician sculptors adorns the façades and the main entrance portal (*Bldr*, 2.5.03, 4.5.07, 2.1.09 and 3.7.09).

Sir Aston Webb's reputation with the government authorities was further enhanced when in 1901 his scheme was placed first in the competition for the improvement of The Mall, SW1, and for a rond-point at Buckingham Palace (*Bldr*, 2.11.01). Those invited to compete were Sir Ernest George, John Belcher and Sir William Emerson from England, Sir Rowand Anderson, Hon. RSA from Scotland, and Sir Thomas Drew from Ireland. Before the design for the setting had been selected, Thomas Brock had already been commissioned for the Queen Victoria Memorial. Aston Webb's design showed a colonnaded and covered walk around the perimeter of the rond-point (*Bldr*, 3.11.06)

Sir Aston Webb, RA: Gonville and Caius College, Cambridge. Twin doorways in St Michael's Court.

Sir Aston Webb, RA: *Above:* Birmingham University, the entrance court. Mosaics by Anning Bell. *Right:* Birmingham University, the Clock Tower.

and a Triumphal Arch at the Trafalgar Square end, with both faces concave to disguise the change of axis at that point. What pleased the authorities was the way Webb had provided offices for the Admiralty in the abutments and attic storey of the arch, so that the Admiralty Arch, as it came to be called, not only symbolised naval activity through the sculptural groups 'Navigation' and 'Gunnery' by Thomas Brock (1910) but also accommodated those engaged in directing it (*Bldr*, 17.6.05 and 30.7.10). Sculpture symbolising the Commonwealth countries on the pedestals surrounding the rond-point was contributed by Alfred Drury and Derwent Wood.

Webb had another card up his sleeve. Some of the designs had suggested a refacing of Blore's dull brown stone façade to Buckingham Palace which Queen Victoria had had built across Nash's open

courtyard to provide more accommodation for her growing family. Since the Palace faces north-east, this façade had reduced the chance of sunlight enlivening the palace front as it had done Nash's open courtyard. Aston Webb delighted the Treasury by omitting the encircling colonnades of his winning design, thus helping to pay for the refacing of the Palace with solid Portland stone. The refacing was done by the builders, Leslie & Co., in *under thirteen weeks*, while the Royal Family had expected it to take a whole year. With his unfailing good sense, King Edward refused to allow the Mall to be renamed 'Processional Way', an expression used persistently by the LCC and the Press (*Observer*, 13.11.10).

Sir Aston Webb, RA: *Right:* The Admiralty Arch, The Mall, SW1. *Below:* The competition design for the setting of the Queen Victoria Memorial in front of Buckingham Palace, SW1, showing the suggested colonnades.

Sir Aston Webb's well-proportioned building, the offices for the Grand Trunk Railway of Canada, in Cockspur Street, SW1 (*Bldr*, 9.5.08), has met a cruel fate; the entire ground floor frontage — wide arches and central doorway, a composition on the lines of the splendid doorway and arches on Norman Shaw's Alliance Chambers in St James's Street — has been swept away so that the whole of this fine stone façade now appears to stand on a plaster shop front. Inside, in a hemicycle, Frank

Brangwyn did a painted frieze illustrating a theme which rings hollow indeed today — 'The Introduction of European Civilisation into the Country of the Red Indian' (since removed; *Bldr*, 2.5.08).

Sir Aston Webb did the Law Courts in Hong Kong in 1904, the year he received his knighthood. He was made CB in 1909, KCVO in 1914 and GCVO in 1925. In 1905 he received the Royal Gold Medal for Architecture and in 1907 the American

Gold Medal. Webb became ARA in 1899, RA in 1903 and PRA 1919—24 (diploma work, 'Proposed Architectural Treatment of the Surroundings to the National Memorial to Queen Victoria in front of Buckingham Palace'). He was made Hon. LLD (Cantab) in 1923 and was President of the RIBA from 1902 to 1904. His portrait by S. J. Solomon is in the National Portrait Gallery and there is a memorial to him in the crypt of St Paul's Cathedral. He took into partnership (as Sir Aston Webb and Son) his son Maurice Webb, architect of Bentall's store at Kingston and of the partial rebuilding of the Army and Navy Stores in Victoria Street (since rebuilt again).

Bldr, 5.8.32, p. 205.

Obit. RIBAJ, 20.9.30, p. 710 *Bldr*, 29.8.30, pp. 329—30 and 333, and 5.9.30, p. 380.

378

WEIR, Robert Weir Schultz (Robert Weir Schultz until 1915)   1861–1951

Robert Schultz Weir was articled to Sir Robert Rowand Anderson, Hon. RSA, in Edinburgh. On coming to London he worked in the offices of R. Norman Shaw and George and Peto, entered the Royal Academy Schools in 1884 and won the Gold Medal and Travelling Studentship in 1887. Schultz Weir began practice in Gray's Inn Square, sharing the same 'pair' of offices with fellow Scot F. W. Troup, who had been with him at Anderson's office. The two were lifelong friends, but never became partners.

Sir Rowand Anderson's clients had included the 4th Marquess of Bute who now became Schultz Weir's chief client. The Marquess had estates in Scotland and was the principal landowner in Cardiff where he gave Cathays Park to the City for the first of the new (and often disappointing) civic centres. For the Marquess in Scotland Schultz Weir did the reconstruction of Wester Kames Tower, Isle of Bute (RA, 1900); Old Palace, Mochrum, Wigtownshire; Dumfries House; and Rothesay Castle. On the Marquess's estates in Wales, he did the Settlement Buildings, Cardiff. In London in 1897, he did alterations to the Marquess's London home, St John's Lodge, Regent's Park, NW1, including the rose garden (RA, 1898; see p. 292); converted into the Sir John Ellerman Hospital for Officers by T. Phillips Figgis.

At the instigation of Lord Bute, Professor Lethaby, Sidney Barnsley and Schultz Weir made study tours of ancient Byzantium on behalf of the Byzantine Research Fund. (Their drawings are in the British Museum.) Weir and Barnsley collaborated on *Byzantine Architecture in Greece* and Weir's studies in this field culminated in the finest work of his career, Khartoum Cathedral. He had already worked with other architects and artists on an original design for the second competition for Liverpool Anglican Cathedral. The team included Troup, Lethaby, Henry Wilson, Stirling Lee and the stained-glass designer Christopher Whall — all members of the Art Workers' Guild and each in turn Master. The design was not beautiful, but, as might be expected of the Guildsmen, it was sincere. In Khartoum Cathedral Weir was able to realise successfully the ideals of honest construction which he shared with his fellow Art Workers. In the Sudan, where he could create the right building for the right climate with none of that bane of the Art Worker, heating installations, there was no call for a highly sophisticated building (*Bldr*, 11.9.09).

Weir did the chapel of St Andrew and the Saints of Scotland in J. F. Bentley's Byzantine Cathedral in Westminster, where low-relief figures are by Thomas Stirling Lee. His earlier church work had included a church at Woolmer Green, Hertfordshire (1899–1900). He also did Knock-en-hair, Dunbar, East Lothian, for Sir Reginald Wingate,

Governor of the Sudan; How Green, Hever, Kent, for M. V. Charrington (*AR*, 1906); Pickenham Hall, Norfolk; The Croft, Winchfield, Hampshire; the Village Hall at Shorne, Kent (*Bldr*, 15.12.06); the South African War Memorial (sculpture by W. Goscombe John) for the Royal Army Medical Corps, Aldershot (*Bldr*, 10.6.05); and St Anne's Hospital, Canford Cliffs, Dorset (1910–12), a seaside convalescent home for the Holloway Sanatorium on which F. W. Troup collaborated.

Like Troup, Weir did excellent small domestic work where the crafts predominated, but the large country house which Norman Shaw could handle with such ease was in his case often clumsy and scarcely redeemed by the introduction of cast lead panels, decorative plasterwork or patterned brickwork.

Schultz Weir was Master of the Art Workers' Guild in 1920. The ideas shared by Weir and his fellow members were presented in a series of lectures given at the Carpenters' Hall, EC2, edited by Raffles Davison and published in 1909 as *The Arts Connected with Building*. Schultz Weir's three lectures were entitled 'Reason in Buildings: or the Commonsense use of Materials'. Weir's and Troup's leadwork is illustrated in *The Builder*, 17.8.01. Schultz Weir and his wife built themselves a house, The Barn, at Hartney Wintney, Hampshire (RA, 1900), where the Lethabys became neighbours.

Ottewill, David, Thesis for MA Degree, Courtauld Institute, University of London 1977

Obit. Bldr, 11.5.51, p. 663.

WELCH, Herbert Arthur   1884–1953

Herbert Welch was born at Seaton, Devon, the son of George Welch. He went to school at Seaton and was articled to Thomas Farrell of Sherborne, Dorset. He studied at University College, London (1905–7) and in 1908 joined the team of architects engaged under Parker and Unwin on the Hampstead Garden Suburb where he designed Wordsworth Walk and Coleridge Walk in the cottage area of the Suburb and many other houses.

In partnership with H. Clifford Hollis, Welch designed the splendid curved terraces of shops and flats in Golders Green Road, NW11 (now lit from light brackets, as in the City of Bath). One is in a vernacular style, the other neo-Georgian, demonstrating the change of taste which occurred over a few years in the early 1900s.

Welch continued to design simple houses in the middle and upper reaches of the Garden Suburb and with Hollis did other buildings in Hendon — the Central Fire Station, NW4 (1912) and United Dairies, Childs Hill, NW11. All his life Welch retained an active interest in the Garden Suburb, where he lived.

381

In 1930, in partnership with N. F. Cachemaille-Day and F. J. Lander (d. 1960) and in association with Frederick Etchells, Welch's firm did the first all steel and glass fronted office building, for Crawfords, in High Holborn, WC1. Three years later they were awarded the London Architecture Medal for St Saviour, Eltham (the scope of the award had been expanded to include any building in the London area).

The firm continues as Welch and Lander.

Obit. Bldr, 20.2.53, p. 314.

WELLS, A. Randall   1877—1942

Randall Wells was the son of an architect, Arthur Wells, of Hastings. Randall Wells's practice began before the force of the Arts and Crafts Movement was spent, but although he was full of innovative ideas, the change in taste, war, and domestic tragedies all combined to hamper his career. He was clerk of works for W. R. Lethaby at All Saints, Brockhampton-by-Ross, Herefordshire, in 1902.

381
382
In the following year, through his brother, Linley Wells, he was engaged by Earl Beauchamp to design the church of St Edward the Confessor and St Mary at Kempley, Gloucestershire, a few miles from Brockhampton. He was to employ direct labour and to order the local materials, stone from the Forest of Dean, timber from the estate, and ironwork from the village blacksmith, Jack Smallman. Wells designed 'Christ the Peacemaker' over the north door for carving by the village carpenter, Walter James. The figures on

Herbert Arthur Welch: houses in Denman Drive, Hampstead Garden Suburb, NW11.

A. Randall Wells: St Edward the Confessor and St Mary, Kempley, Gloucestershire, the interior.

the rood are by David Gibb, a carver of ships' figureheads from the Clyde. Wells wrote of the figures, 'The Bishops had them pulled down but they have since been replaced' (*BA*, 5.3.09). The furnishings are from Gimson's Daneway Workshop at Sapperton, the pews are by Peter Waals, the lectern and candlesticks by Ernest Barnsley, and Laurence Turner did the Virgin and Child. The church clearly derives from Lethaby's Brockhampton church, including the diamond lattice stone frame of the west window.

33
296
Building at Kempley was followed by Voewood (later called Home Place), Kelling, near Holt, Norfolk, which Wells carried out in 1904 for the architect E. S. Prior. This 'rogue' house, built largely of flints, cost the owner, the Rev. Percy Lloyd, £60,000 — a large sum at that time.

In 1906—7 Randall Wells again worked for Prior on St Andrew, Roker, Sunderland, the best church of the Arts and Crafts Movement, for which Wells carved the font. Wells was one of those disciples of William Morris who believed that the architect should be competent both to design and to work in the arts, crafts and trades which embellish his buildings.

Wells designed a prize-winning cottage at Letchworth Garden City and a house for Wyldes Close, Hampstead Garden Suburb, not carried out. In 1914 he prepared a design for government offices which anticipated the more recent 'curtain

A. Randall Wells: St Edward the Confessor and St Mary, Kempley, Gloucestershire. *Above:* the north porch and north aisle. *Below:* the west window.

walling' style. In 1937 he designed St Wilfrid, Halton Hill, Leeds, including the fittings. Eric Gill did the figure of St Wilfrid. Lloyds Bank, Teddington, Middlesex (1930), is equally bold in its geometry. S. Rowland Pierce, joint architect of

Norwich City Hall, worked in his office, having also come from Hastings.

Wells had more than his share of personal tragedy. His daughter was killed in a railway accident; his wife became mentally ill and died in hospital. He died at Oban, Argyllshire.

AR, Oct., 1904, pp. 181−5

Obit. ABN, 4.10.42, p. 18.

WHINNEY, Thomas Bostock 1860−1926

Thomas Whinney was articled to E. A. Grüning in 1877 and entered the Royal Academy Schools in 1878. He won the RIBA Essay Prize in 1886. Whinney was Diocesan Surveyor for Rochester (1894−1904) and Southwark (1904−16). His son, H. G. D. Whinney, and Herbert Austen Hall (*q.v.*) became partners. They did the Bankers Clearing House, 10 Lombard Street, EC3, in the 1920s. The practice continues as the Whinney, Mackay-Lewis Partnership. His daughter was the architectural historian, Margaret Whinney.

Thomas Whinney's principal secular works were for the Midland Bank for which he did branches at Newport in Monmouthshire (1896) and Temple Gate in Birmingham (1898), *and the following from 1900:*

1900	Gloucester
1902	Sutton Coldfield, Warwickshire
1903	Margate, Kent
1904	Brighton, Sussex
1905	Shepherd's Bush, London, W12
1906	Watford, Hertfordshire, and Torquay, Devon

Obit. Bldr, 2.7.26, p. 4.

WHITE, William Henry   1862–1949

Born in Bristol, William White went to Bristol Grammar School and Bristol School of Art (now the West of England Academy). In 1881 he was articled to W. Hartley Price for three years, then joined the office of Edwin Seward and Thomas of Cardiff before coming to London in 1886 and entering the office of George Sherrin. White carried on his studies at the Royal College of Art and became assistant to T. H. Watson.

In 1892 White began practice on his own account, first in Vere Street, W1, and two years later in Cavendish Place. In 1928 two of his sons joined him in partnership.

White devised a happy solution to the problem of the small terrace house, particularly in the Harley Street area where the leases of the eighteenth-century houses were due for renewal and the buildings were thought too monotonous or plain for their purpose. White's façades are elaborately detailed versions of English Renaissance. Some look as if they might be equally at home in Paris or the cities of New England where houses of a similar style occur.

White gave lectures on 'The Development of the Town House' which appeared in the Sessional Papers of the Architectural Association. His houses and business premises, most of them in the Harley Street area of London, include:

1903	78 Great Portland Street
1904	51 and 52 New Bond Street
	101 Harley Street
1905	73 Harley Street (*Bldr*, 27.1.06)
	53, 54, 55 New Bond Street
1906	25 Queen Anne Street
	27 Harley Street
	32 Cavendish Square (demolished; *Bldr*, 27.1.06)
	Holy Trinity Church Hall, Great Portland Street (demolished 1970)
1908	41 Harley Street
1909	112a Harley Street
	Prince's Street
1910	4 Wimpole Street (*Bldr*, 24.9.10)

Obit. RIBAJ, Feb., 1950, p. 160 *Bldr*, 23.12.49, p. 835.

WHITELAW, James Mitchell   1886–1913

J. M. Whitelaw was born in Glasgow in 1886, was articled to Alexander Skirving, studied at the Glasgow School of Art, and worked in the office of Honeyman and Keppie. He won the Alexander ('Greek') Thomson Travelling Studentship and toured Spain and Italy. He entered Sir John Burnet's London office in 1907 and worked on the King Edward VII Galleries of the British Museum.

Whitelaw won the Herbert Batsford Prize of the

James Mitchell Whitelaw: a drawing by this brilliant student, whose style would have provided a nobler Kingsway and a nobler re-building of Regent Street.

Architectural Association, and the RIBA Silver Medal for his measured drawings of Alfred Stevens's Wellington Monument in St Paul's Cathedral, and entered the Royal Academy Schools in 1909. In 1913 he won the Soane Medallion with a design for a railway terminus. In public competitions he submitted a design with Thomas S. Tait for the Marylebone Town Hall, won by Edwin Cooper, and with Tait won the unofficial competition held by *The Builder* for the rebuilding of the Quadrant, Regent Street, W1.

Whitelaw's drawings, which equal the highest standards of the Ecole des Beaux-Arts, present a contrast to those of the brilliant draughtsman E. A. Rickards (*q.v.*). Where Rickards's drawings, like those of Borromini, display an ebullient freehand flourish, Whitelaw's show more use of the T-square and set-square. The neo-neo-Classic style was 'in', and had he lived, Whitelaw would probably have been one of its most outstanding exponents, but his career was tragically cut short when he was drowned at Bournemouth in 1913. It is interesting to speculate how the City banks, the new Kingsway and the new Regent Street might have looked if Whitelaw had had a hand in them. The nearest approach to the Whitelaw style are Nos 204 and 206, 224 and 226 Great Portland Street (*see under* Ferrier, Claude). His friends and colleagues produced a memorial volume of his work: *Designs in Architecture by James Mitchell Whitelaw 1886–1913*, inscribed 'Collected and Published as a Tribute from his Fellow Students and Admirers and as a Memorial to his Life and Work'. It was privately printed and presented to

383

the subscribers to the fund with a note by T. S. Tait and A. G. Shoosmith. Among the subscribers was another brilliant young draughtsman, Alick Horsnell, who did not live to receive his copy, for he was killed in action in France in 1916.

Obit. RIBAJ, 26.7.13, p. 648 *Bldr,* 11.7.13, pp. 30–31

WIDDOWS, George   *floruit c.* 1905

George Widdows was articled in 1887 to John Lacey of Norwich, and was assistant to A. C. Havers of Norwich, W. G. Penty of York, and Bradshaw Gass of Bolton. In 1898 he became head of the architectural department of the Borough Surveyor's Office, Derby, and in 1904 architect to the County Education Committee.

Widdows's schools were among the first to break away from the old 'Hall' type to the open court-yard type of school. His work included the Higher Elementary School, Long Eaton (*Bldr,* 31.7.09), and the Secondary Schools at Heanor and Chesterfield, Derbyshire.

WIGGLESWORTH, Herbert Hardy   1866–1949

H. H. Wigglesworth was articled to James Matthews and A. Marshall Mackenzie of Aberdeen, joined the office of Ernest George and Harold Peto in London and entered the Royal Academy Schools in 1890. From 1893 to 1927 Wigglesworth was in partnership with David Barclay Niven (*q.v.*), and in 1926 he joined in partnership with A. G. R. Mackenzie, son of his former principal.

Obit. RIBAJ, Dec., 1949, p. 72.

WILLINK, William Edward   1856–1924

W. E. Willink was the son of the vicar of St Paul, Tranmere, Liverpool, went to Liverpool College and King's College, Cambridge, and was articled to Alfred Waterhouse, RA. He commenced practice in 1882 and in 1884 P. C. Thicknesse (*q.v.*) became a partner.

The firm did the Queen Victoria Memorial and public convenience, Derby Square, Liverpool, in 1902, in collaboration with F. M. Simpson (*q.v.*). This had sculpture in bronze by C. J. Allen and lead vases by Thomas Elsley.

With Norman Shaw, Willink and Thicknesse did Parr's Bank, Castle Street, Liverpool (1900). The firm also did St Andrew's, Bootle (1903); the Zoology Building, Liverpool University (1905); and an extension to the College of Art (1910). They did the grammar schools at Wallasey and Macclesfield and alterations at Shrewsbury and Uppingham schools.

Willink and Thicknesse designed the interiors of some of the Booth Line ships and the Cunard liners SS *Franconia* and *Laconia* (with Mewès and Davis), and in 1913 they did the Cunard Building on the waterfront of Liverpool, also in conjunction with A. J. Davis, of Mewès and Davis. This building marks the end of an era and the beginning of the age of George V, when published plates of measured drawings supplanted original inspiration. Their design for a Liverpool branch of Harrods Stores was not realised.

On the death of Thicknesse, H. A. Dod (b. 1890), a studio instructor at the School of Architecture, became a partner. To the firm's list of ship interiors were now added those of the Anchor and Donaldson lines.

Obit. Bldr, 28.3.24, p. 503.

William Edward Willink and P. C. Thicknesse. *Left:* **the College of Art, Hope Street, Liverpool.** *Above right:* **the Cunard Building, Pier Head, Liverpool. Although called 'Beauty among the Beasts', collaboration with Arthur J. Davis** (*q.v.*) **did not improve the proportions; neither has the painting of the sashes white, a regrettable practice spoiling important London buildings also.**

384

385

Herbert Winkler Wills ▷ and John Anderson: the Public Baths, Chelsea, SW3.

WILLMOTT, Ernest (Ernest Willmott Sloper until 1907) 1871–1916

Ernest Willmott Sloper went to Taunton School of
Art, worked for Roberts of Taunton and was
engaged on architectural work for the Kingsbridge
Railway, South Devon (1890–6). He then became
manager to Thomas Garner (former partner of
G. F. Bodley) for whom he did the drawings for
the Empire Hotel, Buxton. Sloper set up in practice in 1897. With Stanley Adshead he won the
competition for the Carnegie Free Library, Hawick,
Roxburghshire (RA, 1903). He then became a
partner with Ambrose Poynter (q.v.) and subsequently joined Herbert Baker (q.v.) and Masey
in South Africa, becoming a partner in 1903. With
them he did churches at Parkston, Randfontein,
Johannesburg and Krugersdorp, the tower and
chapel at Bloemfontein Cathedral, and New
Roedean School, Johannesburg. He worked on the
Government Offices, Bloemfontein, and Government House, Pretoria.

385

On his return to England in 1907, Ernest Willmott Sloper set up in practice as E. Willmott, and did houses in the Dutch South African style, one of which was Shorne Hill, near Totton, Hampshire, illustrated in his excellent book, *English House Design* (London, 1911). He also wrote *English Shopfronts Old and New* (London, 1907). His architectural work of this period included Amersfoort, Berkhamsted, Hertfordshire (*Bldr*, 30.11.07); a house at Stanmore, Middlesex (*AR*, 1910); and in the Hampstead Garden Suburb (1909), Nos 79 and 81 Hampstead Way, houses of exceptional distinction among those of a generally high standard. He also supervised some houses in England for Sir Herbert Baker, and did the orphanage at All Saints' Convent, London Colney, Hertfordshire (*Bldr*, 26.11.10), next to Leonard Stokes's building (now the Pastoral Centre).

Obit. *Bldr*, 23.6.16, p. 453.

Ernest Willmott (Sloper): 79 and 81 Hampstead Way, NW11. An early example of brickwork with a recessed joint in a design showing a Lutyens influence.

WILLS, Herbert Winkler   1864–1937

Herbert Wills went to University College, London, won the Donaldson Medal, and was articled to H. C. Boyes and Henry Lowell. He became assistant to Boyes and Arthur Cawston and studied at the South Kensington Schools before leaving for the USA, where he entered the offices of McKim, Mead and White of New York, and Henry Vaughan of Boston, Mass. On his return to London Wills joined the office of George and Peto before going abroad again. He was three years in the Public Works Department in Hong Kong, practised in Vancouver, BC, returned in 1892 and practised in Swansea, Glamorgan.

With John Anderson, formerly of Halliday and Anderson of Cardiff, Wills entered indefatigably for many large architectural competitions and in 1901 won the limited competition for the Registry Offices of the University of South Wales and Monmouthshire, Cathays Park, Cardiff (*RA*, 1905; *Bldr*, 27.2.09). This success was followed in 1902 by the Police Courts and Fire Station, Sunderland, Durham (with W and T. R. Milburn): the Public Baths, Chelsea, SW3, assessed by Norman Shaw, only part of which was executed (*Bldr*, 3.12.04; *AR*, 1907); Public Libraries at Rowley Regis, Staffordshire (*Bldr*, 27.2.07) and at Greenwich, SE10; and additions to the Municipal Buildings, Sunderland (*Bldr*, 7.10.05). The Cardiff building shows the result of Wills's period in the office of McKim, Mead and White, exponents of the new classical style which had its origins in Paris. (The additions of 1933 are by T. Alwyn Lloyd and Alex Gordon.)

Wills was the seventh editor of *The Builder*, succeeding Arthur Stratton in 1913 and resigning in 1918 to become the editor of *The Architect*.

In the 1920s Wills joined in partnership with William Kaula (1871–1953) and did houses in

Herbert Winkler Wills and John Anderson: the University Registry, Cardiff. This and the National Museum of Wales show a change from the baroque of the City Hall to a more classical style.

Weymouth Street and Harley Street, W1, and luxury mansion flats in Mansfield Street and Portland Place in the 'Champs Elysées' style introduced by Frank Verity.

Obit. *RIBAJ*, 20.3.37 p. 517 *Bldr*, 5.2.37, p. 305.

WILSON, Henry   1864–1934

Henry Wilson, brother of the illustrator, Patten Wilson, was born in Liverpool. He went to Kidderminster Art School, was articled in Maidenhead, Berkshire, and then worked in the offices of J. Oldrid Scott, John Belcher and J. D. Sedding. After Sedding's death in 1891 Wilson carried on the practice with the assistance of Charles Nicholson who was Sedding's pupil. The works of Sedding completed by Henry Wilson included the Church of the Holy Redeemer, Exmouth Street, EC1; St Peter, Mount Park Road, Ealing, W5 (1893); the tower of St Clement, Bournemouth; and Holy Trinity, Sloane Street, SW3 (1888–90), a church which was to represent one of the high peaks of Arts and Crafts church building. Wilson also completed the chapel at Welbeck Abbey, Nottinghamshire (1889), for the 6th Duke of Portland, later damaged by fire and reconstructed by Sir Ernest George and Alfred Yeates.

Highgate, N6 — an 1880 church by Sedding, with a tower by Harold Gibbons (1925). Wilson also did work at the cathedrals of Aberdeen, Durham and Ripon (where he did the pulpit of 1913). In Gloucester Cathedral he did the memorial tablet to Canon Evan Evans (1891), the memorial to Canon Tinling (1897) and the clock case in the north transept (1903).

Between 1895 and 1910 Wilson carried out an elaborate scheme of decoration in the huge brick church of St Bartholomew, Brighton (an 1872–4 work by Edmund Scott), adding the baldachino, side altar, pulpit and baptistry. John Harris attributes to Wilson the Dallas-Yorke Memorial Chapel, built in 1901 at Walmsgate Hall and removed (apart from the plaster decoration) to St Hugh, Langworth, Lincolnshire. Henry Wilson was one of the team of artists and architects who submitted a design in competition for the Liver-

Henry Wilson: the sculptured frieze over the entrance to All Saints, London Colney, Hertfordshire, a building by Leonard Stokes.

One of the brightest stars of the Arts and Crafts Movement, Henry Wilson was as gifted in the arts associated with building as he was in architecture. An unusual secular work by him is the Public Library, Ladbroke Grove, W11 (A, 20.6.1890) won in competition in association with T. Phillips Figgis. But, executed in poor materials and ravaged by war and weather, it is now only a shadow of the original Art Nouveau competition design.

After 1890 Wilson directed his energies to the arts and crafts connected with church building — metalwork, sculpture, stained glass and fittings. He did the altar rails, grilles and railings at Sedding's Holy Trinity, Sloane Street, and the bronze south door of St Mary, Nottingham (1904), and was commissioned to do the bronze doors of the Cathedral of St John the Divine in New York. He designed the stone figures for the exterior of Leonard Stokes's All Saints' Convent, London Colney, Hertfordshire (1899), now the Pastoral Centre, and other church work by him occurs at St Mary the Virgin, Norton-sub-Hamdon, Somerset (the font); Holy Trinity, Ilfracombe, Devon (lychgate and vestry); St Mary the Virgin, Lynton, North Devon (new chancel); St Dyfrig, Cardiff; St Mark, Brithdir, Merioneth; St Mark, Rawtenstall, Lancashire; and St Augustine,

339
387

pool Anglican Cathedral in 1901. In 1907 he competed for the new cathedral for Victoria, B.C., won by J. C. M. Keith (*RIBAJ*, 23.2.07).

From 1901 Wilson taught metalwork at the Royal College of Art and at the Central School of Arts and Crafts, WC1. He designed furniture for Charles Trask & Co., Wallpaper for Jeffrey & Co. and fireplaces for Longden & Co. Sedding's son, G. E. Sedding, was a pupil (1901–4), who set up his own workshop in Noel Street, Soho, after studying at the Royal College of Art, but died early as a result of war service. Wilson was a Master of the Art Workers' Guild in 1917, a member of the Northern Art Workers' Guild and President of the Arts and Crafts Exhibition Society (1915–22). He became the first editor of the *Architectural Review* in 1896, succeeded by D. S. McColl in 1901. Wilson spent his last years in France and died at Menton.

AR, 1966, March, pp. 274–77; 'Byzantium in Brighton', by Nicholas Taylor

Harris, Mark, Thesis for the Oxford Architectural History Prize, 1975

Victoria and Albert Museum, exhibition catalogue, *Victorian and Edwardian Decorative Arts*, 1952

Wilson, Henry, *Silverwork and Jewellery*, London, 1903

Obit. RIBAJ, 24.3.34, pp. 539 and 588–9.

WILSON, Thomas Millwood   1879—1957

T. M. Wilson was articled to J. J. Stevenson from 1895 to 1901, entered the office of Harry Redfern and then of Guy Dawber, and became his chief assistant. In 1909 Wilson set up on his own account and designed three of the early cinematograph theatres — at Harrow Road, NW10 (1911), Willesden Green, NW2, and South End Green, Hampstead, NW3 (1912).

Wilson designed seventeen houses in the Hampstead Garden Suburb (1909—13): 1, 2, 3 and 4 Chatham Close; 46 (his own house) and 163 Hampstead Way; 1 Hurst Close; 41 and 43 Meadway; 14 North Square; 14 Turner Close; 3, 4, 5 and 6 Wild Hatch; 5 Willifield Way; and The Studio, North Square.

After the First World War Wilson designed some twenty branches of Lloyds Bank including those at Cranbrook and Sevenoaks, Kent. Wilson won competitions for the Public Baths and for the Public Library at Hendon, NW4; the interior of this has been completely remodelled.

After the death of Sir Guy Dawber, T. M. Wilson with A. R. Fox carried on the practice as Sir Guy Dawber, Wilson and Fox. Wilson retired in 1954.

Obit.   Times, 19.1.57.

WIMPERIS, Edmund Walter   1865—1946

E. W. Wimperis was the son of the painter E. M. Wimperis (1835—1900) and a cousin of the architect J. T. Wimperis (1829—1904). A brother was the actor Arthur Wimperis. Edmund Wimperis carried on a family tradition by designing town houses on the Duke of Westminster's Grosvenor Estate in Mayfair, W1, for J. T. Wimperis had designed much of the estate in the first Duke's day.

With his first partner, J. R. Best, Edmund Wimperis carried out considerable works including the refronting of 45 Grosvenor Square (1902—3), the rebuilding of 1 Upper Brook Street (1907—8) and the first of three stone elevations at 16—18 Upper Brook Street (1907—16). Also with Best, Wimperis designed Thurston's, the billiards firm on the west side of Leicester Square which had a room designed by Frank Brangwyn. The building was destroyed in the Second World War.

In 1910 Wimperis succeeded Col. Eustace Balfour (*q.v.*) as Surveyor to the Grosvenor Estate and in 1913 he was joined in partnership by W. Begg Simpson, a very able designer. Henceforth the character of the work improved further. Simpson first made his mark in 26 Grosvenor Street (1913—16) when the work took on a neo-Georgian flavour deriving to some extent from the work of Sir Edwin Lutyens. In the years after the First World War the neo-Georgian idiom was

continued. Simpson was joined by L. Rome Guthrie, a son-in-law of William Flockhart (*q.v.*), in 1925 when the mammoth Grosvenor House was designed. This replaced the Duke's town house and garden and had Lutyens as consultant.

WITTET, George   1877—1926

George Wittet was articled to Andrew Heiton of Perth and then joined the office of George Washington Browne of Edinburgh. After a period with Walter Brierley in York, Wittet went to India as assistant to John Begg (*q.v.*), Consulting Architect to the Government of Bombay, succeeding Begg in that post in 1907. Wittet's period of service with the Bombay Government had lasting results in the sound basis he laid in the Public Works Department and for architectural education in Bombay. A plaque in his memory is fixed in the Gateway of India, which he built to receive the royal visitors to the Delhi Durbar of 1911. Wittet also built the College of Science, the Custom House and the Agricultural College, Bombay.

Obit.   RIBAJ, 6.11.26, p. 31   *Bldr*, 17.9.26, p. 438.

Edgar Wood: the First Church of Christ Scientist (now the Edgar Wood Centre), Victoria Park, Manchester.

Edgar Wood with Henry Sellers (*q.v.*): Durnsford Street School, Middleton, Manchester.

WOOD, Edgar   1860–1935

Edgar Wood was the sixth of the eight children of Thomas Broadbent Wood, a cotton mill owner and Unitarian, of Middleton, near Manchester. Edgar Wood went to Queen Elizabeth's Grammar School, Middleton, under the Rev. James Jelly, whose daughter he married. He showed an aptitude for painting and did not want to go into his father's business — architecture was a compromise that suited them both. After serving articles with Mills and Murgatroyd, the Manchester architects who had designed his father's house, Wood started practice in his father's disused Park Mill in Suffield Street, Middleton. His first job was the Queen Victoria Jubilee drinking fountain and shelter — the gift of his stepmother — in the Market Place, Middleton (later moved to another site and finally destroyed).

In 1889 Wood did the Manchester and County (now Williams and Glyn's) Bank, Long Street; Temple Street Baptist Church; and *The Guardian* building (now much altered) — all in Middleton. In 1892 he moved his offices to Manchester and did the Manchester and Salford (now also Williams and Glyn's) Bank, Middleton. After this, work flowed in consistently.

In common with his contemporaries, Voysey, Barry Parker, Mackintosh and A. J. Penty, Wood came from a strong nonconformist background and from a district where the hard local building stone led to some severity of treatment. In the north of Britain, not yet invaded by the South

Wealden style, they were fortunate in finding some discerning clients who showed a preference for simple modern houses and plain furniture. Wood's houses of this period included Halecroft, Hale Road, Hale (1891); 37 and 39 Rochdale Road, Middleton (1893); Westdene, Archer Park, Middleton, and Barcroft, Bolton Road, Marland, Rochdale (1894); Fencegate and Redcroft (his home till 1916), Rochdale Road, Middleton, and Briarcourt, Occupation Road, Lindley, Huddersfield (all 1895); Dunarden, Archer Park, Middleton, and a shop and four houses at 34–38 Rochdale Road, Middleton (1898). A few years later Wood joined in practice, although not strictly in partnership, with J. Henry Sellers (*q.v.*) and each influenced the work of the other.

Wood has left a considerable record of houses, churches and schools of refreshing simplicity. Some of his designs anticipated the style that was to be known as Art Deco and he was early in introducing the flat roof — not always with success. His work is mentioned by Muthesius, and a late work, Edgecroft, Manchester Road, Heywood (1921), is illustrated in *Moderne Bauformen* (Vol. 6).

Wood did the Silver Street Chapel in Rochdale in 1893 and the Clergy House, Almondbury, Huddersfield (*BA*, 11.5.1900) in 1898. The Victoria Hotel in Spotland Road, Rochdale (now much altered) is a Wood work of 1897.

In 1909 Wood was left a considerable 'competency'

Edgar Wood: Long Street Wesleyan Church and Schools, Middleton, Manchester.

by his father and was able to indulge his love of painting again. He retired in 1922 and built a house in Italy — Monte Calvario at Port Marizio, Imperia, where he entertained distinguished paying guests, including the sculptor, Epstein, and cultivated a beautiful garden with splendid views which he loved to paint. A slab of black marble marks his grave at Diana Marina there.

Wood also designed furniture and jewellery and was a founder member of the Northern Art Workers' Guild, inaugurated by Walter Crane in 1896. Wood was Master in 1897. For *The Builders' Journal and Architectural Record* (7.3.1900, pp. 73—5), Wood wrote 'An Architect's Experience in the Development of Design' and he read a paper on 'Colour as applied to Architecture' to the RIBA (*RIBAJ*, 19.11.12). When the old Manchester Town Hall was demolished in 1911, the Ionic colonnade was re-erected at Heaton Park according to a scheme prepared by Edgar Wood. *His works include:*

390	1899-1901	Long Street Wesleyan Church and Schools, Middleton (now Methodist) (*Bldr*, 31.12.04, RA, 1904)
	1900	Banney Royd, Halifax Road, Edgerton, Huddersfield (*BA*, 19.2.04), in partnership with Henry Sellers. (This later became the Fire Services Headquarters.)
		Alterations to Newbold Revel, Stretton-under-Fosse, Warwickshire (later St Paul's College)
	1901-2	Clock Tower, Lindley, Huddersfield, with sculpture by Thomas Stirling Lee (RA, 1900)
		Solicitors' offices, King Street, Oldham (RA, 1902)
		Richardson's Estate, Hale, Cheshire
		226, 227 and 229 Hale Road, 119 Park Road and 20 Plane Tree Road, Hale
	1902	Gatehouse (main house not built), Crosland Road, Lindley
	1903	Gatehouse, Cragg Hall, Mytholmroyd, W. Riding.
388 391		First Church of Christ Scientist, Daisybank Road, Victoria Park, Manchester (RA, 1904; *Bldr*, 3.12.04; now the Edgar Wood Centre)
	1904	House at Dore, Sheffield
	1905	Holly Cottage, Holly Road, Bramhall, Stockport
		Bayliss House, Slough, Buckinghamshire (conversion for his brother, W. H. Wood, into a health cure home)
	1906	36 Mellalieu Street, Middleton
		Parsonage House, Thurlstone, Penistone, W. Riding
		Steps and fountain, Jubilee Park, Long Street, Middleton. Now only a sad relic
		Dalnyreed, Barley, Royston, Hertfordshire
	1907	116, 117, 119 and 121 Plane Tree Road, Hale, Cheshire
		Manor Villas, 1092-1104 Middleton Road, Chadderton, Oldham
		22 and 24 Mount Road, Alkrington, Middleton
389	1907-10	Durnsford Street and Elm Street Schools, Middleton (with Henry Sellers, whose influence is evident) (*Bldr*, 9.1.09)
	1908	Upmeads, Newport Road, Stafford
		Pilkington Tiles Pavilion, White City Exhibition in London
		Shops, 33—37 Manchester Road, Middleton
	1909	Design for houses in a hemicycle, Wellgarth Road and Hampstead Way, Hampstead Garden Suburb (not executed; *RA*, 1909; *Bldr*, 12.3.10)
	1913-39	Houses at Fairfield Moravian Settlement, Droylsden, Manchester
	1914	Royd House, 224 Hale Road, Hale, Cheshire (his own house)

AR, Mar., 1976

Archer, J. H. G., 'Edgar Wood: A Notable Manchester Architect', *Transactions of the Lancashire and Cheshire Antiquarian Society*, Vols 73—4 1963—4

Building Design, 24.10.75

Burlington Magazine, Dec., 1975

Manchester City Art Galleries, *Partnership in Style: Edgar Wood and J. Henry Sellers*, exhibition catalogue, 1975

Obit. *Bldr*, 25.10.35, p. 740.

WOOD, Francis Derwent, RA   1871—1926

Derwent Wood, one of the ablest sculptors of the reign of George V, was born at Keswick, Cumberland. His father was American. He went to school at Lausanne and studied at the Karlsruhe School of Art under H. Weltring Götz. In 1887 he came to London and worked as a modeller in potteries and foundries while studying under Professor Lantéri at South Kensington where he won a National Scholarship. He was a student and then an assistant of Alphonse Légros at the Slade

Edgar Wood: Long Street Wesleyan Church and Schools, Middleton, Manchester.

(1890–2) and also of Thomas Brock. He entered the Royal Academy Schools in 1894, winning the Gold Medal and Travelling Studentship with his 'Daedalus and Icarus' in 1895. His 'Maternity' won an honourable mention at the Paris Salon of 1897 and he visited Paris in the same year. Derwent Wood also studied at the Glasgow School of Art from 1897 and was modelling master there until 1901 when he returned to London. He was Professor of Sculpture at the Royal College of Art (1918–23).

During his Glasgow years Derwent Wood carried out a great deal of carving and sculpture on the numerous buildings designed by Salmon, Son and Gillespie, including Mercantile Chambers, 39–69 Bothwell Street (1897–8). In London he assisted Thomas Brock on the Queen Victoria Memorial, Buckingham Palace, and himself did 'Australia' with Kangaroo and Ram on one of the outlying pedestals of the rond-point. His best-known work is the Machine Gun Corps Memorial, Hyde Park Corner, SW1, executed after the First World War and unveiled in 1925. A bronze bust by Wood of the painter Ambrose McEvoy (d. 1927) is in the National Portrait Gallery. He also did the statue of Sir Frederick Henry Royce (d. 1933), the motor car engineer. His portrait bust of the architect C. Harrison Townsend is at the Art Workers' Guild, of which Wood was a member.

Derwent Wood's work continued in the direct line

of Renaissance sculpture, showing most sympathy with the work of Donatello. One of his sculptures stands as his memorial at the Albert Bridge, Chelsea. He was made ARA in 1910 and RA in 1920 (diploma work, 'The Dancer'). He married the Australian singer, Florence Schmidt, in 1903.

WOODHOUSE, John Henry   1847–1929

J. H. Woodhouse studied at Manchester School of Art and started as an improver in the office of Philip and Nunn in 1865. He was also with Royle and Bennett before going into partnership, first with Smith and Willoughby, then with Willoughby and Langham, and then with Corbett and Dean.

As Woodhouse and Willoughby, the partners did the Verdin Grammar School, Winsford, Cheshire (1895); the Stephenson Memorial Hall, Chesterfield, Derbyshire; the Technical College and the Police Courts, Blackburn, Lancashire; and the Art Gallery and Library, Bury, Lancashire (1899–1901; *Bldr*, 12.10.01). As Woodhouse, Willoughby and Langham, they did the Manchester Fire Station and Police Station (1901–6; *Bldr*, 7.12.01) and the Municipal Hall, Colne, Lancashire (1901–2).

As Woodhouse, Corbett and Dean, they did the YMCA Building in St Peter's Street, Manchester (1909). Here the reinforced concrete structure supports a swimming pool in the top floor and is faced in glazed faience. For its date the building

393

shows a form and finish reasonably in sympathy with these new materials, anticipating Burnet's Kodak Building, in Kingsway, WC2, and Troup's Spicers Building, New Bridge Street, EC4 (both of 1911; *Bldr*, 16.12.09 and 10.2.11).

Obit. RIBAJ, 7.6.1930, p. 567.

WOODWARD, William   1846—1927

William Woodward was born in London, and articled to a Mr Reggett, then to Arthur Cates, surveyor to the Crown Estates. He later went into partnership with Eugene Argent, surveyor to the Crown Estates Paving Commissioners.

Woodward's work expanded into a West End practice and included flats in Cleveland Row, St James's, SW1, and Brook's of Regent Street, W1 (since demolished). He also did the little lead-covered 'Bridge of Sighs' — now sadly missing — which spanned Craven Street, Strand, WC2, to connect the Grand Hotel (now offices) to its annexe (*A*, 1903).

63   When he was appointed architect to the newly-formed Piccadilly Hotel Company which had taken a lease from the Crown on a section of Regent Street Quadrant and the site of the St James's Hall and Restaurant, Woodward was caught up in the heated debate surrounding the design for the new Quadrant (*see* p. 77). Collaborating with Woodward was Walter Emden who was succeeded by E. A. Grüning.

William Woodward was Mayor of Hampstead in 1910 and 1911. His sons Charles Woodward (d. 1960), who was resident architect for the Piccadilly Hotel, and Frank Woodward (d. 1958) carried on the practice.

Other works by Woodward are:

1905   Piccadilly Buildings, 166—173 Piccadilly, SW1, on the site of the 'Egyptian Hall'

Shops and chambers at the corner of Piccadilly and Haymarket, SW1, and at the corner of Duke Street and Jermyn Street, SW1 (now demolished)

1906   Shops and chambers at the corner of Jermyn Street and St James's Street, SW1

The International Sleeping Car Co., 20 Cockspur Street, SW1 — a turreted pastiche in Château style

23—29 St James's Street (demolished; the site is now occupied by *The Economist*)

Obit. Bldr, 25.11.27, pp. 805 and 824.

WORTHINGTON, Sir Percy Scott, LittD 1864—1939

Percy Worthington, the son of the architect Thomas Worthington of Manchester, was educated at Clifton College and Corpus Christi, Oxford. He was articled to his father, studied at Manchester School of Art and at University College, London, and entered the Royal Academy Schools in 1888. He was assistant for a time with J. MacVicar Anderson in London and became a partner with his father in 1891 and extended an already large practice. In 1898 they won the competition for the Halifax Royal Infirmary, W. Riding, and a long list of hospitals followed. They also did Ullet Road Unitarian Chapel, Sefton Park, Liverpool (1896—9) and the Hall and Memorial Passage there (1902). In the library and Vestry are wall-paintings by Gerald Moira (1902). Their work for Manchester University included the Faculty of Arts building (1911—19).

Worthington received the Royal Gold Medal for Architecture in 1930 and received a knighthood in in his later years. He was succeeded by his half-brother Hubert Worthington (1886—1963) and his son Shirley Worthington; the firm continues as Thomas Worthington and Sons.

Obit. RIBAJ, 14.8.39, pp. 950—2 and 18.9, p. 983. *Bldr*, 21.7.39, p. 100.

WRATTEN, Edmund Livingstone   d. 1926

E. L. Wratten was a student of the Architectural Association, and in 1893 was articled to George Devey's former chief assistant and successor, James Williams. When Williams retired in 1905, Wratten and Walter Godfrey, another pupil of Williams, carried on the practice (*see under* Godfrey).

Obit. Bldr, 18.12.25, p. 872.

YOUNG, Clyde F.   1871—1948

Clyde Young was the son of the architect William Young (*q.v.*). He studied at Lille, Belgium, at South Kensington and in Italy. He was articled to his father and assisted him on the then New War Office, Whitehall, SW1. After his father's death in 1900 he completed the building in association with Sir John Taylor, the retired Chief Architect of HM Office of Works (*Bldr*, 1.6.07).

Other buildings by Clyde Young were the Imperial Service College, Windsor, Berkshire; University College, Southampton; and King Edward's Horse Hall at the Imperial Service College, Windsor. He also did Westbury Manor, Buckinghamshire (*Bldr*, 17.12.04) and Pyrford Court, Surrey, for Lord Iveagh in 1910.

Young's most recent work was the reinstatement of the marble grand staircase in the National Liberal Club, Whitehall Place, SW1, after destruction by a bomb in the Second World War. In this he was associated with Bernard Engle who continued his practice.

Obit. RIBAJ, June, 1948, p. 373 *Bldr*, 14.5.48, p. 585.

Woodhouse, Corbett and Dean: the Y.M.C.A. building, Peter Street, Manchester. An early reinforced concrete building faced with faience.

YOUNG, Keith Downes   1848–1929

Keith Young went to Tonbridge School and was articled to his father, George Adam Young. He studied at South Kensington and at the Architectural Association. Young became a partner with his father in 1871 and later with a church architect, Henry Hall, in a practice which acquired a reputation for hospitals and school sanatoria. They did the sanatoria at Harrow, Clifton, Shrewsbury and Sherborne Schools, and at Blundell's School, Tiverton, Devon.

The hospitals carried out by Young and Hall included the Derbyshire Royal Infirmary, Derby; the Royal Eye Hospital, Southwark, SE1; the Victoria Hospital for Children, Tite Street, Chelsea, SW3; the Evelina Hospital for Children, Southwark, SE1; the Royal Dental Hospital, Leicester Square, WC2; the East Sussex Hospital, Hastings; and the Great Northern Hospital, Holloway, N19.

In 1905 the firm did the *Evening Standard* building in Shoe Lane, EC4, and in 1909 Dunsley, near Whitby, for F. H. Pyman (*Bldr*, 17.7.09). The practice was joined by Henry Hall's son Alner Hall. Their works after the First World War included the rebuilding of the Middlesex Hospital, W1 (1922–36). After the Second World War the firm did additions to the Royal College of Surgeons, Lincoln's Inn Fields, WC2 (with John Musgrove) and additions to Guy's Hospital Medical School.

Young and Hall's other works include:

1903	54 Ludgate Hill, EC4 (*Bldr*, 26.4.02)
	Hampstead General Hospital, NW3 (demolished 1975; *Bldr*, 31.1.03)
	Bolingbroke Hospital, SW11
	Chelsea Hospital for Women, Dovehouse Street, SW3 (with George Elkington)
	Ear, Nose and Throat Hospital, Gray's Inn Road, WC1
	The Maida Vale Hospital, W9 (RA, 1903; *Bldr*, 22.6.01)
1907	The Chest Hospital, Putney, SW15
1909	Boscombe and West Hants Hospital (with Bligh Livesay; *Bldr*, 10.4.09)
	The Miller Hospital, Greenwich, SE10
	Nurses' Home, City of London Chest Hospital, Victoria Park, E9 (RA, 1904)

Obit. RIBAJ, 25.1.30, p. 207 *Bldr*, 6.12.29, p. 969.

YOUNG, William   1843–1900

William Young was articled to James Lamb of Paisley and entered the office of a Mr Tait in Glasgow. The first office he entered in London was that of the Surrey County Surveyor. Here the resourcefulness and energy of the young Scot showed when he was required to put up a large wooden marquee at Wimbledon Common, SW19, for the National Rifle Brigade: 50,000 sq ft in area,

this was to seat 1,000 at table and have a bar 200 ft long. The order came from Lord Elcho (afterwards Lord Wemyss).

Young's promptitude and success with Lord Elcho's building led to commissions for the design of town and country houses for the nobility and gentry, including a house in Chelsea for Lord Cadogan; improvements to a house in Suffolk for the Maharajah Duleep Singh; a ballroom for Lord Iveagh in Dublin; and, most resplendent of all, Gosford Park, Haddington, East Lothian for Lord Wemyss. Here Young gave special importance to the grand staircase, that essential feature of the large mansion where guests waiting to be announced could see and be seen. J. McK. Brydon said of Young, 'No man knew more the requirements of a great country house or how more effectively to carry them out'.

After a first competition proved abortive, Young entered a design for the Glasgow Municipal Chambers in a second competition assessed by Charles Barry junior. A preliminary contest of sketches was held and ten competitors were selected for the next round, among them Young, George Washington Browne, J. J. Burnet, William Leiper and James Sellars. Young visited Rome and Florence to gather ideas for his design. A condition laid down was that a tower, as suggested in an earlier design by John Carrick, should be the central feature. While Burnet and Sellars ignored the requirement and gave their designs a cupola, Young kept to the rules and won. Begun in 1883 and completed in 1889, the new Glasgow Municipal Chambers vied in magnificence with Manchester's Gothic Town Hall by Alfred Waterhouse. It set the fashion for other such buildings, culminating twenty years later in Sir Alfred Brumwell Thomas's Belfast City Hall where there was also no lack of marbled and vaulted staircases and corridors.

As a result of his Glasgow building and through the many influential people he had served well, Young was given without competition the commission to do the new War Office, Whitehall, replacing the 'Old War Office' in York House and adjacent town houses in Pall Mall — now the site of the Royal Automobile Club. As it was to be next to the Banqueting House, Lord Wemyss had wanted the new War Office to follow Inigo Jones's design for Charles I's Whitehall Palace, but the Government was unwilling to embark on so ambitious a project.

Only the foundations of the new War Office had been completed when Willian Young died at the age of fifty-seven. The Government wanted HM Office of Works to take over the work entirely, but the President of the RIBA interceded on behalf of Young's son and partner, Clyde Young (*q.v.*), who carried on jointly with Sir John Taylor, the retired chief architect of the Office of Works (*Bldr*, 6.1.06). The symbolical sculpture is by Alfred Drury.

William Young: the New (now Old) War Office,
Whitehall, SW1. Lord Wemyss wanted Inigo Jones's
designs for Whitehall Palace to be followed.

It was due largely to the suggestion of William
Young that Kingsway and Aldwych, connecting
Holborn and the Strand, took their present form.
William Young wrote *Town and Country*

Residences and edited a folio edition of
Piranesi's *Italian Architecture, Painting and
Sculpture.* His practice was continued by his
son, Clyde Young (*q.v.*), joined later by Bernard
Engle.

Obit. RIBAJ, 10.11.1900, pp. 21–2 and 44–7 *Bldr*,
10.11.1900, p. 410.

Picture credits

With the exception of those listed below, all the photographs used in this book were taken by Jean and Nicholas Breach, and all the drawings were done by Charlotte Halliday. The author and publishers are grateful to the following for supplying and giving permission to reproduce illustrations.

Adams, Holden and Pearson, pp. 121, 212

Alphabet and Image Ltd, pp. 36 (top), 125, 170, 221, 271

Architectural Association Slide Collection, p. 298

British Architectural Drawings Collection, pp. 223 (top), 224

British Architectural Library, pp. 28, 42 (right), 63 (top), 74, 84, 91, 97, 98, 109, 155, 172, 173, 176, 205 (bottom), 262, 272, 275 (bottom), 277, 280 (top), 288 (top), 305 (top), 340, 363, 366, 375 (top), 378–9 (bottom), 383

John Brookholding-Jones, p. 226

Country Life, p. 242 (top & bottom)

B. D. Elwes, p. 220

Greater London Council, pp. 22 (top & bottom), 57, 166

Hampstead Garden Suburb Archive, p. 27 (top & bottom)

Harrods Press Office, p. 68

London Passenger Transport Board, pp. 48 (top), 76 (top & bottom), 198 (top & bottom)

Mansell Collection, p. 190

Punch, p. 82

Henry Rushton, p. 274, 276

Savoy Hotel Press Office, pp. 58, 59, 60 (top & bottom)

Norman Watkins, p. 372

Abbreviations

A	*The Architect*
AA	*Academy Architecture*
ABJ	*Architects' & Builders' Journal*
ABN	*Architect & Building News*
AJ	*Architects' Journal*
AR	*Architectural Review*
BA	*The British Architect*
Bldng	*Building*
Bldr	*The Builder*
BN	*Building News*
DNB	*Dictionary of National Biography*
RIBAJ	*Journal of the Royal Institute of British Architects*

Index

Wherever possible, buildings, sculptures, etc., have been indexed according to their location. Page numbers in bold type refer to the main entries in the dictionary section; page numbers in italics refer to illustrations. Titles of works of art appear in quotation marks.

Ritz, César, 20, 59, 61, *158*, 259
Robert-Fleury, 142
Roberts-Austen, Sir William, 354
Robertsbridge, Sussex: Scalands, 220; Village Institute, 216
Robertson, J. Murray, 274
Robinson, R., 151
Robinson, William, 13, 36, *81*, 114, 220, 240, 284
Robson, E. R., 97, 312
Robson, Philip Appleby, **312-13**
Rochdale, Lancs.: 'John Bright', 350; chapel, hotel & houses by Edgar Wood, 389; St Mary, 148; Whirriestone, 277
Rochester, Kent: diocese, 208; Foord Almshouses, 163, 263; Shorts' Flying Boat works, 133; Technical Institute, 151, 315
Rock Ferry, Ches.: St Barnabas, 275
Rodin, Auguste, 49, 112, 174, 190, 247, 358, 359, 368
Rodmarton Manor, Cirencester, 102
Rodway, Ernest George, 164
Roker, Sunderland: St Andrew, *see under* Monkwearmouth
Rolland, François, 128
Roll Call, The, 311
Rollins, J. Wenlock, 46, 120, 185, 352
Romaine-Walker, William Henry, 56, **313-14**
Rome: exhibition of 1911, 93; Forum of Nerva, 268; Il Gesu, 110; Gigi's Academy, 220; Palazzo Odescalchi, 93; St Paul-beyond-the-walls, 109; St Peter's Basilica, 109; Sistine Chapel, 223
Ronsdon, Devon, 186
Roosevelt, Franklin D., 360
Rosebery, Lord, 350, 351
Roseneath, Dunbarton: The Inn, *238*, 240
Ross, Alexander, 229
Rossetti, Dante Gabriele, 163
Rosslare, Ireland: house by Parker, 277
Rothenstein, Sir William, 150, 193
Rotherfield, Sussex: Oakdene, 277
Rotherham High School, Yorks., 313
Rothesay Castle, Bute, 380
Rottingdean, Sussex, 108
Rowat, Jessie, 249
Rowley Regis, Staffs.: public library, 386
Rowntree, Colin, 314
Rowntree, Douglas, 314
Rowntree, Fred, 283, **314**, 335
Rowntree, Joseph, 11, 24, 276, 359
Rowntree, Seebohm, 359
Royal Academy Schools, 19, 46, 124, 335
Royal Agricultural College, 321
Royal College of Art, 107, 219, 235
Royal Commission of 1884, 22
Royal Doulton, 122
Royal School of Art Needlework, 366
Royal Society of Arts: lecture, 67
Royal Society of Miniaturists, 271
Royal Veterinary College, 226
Royl and Bennett, 391
'Royce, Sir Henry', 391
Royston, Herts.: Dalnyreed, 390
Royton, Lancs.: St Anne, 265

Rubens, Godfrey, 235
Ruckley Grange, Salop., 186
Rudall, Carte & Co., 59
Rude, Jean-Baptiste, 45
Rufforth, Yorks.: All Saints, 123
Rugby, Warwicks.: engineering works, 154; St Philip, 154
Rugby School, Warwicks., 371
Rugeley, Staffs.: St Augustine, 281
Ruislip, Middx.: Garden Suburb, 92; Kingsend, 284
Rumania, Crown Princess of, 323
Runtz, Ernest Augustus, 54, 55, 56, *57*, 80, 265, **314-15**, *327*
Runtz and Ford, 271
Rushmore Park, Wilts., 314
Rushton, Henry, 274
Rushton, Thomas Johnson, 274
Ruskin, John, 44, 52, 90, 113, 117, 127, 235, 243
Russell, Sir Gordon, 194, 324
Russell, Samuel Bridgman, 151, 188, 255, **315**
Russell, S. Fabian, 203
Russell and Cooper, 230
Russian Ballet, 311
Rutherford, J. H., 123
Rye Harbour, Sussex: Holy Spirit, 335

Sachs, Edwin Otto, 54, **315-16**, 330
Sacred Sites of the Gospels, 372
Safad, Israel: The English Church, 286
Saint, Andrew, 325
St Albans Abbey: 'Passing of Queen Eleanor', 316
St Albans Cathedral: the High Altar, 190
St Andrews, Fife: Mount Melville, 372
St George's Art Society, 43, 234, 294
St Ives, Hunts.: 'Oliver Cromwell', 290
St Margaret's Bay, Kent: Zachary Merton Homes, 89
St Moritz, Switzerland: house at Chasellas, 356; Villa Guardamunt, 356
St Neots, Hunts., 276
St Quintin, Wilts., 291
S. Raphael, France: the English Chapel, 274
Sala, George Augustus, 67
Salamans and Wornum, 254
Salisbury, Frank Owen, 53, 83, **316**
Salisbury, H. J., 316
Salisbury, Rhodesia: Government House, 117
Salisbury diocese, 290
Salmon, James, 19, 192, **316-18**, *316*, *317*
Salmon & Glucksten, 65, 88
Salmon, Son and Gillespie, 49, 209, 391
Salmon and Stendhal, 87
Salt, Titus, 11
Saltaire, nr Leeds, 11
Saltburn, Yorks.: Girls' Grammar School, 151, 315
Salter, Stephen, 60, 84, 294
Salvin, Anthony, 135, 325, 344
Samian Ware, 49
Samuel, Sir Herbert, 92
Samuel, Sir Marcus, 228
Sanderson, Cobden, *114*
Sanderson, Fred, 321
Sanderson & Sons, Arthur, 362
Sanderstead, Surrey: house by Atkinson, 95; house by Keen, 229
Sandgate, Kent: Spade House, *363*
Sandiway, Ches.: St John the

Evangelist, 166
San Domingo, W. Indies: Columbus memorial, 230
Sandon, Staffs.: Dog & Doublet, 162; village hall, 162
Sandringham, Norfolk: 'Persimmon', 228
'Sandys, Lt Col Myles', 367
São Paulo, Brazil, 276; Auto Club, 160
Sapperton, Glos., 195; Coates Manor, 101; The Leasowes, *101*; Upper Dorvel House, 101; village hall, *193*
Sargent, John Singer, 83, 92, 359
Saul and Hardy, *51*, 67
Saunders, C. H., 196
Savage, James, 37
Savage, Rupert, 158
Savernake, Wilts.: 2nd Marchioness of Ailesbury monument, 190
Savernake Estate, Wilts., 290
Sawyer, Joseph, 298
Scarborough, Yorks.: Brackencliffe, 123; Dunollie, 284
Scarborough Technical School, 151, 177
Scarborough Town Hall: 'Lord Leighton', 124
Schaufelberg, E., 315
Schenck, Frederick E. E., 170, *204*, 205, 285, **318**
Schmidt, Florence, 391
school sanatoria by Young and Hall, 394
schools by Sir B. Thomas, 348
Schreiner, Olive, 99
Schussel, Prof. Christian, 83
Scott, Adrian Gilbert, 318, 320, *321*
Scott, A. R., 229
Scott, Charles Marriott Oldrid, **318**
Scott, Sir George Gilbert, 12, 13, 14, 108, 219, 281, 318
Scott, George Gilbert, jnr., 38, 135, 264, 357
Scott, Sir Giles Gilbert, *40*, *42*, 230, 264, 303, **318-21**, *319*, *321*
Scott, J. Oldrid, 289, 318, 387
Scott, Mackay Hugh Baillie, 19, 21, 34, 35, 90, 166, 250, 254, **321-3**, *323*, 343
Scott, Thomas, 318
Scott and Moffatt, 185
Scribner's, 83
Sculptor Speaks, The, 175
Seal Church, Kent, 92
Seale, Barney, 324
Seale, Gilbert, 69, 265, *266*, **324**
Searles-Wood (Appleton), H. D., 267
Secessionists, 34, 92, 122, 222, 212, 249
Secham, W., 347
Sedding, Edmund Harold, **324**
Sedding, G. E., 387
Sedding, John Dando, 38, 39, 40, 100, 114, 179, 193, 273, 299, 324, 326, 387
Seddon, J. P., 137, 139, 303, 362
Seifert, Richard, 95
Selby, Yorks.: Carlton Towers, 109
Selby Abbey, Yorks., 318
Selfridge, Gordon, 66, 67, 95
Sellers, James Henry, **324**, *325*, 389, 394
Selsey Bill, Sussex: bungalow, 151
Selsey-on-Sea, Sussex: Bill House, 323
Semper, Gottfried, 232, 375
Sergent, René, 61, 62
Seth-Smith, William Howard, **324**
Sevenoaks, Kent: hospital by

Ansell, 89; house by Niven, 274; house by Scott, 323; St Thomas of Canterbury, 368
Severn river: electricity generating station, 216
Severn tunnel, 11
Seward and Thomas, 383
Shanghai, China: 'Sir Robert Hart', 282
Shannon, Charles, 182, 371
Sharp, Lewen, 55
Sharpe, Stewart & Co., 108
Shattock, L. H., 110, 216
Shavington Hall, Salop., 273
Shaw, Byam, 69, 83
Shaw, George Bernard, 175
Shaw, Henry, 167
Shaw, John, jnr, 33
Shaw, Richard Norman, 14, 18, 28, 31, 33, 35, 43, 48, 55, 57, 62, *63*, *69*, 70, 79, 80, 86, 88, 95, 101, 113, 114, 126, 127, 132, 142, 167, *168*, *176*, 186, 193, 217, 229, 230, 234, 235, 239, 240, *242*, 243, 244, 246, 253, 257, 258, 260, 272, 275, 290, 294, 315, 320, **325-9**, *326*, *327*, *328*, *329*, 330, 333, 347, 357, 362, 380, 384, 386
Shaw Savill, 326
Shaw Sparrow, W., 262
Shaw, Wilts.: Christ Church, 291
Shedfield, Hants.: New Place, 245
Sheffield, Yorks.: Alliance Insurance, 195; branch libraries, 187; house at Dore, 390; 'King Edward VII', 170; Mappin Art Gallery, 187; Mappin Hall, 207; public baths, 187; Queen Victoria memorial, 357; St John the Evangelist, 187; town hall, 289; University College, 187
Shenley, Herts.: stud farm & cottages, 151
Shenley Hill, Herts., 260
Sherborne, Dorset: houses at Long Burton by Scott, 323
Sherborne School, Dorset, 34, 116; 'Archbishop Temple', 184
Sherfield-on-Loddon, Hants.: North Foreland Lodge, 366
Sherrin, George Campbell, 87, 232, 308, **330**, *330*, 383
Shetland Is., 265
Shields, Frederick, 52
Shillingstone, Dorset: house by Ponting, 291
Shiplake, Oxon.: The White House, 369
Shipley, Sussex: Old Barn, 293
Shirehampton, nr Bristol: Post Office Engineering School, 120; public hall, 120
Shirley, Croydon: All Saints, 200
Shoosmith, A. G., 384
Shorne, Kent: village hall, 380
Shortlands, Kent: St Mary, 260
Sibford Ferris, Oxon., 323
Sickert, Walter, 174
Sidcup, Kent: St John, 298
Sidgwick, Mrs, 99
Sidmouth, Devon: house by Scott, 323
'Siegfried', 102
Sierra Leone: law courts, 154
Silcock and Reay, 126, 176, 202
Simla, Punjab, India: government offices, 217
Simmons, Charles Evelyn, 178, **330**
Simon, Frank Worthington, 202, *258*, 304, **330-1**, 371
Simonds, George Blackall, 46
Simpson, Alexander, 248